THE NEW GOLDEN DOOR TO RETIREMENT AND LIVING IN COSTA RICA

A GUIDE TO INEXPENSIVE LIVING, MAKING MONEY AND FINDING LOVE IN A PEACEFUL TROPICAL PARADISE

WRITTEN BY
CHRISTOPHER HOWARD
WITH THE HELP OF RYAN PIERCY
OF THE ASSOCIATION OF RESIDENTS OF COSTA RICA

THE NEW GOLDEN DOOR TO RETIREMENT AND LIVING IN COSTA RICA

By Christopher Howard

Fifteenth Edition

Printed in Hong Kong

© 2007 Editora de Turismo Nacional, S.A.
Astro Enterprises, Pamama

ISBN 1-881233-65-0

Costa Rica Books
Suite 1 SJO 981
P.O. Box 025216
Miami, FL 33102-5216

www.costaricabooks.com
www.liveincostarica.com
www.amazon.com

"If there be any splendor in peace, let it rest in a country like this..."

Lambert James

"Costa Rica is a proud example of a free people practicing the principals of democracy. And you have done so in good times and in bad, when it was easier and when it required great courage."

Ronald Reagan, 1982

Christopher Howard with Costa Rica's Presidents

Former Costa Rican President, Luis Alberto Monge, receives a copy of Christopher's Bestseller.

Christopher Howard meets with Oscar Arias, Costa Rica's Nobel Peace Prize Winning President

Christopher Howard is interviewed on the NBC Today Show in April 2006

Media Attention and Accolades for Christopher Howard's Costa Rica Retirement Tours

Christopher Howard appears on the International Herald Tribune and CNBC World News in June of 2006

ACKNOWLEDGEMENTS

This edition would not have become a reality without the invaluable help of many people.

I would first like to thank my graphic designers, William *"El Mago"* Morales and Gabriela Watson, for their hard work and patience.

I am also very grateful to Pam and Mary at Blue Jewel Travel.

A special thanks to the following local writers and Costa Rican residents for their contributions to this edition: Martha Bennett, Landy Blank, Lair Davis, Annie Drake, Arnoldo Fournier, David Garrett, Rob Hodel, Guillermo Jiménez, Eric Liljenstrope, Randall Linder, Rudy Mathews, Charles Mills, Lyod Newton, Roger Petersen, Jacqueline Passey, Michael Pierpont, Ryan Piercy, Carlos Morton, Les Nuñez, Martin Rice, Tim Rogers, Todd Staley, JO Stuart, the late Jay Trettien, John Vickery, John Williams, Meg Yamamoto and Abby Danielle of *The Tico Times* and all of the people at Costa Rica Living.

I am also indebted to all the critics whose many favorable reviews made my previous editions a success.

I would like to acknowledge all of the help I have received from the Publishers Marketing Association's and Amazon.com's programs for independent publishers. Thanks to them, this book is now available in the U.S., Canada and rest of the world. A special thanks to my Costa Rican distributor, 7th Street Books, for a job well done.

Finally, I would like to express my eternal gratitude to members of my family, especially my late mother and wife, for their constant support when I needed it the most.

Christopher Howard
San José, Costa Rica

MORE ABOUT THE AUTHOR

Christopher Howard has lived, worked and played in one of the most magical places on earth for more than 20 years. His love for Costa Rica is so great that he became a citizen.

During this time, he has had the opportunity to gather a plethora of information about living, investing and retiring in Costa Rica. It is not surprising that he has first-hand knowledge and insight into all aspects of Costa Rica's culture and its people. Because of his expertise, he is a frequent lecturer at numerous investment seminars.

Mr. Howard has an extensive foreign language background, having earned a Bachelor of Arts in Latin American studies and a Master's degree in Spanish from the University of California. Mr. He also has credentials to teach Spanish at all levels from California State University, San Francisco.

Mr. Howard was the recipient of scholarships for graduate study at the University of the Americas in Puebla, Mexico and the Jesuit University of Guadalajara, Mexico in conjunction with the University of San Diego, California. In 1985, he founded a successful language institute in San José, Costa Rica. Mr. Howard has written three foreign language books including the one-of-a-kind Christopher Howard's

The author lives full-time in Heredia, Costa Rica.

Guide to Costa Rican Spanish It is the only Spanish book that teaches Costa Rican style Spanish.

At present, Chris Howard has been busy working as a paid consultant for *National Geographic Magazine*, published articles and columns in *Costa Rica Today*, *Escape Artist.com*, *Costa Rica Outdoors*, *Inside Costa Rica*, *AM Costa Rica*, for various newsletter about living abroad and working on a feature action movie script to be filmed in Central America.

Mr. Howard also serves as an officer on the Board of Directors of the Association of Residents of Costa Rica.

In 1998 he published the visionary guidebook, *Living and Investing in the New Cuba*. His most recent guidebooks are *Living and Investing in the New Nicaragua* (2000) and *Living and Investing in Panama* (2004).

His forthcoming guidebooks are, *Christopher Howard's Official Guide to Costa Rica Real Estate*, *The Official Guide to the Costa Rican Legal System* and *Christopher Howard's Living and Investing in South America*. They all promise to be the definitive books on their respective subjects.

Due to a multitude of requests from the readers of this guidebook, Christopher Howard began to offer relocation and retirement tours to Costa Rica starting in 1997. Since then he has personally introduced 1000's of people to Costa Rica through his one-of-a-kind monthly tours, seminars and private consultation services. Please see **www. liveincostarica.com** information about his unique tours.

- The Publisher

CONTENTS

FOREWORD

WHY LIVE IN COSTA RICA?

Recently I led a group of prospective residents on a trip around Costa Rica. After a week of traveling and attending a series of informative seminars, most of my clients decided they would like to live here for at least part of the year. Some of them even wanted to invest in real estate. It comes as little surprise that they felt this way. Costa Rica has more Americans per capita than any other country outside the United States. Why do so many people want to live here?

The most obvious reason is the climate. People are tired of freezing winters, scorching summers and the high utility bills that go with them. In Costa Rica they can enjoy one of the best year-round climates in the world (72 degrees average in the Central Valley.) We have only two seasons here, dry and rainy, both with an abundance of sunshine. We rarely need air conditioning and never need heat. Costa Rica has more winter sunshine than Hawaii or Florida and fewer people.

Costa Rica is called "the Switzerland of the Americas" by many due to its neutral political status and spectacular mountains. From the huge, curling waves of the Pacific coast, to the sight of molten rock tumbling down the sides of a volcano, Costa Rica's natural beauty has something for everyone. This unique little country offers a real paradise for the nature lover, fishing enthusiast and water sports fanatic as well as the retiree.

Many come here for the lifestyle. Costa Rica fits the bill for anyone sick of the hustle and bustle, seeking a more laid-back way of life. One of the tour participants remarked, "Costa Rica reminds me of the U.S. about 40 years ago when everything was unspoiled, unhurried and less crowded." It will also appeal to people of all ages seeking to move to a new and exotic land outside the States and Canada, as well as the energetic entrepreneur, the burned-out baby boomer, those sick of long rush-hour commutes and anyone seeking an alternative way of life.

This beautiful country is so appealing because it has the warmth and flavor of Mexico, without anti-Americanism and fear of government expropriations; the physical beauty of Guatemala without a large military presence; and the sophistication of Brazil without the abject poverty and with far less crime.

But Isn't It Expensive?

Although much has been written about the high cost of living here, what you spend depends on your lifestyle. If you must have a luxurious home, drive a late model car and buy imported goods, you will spend as much or more than you would in North America. But if you live more like the locals and watch your spending, you will spend considerably less.

Many Americans living below the poverty line in the United States can live in moderate luxury on a modest retirement or investment income in Costa Rica.

The favorable exchange rate and low rate of inflation let you stretch your dollars here. The cost of food, utilities and entertainment are all substantially lower than in the United States.

Costa Rica's affordable medical care is among the best anywhere. The quality of health care is comparable to North America but the prices are one half or less. Considered by many to be the healthiest country south of Canada, Costa Rica has a longer life-expectancy than the United States (76.3 for men, 79.8 for women), rumored to be the third longest in the world.

In most areas housing costs are less than what you would be accustomed to paying in the United States. I just purchased a new three-bedroom home in San Francisco de Heredia, about five miles from downtown San José, for $85,000. It has a cathedral ceiling, sits on a 270-square- meter lot and is very comfortable for three people and a dog. I have a 15-year mortgage and pay $600 monthly including insurance, with a nine percent loan from a Costa Rican state bank.

Besides our home, I have two cars and a full-time maid. Household help makes life easier. (You can hire a full-time maid for as little as $200 per month or $1 per hour.) My son goes to one of the best private schools in the country. I eat out a few times a week and enjoy various types of entertainment. We spend a week at the beach during Easter and go to the United States every Christmas. Our monthly expenses are about $2,500.

Costa Rica's inexpensive medical care, affordable housing, excellent transportation and communication networks, and abundance of activities with which to stay busy and happy, all contribute to the country's appeal and place it at the top of the list of retirement and expatriate havens.

According to a survey of potential foreign retirement areas in the Robb Report, due to the high quality of life Costa Rica surpasses all countries, including Mexico, Puerto Rico, Spain, Portugal, Australia, the Caribbean Islands and Greece.

What Sets Costa Rica Apart from Its Neighbors?

Nicaragua, Belize, Honduras and Guatemala have lower living costs, but you get what you pay for. The quality of life and lack of infrastructure in those countries leave a lot to be desired. Safety is a concern, especially where paramilitary police have power or where police are corrupt, as in Mexico. Costa Rica is politically stable and is unique in having no army. Although theft occurs, violent crime is minimal.

One expatriate said about Costa Rica. "Costa Rica has one of the most pacifist cultures in the world. Think of it: it has been almost 60 years since Costa Rica outlawed the army. This is the reason that I always return to Costa Rica its lack of an army. When I first arrived here in 1978, they used to boast that they had more teachers than policemen. I don't know if that is still true but they still put more emphasis on education and health than any other Central American country, not to mention the States and many European countries.

So to the person who is wondering about retiring to Costa Rica because it is more expensive than Panama or Belize, I would say research more than just economics because other things in my mind are more important."

A Place to Invest

Costa Rica has a myriad of business opportunities awaiting creative, hard-working individuals. You can run a global business from here by using Internet access, fax machines and cell phones. It is also relatively easy to start a small business on a shoestring. Tax incentives and a government that encourages investments and affords investors the same rights as citizens contribute to a propitious business climate. Many countries either do not permit non-citizens to own property or place restrictions on foreign-owned real estate, but this is not the case in Costa Rica. Anyone may buy real estate with all the legal rights of citizens. Actually, an investment in Costa Rica today is much better than an investment in California real estate was 30 years ago.

What gets people excited about Costa Rica is that it offers some of the best real estate on the planet at affordable prices. The price will eventually go up as the rest of the world catches on. There's only so much beautiful beachfront and prime real estate left in the world. When you consider that almost every bit of coastline in the United States is becoming overcrowded and overpriced, Costa Rica seems like a bargain.

Passive investors will find CD's, second mortgages or other investments that pay 25 to 30 percent in colones annually. These numbers are fantastic when you consider that a million dollars invested in the United States at a standard four to five percent annual rate will generate only $45,000 to $50,000 a year.

A burgeoning global economy and the Internet communications revolution have created unlimited possibilities for doing business in Central and South America. Furthermore, trade pacts between Costa Rica, the United States, Mexico and South America will soon become a reality. These free-trade treaties promise to link all of the nations in the hemisphere in to one trading block.

Costa Rica's current prosperity is being fueled by the immigration of affluent baby boomers from around the world seeking their own piece of paradise and the same engine that has fueled the growth in California for the last 30 years, technology. When Intel decided it needed more capacity, they looked all over the western hemisphere and chose Costa Rica for the very same reasons you will.

Word is getting out about Costa Rica. And that's why now is such a good time to invest.

The Adventure of Starting Over

Some move here to start over and seek adventure in an exotic land. They are tired of dead-end jobs or the rat race and want new challenges, a chance to pursue their dreams and achieve greater personal growth. As a foreigner, you have the challenge of immersing yourself in a new culture and, if you choose, the rewards of learning a foreign language.

Newcomers can make friends easily because foreigners gravitate towards one another. One transplant from Florida told us he had lived in Florida for 20 years and hardly ever had contact with his neighbors.

He claims not to be the most sociable person in the world, nevertheless he has made more than a hundred friends in Costa Rica. He proudly says, "Everywhere I go I bump into people I know."

Why Some People Choose to Live Overseas?

Most citizens of the United States and Canada feel comfortable living where they have always resided. Some are lucky enough to have invested in property and have good retirement programs, affordable health insurance, stocks, bonds or IRAs to ensure a good quality of life during their retirement years.

Others may not have been as fortunate. They realize that they may have not planned well and may be a little short on money to maintain their present lifestyle. A simple solution is to try to lower their standard of living and be more frugal in their own country to compensate for poor financial planning and/or bad investments. They can downsize to a smaller home, move to a more affordable but less suitable area, give up their yearly vacations, fire the gardener and cut back on other areas of their life to just scrape by. But what if they could move to another country with the same amount of income and improve their lifestyle dramatically instead of reducing it?

Living in the right country outside the United States. can make all the difference in the world between just subsisting and maintaining the lifestyle to which you are accustomed. Costa Rica may offer a viable alternative.

The idea of living overseas is not new. The huge number of Americans due to retire is staggering. Currently almost 40 percent of the population of the United States is over 50. By 2020, half the U.S. population will be over 50. Most Americans ages 41 to 59 say they will move when they retire.

Adjusting and Keeping Busy

Adjustment to a new way of life can take many months. However, an open mind, a positive attitude and a willingness to seek out new experiences can make the transition relatively painless.

Costa Rica has come a long way in the last decade. Satellite and Direct TV, private mail service and the Internet make it easier to stay in touch with family and friends in the United States and keep up with what is going on all over the world. If you don't own a computer, you can go to an Internet café.

Costa Rica's modern technology has made life easy for foreign residents. In most areas of the country you can get cash at a local ATM, manage your investments online and read almost any major newspaper in the world the day it comes out.

A friend of ours, a 20-year resident of Costa Rica, said, " My days are so filled with exciting activities and interesting experiences that each day seems like a whole lifetime. I really feel that I have discovered the fountain of youth."

Single men are attracted to the country because it has the reputation of having the most beautiful, flirtatious and accessible women in Latin America. It comes as no surprise that Costa Rican women are highly sought as companions by foreign men of all ages. Single men will have no problem finding love, romance and a second chance in life with a devoted Costa Rican woman.

You will never be bored here unless you choose to be. Costa Rica has something for everyone. In The *Tico Times*, the weekly English-language newspaper, you can find hundreds of interesting activities: movies in English, support groups, computer and bridge clubs — you name it, Costa Rica has it.

Living in Costa Rica can open the door to a new and exciting life. Who knows? You may never want to return home.

One Expatriate's Experience

Michael Pierpont, the founder of Sunburst Coffee, fell in love with Costa Rica a few years ago and knew right away that this was where he wanted to live. You, too, may find that you want to spend more than just a few weeks every year in this delightful country.

"People ask me all the time why I chose Costa Rica," says Michael. "I like this country for several reasons. First, it is a spectacularly beautiful place. Along the Pacific coast you will find rocky outcrops and pounding surf. The beaches look just like those in California, which is where I am from. But you can buy here for one-tenth the cost of California. Inland you'll find a lush jungle Lake Arenal, the Irazú Volcano and coffee plantations and the most beautiful rain forests in the world. In the northwest you will find white-sand beaches, many declared turtle reserves, one of the numerous areas in this country set aside for wildlife research and preservation.

"Second, and important to me, is the cost of living. I can live well in this country on as little as $1,500 per month. You can rent a comfortable house in San José, where I chose to settle, for $500 per month. You can employ a full-time maid for $185 monthly. You will spend $300 per month on groceries, $65 per month on electricity. You can see a movie for $3 and have a nice dinner with drinks for $15.

" Third, I was smitten by the people. Costa Ricans are good-natured and kind, trusting and friendly and extremely beautiful. I knew I'd be happy living and making friends here."

"A few more notes on why I came to Costa Rica: the weather is great, the Spanish colonial history and architecture is delightful, the small expatriate community is welcoming and an extremely interesting bunch. Everyone's got a story. And best of all the taxes are low and easy to deal with. "

Another Resident's View of the Country

There are many reasons why people come to Costa Rica, but here are the reasons I personally hear most frequently:

1) The sweetest people in the world. The *ticos* welcome foreigners and, are affectionate, and sunny.
2) One of the world's best climates. Even in the rainy season, it beats almost anywhere else.
3) Still affordable prices: you can build a simple but pleasant home here for $35 per square foot.
4) A government that allows you to retire here with a modest pension.
5) Almost any part of Costa Rica is cheaper than most parts of the United States and Europe. Exceptions might be Florida, Texas and other southern states.
6) Medical care is excellent and inexpensive.
7) The people here are generally handsome and well groomed. The ladies I emphasize lady, please are pretty, slender, appealing. We do not encourage, however, exploitation although it sometimes happens.
8) There are micro-climates for all tastes. I personally like the higher elevations and mountainous areas where it is cooler and fresher. Others crave beaches, hotter and more humid. There are literally dozens of climates, and you can pick what is comfortable for you.
9) This is both a rustic, primitive country, and an upcoming economy with many amenities, Internet, movies and shopping malls the best of all worlds.
10) Although there is constant petty pilfering here, it is also a gun-free country for the most part, and people feel safer here than in equivalent areas in the United States and abroad. The worst thing that might happen to you is that someone takes your T.V. because they think they need it more than you do."

Actually, Costa Rica is a Lot Like the United States
I've lived in San José for six months and I've found I can get almost anything here that I could get in the United States.

I live in a house with all the same services I had in the United States: electricity, hot water to all my sinks and showers, flush toilets, cable television with US programming, high-speed Internet service, etc. The main difference is that I don't have or need air conditioning or heating and we are able to leave our windows open year-round.

I go shopping at supermarkets, pharmacies, malls, and other stores very similar to the ones in the United States. They close earlier, but stock almost all the same stuff.

Más x Menos and AutoMercado are very similar to U.S. supermarkets, except some of the foods are different and the cash registers and sales displays are actually more advanced than the ones I'd seen in the US. I can also buy liquor in the grocery store which is a nice change from my home state of Washington.

The pharmacies here are well stocked and you can buy many more drugs without a prescription than you can in North America; just tell the pharmacist what is wrong with you, and he or she will hook you up.

Hipermás is bigger than any Wal-Mart I've ever been in. PriceSmart is very similar to Costco or Sam's Club. There are Office Depots here.

The malls here are very much like the malls in the United States, except the VIP theaters in Terra Mall in Cartago are far superior to any movie theater I've been to in the United States.

Cars and gas are more expensive than in the United States but are becoming more common as rising middle-class incomes allow people other than the rich to buy them. There are new car dealerships, used car dealerships, private party sales, etc. just like in the United States.

I have yet to find a service that I used in the United States that isn't available here. Not only are services widely available, they are much cheaper than in the United States. A general rule of thumb is services are cheaper and physical things (especially imports) are more expensive.

I said I have been able to find "almost" everything here. Here are the few things that I have not been able to find (yet):
- Christmas cookie cutters
- Bubble tea
- Foundation and powder in my skin tone (very pale)
- The selection of English-language books is not very big

- Occasionally the brand of shampoo I use is sold out in all the stores at the same time-
- The Sci-Fi Channel is not available on cable here, but all I wanted to watch was Battlestar Galactica and I discovered that I could buy and download the episodes from iTunes

Other than the above I have had no problem obtaining the goods and services necessary to lead an "American lifestyle", for significantly less money than it would cost me to live a similar lifestyle in the US.

Yes, there are some significant differences between the United States and Costa Rica, but these have to do with culture, language, politics, economics and climate — not with the availability of material things. So the people who tell you that you can't life the same sort of lifestyle here as you can in the United States are either a) lying (and who knows what their motives are), b) living way out in the country, or c) very poor.

— Courtesy of Jacqueline Passey. Check out her blog! http://jacquelinepassey.blogs.com/

Why the Author Chose Costa Rica

About 32 years ago I spent a year as an exchange student in Puebla, Mexico. It proved to be the best experience I ever had and the turning point of my life. I truly became enamored with the Latin culture and decided I really wanted to live in a Spanish-speaking country.

I was bareley 20 years old and still had to finish my last year of undergraduate work at UCLA. Nevertheless, I did not give up on my dream. After graduating, I obtained a teaching credential so I would have three months of vacation each year to explore Mexico and the rest of Latin America.

My journey began with Guatemala. Every country I visited in Central and South America had something to offer. But as a whole Costa Rica was by far the leader of the pack. Brazil had Rio and its vibrant culture. Argentina had cosmopolitan Buenos Aires, Mendoza, the Pampas, Patagonia and Bariloche. Chile had its Switzerland-like lake region in the south and Santiago in the center of the country set against the backdrop of the Andes. Peru had Lake Titicaca, pre-colonial Cuzco and Machu Picchu with its rich Incan culture. Ecuador had the Galapagos Islands and colonial Quito. But none of these countries, including beautiful Mexico to the north, came close to Costa Rica as a whole. So, after extensive research and travel I decided the country where I really wanted to live was Costa Rica.

I began to return to Costa Rica every chance I had. My first trip was for two weeks. My next visit was for a month. Each time I found a way to protract my stay. I was living in the San Francisco Bay Area but found myself spending most of my time thinking about Costa Rica. I really felt more at home there than in the United States. Consequently, I decided to follow my heart and move to Costa Rica to pursue my dream. I did not want to wait until I was 65 years old and retired to make the move.

All of my friends and relatives said I was crazy to give up a secure teaching position and move abroad. They just couldn't understand why I would leave the comforts of the good old U.S.A to move to a third world country. Some even asked me if there was a revolution going on in Costa Rica. Obviously they were confusing Costa Rica with Nicaragua and El Salvador of the 1980s.

Needless to say, I made my move twenty-five years ago and have never looked back. I love the country, the culture and the people. My adopted country has been very good to me and I have found success and happiness here.

¡Pura vida!

INTRODUCTION

WELCOME TO BEAUTIFUL COSTA RICA

Costa Rica's friendly 4 million people, or *ticos* as they affectionately call themselves, invite you to come and experience their tranquil country, with its long and beautiful coastlines, alluring Caribbean and Pacific waters, pristine beaches and some of the most picturesque surroundings you have ever laid eyes on.

Many visitors say Costa Rica is even more beautiful than Hawaii, and, best of all, still unspoiled.— In fact, Costa Rica took over Hawaii's place as best adventure destination last year, according to the publication *Pacific Business News*. *Travel Weekly* selected Costa Rica as "the 2004 best destination for tourists traveling from the United States." — Costa Rica has Hawaii's weather, spectacular green mountains, and beaches without the high prices. The country offers more beauty and adventure per acre than any other place in the world.

In the heart of the Central Valley, surrounded by beautiful rolling mountains and volcanoes, sits San José, the capital and largest city in the country. Viewed from above, this area looks like some parts of Switzerland.

Downtown San José is always bustling with activity.

San José is the center of the country's politics and cultural events. It has a mixture of modern and colonial architecture, yet remains charmingly quaint and retains a small-town feel despite being a fairly large city with a slightly international flavor. It feels more like a town that has grown in all directions, rather than a metropolis. Though San José and adjacent suburbs have a population of approximately 1 million, you get a small-town feeling because of the layout of the city. San José and Panama City are considered the most cosmopolitan cities in Central America.

In a 2004 survey by *Mercer Human Resource Consulting*, San José ranked 130 out of 140 cities world wide with respect to cost of living. Tokyo and London were at the head of the list. The British publication *The Economist* ranked San José as the second most affordable city in Latin America. The cost of living is only 45 percent of that of New York.

San José or *Chepe*, as the locals call it, is also the cultural and business center of the country and a mecca for North Americans. There is something for everyone. The city boasts the three largest shopping malls in Central America, with lots of stores to which you are accustomed back home. San José also offers a variety of night life, a wide range of hotels, restaurants serving international cuisine, casinos, quaint cafés, lovely parks, the old National Theater with a wonderful orchestra and lots of outside attractions on a regular basis. Other things of interest are a zoo, art galleries, theaters, museums, parks, two English-language newspapers, places for people watching and much more. Virtually everything in a large U.S. city can be found here. Americans have no trouble feeling at home. It is very easy to find something to do to entertain yourself. At an altitude of just over 3,750 feet above sea level, San José offers year-round spring-like temperatures add to its appeal.

The city is laid out on a grid plan. *Calles* (streets) run north and south and *avenidas* (avenues) run east and west. Avenues to the north of *Avenida Central* have odd numbers and those to the south even numbers. Streets to the east of *Calle Central* have odd numbers and those to the west even.

San José's convenient central location makes any part of the country accessible in a matter of hours by automobile. We recommend you use San José as a gateway, starting point or home base while you explore Costa Rica and look for a permanent place to reside.

Because of the county's small size, it is possible to spend the morning at the beach, visit a volcano by noon and enjoy dinner at a mountain resort overlooking the Central Valley.

COSTA RICA
A country that lives up to its name
by Julie Campbe

"In my capacity as Fashion and Travel Editor of Sports Illustrated magazine, I've produced every one of the magazine's swimsuit issues from 1965 to 1996, thirty-two in all. My annual search for beautiful and unspoiled locations has led me to every continent except Antarctica, and I've walked literally hundreds of miles of beaches, mountain trails, deserts, and even glaciers in order to take our readers to some of the most exotic, and often overlooked, corners of our planet. Sometimes my choice was a resort so new that it could only be envisioned from an architect's blueprint; in other years I've settled on an island or a country or even an entire continent— Australia.

So what brought me to Dominical, Costa Rica? Looking at the map I was struck for the first time by how near a neighbor Central America was, and at the same time how little I knew about it. I had to know more, and when I discovered Costa Rica, the jewel of the Central American chain, and traveled its length and breadth, I knew I had found something very special—a country that truly lives up to its name.

Costa Rica means Coast of Abundance or richness of nature. Its rainforests comprise a virtual cornucopia of flowers, lush vegetation, birds and wildlife—all still unspoiled. Rising from the coastline at Dominical are the majestic green mountains with rushing clear streams leading to crystal waterfalls and swimable fresh-water pools.

Coming down from mountains that were often tucked behind mist and clouds I found myself in a beautiful and varied stretch of coast. One side of the country faces the Pacific and the other the Caribbean. For our shoot I chose the Pacific at a place called Dominical, where one beach is more lovely and dramatic than the next. The diversity was breathtaking. And on these immaculate beaches there is no one to step over you while sunning, and only the sound of tropical birds and rolling surf.

I came to Dominical to take gorgeous pictures of gorgeous models in a gorgeous setting, and indeed I was able to do that. But the real discovery was a small piece of God's Country that I'll want to revisit again and again—and on my own time!

*Courtesy of Sports Illustrated

Costa Rica Love Song
Written by: Lair Davis

I love you, Costa Rica, my home. Let me count the ways.

I love the fact that I have no mailbox, which means I receive no junk mail. I do have a post office box, however. There is never any junk mail in it, either.

I love my neighborhood bar, where they welcomed me effusively and let me run a tab the first time they ever laid eyes on me. Each time I go to that happy place, you would think I am their most regular customer. I've been there three times in the past year.

I love being able to make monthly payments on something the full cost of which is $25.

I love the iguana that lives in the drainage ditch up the block, and that he has become so fat because all the neighbors feed him constantly.

I love never having to think about tomatoes (or other fruits and vegetables) being out of season.

I love the jugglers who entertain you at street intersections in San José while you wait for the light to change.

I love the police — wow! Never thought I'd say that! Costa Rican police really aren't law enforcers so much as peace-keepers and information-givers. They seem so much less full of themselves than police I've encountered elsewhere.

I love those wonderful massages given by the fully accredited physical therapist in my town. It costs $15 for a 90-minute treatment.

I love that the buses will stop to pick up and drop off people anywhere along the road between towns.

I love it that there is a shop where they only repair umbrellas. It costs about a dollar to have one fixed — while you wait.

I love receiving a discount from just about every store and business in the country simply because I smile and say *buenos días* to everyone when I enter. I enjoy watching other gringos in the same stores seriously "get right down to business," having not learned this little touch of Costa Rican social grace — and then watching them pay more everywhere every time. You think cultural differences do not matter? You feel that simple, basic courtesy doesn't pay?

I love the continued tradition in this country of doctors, lawyers and other professionals making "house calls."

I love watching a teenage boy holding hands with his mother while walking through the public park in the center of town in full view of all his friends.

I love never having seen a single child throw a fit in the grocery store. How have these children learned to behave so well in public places, I wonder.

I love never having to trim the fat off the beef.

I love knowing when the national soccer team scores without even watching the game. Everyone else is watching, though. With every goal, the whole community lets out a roar.

I love when I ask someone for directions and he or she completely stops what they are doing in order to escort me personally halfway across town, deliver me to the door, and proudly introduce me to the proprietor.

I love the politeness most teenagers display to people my age. Yesterday I watched a teenage boy leave his friends waiting while he went back across the street and assisted an elderly gentleman in making his way. No snide, smart-alecky remarks greeted the good Samaritan when he returned to his group of friends.

I love not knowing the weather forecast. Actually, I DO know the forecast. Everyone who lives in Costa Rica knows what the weather will be like today.

I love not having to decide what to wear today.

I love not being able to hear the televisions in so many places because of the sound of the rain falling on the tin roofs.

I love when the clouds suddenly roll in and hide that tremendous mountain across the valley, and then just as suddenly roll out again.

I love having sidewalks along country roads.

I love sunsets that take my breath away, and the necklaces of streetlights that sparkle at night up and down the mountains in the distance.

I love being awakened at dawn by the noisiest birds on the planet.

I love having a cup of java at the local coffee shop that is as good as any offered by Starbuck's — at one-fifth the price.

I love when a storekeeper informs me that I am the greatest living customer he has ever had the honor and privilege to humbly serve and that my presence in his establishment has surpassed any possible visit in the future by Her Majesty Queen Elizabeth II of England herself. (A slight exaggeration, I suppose but, hey, it worked — I'll be back!)

I love the smiles on the faces of the taxi drivers as they go about their daily work. I love the fact that tipping taxi drivers is not customary. I love that so many *taxistas* insist that I take back the change from my fare, even when it amounts to less than a nickel.

I love that I am coming to understand the joy of "now." Tomorrow will come — or not — but "now" is this moment's pleasure. *¡Pura vida!* Pure life!

* Printed with the author's permission.

Noble country, our lives
are revered in your flying flag;
For in peace, white and pure,
we live tranquil
beneath the clear limpid blue
of your sky.

And their faces are ruddy with
hard work,
In fields beneath the life
giving sun.
Though are but farm
workers, their labors eternal,
Esteem, renown and honor
have won.

Hail, oh land of our birth!
Hail, oh gracious land we love!

If an enemy seeking to slander
you or
harms your name, then we will
abandon our farms
and arise with fervor to take up arms.

Oh, sweet country, our refuge
and shelter;
How fertile your life giving soil!
May your people contended
and peaceful
unmolested continue their hard
work.

Things to think about before moving to a new country or making foreign investments

◊ What is required to become a legal resident? Can I meet these requirements? What is the cost? How often does residency have to be renewed, what are the conditions of renewal and what is the cost?

◊ What is required to visit, or stay while I'm waiting for residency?

◊ What is the political situation? How stable is the country?

◊ Weather — Will I like the weather year-round?

◊ Income taxes — Will I be taxed on income brought into the country? — Am I allowed to earn income in the country? If yes, how is it taxed?

◊ Other taxes — Sales tax, import duties, exit taxes, vehicle taxes, etc.

◊ How much will it cost in fees, duties and import taxes to bring my personal possessions into the country— cars, boats, appliances, electronic equipment, etc.?

◊ Rental property — How much? Availability?

◊ Purchase property — property taxes, restrictions on foreign ownership of property, expropriation laws, building regulations, squatters rights, etc. Is there a capital gains tax?

◊ Communications — Are there reliable phone and fax lines, cellular phones, beepers, connections to Internet and other computer communication services? Is there good mail service between the country and the rest of the world? Are there private express mail services such as DHL, UPS and FedEx? Are there local newspapers, radio and TV in a language I will understand? Is cable or satellite TV available?

◊ Transportation — How are the roads? Are flights available to places I will want to go? How are the buses and taxis ? How costly is it to travel to and from other international destinations?

◊ Is it difficult for friends and family to visit?

◊ Shopping — Are replacement parts available for the items I have brought from home? If so, what are the costs? If not, how much will it cost to import what I need?

◊ Are the types of food to which I am accustomed readily available in both markets and restaurants?

◊ If I have hobbies, are clubs, supplies and assistance available?

◊ What cultural activities are available — (art, music, theater, museums, etc.)?

◊ What entertainment is available— (sports, movies, nightclubs, dancing, etc.)?

◊ What recreational facilities are available? (golf courses, tennis, health clubs, recreational centers, parks, etc.)?

◊ If I like the beach, are good beaches available? Can they be reached easily? What is the year round temperature of the water?

◊ What is the violent crime rate? Minor crime (theft, car and house break-ins)? What support can be expected from the police? Are the police helpful to foreign residents?

◊ How do local residents treat foreign visitors and residents?

◊ What are the local investment opportunities like? Is there any consumer or protective legislation for investors? What return can I expect from my investments?

◊ Is the banking system safe and reliable? Can banks transfer funds and convert foreign currency, checks, drafts, and transfers? Are checking, savings and other accounts available to foreigners? Is there banking confidentiality? Is there a favorable rate of exchange with the U.S. dollar?

◊ Are good lawyers, accountants, investment advisors and other professionals available?

◊ How difficult is it to start a business? What kinds of opportunities are there?

◊ How is the health care system? Is it affordable? Do they honor U.S. and Canadian health insurance? Are there any dangerous diseases, and if so, does the local health care system address the problem? What is the quality of hospitals, clinics, doctors and dentists? What is the availability of good specialists?

◊ How is the sanitation? Can I drink the water? Do the restaurants have good sanitation standards? Are pasteurized milk and other dairy products available? Do meat, fish and vegetable markets have satisfactory sanitary standards?

◊ If I am interested in domestic staff, what is the cost of cooks, housekeepers and gardeners, etc.? Is the local help reliable? What regulations are involved in hiring employees? What are employers' responsibilities to workers?

◊ What legislation is there to protect foreign residents? What rights do foreign residents have in comparison to citizens?

◊ What natural disasters are there — hurricanes, tornadoes, typhoons, earthquakes, droughts, floods?

◊ Can pets be brought into the country?

◊ Is there religious freedom?

*Courtesy of the Association of Residents of Costa Rica

COSTA RICA'S LAND,
HISTORY AND PEOPLE

The Lay of the Land

Costa Rica occupies a territory of about 20,000 square miles in the southern part of Central America, and includes several small islands, mostly on the Pacific side. It is much like the state of Florida with two long coastlines. The country is only about 200 miles long and 70 miles wide at its narrowest part.

Costa Rica is often compared to Switzerland and Hawaii because of its mountains and forests. The country's three mountain ranges create five geographically diverse areas, the Northern Central Plains, the Northwest Peninsula, the Tropical Lowlands on the Pacific and Caribbean coasts and the Central Valley where 70 percent of the population resides. The country is divided into seven provinces: Alajuela, Cartago, Guanacaste, Heredia, Puntarenas, Limón and San José.

Unlike many areas of Mexico, Central and South America, Costa Rica remains beautiful and warm year-round. This is partly because it borders the Pacific Ocean on the west, the Atlantic Ocean on the east, and has a string of towering volcanoes on the Central Plateau. Combine all this and you have a unique tropical paradise with 11 climatic zones.

COSTA RICA - General Information

Capital	San José
Population	4,000,000
Size	19,730 square miles
Quality of Life	Excellent,(good weather, friendly people, affordable)
Official Language	Spanish (English is widely spoken)
Political System	Democracy
Currency	Colón
Investment Climate	Good-many opportunities
Per capita income	$4,288
Official Religion	Catholicism
Foreign Population (U.S., Canadian and European)	Over 50,000
Longevity	77.49 is almost as high the U.S.
Literacy	95%
Time	Central Standard (U.S.)

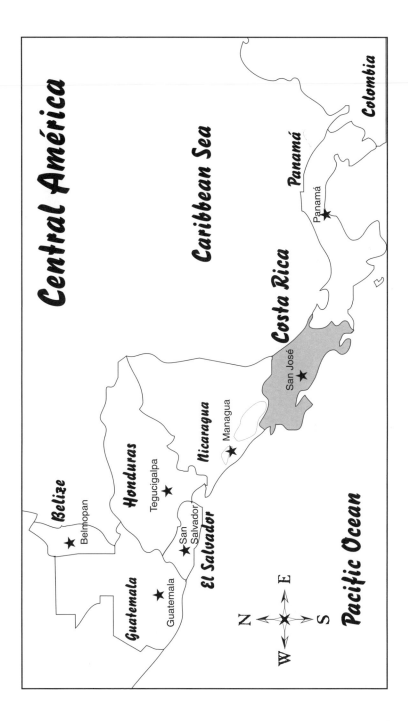

Central América

Caribbean Sea

Colombia

Panamá

Panamá ★

Costa Rica

San José ★

Nicaragua

Managua ★

Honduras

Tegucigalpa ★

Belize

Belmopan ★

San
Salvador ★

El Salvador

Guatemala

Guatemala ★

Pacific Ocean

N
E
S
W

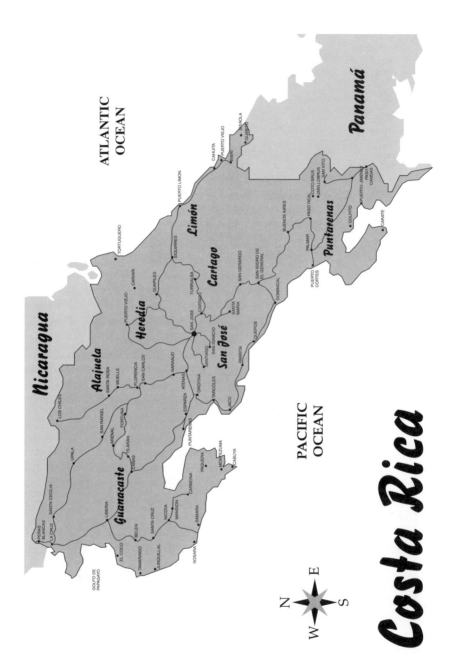

ATLANTIC OCEAN

Nicaragua

Panamá

PACIFIC OCEAN

Costa Rica

PEÑAS BLANCAS
LA CRUZ
SANTA CECILIA
LOS CHILES
UPALA
LIBERIA
EL COCO
BELEN
SANTA CRUZ
TAMARINDO
JUNQUILLAL
NOSARA
SAMARA
MANSION
NICOYA
CARMONA
PAQUERA
MONTEZUMA
CABUYA
GOLFO DE PAPAGAYO
CAÑAS
TILARAN
ARENAL
FORTUNA
SAN RAFAEL
SANTA ROSA
MUELLE
FLORENCIA
SAN CARLOS
NARANJO
ESPARZA
ATENAS
PUNTARENAS
JACO
OROTINA
TARCOLES
SANTIAGO
SAN IGNACIO
PARRITA
QUEPOS
DOMINICAL
PUERTO CORTES
PUERTO VIEJO
HEREDIA
SAN JOSE
CARTAGO
TURRIALBA
SANTA MARIA
SAN GERARDO
SAN ISIDRO DE EL GENERAL
BUENOS AIRES
PALMAR
PASO REAL
COTO BRUS
SABALITO
SAN VITO
PUERTO JIMENEZ
PASO CANOAS
CANOAS
GOLFITO
CARATE
CARIARI
GUAPILES
SIQUIRRES
TORTUGUERO
PUERTO LIMON
CAHUITA
PUERTO VIEJO
GANDOCA
GUABITO
SIXAOLA

Alajuela
Guanacaste
Heredia
San José
Cartago
Limón
Puntarenas

N
E
S
W

Weather

Costa Rica has a tropical climate since it lies so near the equator. The country is famous for having one of the best climates in the world. You dress in lightweight clothing year-round; a jacket may be necessary for higher elevations and cool nights. For the rainy season since U.S.-style rain gear is too warm and cumbersome for the tropics.

Temperatures vary little from season to season and fluctuate with altitude. The higher you go, the colder it gets, and the lower you go the warmer it is. In the Central Valley, spring-like daytime temperatures hover around 72 degrees all year, while lower elevations enjoy temperatures ranging from the upper 70s to the high 80s. Temperatures at sea level fluctuate between the high 80s and low 90s in summer with slightly more humidity than at higher elevations.

Like other tropical places, Costa Rica only has two seasons. The summer, or *verano*, is generally from late December to April with March and April being the warmest months of the year. The rainy season or *invierno*, runs from May to November. January is usually the coolest month. At times, there is an unseasonably dry spell or Indian summer either in July, August or September. The Costa Ricans call this pause in the rainy weather, *veranillo*, or "little summer." A relatively dry period at the end of July is referred to as *canícula* when there is a respite in the May to November rains. Light rains mixed with sunshine characterize this period, which can sometimes extend into August.

Unlike many of the world's tropical areas, almost all mornings are sunny and clear, with only a few hours of rain in the afternoons during the wet season. Since the temperature varies little, the wet months are usually as warm as the dry months. It is unusual to have two or three days of continuous rainy weather in most areas of the country. October is usually the rainiest month of the year. However, the Caribbean coast tends to be wet all year long. For this reason, many foreigners choose to live on the west coast of Costa Rica. This climate, along with a unique geography, is responsible for Costa Rica's lush vegetation and greenness at all elevations, especially during the rainy season.

Foreigners should not let the rain get them down, since there are a variety of indoor activities available. San José's many museums, theaters, malls, casinos, roller skating rinks, Internet cafés and other indoor activities will more than keep you busy when it rains.

Here are several good sites that offer information about Costa Rica's weather: http://costa-rica-guide.com/Weather/WeatherMap. html, http://www.vacationscostarica.com/costa_rica_weather.htm, http://www.fallingrain.com/world/CS/, and www.planetario.ucr.ac.cr, www.imn.ac.cr/prono/prono.htm weather for next five days, www. imn.ac.cr/prono/EXTENDIDO.htm (for the next five days), for 20 costa rica cities www.worldweather.org/171/m171.htm (for 20 cities in Costa Rica) and for sea weather www.imn.ac.cr/marino/MARINO. htm (sea weather).

Costa Rica's Unique History in Brief

Traditionally Costa Rica has been a freedom-loving country living by democratic rules and respecting human rights.

According to archeologists, the northern part of Costa Rica was originally inhabited by the **Chorotegas**, who got their name from an ancient place in Mexico called Cholula. Another group of pre-Columbian people migrated from northern South America. They were skilled gold artisans.

When Columbus set foot on the Atlantic coast at a place called *Cariari* (Puerto Limón) on September 18, 1502, he anticipated finding vast amounts of gold, so he named this area Costa Rica "rich coast" in Spanish. However, unlike Mexico and Peru, Costa Rica had neither advanced indigenous civilizations nor large deposits of gold. The small Indian population offered little resistance to the Spanish and was eventually wiped out by disease. Faced with no source of cheap labor, the Spanish colonists were forced to supply the labor themselves. Consequently, the became quite independent and self-sufficient, and were basically very poor. Thus, a sort of democratic, equalitarian society developed with everyone doing their share of the work, and few becoming very rich or very poor.

For a couple of centuries Costa Rica was almost forgotten by Spain because it lacked trade and wealth. In fact, Costa Rica became so isolated and unimportant to the mother country that it didn't experience the same conquest and domination that took place in countries to the north and to the south. Costa Rica was so far removed from the mainstream that there was no War of Independence from Spain in the early 1800s, as there was in the rest of Latin America. Costa Ricans learned of their newly won independence from a letter that arrived one month after independence was officially granted in October of 1821. During this period, coffee became the leading export and the wealth it brought to the coffee growers allowed them to dominate politics.

In the mid-1800s the country experienced imperialism first-hand when an impish American, named William Walker, tried to establish himself as dictator in Central America. Costa Ricans rallied to defend their sovereignty and soundly beat Walker's mercenary army in a couple of battles. Walker was eventually executed in Honduras when he tried to conquer Central America again.

Coffee continued to be the mainstay of the economy and allowed the rich coffee growers to dominate politics for the rest of the 19th century.

During this time, construction on the railroad was begun from the Atlantic coast and eventually finished in 1890.

Costa Rica's development continued well into the 20th century with only a few minor interruptions. In the 1940s Rafael Angel Calderón Guardia became president and initiated a series of reforms, including a labor code and social security system to protect the rights of workers and citizens. The most notable achievement was the abolition of the army forever in 1948 after a brief civil war. The same year, a new constitution was drafted that laid the groundwork for the most enduring democracy in Latin America. Women received the right to vote and all banks and insurance companies were nationalized. Presidential terms were also limited to prevent dictatorships.

Although the military has frequently threatened democratic institutions throughout the rest of turbulent Latin America, this is not the case in Costa Rica. Costa Rica has a 5,000-man, non-political National Guard or police force under control of the civilian government. Like the police in the United States, they concentrate on enforcing the law and controlling traffic.

Due to a lack of large military expenditures that go with maintaining an army, Costa Rica has put its money into human development and has been able to establish one of the best all-encompassing social security systems in the world. It also developed an excellent public education system, hospitals, housing, modern communication systems and roads. Every school now has at least one computer. As a result, Costa Rica has the largest proportion of middle class citizens in Latin America and a literacy rate of over 90 percent. Furthermore, the prohibition of armed forces guarantees political stability and peace for future generations and reaffirms Costa Rica's dedication to respecting human rights.

Government

Costa Rica's government has been an outstanding example of an enduring democracy for over 50 years. This is quite an achievement when one looks at the rest of the world—particularly Latin America. In an area of the world noted for wars, political chaos and even dictatorships, Costa Rica stands out as a beacon of democratic tranquility.

The World Bank rates Costa Rica and Chile as having the best governments in Latin America.

Costa Rica is compared to Switzerland because of its neutral political posture, with one exception: Costa Rica has no army. As we mentioned earlier, in 1948 Costa Ricans did what no other modern nation has done — it formally abolished its army. That same year, the country limited the power of its presidents, began universal suffrage and dedicated its government to justice and equality for all, thus ending discrimination and making Costa Rica a truly unique nation. Consequently, in Costa Rica you do not see any of the racial tension so prevalent in the United States and some other parts of the world. Non-citizens have the same rights as Costa Ricans. Today there is even a growing women's - rights movement.

Costa Ricans set up the legislative, judicial and executive power structure to prevent any one person or group from gaining too much power in order to ensure the continuity of the democratic process. For example, to eliminate the possibility of a dictatorship, all presidents are limited to four-year non-consecutives terms. In April of 2003 the *Sala IV* constitutional court reinstated Article 132 enabling past heads of state to run for president again eight years after their term expired.

The members of the legislative assembly are limited to a single four-year term and cannot be re-elected. There are 57 seats in the national legislative assembly, elected by proportional representation from seven districts. Seats are allocated to districts by population: San José has 20, Alajuela has 11, Cartago has seven, Heredia, Limón and Puntarenas have five, and Guanacaste has four.

Costa Rica's government is divided into four branches: the Executive (the president and two vice-presidents), the Legislative Branch (Legislative Assembly and 57 legislators), the Elections Tribunal and the Judicial Branch (the Supreme and lower courts).

The court is divided into four sections. The first court, called the *Sala Primera*, decides civil matters. The second court is called the *Sala Segunda*, and is the labor court. The third court, the *Sala Tercera*, is the criminal court. The fourth court is the Constitutional Court, called the *Sala Cuarta*, and by its name it is obvious that it decides constitutional issues and that its decisions can override laws made by any of the lower courts.

The country's two main political parties are the National Liberation Party and the Social Christian Unity Party.

The Costa Rican National Assembly has just inaugurated a new Internet site (**www.asamblea.go.cr**) that you can visit to keep up on new laws and legislation as well as contact local legislators and politicians.

Since Costa Rica is such a small country, voters can participate more directly in the democratic process. Each vote carries more weight, so politicians are more accessible and have more contact with the people. Costa Ricans approach the presidential elections with such enthusiasm that they celebrate Election Day as if it were a big party or national holiday. People wearing party colors, honking cars and, bands playing Latin music all contribute to the festive atmosphere. For the 2002 presidential election the turnout was about 90 percent— a figure that dwarfs dwarf the United States,' meager 50-percent turnout.

In Costa Rica people settle arguments at the ballot box, not on the battlefield. A group of American Quakers established a colony because of this peaceful democratic tradition, and the University of Peace was started and still exists near San José.

In 2006, former president Oscar Arias Sánchez, who during his first presidency was awarded the Nobel Peace Prize in 1987 for his efforts to spread peace and democracy from Costa Rica to the rest of strife-torn Central America, was re-elected to the country's highest office.

Much has been made about corruption in Latin America. According to the *Transparency International Corruption Perceptions Index*, Costa Rica is ranked third in all of Latin America in a list of least corrupt countries. As a whole Costa Rica is considered the 40th least corrupt country in the world. This is a very favorable ranking since there is currently a worldwide corruption crisis.

All government services may be accessed at **Gobiernodigital.org**.

Economy

Because of its endless beauty, natural wonders and peaceful atmosphere, Costa Rica has become very popular with nature lovers, adventurers and others.

Presently, tourism and high technology have replaced coffee and bananas as the main income earners for the country. Costa Rica's reputation as the "destination of the 90s" has helped the economy. Tourism is now the number-one source of income for Costa Rica. From 1993 to present the tourism industry was the prime source of foreign capital. In 2004 Costa Rica's tourism industry had its best year ever, with an estimated 1.5 million foreign visitors. From December 2004 to May 2005 the occupancy rate of hotels was between 85 and 90 percent as compared to the same period in 2004 when it ranged between 75 percent and 90 percent. The average tourist spent $1,938, which is a 23 percent increase over the previous year. In 2005, 1.7 million tourists spent more than one billion dollars. Most of these travelers arrived on an ever-increasing number of flights to the country. Approximately 310,000 came through the new Liberia airport.

The Walt Disney Company recently announced that Costa Rica would be the only country in Latin America selected for their new vacation program called **Adventures by Disney**. The only other countries selected in the world were the United States, Italy, Great Britain, Canada and France. Travelers will view Costa Rica's natural wonders on these highly specialized tours.

U.S. high-tech firms are drawn by Costa Rica's lower costs, educated and bilingual workforce, political stability, tax breaks and proximity. Consequently, the electronic sector, led by multinational microchip manufacturer **Intel**, became one of the country's top foreign currency earners by the end of 1998. The new Intel plant has turned Costa Rica into a leading exporter of computer parts. It produces about one-third of the company's computer chips. In 1999, microchips exported by Intel continued to drive the Costa Rican economy and were responsible for about half of the country's booming 8.3 percent growth (GDP), which gave rise to some of the decade's best economic indicators. Hopefully this will lead to more foreign investment in this area.

Banana exports are the third major source of income. After Ecuador, Costa Rica is the second-largest banana exporter in the world. However, worldwide fluctuations in prices have affected this export in recent years.

Ideal growing conditions have enabled Costa Rica to produce some of the world's best coffee for over a hundred years. Other exports include electrical components, sugar, cacao, papaya, macadamia nuts and ornamental household plants. Some of these non-traditional export items are beginning to rival traditional exports such as bananas, coffee and sugar.

Another surprising source of income for the country is its foreign residents. According to the November 14, 2005, edition of the *Wall Street Journal*, "Costa Rica's retirees contribute significantly to the $1.4 billion a year in direct spending by Americans according to the government. The multiple effects — salaries in health care, construction, retail and other services — could bring the total benefit to $4 billion , nearly 25 percent of Costa Rica's gross domestic product." The waves of almost 70 million baby boomers are sure to increase the figures as Costa Rica becomes even more popular as a retirement haven.

The *2005 Global Outsourcing Report* ranked Costa Rica third in outsourcing potential behind only India and China. This study takes such factors into consideration as cost, reliability and efficiency.

Surprisingly, sportsbooks contribute more than $100 million a year to the Costa Rican economy. More than 100 such firms are presently operating in the country. Local workers make good salaries in the online betting industry. Costa Rica is sometimes referred to as the "Las Vegas of the Internet" because of the number of sportsbooks that operate here. One wealthy sportsbook owner was recently featured on the cover of Forbes magazine.

Recently, new companies have invested in Costa Rica, which should help the domestic and export economy. The California-based wholesale shopping chain **PriceSmart** has opened three warehouse-style stores in the San José area in last several years. The PriceSmart concept has revolutionized shopping in other Central American countries as well. In the wake of this U.S.-style shopping craze, a local company constructed four **Hipermás** mega -markets to rival Price Smart.

The Swiss pharmaceutical giant **Roche** announced it would build its operations center in Costa Rica to service its plants in Central America and the Caribbean. U.S. health products manufacturer **Procter and Gamble** recently opened a business center in Costa Rica. Several U.S. pharmaceutical companies also have opened plants here.

U.S. all-night diner franchise **Denny's** opened its first restaurant in San José and will open several more in coming years. The **GNC** nutritional chain has opened several store in the San José area. Multinational tire manufacturer **Bridgestone Firestone** inaugurated a new plant in April of 1999, promising to double its exports. This wave of new foreign investment will create thousands of jobs for Costa Ricans. **Baskin-Robbins**, **Dunkin' Donuts** and **Cinnabon** all plan to open branches in Costa Rica in the near future.

In 2005 several big players made sizeable investments in Costa Rica. **Wal-Mart** purchased a large portion of **Supermercados Unidos**.

General Electric bought 50 percent of the stock in Banco de San José, one of the country's best private banks. **Steve Case**, co-founder of AOL and of Time Warner fame, purchased $23 millon worth of beach property to build an upscale resort in the Northwest Pacific area. **Wendy's** hamburger chain is expected to open 15 restaurants in Costa Rica over the next five years.

Real estate investment in creased in 2006. Big players **Monroe Capital Corporation**, Steve Case and **Hyatt Regency Hotels** are investing heavily in real estate projects. These events are sure to boost investor confidence in Costa Rica.

According to Costa Rica's Central Bank, foreign investment in Costa Rica topped a $1 billion in 2006.

Despite the new areas of investment and exports just mentioned, Costa Rica is still heavily dependent on foreign investment and loans to help fund its social programs and keep its economy afloat. However, the country no longer receives as much foreign aid as it used to and still has one of the highest per capita debts in the world. The government has, at times, been hard-pressed to meet loan payments from abroad, which take up most export earnings. Foreign debt has hindered economic development to some extent. Gradual currency devaluations have helped the country meet its obligations. Fortunately, these devaluations have been in small increments.

One problem is the number of people employed by the government's massive bureaucratic apparatus. About one of every seven Costa Rican employees works in some way or another for the government. Consequently, large parts of the country's resources goes toward workers' salaries, benefits and operating expenses instead of pressing needs as road repair. Some economists believe one way to help the country progress is to lay off all of the unnecessary government workers.

Hopefully the present growth in tourism and continued foreign investment will help the country's economic future. President Clinton's trip to Costa Rica in May 1997 set the wheels in motion for a free-trade treaty with the Central American countries. It promises to be much like the NAFTA treaty between the U.S., Canada and Mexico.

The Central America Free-Trade Agreement (CAFTA) is expected to be ratified soon by Costa Rica, and many believe it will help all of the Central American counties' economies.

The most salient feature of the new trade pact calls for the partial opening of the government-run telecommunications monopoly by 2007. After January 1, 2007, Costa Rican and foreign companies will be able to offer their telecommunication services, despite the seeming strangle hold of the *Instituto Costarricense de Electricidad*, commonly referred to by its acronym, ICE. Broadband Internet and cellular phone service will be affected by the opening up of telecommunications. The treaty also calls for the complete opening of the country's insurance monopoly or the *Instituto Nacional de Seguros* (INS) by 2011. Costa Rica must allow foreign companies to sell all types of insurance except mandatory policies by 2008.

Other sectors of the economy affected by the new treaty are rice, sugar, beef, chicken drumsticks, pork, oils, ethanol, dairy products, industrial goods, free zones, textiles and intellectual property.

According to the Central Bank, inflation was 22.56 percent in 1995, almost double what the government had hoped for. In 1996 inflation was about 14 percent. It dropped to 11.2 percent in 1997, was around 12.6 percent in late 1998, 10 percent in 1999, 10.3 percent for 2000, 11 percent for 2001, nine percent for the year 2002 and 9.4 percent for 2003. Inflation closed at about 13 percent for 2005. The Central Bank expects inflation to be around 10 percent in 2006.

In an effort to control inflation, the Central Bank of Costa Rica modified its system to establish the rate of exchange in October 2006, by switching from the mini-devaluation one to one in which the rate is allowed to fluctuate between two ranges. Mini-devaluations had been applied for 22 years and they consist basically in a gradual increase of the price of the dollar. In the past it increased an average 13 cents of a *colón* a day. Regarding the control of inflation, the chief executive of the Central Bank, Francisco Gutiérrez, explained that, for example, because it would no longer be possible to forecast devaluation, the chances of transferring it to domestic prices will be greatly reduced.

Gross domestic product grew 3.2 percent in 1997, 4.5 percent in 1998, 8.3 percent in 1999, 2.2 percent in 2000, 0.3 percent for 2001, 5.2 percent in 2003, 4.2 percent in 2004, 3.5 percent in 2005 and an anticipated 3.7 percent in 2006.

Central Bank economic indicators and other financial information are available (in Spanish) on the bank's web site: **www.bccr.fi.cr**.

The People

Besides its excellent weather and natural beauty, Costa Rica's unique people are probably the country's most important resource and one of the main factors in considering Costa Rica as a place to live or retire.

Costa Ricans proudly call themselves *ticos*. They affectionately and playfully use this nickname to set themselves apart from their neighbors. This practice is derived from their habit of adding the diminutive suffix - *ico* to words instead of - *ito*, as done in most Spanish-speaking countries. For example, instead of saying un *ratito* (a little while), *ticos* say un *ratico*.

Foreigners who have traveled in Mexico and other parts of Central America are quick to notice the racial and political differences between Costa Ricans and their neighbors.

Costa Ricans are mostly white and of Spanish origin, with a mixture of German, Italian, English and other Europeans who have settled in Costa Rica over the years. This makes Costa Ricans the most racially homogeneous of all the Central American peoples. More than 90 percent of the population is considered white or *mestizo*. Argentina and Uruguay are the only other countries in Latin America with similar racial compositions.

There is also a small black population of about two percent, mainly living on the Atlantic coast. Indigenous groups in the mountainous areas of the Central Plateau and along the southeastern coast account for one percent of the population. Costa Rica has never had a large indigenous population compared to other countries in the region.

In recent times, the country's stability and prosperity have made it a kind of melting pot for people from less stable Latin American countries, such as neighboring Nicaragua, Colombia, Cuba and Argentina. Many Colombians have sought refuge in Costa Rica because of the strife at home and similarities between the two countries food, culture and language.

Nicaraguans make up 10 percent of the population. About 400,000 Nicaraguan immigrants make their home in Costa Rica. Economic hardship in their own country has caused them to flock to Costa Rica to find work. Most Nicaraguans work as domestics, in construction, picking coffee, cutting sugarcane and in other kinds of manual labor. As prosperity and opportunities have increased, fewer and fewer Costa Ricans will do this type of work.

Most of these new immigrants come to Costa Rica to seek a piece of the so-called, *sueño tico* or "Costa Rican dream," the Latin American equivalent of the American dream.

Unofficially there are about 50,000 North American English-speaking residents living in Costa Rica. Many more North Americans and Europeans live here illegally as tourists. Some are "snow birds" who spend only part of the year in the country.

Survival TipsTen Fun and Useful Things to Know!
By Eric Liljenstolpe, M.A. Ed.

(1) The Kissing Stuff: People greet one another by touching their right cheeks and kissing into the air. People seldom actually kiss one another on the cheek. Hint! Men do not kiss men. As a foreigner, you are forgiven for not doing this, but learning this and some of the other traditions will earn you respect.

(2) At the doorway: When entering a home, it is customary to stand at the door and wait to be invited in, even if the people are good friends. When at the doorway, you might say *"Con Permiso"* (With your permission). Your host will then normally reply, *"Adelante"* or *Pase"* which means come on in. This is a sign or respect and courtesy you are showing to your host.

(3) Coming and going: When entering or leaving a party or gathering, greet or say goodbye to everyone in the room with the appropriate kiss. Of course, if it is a large party that may not be possible or necessary.

(4) Bars on the windows: There are bars on the windows of many homes, but this may not mean that the neighborhood is unsafe or poor. This comes from tradition and from a different sense of private property than Anglo North American countries. However, petty theft is rampant and growing and one must be exceedingly careful of one's home and property.

(5) Business in Costa Rica: When doing business (not retail stores), it is considered good form to greet and "chat" with your customer or client before getting down to business. This can take the form of discussing the weather, the beach, an upcoming vacation or any other neutral subject.

(6)"Watchingman": When parking on the street there will almost always be someone who is guarding the cars. He is called a "watchingman" which is pronounced as one word. He or she is tipped about 200 *colones* (50 cents) for stays of more than half an hour. You can give less if it is a quick in-and-out trip.

7) *Ssst Ssst, Macha! Macha!* It is customary for men to compliment women in public places. These cat calls are called *piropos* and are usually harmless and should not be considered offensive unless they are vulgar. Women are advised to ignore them. Acknowledgment, even with hostility, is often interpreted as an invitation for more of the same. Macha refers to someone with a light complexion.

(8) However did she get into those pants? Women wear much tighter and more revealing clothes in Latin America than in many

parts of the USA or Canada. This does not mean that they are sexually promiscuous.

(9) Let your yes be yes. Costa Ricans have an indirect communication style that is often misunderstood by outsiders. For a Costa Rican, it sounds harsh to come right out and say no. They will use qualified speech such as, "it is complicated" or "it will be difficult" instead of saying no. Sometimes they will even say "yes" to acknowledge that they heard you, but "yes" doesn't always mean an affirmative response.

(10) Get off my back! Costa Ricans have a smaller bubble of 'personal space' than Anglo North Americans and Western Europeans. They are quite comfortable standing closer to one another and touching more often. It is quite common that while standing in line at the bank that the person behind you will stand so close that you can feel his body heat. On a bus, you may be the only passenger, but when a Tico boards, he may sit next to you even when there is plenty of room elsewhere!

Eric Liljenstolpe, M.A. Ed., is the founder and president of GSG and its principal trainer and service provider. His diverse experience in sales, education (elementary, secondary, university and adult) and non-profit administration allow him to understand the unique cultural adjustment needs of such diverse groups as businesspeople, educators, missionaries and students.

Eric's experience in Costa Rica began in 1992 when he came on an international studies program. He was convinced during his time that an intercultural experience held the possibility of powerful personal transformation. He has been a permanent resident for the last four years, first, administering a University experiential learning and cross-cultural training program and later as the founder of the GlobalSolutions Group. Extensive educational experience with the Latino population in California and work experience in Nicaragua, Guatemala and Cuba have helped him to develop a comprehensive understanding of Latin American culture and society.

Politically, Costa Ricans have always been more democratic than their neighbors—especially during the last 45 years. Indeed they should be congratulated for being the only people to make democracy work in such a troubled region.

National Geographic reported several years ago that, when asked why Costa Rica isn't plagued by political instability and wars like its neighbors, a Costa Rican replied, in typical *tico* humor, or *vacilón*, "We are too busy making love and have no time for wars or revolutions."

Because they have the largest middle class of any Central American nation, Costa Ricans love to boast that they have a classless society. Most people share the middle-class mindset and tend to be more upwardly mobile than in other countries of the region.

Although there is some poverty, most Costa Ricans are well-to-do when compared to the many destitute people found in neighboring countries.

Another thing setting Costa Ricans apart from other countries in the region is the cleanliness of its people. Costa Ricans take pride in their personal appearance and are very style-conscious. We know a *tico* of modest means who dresses so well he is often mistaken for a millionaire. Men, women and children all seem to be well-dressed. Above all, you don't see as many ragged beggars and panhandlers as in Mexico and many other Latin American countries.

A Tightly-Knit Costa Rican Family.

Costa Ricans are healthy people and have a life expectancy on par with most first-world countries — 76.3. In fact, they have the highest life expectancy in all Latin America and just about the same as people in the United States. This is primarily due to the country's excellent Social Security System that provides "cradle-to-grave" health care. A recent study by sociologists at the University of Leicester, England, demonstrated that Costa Ricans are the happiest people in Latin America and the 13th happiest in the world. Surely this contributes to their longevity.

The people of Costa Rica place great emphasis on education. Education has been compulsory in Costa Rica since 1869, and the federal government currently spends about 20 percent of its budget on education. Costa Rica's 95 percent literacy rate is among the highest in Latin America. A higher percentage of the population is enrolled in universities than in any other country in Latin America.

Costa Ricans are friendly and outgoing and will often go out of their way to help you even if you do not speak Spanish. They are also very pro-American and love anything American—music, TV, fashion and U.S. culture in general. Because of these close ties to the United States and just the right amount of American influence, Costa Ricans tend to be more like North Americans than any other people in Latin America.

Surprisingly, Costa Ricans, especially the young people of the country, seem to have more liberal attitudes in some areas. Costa Rican women are considered to be some of the most sexually liberated females in Latin America. Their liberation is due in part to the fact that the Catholic Church seems to have less of a foothold in Costa Rica than in some other Latin American countries.

However, you should not get the wrong idea from reading this. The vast majority of the people are Catholic and can be conservative when it comes to such issues as movie censorship. Also, Costa Ricans don't miss the chance to celebrate the many religious holidays that occur throughout the year. (See Chapter 11 for a list of some of the most important holidays.)

Generally speaking, the people of Costa Rica love to have fun, to live with "*gusto*" and know how to enjoy themselves. One has only to go to any local dance hall on a weekend night to see *ticos* out having a good time, or observe entire families picnicking together on any given Sunday—the traditional family day in Costa Rica.

The people of Costa Rica, no matter what their station in life, seem to enjoy themselves with less and do not give as much importance to materialism as do North Americans. Even people who can't afford to seem to be able to eat, drink, be merry and live for today.

Recent polls indicate that the majority of Costa Ricans are happy with their quality of life. Out of 162 countries polled, Costa Rica was in the top 40 when it comes to quality of life. More and more job opportunities, accessibility to education and a state-run health care system are cited as the prime reasons for the country's excellent quality of life.

Basic old-fashioned family values and unity are very important to Costa Ricans. Just as in the rest of Latin America, a strong family unit seems to be the most important element in Costa Rican society. Social life still centers around the home. Much of one's leisure time is usually spent with family. Mother's Day is one of the most important holidays. Parents and relatives go to almost any length to spoil and baby their children. Elderly family members are revered and generally treated better than their counterparts in the United States or Canada. Most are not sent to nursing homes as in North America. Young adult singles, especially women, tend to live with their families until they marry.

Costa Rican families will help each other through hard economic times and in the face of poverty. Some foreigners complain that it is difficult to develop deep friendships with Costa Ricans because the family unit is so strong and predominant.

Nepotism, or using relatives and family connections to get ahead, is the way things work in business and government in Costa Rica. In many instances it doesn't matter what your qualifications are but who your family knows that helps you.

Despite all their admirable qualities, there is a negative side to the character of the Costa Rican people. While similar to North Americans in many ways and with a fondness for some aspects of *gringo* culture, Costa Ricans are distinctly Latin in their temperament. They suffer from many of the same problems common in Latin American societies.

Corruption and bribery are a way of life, bureaucratic ineptitude and red-tape thrive, the concepts of punctuality and logical reasoning are almost non-existent by North American standards, and the "*Mañana Syndrome*"—leaving for tomorrow what can be done today—seems to be the norm rather than the exception.

Unfortunately, as in most Latin American countries, **machismo** (manliness) is prevalent to some degree among Costa Rican males. *Machismo* is the belief in the natural superiority of men in all fields of endeavor. It becomes the obsession and constant preoccupation of many Latin men to demonstrate they are *macho* in a variety of ways. Fortunately, the Costa Rican version of *machismo* is much milder than the type found in Mexico, but it nevertheless exists.

There is no telling to what lengths some men will go in order to demonstrate their virility. A man's virility is measured by the number of seductions or *conquistas* he makes. It is not unusual for married men to have a *querida* or lover. Many even have children with their mistresses. Since many married men do not want to risk having a lover, they sleep with prostitutes or loose women called *zorras*. For this reason many Costa Rican women prefer American men to Costa Rican men. As the *Ticas* say, "Costa Rican men are *machista* and always have to prove it. You marry a Costa Rican man today and tomorrow he is out chasing other women and drinking."

Costa Rica is said to have the highest rate of alcoholism in Central America — an estimated 20 percent of the population are problem drinkers. This should come as no surprise, since drinking is part of the *macho* mentality. Making love, drinking and flirting are the national pastimes of most Costa Rican men.

As we discuss in Chapter 9, foreign women walking along the street will be alarmed by the flirtatious behavior and outrageous comments of some Costa Rican men. Many of these flirtations or *piropos*, as they are called in Spanish, may border on the obscene but are usually harmless forms of flattery to get a female's attention. Foreign women are wise to ignore this and any other manifestations of Costa Rican men's efforts to prove their manliness, or *machismo*.

Sadly, many Costa Ricans have misconceptions about North Americans' wealth. A few people seem to think that all Americans and Canadians are millionaires. It is easy to understand why many *Ticos* think this way because of the heavy influence of U.S. television and movies that depict North Americans as being very affluent. Also, the only contact many Costa Ricans have with Americans is primarily with tourists, who are usually living high on the hog and spending freely while on vacation.

It is therefore not surprising that some individuals will try to take advantage of foreigners by overcharging them for services and goods. Others will use very persuasive means to borrow amounts of money ranging from pocket change to larger sums of money, with no intention of ever paying the debt. Please, take our advice: do not lend money to anyone, however convincing their sob story.

Another thing to be wary about is the "*regálame* mindset" of some Costa Ricans. Basically this term comes from the Spanish verb

One View of Living in Costa Rica
by Martha Bennett

Costa Rica is, quite naturally, very Latin. The *Ticos* are fatalistic and live for the moment. They have extended families which often supply most of their social life. By and large they are a happy people, accepting their lot in life and finding a bright side to dark issues. Music and laughter are common sounds everywhere. For me, these are the positives.

Ticos do things that amuse rather than irritate me, such as shoot off fireworks to celebrate a Virgin's Day. Do virgins like fireworks? On the negative side, I must tolerate what appears to be a total lack of planning. Things happen when they happen no matter what promise has been made. It is not a place where "to do" lists get done. Long lines are common in banks, telephone offices or almost everywhere.

Costa Rica is caught between the old world where oxen still pull *carretas* (carts) and the new world of TV and computers. Because of this, there is apt to be confusion about what North America is like, and problems with computers that don't compute because there is a lack of training of the user.

Ticos seem to have a love-hate relationship with the U.S. They want to be like it, but resent it at the same time. This sometimes produces jaded dealings with *Gringos*, i.e.: special prices for blue eyes. But it doesn't happen all of the time and sometimes they cheat each other too. I am a guest in their country and don't try to tell them how to run it.

Since I used to live in Michigan, I find the climate in Costa Rica perfect. It's the same all year round. The sun shines daily and the rain keeps everything green. The countryside is outrageously beautiful.

Ticos are paranoid about crime and all houses in the cities have bars. Yes there is crime here, but I feel safer here than I did in Detroit.

Driving here can be a nightmare. This combined with some bad roads can ruin your day. *Buses* are cheap and go everywhere.

The cost of living is low if you don't buy a lot of imported stuff. A three-bedroom house can be rented for under $500 in some areas like Heredia. Utilities are a bargain. Food is cheap. Fruits and vegetables are almost free. However, appliances cost almost double. Books are expensive, so bring reference books. Cars are twice the cost to buy or bring in. Group health insurance costs around $600 a year per person.

Spanish is important. It allows you to make many friends. I have been living here four years and never dream of returning to the States. But that's me. To know how it is for you, you'll have to try it.

regalar, which means to give something as a gift with no intention of repayment. The verb *dar* is the correct verb to use when requesting something. People here use *regalar* in a figurative way in everyday conversation when asking for everything from small items in stores to ordering a beer in a bar. Unfortunately, too many people take this verb literally and expect something for nothing. We know of many instances where foreigners have been overly generous to locals. As long as they continued their altruistic ways, they were liked. Once they got wise or decided to curtail their generosity, they were considered cheapskates. The bottom line is not to be too generous or spoil people here. Some people will take advantage of your generosity and misunderstandings inevitably will arise.

There have been cases of foreigners who have married Costa Rican women being taken to the cleaners. Because family ties are so strong in Costa Rica, you can end up supporting your spouse's whole family. We talked to one retired American who could not live on his $2,000-a-month pension because he had to support not only his wife and stepchildren, but his wife's sister's children as well. Furthermore, he had to lend his father-in-law money to pay off a second mortgage because the bank was going to repossess the latter's house. This is an extreme example, and though we have heard many similar stories while living in Costa Rica not all Costa Rican families are like this one.

When doing business with Costa Ricans, you should exercise extreme caution. A few years ago, we had the pleasure of dining with a prominent Costa Rican banker who eventually became the country's Minister of the Interior. We mentioned that we wanted to start a business in Costa Rica. He replied, "Be very careful when doing business with Costa Ricans. This is not to say that all people are dishonest here. Just be cautious with whom you deal."

We suggest that you do not dwell on these negatives and hope you realize how difficult it is to generalize about a group of people. After you have resided in Costa Rica and experienced living with the people, you will be able to make your own judgments. The good qualities of the Costa Rican people far outweigh any shortcomings they may have.

WHERE TO LIVE
IN COSTA RICA

The Central Valley

The Central Valley, or *Meseta Central*, is the center of Costa Rica due to its geographical location, culture and economic activities. The valley lies at an altitude of 3,000 to 4,000 feet above sea level. It is surrounded by mountains and semi-active volcanos such as **Poás** and **Irazú**. Its fertile volcanic soil makes it an ideal place for growing anything, including some of the world's best coffee. It is not surprising that more than half of Costa Rica's 4 million people live in this area because of its almost perfect year-round spring-like climate. The capital city of **San José** is located here as well.

The Central Valley offers a wide range of housing. Decent, affordable housing ranges from $50,000 to $100,000, while mid-range prices are $100,000 to $250,000. Low-end condos in the Escazú area start at $150,000 to $250,000. Luxury apartments in Escazú can cost between $250,000 to $500,000. To many this seems expensive but the same product would cost several times as much or more in some places in the United States.

A recent boom in the construction industry has created a wide variety of affordable new homes from which to choose. Many gated communities have been built in Santa Ana and in the Heredia and

Map of the Central Valley

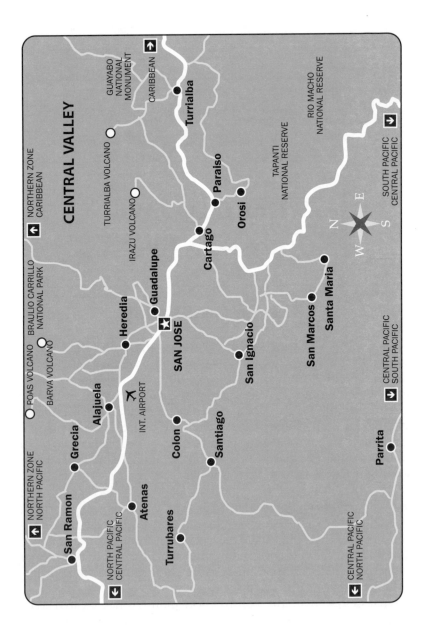

Grecia areas. Older homes also abound and are sometimes a better deal because they often have larger parcels of land.

Deciding where to live in Costa Rica depends on your preferences. If you like the stimulation of urban living and spring-like weather all year, you will probably be happiest living in San José, Heredia or one of the adjacent smaller towns and cities in the Central Valley, such as Alajuela, Escazú or Santa Ana.

As we mention later in this book, there are hundreds of activities for everyone in, around and near San José. The infrastructure is excellent, and the area offers almost all of the amenities of living in the United States.

Retirement is a big change for many people because they find themselves with more free time than usual and sometimes get bored. This should not be a problem if you reside in the San José or the nearby suburbs, since there is a large North American community and it is always easy to find something to do.

Living in San José proper has a couple of drawbacks. Like most cities, San José is crowded, noisy and suffers from some pollution from buses and cars. There is also some crime in the downtown area. If you own a vehicle it is hard to find a place to keep it except for public parking lots. Despite these shortcomings, we do know quite a few Americans who live in the center of town because it is convenient and there is a lot to do to stay busy.

One friend from Florida loves this area because he is right in the thick of the action in the *Gringo* Gulch area. Another American we know likes to spend all day in front of the *Gran Hotel Costa Rica* seated at one of the tables talking with other expatriates and people watching. The latter is a favorite among foreigners in the downtown area. A couple of groups of *gringos* gather for coffee and conversation most days at the McDonald's next to the *Plaza de la Cultura* and National Theater. Newcomers can make some instant friends there.

Recently the municipal authorities announced plans to revamp downtown San José in an effort to draw more people back to the city. The population of the areas which make up the central San José area has dropped from about 70,000 people to 60,000 over the last 20 years, with many people moving to the suburbs. Urban planners intend to transform the city by building more parks and six new pedestrian walkways, similar to the one now found on *Avenida Central*. The National Water and Sewage Institute will improve the city's water, sewage and drainage systems, and the Ministry of Transportation plans to improve traffic in the city by placing major transportation arteries

DOWNTOWN SAN JOSE

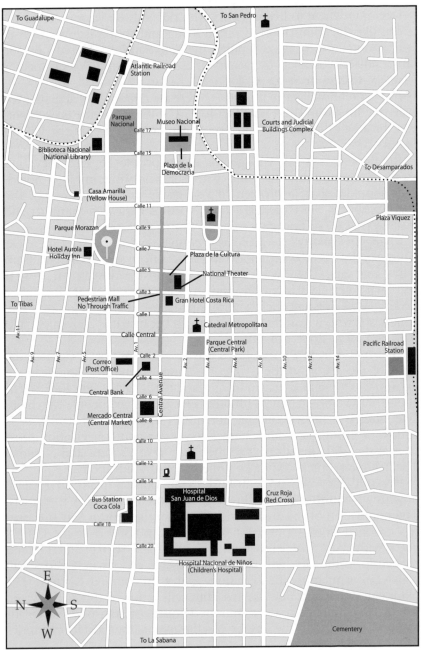

To Guadalupe

To San Pedro

Atlantic Railroad Station

Parque Nacional

Museo Nacional

Courts and Judicial Buildings Complex

Calle 17

Biblioteca Nacional (National Library)

Calle 15

Plaza de la Democracia

To Desamparados

Casa Amarilla (Yellow House)

Calle 11

Plaza Viquez

Parque Morazan

Calle 9

Hotel Aurola Holiday Inn

Calle 7

Plaza de la Cultura

Calle 5

National Theater

Calle 3

Pedestrian Mall No Through Traffic

Gran Hotel Costa Rica

To Tibas

Calle 1

Catedral Metropolitana

Calle Central

Parque Central (Central Park)

Pacific Railroad Station

Av. 11

Av. 9

Av. 7

Av. 5

Av. 3

Av. 1

Calle 2

Correo (Post Office)

Av. 2

Av. 4

Av. 6

Av. 8

Av. 10

Av. 12

Av. 14

Calle 4

Central Bank

Central Avenue

Calle 6

Mercado Central (Central Market)

Calle 8

Calle 10

Calle 12

Calle 14

Hospital San Juan de Dios

Cruz Roja (Red Cross)

Bus Station Coca Cola

Calle 16

Calle 18

Calle 20

Hospital Nacional de Niños (Children's Hospital)

E

N   S

W

Cementery

To La Sabana

outside of the 53 blocks that make up the heart of the city, leaving the downtown area for pedestrians. The electricity company has already placed electrical lines underground.

Here is an expatriate's take on San José: "I find the San Jose's air to be much cleaner than 11 years ago. I go from San Antonio de Coronado to downtown San José everyday Monday through Sunday. I have walked from Sabana Park to the Central Market many days and then all over the downtown area and never had a problem. Today I went to the U.S. Embassy by taking two buses from central San José and then back on another bus. I also did a few errands. Then I took the bus back to my house and was home by 2 pm. I know about 20 words in Spanish. For me the city is great. You could not pay me to return to the little town I came from in the U.S. I have been living here less than a month and have accomplished a lot in a little time — a Costa Rican driver's license, a bank, a post office box and a girl friend. So if a 66-year-old man with no Spanish can do it, anyone can."

Here is another foreign resident's view of the city of San Jose: "I can understand every expat has a different perspective about San José. After living in New York City so many years without a car, I have no intention of buying one to live in the suburbs of San José. The city suits me fine. And buses and taxis are always available if I want to travel outside the city. I have a home just a block north of *Torre Mercedes*, off *Paseo Colón*, and easily walk to most things I need such as the weekend flea market in the *Cementerio* district, theaters and art galleries in San José Centro and Sabana Park.

"A block or less from my house there's a supermarket, several interesting restaurants, a major bank and a few bakeries. I know the neighbors on my little street as well as the guys who knock on the door to offer the daily newspapers or a pushcart full of vegetables."

Many North Americans who do not want to live too far from town reside around the Sabana Park. Most of them live in nearby **Sabana Norte** and **Sabana Sur**. Restaurants, gyms, the new Más x Menos supermarket and a variety of stores and services are all found in this area.

Located at the west end of **Paseo Colón**, the sprawling **Sabana Park** is the largest of Costa Rica's urban parks and is within walking distance of San José and neighboring Rohrmoser. It is right on the outskirts of the center of the city and has nice upscale neighborhoods on the north, south and west. *La Sabana* was originally the site of the country's international airport. It is now covered with tall trees and features a museum, a lake, jogging trails, an Olympic-size pool, soccer

Why I live in Costa Rica?
By Jo Stuart

The quality of life is not measured simply by efficiency nor by material things. For those of you who want to know why I live Costa Rica, here are my reasons why.

(1) I was originally drawn to this country because it has no army, and as a result has developed a peaceful mentality. Costa Ricans do not like confrontations and are not greatly into competition. Perhaps because of this, the minute I arrived, I felt comfortable here.

(2) I was charmed (and still am) because when *ticos* "Thank you," they don't say *"Gracias."* They usually say *"Gracias muy amable,"* which means "Thank you, you're very kind." Being told I am kind often enough makes me see myself as kind and wanting to be more so.

My life here is enhanced each time a tico says, "You're welcome." Here they don't say, as they do in most other Spanish-speaking countries, *"No hay de que"* or *"De nada"* (For nothing). They say *"Con mucho gusto"* (Which much pleasure or, more loosely, The pleasure is mine). My friend Jerry has said more than once that giving and receiving are the same thing, and *Ticos* seem to have recognized this. I have been trying to remember to say both *Gracias, muy amable* and *Con mucho gusto*. Language is a powerful influence on attitude.

(3) Although I have learned that there is a downside to a peace-loving philosophy, a trait called passive-aggressive, I have decided that I can handle passive-aggressive better that I can the downside of a personal freedom-loving philosophy, which seems to be aggresive-aggressive.

(4) I enjoy walking in downtown San José in spite of the traffic and challenging sidewalks. When I first came here and mixed with the people on the streets, I thought there are as many pedestrians here as there are in New York at Christmas time but without the hostility. Instead, I find myself energized and uplifted.

(5) I also noticed that Costa Ricans as a rule have fine postures. It is a pleasure to see them, and seeing them reminds me to straighten up. It is surprising how much better you feel when you walk tall.

(6) I have on a number of occasions, experienced the health care system of Costa Rica, both private and public . The cost here for medical care is far less than in the United States, and I always have felt more cared for and cared about in my experiences here. Even in the overworked and under-supplied public hospitals, I have found attention and compassion. It outweighs the lack of Kleenex. The last time I was in

Calderón Guardia emergency section, they passed out lunches at noon and coffee and snacks in the late afternoon to the waiting patients.

(7) Although business transactions are not always speedy here, how can you not like a country where it is the law that every public building must have a public bathroom? (That doesn't mean they must supply paper.) It is true one spends considerable time waiting in lines. This is where I get a lot of my reading done. I've waited in lines in many countries, and I'll take orderly, friendly queue of *ticos* any day.

(8) There is a custom here that many North Americans have picked up and that is the custom of brushing cheeks when seeing a friend or acquaintance. In the States, after an initial handshake following an introduction, I seldom touch that person again, certainly not my travel agent, my doctor or my landlord. Here, I do. Touching cheeks makes me feel a connectedness to others, and when you think about it, is much more sanitary than a handshake.

(9) On the comfort front, it is hard to beat the climate in the Central Valley of Costa Rica. I have lived where there were 15-foot snowdrifts and where I became accustomed to perspiration dripping down my neck all the time. Living where I need neither air conditioning nor a heater is such a pleasure, and I am sure, far healthier.

(10) Something that is changing here that I regret are the window displays in the stores. Once there was nothing that caught my attention, and I had no desire to buy. I was not lured into being a consumer. Now they are getting both more artistic and more products, and I have found myself stopping and thinking I would like that something.

(11) Because the growing season is so rapid, fresh vegetables and fruits are available most of the year. If one were a vegetarian, one could live very cheaply here.

(12) And finally, what clinched my love affair with Costa Rica was discovering that their national bird is the *yigüirro*. The *yigüirro* (which I can't even pronounce) is very similar to the U.S. robin but smaller, and even less colorful. The *yiguirro* neither threatens anyone's existence (it is certainly not a bird of prey nor is it a rare or endangered bird. It is a common little dun-colored bird, an Every bird, if you will. I think people who choose the *yiguirro* as a national bird has something to say to the rest of the world about peaceful co-existence, humanity, self-esteem and equality.

*Jo Stuart is a regular columnist for the online daily *Am Costa Rica*. See **www.amcostarica.com** for more details.

fields, recreational facilities and many more attractions for the general public.

The fashionable suburb of **Rohrmoser**, on the northwest side of Sabana Park, is very popular with people who want to live in a suburban area close to San José. Living in Rohrmoser is much like having a home near New York's Central Park or San Francisco's Golden Gate Park. The main tree-lined street or Rohrmoser Boulevard runs right through the center of this neighborhood, virtually bisecting it in half. Rohrmoser is bordered on the south by the Pavas Highway. Just about any type of store you might need is found along this busy thoroughfare as well as the U.S. Embassy to the west.

The neighborhood is made up of homes, apartments, condos, a few businesses and has some lovely neighborhood parks. Rohrmoser has many upscale homes owned by wealthy Costa Ricans and is considered very safe, since a large number of well-guarded foreign embassies are found here. Home prices start at about $80,000 on the low end, from $80,000 to $250,000 for a mid-range home and $250,000 plus for an upper-end home. Rent begins at $500. When we lived there a few years ago we paid $600 for a three-bedroom, three-bath penthouse apartment with a panoramic view of the mountains.

A $400,000 + home in the upscale Rohrmoser neighborhood.

Excellent supermarkets, boutiques, international restaurants, the Cemaco department store, an English-language bookstore, pharmacies, bars, discos, doctor's offices, health clubs, movie theaters and the modern Plaza Mayor shopping center are located in and around this upscale neighborhood.

For you nighthawks there is even a 24-hour mini-market at the Shell gas station. The only thing bad about Rohrmoser is that bus service to downtown San José is not good, but you can always take a taxi since they are so affordable.

About five minutes east of downtown San José sits the residential neighborhood of **Los Yoses**. Like all areas east of downtown San José, Los Yoses features a mixture of new and old homes and businesses. Many foreigners live in this area because it is only a short walk to downtown San José. The *Centro Cultural Costarricense-Norteamericano* (Costa Rican-North American Cultural Center) is located in this area so, there are interesting activities to keep a person occupied (there is also a smaller branch in Sabana Norte next to the American Chamber of Commerce). Los Yoses boasts a bowling alley, a supermarket complex, a bookstore and many bars and restaurants. The gigantic San Pedro Mall is found on the eastern edge of this neighborhood.

Barrio Escalante, slightly to the north of Los Yoses, has many older homes and stately mansions. The area provides a glimpse of how the upper crust used to live in Costa Rica. Many foreigners prefer this area since it is so close to downtown and some reasonably priced housing is available. Prices range from about $80,000 on up. Rent starts at about $400 for a small apartment.

Just east of Los Yoses is **San Pedro** — the home of the University of Costa Rica. The campus and surrounding area resemble many U.S. college towns with numerous student hangouts, restaurants, bookstores, nightspots, boutiques and two large shopping malls. You can spend the day sitting at a table at one of the many sidewalk cafés and check out the people as they pass by. A distinctly bohemian ambience fills the air. Some interesting event or cultural activity is always happening in or around the university. During April, the annual University Week celebration takes place. This spectacle includes floats and a carnival-like atmosphere. Low-priced student apartments are available within walking distance of the university.

Another place you might consider living is **Escazú** — a popular suburb where many North Americans reside. It is sometimes referred to as the Beverly Hills of Costa Rica because of its upscale cosmopolitan atmosphere. In the words of one American who lives there, "Escazú is an odd modern conglomeration of micro niches and little islands of green, stitched together by pot-holed roads and pocked with condo complexes, great mansions behind ominous gates and little tin barrios where the wash bakes in the noonday sun."

Escazú is about five miles west of San José, 10 to 15 minutes driving time on the old two-lane road or new autopista (highway). Since most of this suburb is located on hilly terrain, it is especially appealing to those people who like cooler temperatures. In fact, Escazú is one of the more popular places for English-speaking foreigners to live. Bus service is excellent to and from San José. You can catch either a mini-bus or regular bus in the park behind the church in downtown Escazú.

Despite being quaint and country-like, Escazú has all the amenities of any North American suburb: pharmacies, mini-malls, supermarkets, excellent English-speaking private schools, first-class restaurants, trendy shops, a bowling alley, mall, doctors, dentists, a post office and much more. The main entrance to Escazú has so many U.S. franchises, you may find it hard to believe you're not in the States. If you reside here you won't have to go to San José for basic services unless you want to. There is even a beautiful private country club and golf course. Housing is plentiful but expensive, as Escazú is popular with wealthy Costa Ricans and well-to-do foreigners. You can find simple *tico*-style single-family homes, condos, high-rise penthouses and even country estates scattered around this area.

Escazú is the home of many a high-rise condo.

Trejos Montealegre, is a neighborhood just off the highway, boasts many homes, condos and apartments from which to choose. Some upper-end homes in Escazú cost a couple of hundred thousand to a million dollars. However, if you are living on a budget or small pension, you can find more affordable housing in San Antonio de Escazú. Many affordable *tico*-style homes are scattered around this area. Because the area is very exclusive, home prices start at around $100,000. Mid-range homes and condos go for around $150,000 and upper-end prices start at about $300,000. Rent ranges from $800 to $2,500 or more monthly.

Escazú's upper-crust lifestyle isn't for everyone. Here is one local's critical view of present-day Escazú which appeared in the Escazú News. It summarizes what some expatriates feel in a nutshell: "There is no way around it: Escazú has become the Costa Rican Miami. Along the main highway to the west of Escazú, PriceSmart, Office Depot, Payless Shoes and Liz Claiborne can be seen to your left and the Marriott Courtyard Hotel, Outback Steakhouse and Confort Suizo can be seen on your right. The highway ends at the mall, or better said, at the Dadeland of Costa Rica, the glamour capital where people from all walks of life converge.

If you enter Escazú from the old road, it is the same, with Tony Roma's and T.G.I.F. on the right and Häagen-Daz, Bagelmen's, U.S. Laundry and Big Dog,s on the left. As you continue on, just like a tropical Flagler Boulevard, you will see on both sides of the street, KFC, McDonald's, Hollywood Video, TCBY and Hugo Boss.

It seems that the only thing missing in Escazú to make it exactly like Miami is the ocean.

Continuing on, there exists another constellation of luxury shopping centers within Escazú with such chic names as Delights Gourmet, Mommy Basics, Underwear Options and Dry Clean USA. There are sales and clearances every week as well as coffee shops where Perrier is the drink of choice.

It isn't any coincidence, though, that in Escazú you will find the upper-crust North Americans, with the Ambassador's residence leading the group, and where, just like in Miami, there are Venezuelans, Colombians and even a "Little Havana," which is headed by such well known-local Cubans.

The schools have names such as Country Day, Blue Valley, Saint Mary, Mount View. There is even a Spanish School.

The former forest of **Guachipelín** and yellow barks has been turned into condominium complexes that offer a more secure, yet more boring,

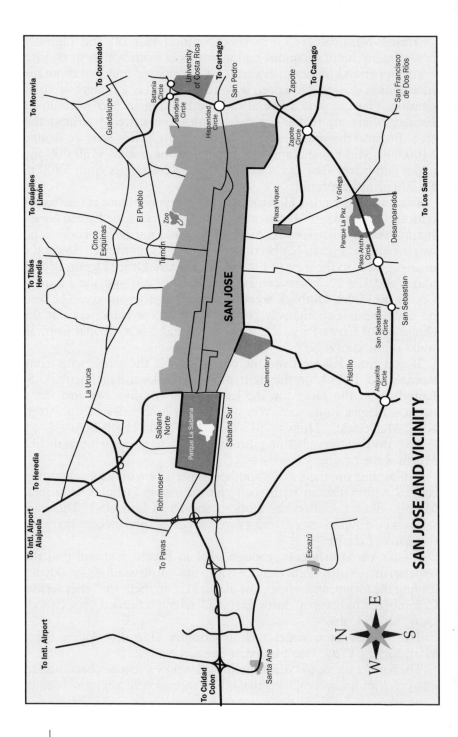

SAN JOSE AND VICINITY

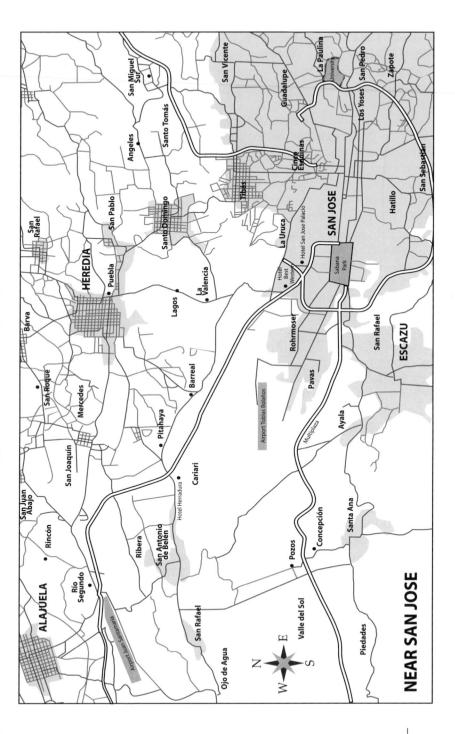

NEAR SAN JOSE

ALAJUELA

Airport Juan Santamaría

Ojo de Agua

Río Segundo

Rincón

San Juan Abajo

Bárva

San Roque

Mercedes

San Joaquín

Ribera

San Antonio de Belén

Hotel Herradura

San Rafael

Valle del Sol

Piedades

HEREDIA

San Rafael

San Pablo

Puebla

Pitahaya

Cariari

Pozos

Concepción

Santa Ana

Angeles

Santo Tomás

Santa Domingo

La Valencia

Lagos

Barreal

Airport Tobías Bolaños

Pavas

Ayala

Multiplaza

San Miguel Sur

San Vicente

La Paulina

University

San Pedro

Zapote

Guadalupe

Los Yoses

Cinco Esquinas

Tibás

La Uruca

Hotel San Jose Palacio

SAN JOSE

San Sebastián

Hatillo

Hotel Best Western

Sabana Park

Rohrmoser

San Rafael

ESCAZU

W N E S

lifestyle. Nowadays, you can't even plant a garden in your backyard, much less have hens to lay fresh eggs every day.

But what really stands out in the center of this big Floridian landscape, erect and upright, the great pioneer of this colony, is the Costa Rica Country Club.

Most of the girls are blonds; they go to the gym and they wear tight, attention-getting clothes. They use Louis Vuitton or Burberry purses, Chopard watches, styled hair and sun visors. The guys drive only the coolest cars, wear only the coolest sunglasses, aerodynamic and galactic, and talk only about business, parties and their trips outside the country.

And to finish off, the Escazu newspaper, as the Miami Herald, has its name in English: *Escazú News*."

Santa Ana, nestled in the "Valley of the Sun," is more rural than Escazú. This fast-growing village is about four miles west of Escazú, and a good mix of Costa Ricans and foreigners resides here. Santa Ana's warm climate makes it an almost perfect place to live. At one time Santa Ana was a popular weekend retreat and summer home for well-to-do Costa Ricans. Many foreigners and ordinary Costa Ricans reside in this town of 2,500 inhabitants now. You can get to Santa Ana by taking the old scenic road from Escazú through the hills or by the new highway.

We recommend checking out this town. Downtown Santa Ana retains a small-town flavor. It is more rural and less developed than Escazú but offers good supermarkets and some shopping. You don't have to go to San José for your essential products. Lately there has been a building boom in the area. Homes here are more reasonably priced than in Escazú. Luxury homes in a secure gated community are a popular choice for middle-to-high-income budgets. An upscale four-bedroom home in a gated community will cost between $225,000 and $450,000.

Ciudad Colón, about 20 minutes beyond Santa Ana, is the farthest western suburb of San José. Some foreigners live here. A new highway from Ciudad Colón to the town of Orotina is in the works and is expected to reduce driving time to the beach from the Central Valley in half.

Beyond Ciudad Colón is the mountain town of **Puriscal**. The cooler mountain climate makes this town appealing. This town is perfect for people seeking affordable housing, more land for their money and rural living. A few properties offer views of both the ocean and Central

Valley. Many people who live in Puriscal commute daily to San José since bus service is good.

A bout five miles northwest of San José is the town of **San Antonio de Belén**. It is a laid-back town behind the airport, just a couple of miles off the main highway west of Cariari, and another good spot to live. This town has experienced a great deal of growth since Intel's mammoth plant opened a few years ago and Marriott built a five-star hotel in the area. A couple of nice gated communities can be found here. Home prices, rent and land cost less than in Escazú, Santa Ana and Cariari. The *Ojo de Agua* recreational complex is also in this area.

Ciudad Cariari, about five miles west of San José and about five minutes before the airport, is an upscale development of mostly newer homes and condos. Housing in this gated community ranges between $130,000 to $750,000. This area is perfect for those interested in country-club living. Within this area are the Cariari Hotel and Costa Rica's oldest golf course, the Cariari Country Club, the Los Arcos neighborhood and the American International School — one of the best English-language schools in the country. A couple of golfer friends of ours live in this area and really like living next to the golf course. Right across the main highway from Cariari sits the Real Cariari Mall.

If you wish to combine an urban life and warmer weather, you can reside in San José's neighboring city **Alajuela**, Costa Rica's second largest city located almost next to the airport. This quiet city is about 30 minutes by bus from downtown San José and has everything you want in a city without the city feeling. The bus service is excellent during the day, so it is easy to commute to San José if necessary. Because of the warm climate, many Americans live in Alajuela, so you can easily make new acquaintances. The city's shady Central Park is a perfect place to sit and relax or socialize with the many locals or fellow expats who gather there in the afternoon. The park is impressive with a lot of tall, ancient trees that are a testament to the city's grandeur. There are other nice parks, movies, restaurants, doctors, supermarkets and more in this city.

The town's Central Market is only a couple of blocks west of the Central Park. Meats, fish, vegetables, fresh fruits and a variety of other odds and ends can be found under one roof. On weekends the city holds a large outdoor farmer's market where a lot of bargains can be found. If nothing else the carnival-like atmosphere of this outdoor market place provides an excellent opportunity to mingle with the locals. Many Americans gather in the bar and restaurant area. Some people say Alajuela is by far the best farmers market in all of Costa

DOWNTOWN ALAJUELA

Plaza Seminario

Liga Soccer Stadium

La Agonia Church

Calle 9

Calle 7

Goodlight Books

Calle 5

Plaza

Calle 3

Calle 1

Alajuela Cathedral

Post Office

Calle Central

Juan Santamaria Museum

Central Park

Av. Central

Park

Av. 2

Calle 4

Av. 4

Juan Santamaria Plaza

Av. 6

Av. 8

Av. 10

To Frailjanes

Hospital San Rafael

Av. 9

Av. 7

Av. 5

Av. 3

Av. 1

Station Wagon Alajuela

Calle 4

Central Market

Calle 6

Calle 8

Old road to Heredia

To Airport

Plaza

Plaza

TUASA Bus Station

Calle 10

School

Calle 12

Gas Station

Park

Farmers Market

La Trinidad

To La Garita

Cementery

N E W S

Rica. Other local attractions are a bird zoo, a butterfly farm, national parks, the spectacular Poás Volcano and much more.

Housing in the Alajuela area is plentiful and very reasonably priced compared to San José. Prices range from about $50,000 to $300,000 and rent begins at about $400.

La Garita, a pleasant area west of the airport on the road to the Central Pacific beach areas of Jacó, Hermosa and Quepos, is said to have one of the best climates in Costa Rica. An average year-round temperature of 72 degrees makes it hard to beat. Many foreigners live in this town. Some large homes come with large parcels of land. We have a friend who rented a home with a pool, a couple of acres of land and a security guard for a very reasonable price. There is also a small zoo and an excellent restaurant called *La Fiesta del Maíz*.

Heredia, the "City of the Flowers," located halfway between San José and Alajuela at the foot of Barva Volcano, is very suitable for living. The surrounding countryside is very beautiful, especially above the city. The hills overlooking the city offer some of the most spectacular views of the Central Valley. The climate is cooler here, especially as you go higher up into the mountains.

This lovely city is only a short distance from San José by car or bus. Three bus lines offer service to San José every five minutes.

We know a lot of foreigners who live in Heredia and commute daily to San José and other neighboring areas.

Heredia's beautiful Central Park.

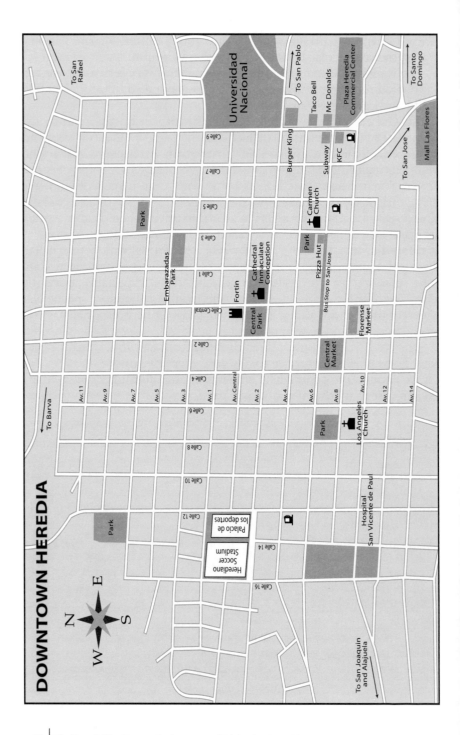

DOWNTOWN HEREDIA

To San Rafael
To Barva

N
E
S
W

To San Joaquin and Alajuela

Universidad Nacional

To San Pablo

Taco Bell
Mc Donalds
Plaza Heredia Commercial Center

To Santo Domingo

Calle 9

Burger King

Subway
KFC

To San Jose

Mall Las Flores

Calle 7

Carmen Church

Calle 5

Park

Calle 3

Embarazadas Park

Cathedral Inmaculate Conception

Park

Pizza Hut

Calle 1

Fortin

Bus Stop to San Jose

Calle Central

Central Park

Florense Market

Calle 2

Central Market

Av. 11
Av. 9
Av. 7
Av. 5
Av. 3
Av. 1
Av. Central
Av. 2
Av. 4
Av. 6
Av. 8
Av. 10
Av. 12
Av. 14

Calle 4

Calle 6

Park

Los Angeles Church

Calle 8

Calle 10

Calle 12

Palacio de los deportes

Herediano Soccer Stadium

Calle 14

Hospital San Vicente de Paul

Calle 16

Heredia is a quaint university town and still retains its rich colonial heritage. Many old Spanish-style buildings made of adobe with tile roofs can still be found near the center of the city. Heredia's beautiful Central Park is one of the finest in the country. It has an imposing old church on one side and a large water fountain. Concerts and music festivals are often held in the park.

Plans call for the construction of a *Paseo de la Cultura*, a cobblestone pedestrian street. This eight-block promenade will run east-west from the National University along the north side of the Central Park and end at the *Palacio de Deportes*. It will pass though the heart of the city's historical district, where many old architectural gems are found.

The new **San Vicente de Paul** public hospital will be finished by 2008. It will replace the old Heredia hospital with the same name.

A group of expatriates hang out at a couple of restaurants in the downtown area. They can be found sitting there every morning. You will find it easy to strike up a conversation. You can meet colorful local characters such as Mr. Goldman, "Search Engine" Bill, Dr. Rick or "Banana Bread" Steve.

In recent years, the city's entertainment and nightlife scene has improved. Bars catering to college students and thrill-seeking tourists dot the area around the National University. Numerous Internet cafés coffee shops and bookstores contribute to the college atmosphere.

Heredia also has unique restaurants offering international fare. **Pane e Vino** is one of the best Italian restaurants in the country. **Paseo de las Flores** is a new shopping mall near the entrance of the city. On Saturday there is a large open-air farmer's market in the south part of the city where you can buy fresh fruits and vegetables at bargain prices.

Many foreign retirees now live in live in Heredia because of the low cost of housing. Here, you may find a lot of affordable homes for less than $100,000. For example, a 1200 square foot home in gated community can be purchased for about $85,000. Our good friend Terry Ortiz purchased a 1,500-square-foot house about two blocks from the huge Hipermás supermarket in San Francisco de Heredia for about $85,000. At present, there is a construction boom in small gated communities on the outskirts of the Heredia area. Heredia is now one of the fastest growing areas in the country.

We know several foreigners who rent nice apartments in downtown Heredia for only a few hundred dollars per month. Carson Sims has a beautiful three-bedroom apartment near the university with all of the amenities. Five or six other Americans live in the same building.

Carson loves his apartment because off its great location. He says, "I can walk around the corner to the pharmacy. I have three supermarkets within four blocks. There are several restaurants and places where my friends gather, all within walking distance. My brother lives in the States and makes more than $500,000 yearly. I would never trade my lifestyle here in Heredia for his."

San Rafael de Heredia is in the hills above the city of Heredia. The most notable feature of this area is the climate, which is considerably cooler than that in San José. Wealthy Costa Ricans and some foreigners live there. The town's most salient feature is a huge church that can be seen from many miles away. The Sunday *feria* or outdoor market is a real plus here.

Our good friend Joe Brennen bought a nice home overlooking San Rafael and the Central Valley for less than $100,000.

If you prefer living in a cooler alpine-like setting, you can find nice homes and cabins all over the pine-covered mountains surrounding the Central Valley. **Los Angeles de Heredia**, to the north of San Rafael, is a favorite with foreigners because of its pastoral setting. The nearby areas around **Monte de la Cruz** and **San José de la Montaña** are all similar but sparsely populated and cooler because of their higher elevation. We know several Americans who live near the mountain towns of **Barva** and **Birrí**.

San Isidro de Heredia is an absolutely spectacular area to the east of Heredia. Gently rolling, verdant hills and meadows surround this Swiss-alpine like town. This area remains green even during the dry season due to its cool climate. Many Americans live in the San Isidro area. Bruce form San Diego just purchased a huge parcel of land with an unbelievable view of the Irazú Volcano. He paid about $80,000 for the land with a farmhouse. He is presently refurbishing it and plans to build his dream home on another part of the property. Our friend Ana Brown built a quaint home in the *Calle Chávez* area of San Isidro.

Another neighboring city, **Cartago**, "just over the hill" from San José, was the former capital of Costa Rica during the colonial period. The city lies 30 minutes to the east of San José, which became the capital after an earthquake destroyed old Cartago. Perhaps the cooler year-round temperatures explain why fewer North Americans reside here. Many Costa Ricans live in Cartago who work in San José, since bus service between the two cities is excellent. The nicest thing about Cartago is its proximity to the beautiful **Orosi Valley**, which lies about 60 minutes east of San José. Viewed from above, this Shangrila-esque valley is breathtaking. The spring-like temperatures on the valley floor

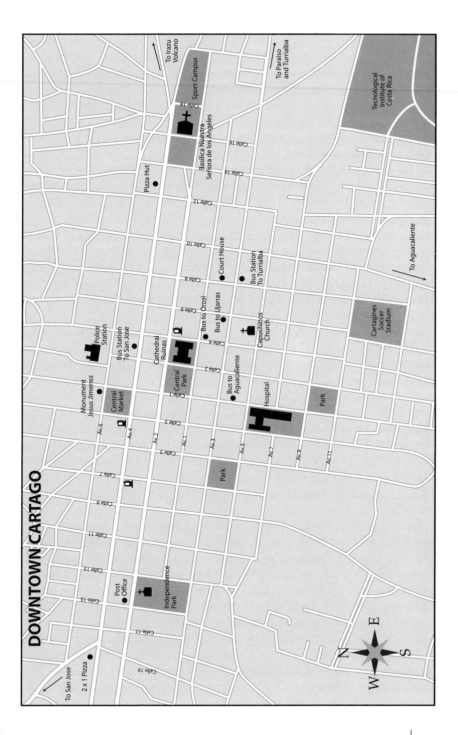

DOWNTOWN CARTAGO

To San Jose

2 x 1 Pizza

Post Office

Independence Park

Monument Jesus Jimenez

Central Market

Central Park

Police Station

Bus Station To San Jose

Cathedral Ruins

Bus to Orosi

Bus to Ujarras

Bus to Aguacaliente

Hospital

Park

Park

Capuchinos Church

Court House

Bus Station To Turrialba

Cartagines Soccer Stadium

Pizza Hut

Basilica Nuestra Señora de los Angeles

Sport Campus

To Irazu Volcano

To Paraiso and Turrialba

Tecnological Institute of Costa Rica

To Aguacaliente

Calle 19
Calle 17
Calle 15
Calle 13
Calle 11
Calle 9
Calle 7
Calle 5
Calle 3
Calle 1
Calle 2
Calle 4
Calle 6
Calle 8
Calle 10
Calle 12
Calle 14
Calle 16
Calle 18

Av. 6
Av. 4
Av. 2
Av. 1
Av. 3
Av. 5
Av. 7
Av. 9
Av. 11

N W E S

stay the same all year. On one end of the valley is a large man-made lake, **Cachí**, and a park where one can participate in many recreational activities, from picnicking to water sports. The lake is fed by the famous **Reventazón** white-water river that runs through the Orosi Valley The area's other main attractions are waterfalls, nature reserves and several hot springs. We consider the Orosí Valley one of the most beautiful spots in the country and are surprised that more foreigners don't choose to live here.

The **Route of the Saints** is an area near Cartago where some foreigners reside. This part of Costa Rica is one of the few places where you can find dairy farms, coffee plantations, log cabins, country inns, pine trees and fresh mountain air. Surrounded by mountains, the towns in this area are all named after different saints, which is how it became known as *La Ruta de los Santos*. Some of the towns are perched precariously on mountainsides while other s are found at the bottom of valleys. **Tarbarca**, **San Ignacio de Acosta**, **San Cristóbal Sur**, **San Marcos de Tarrazú** and **Santa María de Dota** are the major towns along the scenic route.

Grecia, known as the cleanest town in Costa Rica, is also a place worth investigating. The area around the town is absolutely beautiful. Gently rolling, verdant hills and sugarcane fields with a backdrop of spectacular mountains in the distance dominate the surrounding landscape. This tranquil agricultural town, about 30 miles from San José, has a beautiful Central Park, a famous church made of metal panels and an ideal climate. On Sunday evenings many residents stroll around the park just like in the days of old. The hills surrounding the town are full of nice spots to live. Grecia will soon be the home of **Plaza Grecia**, which will house more than 75 shops, a supermarket, food court, movie theaters and be one of the first malls constructed in the area.

Grecia is rapidly becoming a bedroom community for people from San José. Many people choose to live here because of the laid-back lifestyle, cheaper housing prices and other factors. They make the hour-long commute to and from San José by bus or car on weekdays. In the last five years, more than 20 housing projects have been built and close to 1,500 construction permits have been issued in the area around Grecia. There is no indication this trend will change.

Nearby is the town of **Sarchí**, famous for its handicrafts and wood products. Other towns worth checking out for living in the west are **Naranjo**, **San Ramón** and **Palmares**. We know of a few Americans and Europeans who live in and around these laid-back towns and are very happy. Our friend Geno and his Costa Rican wife live on the outskirts of Naranjo in a beautiful 3,000-square-foot home they purchased for less than $100,000.

Some absolutely beautiful areas can be found above the town of San Ramón. Helene from Austria has a hotel and health resort in the **Piedades Sur de San Ramón**. Located in the coastal mountains, it has an absolutely incredible view of the Gulf of Nicoya.

The town of **Palmares** is known for its yearly carnival held every January. The town fills up with Costa Ricans and foreigners in search of a good time.

Nestled in the foothills at the Western edge of the Central Valley at about 2,500 feet in altitude, the picturesque rural town of **Atenas** offers panoramic views of the Central Valley and nearby volcanoes. They town's weather is it's claim to fame. According to National Geographic, Atenas has one the world's best climate.

Atenas has a friendly, small-town, laid-back atmosphere with about 5,000 residents. Another 15,000 people live in the surrounding area. The town is clean with a beautiful central park lined with palm trees. There are schools, banks, several supermarkets, a health care center, an Internet café and good restaurants. About 200 North Americans and Europeans have chosen to live in here. Many Costa Ricans have their country homes in the surrounding Hills. In general, Three-bedroom homes range from $80,000 to $150,000.

Orotina, located over the hill and west of Atenas, is a nice-size little *tico* town. Fruit and nuts is what they do best, but there are plenty of

Downtown Atenas has good shopping.

horse farms and cattle ranches around. This area is gradually developing; there is a lot of land for sale. If you want a quiet Costa Rican town, Orotina could be for you. Few North Americans live here, but there is a bilingual school where some people send kids there from as far away as Jacó Beach.

For those seeking a more relaxed lifestyle, many other small towns and *fincas* (farms) are scattered all over the Central Valley. These places are ideal for people who can do without the excitement found in and around large cities.

The Northern Zone

The quaint mountain town of **Zarcero** is famous for its sculptured bushes. The park in front of Zarcero's church is full of shrubs that have been sculpted into the shapes of arches, animals, people and even an oxcart complete with oxen.

San Carlos, or **Ciudad Quesada** as it is sometimes called, is considered the capital of the country's Northern Zone. We know a few North Americans who own ranches in this area. Almost everything of importance is found within several blocks of the town's main square.

Plaza San Carlos is a new mall with about 143 stores including a supermarket, movie theaters, food court, travel agencies and much more.

Northwest of San Carlos is the beautiful, 48-square-mile, man-made **Lake Arenal**. This area is rapidly becoming popular with foreign residents.

The lake was created to be a reservoir when engineers flooded a large valley. It is surrounded by rolling hills covered with pastures and patches of tropical forest. The very active **Arenal Volcano** can often be seen smoking in the distance.

There are many enjoyable things to do around Arenal. The lake and surrounding area offer excellent fishing, sailing, hiking, windsurfing, mountain biking, bird-watching and other outdoor activities. Land around the lake is readily available. Prices vary per square meter depending on location and views.

Several interesting towns are found in this area. Nearby **Tilarán** is home to a number of foreigners, as are **Nuevo Arenal** and **La Fortuna**. The latter is a quiet town east of the volcano and a good place to view its activity. The *Catarata La Fortuna* is a spectacular waterfall that plummets some 100 feet into a deep pool surrounded by

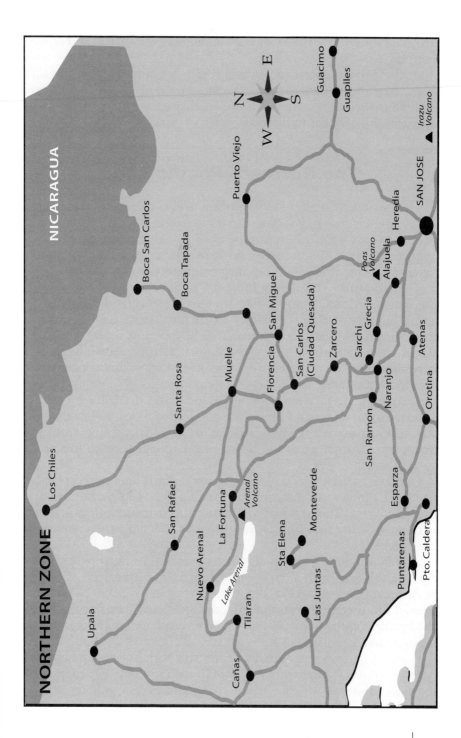

luxuriant foliage. We have met a few foreigners who live in and around Fortuna.

At the **Tabacón Resort** you will find a hot spring in a lush valley at the base of the picture-perfect Arenal Volcano. This is the place to soak your tired bones after a day of participating in one of the many activities this area has to offer.

The Northern Pacific Zone

The northwest region has vast plains and is drier than the Central Valley and central and southern coastal regions. Nevertheless, some of the country's most beautiful beaches, breathtaking views, history, culture and nightlife can be found here. The city of Liberia and the new Tempisque Bridge are the entry points to Guanacaste's beaches.

The capital city of **Liberia**, located 125 miles north of San José on the Pan-American Highway, is considered the heart of **Guanacaste**, and a full-service city. Sometimes called the "white city" because of its architecture, Liberia is considered to be the most colonial of Costa Rica's cities. Due to the area's growing popularity, Liberia is quickly becoming one of the country's largest and most important cities, offering restaurants, hotels, several museums, good shopping, a new mall with movie theaters, a public hospital and the **Daniel Oduber International Airport**. Liberia is a good place to visit while on your way to Guanacaste's many beaches. Our good friend Bud from Las Vegas owns a small farm and is one of the foreigners who live in the Liberia area.

Good news! The Holiday Inn Express recently announced plans to invest $10 million in the construction of a new 120-room hotel and mall in Liberia. The new mall will house approximately 40 stores with parking for 450 cars. Holiday Inn also plans to build a golf course near the hotel.

Another exciting development is the new wild animal park, **Africa Mía**, a 100 -acre open-air zoo with free-roaming animals.

Approximately 40 weekly flights from the United States to Liberia's **Daniel Oduber International Airport** and better infrastructure than the beaches on the southern Nicoya Peninsula have contributed to the development of this area.

A wide range of condos may be found on both isolated and popular beaches. Prices range from $100,000 to $750,000 depending on location. A couple of nice gated communities and golf resorts are

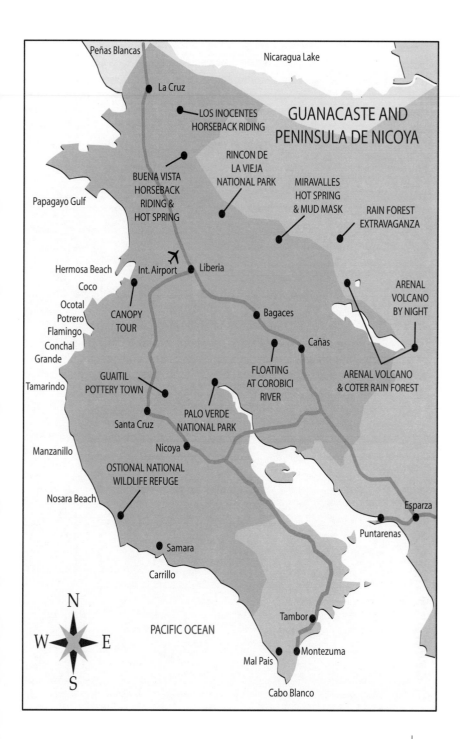

Peñas Blancas

Nicaragua Lake

La Cruz

LOS INOCENTES
HORSEBACK RIDING

GUANACASTE AND
PENINSULA DE NICOYA

RINCON DE
LA VIEJA
NATIONAL PARK

BUENA VISTA
HORSEBACK
RIDING &
HOT SPRING

Papagayo Gulf

MIRAVALLES
HOT SPRING
& MUD MASK

RAIN FOREST
EXTRAVAGANZA

Hermosa Beach

Int. Airport   Liberia

Coco

ARENAL
VOLCANO
BY NIGHT

Ocotal
Potrero
Flamingo
Conchal
Grande

CANOPY
TOUR

Bagaces

Cañas

ARENAL VOLCANO
& COTER RAIN FOREST

Tamarindo

GUAITIL
POTTERY TOWN

FLOATING
AT COROBICI
RIVER

PALO VERDE
NATIONAL PARK

Santa Cruz

Manzanillo

Nicoya

OSTIONAL NATIONAL
WILDLIFE REFUGE

Esparza

Nosara Beach

Puntarenas

Samara

Carrillo

N

W   E

S

PACIFIC OCEAN

Tambor

Montezuma

Mal Pais

Cabo Blanco

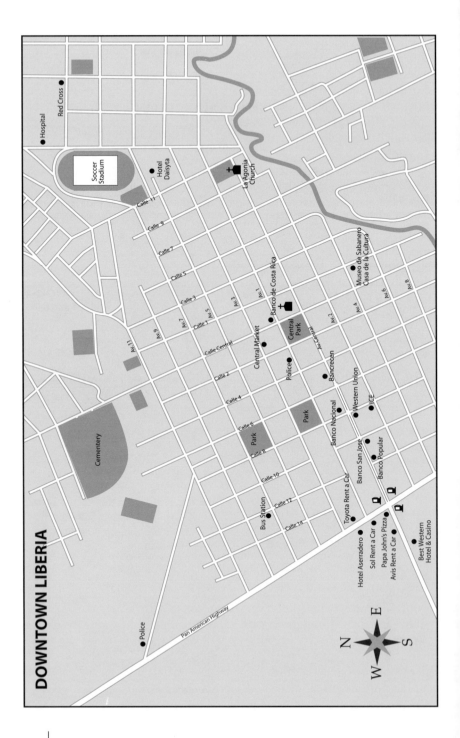

DOWNTOWN LIBERIA

- Red Cross
- Hospital
- Soccer Stadium
- Hotel Daisyta
- La Agonia Church
- Museo de Sabanero Casa de la Cultura
- Calle 11
- Calle 9
- Calle 7
- Calle 5
- Calle 3
- Calle 1
- Av. 1
- Av. 3
- Av. 5
- Av. 7
- Av. 9
- Av. 11
- Av. A
- Av. 2
- Av. 4
- Av. 6
- Av. 8
- Banco de Costa Rica
- Central Market
- Central Park
- Av. Central
- Calle Central
- Police
- Bancrecen
- Calle 2
- Calle 4
- Western Union
- ICE
- Park
- Banco Nacional
- Calle 6
- Park
- Calle 8
- Banco San Jose
- Banco Popular
- Calle 10
- Calle 12
- Bus Station
- Calle 14
- Toyota Rent a Car
- Cementery
- Hotel Aserradero
- Sol Rent a Car
- Papa John's Pizza
- Avis Rent a Car
- Best Western Hotel & Casino
- Police
- Pan American Highway

N E S W

found in this section of the country. Undeveloped beach and ocean-view properties can still be found in some areas.

More than 50 spectacular beaches of all sizes, shapes and colors and clear blue water are found all along the Pacific coast in the Guanacaste Province. This area is sometimes referred to as Costa Rica's "Gold Coast". However, a few of the adjacent beach communities may have too much tranquility for some people or have too much of a resort atmosphere for others.

The area around the peninsula has been the scene of recent development. The spectacular, upscale **Four Seasons Resort** on **Playa Blanca** is found in this area. The new 370-slip **La Marina Papagayo** is being built in Manzanillo Bay in the Gulf of Papagayo. Recently, AOL co-founder Steve Case spent $23 million to build a new 200-acre upscale hotel at nearby **Punta Cacique**. Soon, the construction of the new $15 million Marina Papagayo will begin. It will have 370 slips and will cover about 100 acres.

Playa Hermosa has white sand and offers some of the country's best diving. It lies in the center of a string of four major beaches, all within 30 minutes of each other: **Hermosa**, **Playas del Coco**, **Playa Ocotal** and **Playa Panamá**. Ocean-view lots in the Hermosa area range between $250,000 to $500,000.

Playas del Coco is one of the most developed beach towns in the region but still retains much of its fishing-village atmosphere. It is set in a deep cove with consistently calm waters, making it a safe swimming beach. This charming seaside town is surrounded by emerald-colored hills, offers a variety of water sports and boasts a small international community. The nightlife here is good and includes restaurants, bars, a disco and casinos catering to those looking to have fun. You will also find basic services such as a bank, post office and all kinds of shops. A new marina is planned in this area.

Land in the Coco area ranges from $20 to $200 per square meter. Ocean view lots can be found for under $100,000. Grupo Mapache offers condos for between $50,000 to $75,000 depending on the size and amenities.

Flamingo is one of the finest resort areas in Costa Rica and has the country's second-best full-service marinas, a picture-perfect, mile-long, white-sand beach and turquoise water. It is also Guanacaste's sport fishing capital and offers some of the best sail and marlin fishing in the world. Excellent skin diving and snorkeling are also offered in this area. All of this plus good nightlife and several restaurants have led some to call Flaming the "Acapulco of Costa Rica."

Why Small is Better
By Christopher Howard

The first week of December I visited my home town of Thousand Oaks, California. I had not returned in almost seven years. The first thing I noticed was that a lot had changed dramatically. Due to a construction boom, I could barely recognize some of the areas of town. It seemed like everything had become a great deal more commercial and homogeneous on much larger scale. Everywhere I went there were people driving a whole gamut of Sports Utility Vehicles or as they are more commonly known, SUVS. The streets were filled with gas-guzzling vehicles we rarely see in Costa Rica - the Ford Excursion, the GMC Yukon, the Ford F-250 monster truck and a couple of models of Hummers – to name a few. The latter is similar to military vehicle you see in Iraq which is being blown to pieces by roadside bombs. The version sold in the states is more luxurious with its leather seats, colorful paint and sporty trim. In California it appears that the bigger the vehicle, the better it is and more status a person has. You are defined by what you drive. I guess the car's size reflects the owner's ego. The interesting thing is that very few of the owners use these mammoth vehicles to go off road but only for commuting at a snail's pace on the over crowded freeways, for going to the grocery store and to take the kids to soccer practice.

The freeways are also bigger than ever. They usually have four or five lanes in each direction. Rush hour is almost an all day affair. Traffic begins to get bad at 5:30 in the morning and ends around 8:00 at night. Sprawling, massive, slow-moving traffic jams can extend from Ventura Country in the north to the Mexican border just south of San Diego. These are normal conditions. God forbid if there is an accident! The freeways are indeed bigger but not a faster means of transportation than our pot-hole-filled roads in Costa Rica. Costa Rica's *presas* or traffic jams are small in comparison.

Everything else is super sized up north. There are 24-hour enormous gyms to keep those perfect bodies in shape. Almost every major shopping center and strip mall has a Starbucks, a Subway sandwich shop, a Home Depot, a Wal-Mart, a Target, a big chain vitamin store, a Borders or Barnes & Noble bookstore, a branch of Best Buy and almost every other colossal chain store. There are supermarkets that even dwarf our Hipermás. They have a huge selection of every imaginable food. There are the gigantic bags of potato chips, barrel-sized bottles of soda pop, and a variety of mouth-watering delicacies to stimulate your appetite. No wonder obesity is such a monumental problem in the U.S. Restaurants super size everything. There is even a chain of a pet stores called Pet Co. Most of their stores are as big or larger than a Costa Rican supermarket. I guess most pets are also overweight in the States. It would not surprise me if there is a Weight Watchers for pets.

Then there are the massive Kinkos copy centers. They basically offer every conceivable type of service from making photo copies to using the Internet. Everything is under one roof and they are conveniently opened 24-hours. These stores are extremely handy for the traveling business person. I accessed my e-mail everyday by using one of their computers. I was going to use the local public library's computer services at $5 an hour but there was an hour limit The price at Kinkos proved to be astronomical. I paid $12 per hour to use a state of the art credit card device connected directly to the computer. The cost of the average net café in Costa Rica is about a dollar an hour. However, none of the Internet cafés in Costa Rica that I have seen feature new Dell computers like the ones at Kinkos.

Everything else is geared towards large scale consumption. People seem very happy and caught up in their fast-paced lifestyles of expensive SUVS, the "shop until you drop" mentality and living in their palatial upscale housing tracts which seem like ritzy suburban ghettos where every house looking almost exactly like it had been cut from the same mold.

After a few days of experiencing everything on the large scale, I began to yearn for my simple down-sized lifestyle in petite Costa Rica. People here seem to be a lot happier with much less. The average person here is materially poorer than the average American, but their lives are far more richer. Here people seem to live with *gusto* (enjoyment) and *sabor* (a flavor or spice). In Costa Rica every day can be filled with adventure and exciting activities. Sure we have the malls and a dose of U.S. culture but we also have a lot more little things which truly make life immensely more worthwhile. People up north exist, we live the pure life on a much smaller scale. The phrase, *"¡Pura vida!,"* says it all.

There is an abundance of real estate, including condominiums dotting the surrounding hills. Land prices range from about $150 to $350 per square meter. A 1000 meter square lot can be found for about $500,000.

Golf lovers will be happy here, since there are three golf courses located nearby.

Flamingo attracts retired foreigners as well people with children because of all it has to offer. The Country Day School, one of the country's most prestigious private primary and secondary institutions, operates a school the area.

Neighboring **Portrero** and **Sugar** beaches offer calm waters, ocean views and breathtaking sunsets. Many foreigners reside around these neighboring areas.

Brasilito and **Conchal**, south of Flamingo, are other beaches worth checking out. Conchal is famous for its powdery sand, made of small white seashells. It is also the home of the all-inclusive 18-hole **Playa Conchal Golf Resort**. There are a lot of high-priced condominiums and townhouses for sale at the resort.

Tamarindo ,often referred to now as *"Tamargringo"*, is a beach town overlooking a long stretch of beautiful beach and a popular spot among surfers. It has the most developed tourist infrastructure in Guanacaste. The foreign community has given birth to many restaurants, hotels and a variety of stores for all tastes that line the main road. The town is very cosmopolitan, with residents from all over the world adding a very exciting cultural diversity to the area.

Property and everything else has become rather expensive in the Tamarindo area because of its popularity. Condos and homes can cost from $200,000 to $700,000. Homes about five minutes from town can be purchased for about $150,000 plus.

Plaza Tamarindo is the town's new mall. It will eventually be the largest mall built in a beach community, boasting 50 businesses and a couple of restaurants.

South of Tamarindo is **Hacienda Pinilla Resort**, which has a championship golf course and offers every imaginable water sport. **Junquillal** is another fast-developing area and has a white-sand, Blue-Flag beach. Our good Costa Rican friend, Ricardo Lara, is building a small real estate development in Junquillal.

Nosara is an attractive area to live if you are a nature lover. The white-sand beach stretches for almost two miles. A flourishing expatriate community gives the town a slightly California-like flavor. Small U.S.-style restaurants and services exist for the growing foreign community. A deluxe, world-class yoga retreat is found just outside of town.

Sámara and **Carrillo** south of Nosara, are laid-back beaches really worth exploring. Both beaches are located on bays and good for swimming. Property is still affordable since the area is not as developed as some of the beaches to the north.

Sámara has a small fishing village-like atmosphere with a few good restaurants, hotels and nightlife. Carrillo, the southern most of the two beaches is an exceptionally beautiful, palm-lined, white-sand beach on a curved bay, yet it lacks the development of Sámara.

South of Carrillo there are several unspoiled beaches such as **Playa Coyote**. However, access is very difficult during the rainy season because of the rivers that have to be forded.

Malpaís, immediately northwest of **Cabo Blanco** near the southern tip of the Nicoya Peninsula, is a surfer's paradise. It has been featured in numerous surfing documentaries and magazines and attracts surfers from all over the world. Even Leonardo DiCaprio went there to surf and relax before a recent Academy Awards ceremony.

The word *Malpaís* means "bad country" in Spanish and is a misnomer. Nothing could be further from the truth. There are several beaches at which to swim, dive and snorkel, though the areas main attraction are its unique conditions for surfing. This isolated area is becoming very popular with some foreigners because of its scenery and incredible sunsets. Some foreigners have settled in this small town permanently and opened small businesses catering to tourists.

To the north lies **Playa Santa Teresa**. Its seemingly endless beach is one of the best places for surfing on the entire Nicoya Peninsula. Nearby **Playa Manzanillo** is also becoming popular with surfers and

Samara is one of Costa Rica's most beautiful beaches.

expatriates. We have a German friend who has lived there for several years and really loves the area.

Montezuma, a remote little fishing village near the southern tip of the Nicoya Peninsula, has almost perfect beaches with clear-blue water just right for bodysurfing. There are miles of beaches with tide pools and even a tropical 50-foot waterfall nearby. Fortunately, Montezuma and its surroundings have not been destroyed by developers. The area is teeming with birds, monkeys and all sorts of exotic wildlife.

This cozy town is a magnet for hip and Bohemian types interested in alternative lifestyles. European backpackers, yoga enthusiasts and people in search of something new visit this area. In this town one can either hangout at the beach or at a local restaurant. The Sano Banano is a vegetarian restaurant where many locals and tourists congregate. There is property available in the area. Jimmy, a 45-year old retiree from Boston, told us he moved there 10 years ago and bought a small home because he found living in San José too expensive. He gets by on about $800 or less monthly—beer included.

Tambor is located on a deep circular bay and is good for swimming and other outdoor activities. The all-inclusive **Hotel Barceló Playa Tambor** is located here. The nearby **Delfines Golf Club** also attracts many visitors. We know a few Americans who reside in the Tambor area and there are some excellent real estate buys. Most live at the **Tango Mar** development three miles southwest of Tambor or in and around the newly developed Tambor Hills area.

Two of our good friends from California, have a beautiful home in the Tango Mar development. They lived at the beach for a few years but found it too laid back for them. They now live in a beautiful condo in Escazú with a panoramic of the Central Valley. They rent their beach home and can pay most of their expenses with the money it generates.

The Central Pacific

The Central Pacific is one of Costa Rica's jewels. It extends from Puntarenas in the north to the Barú River in the south. The closest and most accessible beaches to San José are found in this area. The beaches are sunny year-round, the weather is hot and the ocean warm. Whether you want to retire or just live in a tropical paradise, the Central Pacific Coast has something for you. Some of the outdoor activities the area offers are: golfing, sport fishing, yachting, canopy tours, river

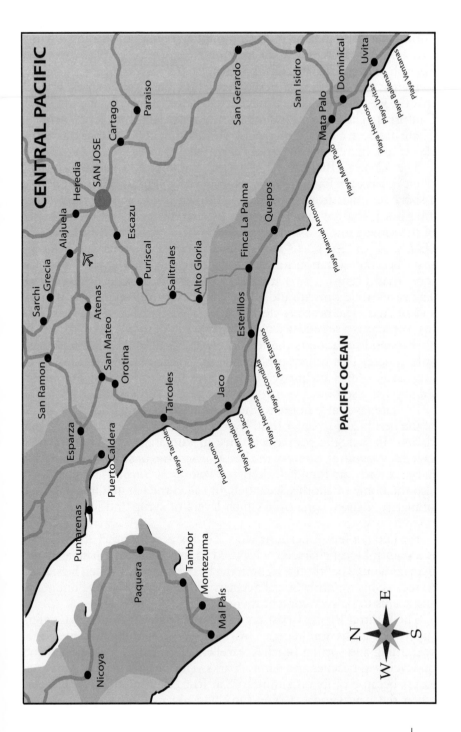

PACIFIC OCEAN

San Gerardo
San Isidro
Dominical
Uvita
Playa Hermosa
Playa Uvitas
Playa Ballenas
Playa Ventanas
Mata Palo
Playa Mata Palo
Paraiso
Cartago
Quepos
Finca La Palma
Playa Manuel Antonio
SAN JOSE
Heredia
Escazu
Puriscal
Salitrales
Alto Gloria
Esterillos
Playa Esterillos
Playa Escondida
Alajuela
Grecia
Sarchi
Atenas
San Mateo
Orotina
Jaco
Playa Hermosa
Playa Jaco
Playa Herradura
Punta Leona
Tarcoles
Playa Tarcoles
San Ramon
Esparza
Puerto Caldera
Puntarenas
Paquera
Tambor
Montezuma
Mal País
Nicoya

N E
W S

rafting, parasailing, hang gliding, mountain biking, snorkeling, diving, kayaking, bird watching and a lot more. There are even places to study Spanish and practice yoga in this area.

Here is one expat's take on the Central Pacific: "It was our experience that the west coast was very much like where we came from San Diego, California. The ocean was similar to that of California (but warmer). There has been a lot of American-style investment here. Prices, as you'd expect, are higher as you get closer to the water. "

The Central Pacific's largest city, Puntarenas (meaning "sandy point"), sits on a long, narrow peninsula or spit in the Gulf of Nicoya, a short 62 miles from San José. The town itself is about three miles long but just a few blocks wide. It is also the capital of the province of the same name. Costa Ricans affectionately refer to **Puntarenas** as "*El Puerto*" or "the port." Due to its closeness Puntarenas has been the main beach destination for Costa Ricans from the Central Valley for more than a century. *Ticos* still flock here to spend the day or weekend. The seven-mile brown-sand, Blue Flag beach runs along the narrow spit of land. The beach is cleaned and raked every day. The **Paseo de los Turistas** is a seaside walkway with a series of souvenir kiosks, open-air bars and restaurants that dot the waterfront and add to the city's atmosphere. This tourist promenade is also the place where dozens of huge cruise ships anchor yearly. It buzzes with activity day and night. Puntarenas also boasts year-round spectacular sunsets.

Puntarenas is also home to the country's only aquarium, and is one of the best places to savor fresh seafood, including *chuchecas* (ink-black clams). In fact, the people who live in Puntarenas are affectionately called *chuchequeros*. Some of the best *marisquerías* or seafood restaurants in the country are found all along the *Paseo de los Turistas*. Puntarenas is also the home of another local delight called the Churchill, a beverage similar to a snow cone over which layers of syrup and ice cream are poured.

We know a few Americans who call this port city their home. Bill, is a colorful local character who used to live in the San José area and manage a huge penthouse right in the heart of the city. When he started to receive his monthly Social Security checks he moved to Puntarenas and seems to be very content there.

The Central Pacific Coast region to the south of Puntarenas offers superb locations for living. This area has something for everyone: swimming and surfing beaches, excellent sport fishing, developed and undeveloped beaches and natural parks. The area is a magnet for beach lovers because of its proximity to San José. Its attraction will increase when the new Ciudad Colón-Orotina-Caldera Highway is finished.

Construction of this 18-mile highway is scheduled to begin soon. The new highway should reduce the driving time from San José to the Central Pacific beaches by about an hour.

Four miles north of Jacó, at Bahía Herradura, is the upscale **Los Sueños Marriott Ocean and Golf Resort**, considered the premier resort and marina in the area. Los Sueños is set on a 1,100-acre property surrounded by protected rainforest. The largest full-service marina between Mexico and Chile is found here. This 200-slip marina can accommodate vessels from 20 to 200 feet with all of the amenities international boaters expect. For more information about the marina, call 1-866-865-9759 toll-free or see **www.lsrm.com**.

In addition to the boat facilities, the marina offers restaurants, bars, a supermarket, gift shop, marine supplies and concessions for jet skis, kayaks, water skiing, scuba diving, snorkeling and other recreational activities. There is also an 18-hole, par-72 championship golf course, a 201-room palatial Marriott Hotel, home sites and deluxe condominiums for sale and a number of nature walks. All of the condos and hotel feature are done in elegant Spanish colonial-style architecture. Condo prices start at about $500,000 and are rising. Some affluent visitors have been known to visit Los Sueños and like it so much they never left.

If you like a lot of action, good waves and partying, we recommend **Jacó Beach**. Lately, it has be come known as "*Jacopulco*" due to the many high-rise condominiums under construction.

Jacó is conveniently located just 72 miles from San José. This Key-West-like town is a very popular weekend retreat with both *ticos* and foreigners since it is only about two hours from San José. With a floating population of about 40,000, it is by far the most developed beach town in the Central Pacific region and has excellent tourist infrastructure. An eclectic mixture of foreigners and locals gives Jacó a sort of cosmopolitan feeling.

Because of its fame, Jacó is usually packed on most summer weekends, holidays such as Easter Week and special occasions such as surf tournaments. Lodging ranges from four-star hotels to small, inexpensive cabins for locals on a tight budget. Boredom will not be a factor here.

There are pizza parlors, international restaurants, handicraft shops, bars, discos and late-night spot where you can party until the wee hours of the morning. Water sports, especially surfing and sport fishing, attract scores of people to the area. You can also explore the natural wonders of nearby forests on foot, horseback or a canopy ride through the treetops.

The Jacó community's new **Plaza Coral Mall** features 60 stores, a three-screen international movie theater, a food court and two formal restaurants. The new mall will cater to both tourists and local residents. A new condo generally costs around $200,000 to $400,000.

Just two miles down the coast from Jacó lies **Playa Hermosa**. Do not confuse this idyllic surf community with the beach with the same name in Guanacaste. *Hermosa* ("Beautiful"), as it s name indicates, is protected as a national wild life refuge. Because of good year-round waves, most people come to Hermosa to surf. Many international surfing tournaments are held here every year. However, there is plenty to keep non-surfers busy, especially at nearby bustling Jacó.

There has been a lot of building in this area, especially 10 miles south in **Esterillos Este**. This area has long, uncrowded beaches surrounded by African palm trees, estuaries and mangroves. **Del Pacifico** is a huge project in the Esterillos Este vicinity. Other nice beaches between Esterillos Este and Quepos are **Bejuco**, **La Palma**, **Banderas** and **Palo Seco**. The town of **Parrita**, where you can find almost any service you may need, is also found to the south of Esterillos Este. Parrita boasts a long seven-mile beach. There are a few new housing developments being touted in this area.

The **Quepos** and adjoining **Manuel Antonio** area is one of the country's most popular tourist destinations, and offers some of the most beautiful beach resorts in the world. Few other places in Costa Rica offer so much in one spot. You will find endless activities to keep you busy in this quaint beach town. Some of the areas most prominent features are white sand, paradise - like beaches, beautiful hidden coves, abundant wildlife, good nightlife, fine cuisine, unforgettable sunsets from many vantage points and even a chance to mingle with the Hollywood crowd at a five-star hotel. The area offers other activities such as rafting on either the Naranjo or Savegre rivers, horseback riding, four-wheeling, hiking and canopy tours in the incredible mountains that serve as a backdrop to the area.

Most foreigners live in and around the town of Quepos and along the road leading to **Manuel Antonio National Park**, just a few kilometers south and over the hill. The park is nestled on some 682-plus hectares of land. The park receives more visitors than any other park or reserve in the country. If you are a nature lover you can always explore the national park or go to one of its pristine white-sand beaches that slope down from tropical forests into the clear blue waters of the Pacific Ocean. The park teems with paradisiacal flora and fauna.

Downtown Quepos is a charming beach community surrounded by forested hills facing the Pacific Ocean. It is replete with bars, boutiques, eateries, a mini-bookstore, good nightlife and a whole lot more to keep local foreigners entertained. Quepos is also known for its sport fishing scene and is the site of several yearly tournaments. Hotels, businesses and even an old airplane converted into a restaurant are scattered around the hills and line the highway between Quepos and Manuel Antonio. Many of the hotels are situated on large properties that extend into the forest. It comes as no surprise that the area's beauty, popularity and abundant activities have made real estate very expensive. Land prices are high due to the popularity of the area.

The infrastructure is good here with a public hospital, an airport for small planes and limited docking facilities. Construction of a new 200- slip $11 million marina began in 2006. On the downside, the area between Quepos and Manuel Antonio National Park has been over built and there is little land available near the coast. Consequently, more and more people are purchasing land in the spectacular foothills and mountains to the east.

One of the best opportunities we have seen are the spectacular ocean view lots in **Manuel Antonio Heights**. For more information call toll-free **1-888-581-1786** or e-mail **robert@ costaricaretirementvacationproperties.com**.

Matapalo located about 15 miles south of Quepos, between Quepos and Dominical, is a little town with a laid-back beach community and a virtually unspoiled beach. The long beach is perfect for walking, horseback riding or just soaking up the rays. A lot of beachfront property can still be this area. There are also many beautiful homes and lots with ocean views in the foothills behind Matapalo.The town has a few hotels, restaurants and places to buy basic groceries.

We know quite a few foreigners who live here. Our good friend Robert Klenz has built a large equestrian development called the **Hills of Portalón** in this mountains high above this area.

All of the property between Quepos and Dominical will increase dramatically in value when the last unpaved stretch of the costal highway is finally paved with two years.

The South Pacific

The area extending from Dominical to the Osa Peninsula all the way to the Panamanian border on the Pacific coast is called the South Pacific. The spectacular **Corcovado National Park**, **Drake's Bay** and **Isla del Caño** are a few of this areas salient features.

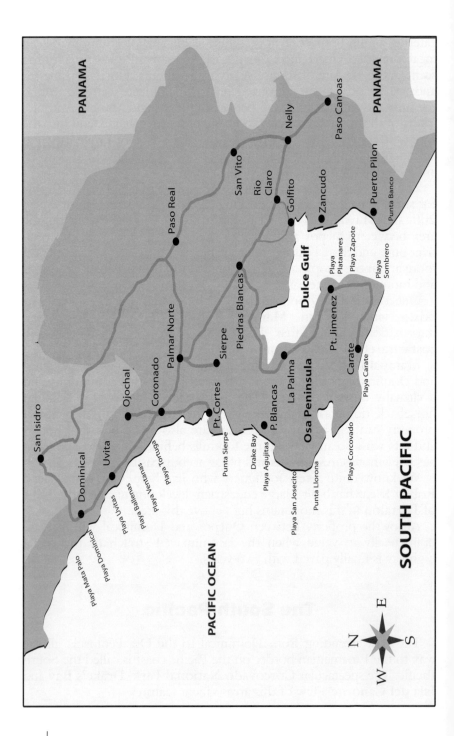

A new international airport intended to boost tourism in this region of Costa Rica will be constructed in the community of Sierpe at the entrance to the Osa Peninsula or in Palmar Sur, the *Coordinador General de Aeropuertos* announced recently. The government expects the airport, whatever its exact location, to invigorate the entire region. The government wants to promote economic, commercial and mostly tourism development. Once the airport is built here, more people will come, just like what happened when Daniel Oduber Airport was built in Liberia, Guanacaste.

Another exciting development designed to improve the area's infrastructure is the construction of the new 28-mile stretch of the coastal highway between Quepos and Dominical scheduled to start in 2006. It will have three and four lanes in some places and a bike path. Once this stretch is completed, more people will come to the area and property values will increase, so now is a good time to invest.

Dominical, located 46 kilometers (30 miles) south of Quepos, is a tiny laid-back resort town surrounded by some of the most breathtaking coastal scenery Costa Rica has to offer. The beautiful **Barú River** winds its way down from the surrounding mountains and empties into the sea at the north end of town.

This area is reminiscent of California's Big Sur because of its spectacular coastline and towering mountains that meet the sea. Dominical is also famous for its long beach, spectacular shoreline, mountain backdrop, panoramic views and excellent surfing. One of the area's claims to fame is that it was used as a backdrop to shoot the 1996 Sport's Illustrated swim suite issue.

Spectacular Playa Dominical

There are unlimited options for adventure and sight-seeing in this pristine area of Costa Rica. Several spectacular jungle waterfalls are found here. **Pozo Azul** is a 30-foot waterfall close to the village of **Dominicalito**. The Barú River Falls, also known as **Santo Cristo** or **Nauyaca Falls**, is located in the mountains above Dominical. This series of waterfalls is considered one of the most picturesque in Costa Rica, if not all of Central America. It cascades down into a huge natural pool that is 20 feet deep and perfect for swimming. The surrounding area is verdant rainforest with abundant wildlife. The mountains between Dominical and Ojochal are filled with dozens of smaller waterfalls. Some properties in this area have their own private waterfall.

The town of **Dominical** is less developed than the beaches in the Central Pacific area, but this is changing quickly. Dominical itself is a small laid-back town with an unpaved main street, which runs right down to the ocean. On either side of the street are a few restaurants and bars, such as the **San Clemente Bar and Grill**, some of which offer limited entertainment. Much like Montezuma, this town attracts those seeking an alternative lifestyle. It is not unusual to see people practicing the Oriental art of tai chi or yoga on the beach. Dominical is a charming little town with friendly people who say hello and greet you with smiles.

Land prices are lower than the Quepos-Manuel Antonio area but are rising fast. There are large homes with incredible views that cost in the hundreds of thousands of dollars dotting the steep hills above the beach. Many expatriates have started businesses or are buying land in the area.

Dominicalito Beach has calm water for swimming. Spectacular views of the coastline may be seen from nearby Punta Dominical.

Just nine miles to the south of Dominical is **Uvita**. A smaller and slower-paced town than Dominical with a good swimming beach. At low tide you can walk out to the point the shape of a whale's tail. Many foreigners live in the hills above **Punta Uvita**, just as they do in Dominical. The setting with mountains in the background is very similar to Dominical. The highway was just paved from Dominical all the way to Palmar Norte, making this once virgin part of the coast very accessible. Prices are still affordable and there are plenty of mountainside homes and lots with spectacular views. We have a friend who just purchased a beautiful mountaintop home overlooking the beach.

Some of the activities available in the Uvita area are kayaking, snorkeling, horseback riding, waterfall and jungle hikes, beachcombing and a lot more.

About 10 years ago I moved to Costa Rica. Initially I found work as a tour guide in the San Jose area. Eventually my work took me to all corners of the country. On one of my tours I visited Dominical and the areas to the south. I was overwhelmed by the sheer beauty of the area. Unlike Guanacaste in the north this area stays green and tropical all year. It is set against a backdrop of towering mountains covered with a lush tropical rain forest that come down to the sea. The surrounding area is teeming with wildlife, has several spectacular waterfalls and abundant fauna.

Eventually I discovered the hamlet of Ojochal. Since the village is set off the highway you could drive by and never know it existed. At the turnoff to the town there is a small general store, real estate office and police station. As you drive along the bumpy dirt road about two kilometers the town starts to emerge. There is a small river on the left with homes and restaurants along both sides of the road. There is even an internet café and a couple of small hotels.

I spent some time there and absolutely feel in love with the area. The town has a thriving community of Costa Ricans, French Canadians, Europeans and Americans. There are actually people form 19 countries living here. The town literally has an international flavor. Foreigners have opened a score of excellent restaurants. A gourmet would be in heaven. There is even a houseboat restaurant where you can dine at the mouth of a nearby river. The cook is from Belgium and the food is absolutely incredible. My friends and I go there to waych the sunset and to eat dinner.

Exo-tica restaurant in Ojochal is another real treat. The place only seats about 25 people but it so popular with the locals that without a reservation, you'll be turned away. I take all of my tour groups there and they leave saying it was one of the best meals they ever tasted.

It didn't take me long to find great house with a view and pool which I decided to buy. It also has another large building lot above it. As time goes buy my love for Ojochal and the surrounding area has grown even bigger. I've been working as a tour guide and really know the area inside out. In fact, I now consider my self an expert. People come to me when they want private tours or want orientation.

The best part of living in my village a re the great people and sense of a tight-knit community. We share and do so much together from community projects to a myriad of group activities. One night we may gather at the local pizza parlor. Another time we get together at somebody's home for a game of Trivial Pursuit. On other occasions we may have a Latin Dance night. We even have a rodeo once a year. Not only do we share activities with the people in Ojochal but get to get together with friends in the neighboring towns of Dominical and Uvita a few kilometers to the North.

We never get bored here. Outdoor activities abound. There is good swimming at nearby Pinuela and Ventanas beaches. The latter is in a secluded cove with rock formation which have five giant blow holes. At Tortuga Beach you can see turtles lay their eggs on the shore. The area is also good for whale watching at certain times of the year. If the ocean isn't your cup of tea you can swim in one offthe mountain streams and soak under a gushing waterfall. There is a lot more to do here. Hiking, fishing, kayaking, snorkeling, bird-watching, hiking and excellent surfing are just a few of the many activities from which to choose. You can even take a boat trip up the Sierpe and Terraba Rivers or to to Caño Island 17 kilometers off shore. The island has coral reefs and is good for snorkeling. The waters teem with all sorts of creatures like moray eel, tropical fish, dolphins, sperm, pilot and humpback whales.

The new highway from Dominical south links all of our communities and makes travel easy. Everyday the local infrastructure improves. New businesses like hardware stores small supermarkets, restaurants, gas station and small hotel have sprung up in the area.

For essentials we either travel forty-five minutes north through the beautiful mountains to the town of San Isidro or south to Palmar Norte or Puerto Cortez. Panam is only a couple of hours to the south and has excellent shopping.

Plans call for an International Airport to be somewhere to the south of us in the not too distant future. Also the lst stretch of the costal highway from Quepos to Dominical will be completed soon. All of these improvements should makeour area more accessible, really spur development and boost property values.

Just to the south of Uvita is the new **South Pacific Hospitality Center** and **South Pacific Real Estate Services** office. They are about 200 meters south of the new shopping complex. The people there will answer any of your questions about the area and give you a free orientation.

The **Tortuga/Ojochal/Cinco Ventanas** area is also suited for living. Ojochal, about 20 miles south of Dominical, is a quaint country village with a nice mixture of *ticos*, French-Canadians and other foreigners. The town is set offf the highway and easy to miss. The village has a surprising number of excellent restaurants owned by locals from all over the world. **Exotica Restaurant**, virtually in the middle of the jungle, has some of the best cuisine I have ever tasted in all of my travels. The owners are French Canadian and really take pride in the gourmet food they prepare. The **Manglar Sur** is a restaurant on a houseboat in this area and serves food that is just as good. The clients on my tours have eaten at both of these restaurants and say the food is as good as you'll find in any first-class restaurant back home.

Although this area is somewhat off the beaten track, DirectTV and other forms of entertainment are available. The members of this community are tight-knit and share many joint activities together. Annie Drake, a local tour expert and resident says, "There is something happening almost every night here. There is a pot luck dinner, party or 'get-to-gether' once or twice a week."

Steep coastal mountains with tropical rainforest serve as a backdrop for this beautiful part of the country. The area's popularity is growing as word spreads about all the natural wonders it has to offer. The beach at *Cinco Ventanas* got it's name because of five spectacular 50-foot, tunnel-like blow holes in the rocks. This beach is truly a work of nature and has to be seen to be believed. **Playa Tortuga**, **Playa Hermosa** and **Playa Ballena** are other spectacular beaches in the area.

Area activities include good fishing, snorkeling, boat and river tours, bird watching, horseback riding, kayaking and boat trips to **Caño Island** and nearby **Drake Bay**. You can even watch whales and see turtles lay their eggs on the beach.

Land prices in this area of Costa Rica start at about $100,000 per acre depending on the proximity to the beach.

San Isidro de El General, a half-hour inland from Dominical and located along the Pan-American Highway, offers a warm climate and inexpensive housing. It is considered the fastest-growing city in Central America. **Monte General** is the city's new shopping mall. It has a Megasuper supermarket, Universal department store, three movie

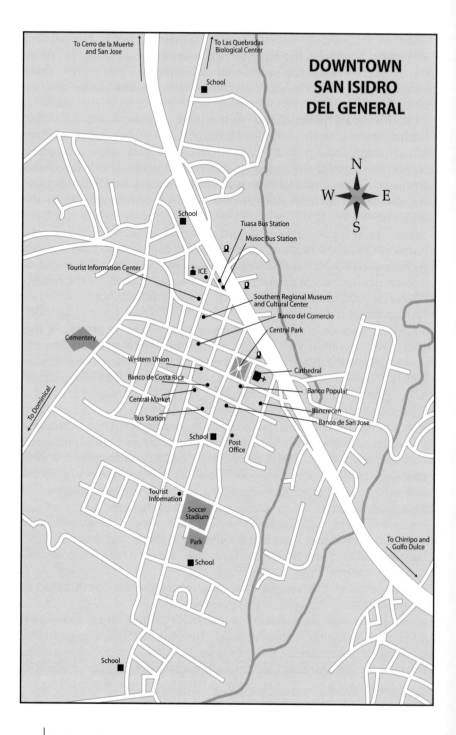

To Cerro de la Muerte and San Jose

To Las Quebradas Biological Center

DOWNTOWN SAN ISIDRO DEL GENERAL

N
W E
S

School

School

Tourist Information Center

Tuasa Bus Station

Musoc Bus Station

ICE

Southern Regional Museum and Cultural Center

Banco del Comercio

Central Park

Cementery

Western Union

Banco de Costa Rica

Central Market

Bus Station

To Dominical

Cathedral

Banco Popular

Bancrecen

Banco de San Jose

School

Post Office

Tourist Information

Soccer Stadium

Park

School

To Chirripo and Golfo Dulce

School

screens, nine restaurants in a food court, a Scotia Bank, 60 stores and 220 parking spaces. The mall is the anchor for the large Monte General residential community adjacent to it.

San Isidro is off the beaten path, but some foreigners make this small city their permanent home. Real estate is reasonably priced in comparison with some of the areas in the Central Valley. There are many ocean-view properties in the mountains along the highway between San Isidro and Dominical.

Despite being small and laid back, **Puerto Jiménez** is the largest town on the Osa Peninsula. It has a population of about 6,000. During the gold rush, 1980s Puerto Jiménez resembled a town out of the Wild West. Nowadays thing have calmed down and the town has become popular with the backpacking set, surfers, lovers of adventure tourism and devotees of ecotourism. Its location on the **Golfo Dulce** Puerto Jiménez and its environs makes perfect for snorkeling, scuba diving and kayaking. One of the nearby attractions is **Corcovado National Park**. *National Geographic* claims it is one of two places in the word with the most biological diversity.

There are a few expats living in and around Puerto Jiménez. With the exception of a few small hotels, bars, restaurants, Internet services and public transportation, there is not much infrastructure found here. The roads are in very bad shape.

San Isidro is the largest city in southern Costa Rica.

Some expatriates live around the port of **Golfito** on Golfo Dulce Bay. The town is sort of drab and somewhat abandoned. However, the surrounding scenery is beautiful. There are several restaurants and gringo hangouts in town where you can strike up a conversation with local expats. Sport fishing and surfing attract many tourists to this area. As one local foreign resident points out, "The town does have basic services like banks, a hospital, courthouse, a couple of supermarkets, butchers and doctor's offices. Transportation is decent with a small airfield ferry transportation to Puerto Jiménez and Zancudo and plenty of taxis and buses. Panama is not far away and a great place to find good shopping."

Golfito started out as a banana port but was abandoned when the United Fruit Company closed down its operation. Over the years, the government has made attempts to help the local economy. In 1990 it opened the **Depósito Libre** or Free Trade Zone. Many *ticos* make the long journey to Golfito since appliances and other items may be purchased for much less than in San José. Foreign residents and tourists with a passport can also purchase an ample variety of goods at the duty-free warehouses.

Plans call for a world-class marina and condo complex that will improve infrastructure and change the face of this area. Local residents have a lot to be excited about. The Costa Rican Tourism Institute (ICT) and the Commission for Marinas approved the installation of two marinas in the southern Pacific port of Golfito. The **Banana Bay Marina** will have 16 slips and the **Bahía Escondida** or **Golfito Marina** will have 217 slips for boats up to 150 feet. This marina will have a hotel, stores, two restaurants, a health club, a yacht club, 84 condominiums with prices ranging from $300,000 to $800,000 and 280 residential units. The ICT approval is long awaited and a big boost for the economy of the struggling port town of Golfito.

Because of this some people expect the Golfito area and the town of Puerto Jiménez to be the sites of the next land boom in Costa Rica. The ICT also considers the Puerto Jiménez area suitable for a future marina project.

Playa Zancudo ("mosquito beach" in Spanish), a slow-paced beach community about 20 kilometers south of Golfito, is home to some foreigners. However, you'll need about two-hours to make the drive over an unpaved road. During the rainy season you will need a four-wheel-drive-vehicle. Some foreigners come only for the winter months while others live in the area year-round. Several bars and open-air restaurants serve as gathering places for expats. Zancudo's uncrowded beach has gentle surf and is very good for swimming. Medium-priced housing may be found here.

Jim, our friend from Baltimore, makes this town his winter home. He has built a small house and even has DirectTV. When he leaves to go back to work in the United States, he has a caretaker oversee his home.

Pavones, 40 kilometers south of Golfito, is a surfer's mecca, renowned for having the longest left-breaking waves in the world. The surrounding scenery is down-right spectacular. Surfers from all over the world are attracted to this area. Everything including the nightlife revolves around the surfing scene. Numerous North Americans and foreigners own large *fincas* (ranches or farms) in this area while others live in the more isolated areas. Our Costa Rican dentist, a sometimes surfer, has a vacation home in Pavones. Because of the excellent surf some say Pavones has the potential to become another Jacó.

The Caribbean Zone

The 150-mile Caribbean coast extends from the border with Nicaragua in the north to the border with Panama in the south.

Puerto Limón is one of Costa Rica's two important ports. It is the cradle of the country's Afro-Caribbean culture and its Creole language. Few Americans live in this city.

The Caribbean coast below Puerto Limón has many places to live. This area particularly appeals to young people who like beautiful tropical settings, surfing, reggae music and the Afro-Caribbean culture. A large colony of foreigners from Europe and the United States live here.

The village of **Cahuita**, about 25 miles south of the city of Limón, is one of the most popular spots on the Atlantic coast. It lies next to **Cahuita National Park** and has one of the best beaches in the country. Despite a rising crime rate, it is still considered one of the most laid-back places anywhere in Costa Rica. Many Europeans own or operate hotels in and around Cahuita.

Puerto Viejo, about 12 miles south of Cahuita, is a funky town with a Jamaican-like ambience. It is a great place for lovers of the Caribbean lifestyle and ocean activities such as snorkeling and surfing. There are some lovely swimming beaches in this area with good waves and crystal- clear water. A large number of Europeans and a few Americans live here.

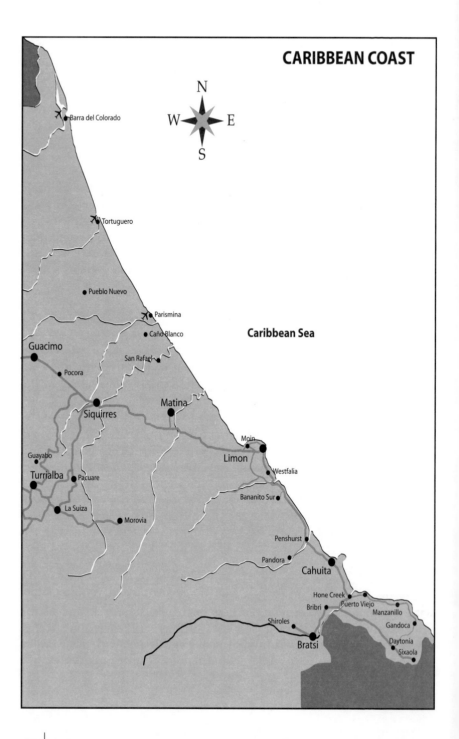

CARIBBEAN COAST

N
W · E
S

Barra del Colorado

Tortuguero

Pueblo Nuevo

Parismina

Caño Blanco

San Rafael

Caribbean Sea

Guacimo

Pocora

Siquirres

Matina

Moin

Limon

Westfalia

Guayabo

Turrialba

Pacuare

Bananito Sur

La Suiza

Morovia

Penshurst

Pandora

Cahuita

Hone Creek

Bribri

Puerto Viejo

Manzanillo

Gandoca

Shiroles

Daytonia

Sixaola

Bratsi

Land prices start at about $100 per square meter and are rising in value. Nice homes can be found for $150,000. There are no condo projects in this area.

A few kilometers south are **Punta Uva**, with a gorgeous beach for swimming, and the fishing village of **Manzanillo**.

The surrounding landscape is lushly tropical, and wildlife such as howler monkeys and iguanas abound. This area is spectacular and undeveloped—but not for long.

The Caribbean coast sounds very enticing; however, the abundant year-round rainfall and humidity make most North Americans, Canadians and other foreigners choose to live on the drier west coast.

If you live in a beach or rural area, life is generally less expensive and more tranquil than in San José. People living on a small budget might consider this factor before choosing a permanent place to settle.

In this section we have tried to give an idea of the more desirable places to live in Costa Rica. Since there are so many other great areas from which to choose—it is impossible to describe all of them here—we suggest you read some of the guide books listed in the back of this book to get a better picture of what Costa Rica has to offer. Then you should plan to visit the places where you think you may want to live. The best guidebook of the bunch is *Moon Publication's Costa Rica Handbook* by the award-winning travel writer Christopher Baker. We highly recommend this great book.

One-of-a-Kind Tours for Those Who Want to Move to Costa Rica

"Tours that Change People's Lives"

One way to see Costa Rica that we highly recommend is to take one of the introductory tours operated by **Christopher Howard's Live in Costa Rica Tours**. No more than the cost of a guided tour. You could NOT possibly do a tour like this by yourself and gain the same knowledge, contacts and information about living or retiring in Costa Rica. NOBODY else offers a tour like this.

What you learn from this personalized tour:
• What it took Christopher Howard 25 years to learn.
• The BEST locations suited for your lifestyle and specific needs.

- You will see a SAMPLING of Costa Rican homes in the PATH OF PROGRESS with high RESALE VALUE and not in REMOTE areas. ALL properties in the Central Valley are in neighborhoods with HIGH SPEED INTERNET ACCESS and near the BEST PRIVATE HOSPITALS in case of a serious medical EMERGENCY. You won't find any of theses INDISPENSABLE amenities in the outlaying areas.
- A two-day highly INFORMATIVE seminar with experts in the fields of real estate, law, moving to Costa Rica, health care, banking, insurance and more. How it really is to reside in Costa Rica.
- You will meet people who have actually moved here and hear about their experiences and make VALUABLE contacts to help ensure your success here.
- Find out how to access INEXPENSIVE health care.
- For the investor, INSIDER information, tips and how to really make money and opportunities that are can be compared to Hawaii 60 years ago.
- How the banking system will work to your advantage
- Time-proven shortcuts for learning Spanish by Christopher Howard, the author of the popular one-of-a-kind Guide to Costa Rican Spanish.
- What to expect when you first arrive
- Learn about the EXCITING lifestyle you can have by living in Costa Rica.
- This tour has NO hidden agendas.

Here is what people are saying about this tour:

"If you're fantasizing about living in Costa Rica, Christopher Howard is the go-to guy. His tour of the beaches is worth taking just for the food and scenery. Chris knows where to find the most delicious meals and gorgeous beaches, and is a fountain of information about what you'll encounter as an expatriate. His tours are a great way to learn if Costa Rica is for you. And they're fun!" - *Sara Davidson, contributing editor of Oprah magazine, October 2005*

"Visit early and often. To help you choose a country for retirement, companies like liveincostarica.com offer pre-retirement tours. It's sort of like a vacation but you may end up staying forever." - *Linda Stern, Newsweek, March 2005*

"This was the tour of a lifetime for us" - **Dan and Lani Curtis,** *Camarillo, California*

"I took your retirement tour in June of 2005. First, let me say it was one of the BEST INVESTMENTS I have ever made. I could not have seen the Central Valley on my own for twice the money and had someone to explain all the wonders of Costa Rica. ANYONE thinking of moving to Costa Rica to TAKE the TOUR, have an open mind and a dream in their heart. - **Don Autry Okemah,** *Oklahoma, csiok@ netzero.net*

TOUR -1
Five-Day Central Valley (Inland) Tour

Below is a sample itinerary from our one-of-a-kind five-day Central Valley tour.

Wednesday:
Day 1
Arrival. Ground transportation from the airport to the Hotel Torremolinos in downtown San José.

Thursday:
Day 2
Breakfast at the hotel
First day of Association of Residents of Costa Rica (ARCR) highly informative all-day seminar featuring:
8:10 Welcome by the President of the ARCR
8:20 Real Estate - Buying, Selling and Renting by Mercedes Castro or Les Nuñez (First Reality)
9:00 Questions about real estate
9:20 Costa Rican Laws and Regulations by Lic. José Carter
10:00 Questions about Costa Rican laws
10:30 BREAK FOR COFFEE
10:55 Moving and Customs by Charles Zeller (ABC Mudanzas)
11:35 Questions about moving and customs
12:05 BREAK FOR LUNCH (included in tour)
1:00 Investing in Costa Rica and Abroad by Alan Weeks Marketing Consultant
1:35 Questions about funds
1:45 Residency by ARCR Legal Residence Advisors
2:10 Questions about residency

2:30 About the ARCR by Ryan Piercy (manager)
3:00 Questions about the ARCR
3:10 The Move to Costa Rica, by Jerry Ledin (ARCR member)
3:30 Questions about moving to Costa Rica
4:00 HAPPY HOUR!

Friday: Day 3
Breakfast at the hotel
Second day of the ARCR's highly informative, all-day seminar featuring:
8:10 Welcome by the President of the ARCR
8:20 CCSS Public Health System in Costa Rica by Ryan Piercy (ARCR)
8:40 Questions about the CCSS (Public Health System)
8:50 Health Care Quality by Dr. C. Alpízar (Cima Hospital)
9:20 Questions about health care
9:35 BREAK FOR COFFEE
9:50 INS and Insurance in Costa Rica, by a representative of a local insurance company
10:20 Questions about insurance
10:30 International Health Insurance by Brad Cook (Clínica Bíblica)
10:40 Questions about insurance
10:50 Learning Spanish, by Christopher Howard (Author and Guide)
11:10 Questions about learning Spanish
11:25 Internet and Communication
11:45 Questions about Internet
12:00 BREAK FOR LUNCH (included in tour)
1:05 Investing from Costa Rica
1:20 Questions about services
1:35 Banking
2:05 Questions about banking
2:10 Culture of Costa Rica by Eric Liljenstolpe
2:30 Questions about culture
2:40 Living in Costa Rica by Ryan Piercy (ARCR manager)
3:30 Closing remarks for the two-day seminar
6:00 Dinner at a world famous restaurant or at a local resident's home.

Saturday:
Day 4
Tour of the city of San José including: Clínica Bíblica Hospital, markets, San Perdro Mall, University of Costa Rica, Hipermás superstore, neighborhoods where Americans live (Los Yoses, Barrio Escalante, Sabana Norte, Sabana Sur, Rohrmoser and Escazú), Hospital Cima and Multiplaza Mall. Continue tour around the Central Valley to see the other choice areas where foreigners reside: Escazú, Santa Ana, San Antonio de Belén, Ciudad Cariari, Alajuela, Heredia and Moravia. Lunch at La Cocina de Doña Lela where they serve authentic Costa Rican cuisine. Free night.

Sunday:
Day 5
Breakfast at the hotel. Tour the best areas for living west of San José including the city of Atenas famous for having the "best climate in the world," according to National Geographic," the charming town of Grecia, known as the "cleanest city in Costa Rica," Alajuela, Costa Rica's second largest city with its thriving expatriate community and finally the area of Santa Bárbara and San Joaquín de Heredia. You will view the inside of several homes and developments after a mouth-watering lunch at one of Costa Rica's best restaurant. Final questions, answers and other concerns.

Monday:
Day 6
Breakfast at hotel. Transportation to the airport. This is an excellent tour to get to know the country, especially the infrastructure. $1299 per person Airfare is not included.

TOUR 2
Eight -Day Central Pacific Beach Tour

Saturday:
Day 1
Arrive in San José. We will meet you at the airport and transport you to the Hotel. Torremolinos
Sunday:
Day 2

A buffet breakfast at the hotel. Then a 7:30 departure for Jacó Beach where you will stay at the beachfront Arenal Pacífico Lodge. On the way, you will receive a packet of materials and orientation about the tour. Prior to arriving at the hotel we will stop at the Nativa Resort and then tour the five-star Marriott Los Sueños resort, marina and golf course. Lunch will be served at the Barco de Mariscos in downtown Jacó Beach. After lunch we will visit the new Del Pacífico Development in Esterillos Este and Faro Escondido. To end the day on a fantastic note, you will view one of the most beautiful sunsets in the world from a Greek-style amphitheater on a hilltop at the Hotel Villas Caletas. The view alone is enough to make you want to live in Costa Rica. Dinner will be at the Colonial Restaurant in Jacó.

Monday:
Day 3
After breakfast we will depart at 7:30 for the Dominical -Tortuga beaches. On the way, we will pass through the towns of Parrita and Quepos. We will take a break in Quepos/Manuel Antonio before continuing to Dominical to meet our local contacts and have lunch. Because the mountains meet the sea in Dominical, it is called a "tropical Big Sur." Next, we will have lunch and then travel along the pristine coast with its beautiful seaside rock formations and tropical rain forest as a backdrop to the beautiful Ojochal/Tortuga area. On the way you will see the areas where whales can be observed during most of the year. This sight is spectacular. This part of Costa Rica just recently became accessible when the new coastal highway was finished. A world of possibilities now exists here to live or retire. During the rest of the day, we will explore the area and learn about the amenities, unique lifestyle and activities it has to offer: waterfalls, tropical rain forests, birdwatching, fishing, diving, horseback riding, hiking, boating, kayaking, surfing and much more.

Tuesday:
Day 4
An early breakfast. Then we will hook up with a local guide and see more of the area and its infrastructure and sample some of the properties. We will have lunch on a house boat/restaurant. You will also have the chance to meet some of the Americans who live and have retired in this part of the country. In the afternoon there will be a visit to Cinco Ventanas, a beach with a rock formation featuring five tunnel-like blow holes. Finally, to end a great day we will have an

unforgettable dinner at Exotica, the area's premier restaurant. Your taste buds will never recover!

Wednesday:

Day 5

Breakfast at the hotel and a 7:30 departure for San José. We will travel along the Barú River through the beautiful coastal mountains to the city of San Isidro, "the fastest growing city in Central America." After a brief stop to rest, we will take the Pan-American Highway over the country's most spectacular mountains on our way to San José, where you will stay at the Hotel Torremolinos again. Free afternoon and evening.

Thursday:

Day 6

Breakfast at the hotel. At 8:00 the first day of a highly-informative relocation, living and retirement seminar sponsored by the Association of Residents of Costa Rica. See the Inland Tour on a previous page for a list of speakers and topics. Free evening.

Friday:

Day 7

Second day of the seminar with lunch included. You will hear more from Costa Rica's experts, including your retirement tour guide, Christopher Howard. See the Inland Tour on a previous page for a list of speakers and topics. Happy Hour is scheduled after the seminar. Surprise group dinner at a local restaurant or a resident's home.

Saturday:

Day 8

Transportation to the airport included.

This tour is for those who are certain they want to explore only the beach as their option. It includes the majority of your meals and all of your transportation while in Costa Rica. Hotel and continental breakfasts are included. $1949. Airfare is not included. Reserve now and see why the baby-boomer generation is choosing Costa Rica as a favorite tropical place to live and retire!

TOUR 3
Combination Tour
(Beach and Central Valley Tour)

*This tour is our most popular. It allows you to see both the beach and the Inland Valley extensively. Airfare is not included.

Saturday:
Day 1
Arrive in San José. We will meet you at the airport and transport you to the Hotel. Torremolinos

Sunday:
Day 2
A buffet breakfast at the hotel. Then a 7:30 departure for Jacó Beach where you will stay at the beachfront Arenal Pacífico Lodge. On the way you will receive a packet of materials and orientation about the tour. Prior to arriving at the hotel we will stop at the Nativa Resort and then tour the five star Marriott Los Sueños resort, marina and golf course. Lunch will be served at the Barco de Mariscos in downtown Jacó Beach. After lunch we will visit the new Del Pacífico Development in Esterillos Este and Faro Escondido. To end the day on a fantastic note, you will view one of the most beautiful sunsets in the world from a Greek-style amphitheater on a hilltop at the Hotel Villas Caletas. The view alone is enough to make you want to live in Costa Rica. Dinner will be at the Colonial Restaurant in Jacó.

Monday:
Day 3
After breakfast we will depart at 7:30 for the Dominical -Tortuga beaches. On the way, we will pass through the towns of Parrita and Quepos. We will take a break in Quepos/Manuel Antonio before continuing to Dominical to meet our local contacts and have lunch. Because the mountains meet the sea in Dominical, it is called a "tropical big sur." Next, we will have lunch and then travel along the pristine coast with its beautiful seaside rock formations and tropical rain forest as a backdrop to the beautiful Ojochal/Tortuga area. On the way, you will see the areas where whales can be observed during most of the year. This sight is spectacular. This part of Costa Rica just recently became accessible when the new coastal highway was finished. A world of possibilities now exists here to live or retire. During the rest of the

day, we will explore the area and learn about the amenities, unique lifestyle and activities it has to offer: waterfalls, tropical rain forests, birdwatching, fishing, diving, horseback riding, hiking, boating, kayaking, surfing and much more.

Tuesday:
Day 4
An early breakfast. Then we will hook up with a local guide and see more of the area and its infrastructure and sample some of the properties. We will have lunch on a house boat/restaurant. You will also have the chance to meet some of the Americans who live and have retired in this part of the country. In the afternoon there will be a visit to Cinco Ventanas a beach with a rock formation featuring five tunnel-like blow holes. Finally, to end a great day we will have an unforgettable dinner at Exotica the area's premier restaurant. Your taste buds will never recover!

Wednesday:
Day 5
Breakfast at the hotel and a 7:30 departure for San José. We will travel along the Barú river through the beautiful costal mountains to the city of San Isidro, "the fastest growing city in Central America." After a brief stop to rest, we will take the Pan-American Highway over the country's most spectacular mountains on our way to San José, where you will stay at the Hotel Torremolinos again. Free afternoon and evening

Thursday:
Day 6
Breakfast at the hotel. At 8:00 the first day of a highly-informative relocation, living and retirement seminar sponsored by the Association of Residents of Costa Rica. See the Inland Tour on a previous page for a list of speakers and topics. Happy Hour is scheduled after the seminar. Free evening.

Friday:
Day 7
Second day of the seminar with lunch included. You will hear more from Costa Rica's experts including your retirement tour guide, Christopher Howard. See the Inland Tour on a previous page for a

list of speakers and topics. Surprise group dinner at a local restaurant. Free evening.

Saturday:
Day 8
Tour of the city of San José including: Clínica Bíblica Hospital, markets, San Pedro Mall, University of Costa Rica, Hipermás superstore, neighborhoods where Americans live (Los Yoses, Barrio Escalante, Sabana Norte, Sabana Sur, Rohrmoser and Escazú, Hospital Cima and Multiplaza Mall. Continue tour around the Central Valley to see the other choice areas where foreigners reside: Escazú, Santa Ana, San Antonio de Belén, Ciudad Cariari, Alajuela, Heredia and Moravia. Lunch at La Cocina de Doña Lela where they serve authentic Costa Rican cuisine. Free night.

Sunday:
Day 9
Breakfast at the hotel. Tour the best areas for living west of San José, including the city of Atenas famous, for having the "best climate in the world," according to National Geographic," the charming town of Grecia, known as the "cleanest city in Costa Rica," Alajuela, Costa Rica's second largest city with its thriving expatriate community, and finally the area of Santa Bárbara and San Joaquín de Heredia. You will view the inside of several homes and developments after a mouth-watering lunch at one of Costa Rica's best restaurants. Final questions, answers and other concerns.

Monday:
Day 10
Breakfast at hotel. Transportation to the airport. This is an excellent tour to get to know the country, especially the infrastructure . $2399.00 per person Airfare is not included.
*The above itinerary is subject to change.

TOUR 4 Guanacaste Tour
(This tour is only given occasionally)

Located in the North Pacific region of Costa Rica, Guanacaste is famous for it's string of beautiful beaches. Many of the beaches have white sand, excellent surf breaks, world-class sportfishing, skin diving and unparalleled beauty. Sunshine is year-round and the area receives less rainfall than the beaches in the Central Pacific area. Numerous daily flights to Liberia's Daniel Oduber International Airport have contributed to the development of this area.

The Guanacaste area has experienced a building boom, especially around the Gulf of Papagayo. The Four Seasons chain just built a mammoth resort here.

Saturday - Arrival

Sunday
Day 1 - Coco, Ocotal Hermosa
Playa Hermosa has some of the country's best diving. It lies in the center of a string of four major beaches, all within 30 minutes of each other: Hermosa, Playa del Coco, Playa Ocotal and Playa Panama. Playa del Coco is a colorful beach town with an active nightlife and a small international community. It is set in a deep cove with consistently calm waters, making it a safe swimming beach. This charming seaside community is surrounded by emerald colored hills and offers a variety of water sports, and various forms of entertainment including restaurants a disco, and casinos. You will also find a bank, post office and all kinds of shops.

Monday
Day 2 Finish Coco, Ocotal Hermosa in the morning.
Afternoon: Flamingo is one of the finest resort areas in Costa Rica and has the country's second best full-service marinas and a beautiful white-sand beach. It is Guanacaste's sport fishing capital and offers some of the best sail and marlin fishing in the world. There is an abundance of real estate, including condominiums which dot the surrounding hills. Check into hotel in Tamarindo.

Tuesday
Day -3
Tamarindo is a laid-back beach town overlooking a long stretch of beautiful beach and a popular spot among surfers. It has the most developed tourist infrastructure in Guanacaste. The small foreign community has given birth to many restaurants, hotels, as well as a variety of stores for all tastes. The town itself is very cosmopolitan with

residents from all over the world which adds a very exciting cultural diversity to the area.

Wednesday
Day 4 - Return to San José

Thursday Day - 5 Breakfast at the hotel. At 8:00 the first day of a highly-informative Seminar sponsored by the Association of Residents of Costa Rica. You will hear from some of the country's foremost authorities in the fields of real estate, law, health care, moving, medical care, insurance, learning the language and more. A few people who have moved to Costa Rica will share their experiences with you. You will make new friends and begin to make a network of valuable contacts. A delicious buffet lunch is included.

Friday
Day - 6
Second day of the seminar with lunch included. You will hear more from the rest of Costa Rica's experts including your tour guide Christopher Howard. Surprise group dinner at a local restaurant or party.

Saturday
Day -7 Return home or stay for the Central Valley Tour.*
This tour may also be combined with our Central Valley Tour by adding two days at the end.

All trips are led by Christopher Howard the author of this guidebook and expert on living and investing in Costa Rica. For additional information contact Live in Costa Rica Tours toll free at: 800 365-2342, e-mail: **liveincostarica@cox.net** or **christopher@costaricabooks. com** or go to **www.liveincostarica.com**. In addition to the tours listed above we offer Private Consultations or Tailor-Made Tours for individuals, couples and small groups short on time or whose schedule does not coincide with the regular fixed-date tours. All tours include a two-day seminar given by experts in real estate, law, banking, health care, investing and more.

*The above itinerary is subject to change.

Some of Our Happy Tour Participants

Our Adventure in Paradise
By Carol Burch

"Oh that's far too beautiful to be real," I muttered to myself, while examining the photographs in Christopher Howard's latest book. "These photos can't be real, I'm sure," I commented cynically. It was October, a comfortable autumn day. But the days were getting shorter and the nights colder. Cold, windy, bleak, winter days were just around the corner. Summer and fall are enjoyable seasons in northeast Ohio. And then there's winter...my thoughts drifted to the ice storm of 1991. Downed trees and powerlines closed many roads. Driving was trecherous. Stores were closed, schools too, and cable TV was out. "How would you like to see Costa Rica?" my husband Jim's question interrupted my thoughts. "Christopher Howard is leading a tour in January," Jim remarked. "Do you think you could get time off? "What are Costa Rica winters like?" I asked. "January is their summer, and in the Central Valley it's 72 degrees year round," he replied. "If you like it we could live there comfortably on my pension. You wouldn't have to work, it would be optional." "Even with the two children," I asked. "Yes," was his reply.

We departed from Cleveland and had an enjoyable, uneventful flight to San José. Jim and I were weary of customs, but it proved to be easier than car trips to Canada. Costa Rican warmth and hospitality were immediately evident; we felt welcome. Someone from the tour company was expected to meet us, but we were flattered and amazed this it was Christopher Howard! Our Costa Rica adventure had begun.

On the way to our hotel Chris helped us get our bearings and was more than willing to answer our many questions. I was immediately struck by the absolute beauty of the country. Such contrasts! It is even more beautiful that the photographs.

The Hotel Torremolinos was convenient and comfortable. The location was perfect for touring the city on our own. Meals were delicious and reasonable, and in close proximity to numerous "sodas" (small cafés), souvenir shops, a museum, the Central Market and casinos. Hotel security watched over us. We were able to mail our postcards and exchange money at the hotel. They also gave directions and called taxis for us. Imagine that at a Holiday Inn. The streets felt safe too, unlike big cities in the States. We enjoyed the tour of the different neighborhoods in the Central Valley. We were able to have a good sampling of how people actually live and even see a couple of homes. We were also able to see hospitals, malls, supermarkets and get a good idea of the infrastructure in the area.

We also loved the Banco de Mariscos restaurant in Heredia. It is touted as the best seafood restaurant in the country. Their dishes are absolutely delicious and a bargain. Tiny's American Sports bar was great fun. We had a group luncheon there and enjoyed hamburgers and fries Costa Rica style.

The two days of lectures and seminars were helpful and informative, especially the representative from the Residents Association of Costa Rica. We have been in touch with several speakers from the tour since our return to the States. Without Chris, we would have never met the realtors, movers, a business consultant, attorneys and other contacts. We could have NEVER done this on our own.

The Clinica Bíblica Hospital offers great medical care. Not wanting to miss any of the tour, I saw a doctor there for a minor problem. The doctors and nurses speak great English. Bedside manner far exceeds what I'm accustomed to. The wait was short, care great and fee minimal. When we departed paradise, our flight from New Jersey was cancelled due to the weather. The next flight was delayed for hours while all planes de-iced. Both at the airport and at home we shoveled snow. Sniff, sniff, good-bye for now, paradise.

Update: We are now in the process of selling our two homes in the States and plan to move with the kids to Costa Rica before the new millennium. It came down to a choice between Costa Rica and Florida and the former won out easily. Florida's sweltering summers cannot compete with Costa Rica's spring-like climate.

Our Concierge Services

For more than 20 years we have helped people move successfully to Costa Rica. Our monthly time-proven tours and seminars have been the first logical step to moving here. To complement our tours we now offer the very best concierge services to our clients.

We know that moving to a new country and dealing with a new culture and language can be difficult for the average person. We will provide you with all of the necessary contacts and information you will need to adjust successfully to a new culture. We strive to make this process as easy as possible. In no time you will feel at home in your new surroundings.

Our associates will show you how to do all daily tasks from A to Z. They will guide you every step of the way to significantly shortening the time it takes to get acclimated to your new country.

Our associates will charge you accordingly for their time. The organizations with which we work come highly recommended and have excellent track records. Please let us know your specific needs and we will connect you with the organizations who provide the services below.

- Airport pick up
- Assistance in dealing with various government departments in Costa Rica.
- Attorneys
- Banking procedures
- Buying furniture
- Cable TV
- Car, home and health insurance
- Computer repair
- Cosmetic Surgery
- Courier service
- Culture shock awareness
- Daily errands
- Doctors, dentists and hospitals
- Expert legal advice from the best lawyers in Costa Rica
- Finding a mechanic
- Finding a maid
- Finding a rental in San José or at the beach
- Finding a school for your children
- Getting a phone
- Home finding
- Home repairs
- Home security system
- Household maintenance program
- How to use Costa Rica's taxis
- Immigration

- Importing your pets
- Insurance for automobile and homeowners
- Locating hard to find items
- Medical plans
- Moving of household items and assistance with shipping and customs
- Obtaining a Costa Rican P.O. box
- Obtaining a gun permit
- Offshore corporations to protect your assets
- Opening a bank account
- Paying utilities
- Pet transportation
- Photocopies
- Placing ads in local newspapers
- Private mail service
- Private taxi driver
- Psychiatric services
- Purchasing a car
- Real estate brokers
- Receiving your Social Security benefits in Costa Rica
- Residency
- Residency renewals
- Safe real estate investments
- Satellite TV
- Shopping
- Social activities
- Spanish schools
- Supermarkets
- Tax and accounting assistance
- Translations, fax and Internet services.
- Understanding the bus system
- Vehicle and property title searches
- Veterinary service
- Work permits for foreign domestic staff.

To Contact us:
Locally 261-8892
International toll-free 1-877-322-4690
E-mail: christopher@costaricabooks.com

SAVING MONEY
IN COSTA RICA

How Much Does it
Cost to Live in Costa Rica?

An important factor that determines the cost of living for foreigners in Costa Rica is their lifestyle. If you are used to a wealthy lifestyle, you'll spend more than someone accustomed to living frugally. Either way, you will still find Costa Rica to be a bargain.

Despite having one of the highest standards of living in Latin America, purchasing power is greater in Costa Rica than in the United States or Canada.

San José's cost of living ranks close to last when compared to 144 cities worldwide. To see where Costa Rica ranks, see http://www. finfacts.com/costofliving3.htm. The cost of living in Guatemala City or Panama City is about 14 percent higher than in San José. Corporate Resource Consulting, a firm that compares costs of goods and services, rates San José among the least expensive cost-of -living cities in the world. It is second to Quito, Ecuador, in the Americas in terms of afford ability. CNN reports that Mercer Human Resource Consulting also finds Costa Rica an inexpensive place to live.

In most areas, housing costs less than what it does in the United States and hired help is a steal. Utilities (telephone service, electricity, and water) are cheaper than in North America. You never need to heat your home or apartment since Costa Rica's climate is warm. You need not cook with gas, since most stoves are electric. These services cost about 30 percent of what they do at home. Bills for heating in the winter and air conditioning in the summer can cost hundreds of dollars in the United States, neither of which is necessary in the Central Valley. Public transportation is also inexpensive. San José and surrounding suburbs occupy a small area. A bus ride across town or to the suburbs usually costs $0.25 to $0.50. Bus fares to the provinces costs no more than $10 to the farthest part of the country (see Chapter 10). Taxi travel around San José is also inexpensive.

A gallon of regular gasoline costs about $4.20, making Costa Rica's gasoline prices among the lowest in the Americas (To figure out the cost of gasoline per gallon in dollars take the actual price per liter in *colones*, divide it by the exchange rate in *colones* and then multiply by 3.8). Only oil-exporting countries such as Mexico and Venezuela have cheaper gasoline. However, you do not really need a car because public transportation is so inexpensive and accessible. If you must have a new car, remember that they are very expensive here due to high import duties. In Costa Rica people tend to keep their cars for a long time and take good care of them. We recommend buying used cars since they are usually in good mechanical condition and their resale value is excellent. Food, continuing education, entertainment (movies cost about $3) and, above all, health care, are surprisingly affordable. Both new and second-hand furniture is priced very low. You will more about these benefits later on.

When you have lived in Costa Rica a while, learned the ins-and-outs and made some friends and contacts, you can cut your living costs more by sharing a house or apartment, house-sitting in exchange for free rent, investing in high-interest yielding accounts in one of Costa Rica's many banks, working full or part-time (if you can find legal work), starting a small business or bartering within the expatriate community. Doing without packaged and canned imported brand-name foods and buying local products, eating in small *cafés* or *sodas* instead of expensive restaurants and buying fresh foods in bulk at the Central Market like Costa Ricans do can also reduce your living costs. You can also help yourself by learning how to get a better rate of exchange on your money and by learning Spanish so you can bargain and get lower prices when shopping.

If you take lessons from the locals and live a modest *tico* lifestyle, you can save a lot of money and still enjoy yourself. By not following a U.S.-"shop-till-you-drop" mentality, you can live reasonably. Taking all of the aforementioned and personal lifestyle into consideration, the minimum needed for a decent standard of living for a single person ranges from $1,200 to $1,500 monthly. A person can indeed live for as little as $35 a day, excluding housing. Some single people scrape by on considerably less and others spend hundreds of dollars more, again depending on what one is accustomed to. A couple can live well on $1,500 per month, and live better on $2,000. Couples with husband and wife both receiving good pensions can live even better. Remember, two in Costa Rica can often live as cheaply as one. Any way you look at it, you will enjoy a higher standard of living in Costa Rica and get more for your money. Considering that the minimum monthly wage is $287 and the average Costa Rican earns only $250 to $350 a month, you should be able to live well.

Here one expats views of the cost of living here: "If you go completely native, you can even live on $400 a month, counting $75 a month to rent a room with no bath but kitchen privileges where there is no hot water to disinfect the communal dishes. But would you like it?

"Most Costa Ricans eat small amounts of meat, rice and beans, and mostly fruits. They dress cleanly and neat if not stylish. They do not, at this salary, have cars. Their homes are not plumbed for hot water, nor do they seem to miss it. Their children are not given textbooks in their public schools. They ride the bus, they seem happy, their clothes are often homemade, they own miniature washers and hang their clothes out to dry. They often share housing, with several earning family members occupying the same house, making for crowded conditions. The older generations leave a piece of their backyard to the newer generations. When they can scrape together the money, they build a house for the new bride and groom.

"On the other hand, wealthy Costa Ricans, live on what seems to be, by observing their restaurant eating habits, their clothing and their large 4 x 4's, in excess of $4000 per month. They buy CD's, eat at restaurants where the tab is often more than $20 per plate, send their kids to expensive private schools costing up to $500 per month, have country places and live in $300,000 homes."

One American retiree stated, "Most Americans I know in Costa Rica are frugal, live on a fixed income, drive older cars, and are just getting by. Many have had to get temporary jobs or start their own small businesses. They live on $1,500 a month. You need to realize that this may exclude many perks that we as Americans are accustomed to having: good quality clothes, travel, electronic toys, eating in steak houses rather than beans-and-rice places, using imported condiments and other nice imported foods that double your food bill."

Another foreigner said, "The long and the short of it is, it can be hugely cheaper to live in Costa Rica. Like others have said, the average *tico* family lives on $4,800 a year. They're not wallowing in abject poverty, either. They have plenty to eat, attractive clothing and a clean appearance. They also have a TV, they own their own home and they might have a computer. Nothing is stopping us from also living on $4,800 a year.

"The question is how you want to live. It is no different in Costa Rica than in the United States. There are families who live quite comfortably on $30,000 or $40,000 a year, and families that wouldn't feel comfortable spending less than $80,000 (or $100,000 or $150,000, etc.). Some things are more expensive in Costa Rica (goods), some are less (services). You can live very well here for less money than would buy you "good living" in the United States, but it may not be the same kind of 'good living' you'd enjoy in the States. Costa Rica is a different country; adjustments are always required.

"If you are prepared to shed some of the luxuries you enjoyed back home (i.e., big kitchens, nice bed linens, long luxurious baths, fast food [if you consider that a luxury], high-quality spices, etc.), then you can live very inexpensively. But you will live like a *tico*, and *ticos* live in a third-world country. Prepare for the differences, embrace your new life and enjoy every minute of the *pura vida*, and you can live the good life *a la tica* (Costa Rican style) for less money than you ever could in the United States."

When you take into account all these factors and others, such as good year-round weather, the friendly Costa Rican people, the lack of political strife and a more peaceful way of life—no price is too high to pay to live in a unique, tropical paradise like Costa Rica.

Jim, a fellow expat remarked, "Costa Rica is a place where one can live whatever lifestyle one desires and can afford to live. I am a 72-year-old *pensionado* who has been living in Costa Rica for more than three years now. I am retired on Social Security and live on less, yes, I said less, than $700 per month. I do not feel that my lifestyle is much better or worse than it was in California. In the United States I lived on more than $25,000 a year. Now I own a small plot of land on which I have built a small (750 square feet) Swiss chalet-style log cabin and have a view that many of my California friends would literally die for."

Here is what another expatriate wrote to an on-line forum: "I am discovering that it is actually much easier than I would have dreamed

How to Get By on a Shoestring in Costa Rica: The Story of Banana Bread Steve
By Christopher Howard

This purpose of this article is to show one person's resourcefulness and courage in the face of adversity. The author is not advocating moving to Costa Rica with little or no money.

About three years ago I met Steve who had lived in Hawaii for many years. He moved here because Hawaii had become very expensive and he wanted to make his early retirement "nest egg" go farther. Steve had always been used to living frugally and in the process amassed a few hundred thousand dollars.

Within a few months of moving here Steve invested his life savings in two high interest -yielding investments with the idea of doubling his money in a few years. This was his game plan but unfortunately both of his investments went "belly up." Steve was left with only a few thousand dollars to his name. As we mentioned Steve had mastered the art of living on very little money but had never been faced with having no resources and living in a foreign country. He knew that he would not be able to draw his pension for four more years. Steve thought of returning to the States to work and then moving back to Costa Rica when he got back on his feet. However, he became involved with a nice Costa Rican woman and had also fallen in love with the country.

His close friends provided him with a place to live for free, but he still had to find a way to generate and income. Since he was born with the ability to repair almost anything, he did odd jobs in exchange for small sums of money and food.

After a while he figured that the only way he could continue to live in Costa Rica was to start a business. Steve had one big problem; no money with which to start a business. His pride kept him for asking for a loan from friends. He started to look at local small business and do research on the Internet. It did not take him long to come up with a good idea for a small business. He came across a good recipe for banana bread and his business was born.

At present he sells he bread to tourists and his many friends in the city of Heredia where he lives. He has purchased a mixing machine, an oven and his lady friend is helping him.

Steve is a born survivor. All of his friends are sure he will continue to do well and continue to enjoy living in the country he has adopted as his home.

to live in Costa Rica on Social Security benefits alone, even though mine are quite meager. I am astonished when I realize that I am living a comfortable middle-class life on less than $1,000 a month. That includes traveling around the country and paying to stay in hotels when friends come to visit occasionally. I am actually saving money while living on Social Security and haven't had to touch my savings. I did come with the intention of simplifying my life, which I have done. I do not own a car. I enjoy taking public transportation. I do not buy every electronic gadget and gizmo that comes down the pike. And you know, I am not missing anything. I feel richer than ever."

Another American stated something similar: "I've been living here now for one year (exactly), and I have spent more than $1,000 per month in only one month so far. I didn't expect to live so cheaply. I do not deprive myself of much of anything. For amusement, I travel about the country quite a bit, staying in fairly nice hotels. I eat well. I rent a two-bedroom, gringo-style apartment and have all modern conveniences. I also have a serious book- and CD-buying habit that I support.

"The big money-saver for me is not owning an auto. Instead, whenever I want or need, I rent a car or truck and its driver, — for the hour or for the day. I also use public transportation — buses, of course, and taxis, — a lot! I go where I want, when I want but I don't worry about auto repairs, buying gas or insurance, or getting a vehicle inspected every year. I promise that at the end of the month, my transportation costs are way lower than the transportation costs of all my auto-addicted friends. Of course, your mileage may vary, particularly if you cannot imagine living without a car in order to drive to the corner *pulpería*.

"Besides, I've lost 20 pounds in the past year, which I attribute to walking. Remember walking? What a concept! The only problem is trying to walk in places where you can avoid the autos!

"I was bragging to some friends about living on less than $1,000 per month. Two of those friends accused me of being a 'spendthrift.' Both have lived here for more than 10 years, and neither spends more than about $600 per month."

Before closing this section, we want to emphasize that you should not be alarmed by high real estate prices you may hear about or see advertised in English-language publications such as *Costa Rica Today* or the *The Tico Times*. This recent rise in land prices is a result of the current land boom and increasing popularity of Costa Rica. Inflated real estate prices do not reflect the real cost of living in Costa Rica, which is still relatively low when compared to North America and Europe . Even more important, the Costa Rican government must keep the cost of goods and services affordable for the Costa Rican people in order to avoid the social problems found in most other Latin American countries.

Approximate Cost of Living and Prices as of January 2007 in Dollars*

Rentals - Monthly
House (small, unfurnished) $400
House (large, luxurious)..$1000–1500
Apartment (small, 1–2 bedrooms, unfurnished)........................... $300+
Apartment (large, luxurious) .... $700+
Property Taxes (a year on a small home) $100

Home Prices
House (small).. $50,000+
House (large) .... $85,000+

Miscellaneous Monthly
Electric Bill (apt.)...$15–25
Water-Sewage (apt.) $8
Telephone (850 impulses).. $13
Telephone (cell 200 minutes)... $24
Cable TV.. $27

Taxi .... ¢365 first kilometer,
                         and ¢340 thereafter per kilometer (Jan. 2007)
Bus Fares (around city) .... $.45
Gasoline (regular gas per gallon).. $3.94
Gasoline (super per gallon).. $4.11
Gasoline (diesel per gallon).. $2.80
Maid/Gardener (per hour).. $1.25
Restaurant Meal (inexpensive)... $5.00+
Soda (a diner or coffee shop) Meal $2.00
Restaurant (mid-range).. $10.00

Banana .... $.05
Soft drink .... $.50
Pineapple... $1.00

Papaya	$.70
Avocado (large)	$.50
Lettuce	$.30
Cereal (large box of corn flakes)	$3.50
Bread (loaf)	$1.00
Tuna (small can)	$.75
Orange	$.08
Rice (1lb.)	$.45
Steak	$4.60 lb.
Quart of Milk	$.95
Beer	$.85
Airmail Letter around	$.33 to the U.S.
Doctor's Visit	$25–35
National Health Insurance (yearly for permanent residents)	$450.00
New Automobile	$15,000–$50,000

* These prices are subject to fluctuations.

Money

The *colón*, named for Christopher Columbus, is Costa Rica's official currency. One of the most stable currencies in Latin America, the *colón* has recently been somewhat shaky because of devaluations. Fortunately, the devaluations are relatively small when compared to the mega-devaluations and run away inflation rampant in other Latin American countries. Since your main source of income will probably be in dollars, you should not worry too much about devaluations unless you have large amounts of money in *colones*, which is not advisable for long-term investments. Devaluations can be good because they increase your purchasing power until prices catch up.

Coins come in denominations of 5, 10, 20, 25, 50, 100 and 500 *colones*. Bills come in 1000 (called *rojos* in slang), 2,000, 5000 (called *tucanes* in slang) and 10,000 (called *pumas* in slang) *colón* denominations. The rate of exchange, which is set by the Central Bank, was around 520 *colones* to the dollar as of October 2006. The older, silver-colored 5, 10 and 20 *colón* coins are the only ones you can use in coin-operated public pay phones.

You can exchange money at most banks between 9 a.m. and 4 p.m., Monday through Friday. Some banks are now open even later,

Costa Rican Coins and Bills

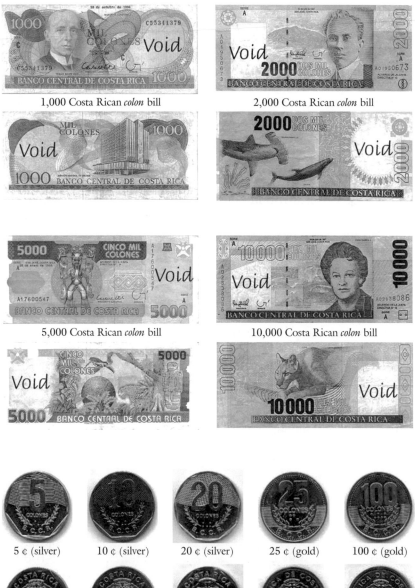

1,000 Costa Rican *colon* bill

2,000 Costa Rican *colon* bill

5,000 Costa Rican *colon* bill

10,000 Costa Rican *colon* bill

5 ¢ (silver) 10 ¢ (silver) 20 ¢ (silver) 25 ¢ (gold) 100 ¢ (gold)

and some are open Saturday mornings as well. Remember to bring only U.S. currency, since other monies are difficult and expensive to exchange. When you exchange money at a bank, do so early in the morning because lines can be long later in the day and you may have to wait for what seems like an eternity. You should always carry your passport, a certified copy of your passport or *pensionado* or resident I.D. when exchanging money or for other banking transactions.

Banks, businesses and most money changers do not accept damaged or torn foreign currency. There is really no need to worry about changing money since a large number of businesses in Costa Rica will accept U.S. dollars. However, some may be reluctant to accept $50 or $100 bills.

Money can also be changed on the street, where you get the same rate of exchange as in the banks. We advise against this because many slick change artists distribute counterfeit bills or attempt to shortchange you.

To see the actual rate of exchange or convert currency, go to **http:// www.xe.com/**.

Banking

Before selecting a bank it is necessary to decide what services you will need.

There are branches of Costa Rica's state-owned banks in San José and in other large cities and towns. The headquarters of Costa Rica's largest banks: **Banco Nacional**, **El Banco de Costa Rica** and **Banco Crédito Agrícola** are in downtown San José near the Central Post Office. The government guarantees all monies deposited in these state banks.

Here is a list of banks:

BAC San José (private).. Tel: 295-9595
Banco Promérica (private)
    E-mail: solucion@promerica.fi.cr.................... Tel: 296-4848
Banco Banex (private). .... Tel: 287-1000
Banco Bantec (private) .... Tel: 242-2222
Banco Cathay (private)... Tel: 290-2233
Banco Central de Costa Rica
    E-mail: webmaster@bccr.fi.cr. .... Tel: 243-3333

Banking Terms

account .... *la cuenta*
application .... *solicitud*
ATM .... *cajero automático*
bank .... *el banco*
bank book .... *la libreta de depósitos*
fixed .... *fijo*
balance .... *saldo*
bill .... *billete*
bond .... *bono*
cash .... *dinero en efectivo*
to cash .... *cobrar, cambiar*
cashier, teller .... *cajero/a*
change .... *cambio*
to change .... *cambiar*
check .... *cheque*
check book .... *la chequera*
checking account .... *cuenta corriente*
coin .... *moneda*
compound interest .... *interés compuesto*
credit card .... *tarjeta de crédito*
customer .... *cliente*
debit .... *débito*
debit card .... *tarjeta de débito*
debt .... *deuda*
deposit .... *depósito*
deposit slip .... *hoja de depósito*
to deposit .... *depositar*
dollar .... *dólar*
draft .... *giro bancario*
endorso .... *endoso*
to endorse .... *endosar*
foreign exchange .... *divisas*
income .... *ingresos*

insured	*asegurado*
interest	*interés*
interest rate	*tasa de interés*
invest	*invertir*
line	*fila*
loan	*préstamo*
manager	*gerente*
money	*dinero/plata*
money order	*giro baancario*
mortgage	*hipoteca*
to mortage	*hipotecar*
payment	*pago, abono*
to pay	*pagar*
pay off debts	*saldar las deudas*
profit	*ganancia*
receipt	*recibo*
safe	*caja fuerte*
salary	*sueldo/salario*
savings	*ahorros*
savings bank	*caja de ahorros*
savings account	*cuenta de ahorros*
to save	*ahorrar*
securities	*valores*
stock, share	*acción*
tax	*impuesto*
taxable	*gravable, sujeto a impuesto*
to tax	*gravar*
teller's window	*la ventanilla*
traveler's check	*cheque de viajero*
withdraw	*retirar, sacar dinero*
withdrawl	*retiro*
withdrawl	*slip hoja de retiro*
to withdraw	*retirar*
vault	*bóveda*

Banco Crédito Agrícola de Cartago	Tel: 550-0202
Banco Cuscatlán (private)	Tel: 299-0299
Banco de Costa Rica E-mail: bancobcr@bancobcr.com	Tel: 287-9088
Banco Interfín (private)	Tel: 210-4000
Banco Nacional	Tel: 212-2000
Banco Popular	Tel: 257-5797
Citibank (private)	Tel: 201-0800
Mutual de Alajuela (private)	Tel: 437-0865
Scotia bank (private) E-mail: scotiacr@scotiabank.com	Tel: 287-8700

When making deposits in national banks, you should consider the following. Checks from outside Costa Rica, including bank cashiers checks, require 30 to 45 working days minimum before funds will be usable after they are deposited. Checks issued by Costa Rican private banks will usually take a couple of working days before the funds will be available. Checks deposited from the same bank and branch are usually available the same day. Wire transfers are usually available in 2 to 4 days.

There are also numerous private banks affiliated with international banks. In the last few years there has been a trend toward privatization. Now private banks can offer many of the same services the state banks do. When the minimum deposit is not maintained, service charges for account operations at private banks can sometimes be higher than at the national banks.

Costa Rican Banks offer a full range of services.

Many private banks pay higher interest than state banks but cannot guarantee your deposits as the government banks do. Remember, the higher the interest, the more the risk. In the mid-1980s private finance companies were offering up to 45 percent interest in *colones*. As recently as 2002, several other companies were paying as much as three percent monthly. Needless to say they all failed and the investors lost everything.

Some of the better private banks are **BAC**, **Scotiabank**, **Banco Interfín**, **Bancrecen**, **Cuscatlán** and **Banex**. Check the yellow pages for more private banks. It is advisable to open an account at one of these banks or state banks so you can have a dollar account to protect against unexpected currency devaluations, cash personal checks, obtain a safety deposit box for your valuables and facilitate having money sent to you from abroad.

Regarding the latter, you should make sure that the bank you choose works with a U.S. correspondent bank to avoid untimely delays in cashing checks.

Warning: Be careful of **Scotiabank**. We have heard many foreign residents complain about unfair treatment at this bank. They complain about having to open their safety boxes for random inspections (which is illegal without a court order) and general lack of privacy at this overly intrusive bank. **Banex** also seems to be making it extremely difficult for foreigners to open accounts, and asks for extensive paperwork.

Here is what one resident said about **Scotiabank**, "I was with Scotiabank for over a year. They were awful. And I mean bad. Their statements were impossible to read. But worse is they didn't know how to read them and often took two months to research the problems. The worst was telling me they would have a decision for a home loan in two weeks and then taking three months. In the end they said the property was worth $4 per square meter when all other sales in the neighborhood are $25 to $35. I moved to **Promerica** and they have been tons better. Not to say they are perfect. But compared to Scotiabank, they are amazing."

Another local who works in the real estate business said about Scotiabank: "Atrocious service, and they outright mislead. I have seen them pull the rug out of a sale at the last minute, when sellers and buyers both had their house packed up to go. No good reason. I have heard this tale from others, too. Overall, I regard them as the worst because they seem so up-to-date and modern with the fancy air conditioning and slick offices. I avoid them like the plague and have no clue why they behave this way."

This is another bad experience a local resident had at Scotiabank. "I have a good excuse to report an experience at Scotiabank from several years ago (downtown branch). I withdrew some money, which the teller gave me after opening an unusual number of drawers (not all at his window) and roaming about a lot. Within 10 minutes of leaving the bank, I discovered I had been given a $100 counterfeit bill. I returned and they wouldn't do anything about it saying, of course, "You left the bank." Whenever I had occasion to be in the bank, I would look at him in passing and he would duck his head and look away. I think he was just waiting for someone to pass it to. I avoid Scotiabank every opportunity I get."

We have a safety deposit box at **Banco Nacional** that is readily accessible during working hours. We also have a dollar account, certificates of deposit and an ATM card. Our only complaint is that service in state run banks tends to be very slow. You can spend up to an hour in the bank waiting to make a simple transaction.

ATMs are found all over the country in banks, supermarkets and other convenient locations. These 24-hour automated tellers disperse a few hundred dollars at a time from your account, cash advance in colones only. When using one of these machines, be sure to exercise the following precautions:

1. Look for an ATM that is not isolated or unknown.
2. Use ATMs located in well-lit area with good visibility.
3. Use an ATM that allows you entry and a door to lock rather than one on an open sidewalk.
4. Cancel the transaction at the first sign of suspicious activity.
5. Take all paperwork with you and do not throw away anything that has your account number printed on it.
6. Do not carry your ATM card with you unless you are going to use it.
7. Don't go alone.
8. RESIDENCY — ATM receipts will NOT work as proof of exchange.

Other banking services are high-yield certificates of deposit in *colones*, certificates of deposit in dollars on par with U.S. interest rates and credit card related services.

All banks have different requirements for opening accounts or obtaining credit cards, possibly entailing banking or personal references, identification and most certainly minimum deposits. Requirements will vary slightly from bank to bank, so check with the banking institution of your choice.

Permanent and non-residents may open a savings account in state and private banks. All that is needed is a minimum deposit, in some cases a letter of reference and a passport or *cédula*. To open a local checking account, you have to be a resident and may be asked to provide a Costa Rican ID card or passport as a form of identification.

You may be asked to show your water, telephone and electric bills in your name to prove you live here. If you cannot provide these documents you will need two references from banks in the United States or from two account holders in the same bank where you wish to open your account. If opening a checking account in local currency you will need an initial deposit of about $500. A local dollar checking account may require an initial deposit of $2,000.

If you have a Costa Rican corporation, you may also open a local corporate checking account, or *cuenta corriente empresarial*. You'll have to provide the following: passport or *cédula* (Costa Rican ID), the name of the corporation or *personería jurídica*, proof that it is active, a letter from the person who has general power of attorney of your corporation authorizing who can sign on the account, along with their ID numbers, and an initial deposit of about $1,000 for an account in local currency or $2,000 for a local dollar account.

International dollar checking accounts are offered through the **BAC**. Individuals and corporations may open these accounts, but specific requirements must be met. Check with the bank of your choice.

Most banks are normally open from 9 a.m. to 5 p.m., Monday through Friday. Two branches of the **Banco Nacional** in downtown San José open at 7:30 a.m. A few branch offices such as the one in Plaza Mayor in Rohrmoser, don't open until 10:30 a.m. The Banco Nacional in the San Pedro Mall and a few of the private banks open on Saturdays. **Mutual de Alajuela** has a new service called **SERVICAJA**. Some of its branches are open after regular banking hours, on Saturdays, Sundays and holidays.

Warning: Never plan to do any banking on the second or last Friday of the month; this is payday for most Costa Rican workers and lines sometimes extend outside the bank.

The state banks are also very crowded after holidays and on Monday and Friday mornings. It is always best to get to the bank at least a half-hour before it opens to get a good place in line. Bring some good reading material, since the lines often move at a snail's pace.

Tipping

A 15 percent sales tax, as well as a three percent tourist tax is added to all hotel bills. *Cafés* and restaurants include a 10 percent service charge or tip, so tipping above that amount is optional. Employees such as bellhops and taxi drivers are appreciative of any additional gratuity for excellent service. It is also customary to give a small tip to the parking attendants who watch your car on the street, called *cuidacarros*. One hundred *colones* is usually sufficient.

Supermarket box boys should be tipped for carrying groceries to your car, since they do not receive a salary. If you live nearby, they will even take your bags to your home. We used to live four blocks from the supermarket at Plaza Mayor in Rohrmoser and liked to walk to the market. Our favorite box boy delivered our food to our front door for about $0.75 cents.

Paying Bills

Although your bills are sent to your home or post office box, the procedure for paying bills is different than in the United States and Canada. In Costa Rica you may pay your phone, electricity, water and cable TV bills at any supermarket, at some banks or by going directly to the company that issues the bill. Nobody sends a check by mail to pay bills in Costa Rica. Some banks are starting to allow you to pay bills online. Check with your local bank to see if it offers this service.

Housing and Real Estate Investments

Rentals

Housing is affordable and plentiful in Costa Rica. Rental prices vary just as in your hometown. With the exception of downtown San José, rent for houses or apartments is reasonable (half or less the cost in the United States). Depending on location and personal taste, a small house or large apartment usually rents for a few hundred dollars per month. A luxurious house or apartment will go for $800 to $1,500 per month or more. Most of these upper-end houses and apartments have all the amenities of home: large bedrooms, a spectacular view, pools, gardens with fruit trees, bathrooms with hot water, kitchens, dining rooms, a laundry room and even maid's quarters, since help is so inexpensive in Costa Rica.

In the lower range—from $300 to $700—you can expect to find a two-to three-bedroom house or apartment in a middle-class neighborhood. Since most Costa Ricans pay less than $150 monthly for rent, a few hundred dollars should rent a nice place to live. Most affordable houses and apartments are unfurnished. However, you can usually buy a complete household of furniture from someone who is leaving the country. This way you can save money. Most of the cheaper places will not have hot water. In the shower there will probably be an electric device that heats the water. If the shower doesn't have of these devices, you can buy one for about $30 and have it installed for a few dollars.

When looking for a place, remember to check the phone, the shower, closet space, kitchen cabinets, electrical outlets, light fixtures, the toilet, faucets and water pressure, locks, general security of the building, windows and the condition of the stove, refrigerator and furniture, if furnished. Look at the ceilings for telltale signs of leaks and stains.

Also, check for traffic noise, signs of insects and rodents and what the neighbors are like. Ask about the proximity of buses and availability of taxis.

Here are some more tips a local real estate expert recently wrote:

1. Be clear on what you are looking for and what you can pay. Better rental equals more money.
2. Ask your agent to negotiate the rent down for you. Some landlords will.
3. Try prepaying the rent a few months to get a better rent. Some landlords like this.
4. Widen your choices by furnishing it yourself. We have a real shortage right now of furnished places.
5. Be a good tenant. Costa Rican landlords have become accustomed to bad renters, slow pay, fussy, "please come over and change my light bulb." Make yourself a model renter, the one you would want to rent to, if you were a landlord. This gives you moral and economic leverage. It just makes sense."

Have anything you sign translated into English before you sign it. **Don't sign anything you don't understand based on the landlord's word of honor**. You should be aware that by law landlords can raise rents where the contract is in *colones* a maximum of 15 percent annually.

Opening a Real Estate Company in Costa Rica
By Lester Núñez

I originally came to Costa Rica from Victoria, British Columbia where I was licensed as a broker and worked both residential and commercial real estate sales for over fifteen years. My interest grew in Costa Rica because of the country's weather and culture. Bascially, I guess I just wanted to seek my Hispanic roots.

My plan was to open a real estate office in Costa Rica. Shortly after arriving I met my present partner, Mercedes Castro, who had been working as an independent real estate agent here. My goal was to provide excellent service combined with professionalism and integrity, just like North Americans are accustomed to back home. However, much to my surprise I soon discovered that the local real estate scene was very disorganized. There was no licensing of agents, no formal training and little regulation. Anyone was permitted to sell anything. Now all of this has changed.

I quickly aligned our real estate franchise with the Costa Rican Chamber of Real Estate (CCBR). My partner and I have worked very closely with them over the last five years to formalize real estate training and licensing as in the States and Canada. This has mainly been achieved by educational courses, creation of an Internet-based multiple listing system and licensing requirements.

The Costa Rican Chamber of Real Estate in conjunction with UNED University have created a twenty-two unit course which takes six months to complete and trains future agents.

Multiple listings were also created to further modernize the local real estate profession. The local multiple listing system is now affiliated with MLS Today which has its base in the U.S. and Canada. Combine this with my franchise's worldwide multiple listing system and both the agent and client are now better off. Also, there is legislation pending to regulate the real estate business. All the government has to do is give its approval.

It initially took us a couple of years to get our business off the ground. Our international listings and advertising have been our "bread and butter." It is well-nigh impossible to make a living off the local market alone.

I love Costa Rica because of the climate, inexpensive health care, tax benefits for foreign residents, Spanish culture and much more. You really couldn't get me to return to Canada for anything in this world.

On the other hand, contracts in dollars may be raised only once every three years. A publication can be purchased that explains in detail how the country's rental laws work (*La Ley General de Arrendamientos Urbanos y Suburbanos Ley 7527*). A Spanish version is available at **www.asamblea.go.cr**. You can soon find an English version at **www.rent.co.cr**.

Principal points of the rental law:

1. A rental contract can be either verbal or written.
2. No matter what a contract says, a renter who duly accomplishes the terms of a rental agreement, can stay for three years minimum, no matter what. If the period of the contract is more than three years, the higher term takes priority.
3. At the end of the term, if the landlord wants the rental property back, he or she needs to notify the tenant at least three months before the term expires. Otherwise the term is automatically renewed for another three years or whatever the original term of the contract states.
4. When property is rented to an individual as a home and in *colones*, Costa Rica's currency, the rent amount increases automatically 15 percent every year. When the rental price is agreed to in any other currency, the automatic increase does not apply. Usually rent is stated in colones or U.S. dollars in Costa Rica, but they can be negotiated using any worldwide currency. Businesses can negotiate any payment method and/or yearly adjustments agreeable to both parties.
5. Public services and utilities are to be paid by the tenant except for property taxes, which are the responsibility of the landlord.
6. If a property is sold or otherwise transferred, it should not affect the tenant's rights and the new landlord must respect any existing contract.
7. Any improvements made by a tenant automatically become the property of the landlord.
8. A tenant can not change the original, agreed-upon use of a property. For example, a home cannot be turned into a pet store or a pet store into a bar.
9. Landlords have the right to inspect their property once a month.
10. Tenants have the legal right to pay rent up to seven days after it is due.
11. In negotiating a rental contract, a landlord can request any guarantee deposit they deem necessary to protect their interests.
12. Tenants can not sublet/lease a property.

Rooms in homes usually rent for about $100 monthly. We know of several foreigners who live this way to save money.

As we mention later on, before deciding to live in Costa Rica permanently, it is a good idea to rent a place first or find a real estate agent who can show you around and guide you through the buying process. As you have just seen, a variety of rental options and price ranges is available to match almost any taste or budget. However, for *gringos*, the prices are generally much higher.

You will need a map of San José and the suburbs. The *Tico Times* and *Costa Rica Today* are two places to start looking. *La Nación* is the most prestigious Spanish-language daily with ads. It has an excellent real estate section on Saturdays. However, relying solely on classified ads in newspapers is a mistake and can prove to be misleading. Some places are outright disappointing when compared to the way they are described in ads.

Other sources for finding an apartment are supermarket bulletin boards and word of mouth. Tell everyone you know you're hunting, and ask them to tell everyone they know, and so on. The Blue Marlin Bar, in the Hotel Del Rey, McDonald's in San José, around the Central Park in Heredia and other *gringo* hangouts are other places to inquire about rentals.

When hunting for an apartment or house to rent, contact the **Association of Residents of Costa Rica** (ARCR), Tel: (506) 233-8068 or 221-2053, Fax: (506) 255-0061, www.arca.net. They will help you look in those areas that suit your personal needs and help take the headaches out of finding a place to live.

When reading the ads in the Spanish-language newspapers you should be familiar with the following words:

Air conditioning	*aire acondicionado*
Apartment	*Apartamento*
Backyard	*Patio*
Balcony	*Balcón*
Bars (window)	*Verjas*
Bathroom	*Baño*
Beach	*Playa*
Bedroom	*Dormitorio*
Building	*Edificio*
Carpeted	*Alfombrado*
Cable TV	*Televisión por cable*
Condominium	*Condominio*

Contract	*Contrato*
Deposit	*Depósito*
Dining room	*Comedor*
Dryer	*Secadora*
Elevator	*Elevador, ascensor*
Farm	*finca*
Floor	*El piso, La planta*
Furnished	*Amueblado*
For rent	*Se alquila, en alquiler*
For sale	*Se vende*
Garage	*Cochera, garaje*
Garden	*Jardín*
Grassy area	*Zona verde*
Ground floor	*Planta baja*
Guard	*Guarda*
High speed internet	*Internet de alta velocidad*
Hot water	*Agua caliente*
House	*Casa*
Kitchen	*Cocina*
Laundry room	*Cuarto de pilas*
Living room	*Sala*
Lower floor	*Planta baja*
Maid's quarters	*Cuarto de servicio*
Parking lot	*Parqueo*
Patio	*Patio*
Peaceful, quiet	*Tranquilo*
Refrigerator	*Refrrigeradora, refri*
Rent	*Alquiler*
Rooms	*Habitaciónes, cuartos*
Safe	*Seguro*
Shower	*Ducha*
Stove	*Cocina*
Swimming pool	*Piscina*
Telephone	*Teléfono*
Tub	*Bañera*
Unfurnished	*Sin muebles*
View	*La vista*

Finding a Temporary
Place to Stay

While exploring Costa Rica or looking for an apartment, house or other type of residence in the San José area, you may choose to stay at one of the many accommodations listed below.

If staying in downtown San José, we recommend the **Dunn Inn** (222-3232). It is run by North Americans and is a very popular gringo hangout. The service is excellent and you can make some good contacts. At night the new bar is a happening place. Around the corner the **Posada Amón** (222-6700) is another quaint place to stay in Barrio Amón. The **Hotel Torremolinos** (222-5266) is where we book most of our tour participants. We recommend it highly. The **Hotel Presidente** (222-2034) has reasonable rates, good service and free breakfast included.

In the beautiful city of Heredia we highly recommend the **Hotel America** (260-9292) E-mail: info@hamerica.net, www.hamerica.net. The owners also operate three other quaint and affordable places in the same area: **Hotel Ceos** (262-2628), **Hotel Heredia** (238-0880) and **Hotel D'Cristina** (237-3036).

There are other accommodations for all tastes and budgets in the metropolitan area. The price range is from a few hundred dollars at the top end to less than $20 at the lower end of the scale. We don't have the space to list every hotel, motel, *pensión*, aparthotel and bed-and-breakfast in the section below. If you want a more extensive list we suggest you purchase *Christopher Baker's Cost Rica Handbook* or any of the guides listed in the last chapter of this book.

Vacation Rental Homes

Located in Heredia, known in Costa Rica as the City of Flowers, and only 10 minutes from the airport, are **Rudy's Vacation Rental Homes**. Both are fully furnished, 1,500 square-foot-homes with three bedrooms and two full baths. Each home has cable TV, Internet, a fully-equipped kitchen, laundry room, phone and much more. To find out more contact **Rudy Matthews** at 262-2083 or 839-6961, E-mail: rkmno@aol.com.

Aparthotels

Aparthotels, a cross between an apartment and a hotel, are a good first option because they are furnished, completely equipped and have phone access as well as bilingual management. From there you can comfortably survey the market. If you are living in Costa Rica only on a seasonal basis, an aparthotel is probably your best bet. Most have a kitchenette or other cooking facilities. Usually they are less expensive than hotels with similar amenities, but more expensive than apartments. The **Don Carlos** and **Los Yoses** are centrally located and have nice accommodations. **Aparthotel Castilla** (222-2113), **Aparthotel La Sabana** (220-2422) and **Aparthotel El Sesteo** (296-1805) round out the list.

Bed & Breakfasts

Bed-and-Breakfasts, or b-and-b's as they are sometimes called, have sprouted up all over Costa Rica in recent years. Most of these establishments are smaller and in many cases less expensive than hotels. What sets them apart from other lodging is their home-like, quaint ambience. Many have a live-in host or owner on the premises and some are downtown. Most b-and-b's advertise in the local English-language newspapers, but there is now a service to help you find the "right" b-and-b for you. Call or fax the **Bed-and-Breakfast Association** at 228-9200. To make a reservation, call, 223-4168.

Homestays

Home stays provide a great introduction to the Costa Rican way of life and provide the opportunity for you to improve your Spanish. We highly recommend **Bell's Home Hospitality**, 225-4752, Fax: 224-5884, E-mail: home-stay@racsa.co.cr.

Apartments

Here are three apartments that cater to foreigners, are located in or near downtown San José and offer kitchens, a telephone, cable TV and are furnished. **Apartments Scotland** (Tel: 223-0833, Fax: 257-5317), **Apartments Sudamer** (Tel:221-0247, Fax: 222-2195) and **Apartments Van Fossen** (Tel: 253-9586).

Buying Real Estate

If you can't afford to buy a house in the United States or Canada, prices for decent homes in Costa Rica begin at about $50,000 with financing available for new homes if you become a resident. In 2003 we purchased a new $85,000 home in Heredia with 80 percent financing. Our payments are about $560 monthly on a 15-year, 7.0 percent loan—$150 less than we used to pay for rent in Rohrmoser. The monthly payment includes a life insurance policy that pays off the loan in full in the event of death of the owner.

You do not have to be a resident of Costa Rica to own property and you are entitled to the same ownership rights as citizens of Costa Rica. Ownership of real estate in Costa Rica is fully guaranteed by the constitution to all foreigners. This means your purchase here can be fully secured and safe.

Beach Property

The value of beach property has skyrocketed over the last decade due to the country's increased popularity. Many people want to realize their dream of owning a beachfront lot in a tropical paradise.

For most foreigners, the main beach development areas that are worth considering for retirement and/or vacation homes can be found in Guanacaste areas such as Flamingo, Junquillal and Tamarindo. The Central Pacific beach areas around the towns of Jacó Beach, Quepos and Manuel Antonio are also attractive. The Central Pacific area has great potential, as it is much closer to the Central Valley and San José. The new Ciudad Colón-Orotina and Quepos-Dominical highways will have a huge effect on real estate values in this area, as it will reduce driving time to the Central and South Pacific areas.

Unlike Mexico, some beachfront property may be purchased. However, the 200-meter strip of land along the seacoasts is owned by the government and for public use. It is prohibited to build anything within the first 50 meters of the high-tide line.

This zone is for the public and cannot be turned into a private beach. Also, you can no longer build within the next 50 to 200 meters of the high tide line—this is called the Maritime Zone, or *Zona Marítima*, —unless there is existing housing or a new tourism project involved. If this is the case, you can lease the land from the municipality, which is overseen by the **Costa Rican Tourism Institute** (ICT).

In theory, foreigners cannot lease this land, but there are loopholes in this law. One of the ways to circumvent this regulation is by obtaining a lease through a corporation owned mainly by a Costa Rican. Check with a lawyer to find out how this works.

For your information, beachfront property is being bought-up fast, and the price of this and other prime real estate is soaring.

Before you move to the beach, you should know that for some people the novelty of living at the beach wears off fast. Visiting the beach for a few days or weeks is very different from living there full-time. The humidity, boredom, bugs, lack of emergency medical facilities in a few areas and the occasional inconveniences of living in an often out-of-the-way area are factors that might deter some from moving to any beach

Buying or Building a House in Costa Rica is Different
By Rudy Matthews

Having said that - Should you buy? Absolutely!

If you have a serious interest or have definitely already decided to invest in Costa Rica real estate, go ahead and do it! Costa Rica is a remarkably beautiful country. The beaches and mountains would be hard to duplicate anywhere in the world. I really love it here.

My name is Rudy Matthews, I have a home in Heredia which is just north of the capital city of San José. Thanks to successful real estate investing in the United States I am able live here in Costa Rica.

After dealing with a variety of lawyers, construction companies and banks in Costa Rica I am on a mission to inform and advise anyone thinking of , or in the process of buying Costa Rican real estate.

You may have heard of a horror story or two about Costa Rica real estate and some people who have been taken advantage of. There is no need to dwell on the negative. Instead you should become an educated, well-informed person who learns how to make intelligent decisions before and during a real estate transaction.

You should gather as much information as you can, become informed and if you wish, talk to me. preventative knowledge is better than remedial. Remedial is where you lose your money.. as I stated above, if you are seriously thinking about purchasing real estate in Costa Rica - do it carefully.

I have more than twenty years experience buying, selling, managing and building houses and apartments. As an independent personal consultant, my main objective is to protect you, save you money and eliminate frustration. My knowledge of negotiation, contract clauses that protect you, construction and improvements will be an invaluable service . My understanding of Costa Rican real estate will protect you.

Hard work, honesty and integrity are virtues I have lived by and will maintain for my clients in Costa Rica.

I am NOT a broker nor do I sell property, so I have NO hidden agendas. I am paid by my clients and NOT by realtors or sellers. My fees are reasonable.

Rudy works with **Costa Rica Retirement, Vacation and Investment Properties**. See **www.costaricaretirementvacationproperties.com** or call TOLL FREE 1-888-581-1786 area. However, in general the positives of beach living far outweigh any negatives. Due to Costa Rica's increasing popularity and improving infrastructure, beach property can be an excellent investment.

Besides beach property, there are also homes, condominiums, farms, lots and ranches for sale at reasonable prices, depending on their location. See the section entitled "Where to Live" in Chapter 2 for a description of the areas where many foreigners reside.

Purchasing Property

Purchasing property in Costa Rica is very different from making a similar purchase in your home country. The laws of Costa Rica and the property registration process can be somewhat confusing to a foreigner. Your best bet is to work with a broker (brokers are licensed in Costa Rica) or real estate consultant when looking for property, such as the people we recommend in the section, "Finding a Broker." When you find a property, your broker can help you negotiate the price and explain your financing options.

If you decide to buy real estate, an attorney is absolutely necessary to do the legal work. We strongly recommend that a competent, English-speaking lawyer do a thorough search of all records before you make your purchase to make sure there are no encumbrances (*gravámenes*) on it. One of the biggest errors made by foreigners buying real estate is not properly researching the title for liens. You can obtain information about property at the *Registro de la Propiedad* (like our land title office) in the suburb of Zapote, about five minutes from downtown San José by car or taxi. Because Costa Rica is so small, all land records are kept at this office.

You can also find the status and ownership of a piece of property and get any title documents and surveys you may need at the *registro*. If the property is registered in the name of a corporation, the legal representatives must be verified, since they have power of attorney to make the sale. Information may also be obtained from the registry's website at **www.registronacional.go.cr**.

Your specific property can be researched by using the owner's name, *cédula* (national ID card) or registration number, called a *folio real*. The more information you obtain the better.

The first information that appears should be the owner and registration number. If the registration number ends in 000, chances are you are dealing with an individual owner. If there is another number within the 000, there are probably co-owners. For example, a husband will have the number 001. If a 002 appears, this indicates the property has two different, non-married owners.

The printout you receive will give you the following information in Spanish. You may need someone to translate.

(a) The description of the property and the name of the province where it is located.

(b) The boundaries of the property

(c) The area in square meters (make sure the property you are buying really is the same size).

(d) The survey number of record.

(e) Origin of land or history (perhaps it was a farm before, etc.)

(f) Government assessment for transfer purposes

(g) Data concerning the owners— whether an individual, individuals or a corporation.

(h) *Cédula* (ID) of the owner(s) or corporation

(i) Estimated price (this can vary in Costa Rica; there is sometimes a difference between what is paid and what is actually recorded).

(j) Statement of full ownership

(k) The number that was recorded in the registry when the owner took over the property.

(l) Date registered.

Beach property is in high demand.

(m) *Anotaciones*—this is very important point since there may be pending activity concerning the property.

(n) *Gravámenes*— has to do with liens, mortgages and encumbrances.

Deposits and Escrows

Let us hear what Rudy Matthews of Costa Rica Retirement Vacation properties has to say about this subject: "In Costa Rica a real estate transaction is different. I have read various Internet articles about "crooked" real estate transactions in Costa Rica. The first step in protecting yourself here in a real estate transaction is to realize you are in a different country governed by a different legal system and you fall under the umbrella of the way things are done here and not the way they are done in the United States. For instance, real estate deposits and escrows here are very different. Escrow accounts are virtually non-existent unless you are dealing with a company like Stuart Title or have a legal arrangement with your lawyer. I will focus on deposits, since you definitely need to be aware of how they work in Costa Rica.

"The majority of the time the deposit is going to be held by the seller. Instead of 'held,' I should have said 'given' to the seller. I do not think many sellers in Costa Rica hold deposits very long. Therefore, you should place as little money as possible in the hands of the seller. Five percent is a start, with a maximum of 10 percent. When asked how much I would like to deposit, I usually say, 'the least amount of money possible.' Then, when the seller names a figure I always say it is too much. What is the least amount possible? It is amazing how much sellers will come down to initiate a sale.

"If you back out as a buyer, the seller who already has your deposit will most likely keep it. I would venture to say in Costa Rica, in many cases the seller has already spent the deposit money. You can put a protective clause in your contract, but the bottom line is, that deposits, once lost, are hard to recover here. The one clause I advise clients to put in the contract is that if the seller does not honor the contract or other unforeseen circumstances occur, the buyer will be returned double the original deposit. I do not think this clause scares away anyone, but it might help you in another situation. It is not uncommon for the seller to sell the property to someone else if they offer a higher price.

"You may think that if you lose your deposit you can take the seller to court to recover it. The legal process can sometimes take years.

"Concerning monies, I advise clients never to use cash because there is no paper trail and cash can do funny things to people. Certified or regular checks from the United States can take a long time to clear. It is better to open an account here, wire your money and get a certified check from your bank in Costa Rica."

Transferring Title

If a property appears free and clear of encumbrances, the lawyer can then proceed. Your lawyer should then draft a transfer deed or *escritura de traspaso* to move the ownership from seller to buyer. The transfer deed should include details about financing of the property. In Costa Rica the buyer and the seller usually share the closing costs, which normally run about four to five of the total purchase. A small real estate transfer tax, or 1.5 percent of the actual value, is included, as well as a registration fee, stamps and notary fees, which vary depending on the price of the sale. Title insurance is optional but advisable. It is common practice with many lawyers in Costa Rica to lower the actual amount paid on a sale to a much lower sum on paper to reduce land transfer tax. This can be risky and problems may arise later on. Make sure you understand what you are expected to pay.

Property may be purchased individually, between several people or in the name of a corporation (*sociedad anónima*). Buying and registering a property in a corporation has many advantages, mainly, asset protection in the event of a divorce or a lawsuit. When a corporation owns the property, the sale or purchase of the company can be negotiated so you don't have to pay property taxes or stamp fees. All you have to

A $175,000 + home in a middle-class neighborhood.

do is change the board of directors, the legal representatives of the corporation, and transfer the shares.

Do not hire the same lawyer used by the seller of the property. In Costa Rica an attorney can legally represent both parties. Also, do not forget to check that you are buying the land from its rightful owner. Some owners have sold their land to several buyers. You can protect your real estate investment further if you talk with neighbors about water shortages, safety and burglaries in the area.

Remember, always see the property in person and never buy sight unseen. Don't forget to check if you need special permits to build. Be sure to check the comparative land values in your area to see if you are getting a good deal. If you are thinking of living in a remote area, check to be sure that roads, electricity and telephone service are available.

Property Taxes

You will be pleased to know that no capital gains taxes on real estate exist in Costa Rica, so it is an excellent investment. You do have to pay yearly taxes, but they are low by U.S. standards. Yearly property taxes are on a sliding scale up to .25 percent of the stated value of a particular property. So on a house valued at $100,000 you pay about $250 yearly. This is a bargain compared to what most people pay in the United States.

Property taxes are collected by the local municipal government, which also collects a separate tax for garbage. The latter has to be paid when you pay your property tax. Every year I go through this painless procedure at the *Palacio Municipal de Heredia*. The taxes on my home run about $280 including garbage. I have found the clerks at the city offices to be very courteous and helpful.

Squatters

Squatters, or *precaristas*, as they are known in Costa Rica, can be a real problem.

In Costa Rica squatters have certain rights. The laws that protect them were originally passed to prevent wealthy people from acquiring too much land, as in some Latin American countries. Land ownership here is an active process — stop taking care of it and it will go to someone who will. It is the law and the intent of the law. Costa Rica did not establish its law so that foreigners could buy large chunks of land and leave it idle as a future investment. They established their law originally so that they wouldn't have a large class of people denied land because a few very rich owned it.

Undeveloped land is a prime target for squatter invasions. Once they establish themselves on your land, it is difficult to get rid of them. If they occupy the land for less than a year, it is fairly easy to have them removed, especially during the first three months. The sooner you get them off the land, the fewer problems you will have. Be careful! After a certain period of time they can claim the land as their own.

The best way to avoid squatters is to prevent them from settling on your land. Visit the land periodically to help prevent people from settling on it. If you cannot live on your property year-round, then you will have to hire a guard, caretaker or a reliable house sitter to watch it for you. If you have a caretaker make sure to obtain a receipt each time you pay him. Have your lawyer or some other person keep an eye on your caretaker. There have been cases in which caretakers have tried to squat on land.

Also, make sure boundary fences and limit signs are well maintained and visible. If you have to be an absentee owner, you can have a friend or attorney stop by to check your property periodically.

There is a trustworthy professional house-sitting agency in San José that will watch your home while you are away. It is bonded and will provide references upon request. You may contact the agency at 256-7890.

For some people it is better to rent for at least six months. However, whether you rent or buy first really depends on your comfort level. Make sure to buy where it's easy to rent or sell your home or condominium in case you change your plans, or in the event of a personal emergency. If you choose to purchase in a popular area in the path of progress you should not have a problem selling your home if it is priced correctly.

Finding a Broker

You are advised to use the services of a real estate broker to buy or sell property in Costa Rica. Real estate agents normally collect a five or six percent commission on the sale of a home and up to 10 percent commission on the sale of raw land. This commission is paid by the seller of the property to the realtor.

In order to find a competent, honest broker, it is wise to talk to other expatriates or contact the local **Chamber of Real Estate Brokers** or *Cámara Costarricense de Bienes Raíces*.

Here is why it is important to work with a good broker.
1. A good broker can help you find a fair-priced property.

2. Only a small percentage of properties for sale are in the newspaper. A lot of brokers have their own listings, which they don't share with other brokers.
3. A broker can save you time and aggravation by showing you just what you want. He will do this by pre-qualifying you.
4. Good brokers have excellent contacts and will help you with every step of the process.
5. A good broker will know all of the good areas and will not waste your time showing you undesirable neighborhoods. A broker who knows you are working faithfully with him will go all out to help you find what you want. Be sure and to tell your broker from the beginning if you are working with other agents.
6. A good broker can form a relationship with you and truly understand your specific needs.
7. Working with a broker in Costa Rica is similar to working with a broker back home. If you are patient, loyal and have confidence in your broker, you will find what you want.
8. Brokers offer a wide range of properties. They sell a little bit of everything.: houses, lots, commercial property, condos, and even *fincas* (farms). Therefore, it is best to find a broker who specializes inexactly what you are looking for. A person who sells at the beach cannot possibly be an expert in properties in the Central Valley.

Be careful because the real estate industry is not regulated as in the United States. Therefore, we recommend contacting **Costa Rica Retirement Vacation Properties** toll-free 1-888-581-1786, E-mail: **robert@costaricaretirementvacationproperties.com**, **christas@ racsa.co.cr** or **www.costaricaretiementvacationproperties.com** or **www.primecostaricaproperty.com**. This company has more than 35 years of combined experience in the retirement/investment market, and has helped thousands of people make their retirement and investment dreams come true.

How to Locate a Property
To find a house or land to purchase, look for a well-recommended realtor who can identify true market value like the real estate agencies we list in this section. You may also want to see the listings in the back of the *The Tico Times*. If you want to save money, look in the daily Spanish-language newspapers *La Nación* or *La República*, because prices are more realistic. Also, look around; go door-to-door in areas you like, and talk to other expats. If you drive around an area you like,

you are bound to see a number of for-sale signs for properties not listed in the newspaper.

Keep in mind that housing costs are much higher in *gringo* enclaves such as Escazú and Rohrmoser. Be sure to remember that the farther away you live from San José and other cities the more you get for your money.

The pricing of land in Costa Rica can be relative. One way to find out is to hang out with the locals and see what land is really going for in an area. By cross-referencing one can usually arrive at the real value of property in a specific area. Another method of pricing is to put a value on it according to what they need. A property may be worth only $10,000, but the owner needs $15,000. So he puts an arbitrary asking price of $15,000 on the property. The best way to find the true value is to compare the price of similar properties in the area, look for a motivated seller and work with a competent broker who knows the area. Many established brokers have sold properties in the area and keep a list of their previous sales. Some foreigners, including North Americans, charge outrageous prices to make a quick buck. So, be careful with whom you deal.

To find a good buy, you should study the market. It is also a good idea to negotiate in colones since you will come out ahead in the long run as the *colón* continues to devaluate. This will make your home appreciate over time. Don't depend too much on the newspaper. Talk to as many people as you can. Nothing works better than word of mouth for finding good deals. Practice your negotiating skills. *Ticos* love to haggle. You may be better off having a trustworthy, bilingual Costa Rican search for you and do your negotiating. Your realtor or lawyer should also be able to assist you.

Stewart Title (Tel: 258-5600, Fax: 222-7936, see www.stewarttitle. com) can assist you with title searches and full title guarantee. American Title also has a representative in Costa Rica.

Recently the **Costa Rica Realtors' Chamber** opened the country's first out-of-court conflict resolution center specializing in property disputes. It specializes in solving property disputes for both sellers and buyers within six months. The same process in the courts can often take up to 10 years or more to get to trial. Anyone in need of such services may contact them at Tel: 283-2891, Fax: 283-0347, or E-mail: **caccbr@racsa.co.cr.**

Tips before you actually
make the purchase

Once you have found the property or home you like, there are a few precautions you need to take.

1. Make sure you know the real value of the property.
2. Do not assume the seller or broker is trustworthy just because they speak English. This is a common pitfall.
3. Make sure the property you are about to purchase in not part of a national park or subject to restricted use. There are areas near Dominical, for example, that abut a rainforest where it is forbidden to cut any trees.
4. If you purchase raw land, be sure to get a soil sample and hire an engineer, especially if your lot has been cut out of a hillside. We know of one man who built a million-dollar home on a bluff overlooking the beach. About a year later he had to spend $100,000 to build a retaining wall because the rain started to undermine his lot.
5. If you buy in a remote region make sure you can bring electricity to the land. This can be expensive. Also check to see if the water supply is good in the area.
6. Do not rely on a verbal contract if you decide to make an offer. Get everything in writing.
7. Check out your neighbors. There is nothing worse than buying property and finding out later that you have bad neighbors.

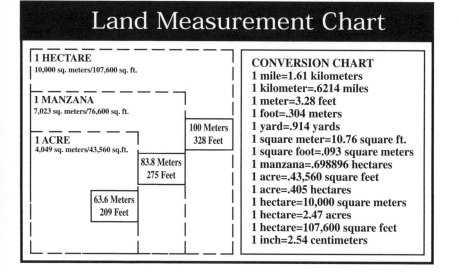

Land Measurement Chart

1 HECTARE
10,000 sq. meters/107,600 sq. ft.

1 MANZANA
7,023 sq. meters/76,600 sq. ft.

1 ACRE
4,049 sq. meters/43,560 sq.ft.

100 Meters
328 Feet

83.8 Meters
275 Feet

63.6 Meters
209 Feet

CONVERSION CHART
1 mile=1.61 kilometers
1 kilometer=.6214 miles
1 meter=3.28 feet
1 foot=.304 meters
1 yard=.914 yards
1 square meter=10.76 square ft.
1 square foot=.093 square meters
1 manzana=.698896 hectares
1 acre=.43,560 square feet
1 acre=.405 hectares
1 hectare=10,000 square meters
1 hectare=2.47 acres
1 hectare=107,600 square feet
1 inch=2.54 centimeters

8. If buying in the city or near a major street, check the noise level. Make sure there are no dancehalls, bars, rowdy neighbors or noisy buses.
9. If you purchase a home, have an engineer make sure it is structurally sound. Also, check the plumbing, wiring, roof for leaks, water pressure and septic or sewage system.
10. If buying in the city it is extremely important to be familiar with the neighborhood where you decide to buy. Make sure you are not buying in a crime-ridden area. There are a few areas around San José where you would not like to live. A good broker and doing your homework can help you avoid this disaster.

Building A Home

In Costa Rica you can build your retirement dream house since land, labor and materials are inexpensive. However, think twice about undertaking such a project because you could be flirting with disaster. Many foreigners who have built homes complain that it sounds easier than it really is. They would not do it again because of costly delays, unreliable labor, fussy building inspectors, different laws and building codes and many other unforeseen problems. Be sure to talk with foreigners who have built homes to see what obstacles they encountered. Costs depend on location, materials and the size of the home you want to build. You generally pay $500 to $1,000 a square meter or $45 to $90 a square foot.

One common mistake some newcomers make is to hurry to build their dream home while they are still on their "honeymoon" with the country. Many have been shocked by substantial cost overruns. Months or years later, they realize too much of their capital has been spent on their new home.

If you do decide to build a home on your land, there are several steps required. First, conduct a preliminary study, which should be completed before you buy the land. Also, be sure to see if your lot has access to water, drainage, electricity and telephone services.

The law says you have to hire an architect or civil engineer to file all of your construction permits.

A building permit must be obtained from the municipality where you plan to build. An architect can usually handle building permits and work jointly with the contractor to supervise the construction. It may take a couple of months or longer to get all of the permits in order. A reliable contractor will also have to be hired. You should get several bids and ask for references. Expect to visit the construction site almost everyday to ensure things are getting done. If you cannot be there, have a reliable person inspect the construction site for you on a daily basis.

According to one local realtor, this is how you can lose money while building a home:

1. Give money to a real nice and friendly contractor and then leave the country and tell him you will be back in a couple of months.
2. Take the first bid you get because it seems so incredibly cheap, far cheaper than anyone else's. Halfway through, when the real price emerges, it is nearly impossible to get a second contractor to come in and finish what the first one started. So, you are stuck with him and have to pay the real price to build, but now you are working with someone you do not trust.
3. Pay no attention to the amount of cinder-blocks delivered to your construction site.
4. Live in the city while building in the country and only drive out on weekends.
5. Give the power of attorney to almost anyone. There is a special trick here for people getting your deed number (*escritura*), and suddenly you don't own the property anymore.
6. Ignore the advice of experienced people because the taxi driver and the guy on the bar stool are "locals" and must give good advice.

In short, I buy my materials directly through local hardware stores (*ferreterías*), get receipts, place orders by phone and live on the land while building on it. Some people do it by contract. I pay the workers once a week, pay my building supplies once a month and use a hardware store I know and trust. The contractor supervising the project gets a bonus of about 10 percent of the total building cost.

One Local Residents Experience
Building a Home in Costa Rica

"Lots of folks seem interested in building a house in Costa Rica. My wife and I have done this twice and thought that maybe knowing about some of our experiences might prove useful to others.

"Because we're focusing on building here, I won't talk about buying land. I'll assume that you've already acquired the land you want to use.

"We arrived here with plans we had purchased in the States. We found them in one of a myriad of home plan books that you can buy at bookstores. When we made our decision, we sent off for the plans.

"Although we loved the plans, we had to make a lot of necessary changes to make the construction suitable for Costa Rica. For example, we didn't want the house built with wooden studs and sheet rock. We decided to use concrete block and stucco.

"Clearly we needed an architect to help us with all this. So we asked the realtors from whom we had bought the land if they could recommend one. They had someone they had worked with in the past and highly recommended. After twice meeting with the architect, we asked him for a quote, found it reasonable, and contracted him to make the modifications.

"Of course we weren't contracting him to design the house from scratch by any means. Had we been doing that, the process would have been different. In any case, if you're going to build a house, you must have some relationship with an architect so that the plans you submit for approval are properly stamped by a professional architect in good standing in Costa Rica. You will also use the architect to obtain the building permits for you.

"Make no mistake about it: you must get your building permits. I can't tell you how many times I have heard of people who had their building projects stopped dead in the water because they had no permits. The interesting thing is that after you've submitted your plans and received your permits, there's not a lot of checking that goes on to make sure that what you're building agrees with the plans. Personally, however, I would not take the chance of submitting plans that are not what you're going to build.

"Also in our agreement we contracted him to be the supervising architect, that is, he would submit the plans, as mentioned above, would do all the paper work, keep the on-site log required by law, work closely with the builder, etc. We paid him $10,000 for all of that. The funds were paid over the course of the project, according to an agreed-upon schedule.

"We had already found a builder. He lived right in our little town. In fact, our property was part of a huge farm his father had once owned. He had built a lot of the houses for our neighbors, and we examined those very closely. We also looked very closely at houses in the neighborhood built by others. Our guy's work was really superior, plus he had an excellent reputation with our friends and neighbors, almost all North Americans. We never regretted our decision to go with him.

"When the architect had the plans ready, we gave them to the builder and two weeks later he came back with a price for all labor and materials. The price was more than we had expected. We now know that the reason for this was that he was concerned because the house was more complex than anything he had ever built before, and he was padding considerably to help ensure that he didn't lose money. The fellow did everything on scraps of paper and didn't have any kind of estimating system of any sophistication at all; he didn't even have a computer. Some houses he made money on, on others he lost money.

"Although the price was higher than we wanted, it was not unreasonable by any means. We both made some adjustments and soon agreed on a price. One thing should be stressed here; the price was for all labor and materials, that is, it was a fixed price. I'll talk about alternatives later. It was agreed, of course, that any changes we wanted to make would cost extra. As it turned out, we did, indeed, make a handful of changes, one of which was significant and the others rather minor. But for each one we agreed beforehand on the cost so that we knew all along what the project was costing us.

"Three things we talked about quite a bit before signing our agreement had to do with allowances, infrastructure improvements, and payment structure.

"The question of allowances is extremely important in a deal such as this, that is, where there's a fixed price. Clearly you, the owner are going to select things such as finishes (tiles, floors, counter-tops, for example), paint, light fixtures, plumbing fixtures, doors, windows, cabinets, shelving and many other things.

"The builder has already estimated what these are going to cost him, otherwise he couldn't give you a fixed price. So you have to know what he estimated so that when you pick things out you'll know whether you're right on the money or whether you're going over budget, in which case you'll owe the builder if you decide to purchase these things anyway, or whether you're under budget, in which case he will owe you money.

"The question of infrastructure is important, too. One must make sure, for example, that the price includes bringing water to the property. In the rural areas where we built both times, there's no such thing as 'city water.' What about telephone lines to the property? What about electricity? All of this has to be planned beforehand, and there are costs the builder isn't responsible for.

"For example, both times we built, although there was electricity available, there was no transformer on the road from which to supply our houses. So we had to pay the electric company for buying and installing a transformer. We had no phones where we first built, so there was no problem about installation. At our second house, telephone service was available, but the nearest pole was a kilometer away. We were responsible for paying for poles and cable and having the work done to bring the lines from that last pole to our house.

"These things about electricity and phone might strike you as being strange or unusual. But if you live out in the country in Costa Rica, that's the way it's done.

"Finally there was the question of payment. We worked out a schedule of how much we needed to give the builder and at what intervals. That made it easy for both of us to watch our cash flow.

"Another important consideration while building is where you will be while the building is going on. The first time we built a large house, we were living in a small guest house right on the property and were always right there. Indeed, every day the foreman (who, by the way, was fantastic) would consult with us numerous times as did the subcontractors. Living on site is the absolutely best arrangement. It's even better when, as in this case, the builder lives right in the neighborhood.

"When we built the second house, we were living in a rental house that was exactly a 20-minute drive from the building site. In addition, the architect/builder lived in San José. What a difference that made. We were obviously not always available to the foreman and subcontractors. We had to schedule regular meetings at exact times on certain days with the builder who had to travel about an hour and a half to get to the site. Although it was doable, it was far from ideal.

"We have friends who continued to live in the States while their houses were being built. In most cases this resulted in large problems and great frustration.

"All in all, the building of our first house went extremely well. The house itself was magnificent, we had all the input anyone could ask for and at the end of the day we still had a fine relationship with the builder.

"I wish I could say that after the first experience, the second was even better because of all we had learned the first time. But the second time we did it differently and I must say that even though in the end, we were extremely pleased with the house, getting to that point was much more difficult than our first venture.

"In this case, we didn't start with pre-drawn plans, but we did have a highly detailed plan that my wife worked out with just a little bit of help from me. Then she built a model that would have done her proud in any school of architecture.

"We met the builder by calling him after seeing his full-page ad in an upscale Costa Rican home and building publication. He was an extremely bright young man who built only log homes, which is what we wanted. There are other log home builders in Costa Rica and we investigated them all. But the type of homes they built were not what we were looking for.

"What we did was to have a series of meetings with the architect at which we would present our ideas, he would make sketches, we'd come back, look at what he did, discuss it and then go to the next round. The purpose of this was to end up with a plan, on paper, with drawings (but not final blue prints) of what we would go ahead with. He charged us a set price for the series of meetings that was quite reasonable, less than $1,000.

"Eventually we agreed on a plan about which we were quite excited. At that point, we contracted, but on an entirely different basis than we did during the first project. This time there was a fixed cost for plans, labor and labor supervision. The idea here is that if they don't meet the deadline for completion, we don't pay anything extra regardless of how long they take.

"The architect's company was also the builder. Materials, however, were only estimated and we would pay for the materials as we went. In most cases they would buy the materials and I would pay the invoices directly to the vendors, unless the architect had already paid for them and gave me a cancelled invoice, in which case I would reimburse him.

"All the things that are normally considered allowances, that is, the things the client picks, we ourselves would just pick and buy, since there was no set price for materials.

"There are two potential dangers in doing this. The first is that the estimate made by the architect/builder is way off, in which case you could go way over budget on materials. The second is that the architect/builder could be in cahoots with the suppliers and we could be overcharged, with them getting a 'commission.'

"The latter was not the case. I was convinced at the time that these were honest people and even after all the difficulties we later had, I still believe them to be honest men. But ... that's the only thing that went well.

"We had the estimate for materials and a completion date five months out. They spent a great deal of time explaining to us why we could be sure that the estimated materials cost was right on the money and the job was going to be on time. Unlike our first builder, these folks were highly computerized—which just goes to show that the old saw about garbage in, garbage out, as far as computers are concerned is absolutely right.

"They were to start working on January 3 or 4 and were to finish on May 30. I fired all of them about early April because it was clear that at this point they had no real idea of when the house was going to be done -- I estimated that it was about 90 percent done.

"At that point we were a good 20 percent over budget and I was having a hard time getting a fix on what was to come. As you can imagine, there was a lot of other stuff going on that contributed to my reaching the point of firing him. One significant problem was, as I mentioned, that they were from San José and weren't here nearly as often as they needed to be, and the foreman here was as bad as our first foreman was great. Additionally, they were always late on their estimates about when we, the clients, had to make certain materials choices. This, in turn, resulted in either falling further and further behind schedule or our settling for something that wasn't our first choice.

"Eventually, after I fired them, the job was finished by a terrific local guy. Before we started the house, he had been the architect and supervisor for a large stable, a nice little house for our workers, a large gate, water system, etc. He had done a great job and he's extremely competent and, in general, an exceedingly nice and honorable young man. We didn't consider him for the main house because we wanted someone with experience in building log homes. That was a mistake.

"He did a fantastic job in getting the house and remaining infrastructure work done and had an extremely efficient crew of local workers. Man, what a difference between using local workers and workers who have no tie to the community.

"Clearly, the first arrangement with a fixed price was far superior to this open-ended material purchasing arrangement. We'd certainly never go into an arrangement such as the second one again.

"Concerning prices per square-meter for building, there is a great, great range of prices, so it is difficult to speak generally. The variables involved are many. For example, a huge part of cost of materials is based on transportation charges. Thus, if you're far away from the suppliers your materials cost can easily increase by as much as 30 percent. At times, I've had delivery charges that were 50 percent of the value of the materials delivered.

"Labor costs, especially unskilled labor, vary from builder to builder, regardless of what the law says. This, too, tends to be influenced by location. If you're building in a generally economically depressed area, the builder will pay the workers less than in an urban area where there might be more work available.

"The type of house you're building will make a great difference in cost per square meter as well. For example, the log and stone house of the second project required much more hand crafting than a block, concrete and stucco house, such as the first one we built. But then comes design. The first one had many curved walls, niches, a curved stairway to the second floor, etc. All of this takes a lot more time to do and thus results in great labor charges.

"In the second project, in addition to the house, we built a large stable, a small house for animal rehabilitation, a large flight cage for un-releasable bats we've rehabilitated, a small house for our workers and a large storage facility. All the prices per square-meter varied greatly, not only because of the usual variables but also because we used several different builders for the several projects.

"But, just to give a general idea, a very good price for a simple home would be between $270 and $323 per square meter ($25 to $30 per square foot). A simple house would be basically a one-story, rectangular structure with straight walls and a simple roof line built with block, concrete, and stucco. Some people refer to this type of design as a "*tico* house."

"On the other hand, you should be able to build just about anything you want, regardless of how complex and complete, for between $540 to $645 per square meter ($50 to $60 per square foot).

"If you're building a simple block and concrete house and you're paying between $40 and $45 per square foot, you're probably paying quite a bit too much.

"And if you're building anything for $65 per square foot and above, you're probably building a mini Taj Mahal."

Long-time Costa Rican resident Martin Rice is the author of A*t Home in Costa Rica* ISBN 1413460283.

Commercial Real Estate

There is commercial real estate for anyone thinking of starting a retail business or looking for office space. Office space in and around San José can be leased for anywhere from $7 to $20 per square meter, depending on the location.

Downtown San José has outgrown itself. The majority of office space is now found west of the city. More and more tenants are moving into new buildings on the outskirts of town. The new **Torre Mercedes**

Real Estate Terms

amortization	*amortización*
appraisal	*el avalúo*
apreciation	*apreciación*
back yard	*el patio*
bathroom	*el baño*
bedroom	*el dormitorio*
borrower	*el prestatario*
to borrow	*pedir prestado*
buyer	*el comprador*
cash price	*precio al contado*
closing	*el cierre*
collateral	*la garantía*
clear title	*título libre de gravamenes*
closing	*costo de los gastos de cierre*
compound interest	*interés compuesto*
condo	*condominio*
contract	*el contrato*
counter offer	*contraoferta*
credit rating	*el historial crediticio*
debt	*deuda*
declared value	*el valor declarado*
deed	*el título de propiedad*
depreciation	*depreciación, desvalorización*
down payment	*la prima, pago inicial, enganche*
easement	*servidumbre*
encumbrance, lien	*el gravamen*
equity	*el activo neto*
extensión of time	*la prórroga*
extensión of credit	*concesión de crédito*
farm	*la finca*
first mortage	*hipoteca en primer grado*
fixed-rate mortgage	*hipoteca con tasa de interés fija*
fixed term	*plazo fijo*

for sale ....*en venta, se vende*
gated community ....*residencial amurallado*
Hall of Records for property ....*El Registro de Propiedad*
hectare (25 acres) ....*la hectárea*
house ....*la casa*
interest rate ....*la tasa de interés*
investment..*la inversión*
joint tenancy ....*tenencia conjunta*
kitchen ....*la cocina*
landlord...*el casero*
lease ....*el contrato de arrendamiento*
lender...*el prestamista*
letter of credit..*carta de crédito*
line of credit ....*la línea de crédito*
list price ....*precio de lista*
loan..*el préstamo*
market value...*el valor de mercado*
mortgage...*la hipoteca*
to mortgage ....*hipotecar*
offer ....*la oferta*
permit ....*el permiso*
pool ....*la piscina*
prime interest rate ....*la tasa de interés preferencial*
property...*la propiedad, bienes inmuebles*
property tax...*impuesto territorial*
real estate ....*bienes raíces*
real estate broker ....*corredor de bienes y raíces*
rea l price ....*precio real*
rent ....*el alquiler*
to rent ....*alquilar*
second mortage ....*hipoteca en segundo grado*
sold ....*vendido*
tenent...*el inquilino*
tax...*el impuesto*
title ....*el título*

and **Centro Colón** are huge office buildings west of downtown. **Oficentro** is a huge complex of five office buildings, to the south of Sabana Park. About five minutes to the west is **Plaza Roble**, located next to Multiplaza Mall. In Santa Ana, the newly constructed **Plaza Forum Center** has abundant office space.

Many large homes in the Rohrmoser area have been turned into businesses because of the lack of adequate space and office facilities in San José. All of the growth toward the west has happened because many Costa Rican landlords have not refurbished buildings in the downtown area.

Financing

Until about 10 years ago it was difficult for anyone to obtain financing here. The only thing available was owner financing. Now all of that has changed. Costa Rica Costa Ricans and foreigners may now apply for loans from public and private banks. However, foreigners need to have a residency permit and/or a job. Interest on the loan and requirements may vary from bank to bank. Please see the next page for details about financing.

A well-kept secret is that foreigners may use pre-tax IRAs from the United States to purchase property here (see the section in this book about IRAs). This procedure is perfectly legal. They can also take out a line on credit of the equity of their home in the United States. We also know of some people who have obtained financing in Costa Rica without being residents as long as their credit rating is good in their home country.

Now you can be part of bigger things by participating in joint venture investor groups. This is not a solicitation for investments, but for those who wish to join forces with other like-minded people seeking larger tracts of land.

For information about financing and joint venture investor groups, contact **Costa Rica Retirement/Investment Properties** toll-free at 1-888-581-1786 E-mail: **robert@ costaricaretirementvacationproperties.com**.

Speculating

If you are interested in purchasing real estate for investment purposes, you will be pleased to know that the government welcomes your investment. If you choose to speculate in real estate, there are some prime areas to choose from in the Central Valley. This area offers a lot more potential because of its proximity to San José, the large

A Sample of Requirements for Obtaining a Loan

Private Banks

Banco Interfin (www.interfin.fi.cr)
INTEREST RATES IN DOLLAR S$9
INTEREST RATES IN COLONES ¢22%
TERM 15 years
MINIMUM LOAN AMOUNT $30,000
MAXIMUM LOAN AMOUNT (% OF APPRAISAL VALUE) . $70%, ¢80%
COMMISSION FEES 3.5% commission; 1.69% legal fees; appraisal fees.
WHO QUALIFIES Residents and non-residents who have lived in the country for at least a year*

Banco Banex (www.banex.co.cr)
INTEREST RATES IN DOLLARS $8.5% revised
INTEREST RATES IN COLONES ¢25%
TERM 0 years
MINIMUM LOAN AMOUNT $30,000
MAXIMUM LOAN AMOUNT (% OF APPRAISAL VALUE) 80%
COMMISSION FEES Approximately 6% including legal fees, bank commission and first month's insurance.
WHO QUALIFIES Residents and non- residents who have lived in the country for at least a year

Banco San José (www.bancosanjose.com)
INTEREST RATES IN DOLLARS Prime rate or 8% minimum, revised quarterly
INTEREST RATE IN COLONES Not available
TERM 15 years
MINIMUM LOAN AMOUNT $30,000
MAXIMUM LOAN AMOUNT (% OF APPRAISAL VALUE) 70% $400,000 maximum
COMMISSION FEES Approximately 10%
WHO QUALIFIES Residents only

Scotiabank (www.scotiabank.com)
INTEREST RATES IN DOLLARS From 7.25% for residents. From 8.25% for non-residents.
INTEREST RATES IN COLONES 19.95% 1st year, options start at 22.5%

TERM Up to 30 years
MINIMUM LOAN AMOUNT None
MAXIMUM LOAN AMOUNT (% OF APPRAISAL VALUE) 75% for living
purposes 65% recreational or rental purposes
COMMISSION FEES From 5 to 10%
WHO QUALIFIES Residents and foreigners/non-residents who must
have two types of ID (including passport), SSN, income tax statements
from last three quarters, last bank and credit card statements certification
of ownership of house, car, etc. Legalized by the Costarican Consulate or
Embassy in US (or Homeland)

Public Banks

Banco Nacional (www.bncr.fi.cr)
INTEREST RATES IN DOLLARS $7,5% fixed first year, variable from
9% minimum subsequent years (currently 9.25%)
INTEREST RATES IN COLONES ¢20% fixed first years, periodically
adjustable subsequent years (currently 24,5%)
TERM $Up to 20 years ¢Up to 30 years
MINIMUM LOAN AMOUNT $1
MAXIMUM LOAN AMOUNT (% OF APPRAISAL VALUE) $80 % ¢ 90%
$200,000 maximum
COMMISSION FEES 2% Comission: appraisal fees (vary with
amount); various other fees
WHO QUALIFIES Residents Only

Banco de Costa Rica (www.bancobcr.com)
INTEREST RATES $9,5% ¢23.5%
TERM 15 years
MINIMUM LOAN AMOUNT $40,000
MAXIMUM LOAN AMOUNT (% OF APPRAISAL VALUE) $70% $80%
COMMISSION FEES Approximately 10%
WHO QUALIFIES Residents Only

Banco de Crédito Agrícola (www.bancocreditocr.com)
INTEREST RATES In DOLLARS $9,5%
TERM 20 years
MINIMUM LOAN AMOUNT $30,000
MAXIMUM LOAN AMOUNT(% OF APPRAISAL VALUE) $75%, ¢80%
COMMISSION FEES Aproximmately 9%
WHO QUALIFIES Residents Only

number of services available and excellent infrastructure. The towns of Escazú, San Rafael de Heredia, Santa Ana, Ciudad Colón, Alajuela (Costa Rica's second city) and San José's suburbs of Rohrmoser, Los Yoses and San Pedro are all hot spots.

Homes range from about $30,000 in some *tico* neighborhoods to a couple of hundred thousand dollars in high-scale areas such as Rohrmoser and Escazú. It is best to speculate in middle and lower-end properties since they are more affordable for the average Costa Rican and financing is available. A standard rule of thumb is the farther from town you go, the lower the price.

The current housing shortage, the popularity of the Costa Rica and the Central Valley's weather assure excellent investment opportunities. Whether you are buying a home or an investment property, you are bound to make money if you hang on to your property. Real estate values are expected to double over the next decade or two. During the last 10 years some property values have risen 10 times. There is limited land in some urban areas, so the resale value goes up as population grows. Beach property is a good investment because of the demand.

Presently there is a building and investment boom in Costa Rica's Central Pacific and Guanacaste beach areas. Infrastructure continues to improve in these once inaccessible areas. The Central Pacific area is like Hawaii or California, but only a fraction of the price. If you cannot afford to live in a prime coastal area in the United States, you may be able to find the property of your dreams in Costa Rica in a much more spectacular setting.

Remember this when thinking of investing in Costa Rican property. Real estate will not become more plentiful in Costa Rica and the demand will increase based on the number of retirees world-wide. Furthermore, the exodus from the United States due to government policies will increase the world wide demand created by North Americans looking for a simpler lifestyle.

Another excellent investment is Costa Rica's nascent Real Estate Investment Trust Market. Briefly, a **Real Estate Investment Trust** (*fondo inmobiliario*) or **REIT** is a type of public investment fund that buys and rents out real estate and distributes the profits among investors. Depending on the fund, dividends are paid on a monthly, quarterly or yearly basis. Revenues for these types of funds depend mainly on the price at which the property was bought and the price at which it rents. For more information, contact **Costa Rica Retirement Vacation Properties** at E-mail: **robert@**

costaricaretirementvacationproperties.com, christas@racsa.co.cr or call toll free 1-888-581-1786.

Banks offer properties that were collateral for a mortgage loan and were legally repossessed by the bank after the client defaulted on the loan. Properties are awarded to the highest bidder. Most banks require a five percent security deposit when making a bid. Some good deals may be found by checking with a local bank.

Property management companies are available to take the hassles out of home ownership. Most property management companies charge a monthly fee to cover general maintenance, security and upkeep costs. The fee ranges from $50 to $150 monthly. If you have a rental in the Central Pacific or Guanacaste beach areas, one of these companies is essential. A list of property management companies can be found in the local Yellow Pages under *"Administración de Condominios."* In addition, many real estate companies have partnerships with property management companies. We have friends who own a rental property in an exclusive gated community in the Central Pacific area who use a local realtor to manage their condo. They are very pleased with this service.

Helpful Real Estate Publications

Before buying a home or making any other real estate investment, we suggest you educate yourself by studying the Costa Rican real estate market. Fortunately, there are excellent guidebooks available to assist you and answer most of your questions.

Christopher Howard's Official Guide to Costa Rican Real Estate, promises to be the definitive work on the subject. Costa Rica's top real estate minds collaborated to write this one-of-a-kind guidebook. It leaves no stone unturned. To order contact **Costa Rica Books** toll-free at 1-800-365-2342, liveincostarica@cox.net, visit Amazon.com or obtain it through your local bookstore. It will be available in April of 2007.

Another good source of information is the *The Tico Times* biannual *Real Estate and Investment Supplement*. It is packed with useful articles and advice. Reading this guide will keep you up on the local real estate scene. It is also filled with ads from local real estate brokers.

Costa Rica Real Estate Magazine is an informative publication that lists numerous properties for sale as well as brokers. To subscribe, see **www.thecostaricaguide.com**.

Affordable Hired Help

As you know, full or part-time domestic help is hard to find and prohibitively expensive for the average person, not to mention a retiree, in the United States. This is not the case in Costa Rica. A live-in maid or other full-time help usually costs between $150 and $200 per month. Often you can hire a couple for a bargain price, with the woman working as a maid and the man working as a full-time gardener and watchman. Before hiring any employee, be aware of all your requirements as an employer. Contact the ARCR for up to date information.

In Costa Rica, a maid usually does everything from washing clothes to taking care of small children. You can also use your maid to stand in line for you or run errands and bargain for you in stores, since foreigners often pay more for some items because of their naiveté and poor language skills.

After you have had an employee for a number of years, they begin to think of you as a parental figure. As a result, it is not unusual for an employee to ask for loans, advances, help with money for family members who wish to build a home, furnish their house, provide school clothes for their children, or provide medical care and medications for family members.

General handymen and carpenters are also inexpensive. If you are infirm, one of the above people can assist you with many daily tasks. To find quality help, check with other retirees for references or look in local newspapers (*The Tico Times*, *La República* or *La Nación*).

Unless your business is going to be a one-man operation, you will need to hire employees. Be very careful, because the labor laws are stringent and there are minimum salaries depending on the type of work. Ignoring these regulations can be very expensive for you if you get caught in violation.

Costa Rica's labor laws for domestic workers are even stricter, and difficult to interpret. All full time domestic employees have the right to Social Security benefits from the *Caja Costarricense de Seguro Social* (roughly the equivalent of the U.S. Social Security System). This important institution pays for sick leave, general health care, pension funds, disability pensions and maternity care.

It is the employer's responsibility to pay monthly Social Security payments for each employee. The employer must make monthly payments of about 22 percent of the worker's monthly wage, and an additional nine percent is deducted from the employee's earnings. In return, the worker is entitled to the Social Security services mentioned above.

New employees must be registered with Social Security within a week of being hired. All new employees must register in an office in downtown San José (223-9890). There is an automatic trial period of one month for domestic help, during which time an employee may be released without notice or termination pay.

It is also mandatory to insure employees against work-related accidents (*seguro contra riesgos de trabajo*). This type of worker's compensation costs 8,000 colones monthly for domestic employees and must be reapplied for annually.

Employers must also pay minimum wage to employees. This wage is set by the **Ministry of Labor** (223-7166) and depends on the job and skills required. Average wages for unskilled workers start at about $120 per month. Live-in help can receive an additional 50 percent more that is not actually paid to them but is used when computing certain benefits and bonuses.

Live-in domestic help cannot be required to work more than 12 hours a day, although few expect this. Live-in workers usually work eight hours a day like other workers. Most regular employees work an eight-hour day, five days per week. Live-in employees can work more than this but have to be given some time off.

Furthermore, employees are entitled to a paid vacation depending on their length of employment and whether they are full-or part-time.

Domestic help is affordable in Costa Rica.

The law requires one day of vacation for every month of employment. A two-week vacation is due after 50 weeks of work. The employer can choose the time the vacation is taken and can require that half be taken at two different times, but they must be granted within 15 weeks of the time when they were due. Upon termination of the employment contract, unused vacation time should be paid using as a base the average of salary earned during the last six months.

Employers must also pay *aguinaldo* (end-of-year bonus) if an employee has worked from December 1 through November 30, or an amount proportionate to the time worked, if less than a year. The amount is the equivalent of one month's salary. This bonus should be paid in early December. Do not forget that live-in employees receive an additional 50 percent year-end bonus. Employees must also be paid for eight official holidays.

Paid holidays are January 1, Easter Thursday and Friday, April 11, May 1, July 25, August 15, September 15 and December 25.

A maternity leave of one month before a baby's birth is required; the employee receives 50 percent of her normal salary. Dismissal of a pregnant employee is also a bad idea, as it is frowned upon and could be very costly to the employer.

Maternity leave is a total of four months, one month before birth and three after. I believe it is at 60 percent pay, but am not sure on that. New mothers are entitled to up to a year of *lactancia*—an hour for breast-feeding. In practice, I've seen most people leave an hour early— I don't recall anyone taking it at lunchtime. I believe this is granted by your doctor for three months intervals (although I've never asked anyone how they decide if you are entitled to three more months). I don't believe there are any restrictions as to, length of time at work, etc.

In some cases, when a worker is terminated, it is the employer's responsibility to pay severance pay, all unused vacation time, the proportionate *aguinaldo*, and any wages due.

An employee must be given notice prior to being laid off. Severance pay, or *cesantía*, is usually one month's salary for each year worked. If an employee resigns voluntarily, the employer does not owe severance pay.

After three months of employment, an employee has the right to receive notice in the event of termination of employment without just cause by the employer (if notice is not given, he must be paid one month's salary, or a fraction if he has been employed for less than one year).

If the worker is fired without justification after at least three months of service, the employer has to pay a severance payment, the amount of which increases in accordance with the time served and could be up to 22 days per year worked, with a maximum calculated on the basis of eight years, all according to a specific calculation table indicated by the Labor Code.

We have touched only briefly on the main points of Costa Rican labor law because it is very complex. If you have any questions, we advise you to contact the Ministry of Labor (223-7166) or better yet your attorney. Have your lawyer help with any labor related matters to avoid unnecessary problems arising between you and your hired help. Information about Costa Rica's labor law in Spanish at **www. leylaboral.com.**

Two new books can help you communicate better with your hired help: *Crown Publishers' Home Maid Spanish* and *Barron's Household Spanish*. Both books enable you to converse with your Spanish-speaking help without being fluent in the language. They are filled with all of the essential words and phrases you need to know.

Monthly minimum salaries are reviewed by the government every six months (January 1 and June 1). Costa Rica strictly regulates salaries. While countries such as the United States and Canada have standard minimum wages, Costa Rica has a separate minimum wage for nearly every type of job. And the salaries change continuously, thanks to constant devaluation of the *colón*.

Every six months, the government negotiates salary increases with various employee unions. If the negotiations fail, as they do from time to time, the president may issue a decree setting the new salaries in conjunction with the **Consejo Nacional de Salarios**.

Unskilled workers earn about $230, semi-skilled workers $260, skilled workers $285, technicians $290, technicians with higher education $450 and employees with a university degree $530. To give you a more precise idea of what salaries are like in Costa Rica, here are some samples of the approximate starting minimum monthly wages as established by the Labor Ministry or *Ministerio de Trabajo y Seguridad Social*: accountant $400, bartender $240, bus driver $250, carpenter $240, chauffeur $175, clerk $175, computer operator $300, dentist or doctor $1000, other professionals $430, farm hand $125, domestic worker (maid) $146 plus food, executive bilingual secretary $375, guard $180.00, journalist $550.00, messenger $175, nurse $375, plant supervisor $400, phone operator $170, secretary $295, tour guide $250 and unskilled laborer $120.

Only inexperienced workers receive these starting salaries. Experienced workers command higher wages. Keep in mind that these figures vary and are subject to change at any time. Such factors as bonuses and other perks also increase actual salaries.

A list of minimum salaries is available at legal bookstores and some newsstands. The Labor Ministry has many more job classifications and specific minimum salaries that don't appear in the book you can buy.

Many professionals work for salaries established by their *colegios* or trade organizations. For instance, a lawyer is supposed to get 10 percent of the value of any contract he or she prepares.

Companies try to pay about the legal minimum, although more enlightened ones reward good employees with higher salaries. Although the salaries appear low by North American standards, they are good for Latin America, and employees here have perks such as pensions, free medical care and other benefits in additional to their salaries.

This site provides you a list of all of the basic salaries http://www.mtss.go.cr/Macros/Salario/Salarios%20Minimos.htm

Health Care

Staying Healthy

Costa Rica is a very healthy country. Costa Rica's health status is comparable to that of developed nations. The country's private health clinics have international fame and attract people from around the world for everything from dental care and ocular laser surgery to major cosmetic surgery and life extension treatments.

Unlike other countries in Latin America, especially Mexico, Costa Rica's water supply is good and perfectly safe to drink in San José and in the majority of small towns. In most places, you can drink the water without fear of Montezuma's Revenge (diarrhea) or other intestinal problems. However, be careful when you drink water in the countryside. We have lived in Costa Rica for years and have not heard many people complain about the quality of the country's water. If you prefer, bottled water is available. Just as in the United States, there are about 20 brands of bottled water in different-size containers sold at the supermarkets. You will be pleased that Costa Rica's water is soft for bathing and washing your hair.

Although the Costa Rican government takes precautions to monitor the quality of the water and the country has high sanitation standards, there are some precautions you should take. Wash and peel all fresh fruits and vegetables. Avoid drinking water-based fruit drinks sold in stands on the street. You should also watch out for raw seafood dishes, such as *ceviche*, served in some bars and restaurants. This type of seafood is soaked in lemon juice and not cooked with heat. In general, restaurants are clean so you shouldn't have to worry what you eat. Low-end establishments display chicken and other food under lamps to keep it warm. If the food doesn't look fresh, use your judgment.

Costa Ricans are proud of their nation's achievements in the field of health care. Their up-to-date, affordable, state-run "cradle to grave" health care system reaches all levels of society by offering the same medical treatment to the poor as those with greater resources. Hospitals, clinics and complete medical services are available in all major cities and some small towns. More than 90 percent of the population is covered by the Social Security System.

There is either a public clinic or hospital in almost every area of the country, making medical care accessible to everyone including foreigners. We know a U.S. couple near Dominical, on the southern Pacific coast, who either use the public hospital in San Isidro or the one in Ciudad Cortez. The wife told us her husband fell when he was working on their house and sustained a compound fracture of the wrist. He was treated at the public hospital in Ciudad Cortez and was very pleased with the emergency treatment he received.

Many international medical authorities rate Costa Rica as having one of the best low-cost medical care systems in the world, when preventive and curative medicines are considered. The United Nations consistently ranks Costa Rica's public health system as the best in Latin America and one of the top 20 in the world.

It is no wonder a large number of foreigners are attracted to Costa Rica because of its affordable health care. In the United States, for example, millions of people do not have health insurance because it is prohibitively expensive. For this reason, Costa Rica attracts many retirees from North America. It doesn't matter if you are a legal resident or a traveler. Everyone is entitled to emergency care at a government hospital.

Costa Ricans are a healthy people. The infant mortality rate of less than 11 in 100,000 live births is lower than that in the United States. This figure is on par with any industrialized country in the world. Life expectancy is 76.3 years for men and 79.8 years for women. Today, an 80-year-old man has a life expectancy of at least eight (actually, 8.4) years. This puts Costa Rica in first place in the world for life expectancy from this age up. Iceland and Japan follow with 7.7 years. Costa Rican women at age 80 are expected to live longer than men of the same age, 9.5 years, slightly behind the women of Japan and France.

Hospitals have the latest equipment, and laboratories are excellent. You can feel safe having most operations without returning to the United States or Canada. Most surgical procedures cost only a fraction of what they do in the United States. For example, a heart bypass operations costs about a third of what it does in the United States.

Even if you are in good health, the probability of needing medical care increases with age. The security of knowing that good health services are available represents an enormous relief.

Costa Rican Doctors

Most Costa Rican doctors are excellent and have been trained in Europe or North America. If you don't speak Spanish, you don't have to worry. Many local doctors speak English, but most receptionists and nurses do not. Doctor's fees for office visits vary. A good private specialist usually charges between $30 and $40 for each visit, although some doctors charge a little more and others a little less.

Unlike many other places, doctors in Costa Rica take time with patients to answer questions and listen. Doctors usually give you their office, home and cell phone numbers as well as pager number. It is not unusual for doctors to call their patients at home to follow-up on care and medications, and they will make house calls.

Doctors here are much less interested in making a profit than serving the people. Considering there are no high malpractice premiums to pay, physicians can make a good living without charging exorbitant prices.

If you join Costa Rica's national health care system, you do not have to pay for each office visit, only a small monthly membership fee. If you have any questions about medical fees or doctors, you should direct them to the *Colegio de Médicos*, which is the Costa Rican equivalent of the AMA.

To find a good English-speaking physician or specialist, talk to other retirees, look in the Yellow Pages under *Médicos*, look for doctor's ads in the *The Tico Times* or see the list at the end of this section.

Hospitals and Medical Facilities

Public medical facilities are so good that you don't usually need private care. Most private specialists are required by law to work part-time in public hospitals. However, private clinics and hospitals provide

Medical Care Cost Comparison
by Martin Rice

Just got a really rude awakening that I thought I might share with you, given the fact that there's been quite a bit of discussion about medical care here lately.

Robin and I went to the States for two weeks over Christmas. While there, I had to go to the emergency room in Knoxville, TN where we were visiting family. The hospital, Baptist Hospital, West, is a brand new (1 1/2 years) super impressive place. They took great care of me in the emergency room -- all the speedy intense care you would expect with chest pains. The reason it was a bit more scary than it might have been is that just three months ago I had an angioplasty here at CIMA.

After they saw that I was doing OK and all the signs were on the money, they said that I had to have a stress test. The kind of stress test I get is a chemical one in the Department of Nuclear Medicine. I had one at CIMA before the angioplasty. It's this that tells them whether you need to have the angioplasty done. Here comes the first cost comparison: The doctor said that based on the results of the stress test, they'd decide whether I'd need another angioplasty. I told him that if all possible I'd prefer to go back to CR to have it done because there it cost me about $13,000 in total and I figured in the States it'd be about $25,000. He laughed and said "more like $40,000 or $50,000!" Now THAT almost gave me a heart attack.

At any rate, the results of the stress test were great and I didn't need anything else at all. When the doctor told me that, he said that I'd be able to leave right then. At this point I had spent a night at the hospital and about a total of 24 hours.

That same stress test at CIMA cost me $750. There was also some compleblood work done which was another $150. I did it on an out-patient basis, but I know that a nice room at CIMA, with a sitting room attached is about $150 per night. No emergency care, but, again from experience there, I'd estimate that what I had done at the ER in the States would have been about $1,000 to $1,500. So a total of about $2,550.00.

What was the bill at the hospital in the United States? $8,000! One night in the hospital and no operation or any other kind of invasive procedure. Is that sick or what? Talk about a broken system. So when people talk about the high cost of private medicine here and at hospitals such as CIMA, remember all is relative, extremely relative.

Anyway, I'm doing just great now and feel fine.

quicker services with more privacy, enabling you to avoid long lines and the bureaucracy of the public system.

In Costa Rica, the term *clínica* is used for private institutions that generally include inpatient medical/surgical facilities, doctor's offices, laboratories, radiology, pharmacy and outpatient services. *Hospital* generally refers to public inpatient medical/surgical facilities that also provide laboratory, radiology, pharmacy and related services.

Most Costa Ricans find the cost of private clinics too expensive. However, foreigners will find private clinics very reasonable compared to similar institutions back home.

You will be happy to know you can receive first-rate care at any of San José's three largest private hospitals.

If you have to enter a private hospital, costs will generally be well under a $100 a day. This includes a spacious private room with bathroom and cable TV with English channels. Private and semi-private rooms often have an extra bed or *sofa* bed so a relative may spend the night, if necessary. It is important to know that the doctor's bill will always be separate from the hospital bill.

Our son was just operated on for an appendectomy at the Clínica Bíblica. The total cost including the surgeon's fee was under $1,000. Our INS insurance covered all but $140.

We know an American who spent a couple of days in the private Clínica Católica hospital and said, "The attention was first-class, the food was as good as home cooking, and the same care would have cost thousands of dollars in the States." It is important to know that payment can be made at most hospitals and clinics with any major credit card. Foreign medical insurance is not accepted, but you may get a reimbursement from your health insurance company if they cover you abroad. In some cases, especially if arranged in advance, your foreign insurance can be used so you can pay the deductible. Talk to your private hospital.

The **Clinica Bíblica** (Tel: 257-5252, 800-911-0800, Fax: 255-4947, E-mail:asoserme@racsa.co.cr, www.clinicabiblica.com) in downtown San José is now affiliated with the Blue Cross and Blue Shield network. By 2007 or 2008 it expects to be affiliated with Medicare. A first-class private hospital with an excellent coronary unit, this fine facility is staffed with highly trained doctors. Complete hospital services including maternity, an ER room, MRI equipment and lab work are available. I have used the lab on many occasions and found the service to be excellent.

In order to keep pace with country's needs for first-rate private care, the hospital recently acquired a new multistoried building in the next block and is adding a large wing to the main hospital.

In addition to the main branch in downtown San José, the Clínica Bíbilica has smaller satellite branches with a doctor on duty, pharmacies and express delivery of medicines in Heredia (260-4959), Cartago (551-0511), San Francisco de Dos Ríos (218-0035), and in the San Pedro Mall (283-6058). Since I live in Heredia, I have used the local Heredia branch of the Clínica Bíblica on several occasions for minor ailments and tests. The service has been very good and fast.

The **Clínica Católica** (246-3006, E-mail: info@clinicacatolica. com, www.clinicacatolica.com) in Guadalupe, a suburb of San José, is another fine private hospital with complete hospital and emergency services 24-hours a day, 365 days a year. It is not as popular with foreigners as the Clínica Bíblica or Hospital CIMA.

This facility takes private INS insurance, Blue Shield and Blue Cross. During an acute asthma episode, I spent three days in this hospital and found the care very good.

Hospital CIMA (Tel: 231- 2781, E-mail cimahsj@racsa.co.cr, www.hospitalsanjose.net) in Escazú, right off the highway, is the newest private hospital in the San José area and is affiliated with the Baylor University Medical Center in Dallas, Texas, and managed by International Hospital Corporation of Dallas. It is a full-service hospital that boasts the latest health care technology, state-of-the-art medical equipment and the most sophisticated physical plant in Central America. It offers complete services including X-ray, ultrasound, emergency and intensive care, as well as an advanced coronary unit.

The average cost of a room per day is between $130 and $140, very reasonable compared to the cost of a hospital in the United States. An adjacent seven-story medical office building houses the offices of more than 100 specialists.

Hospital CIMA (208-1800) recently opened a smaller branch in the eastern suburb of Los Yoses, about 100 meters west of San Pedro Mall. It also plans to open a full-service branch near Flamingo Beach in Guanacaste.

The **Clínica Santa Rita** (221-6433), near the court buildings, has an excellent maternity center and is used for cosmetic surgery procedures. The **Hospital Cristiano Jerusalem** (285-0202), in Alto de Guadalupe, offers limited services. Although not a hospital, the **Clínica Americana** (222-1010), next to Clínica Bíblica, offers private out-patient service and U.S.-trained doctors on call 24-hours a day.

Hospital Clínica Santa María, (Tel: 523-6000, Fax: 523-6060, E-mail: servicioalcliente@hospitalcsantamaria.com), offers a variety of high-quality services in downtown San José.

Hospital Universitario de La Universidad Iberoaméricana, (Tel: 297-2242, Fax: 236-0426, E-mail: admisiones@unibe.ac.cr), located in San José's suburb of Tibás, is the country's newest private hospital. It is a full-service university hospital where specialists treat all patients with students as observers.

C.A.R.E. 353-7456 or 282-2626 (beeper) or 637-8606 (Los Sueños Resort) or 643-1690 is a private emergency medical center in the Jaco Beach area. It offers medical consultation, an advanced life support ambulance, minor surgery and special events coverage. The clinic's regular hours are from 8 a.m. to 6 p.m.

Emergencias Médicas (290-4444) is a private company offering quick ambulance service. For a small yearly fee you can take advantage of its first-rate service. **Emergencias Metro** (263-2983, emergenciasmetro@yahoo.com) is another company offering emergency medical transportation and care. **Costa Rica Life Guard** (824-5227) offers emergency transportation by airplane.

The Clínica Bíblica is one of Costa Rica's better private hospitals.

Public Hospitals

As you already know, public hospitals and clinics are found in most parts of the country, with the three major facilities in the San José area. Although public hospitals are generally crowded and waits can be long for appointments, there is no problem when it comes to emergency treatment.

I can personally vouch for the care at Costa Rica's public hospitals. After many hours in labor my wife gave birth to my son by cesarean section at San Juan de Dios Hospital. He was taken to the Children's Hospital next door because he required some special care and was placed in an incubator while my wife recovered. About three days later both mother and baby were released without any complications. Today I have a healthy 18-year old son.

The country's three major public medical centers in San José are:

Hospital San Juan de Dios .... Tel: 257-6282
Hospital Calderón Guardia .... Tel: 257-7299
Hospital México .... Tel: 232-6122
Hospital de Niños (Children's Hospital) .... Tel: 222-0122

Major public medical facilities in other areas of the country:

Heredia
San Vicente de Paul .... Tel: 237-5944

Alajuela
Hospital San Rafael .... Tel: 440-1333

Cartago
Hospital Max Peralta .... Tel: 550-1999

Guanacaste
Hospital Dr. Enrique Baltodano .... Tel: 666-0011

Limón
Hospital Dr. Tony Facio .... Tel: 758-2222

Puntarenas
Hospital Monseñor Sanabria .... Tel: 663-0033

Health Care for Veteran's in Costa Rica

The Clínica Bíblica now accepts medical coverage through Tri Care Latin America and CHAMPUS for hospital and pharmacy services.

Here are the requirements for medical benefits for **U.S. military retirees** and their families:

1. A current U.S. military retiree ID card (20 years of active duty)
2. 65 years or over and have Medicare Part B.
3. Current ID cards for all dependents under 21 years of age if in college with proof of enrollment
4. Unmarried widows must have the related documents above for their husband.

Medical benefits for **U.S. veterans**:

The disabled veteran can only be treated for the disabilities listed on the Treatment Authorization Sheet from the VA. If the veteran is 100 percent disabled, all dependents will receive total health care, not including dental and glasses. The following documents are required:

1. Current CHAMPUS VA card.
2. Current ID card for all dependents under the age of 21 and up to 23 years of age if in college with proof of enrollment.
4. Copy of DD 214
5. Unmarried widows must have the related documents above for their husband.

To find out about benefits for military retirees and their families and for disabled veterans, call **522-1500/221-7717** or E-mail: seguros@clinicabiblica.com.

Low-Cost Medical Insurance

Costa Rica's health care system is available to retirees (*pensionados* and *rentistas*) and other foreign residents. Residents may join the *Caja Costarricense de Seguro Social* (Costa Rican Social Security System) and enjoy the same inexpensive medical coverage as most Costa Ricans do. Most foreigners do not enroll in this system because of the long waits for medical appointments, some medications and other delays. However, despite being overburdened, the emergency care provided is very good. There are also clinics all over the country. At a low cost of no more than $60 monthly, the *Caja* is a good deal for foreigners.

The cost to affiliate directly is about 13 percent of your monthly income by law; however the **ARCR** (www.arcr.net) has a legal contract with the *Caja* to affiliate at a very reasonable price.

As we just stated, according to the law you must pay 11 to 13 percent of your income to the *Caja* for voluntary medical insurance. We know of some foreigners who try to get around this by lying about their income and paying the minimum of about $25 monthly. If they are legal residents, the government will know they have at least an income of $600 per month and should be paying about $70 monthly. If they are caught underpaying, they can be fined and ordered to pay the difference in what was not paid in the first place. You shouldn't try to cut corners.

Most foreigners and retirees opt for the medical insurance offered by the government's insurance company—the National Insurance Institute or INS. Everyone is eligible to apply, including permanent residents, *pensionados* and even tourists. Elderly people have to submit to a physical before they can be insured. The medical policy covers expenses resulting from illness, accidents, hospitalization, office visits, lab work, medicines and medical costs in foreign countries. However, if you incur medical expenses abroad, INS will pay only the amount equivalent to the same treatment in Costa Rica and you have to pay the difference.

When you purchase a policy, INS will supply you with an identification card and a booklet that lists the names of affiliated groups such as hospitals, doctors, labs and pharmacies. Most surgical procedures are covered 100 percent. You pay a small deductible for office visits, labs, medicines and treatments. If you seek medical services not affiliated with INS, you have to pay up front. You then submit a claim to INS and will be reimbursed in a few weeks.

Depending on age and sex, the annual cost of this insurance is about $800 for a man 50 to 69. For example, rates for a man 18-39 year s old run about $250 per year; $1,800 for a 70-year old man ; and women of all ages pay an average annual rate of about $1,500. Women of childbearing age pay slightly more than men. There is a discount if more than one person is insured on the same policy. It is easy to enroll an entire family for a low monthly rate. If you belong to a group of 15 or more people—such as the Association of Residents (ARCR) or the American Legion— you can obtain an approximately a five percent discount.

There is a ceiling of around $17,000 per individual. Since medical costs are so low in Costa Rica, this policy is more than enough to take care of your medical needs. Retirees and other residents need not worry about lacking adequate medical coverage in Costa Rica. For information, go to the **ARCR** or contact them at: (Tel: 233-8068,

Fax: 011-(506) 222-7862) or see www.arcr.net. You can reach the **National Insurance Institute** at 223-5800.

INS now offers a new international insurance policy that covers your needs in Costa Rica and the rest of the world. This new medical policy covers medical expenses resulting from accident or sickness. Here are some of the items covered: hospitalization and ambulance expenses, maternity, prosthesis, organ transplants, air evacuation, repatriation of remains, funeral costs and a yearly check-up and eye test. The rates are high but the coverage is very complete.

Mixed Medicine

This method of combining both public and private health care can work in several ways. Some Costa Ricans and many foreigners use the *Caja* as a type of back up insurance for extra protection. They utilize a private doctor for minor ailments and the *Caja* for major problems, while others use the *Caja* for certain tests and expensive medicines and minor illnesses. Another way to do it is to use a private physician for problems that require a long wait through the *Caja*. The waits for some tests and procedures can take months, so people with cancer and other serious problems often go to a private lab to get faster test results.

Many doctors who have a private practice and also work in the public system will operate on their patients in a public hospital to reduce costs.

Be careful of so-called *biombo*. A *biombo* is a medical practice that has been used from time to time by some unscrupulous individuals in the medical profession. For example, a couple of medical professionals employed by the *Caja* were just arrested for taking samples of blood at their own private laboratory and then using equipment at a public hospital to do the analysis.

Comparing Costa Rica's Health Care Plans

Here is a brief comparison of the *Caja* and the INS medical plans available in Costa Rica.

Caja — National socialized system.
1. Covers doctor's visits, medications, examinations and hospitalization.
2. Doctors are assigned to the patient.
3. Covers pre-existing conditions.
4. Covers all medications including dental and eyes.

Some reasons to consider this plan:

1. Have pre-existing health condition and do not qualify for INS insurance.
2. Take medication on a regular basis.
3. Have it as major medical in case of serious illness.

Monthly premiums cover all illnesses for the member and his immediate family for that month. The cost through the ARCR if younger than 55 years old is $58 per month; $37 per month if 55 years or older.

INS — The semi-autonomous government insurance company.

1. Covers 75 percent of the cost of doctor's visits, medications, examinations and hospitalization.
2. Individual chooses the doctor.
3. Does not cover any pre-existing medical condition.
4. Does not cover most dental or eye exams, treatments or glasses, preventive medical check-up, illness or disorders related to female reproductive organs during the first 12 months of coverage, or birth of a baby during the first six months of coverage.

Some reasons ARCR members have the INS plan.

1. Can choose a doctor.
2. Can make doctor's appointments with less red tape.

Rates of coverage depend on age and sex; 20 percent deductible for each doctor's visit.

NEW Changes to the "Plan 16" Medical Insurance Policy

"Plan 16" is the medical insurance policy INS has been selling since 1990, and a lot of people from the foreign community have obtained coverage through the Canadian Club, the American Legion and the ARCR. INS advised that, starting with the renewal at January 1, 2005, some new rules apply to this policy. Some of them look good, some not so good, but, in balance, the changes iron out some of the "bugs." At the same time, the premium rates, which are in colones, have increased by about 20 percent, which is reasonable just a tad above what inflation will probably rack up to in calendar year 2004.

Outlined below are the nuts and bolts of Plan 16. After each paragraph, in CAPITAL LETTERS, are comments regarding the changes INS has made.

WHO CAN BE INSURED? Anyone up to age 100, regardless of legal status in Costa Rica. Applicants over 69 must undergo an examination by an INS doctor. It takes INS about three weeks to study applications; you can't pay until your application is accepted. The policy goes with the calendar year; if someone applies and is accepted part way through the year, the yearly premium is prorated. NO CHANGES.

WHAT DOES THE POLICY PAY FOR? It covers expenses due to sickness, accident or childbirth. Outpatient services are paid for up to 10 percent of the insured amount, per year. The rest of the policy, the other 90 percent, is for hospitalization, surgery, pre- and post-operative care, private room, food, support systems, intensive care, rehabilitation, ambulances, home care, therapy, medication, etc. In case of death, 50 percent of the insured amount is paid to named beneficiary. Please note that there is no payment for checkups or "preventive maintenance," NO CHANGES.

WHAT DOES IT EXCLUDE? Pre-existing conditions. Non-prescribed expenses. AIDS. VD. Medical expenses as a result of cataclysmic events, fighting except in self-defense, tournament sports, martial arts and other dangerous activities. Accidents when under the influence of alcohol or drugs. Mental or nervous disorders. Checkups. Allergies. Stress. Plastic surgery. Only accident related eyeglasses, dentist's bills or reconstructive surgery are paid. Some ailments (e.g. glaucoma, cataracts, ENT, women's reproductive organs, breasts, asthma, hernias, pregnancy, prostates, stones, osteoporosis) have a 12-month moratorium during which claims are not allowed. HERE WE SEE A CHANGE: GLAUCOMA AND CATARACTS WERE NOT PREVIOUSLY SUBJECT TO THE MORATORIUM.

HOW MUCH DOES IT COST? You can choose from three levels of insurance. The insured amount refers to the maximum amount INS will pay for your health in the calendar year. Premiums depend on the level of insurance, and on the age and sex of the insured. THESE RATES REFLECT THE 20 PERCENT INCREASE – HOWEVER, IT IS NOT EXACTLY 20 PERCENT, AS FIGURES HAVE BEEN ROUNDED.

Group policies for companies cost about 12 percent less. Associations or clubs, (ARCR, American Legion, etc.) get about 6 percent off. Cost of renewal may increase if there is a high claim/premium ratio. ANOTHER CHANGE HERE: DISCOUNTS FOR GROUP POLICIES USED TO BE GREATER.

HOW DOES THE POLICY WORK? In case of ambulatory care (when hospitalization is not needed), you must pay for your care and later submit an INS claim form signed by you and your main doctor, attaching original receipts and corresponding prescriptions for medicines, treatments and lab tests. Your agent will push your claim through INS, which usually pays after three to six weeks, based on usual and reasonable charges. If you require hospitalization, a week before you go into hospital, through your agent you should obtain a "pre authorization" from INS, which will negotiate prices with your care giver. When released from hospital, you must show your insurance card and so pay the deductible only. If you didn't get the "pre authorization," you must pay the entire bill and make a claim as described above. IMPORTANT CHANGES HERE: A NETWORK OF PROVIDERS USED TO ACCEPT PATIENTS' INSURANCE CARDS AND COLLECT ONLY THE DEDUCTIBLE FROM THEM, AND THE NETWORK PROVIDERS WERE SUPPOSED TO ABIDE BY A PRICE LIST IMPOSED BY INS. NOW, THERE ARE NO NETWORK PROVIDERS, THERE IS NO OFFICIAL PRICE LIST, PAYMENT OF CLAIMS IS BASED ON "USUAL AND CUSTOMARY PRICES," AND INSURANCE CARDS CAN BE USED ONLY FOR AILMENTS REQUIRING HOSPITALIZATION IN CASES WHERE PRIOR APPROVAL ("PREAUTHORIZATION") HAS BEEN OBTAINED FROM INS.

DEDUCTIBLE? The general deductible is 25 percent. In some cases, such as claims from abroad, or if you buy a patented medicine when a generic equivalent is available, the deductible can be 30%. -- MORE CHANGES: GENERAL DEDUCTIBLE USED TO BE 30 PERCENT; THERE WAS NO DIFFERENCE BETWEEN PATENT AND GENERIC MEDICINES; AND THERE WAS NO DEDUCTIBLE ON SURGEON'S FEES.

For additional information contact the author of this last section, **David Garrett**, at 233-2455 or E-mail: **info@segurosgarrett.com**.

INS Medical Regional

The INS Medical Regional is an alternative to Plan 16 and provides broader coverage.

Who Can Be Insured?

Residents of Costa Rica ages 18 to 65 can apply. Sometimes people up to 70 have been accepted. Once insured, INS will renew indefinitely so long as the premium is paid. Dependents from birth up to age 24 can also be insured.

What is Covered?

Medical expenses due to accident, sickness or maternity, up to $200,000 per year. For people over 69, the coverage is reduced to $60,000 per year. The policy will also pay for an eye test and checkup, as of the second year. It covers hospital care and ambulatory care. Subject to sub-limits, also maternity, cancer, epidemic diseases, prosthesis, organ transplants, ophthalmic care, air ambulance if treatment can only be administered abroad, repatriation of remains, death benefit for burial, etc. By means of surcharges you can increase the cancer coverage, and coverage for severe medical conditions, to $400,000.

Where?

Worldwide coverage. But the policy is designed for and works best in Central America.

Main Exclusions

Conditions existing when the insurance is bought. Treatments for obesity, cosmetic surgery, sterility, congenital conditions, dental care, sex change, insemination, mental disease, addictions, attempted suicide, self-inflicted lesions, pregnancy of dependents except spouse, accidents when the insured was under the influence of drugs or alcohol, correction of vision, for AIDS and HIV positive, erectile dysfunction, chiropractic and podiatrist care, tranquilizers, antidepressants, vitamins, non-prescribed expenses, experimental treatments, accidents while practicing high-risk or speed sports, medical expenses as a result of cataclysmic events, terrorism, civil insurrection or war.

Pre-existing Conditions

Chronic conditions, at the discretion of INS, can be covered if the applicant has had no symptoms in the last two years.

Claims and Deductible

In Central America there is a network of providers (doctors, hospitals, labs, clinics and pharmacies), which includes Clínica Biblica, Hospital CIMA, Clínica Católica and others, where you will pay less because they are bound to a price limitation imposed by INS, and you will get a lower deductible. Also, for hospital care you use your insurance card to cover the balance. With preferred providers, for hospital care you pay for one day of hospital room, plus 10 percent of the following $5,000; for ambulatory care you pay $10 per doctors' visit, plus 10 percent of other prescribed expenses. With outside providers, for hospital care you will pay for one day of hospital room with a minimum of $200, plus 20 percent of the next $20,000; for ambulatory care, you pay $20 per doctor's visit, plus 20 percent of other prescribed expenses.

How Much Does It Cost?

You can choose from three levels of insurance. Premiums depend on the level, and on age and sex of applicants (costs shown in U.S. dollars). Some averages of yearly premiums:

Adults

Age	Men	Women
0-18	US$ 448	US$ 524
19-25	470	562
26-29	498	602
30-34	553	678
35-39	640	783
40-44	692	865
45-49	829	931
50-54	953	1,086
55-59	1,068	1,179
60-64	1,348	1,364
65-69	1,625	1,599
70-75	2,090	2,046

Children to 10 years.

Both genders

1 kid	US$ 226
2 kids	291
3 kids +	376

Applications

No medical examination is normally necessary. For bureaucratic reasons, policy applications are best filled out by an agent. You must pay the first premium at the time of applying. The policy comes into effect 30 days later. Some medical conditions have a 10-month moratorium.

What numbers do I phone for medical assistance when I am away from Costa Rica ?

• Within the United States: 1-866-543-6307 (toll free)
• Any other country except Costa Rica: +1 (305) 463 9635 (you may call collect)

Disclaimer: This document is intended as a summary of most relevant points of the insurance policy; as such, it does not contain every provision stated therein.

Courtesy 2005 Garrett & Associates, www.segurosgarrett.com

INS Medical International

Who Can Be Insured?

Residents of Costa Rica ages 18 to 65 can apply. Applications from people up to 70 have sometimes been accepted. INS will renew indefinitely so long as the premium is paid. Dependents from birth to age 24 can also be insured.

What Is Covered?

Medical expenses resulting from accident, sickness or maternity, up to $2 million per year. For people over 69, coverage is reduced to $600,000 per year. The policy will also pay for a yearly eye test and checkup, as of the second year. Covers hospital and ambulatory care. Subject to sub-limits, maternity, cancer, epidemic diseases, prosthesis, transplants, ophthalmic care, air ambulance if medically required, repatriation of remains, death benefit for burial, etc.

Where?

Worldwide coverage.

Main Exclusions

Conditions existing when the insurance is bought. Treatments for obesity, cosmetic surgery, sterility, congenital conditions, dental care, sex change, insemination, mental disease, addictions, attempted suicide, self-inflicted lesions, pregnancy of dependents except spouse, accidents when the insured was under the influence of drugs or alcohol, correction of vision, treatment for AIDS and HIV positive, erectile dysfunction, chiropractic and podiatrist care, tranquilizers, antidepressants, vitamins, non-prescribed expenses, experimental treatments, accidents while practicing high-risk or speed sports, medical expenses as a result of cataclysmic events, terrorism, civil insurrection or war.

Pre-existing Conditions

At the discretion of INS, these can be covered if the applicant has had no symptoms in the two years before an application is submitted.

Claims and Deductible

In Central and North America there is a network of providers (doctors, hospitals, labs, clinics and pharmacies) where you will pay less because they are bound to a price list imposed by INS — and you will get a lower deductible. Also, you use your insurance card to cover the balance for hospital care. (You can also get this insurance with a blanket, per-year deductible, where you accumulate your medical expenses and, if in the policy year they exceed the limit, you can claim for the excess.) With preferred providers, for hospital care you pay for one day of hospital room, plus 10 percent of the following $5,000; for ambulatory care you pay $10 per doctor's visit, plus 10 percent of other prescribed expenses. With outside providers, for hospital care you will pay for one day of hospital room with a minimum of $200, plus 20 percent of the next $20,000; for ambulatory care, you will pay $20 per doctor's visit, plus 20 percent of other prescribed expenses.

How Much Does It Cost?

You can choose from three levels of insurance. Premiums depend on the level, and on age and sex of applicants (costs shown in US dollars).

Applications

No medical examination is normally necessary. For bureaucratic reasons, policy applications are best filled out by an agent. You must pay the first premium at the time of applying. The policy comes into effect 30 days later. Some medical conditions have a 10-month moratorium.

What numbers do I phone for medical assistance when I am away from Costa Rica ?

• Within the United States: 1-866-543-6307 (toll-free)

• Any other country except Costa Rica: +1 (305) 463 9635 (you may call collect)

Courtesy of 2005 Garrett & Associates www.segurosgarrett.com

Alternative International Medical Plans

Costa Rican medical plans mentioned above. Companies such as **Blue Shield** and **Blue Cross** offer international coverage for their policy holders. The majority of private clinics in Costa Rica work with companies offering international medical coverage.

With some of these policies you may have to pay out of your own pocket and provide receipts for reimbursement at a later date. Other companies will pay "right on the spot." It is a good idea to have a policy that provides international evacuation which in some cases may be a viable option. A friend of ours went on a trip from Costa Rica to Nicaragua and became very ill while there. He developed a problem with internal bleeding. Because he had an international evacuation policy, he was flown to New Orleans. He was unconscious for several days but eventually recovered fully. Needless to say, he would have probably died without this policy that allowed him to go to the United States for specialized treatment.

I.M.C. Asociados, S.A. offers BUPA International's health plan in Costa Rica. They have health care plans specifically designed for residents of Central America with worldwide coverage wherever and whenever needed. They guarantee lifetime coverage without excessive increases in premiums with age. Contact them at: Tel: 256-5848 or E-mail: imccr2002@yahoo.com.

Global Insurance offers medical plans for people living abroad. You may contact them at: Tel: (305)-274-0284, Fax: (305)-675-6134, toll-free 1-800-975-7363, E-mail: cperez@globalinsurancenet.com or www.globalinsurancenet.com.

Medibroker (Tel: 0-191-297-2411/44-191-297-2411, Fax: 0-191-251-6424, www.medibroaker.com, e-mail: medibroker@aol.com offers medical coverage for retirees, expats and others living abroad. They have various plans from which to choose.

The **AARP** supposedly offers a program for foreign coverage.

While checking out Costa Rica, to see if it is the place for you to settle, you can get temporary medical insurance as a tourist through the Costa Rican Social Security office and the **International Organization of Cultural Interchanges** (O.I.C.I.). Contact them at 222-7867.

Medicines and Pharmacies

Pharmacies are numerous in Costa Rica and they stock most standard medicines available in Europe, Canada and the United States. In general, the cost of most medicines is lower than in the U.S. However, it pays to shop around. There has been a continuous price war going on among most of the pharmacy chains. So, good bargains may be found.

Most drugs requiring a prescription in North America are freely available "over the counter" in any Costa Rican *farmacia*. Exceptions are strong pain relievers and narcotics that require a special prescription. In Costa Rica, pharmacists are permitted to prescribe medicines as well as administer on-the-spot injections. They are also available to answer your questions and give free medical advice about less complex conditions. In general, Costa Rican pharmacists usually will give you the correct advice and appropriate medication. This can save you a trip to the doctor's office.

Foreigners who can't find their specific medication will have no problem. Pharmacists have a thick medical guide listing most medicines in the world and their generic equivalents. Some caution should be taken when figuring out the specific dose. I have a friend form Fort Lauderdale, Florida, who mistakenly purchased blood pressure medicine that was twice as strong as what he needed. He ended up feeling very ill and had to be taken to a local hospital. The problem was quickly resolved when the doctor realized the dosage was incorrect.

Some pharmacies open 24-hours a day are in downtown San José at **Clínica Bíblica**, 223-6422; at the **Clínica Católica**, 225-9095; and the **Farmacia del Este** in San Pedro (253-5121).

The **Farmacia Alvarez** (237-5425 , E-mail: farmacia@rxcr.com or see www.farmacia-alvarez.com) in downtown Heredia offers some of the best prices in Costa Rica. In some cases you can save up to 80 percent of what you would pay in the United States. They also have bilingual employees to help you.

The main branch of the **Fischel pharmacy** (223-0909), across from the main post office in San José, has a doctor on duty to give medical advice. Fischel will deliver medicine and prescriptions in most areas. Many of their employees speak English. They also have smaller pharmacies in other locations around San José and in Heredia, Alajuela, Cartago and Puntarenas.

Pharmacy

For home delivery call them toll-free at 800 Fischel (800-347-2435). Recently, Fischel opened the country's first online pharmacy. They offer the sale of prescriptions and over-the-counter products. In addition, their staff of pharmacists and doctors will answer your questions. Their site also provides general information on topics such as proper use and storage of medicines. You may view their site at **www.fishel.co.cr**. Fishhel doesn't give very good discounts. You can find the price of most medicines by accessing their site at:**www.fischel. co.cr/Default.asp?Usu=Anonimo.**

Farmacia Sucre and **Farmacia Catedral** are other large pharmacy chains in the Central Valley.

The newest concept in pharmacies is **Farmacia Rx Express 800-MEDICINA** (800-633-4246). They offer 24-hour home delivery seven days a week and don't close for holidays. They have 14 locations and plan to open more. Contact them to find out about their discount programs.

Dental Care

Many tourists come to Costa Rica to have their cosmetic dental work done inexpensively. The quality of dental work in Costa Rica is equal to that found in Europe, Canada or the United States. On the average, dental work costs about 25 to 30 percent less than in the United States. Most dentists charge about $35 for an initial exam. The approximate costs of the most common cosmetic procedures are: wisdom tooth surgery $175, single root canal $150, new crown $250, implants $750, fillings about $30 per tooth, and regular tooth extraction $40. If you have children, orthodontics are very affordable. Check prices with the dentist of your choice, since rates vary.

Costa Rican dentists offer the following services: implants, gum treatment, root canals, whitening, oral surgery, crowns, bridges and nitrous oxide sedation.

Orthodontics for children and adults are available and affordable in Costa Rica. Our son has braces. The total cost for a two-year treatment is about $1,500 which can be paid in monthly installments of $45.

One word of caution for foreigners, some Costa Rican dentists advertise in English-language publications and cater almost exclusively to foreigners. Patients will sometimes pay more for the dental services these doctors provide. It's a good idea to shop around and ask for recommendations. **The Costa Rican Surgeons and Dentists Association** (Tel/Fax: 256-3100, E-mail: dentista@racsa.co.cr, www. colegiodentists.co.cr) will give you a list of dentists practicing in Costa

Do Not Hesitate to ask
Who's Who in Costa Rica
By Dr. John Williams

When trying to find a competent doctor, lawyer, dentist or other professional in Costa Rica, it's best to make sure you are in the right hands. Just beacuse someone knows how to market their services, doesn't guarantee quality work or customer satisfaction.

When I strarted placing dental implants in my patients way back in 1982 my colleagues thought I was crazy! Very little information about the procedure had been published and dental schools offered no implant courses. Early ideas were exchanged only in whispers within the dental underground. By the early 1980s two pioneer implantologists, Dr. Linkow and Dr. Weiss, had made available insertable blades as a base structure to support prosthetic work. New companies emerged like Oratronics and supplied the new industry. Blades quickly became the method of choice. Dr. Babbush published his first book regarding implants in 1980. The American Academy of Implant Dentistry and The Alabama Implant Study group soon became major information sources. Dr. Branemark then published his studies on osseous integrated implants. This important system was slow to catch on due to its start-up costs.

My personal break-through came when visiting Dr. Lazzarra in Palm Beach who took time out of his practice to show this Costa Rican dentist all about his new system. The lights came on and I immediately adopted his superior methodology. Today Dr. Lazzarra heads Implant Inovation Inc.(3i), theworld's leading implant supplier organization. I subscribe to 3i due to their use of certified high grade titanium and state-of-the-art precision fittings. Their prescribed dental rehabilitation procedures are most reliable, fully functional, and esthetically beautiful.

Currently our team offers the implant patient highly qualified professional services ranging from oral surgery to an American-board certified periodontist and endodontist. I personally do the treatment planning, team coordination and the final prosthetic work. Starting very young, twenty years ago, in the implant field has given me great experience and sufficient knowledge to treat both the most complicated cases and the routine with great confidence. Our lab work is all done with certified high noble alloys and vita porcelain which are worked by an Italian artist of international repute.

To combine dental work, cosmetic surgery or a language study vacation with **Christopher Howard's Retirement Tour.**

Rica. Check with other residents for recommendations. Above all, be sure to find out if the dentist you are considering is practicing legally.

You may now combine a dental vacation with one of **Christopher Howard's Relocation/Retirement Tours**. Please see www.travel. costaricabooks.com for all details or call toll-free 800-365-2342.

Cosmetic Surgery

Costa Rica has long been the destination for those in search of the "Fountain of Youth." People from all over the world flock to Costa Rica for cosmetic surgery because prices are lower than in the United States for comparable procedures. Costa Rica's surgeons are among the world's best. Most of Costa Rica's plastic surgeons are trained in the United States or Europe. They keep up-to-date on new trends and methods in their field and attend professional seminars regularly. Rates for different operations vary from doctor to doctor. You can combine several procedures to reduce the price substantially. There are even package prices that combine surgery, hotel and hospitalization.

In general, prices average 25 to 60 percent less than in the United States, although the final cost is open to negotiation with the surgeon. The low cost of cosmetic surgery should not, however, be interpreted as a sacrifice of quality for affordability. The cost of a full-face lift is between $2,000 and $3,500 (add a few hundred dollars per day in the hospital to recuperate from the surgery); nose surgery about $2,000; liposuction $800 to $1,500; with a tummy tuck, $2,000 to $3,000, breast implant $2,500 to $3,500 and eyelid surgery between $800 to $1,500. Many doctors send their patients to special recovery houses for about $70 a day. Rates vary from surgeon to surgeon. We suggest you contact **Dr. Arnoldo Fournier** (please see the article in this section). They are the best plastic surgeons in Costa Rica and will be more than happy to send a brochure and answer any of your questions. For information about travel arrangements or cosmetic surgery vacations see **Unique Costa Rica Tours** at **www.travel.costaricabooks.com**. You may combine cosmetic surgery, dental work or language study vacation with Christopher Howard's Retirement Tour.

One quick word about cosmetic surgery in Costa Rica. There are a couple of doctors who advertise their services as cosmetic surgeons but have no specialized training in the field. Therefore to get the best results from your surgery, we suggest you do the following:

(1) Ask the U.S. Embassy for a list of certified plastic surgeons; (2) Also check with the *Colegio de Médicos* (the local equivalent of the A.M.A.) to see if a particular doctor is trained as a plastic surgeon.

Plastic Surgery in Costa Rica
By Arnoldo Fournier M.D.

Within the American Continent, Costa Rican Cosmetic, Plastic and Reconstructive surgeons, has been more and more recognized for their natural post-surgical results.

These surgeons, most likely, are fluent in more than two languages because they have earned the opportunity to study abroad for their post-medical graduate studies in cosmetic procedures.

For the last ten years, cosmetic tourism has increased significantly. One of the pioneers in this field is Arnoldo Fournier, M.D., F.A.C.S., Founder and Board Member of the Society of Plastic Surgeons in Costa Rica, Correspondent Member of the American Society of Plastic Surgeons, and the American Aesthetic of Plastic Surgery. "When I came back to Costa Rica (more than twenty years ago) from St. Luke Hospital in New York, I was told by a former Plastic Surgeon, that cosmetic procedures were not in demand by Costa Ricans."

As a result, this stubborn Surgeon decided that if he was not going to have Costa Rican clientele, he was going to open a market outside the borders of Costa Rica. He placed his first advertisement in the Tico Times (a national English Spoken newspaper) offering his services for Cosmetic, Reconstructive and Plastic Surgery. As time went by, he also placed more advertisements in other well know magazines such as LACSA Magazine, Eastern Magazine, Skyword Magazine, Passages Magazines, etc. "I was the seventh Cosmetic Surgeon in the world who owned a website when the era of the internet began".

The majority of his patients come from overseas, specially from the United States. Cosmetic Surgery Vacations have become more an more attractive, due to the natural beauty of Costa Rica. Most people come to Costa Rica, and tour around for one week, and then have their procedures done. Others, simply come for their procedure, relax during their post surgical recovery, and do day tours to nearby volcanoes, National Parks, etc. Costa Rica's wonderful year round weather (75 F year round!), is an adequate place to recover. Its not to hot, and not to cold, and it has the humidity every skin desires.

One of the most attractive things about the Cosmetic Vacations, are their affordable costs, excellent quality surgery, and safety. "Within the U.S., you can find rates that vary from $10, 000 to $15,000. In Costa Rica, for the same procedures, I offer rates that are as high as $3,000 and lower", says Dr. Fournier.

The Secretary of Health, yearly supervises several public and private hospitals in Costa Rica. They all need to have the appropriate, and updated equipment for the procedures performed at hospital's operating rooms. A requirement for the patients is to have their pre-surgical medical exams results prior any procedure, and antibiotics. The procedures are done with local anesthesia and sedation to reduce the risk of general anesthesia. "This means, that the patients are given pills for sedation prior and during the procedures, and intravenous medication given by an anesthesiologist". Therefore, the patients will not be aware or awake during the procedures.

His surgery team is lead by Dr. Fournier, and presided by his assistant, anesthesiologist, and two certified nurses. As time goes by, more an more patients call him and write him from around the world for his services. He is known for his personal care with every patient. "I do one to two procedures a day during the morning time. I perform all procedures". Dr. Fournier, says that he likes to work first time in the morning because he feels fresh, clear and energetic for the procedures he performs. "It is better to do one or two procedures a day, than five or twenty supervised or half way done. As a result, I can explain the patient precisely know how the procedure will be or was done at the operating room".

You will notice, that he personally answers all the emails and telephone calls he receives from his patients. He personally visits them at their hospital rooms, and accompanies them throughout their post-operatory period. Patients area asked to stay in San José for a few days at any Recovery Homes after their surgeries. During this time, he sets up appointments at his office several times a week, and revise the recovery in every patient.

Today, his best advertising is the "Word of Mouth". His former patients "spread around" the good things of DR. Fournier whom has "The hands of an Surgeon, the eyes of an Artist, and the heart of a Friend".

For more information you can visit his website at www.drfounier.com, E-mail at: fournier@racsa.co.cr , or call him at 011-506-223-7314.

To combine cosmetic surgery, dental work, or a language study vacation with **Christopher Howard's Retirement Tour** see www.ravel.costaricabooks.com or call toll free 800 365-2342.

All doctors in Costa Rica must be registered with the **Costa Rican Doctor's Association** or *Colegio de Médicos* (Tel: 232-3433, Fax: 232-2406, E-mail: medicos@racsa.co.cr, www.medicos.sa.cr). Only registered plastic surgeons may advertise their services; (3) Ask a local family doctor for a recommendation of a good plastic surgeon. (4) Talk with former patients of the doctor of your choice before you make a decision and find out if they are pleased with the results of their surgery (5) Just because some cosmetic surgeons advertise in English-language publications doesn't mean they offer the best quality or prices. Contact the **Costa Rican Plastic Surgery Association** (Tel: 258-0396, Fax: 257-9413, E-mail: drmacaya@msn.com) for additional information.

Ophtalmology

Costa Rica has excellent ophthalmologists. **Lasik Surgery** costs $800 to $1200. Johan Fernández runs the **Oftalmología Laser Center** (258-3031 or 522-1000 ext. 2430) or see www.OftalmologiaLaserCenter. com. His email is: JFernandezJ@ClinicaBiblica.com. He has an English- speaking staff. His office is located in the Torre Médica Omega, Clínica Bíblica, 8th floor in downtown San José. See the Yellow Pages for more *"Oftamólogos."*

Care for the Elderly

Although the Costa Rican government funds homes for the elderly, foreigners are probably better off in a private facility. Full-service custodial health care is available in Costa Rica for the elderly at a very low cost. Care for less independent senior citizens is about $1,500 per month. **Retirement Centers International** offers comprehensive medical care and assistance that includes all medicines, lab work, dental care, physical therapy, rehabilitation and special diets.

Villa Alegría (Tel:433-8590 or 372-1244, E-mail: info@ costaricanursinghomes .com, www.costaricanursinghomes.com) is another full-service facility for the elderly. The staff with more than 15 years of experience is specialized in elderly illnesses such as Parkinson and Alzheimer's. This makes Villa Alegría a unique facility in Costa Rica. Love and dedication are the main ingredients that inspire this group of professional caregivers.

These programs are some of Central America's best and are considerably less expensive than in the United States. However, if these facilities are beyond an elderly person's means, a full-time, live-in domestic worker can be hired as a nurse for a couple of hundred dollars monthly. In addition to caring for an elderly person this worker can manage other household chores.

*Once again, to find a good physician or specialist talk to other retirees, look in the Yellow Pages under *MEDICOS* or look for doctors' ads in *The Tico Times* and *Central America Weekly*. Below are the names of some English speaking physicians.

Dr. John Longworth, M.D.— Family Medicine
(English-speaking , excellent doctor with a good bedside manner)
Clínica Bíblica
Tel: 221-3922 or 221-3064

Dr. Ricky Brown, BS, DC, NMD — Chiropractor
(English-speaking) in Heredia
Tel: 560-0424 E-mail: rickbrowndc@gmail.com

Dr. Jason Ramke, D.C. — Chiropractor
Tel: 220-3041, www. quiropraticafamiliar.com

Dr. Arieh Grunhaus z. —Urology
Apartado334-1260, Plaza Colonial, Escazú
Tel: 208-1716 Fax: 208-1736
E-mail: a grunhause@hospitalcima.com

Dr. Stephen Kogel—Physician/Psychiatrist
A U.S.-born doctor who has helped many American clients with alcohol and drug problems.
Tel: 224-6176

Dr. Manuel Trimiño Vásquez—Physician/Psychiatrist
He has many clients from the United States and is bilingual.
He has helped many foreigners adjust to living in Costa Rica.
Tel: 221-6140 or 233-3333

For the names of more doctors and dentists, see the section in the back of this book titled " More Phone Numbers." Also there is a publication called *Guía Integral de la Salud* that lists hundreds of health- related services including doctors, laboratories, hospitals and clinics. Please see the "Suggested Reading" section in Chapter 10 for additional information.

Alternative Healing

Costa Rica has more than a hundred chiropractors, homeopathic doctors, massage specialists and natural health practitioners. Check *The Tico Times*, talk to other foreigners, health-food-stores, the Yellow Pages.

Taxes

You will have many tax advantages in Costa Rica. Investors pay no capital gains taxes on real estate investments. High interest-bearing bank accounts are also tax -free. The maximum Costa Rican tax rate is around 30 percent with no city or state taxes and low property taxes. There is no personal income tax on a salary of less than $750 monthly. Self-employed people can earn up to $3000 a year without paying taxes. The most a corporation has to pay in taxes is 30 percent on an income of more than $100,000 (tax percentage is applied to net income after all expenses). However, it is easy to form a Costa Rican "offshore" corporation, or *Sociedad Anónima*, to shelter earnings and pay significantly fewer taxes. There are also many write offs to lessen taxes. Tax information is available in Spanish from a government website: **www.hacienda.go.cr**.

Briefly, a *Sociedad Anónima* is an anonymous corporation anyone, even tourists, can set up without their names appearing on any records. The initials S.A. will appear after a corporation's name instead of Inc.. A Costa Rican corporation is similar to its U.S. counterpart in having a board of directors, shareholders and shares that can be bought and sold freely. You control all the stock in the corporation but your identity remains unknown. This practice is illegal in the United States. but not in Costa Rica. Thus you are able to maintain some degree of secrecy in financial matters and protect yourself from some tax problems.

Each corporation has a set of six legal books in which changes may be made. Many corporations never even use their books because they never engage in any commercial activity, existing only to hold vehicles or real estate and other investments.

These offshore corporations are used in most business transactions in Costa Rica and abroad. Because they are foreign corporations they are not subject to U.S. taxes. Furthermore, Costa Rican corporations pay only minimal taxes in Costa Rica, or none at all.

There are additional benefits to establishing an "offshore" corporation. If you put your property in your corporation's name, it

Living in Costa Rica and U.S. Taxation
By Randall J. Linder E.A.

For U.S. citizens living in a foreign country, there is little or no relief in income tax filing requirements. Often we are faced with new requirements, new situations, and given wrong advice from fellow citizens.

As a professional U.S. Income Tax preparer specializing in U.S. citizens living in a foreign country, I have personally provided answers to some of the most frequently asked questions.

Now that I am living in Costa Rica, do I need to file a U.S. income tax? Most U.S. citizens must file an annual income tax return on their worldwide income. As a general rule, if you wereliving in the U.S., and think you need to file a return there, you should probably file one here. It is better to file tha not.

My only income is from a Costa Rica company and I pay taxes in Costa Rica. Do I have to include this income on my U.S. tax return? U.S. citizens must include worldwide income on thier tax returns. This income could qualify for the $80,000 foreign earned income exclusion, but the exclusion in not automatic. You must include the income on your tax return and then exclude it by using the IRS form 2555. If you do not meet the requirements for the exclusion, then the tax you paaid in Costa Rica could be possiblky taken as foreign tax credit.

I live in Costa Rica and work for a U.S. Company Does this income qualify for the $80,000 foreign earned income tax exclussion? If you meet the other requirements for the foreign earned income exclusion, the wages you receive from your U.S. employer can also be excluded. Your employer is still required to withold Social Security and Medicare on your wages.

I have my own business in Costa Rica and work as a self-employed person. My business is not incorporated. Does this income qualify for the foreign earned income exclusion? Yes. This income can qualify for the exclusion just as if you were working for a U.S. employer. Caution: The exclusion is for federal income tax only. You will still be required to pay self-employment tax (Socila Security and Medicare taxes) on your profits.

I have dividends from a Costa Rican company. Are the dividends "foreign earned income" and do they qualify for exclusion? No The foreign earned income exclusion does not apply to income such as interest, dividends, capital gains, pensions, annuities and gambling.

Thexculsion applies strictly to earned income. Note: If you own 10% or more of a foreign corporation, you are required to file wwith your individual income tax return IRS form 5471.

I receive interest frommy Costa Rican bank account, Do I have to report this interest on my U.S. income tax return? Yes, U.S. citizens must include in their income monies received worldwide. This includes interest and dividend income. In addition, if the aggregate value of your foreign accounts is greater than $10,000, at any time during the year, A Report of Foreign Bank and Financial Accounts must be submitted to the U.S. Treasury Department.

I transferred money from the U.S. to Costa Rica, Is there anything special that I need to do? If a U.S. citizen has a financial interest in, or signature authority over any financial accounts, including bank, securities or other types of financial accounts in a foreign country, and if the aggregate value of these accounts exceeds $10,000 at ant time during the year, the accounts must be reported the the U.S. Department of the Treasury.

Last year I got marrried to a Costa Rican citizen. Can I file a joint return with my spouse who is not a U.S. citizen? Yes, but in doing so, you make the choice of reporting your income and your spouse's income worldwide. *

My Costa Rica wife has a child from a previous marriage. The child is living with us. Can I claim the child as a dependent on my tax return? To be claimed as a dependent, the dependent must be a U.S. citizen or a resident of the U.S., or in certain cases a legally adopted child of a U.S. citizzen.

I have been living in Costa Rica for years and haave not filed a tax return. What Should I do? It is to your advantage to seek professional help to determine whether or not you need to file.

My business is incorporated as a Costa Rican S.A. (*sociedad anónima*). Currently it is not making a profit, and I am not receiving a paycheck. Does this have to be included in my tax return? Yes. if you own 10% or more of a foreign corporation, you are required to file with your individual income tax return IRS form 5471 (Information Return of U.S. Persons With Respect to Certain Foreign Corporations). This includes inactive S.A.'s and corporations not making a profit.

* Courtesy of **Randall Linder**, U.S. Tax & Accounting Service, Tel: 011-506-288-2201, Cell: 011-506-839-9970, Fax: 011-506-288-0120, e-mail: ustax@lawyer.com.

is easier to transfer title. All one has to do is exchange the company's stocks. This way your assets can be transferred or sold by simply giving your shares to the new owner or vice versa. Owning one of these corporations entitles you to start a business and open a checking account in the company's name, even though you are not a legal resident or citizen. If you have relatives on the board of directors of your company, there will be no probate taxes in the event of your death. It is almost impossible to find out whose name appears in the public records since ownership is confidential. Furthermore, if you get involved in any serious litigation, it will be difficult to sue you directly. You will be protected against most judgments and liens. This affords your assets greater protection. If you are a non-resident foreigner, you must have one of these corporations to own a business.

Contact your attorney if you are seriously thinking about forming one of these anonymous corporations. Your lawyer can explain how they work and their advantages and disadvantages. The fee for starting one of these corporations is usually between $300 and $1,000. It will usually take a few months to finish all of the paperwork, depending on how fast your lawyer works.

In order to form a corporation, your attorney will have to make sure there are no other corporations with the same name as your company. The name of your company will have to be in Spanish, not English. Your corporation must have a minimum number of shareholders. It also must have a board of directors, consisting of a president, secretary and treasurer—all of whom have the option of being shareholders. The final steps are preparing a set of books, registering your company, establishing a charter and advertising the charter in the local newspaper.

Be forewarned: Many individuals have lost large amounts of money and property by not understanding fully how the corporate structure works, and therefore have been defrauded by their lawyer or other persons (often foreigners). Please contact Ryan Piercy at 257-6646 to obtain an appointment if you wish to better understand this structure.

Costa Rica's bank secrecy is not "foolproof." This is especially true since the September 11, 2001 terrorist incident in the United States. If you attempt to use your corporation for fraudulent purposes, you are asking for big trouble. Fortunately the IRS usually will not go after you unless you are a "big fish" who has done something obvious to attract their attention. This rarely happens, since the country's banks are not very cooperative with U.S. authorities in such matters. Furthermore, the U.S. also has to obtain the authorization of a Costa Rican judge in such matters, which is difficult.

If you desire better protection for your assets or business, we suggest you form a Panamanian corporation. Many savvy investors put their Costa Rica corporation in a Panamanian corporation. This way they are guaranteed maximum protection of their assets. Since we do not know all of the nuances of setting up one of these corporations, we suggest you contact one of the companies listed at the end of the next section.

Foreign income is exempt from taxation in Costa Rica. You will have to pay taxes on income earned in Costa Rica. *La Tributación Directa*, the local equivalent of the IRS, is in charge of collecting taxes, but is far less efficient.

However, if you go into business in Costa Rica and form a tax-sheltered corporation, many of your expenses can be written off. You will pay an income tax on your company's earnings during the prior fiscal year, or *año económico* which runs from October through September 30. Corporations are taxed only on the income earned within Costa Rica. Every company needs to file form D110 in March. If your corporation owns property, there are a couple of property taxes to be paid. Corporations that are inactive pay a small tax.

You must report all income made in Costa Rica. All net income is subject to taxation. Current taxes for salaried employees run from about zero to 15 percent on a monthly income above $900. Taxes for the self-employed go from zero to $3,000 annually to 25 percent above $15,000 annually. Small companies pay from 10 percent to 30 percent depending on their profits. Though it must be declared, bank interest is tax free to the depositor (therefore deducted as non-taxable income), as the rate offered at the bank in net interest.

Due to the need for more revenue, the government has cracked down on individuals and businesses that attempt to evade their fiscal responsibilities. With the help of the U.S. Internal Revenue Service, Costa Rica is getting better at collecting taxes. Under the new tax law, evaders are now subject to big fines, interest, penalties and possible prison terms. Don't panic! A good accountant or tax lawyer can help you minimize your taxes and avoid problems later on.

Also, unlike some other places, a foreign retiree is not required to pay Costa Rican taxes on his external income (income generated abroad), so you can see why Costa Rica is considered a tax-haven by many people.

There is a yearly municipal property tax of 0.25% on your land or home and a sales tax of 13 percent paid for goods and service. In addition to paying your property taxes at the municipality, you may also pay them at the **Banco Nacional**. If you have an account at the Banco Nacional and use Internet banking, you can see what you owe in property taxes by typing in the *cédula* number of the owner of the property or corporation. Then go pay in person and be sure to get a receipt. Don't forget to save the receipt if the municipality has a dispute.

U.S. citizens are subject to income tax wherever they are living. You must file your U.S. income tax returns yearly through the U.S. Embassy. You have to declare all income earned abroad but you may claim a tax exemption up to $ 80,000 on overseas-earned gross income. The $80,000 applies to individual, unmarried taxpayers. If you are married, you and your spouse may exclude up to $144,000 of foreign income, but you cannot combine the two exemptions. This exclusion does not apply to passive income such as interest, dividends, capital gains or overseas pensions. It only applies to a foreign earned income. You must reside outside of the United States for at least 330 days a year or be a legal resident of a foreign country to qualify for this exemption. Your primary business must also be located abroad to qualify for the foreign-earned income exemption.

Fortunately, if you live outside the United States you qualify for a two-month extension and may wait to file your taxes until June 15. However, if you mail your return from outside the United States, it is best to mail your return at least two weeks before the due date. You can speed this up by using DHL, FedEx or UPS. You need to use a U.S. tax form 2555 to apply for this extension. Even if you earn no income in Costa Rica, it is imperative to file a standard 1040 tax form to avoid problems. The biggest mistake made by individuals is assuming that since their income is under the exclusionary amount, they do not have to file a return. Payment of taxes, interest and penalties can now be done by credit card by dialing 1-888-2PAY-TAX.

If you have any tax questions, contact the U.S. Embassy or IRS. Call either the Consular Section of the U.S. Embassy (220-3939) or the nearest IRS office in Mexico City at (525) 211-0042, ext. 3557. You may consult the IRS Web sites at www.irs.gov or www.irs.gov/faqs/faq13.html.

There is also book titled *The Expats Guide to U.S. Taxes*. It may be purchased through www.amazon.com. Another good resource is found at www.filetax.com/expat.html.

If you need help with your tax forms and returns while living in Costa Rica, contact **U.S. Tax and Accounting** 383-7043, E-mail: ustax@lawyer.com and **David Houseman** at 257-1655 or 239-2005, fax: 223-7997 or 293- 2437, for income tax assistance or for help with IRS problems.

Don D. Nelson, Attorney at Law and CPA, specializes in expatriate tax services. You may call him toll-free (866) 712-0320 or E-mail him at: don@taxmeless.com. You may view his website at www.taxmelesss.com.

If Canadians want to be exempt from income taxes in Canada they need to have severed major residency ties for at least two years. These "residency ties" can include an un-leased house, Canadian health coverage, automobile registration, spouse or child support in Canada, banking or investment ties.

A foreign tax credit is often available for taxpayers who pay tax in another country, i.e. Costa Rica. To find out your tax status, consult form IT221R3 on the Canadian Customs and Revenue Agency Web site: www.ccraedrc.gc.ca. Canadian tax returns should be in by April 30. Self-employed people have until June 15.

Canadians will have to contact **Revenue Canada** concerning their tax obligations while living abroad.

Panamanian (Offshore) Corporations

Offshore corporations enable you to act as an international citizen with complete confidentiality, privacy and safety. Offshore corporations can legally open offshore bank accounts, brokerage accounts, hold credit cards, own property, stocks etc., and in many cases completely exempt you from any tax reporting requirements and with complete confidentiality.

Why Panama?
For many years Panama has been recognized worldwide as a major international offshore banking center that offers very attractive legal and tax incentives to Panamanian corporations. For example, Panamanian law allows Panamanian corporations to issue "bearer" stock certificates. This means the owners who control the corporation do not have to be named in any public record, since ownership is through physical possession of the "bearer" shares. Panamanian corporations are not subject to Panamanian tax on income earned outside of Panama.

Also, Panama allows you to name your corporation with an English name. This gives you many advantages when using your Panamanian Corporation in English speaking countries. These are just a few of the more important reasons why Panamanian corporations are so popular.

Forming a Panamanian Corporation:

First, we recommend you select a name in English followed by: Corp., Corporation Inc. or Incorporated. You cannot use the words Bank, Trust, Foundation or Insurance in the name of your corporation. You may use any name as long as it is not being currently used in Panama. If you own a U.S. corporation, you may find some advantages in using the same name for your Panamanian corporation, if available. This would allow you to have identically named offshore and onshore bank accounts as well as other similar advantages.

Panamanian corporations are typically formed with nominee directors, president, secretary and treasurer. These are Panamanian citizens who are modestly paid officer workers. If you wish, you may select your own directors and officers. However, the original directors and officers selected are registered with the Panamanian public registry, and it becomes public information available to anyone who inquires. Therefore, if you wish confidentiality, we recommend that you select the nominee director option. Officers and directors can always be changed later.

Panamanian law allows corporate shares to be issued in "bearer" form. This means that whoever physically possesses the shares, owns the company. This allows for total confidentiality of ownership, since the person who physically possesses the shares is not identified in any public or even private record. Having a Panamanian corporation with "bearer" shares also makes transfer of ownership completely private and not a matter of public record, since transfer of ownership is a simple process of physically transferring the "bearer" shares to a new owner very similar to passing a $20 bill to someone else versus writing them a check. This feature makes it very easy to sell or transfer properties confidentially by simply transferring the "bearer" shares and ownership of the Panamanian corporation. Thus you may avoid many forms of taxes and closing costs because title to the property remains in the name of the Panamanian corporation. Essentially you are simply selling the corporation that owns the property.

Your Panamanian Corporation comes with a notarized General Power of Attorney (in English) signed by two officers named in the articles of incorporation. This power of attorney provides a blank space for you to fill in the name of any person you want to act as the legal agent for the corporation with the authority to open and sign on corporate bank accounts, enter into contracts for the corporation, sign and transfer assets for the corporation, etc. Although you fill in your name or another person's name as having Power of Attorney, this is not evidence of ownership.

The person named is simply an agent, similar to an employee empowered to act for the corporation. You may order as many additional Power of Attorney forms as you wish.

As you can see there is a world market for Panamanian corporations because they are extremely popular. Older Panamanian corporations with established bank accounts sell for thousands of dollars or more. Selling your Panamanian corporation is a matter of physically transferring the "bearer" stock certificate together with the other corporate records to the new owner.

The one-time cost for setting up a simple Panamanian Corporation is about $1600. You will have to pay an annual Registered Agent and Director's fee of $595 yearly, due one month before the anniversary date of the corporation.

For forming a Panamanian corporation or foundation, we highly recommend **Roberto I. Guardia**. A number of Americans we interviewed speak very well of him. You can contact him at: Tel: (507) 263-3917, Fax: (507) 263-3924 Cel: 612-5429 E-mail: rig@orcag. com, www.orcag.com.

Insurance

The *Instituto Nacional de Seguros*, or INS, is a state-run insurance company that controls all insurance in Costa Rica. They will handle all of your insurance needs. INS has a new English section on their website at www.ins-cr.com or www.ins.go.cr.

All insurance is less expensive in Costa Rica than in the United States. Auto, fire and theft insurance will cost less than half the U.S. premium. All vehicles in Costa Rica have Obligatory Insurance or *Seguro Obligatorio*, which comes automatically with your vehicle registration. It is renewed every December when you pay your car's road tax (*marchamo*). This insurance gives you a small amount of personal liability coverage, which is the type that protects you if you hurt, kill or maim another person when you are driving your car.

About 65 percent of cars have only the obligatory insurance which is not really complete coverage. If you want real coverage you must buy a supplementary policy. For an additional cost, supplemental insurance policies provide broader coverage than the basic compulsory policy. Your car's value determines the price of your premium. These supplemental policies are paid in full every six months. They cannot be paid in monthly premiums as in the United States. Also, as in the States, premiums are increased when you have an accident. However, these increases are not as big as in the United States. It doesn't matter if it was your fault or not.

When considering coverage, remember the general rule of thumb: Insure against everything you would find yourself hard-pressed to overcome financially. The essential coverages are A and C; if you don't get those, INS won't sell you any of the others. For coverage F or H, you must also have D. (By the way, coverages B and G have never existed). Rates are determined by the vehicle's and applicant's characteristics.

Here is a breakdown of the basic automobile coverages in Costa Rica:

(A) PERSONAL LIABILITY — Covers liability established by the courts as a result of death or injury caused by an accident for which the driver of your vehicle was guilty. The benefits are paid once the Obligatory Insurance is used up and does not cover injury or death of family members or employees of the policyholder or driver.

(C) PROPERTY DAMAGE — Covers damage to property (car, house, etc.) belonging to other people if the accident was the fault of the driver of your vehicle. Excludes items being transported by your vehicle.

(D) COLLISION — In case of collision with another vehicle, persons, or property belonging to someone else, this policy pays for damage sustained by your vehicle: (a) if the accident was not the fault of your driver, or (b) if the accident was not the fault of your driver but the other vehicle has no insurance and the owner cannot pay.

(E) FIRE — Covers damage to your vehicle caused by fire due to either internal factors such as short circuit, or to external factors such as lightning, or if the place where the vehicle is parked burns.

(F) THEFT — Covers total theft of the vehicle or loss derived from the total theft. If it is not recovered, policy pays for damage and/or missing parts. If not recovered within a month, the insured amount is paid or the vehicle is replaced.

(H) ADDITIONAL RISKS — Covers damage resulting from overturning, running off the road, vandalism, floods, hurricanes, quakes, explosions, collisions with birds, falling objects, accidents within parking lots or private property, riots, etc.

OTHER CONSIDERATIONS

Insured values — Cars should be insured at their market value in Costa Rica, and it is up to the policy applicant to determine it. To determine values of vehicles, it is sometimes best to use the newspaper classified ads. Only you can change the value on your policy; INS will not automatically reduce the insured values on vehicles as they depreciate.

Renewals — Auto insurance is normally for six months, after which you have a grace period of 10 working days to pay for renewal. After that, you would have to apply for new insurance or reinstatement.

Coverage outside of Costa Rica — For cars with Costa Rican registration, coverage extends to all of Central America and Panama.

Deductibles — All coverages except "A" have standard deductibles. "A" has no deductible. Double deductible if the driver is under 22, in cases of vandalism, birds or accidents on private property.

Alcohol — Policies will not pay for accidents to vehicles being driven by people under the influence of alcohol or drugs, even if the condition did not cause the accident. An alcohol count of 50 mg or more in 100 cc of blood will invalidate insurance coverage, except for liability coverages A and C.

Roadside Assistance — This comes free for vehicles less than 15 years old that have coverage "D". Call 800-800-7000(toll-free) if you have a flat tire, dead battery, are out of gas, or need a tow truck.

Special Notes for Tourists— When you bring a car into Costa Rica, you will be given a permit to drive the car into the country. The permit is usually for three months, renewable once. For issuance of the permit you must state who is going to drive the car— they allow the owner and one other person, usually one's spouse. If you don't have Costa Rican plates on your automobile, you can't cover it against collision or theft. All other coverages are available under these circumstances. However, in most cases, after 180 days you can get Costa Rican plates when you pay the corresponding taxes on your vehicle.

(I) HOMEOWNERS INSURANCE — A homeowners insurance policy is called *Hogar Comprensivo* in Spanish. It protects your home against fire and natural disaster. The home fire policy has four sub-coverages: "A" is for fire and lightening; "B" covers damage caused by strikes, vandalism, hurricane, cyclone, explosion, smoke, falling objects and vehicles; "C" pays for damage caused by floods and landslides; "D" covers natural disasters: earthquakes, tremors, volcanoes, etc. You can take coverage A by itself, A+B, A+CD or complete coverage A+B+CD. Rates are based on a percentage of the value of the building and include a 13 percent tax and an inflationary factory whereby there is a small yearly increase. Depreciation is also factored in at a rate of one to two percent yearly.

If you have one of these policies you will have to insure your house's contents as well as the house itself. You will have to submit a complete list of household effects with the value of each item, and the respective brand name, model and serial numbers. If you want to insure the contents of your home, you must put a value on the objects based on depreciated value. The same rate for the house applies to the contents. You should have your house appraised so you can carry enough coverage.

Some people doubt whether INS would be able to settle claims from a major earthquake or hurricane. INS is by far the largest insurance company in Central America. In fact, INS is one of the largest insurance companies in Latin America, is financially solid and most importantly, it re-insures worldwide a large percentage of the risk.

We have already mentioned the affordability of medical insurance in Costa Rica in the section titled "Medical Care." Because not everyone's insurance needs are the same and because laws and coverages work differently in Costa Rica, we suggest you consult your attorney or the English-speaking insurance agent, Dave Garrett, we have listed below.

Garrett y Asociados
SJO 450
Miami, FL 33102-5216
Tel: 233-2455 Fax: 222-0007
E-mail: info@segurosgarrett.com
www.segurosgarrett.com

A Summary of Reasons to Live or Invest in Costa Rica

- Year-round spring-like weather in the Central Valley.
- Untarnished international image. How often do you hear bad things in the news about Costa Rica. Only good news!
- Latin America's oldest democracy.
- NO army and NO terrorism. Costa Rica has NO enemies.
- Excellent health care at a fraction of the price you would pay at home.
- Good real estate investments. Costa Rica is considered one of the world's best emerging real estate markets. Many properties are in locations with breathtaking views.
- More North American residents proportionately than any country in the world.
- A tightly-knit expatriate community.
- Time-tested organizations in place to help you with everything you need to make the move from A to Z.
- Excellent quality of life.
- Good communications with high-speed internet in many areas.
- Tax savings.
- Opportunities for entrepreneurs.
- Affordable utilities.
- Friendly people.
- Many people who speak English.
- 1000s of activities to stay busy and happy.
- A nature lovers Disneyland.
- Affordable hired help.
- The beauty of the country.
- Fantastic beaches with warm water.
- Latin America's #1 tourist destination according to Travel Weekly magazine.
- Many American products and services available.
- Fruits and vegetable all year.
- Good public transportation.
- And many intangibles more.

4

MAKING MONEY
IN COSTA RICA

Investing in Costa Rica

A recent study by the *Miami Herald* rated Costa Rica the 27th safest country for investment of 140 countries surveyed. If you are not impressed by Costa Rica's ranking, consider that the United States was ranked only 22nd. Another recent study found Costa Rica to be the least corrupt country in Latin America.

In addition, U.S. business magazine Fortune ranked San José Latin America's fifth best city in which to do business and placed it within the 25 best cities in the world. According to the report, Fortune considered the city's ability to create opportunity for its residents, its business climate and how well it can satisfy the business needs of companies that invest here. San José ranked tops in the quality of its labor force, its business environment and the lifestyle it offers resident executives and investors.

Let us review a few of the reasons why Costa Rica has such magnetism for qualified foreign investors. First, and perhaps most important, is the enduring political stability. As you already know, Costa Rica has had a strong, democratic government without interruption since the 1940s and an excellent centralized banking system. The trend towards an open economy and possible trade pacts with such nations as the United States and Mexico are conducive to investment in Costa Rica. Privatization of many state-run institutions will undoubtedly help economic growth in the future. There are also no government expropriations or interference, unlike in many Latin American countries.

Costa Rica is easily accessible from all parts of the world by land, sea or air. Outstanding phone and Internet systems link Costa Rica internationally to other parts of the world. Also, let's remember that investors in Costa Rica have equal rights and laws to protect them. Regulations for conducting business in Costa Rica are the same for both local and foreign corporations. Both can fully own and control local corporations, as well as real estate without any access limitations or restrictions. Many opportunities await foreigners who start new businesses previously nonexistent in Costa Rica. In addition, the cost of labor is low.

Additional reasons for investing in Costa Rica are: asset protection (creditors, judgments, liens, bankruptcy and divorce), privacy from individuals and governments and fewer taxes (income tax, inheritance tax, estate taxes and probate fees).

Many attractive incentives are available to foreigners investing in Costa Rica. Investments of $50,000 or more in an approved project qualify the investor for legal residency. However, it is not necessary to become a resident to own or manage a business. Anyone who owns a business can import some items used to operate it and get a tax break on some of the usual duties. Contact the incentive section of the **Costa Rican Tourism Institute** (ICT) for more information about incentive programs.

Tourism is now the leading industry in Costa Rica. Numerous opportunities exist in this field. However, sometimes there can be a lot of red tape and competition. Small hotels and bread-and-breakfasts were good investments a few years ago, but there may be a surplus of them now. We have a good friend who refurbished an old building and turned it into a small hotel in 1990. He has done very well only because he has been in the country for a while, knows all the ropes, and was a pioneer in the field.

Foreigners can invest with Costa Rica's nationalized banking system or private banks. Interest rates are higher than in the United States (22 percent or even higher in colones and over 5.75 percent in dollars) and there are many attractive savings accounts and time deposit programs from which to choose. Presently there is no tax on interest from bank accounts. However, when investing in *colón* accounts, you have to figure

Costa Rica Most Stable Country in Latin America

A World Bank study released in May aims to provide a "set of governance indicators that can help depoliticize efforts to track the quality of institutions, support capacity building, improve governance and address corruption."

The index, which analyzed 209 countries between 1996 to 2004, focuses on six components of good governance: political, civil and human rights; political stability and violence; government effectiveness; the incidence of unfriendly market policies; rule of law; and control of corruption.

"On average the quality of governance around the world has remained stagnant, highlighting the urgent need for more determined progress in this area in order to accelerate poverty reduction," said the World Bank.

The percentile ranks below indicate the percentage of countries worldwide that rank below the selected country. For example, 83 percent of countries studied worldwide have less political stability than Costa Rica, meaning that according to this study, it is the most stable country in Latin America.

CountryPercentile
Costa Rica83.0
Chile76.7
Uruguay62.1
Panama.55.3
Dominican Republic .48.1
Mexico43.7
Brazil43.7
Nicaragua43.7
El Salvador.39.8
Argentina38.3
Bolivia28.6
Peru.27.2
Honduras.26.7
Paraguay.25.7
Ecaudor.23.3
Guatemala.21.8
Venezuela.13.6
Colombia5.8

Costa Rica Number One in Latin America in Economic Freedom

Costa Rica and Chile are tied for first in the area of Economic freedom in Latin America. Hong Kong offers the most economic freedom in the world with Costa Rica and Chile in nineteenth place. One hundred twenty-seven countries were studied in the survey.

Factors such as the flexibility of the labor force, monetary regulation and more were studied in order to determine a country's ranking.

Other Countries in the region:

Country Ranking
Costa Rica19
Chile19
Panamá24
El Salvador29
Uruguay44
Guatemala53
Perú38
Honduras59
Bolivia59
Mexico.59
Paraguay65
Dominican Republic68
Nicaragua68
Ecuador86
Brazil86
Haití86
Argentina92
Colombia101
Venezuela120

in yearly inflation to see if you are really getting a good deal. There are some degrees of bank secrecy, liberal money transfer regulations, and favorable tax laws for foreigners (see the section in this Chapter 3 entitled "Taxes").

Foreigners can also invest in the local stock exchange (*Bolsa Nacional de Valores*) to get better returns than from traditional financial systems. The stock market presents a safe investment alternative with great opportunities for the investment to grow through stock appreciation, dividends, stock splits, mergers and acquisitions.

Costa Rica has the largest stock exchange in Central America. Approximately 29 firms or *puestos de bolsa* are registered with the National Stock Exchange. Costa Rican stockbrokers can study economic trends and give you advice on investing in government bonds, real estate, time deposits and other investments. The Costa Rican Stock Exchange is regulated by the National Securities Commission or *Superintendencia Nacional de Valores de Costa Rica* (SUGEVAL), which is the counterpart of the U.S. Securities and Exchange Commission. They can give you information about the reliability of firms and brokers. There exists a strong possibility that the local exchange will be linked with other Latin American trade blocks in the very near future. For more information about the Costa Rican stock market, contact **Grupo Busátil Aldesa** at 1-888-5-ALDESA (United States only) or 223-1022, or E-mail: grupo@aldesa.com. Investors can find additional information about the local stock market at www.capitales.com.

You may also invest profitably in blue-chip, offshore mutual funds. Most people do this to protect their assets from creditors, judgments, liens, bankruptcy, malpractice claims, divorce and separation claims, liability claims not covered by insurance and seizure by the U.S. government.

AmCham's Guide to Investing and Doing Business in Costa Rica is another source of information for the potential investor. It is available through the **Costa Rican-American Chamber of Commerce, or AMCHAM**. The Chamber of Commerce also publishes a monthly magazine entitled Business in Costa Rica that has advice on how to invest in Costa Rica. You may also want to attend a meeting of the Investors Club of Costa Rica. For information, call 240-2240 or 222-5601. This is a good way to meet people with common interests.

RELOCATION, INVESTMENT and **RETIREMENT CONSULTANTS** is a firm we highly recommend to any newcomer or potential investor. Its consultants have many years of experience, will steer you in the right direction and will save you a lot of headaches

Costa Rica: Bright Outlook

Costa Rica's economic outlook is bright, thanks to an attractive environment for business, a new pro-trade government and a planned free trade agreement with the United States. (Courtesy of Latin Business Chronicle)

BY CHRONICLE STAFF

During the 1980s, when Central America was dominated by political violence and armed conflicts, Costa Rica provided an oasis of peaceful stability and was often referred to as "the Switzerland of Central America." While the area subsequently has returned to normalcy, Costa Rica remains an attractive destination not only in Central America, but also compared with the rest of Latin America.

Foreign investors emphasize the country's democratic system as one of the key benefits of Costa Rica. The Central American nation is only one of three countries in Latin America with a perfect score in terms of political and civil rights, according to Freedom House (the others are Chile and Uruguay).

"It's a longstanding democracy," was among the first things Peter Cardinal said when asked about the advantages of doing business in Costa Rica. Cardinal is the executive vice president for Latin America for Canada-based Scotiabank, which acquired Costa Rica's largest bank, Interfin, in July of 2006.

Jose Antonio Rios, international president for Global Crossing, also emphasizes the democratic credentials of Costa Rica. "It's a very democratic country that also calls for stability of institutions in the longterm," he says. "The way they have handled that has been incredible." Global Crossing last month announced plans to extend its core network to Costa Rica.

Costa Rica's democracy was further strengthened with the peaceful handover of power last month to Oscar Arias, an economist and Nobel peace prize winner who also ran Costa Rica in the late 1980s. Arias succeeded Abel Pacheco, a medical doctor who assumed the presidency in 2002..

ATTRACTIVE BUSINESS CLIMATE
But Costa Rica wouldn't be garnering all that attention from investors if a strong democracy was the only thing it could offer. "They

have a clear and aggressive tax benefit program for companies that invest there," says Rui da Costa, managing director for Latin America and Caribbean for U.S. computer giant HP, which employs almost 1,800 people in the country, making it home to its largest number of employees in Latin America. "They have a very updated infrastructure in terms of telecommunications, very good level of education - in terms of tech skills and also in terms of language. And it's also a more secure area. There's not as much violence as other places."

Thanks to high penetration rates of Internet, PC and wireless and fixed telecommunications, Costa Rica ranks second in Latin America in technology level, according to the Latin Business Index published by *Latin Business Chronicle*. Costa Rica has a fixed line telephony rate of 31.6 percent, and a PC penetration rate of 23.9 percent - both the highest in Latin America, while its Internet penetration rate of 23.5 percent is the second-highest in the region, according to 2004 data from the ITU (the latest available).

Costa Rica has one of the highest education levels in Latin America and ranks fourth in the region on the latest UN Human Development Index, which measures the adult literacy rate and combined gross enrolment ratio for primary, secondary and tertiary schools as well as health conditions and purchasing power. And Costa Rican capital San Jose is among the three safest cities in Latin America, according to a ranking published in the pan-regional business magazine America Economia recently.

In terms of competitiveness, Costa Rica ranks third in Latin America (behind Chile and Argentina), according to the 2006 Latin America Competitiveness Review from the World Economic Forum, while it also came in third (behind Panama and the Dominican Republic) on the Latin American Globalization Index published by Latin Business Chronicle.

ECONOMIC FREEDOM
And Costa Rica's economy is among the freest in Latin America. It came in third on the 2006 Heritage Foundation/Wall Street Journal survey of economic freedom in the world. Costa Rica shared the third place with Uruguay and was only beaten by Chile and El Salvador. Finally, Costa Rica also ranked third on the FTAA Readiness Indicator developed by the Institute for International Economics in 2001. The indicator measures how prepared Latin American countries are for the Free Trade Area of the Americas (FTAA).

As a result of its high scores in business, political and economic environment, Costa Rica came in third on the Latin Business Index (behind Chile and Mexico).

Apart from investors like Scotiabank, Global Crossing and HP, Costa Rica has attracted significant investment from US-based chip giant Intel, which employs 2,200 people and has become the top exporter. Intel operates two micro chip factories and a distribution center at Heredia, 19 kilometers (12 miles) west of San Jose.

"Costa Rica was originally selected for its export-oriented infrastructure, reliable power and advanced telecommunications, as well as its talented and educated workforce, high literacy rate (95.5 percent) and supportive business environment," Intel says on its web site.

The chip giant, which has operated in Costa Rica since 1998, also chose the Central American country over other candidates such as Mexico due to lower corruption, according to Intel officials. Costa Rica is the third-most transparent country in Latin America, way ahead of countries like Mexico and Brazil, according to Transparency International.

MOTOROLA AND MICROSOFT

Other key investors in Costa Rica include Microsoft, Motorola and pharmaceuticals like Baxter International Inc. and Boston Scientific. "It's very open to investment [and] open to people," Rios says.

Costa Rica is one of the leading tourism destinations in Latin America. In 2004, the number of visitors to the country reached 1.4 million, an increase of 17.3 percent from 2003, according to the World Tourism Organisation (UNWTO). While it ranked eight in the region in terms of visitors, it came in fifth in terms of receipts: $1.3 billion.

And Costa Rica can also boast a significant expat community of both retirees and current workers, which in turn is helping drive demand for real estate. "On the plane down there, you see a lot of people not just visiting for meetings, but living there or visiting people living there," Rios says. "There are now direct flights from [and to] the West Coast of Costa Rica and not just from capital San Jose."

WAITING FOR CAFTA

There is now much anticipation surrounding the implementation of a free trade agreement with the United States. Costa Rica was one of five Central American countries that signed the Central American Free Trade Agreement (CAFTA) with the United States in May 2004, but is the only one that has yet to ratify it. (El Salvador, Honduras and Nicaragua have implemented it, while implementation is pending in Guatemala. The Dominican Republic signed the pact later and is also awaiting implementation.)

Pacheco delayed sending CAFTA to the local legislature for approval until October last year. And there has been strong opposition to the pact from local unions and other interest groups. However, Arias has made the ratification one of his top priorities.

"The president is committed to going into the CAFTA with the US," Cardinal says.

Arias, who narrowly won the presidential election in February, named Marco Vinicio Ruiz as commerce minister. Ruiz was a business leader who led Costa Rican private sector efforts to support CAFTA. In a meeting with US investors at the Council of the Americas last year Arias pledged support for open markets and private investment.

At the same time, Costa Rica will benefit from a free trade agreement between Central America and the European Union. Negotiations for such a pact were announced in Vienna in May, although talks will likely take some time and result in implementation after 2008, some experts predict.

Costa Rica's total trade grew by 13.4 percent last year to $20.1 billion, according to the United Nations Economic Commission for Latin America and the Caribbean (ECLAC). Exports increased by 13.3 percent to $9.7 billion, while imports grew by 13.4 percent to $10.4 billion.

KEY US PARTNER

Trade with the United States grew by 5.6 percent last year to $7.0 billion, according to US Census Bureau data. That was the strongest growth of any Central American country except Nicaragua. Exports to the United States grew by 2.5 percent to $3.4 billion, while imports from the United States increased by 8.8 percent to $3.6 billion. The United States is Costa Rica's top trading partner and Costa Rica is the top US trading partner in Central America.

Meanwhile, trade with the European Union grew by 0.7 percent to 3.8 billion euro (approximately $4.7 billion). Costa Rican exports to the EU fell by 1.1 percent to 3.0 billion euro, but imports from the EU grew by 8.0 percent to 809 million euro, according to Eurostat.

This year, total trade is expected to grow even stronger than last year. Exports during the first five months were up 17.4 percent compared with the same period last year, according to Costa Rican data quoted by Bear Stearns. Top export items were microchips, bananas and textiles.

This year, GDP growth is picking up. In April, the economy grew by 6.3 percent and growth of more than 5 percent during each of the first four months of the year has taken the 12-month rate of expansion through April to 5.5 percent, its highest level since July 2004.

and money. Their expertise, network of reliable contacts and insider information have already helped hundreds of people find success, prosperity and happiness in Costa Rica. Most important, they can show you how to really make money in Costa Rica by hooking you up with time-tested investments. You may contact them at Tel/Fax: 011-(506)-261-8968 or through: E-mail: **crbooks@racsa.co.cr**.

Before investing or starting a business, you should take the time to do your homework. Under no circumstances should you invest right off the plane, that is to say, on your first trip to Costa Rica. Unscrupulous individuals and scamsters will always prey on impulsive buyers anywhere in the world. Be wary of any salesmen who try to pressure you into investing. Remember, it is hard to start a business in your own home country; don't imagine it will be any easier in Costa Rica, where both language and customs are different. **The Better Business Bureau of Costa Rica** will help you find reliable businesses and services.

We also suggest you ask a lot of questions and get information and assistance from any of the organizations listed below in order to thoroughly understand the business climate of the country. However, don't solely depend on the help of these organizations. You'll have to garner a lot of information and learn on your own by some trial and error. This way you can find out what works best for your particular situation.

Costa Rican-American Chamber of Commerce of Costa Rica: (AMCHAM)
Address in Costa Rica:
P.O. Box 4946-1000
San José, Costa Rica
Address in United States:
Amcham SJO 1576
P.O. Box 025216
Miami, FL 33102-5216
Tel: 220-2200
Fax: 220-233-0969
E-mail: chamber@amcham.co.cr

Coalition for Investment Initiatives-(CINDE)
P.O. Box 7170
San José, Costa Rica
Tel: 220-0036

Fax: 220-4750
E-mail: aheilbron@cinde.or.cr

Export Promotion Center (CENPRO)
P.O. Box 5418
San José, Costa Rica
Tel: 0i1-(506) 220-0066
Fax: 011-(506) 223-5722

The Costa Rican Stock Exchange (*Bolsa de Valores*)
Bolsa Nacional de Valores
P.O. Box 1756
San José, Costa Rica
Tel: 222-8011
Fax: 255-0531

National Securities Commission
P.O. Box 10058
San José, Costa Rica
Tel: 233-2840;
Fax: 233-0969

Canada Costa Rica Chamber of Commerce
Tel: 257-4466

Investment Opportunities According to Risk

(1) **Certificates of Deposit** in dollars through a state-run bank paying about 3 to 3.6 percent annually. Advantage: Your money is insured by the Costa Rican government and earns tax-free interest.

(2) **Real Estate Advantages**: If purchased at the right place and in the right location, you are assured your property will double or triple over the next 10 years. Areas such as the Central and Southern Pacific are booming. Real Estate Investment Trusts are also a good bet. Disadvantages: Overpaying or purchasing in a bad location. See the section in Chapter 3 and this chapter about investing in Costa Rican real estate.

(3) **Certificates of Deposit** in *colones* (local currency) from a government bank. Advantage: Pay about 20 percent annually and are

insured. Disadvantage: Mini-devaluations give you a net annual yield of about 10 percent at the most. If there is a huge devaluation, you will lose a lot of money. This hasn't happened since 1982. The mini-devaluations exist as a measure to prevent large devaluations.

(4) **Personal Loans on Secured Property** in dollars or *colones*. Advantage: Can earn up to 3 percent monthly in colones and hold a note on the property. Disadvantage: If borrower defaults, you might have to go to court to recover your property.

(5) **Certificate of Deposit** from a private bank in an offshore account. Advantage: You can earn a little more interest than through the state- run banks and investment is tax-free. Disadvantage: Your money will not be insured. Several private banks offer these types of investments. It is best to visit different banks and to shop around for the best interest rate.

(6) **Starting a Foreign-Based Business**. Advantages: You don't have to depend on the small local economy. Dependence on a larger market. You have a low U.S. tax liability if you use a Costa Rican or Panamanian corporation. An example of this would be an export or Internet-based business. Disadvantage: Not doing your homework and choosing the wrong business.

(7) **Starting a Local-Based Business**. Advantages: There are a lot of opportunities for entrepreneurs here. It is highly advisable to have prior experience in the venture you undertake. You should do a thorough feasibility study. Disadvantages: Not understanding the local economy, not doing your homework and thinking that what works abroad will work here. On the average, only three of 10 foreigners succeed here for a variety of reasons. There is a section in this chapter with details and advice about going into business in Costa Rica, including success stories and failures.

(8) **Offshore Mutual Funds**. Advantages: All the wonderful benefits of investing offshore with the peace of mind of knowing your assets are held safe and secure with a major New York Stock Exchange firm. By moving liquid assets offshore, you also achieve substantial protection from illegitimate creditors and financial predators and limit your tax liability. Disadvantages: Although mutual funds have more built-in safeguards than regular stocks, they are still subject to fluctuations in the market.

The Case for Costa Rica
By Barry Strudwich

In 2006 the first Baby Boomers turned 60. Behind this first wave is a virtual tsunami of graying, affluent soon-to-be-retirees desperately seeking some affordable sunshine. And it's not only Americans. Swedes, Germans, Brits, Canadians, and others are all looking to escape cold weather, dark skies and their dreary, over-regulated, under-performing economies.

So where are you (and your global counterparts) going to land? Have you priced real estate in Arizona, Florida, or Southern California lately? Do you want to risk building your dream home on the Gulf Coast only to have it flattened by Hurricane Katrina's uglier, meaner sister? Look around the rest of the investment landscape and you can be just as depressed. Even Wall Street's deep thinkers will tell you that we're most likely in for decades of tepid, single-digit returns in stocks. Don't even think about living off your fixed-income investments either.

A savvy, soon to retire investor with a few bucks tucked away might look at it this way:

Thedollar is weak and will continue to fall; wars, record deficits and morewill keep the pressure on

The USgovernments will be staring at a colossal tax increase in just a few yearsto fund social security and Medicaid benefits for the flood of retirees

U.S.real estate is massively over-priced and any rise in interest rates couldpop the bubble

Diversifyingout of a falling currency and into hard assets outside the U.S. just mightbe the only way to protect your hard-earned wealth— and enjoy the lifestyle you want .

Is there an investment way to profit from these irreversible waves? Consider your options, run the numbers, and think about everything you'll need: an ideal climate, accessibility, advanced infrastructure, excellent healthcare, and so on. Over and over again—Costa Rica is the brightest blip on the radar.

The Rush to Paradise is Just Beginning
But great vacations are only part of the story. The real secret of Costa Rica today is how easy it is to live and work there. The next wave is for retiring boomers to move "way South" for at least part of the year. Telecom is much better than people realize. With a laptop, cell phone, VPN (virtual private network) and the latest VOIP (voice-over Internet

protocol) phone services, you can stay in touch more cheaply than ever. Costa Rica is easily reachable from major U.S. airports. Health care is superior. The people are friendly and welcoming. English is widely spoken. The Costa Rican government has made a major commitment to protecting and enhancing its spectacular natural environment.

Barry's Top-10 Reasons Why You'll Love Costa Rica
1. The people are welcoming and friendly
2. Surfing and fishing are both spectacular
3. Costa Rica is not a Banana Republic. Intel makes all its Pentium chips here
4. Costa Rica is easy to get to with non-stops daily from 22 US cities
5. Costa Rica abolished their Army in 1949
6. Cell phones are only $10 a month and long distance calls to the U.S. are less than $0.20 a minute. New VOIP rates are less than a nickel a minute
7. 80% OF THE people live in San Jose which means the beautiful coasts are deserted
8. The Pacific Coast is protected from hurricanes by the mountains
9. Prime real estate is still affordable
10. It's the last place in the world they still like Americans

The Perfect Wave is Heading for the Central Pacific Coast
Costa Rica's Central Pacific Coast is pristine and unspoiled. You'll find the most spectacular scenery, the best surfing, superb sport fishing, endless empty beaches, and as much privacy as you want. Even better, it's getting easier and easier to reach this slice of heaven. A new toll road means that you can drive from San Jose to Esterillos Este in just one and a half hours. Without question, over the next five years the Pacific Coast of Costa Rica will be the sweet spot for investors.

Using the analogy of a commercial center, the Central Pacific region of Costa Rica is anchored by the Marriott Los Suenos Resort and 40 miles to the south by Costa Rica's crown jewel, the Manuel Antonio National Park. Both of these anchors are geographically constrained and the logical path of future growth is towards the center.

From a practical perspective, this will be in the area of Esterillos Este as it is thelast high ground between the two anchors. Our reputation for successful development in the area as well as our extensive local ties has created numerous opportunities with local land holders who wish to sell land. In the past several years we have acquired over 2000 acres in this prime growth corridor.

The Del Pacifico at Esterillos Story

Our investment recommendations for Costa Rica aren't just theories. We've made a substantial bet on the soon to boom Central Pacific Coast with the master-planned community of Del Pacifico and our private land banking partnership.

Del Pacifico is 1,000 acres with one-half mile of private beachfront. All residents will have access to the golf course and the Beach Club and Wellness Center. The starting point for the area's finest eco-tourism is the Equestrian and Ecology Center.

No matter where you are on the property, it's an easy walk to the shops and restaurants of La Prada Town Center. Every aspect of our community is designed to meet the highest expectations of sophisticated North American and European investors and vacationers. The 18-hole championship golf course will feature a beachfront nine and a mountain nine. The course is designed by Billy Casper Golf.

There are several ownership and rental options from one-bedroom Town Square condominiums ideal for the fisherman, golfer, or the adventure-loving couple to larger, detached condo-cottages designed for the traveling family. Luxury condominiums and villa sites are available for people who expect to spend extended periods in residence. To learn more about investment opportunities contact: **Costa Rica Retirement Vacation Properties** toll free 800-888-581-1786, E-mail: **carla@costaricaretirementvacationproperties.com** or see **www.primecostaricaproperty.com**

How to Become a Costa Rican Land Baron (or Baroness)

The first way is also the easiest because you don't even have to leave the country. You do this by purchasing shares in a "private land bank". Similar to a mutual fund, this is a professionally managed diversified portfolio of undeveloped land and investments in resort developments. Owning shares in a land bank allows you to participate in locking up large tracts of cheap land today to sell in a few years when the North American *"gringo"* developers start showing up in force. Look for a 5 to 7 year investment horizon and a minimum investment of only $50,000 with a well structured partnership. Your shares can also be purchased with your IRA account. Private land partnerships are only available to "accredited investors" and of course you'll want to check out the track record of the general partner.

Or you can buy your property outright and use it as you see fit. In fact, investing can be almost as easy as purchasing a mutual fund or a stock. Here's why: When you purchase a condo or even a beach front lot, the title for the real estate is usually registered in the name of a private company which actually owns the real estate. By purchasing 100% of the private company shares, you acquire the real estate while avoiding paying real estate transfer taxes twice.

The IRA option is especially powerful here. When you purchase real estate structured as stock transactions, you can purchase the shares inside your IRA account with pre-tax dollars. This also means, when the time comes to cash out at a profit, you can sell tax free as well.

Del Pacifico has been pre-approved by specialty IRA custodians. Current IRA approved investment opportunities include ocean view and golf course condominiums at "pre-construction" prices as well as some spectacular "ocean view" single family lots. Currently, comparable condos at the nearby Marriott Los Suenos resort command rental rates of $700/day, not to mention a resale price of over $1.3 million. Condo prices have been escalating rapidly and will continue to do so as the baby boomers march to retirement.

Check Out This Tropical Eden Before It's Too Late

If you want a fun way to perform your "due diligence", join us for a long weekend. This way you can experience Costa Rica's amazing natural beauty and to learn about this delightful country's people and culture first hand. Experience a zipline, go horseback riding or take a stroll on the beach—and at the end of the day sip a cool drink and watch one more spectacular sunset. Investing doesn't get any better than this. Give Chris Howard a call and he'll help arrange your itinerary.

Barry Strudwick is the developer of The Del Pacifico Surf & Golf Resort and several land banking partnerships holding over 2,000 acres of land in Costa Rica. He serves an international client base from his offices in Maryland and Costa Rica.

Finding Work

Foreigners can only work when they are legal residents, depending on the type of residency. They don't need a work permit. The only exception to this rule is when you can do a job a Costa Rican is unqualified to do. In this case, you can obtain a work permit (see Chapter 5). However, jobs that will qualify you for a work permit are very scarce. If you do obtain a work permit, it must be renewed annually. *Pensionados, rentistas* and foreigners without permanent residency may only own a company, invest or start a business. If you have questions about work permits, contact the **Costa Rican Immigration** at 220-1860.

We have some discouraging news for those living on small pensions and hoping to supplement their income with a part- or full-time job or for others who need to work just to keep busy. Finding work can be difficult, but it is not impossible. In the first place, it is not easy for a Costa Rican, not to mention foreigners who do not speak fluent Spanish, to find permanent work.

If you are one of the few foreigners who have mastered Spanish, you will probably have a fair chance of finding work in tourism or some other related field. However, your best bet may be to find employment with a North American firm doing business in Costa Rica. The best-paying jobs are with multinational corporations.

It is best to contact one of these companies before moving to Costa Rica. Depending on your qualifications, you may be able to find a job as a salesman, an executive or a representative.

When local companies hire foreigners, they are generally looking for a solid educational background and an entrepreneurial spirit that some companies find lacking in Costa Ricans. It helps to have a degree, preferably an MBA, from a well-known U.S. university.

Even if you speak little or no Spanish, you have a chance of finding work as an English teacher at a language institute in San José. Do not expect to earn more than a survival salary from one of these jobs because the minimum wage in Costa Rica is low. Working as a full-time language instructor will not bring you more than a few hundred dollars monthly.

As supplemental income or busywork, this is fine, but you won't make a living on apar with the kind of lifestyle to which you are probably accustomed. If you can find work at a private bilingual school, you can earn more than $1000 a month. The competition for these jobs is very stiff; preference is given to bilingual Costa Ricans and most foreigners hang on to these coveted positions.

There is some work available for English speakers in the sportsbook industry. However, some sportsbooks may be forced to move to other countries because of a change in regulation here.

Try putting one of your skills to use by providing some service to the large expatriate community in Costa Rica. Everyone has a talent or specialty they can offer. For example, if you are a writer, journalist or have experience in advertising, you might look for work at one of Costa Rica's two English-language newspapers. Unfortunately, if you are a retired professional such as a doctor or lawyer, you cannot practice in Costa Rica because of certain restrictions, but you can offer your services as a consultant to other foreigners and retirees.

As if finding work were not hard enough in Costa Rica, a work permit or residency is required before foreigners can work legally. Labor laws are very strict and the government does not want foreigners taking jobs away from Costa Ricans. In theory, companies are not allowed to have more than 10 percent foreign labor. It is actually much lower in practice. You are only allowed to work if you can perform specialized work that a Costa Rican cannot do. However, many foreigners work for under-the-table pay without a work permit.

If you do not seek remuneration, you can always find volunteer work to keep yourself busy. Volunteer work is legal, so you will not need a work permit or run the risk of being deported for working illegally.

An American working at a private highschool.

A Sample of Jobs for English Speakers

Rawlings
RAWLINGS DE COSTA RICA S.A.

A Baseball and Apparel Company in Turrialba

Is looking for:

1. Manufacturing and production supervisor for the baseball area

- Four years university degree in Industrial Engineering
- Bilingual (100% Spanish-English)
- Have full command of MS Office applications
- Be proactive, fast learner, team player, and quality oriented
- Be willing to live in Turrialba

2. Supervisor de Planta de producción para el área textil

- Mínimo cinco años de experiencia en puestos similares en el área textil
- Facilidad para trabajar en equipo
- Conocimientos en el uso de diferentes máquinas industriales de coser.
- Experiencia en la elaboración y construcción de muestras de prendas.
- Conocimiento en telas, hilos y materiales necesarios en la confección de prendas.
- Disponibilidad de vivir en Turrialba.

The company offers a competitive salary, excellent working environment and the necessary training will be given.

Los interesados enviar su oferta de servicios a.sgomez@rawlings.com especificando el puesto al que aplican.

BROKERS
First Year Income
$90 To $100 K
For the Right Individual

IF YOU HAVE A BURNING DESIRE TO SUCCEED, AND ARE A SELF-STARTER, WITH FULL UNDERSTANDING AND PERFECT PRONUNCIATION OF THE ENGLISH LANGUAGE. WE WANT TO TALK TO YOU TODAY!

Company Offers:
- Paid Training
- No Cold Calls
- Top Industry Pay
- Fresh Leads

E-mail resume in English to Kathia@wellingtoncr.com or fax your resume to
(506) 291-7074

On your response, please spe[...]
BROKERS

WESTERN UNION

Exciting opportunity to join a multinational industry leader appointed to provide a fast and reliable money transfer service all over the world. We have a challenging job for a:

GENERAL DIRECTOR OF CONTACT CENTER OPERATIONS

This position has the responsibility of leading a Contact Center team of 600+ employees in areas related to Customer Service. The candidate will be actively involved in defining strategies for the business by providing decision, support and analysis to the [...]

[...] performance improvement to ensure [...]lationships with internal and external

[...]nagerial role in a Call Center environ[...]lls to manage talent in a proper way. [...]rder to adapt to business needs, and [...]ship skills. MBA with an International [...]guage is highly desirable.

[...]s package and the opportunity to work

[...]icating your salary expectations, to the [...]ternunion.com

WE ARE SEEKING CANDIDATES FOR OUR
Global Procurement Organization

Project Leader
- Professional in Industrial Engineering, Business Administration or any other administrative-related career. MBA is a plus.
- Experience required 4-6 years in financial analysis, process controls, quality [...] positions
  - a U.S. - based commercial [...] 2, 1D tdwards or similar ERP's
  - software company is now [...] applications, a plus.
  - hiring full-time professionals [...] promote teamwork.
  - [...] self-motivated.

aplicor

Senior Software Developers

- 5+ years professional software development experience
- 2+ years full-time experience programming using .NET
- Technologies: ASP .NET, Dynamic HTML; JavaScript; Ajax, Multi-Tiered Architecture, Patterns, SQL, OLAP, Reporting
- Good spoken and written English is required

We are seeking self-directed professionals with deep technical expertise interested in creating enterprise-grade commercial software solutions.

We offer an **excellent work environment, stability, regular schedule,** and **extremely competitive salaries, paid in US Dollars.**

Please visit our web site at http://www.aplicor.com and submit a letter of interest and your current resume (in English, please) to: hr@aplicor.com

We Are Hiring Now Experienced
Sales Executives

We are an established international company with offices worldwide

Come work in an exciting, fast paced, fun, English speaking USA call center environment. [Work with music surrounds sound, lunch barbecues, beach trips, and after parties].

- **Excellent base monthly salary $1.500/$2.000 plus daily bonuses, weekly team bonuses daily prizes and monthly commissions.**

Requirements:
- Experience in Call Center Sales Environment (Sportsbook, Tylex, ITS)
- Exceeding monthly sales team quotas
- Excellent verbal and written English skills [100% Fluent]
- Strong computer, customer data entry & Internet skills

To apply, please send us your resume
in ENGLISH Attn: HR/Director of Human
Resources LexingtonGroup@Gmail.com

Grow with us! FUJITSU

TECHNICAL SUPPORT REPRESENTATIVES (SCHEDULE FLEXIBILITY REQUIRED)
Provide professional technical assistance to customers.

CUSTOMER SERVICE REPRESENTATIVES (SCHEDULE FLEXIBILITY REQUIRED)
Provide accurate information and assistance to customers.

CALL CENTER MOD (Manager on Duty) (SCHEDULE FLEXIBILITY REQUIRED)
Previous experience as Call Center MOD - Real Time monitoring is a must.

We offer:
- Paid training
- Competitive compensation in US dollars
- Bonus opportunity
- Transportation
- Employee-focused work environment
- Professional development
- Advancement opportunity
- Asociación Solidarista

Fujitsu Consulting, a $45 billion global technology leader, is expanding its services in Costa Rica. We seek talented, enthusiastic, candidates for several key positions.

All positions require:
- Full bilingual skills with 100% English fluency.
- Proficient in Internet and Microsoft Office tools.
- Customer service and call center experience a plus.
- Ability to work in a fast-paced, high growth environment.

Fujitsu - The possibili[...]

Villas Sol
Hotel & Beach Resort

IS LOOKING FOR STAFF TO FILL SEVERAL POSITIONS

Would you like to work at the Beach in Guanacaste?
This is a once in a lifetime opportunity

Requirements
- Over 19 years old
- Full English
- Excellent personal grooming
- Great communication skills

We offer
- Excellent compensation
- Opportunity to grow
- Training
- Great working environment

IF YOU ARE INTERESTED
Please APPLY IN PERSON from 8 a.m. to 5 p.m., Monday 28 and Tuesday 29, at the office of Villas Sol, 400 m north the Centro Colón.

U.S. PEACE CORPS IS LOOKING FOR A

SAFETY AND SECURITY COORDINATOR

Responsible for supporting the Country Director and Senior Staff to insure the safety and security of Peace Corps Volunteers and Trainees in Costa Rica in compliance with the guidelines.

Qualifications
- B.S., B.A. or equivalent college or professional training
- Fully bilingual in Spanish/English.
- Strong computer skills, especially using Windows, Excel, Word, and database software.
- Experience in conducting training sessions.
- Strong written and verbal communication, office organization and information processing skills.
- Ability to analyze situations of potential risk and develop contingency plans.
- Highly developed interpersonal skills, willingness to travel country wide when required, team player, professional attitude and individual commitment to excellence.
- Valid driver's license.

Also Desirable: Knowledge or experience in emergency response and/or safety and security issues. Bicultural experience.

Interested applicants may obtain a full position description and instructions for applying by sending an e-mail inquiry to:

PCTrabajo@cr.peacecorps.gov
Deadline for application: 4:30 p.m. - Monday, February 27, 2006

International Sales Professionals

Requirements
Experience working overseas. Have a strong knowledge of the US Financial Markets. Money Motivated. Willingness to work odd hours

Ideal Personal Profile
- Candidate must possess outstanding verbal and communication skills
- Candidate will be a strong team player who is self-motivated and money motivated.
- Strong interest in fixed income markets and portfolio management techniques
- Be driven by a willingness to grow our business throughout Europe.
- Exhibits strong conceptual aptitude.
- Professional approach, with the ability to deal with all levels within the organization.

Only serious experienced candidates need apply. If that's you, call Gabriela 250-0040.

Qualified candidates, PLEASE EMAIL TO: CAREERSCR@US.FUJITSU.COM PLEASE INDICATE POSITION YOU A IN THE SUBJECT.
One page resume.

doris peters
Our client, a global company in the automotive leather industry with facilities throughout the Americas, Europe, Asia and South Africa is currently looking for :

GLOBAL LOGISTICS MANAGER

- The successful candidate will have a minimum of a Bachelor's Degree and 5 years experience in overall logistics management, working for a global organization in a truly global capacity.
- The individual should have experience in dealing with Purchasing, Product Planning, Customer Service and Sales Departments in a Demand-Based, Just-in-Time Manufacturing environment, and should be experienced in freight negotiations with freight forwarders, airlines and steamship companies.
- The individual must be a hands-on, detail-oriented, self-starter with the ability to communicate verbally and in writing with all levels of management.
- English proficiency and excellent computer skills a must.

For immediate consideration please send resume to:

DORIS PETERS & ASOCIADOS, S.A.
Oficentro Centauro, 3er piso, oficina 7, Guadalupe
E-mail: doris.rodriguez@dorispeters.com

American Company is seeking for:
ACCOUNTANT

- 3 years experience minimum
- Full experience in the whole Accounting Cycle
- Knowledge in Quickbooks Software or similar Accounting Systems

If you fulfill 100% of these require[...]

Bilingual Customer Service Representatives
QUALFON

Requirements:
- 100% English conversational skills: comprehensive, oral, written and reading areas.
- Computer literate.
- Customer service experience preferable.
- Availability to work 6 days a week, weekends and holidays.
- Updated ID documents.

We offer:
- Positive working atmosphere
- Job stability
- Growth opportunities within the company
- Social guarantees
- Cafetería / Transportation.

If you are interested please call us at: 295-1133, Ext. 16 or send your resume to: reclutamiento@qualfoncr.com

Language Institute needs:
English Teachers

For Greater Metropolitan Area
We Offer:
- Competitive salaries
- Training opportunities
- Pleasant working conditions
We require:
- Full command of English
- Costa Rican or resident

Telephone: 281-1818

Check out **www.ticotrabajos.com** and the Sunday classified job ads in *La Nación* for possible jobs. You will see some firms are seeking English speakers for sales, call centers and sportsbooks.

Starting a Business

Of 115 countries, Costa Rica came in first in Latin America and ninth in the world with respect to nations offering greatest commercial freedom and protection for private business, according to Freedom and Development, a Chilean research institute.

As a foreigner, you can invest in Costa Rica and even start your own business with only a few restrictions.

If you plan to go into business here, it is very important to be aware of the local consumer market in order to succeed. Most of the country's purchasing power is located in the Central Valley. A total of 75 percent of the country's population resides in the central provinces of San José, Alajuela, Heredia and Cartago. About 60 percent of the population is under than 30 years old. Intelligent business people will try to meet the needs of this group.

You may also think about targeting tourists and upper-class Costa Ricans. A wealth of opportunities is available in tourist-related businesses. Upper-class *ticos* have a lot of disposable income and the greatest purchasing power. They do not mind spending a little more on good quality products. Just look at their expensive designer clothing, their expensive imported automobiles and many palatial homes.

The majority of the country's middle-class consumer values are now more akin to their U.S. counterparts. You can see this starting to take hold with a number of shopping malls being built around the Central Valley and the popularity of stores such as Radio Shack and megawarehouses like PriceSmart and Hipermás. Middle and upper lower class Costa Ricans seem to want all of the goodies so much that sales of cellular telephones have temporarily exceeded the availability of cellular phone lines.

One group to target is the lucrative foreign-resident market. There are approximately 50,000 full-time foreigners living in Costa Rica. All you have to do is look for a product to fill their needs. Most yearn for hard -to-find-products from home and would rather buy them in Costa Rica than go to the United States to shop.

Costa Rica is ripe for innovative foreigners willing to take a risk and start businesses that have not previously existed. Start up costs for

What brings younger people to Costa Rica?
By Jacqueline Passey

Costa Rica is not just for retirees! Younger people move to Costa Rica as well, and many of us can be found via the Young Expats of Costa Rica club (**http://www.youngexpatsofcostarica.org/**). Younger folk move to Costa Rica for many of the same reasons older people do – the climate, the natural beauty, the lower cost of living, the culture and lifestyle, or to start a new life somewhere new. However, they usually move here without as many assets as older people possess and thus are not ready to retire or invest a substantial amount in a local business. So most come here as students, volunteers, teachers, employees of multinational companies, freelancers or self-employed businesspeople, with their parents, or as spouses of *Ticos*.

Costa Rica is a very popular destination for studying Spanish, tropical biology, and Latin American culture, politics, and economics. There are a variety of university exchange programs and short term Spanish language programs as well as the University for Peace (a graduate school with programs taught in English). Many of these schools are also linked with environmental or economic development service learning volunteer programs.

Many younger people who visit Costa Rica as tourists, students, or volunteers like the country so much that they want to stay. One of the easiest legal ways to do this is to teach English or teach in an international school. Although it doesn't pay very well (frequently not enough to pay off debts or save for a house or retirement in their home countries) many people find it to be enough to live on here, and teachers with more qualifications (degrees, teaching certificates, experience) make a lot more and have more job opportunities than less qualified teachers. Anecdotally from our club members, it seems that most teachers at bilingual grade and high schools arrange for their jobs in advance whereas most English teachers for adults come here first and then find employment.

Globalization and the internet are bringing more and more multinational businesses to Costa Rica. Many companies have set up customer support offices in Costa Rica employing a mix of English-speaking Ticos and foreign consultants. In particular, the internet gambling industry (online sports books, casinos, and poker rooms) employs many foreigners as consultants, managers, specialists, etc.

The internet is also making it possible for many freelancers and self-employed people to move here as well. Writers, artists, graphic designers, webmasters, computer programmers, internet marketers, professional gamblers and other knowledge workers can now work and sell their services online from anywhere in the world and many of them choose to do it here. They find that self-employment or freelancing via the internet is a great way to make money at North American rates while only spending it at Costa Rican rates, often allowing them to save money or support themselves with only part time work. Of those who have enough money to start a more traditional business in Costa Rica many choose to go into tourism or agriculture.

Family and romance also brings younger people to Costa Rica. Many children, teens, and young adults tag along when their parents move to Costa Rica for retirement or business. Also, with so many travelers to and from Costa Rica there are many opportunities for international romance. Many of these mixed couples choose to settle in Costa Rica after marriage so that they can raise their children in a culture that places a high priority on family.

As you can see, there are many opportunities to live in Costa Rica even if you're not ready to retire yet!

Jacqueline Passey is a 27-year-old professional blogger and gambler living part time in San Jose, Costa Rica and the founder of the **Young Expats of Costa Rica** social club. She can be found on the web at **http://www.JacquelinePassey.com/**

small businesses are less than in the United States or Canada. Many of the same types of businesses that have been successful in the North America will work if researched correctly. There is definitely a need for these types of businesses. You just have to do your homework and explore the market. Be aware that not everything that works in the United States will work here. Also you may have to adapt your idea due to the vagaries of the local market and different purchasing power. Don't get any grandiose ideas since the country only has about 4 million people. You cannot expect to market products on a large scale as in North America.

Costa Rica's local artisans make scores of beautiful handcrafted products such as furniture, pottery and cloth. With so many choices, a smart person can find something to sell back home.

These are some potential business opportunities worth exploring: building and selling of small homes for middle-class Costa Ricans or foreigners, an import-export business, desktop publishing, computer services and support, U.S. franchises, importing new foods, specialty bookstores, restaurants and bars, an auto body and paint shop, consulting or specialty shops catering to North Americans and upper-class Costa Ricans.

Costa Ricans love anything novel from North America. Many stores sell both new and used trendy U.S.-style clothing. Costa Rican teenagers dress like their counterparts in the United States and even watch MTV. U.S. fast-food restaurants such as Taco Bell, Burger King, Pizza Hut and McDonald's are extremely popular. Real estate speculation can be lucrative if you have the know-how and capital.

Common Business Sense in Costa Rica

It is important to keep in mind that running a business in Costa Rica is not like managing a business in the United States because of unusual labor laws, the Costa Rican work ethic and the Costa Rican way of doing business.

In order for a foreigner to own a business, a Costa Rican corporation or *sociedad anónima* must be formed (see the section entitled "Taxes" in the last chapter).

If you do choose to establish your own business, keep in mind that you can be limited to managerial or supervisory duties and will have to hire Costa Ricans to do the bulk of everyday work. We also recommend

Success Stories in Costa Rica
By Chris Howard

A Coffee Baron

Cafe Britt was founded by American Steve Aronson. Today the company has gone international with their many products available all over the world. They grow, roast and sell some of the best "Mountain Grown" coffeee in the world. They even make a cafe liqueur. Their coffee farm tour is one of the most entertaining half-days you will spend in Costa Rica. It takes place on a beautiful farm nestled in the verdant hills of Heredia. You will learn about the history of coffee, see how it is grown and purchase many interesting products in their gift shop at the conclusion of the tour.

A Service for Expats

About 10 years ago, Jim Fendell realized the need for a fast reliable mail service as an alternative to the regular Costa Rican mail system. Thus **Aerocasillas** was born. Today they offer similar services in Panama and several other countries in the region. Please see Chapter 6 for more details about the history of this comapny and the services they offer.

A Company thich Protects Nature

In 1978 Michael Kaye founded the first white water tour company,

Costa Rica Expeditions, when tourism was in its infancy. The company was started to help the sophisticated traveller explore Costa Rica - its flora and fauna, its people and culture, its wildlife and beautiful places. Their goal is to create unique travel experiences.

An American-Style School

Country Day School was started by American Woodson Brown around twenty years ago. The present campus is located in the hills of Escazú overlooking San José. You canbot beat the school's beautiful setting. The actual campus evolved from a few buildings into a huge complex which rivals any U.S. private school. The owner is a visionary who recognized the need for a first-rate U.S. type English-speaking school to cater to both the local and foreign population.

A Newspaper for Foreigners

Many years ago the late American journalist Richard Dyer founded **The Tico Times** newspaper. It has become Central America's leading independent weekly covering news, business, tourism, culture and developments in Costa Rica and Central America. The classified ad section is very complete, and there is now an on-line version of the paper. Fifteen thousand copies are printed weekly with some being shipped overseas.

Satellite TV

Reiny and Kathy have lived in Costa Rica for 14 years. After having visited 43 countries on a two-year trip around the world, they decided Costa Rica was the place to live. For years the ran a small restaurant in Jacó Beach. However, 4 years ago they started **Sun Sat TV** Services, a satellite dish company, which offers American TV programs to people living in Costa Rica. Now viewers can watch their favorite TV shows including NBC, CBS, ABC, FOX, ESPN, HBO and a whole lot more.

A Hotel Fit for a King

An enterprising American runs perhaps San José's most successful hotel. He spent a couple of years and a lot of money refurbishing the old building. His hard work paid off. Today his downtown hotel boasts one of the highest occupancy rate in the country. It is a haven for fishermen, tourists, expatriates and many local characters. The bar on the first floor is the most successful operation in Central America. At night the place really heats up. The ladies of the night are the big draw and mostly responsible for the hotel's success.

A Place to Learn Languages

American David Kaufman is the founder of **Conversa**, Costa Rica's oldest and most successful language school. David earned a Masters Degree in linguistics and served in the Peace Corps in the Dominican Republic. At his school's two campuses, Spanish is taught to foreigners and English to Costa Ricans. Please see more about Conversa in Chapter 3.

The Local Tax Man

Gordon F. is a former U.S. tax attorney from California. Currently he helps foreigners with business matters, tax returns and other related matters. His services are very high in demand due to his expertise. In addition, he and his wife run **Posada Quijote** in the Bello Horizonte hills section of Escazú. The view is just spectacular. This small hotel is in a beautiful Spanish colonial home, which has been totally renovated and exquisitely decorated.

that you do a thorough feasibility study. Spend at least a few months thoroughly analyzing its potential. Do not assume that what works in the United States will work in Costa Rica.

Check out restrictions and the tax situation. And, most important, choose a business in which you have prior experience. It's much more difficult to familiarize yourself with a new type of business in a foreign country.

Remember, a trustworthy partner or manager can mean the difference between success and failure. Make sure you choose a partner with local experience. Do not trust anyone until you know him or her and have seen them perform in the workplace.

You will be doomed to failure if you intend to be an absentee owner. We know of someone who founded an English-language book distribution business that initially did very well.

However, the person moved back to the United States and put a couple of employees in charge, and everything eventually fell apart: sales began to lag, money went uncollected, checks began to bounce, expenses were unaccounted for and incompetent salesmen were hired. Their potentially successful business just could not be run from abroad.

You have to stay on top of your business affairs. At times it is hard to find reliable labor, and the bureaucracy can be stifling. If you have a business with employees, be aware of your duties and responsibilities as an employer. To avoid problems, know what benefits you need to pay in addition to salary to avoid problems. Remember that the more employees you have, the more headaches.

In case things get rough, be sure you have enough money in reserve, in case of an emergency. You should have an ample reserve of capital to fall back on during the initial stage of your business.

Newcomers should not count on obtaining financing in Costa Rica for a new business. If you become a resident, you may be able to obtain some type of financing. Neophytes should learn not only the language but also the rules of the game.

One option is to buy an existing business from someone else.

In principal, this can save you lots of time and trouble, which means you can bypass most of the cumbersome start-up procedures and usually save a lot of time and energy.

While this is a definite advantage over starting a business from scratch, there is a downside. You can be taken advantage of by an unscrupulous seller trying to dump his problems on you. These problems may include unpaid back wages to employees, loss of a license or lease, or other legal problems that may not be apparent at first.

The best thing to do is to have a good lawyer check into the legal status of the proposed purchase and investigate potential problem areas. He can then tell you whether he thinks the business is feasible and if there is any unwanted baggage. You will also need to have a good accountant do a complete inspection of the books and records, and perhaps even conduct a complete audit to make sure all taxes, wages and Social Security payments are up-to-date.

Any one of these items could cause untold headaches if not detected before you buy the business. Taking care of these matters is the best investment you could possibly make.

Talk to people, especially the "old-timers," who have been successful in business, and learn from them. Profit from their mistakes, experiences and wisdom. Do not rush into anything that seems too good to be true. Trust your intuition and gut feeling at times. However, the best strategy and rule of thumb is, "Test before you invest."

Newcomers find themselves seduced by the country's beauty and friendly people and are often lured into business and investment opportunities that seem too good to be true, and often are.

When it comes to making money in Costa Rica, it has been said: "The best way to leave Costa Rica with a million dollars is to bring two." In the case of some foreigners, this statement is true. During

Long-time Costa Rican resident, Mark, runs a successful
travel bookstore in downtown San José.

the time we have lived in Costa Rica, we have seen many foreigners succeed and fail in business ventures. Only about three in 10 foreigners succeed in business in Costa Rica. There are few success stories and a lot of failures, in areas as diverse as bars, restaurants, car-painting shops, language schools, real estate, tourism, and bed-and- breakfasts to name a few. People have impossible dreams about what business will be like in Costa Rica. It is a gigantic mistake to assume that success comes easily in here. Initially, starting any business usually takes more time and more money. Also, many unforeseen problems are surely, to arise.

If you decide to purchase an existing business, make sure it is not over-priced. Try to find out the owner's real motives for selling it. Make sure you are not buying a "pink elephant." Ask to see the books and talk to clients if you can. To ferret out a good deal, look for someone who is desperate to sell his business. Check the newspapers and ask everyone you know if they know of someone selling a business. Finally, make sure there are no lawsuits, debts, unpaid creditors or liens against the business.

There are some benefits to investing in certain businesses in Costa Rica. As we mention in Chapter 6, you can obtain Costa Rican residency by investing in tourism or a reforestation project. Also, part of your profits can be sheltered in your corporation.

Business tip: dealing with people is always the best way to deal with people here, develop a business relationship here. All business in Costa Rica is based on friendships and mutually respectful behavior. In fact, when dealing with all government officials it is a good idea to treat them to a snack, a drink and chat. You will be amazed at the difference.

After reading the above information, if you still have questions or are confused, we advise you to consult a knowledgeable Costa Rican attorney for further information. If you plan to invest or do business in a Spanish-speaking country, you should definitely purchase *Wiley's English-Spanish Dictionary*, *Barron's Talking Business in Spanish*, or *Passport Books Just Enough Business Spanish*. All of these guides contain hundreds of useful business terms and phrases.

Beware of the So-called Experts and Overnight Gurus

Costa Rica's popularity and good business climate has brought with it a whole slew of enterprising foreigners. Unfortunately, some of these people lack qualifications in their fields of endeavor.

In Costa Rica, the word "expert" is sometimes used very loosely in the expatriate community, on numerous websites, English publications and on business cards.

Do not get me wrong; there are some highly qualified English speakers here. Nevertheless, one should be extremely cautious when dealing with foreigners who consider themselves experts in Costa Rica. Just because a person was a professional in his home country or has gone through the process of moving here does NOT qualify him to be an expert here. Some foreigners consider themselves experts just because they have lived here for a short time. Remember, anyone can build a website and say anything about themselves.

We know people who move here, and go into business and miraculously become experts overnight. Costa Rica is indeed a magical country!

Many naive newcomers have been taken advantage of by other foreigners who call themselves "experts," but are really incompetent imposters. So, be careful!

We suggest that if you happen to come into contact with any foreigner who calls himself an "expert," no matter how convincing he may be, do all of the following:

1. Ask for references from other foreign residents who have used the expert's services. Don't rely on the testimonials that appear on a person's website. They may be slanted. If your expert will not give you any references, you will know immediately you are being duped or sold shoddy second-rate services. Also, try to contact the person's last employer before they moved to Costa Rica. Again, if they will not give you the contact information, you can bet the person is hiding something. If a person who is not of retirement age claims to have been highly successful in his or her former country, they may be trying to cover up something about their background.

2. Check with the Association of Residents of Costa Rica to see if they are familiar with the person's services.

3. Enter the person's name in a search engine such as Google to see what comes up. There are even companies you can pay to do a background check if you suspect something.

4. Ask how long the person has lived in Costa Rica. If they have been here for less than 10 years, be careful. It takes years to understand this country. It takes more than a year or two to know the ropes. Many of these neophyte relocation gurus and entrepreneurs mean well but just don't have enough experience under their belt.

5. Find out what the person's educational background was when they lived in their home country and if they have any formal training in the Latin American culture, studies or foreign investments. If someone was a plumber, janitor, welder or doctor, for example, prior to moving here, this does not qualify them to give professional advice in Costa Rica.

6. Beware of colorful, well-designed web sites built by the so-called experts to express their admiration for the country to attract naive foreigners.

7. Be cautious of publications that appear to be helpful on the surface but incessantly hype the services of the person(s) or organization behind them.

8. Over the years we have run into so-called foreign experts who live comfortably in upscale in "Ivory Towers" and gated communities in *gringo* enclaves such as Escazú. The majority of their friends are other English speakers, so they have never have really immersed themselves in the local culture. They are virtually still foreigners living among other foreigners. These people live in virtual isolation from the real Costa Rica. Few of them have any contact with Costa Ricans except for their maids and servants and rich Costa Rican friends from the country-club set. They rarely venture out of their safe environment to gather the necessary experience to confront real life situations here. Most live as if they were still in their home country, and give advice about a country and culture they really don't know.

9. Most important find out if the person is truly fluent in Spanish. There is no way a person can have expertise unless he or she can communicate with the locals and understand the nuances of the local humor, culture and language. **Beware**: there are many foreigners who say they speak fluent Spanish with a vocabulary of only a couple of hundred words. I have run into many of them in my 25 years here.

How I Came to Open a Language School
By David Hansen

The year was 1978 and I had just come back from an incredible junior year abroad in Madrid, Spain. I was looking for someone who spoke Spanish and wore high-heeled shoes. One particular morning in late September my roommate and I drove to American Univesity and when we arrived for our 11am classes we looked at our watches and saw it was only 10am. We had no idea why we were there one hour early. We just couldn't figure it out. You never arrive an hour early for anyting much less a morning class at the university. Since we had some time to kill we decided to go to the *cafeteria* for a cup of coffee. As soon as we walked in my roommate spotted, Zaida, his Costa Rican housemate from the previous year. We got talking and as they say, the rest is history. (She did wear high-heeled shoes back then.)

After coming to Costa Rica a couple of times on extended vacations in the early 80's I really wanted to move down here. Zaida, my wife by then, didn't really want to go back home, been there done that. Also, living in DC was very exciting back then for a couple of 23 year olds. However, the president of Costa Rica at that time threw out the IMF and the World Bank and the international credits dried up very quickly and the local economy went into a tail spin. Zaida's dad, who was one of the most exceptional people I have ever met, was a pilot and had a small, two plane air-taxi service that went down along with everything else in the economy. So at that point she was ready to come down and help out her parents for a couple of years in 1983 Well, we are still here.

I love it. We run the IPED language school in Heredia where we teach English to the Costa Ricans and Spanish to people from all over the world. It is the best of both worlds. I live in a great town where I know many of the locals and spend my days with really interesting people from Asia, Africa, Europe, North America and the Carribean. They live with lovely Costa Rican families, study Spanish, go to some amazing nearby attractions like the Coffee Tour, the Waterfall Gardens, InBio Park, ZooAve or the Poas or Irazu Vaolcanoes during the week. In the afternoons their senses are delighted by the great dance classes and delicious cooking classes. At night they have dinner with thier family and talk and practice Spanish with them and then study a little. If they still feel like it we go out to the great places around Heredia to meet the locals and go dancing or listen to music. On the weekends they go to all of the wonderful, beaches, volcanoes and rain forests around the country.

It is *Pura Vida* (Pure Life) in Costa Rica.

Would You Buy Real Estate from a Tourist?

Again and again I hear stories about people making mistakes when purchasing property in Costa Rica. I really feel it is my responsibility to share the following with my readers.

As you probably know, by now Costa Rica has become very popular over the last couple of years. From all indications, interest in the country is not going to wane for some time to come. Recently, one economist told me the local boom could last for up to 10 years more.

Therefore, it is not surprising that investors are pouring into the country to purchase all kinds of homes and land. Unfortunately, in many cases they are not using their common sense.

Scores of would-be entrepreneurs have set up shop here. Most have eye-catching web sites proclaiming their expertise and real estate offices. The problem is that some of these people are little more that modern day carpetbaggers with no credibility trying to cash in on the real estate gold rush. They are here to get what they can take and ride happily off into the sunset.

A large number of these JCLs or "Johnny Come Latelys," are not even legal Costa Rican residents but tourists. Would you buy real estate in your hometown from a tourist? Of course not! Only a fool would do it. A realtor friend of ours had the immigration department run a check to see what the status was of foreigners selling real estate in a certain beach area of Costa Rica. The results were frightening. Many of the realtors in the area turned out to be tourists living here illegally. Furthermore, the Costa Rican government prohibits anyone from working here who is not a resident.

So, when looking for real estate in Costa Rica you should only deal with time-tested real estate agencies and people who are legal residents of the country. Do your homework, ask a lot of questions and don't "leave your brain on the plane."

One of the Best Ways to Make Money in Costa Rica

Until 2003, a large number of North Americans living in Costa Rica earned "high returns" on their money by investing in private finance companies. In general, these returns in dollars ranged between 13 to 42 percent, depending on the duration and amount of the investment.

Some foreigners had been in these programs for many years with no complaints and never a single problem. The most successful of these unregulated companies operated for 20 years without missing a single payment to its creditors. Other companies sprung up, but they were basically riding the success and credibility of the company with the longest track record.

Unfortunately, this bonanza came to an abrupt halt with a major change in the financial climate of the country. The private banking industry could not compete with these private finance companies. So, with the help of their ally the Costa Rican government, they managed to surreptitiously undermine all unregulated investment in the country.

Let me tell you a little about these finance companies and why they were able to pay you more on your dollar accounts than the average bank. This will come as a surprise to most of you, but, in fact, the market interest rate for dollar accounts is much, much higher in other countries than what you may be getting from the banks in your country.

The loans these private finance companies made were considerably less risk than the loans made by many banks in countries where the banks are heavily regulated by the government. Government-regulated banks rely more on government insurance for their loan security rather than on sound business judgment when making loans. I am sure you have read about the numerous bank frauds in the United States. Who ends up paying the bill? You do, with high income taxes and the low interest rates paid on your savings. Somebody always has to pay.

The high rates the companies were able to receive on making very secure loans in dollars have more to do with supply and demand for dollars in Central American countries. These countries have very high rates of devaluation in their local currencies, and most businesses here need U.S. dollars to buy products from the United States, so there is a big business demand for U.S. dollars. Dollars are scarce here, so the private lending companies can get big returns making loans in U.S. dollars. Why? Simple supply and demand; big demand for U.S. dollars, small supply of U.S. dollars.

Why is it that local banks do not have much money? Would you put your money in a bank paying 7 percent, per year if your local currency lost 20 percent, per year in value against the dollar. Probably not. The result is that the banks do not have enough money to supply the credit demand of a healthy economy, such as Costa Rica's. This means the banks here do not have the money to finance various types of short-term business loans. In addition, there is a lot of paper work and endless delays when trying to borrow money from a bank in Costa Rica. So where did some people and companies go to borrow money? They went to private lending companies that had the money and were easy to work with. A couple private lending companies had been operating for decades in Costa Rica and were very, very profitable. Costa Rica is very unique, since it has an extremely stable government, no military, very low wages and one of the highest standards of living in Central and South America, but very little money in the banks with which to work.

Private lending companies were not government-regulated institutions. They loaned money to large Central American corporations and businesses. In Costa Rica, they paid excellent monthly returns on making short-term loans to businesses that put up more than enough collateral to pay the loan amount several times over.

Most businesses here own their buildings and land free of debt. So the private lending companies never needed to loan more than 20 to 30 percent of the liquidation value of the collateral the borrowers put up, which is typically land and buildings. Consequently, the private lending companies were able to profitably pay their private clients very good rates of return on their deposits.

For example, a large coffee farm had to put up a $10 million coffee farm as collateral to borrow $200,000 at six percent per month for two or three months. Typically, at the end of their harvest season, they would run out of money. So, once a year, they would borrow to pay their employees and expenses until the coffee beans were sold . Needless to say, they always paid the loan off. Even if something went wrong and they did not get paid for their coffee beans, they would sell off part of the farm to pay off the loan rather than lose the entire farm.

Large department stores here would also borrow dollars from these private lending companies at six percent per month to buy electrical home appliances and other products from the United States.

When a large company negotiates a big loan from a bank here it usually takes two to three months after the loan approval for the bank to pay out the money. In the meantime, the big company would borrow from a private lending company at six percent per month until the bank paid out the money on their approved loan.

Factories here must give their retail store customers terms of 60 to 90 days to pay for products shipped, because the stores need 60 to 90 days to sell the products and collect the money from their customers. Most factories were happy to pay six percent per month to get their money sooner so they could manufacture more products. They simply add this cost to the products they ship to the retail stores. Who pays? The consumer does.

However, the days of these unregulated high-yield investments all came to an end due to the Costa Rican government's change of policy and a few unscrupulous individuals.

Fortunately, now there are even more secure investments available in Costa Rica. The hot investment area is real estate on Costa Rica's spectacular Pacific coast. According to a recent article in the country's, financial daily, *La República*, property in the Central Pacific region has risen 250 percent in value over the last six years. In addition, with the paving of two new sections of the Costal Highway, the driving time between the country's capital, San José and the nearest beach resorts will be reduced by half. The first stage of the new highway will link Ciudad Colón in the Central Valley to the town of Orotina near the Central Pacific Coast. The other section of new highway will link the towns of Quepos and Dominical to the south. Furthermore, there are plans for a major marina in Quepos, a water park with artificial waves between Quepos and Dominical and a new international airport in the town of Palmares. All of this will combine to make real estate values soar even more.

As an example of this boom, the **Marriott Corporation** built its crown jewel of Central America, "**Los Sueños Resort**" and pre-sold 50 condominium units of 2,000 square feet each for $250,000. The next year they sold another 50 at $350,000 and this year's upper-end units sold between $600,000 to $950,000. And there is a waiting list!

South of Jacó Beach at the **Del Pacífico development**, the owners say investments will yield at least 25 to 30 percent, in yearly appreciation. Obviously this area is the place to find secure investments with a high rate of return. Liquidity is not a problem since land is in demand.

Let us look at why this real estate boom is happening. The simple fact that almost every bit of coastline worldwide is becoming over crowded, overpriced and more scarce contributes to a high level of interest Costa Rica's beach areas. The U.S. National Association of Realtors says Americans are buying second homes in record numbers, thus driving up the cost of vacation homes everywhere in the country. A recent newspaper article stated one in every seven people in the Untied States now lives in areas bordering the coast. This trend is driving the great baby-boomer migration. As a result, land in prime sunbelt areas of the United States has, become prohibitively expensive and hard to find. This is not the case in Costa Rica.

Savvy people with a thirst for adventure, fun and profitable investments are now taking a closer look at Costa Rica. Actually, an investment in real estate in Costa Rica's Central Pacific is much better than an investment in California real estate 30 years ago.

Along Costa Rica's Central Pacific Coast, you will find wide white- and dark-sand beaches, rocky outcrops and clear water set against a tropical backdrop of primary rain forest. The beaches are reminiscent of those in California and Hawaii, but you can buy here for one-tenth the cost. For a very reasonable price, you may purchase a couple of acres of land with an ocean view. You can have a spectacular home perched on a hill, complete with custom tiles and finished in mahogany, teak and precious woods you never knew existed. The geography looks like California or Hawaii years ago.

Getting in before the crowd has always been the secret to making a lot of money with real estate investments. People who took a chance and invested in real estate in beach property in California, Hawaii and some parts of Florida were ahead of their time. They saw opportunity where others saw nothing. They took well-planned risks and were paid handsomely for their investments and created better lives for themselves and their families. What really gets people excited about Costa Rica is that it offers some of the most undervalued prime beach real estate in the world. As the rest of the world finds out about Costa Rica, prices will only go up.

Local real estate expert Rudy Mathews shares his perspective on the future of Costa Rican Real estate: " One has only to look here in Costa Rica, and see what has happened in the last five years. Now the baby boomers are coming and the market should continue to improve."

By the way, you can legally use your pre-tax IRA to purchase real estate in Costa Rica. The company listed below can help you with this. Depending on your particular situation, it also has the contacts to help you obtain partial financing in Costa Rica.

Now you can be part of bigger things by participating in joint venture groups. This is not a solicitation for investments, but for those who wish to join forces with other like-minded people seeking larger tracts of land.

To find out about these opportunities contact: **Retirement and Vacation Properties** at E-mail: **robert@ costaricaretirementvacationproperties.com** or call toll-free from the United States or Canada, 1-877-815-1535. You may view some of these incredible properties at, **www.costaricaretirementvacationproperties. com**.

The Yanquis Are Coming!
By Coley Hudgins

08/18 In the run-up to last month's passage of the Central American Free-Trade Agreement (CAFTA), the anti-globalization doomsayers were out in force with bold predictions about the "final blow" the deal would mean to the economies of Central American countries. Pro free-traders argued just as vehemently that CAFTA was a major step in building the foundations for a democratic community of nations in our hemisphere.

What's largely been overlooked from both sides, however, may have little to do with CAFTA at all. Instead, one of the biggest economic forces reshaping Central America in the coming years may be a demographic shift occurring right here in the Unites States, spurred by the massive retirement of the baby boomer generation.

According to a recent *New York Times* story, starting in January of next year baby boomers — defined as those born between 1946 and 1964 — will start turning 60 at a rate of more than 4 million a year. The leading edge of the baby boomers is now beginning to turn 59 now — the age when Americans can start collecting certain retirement benefits without penalty. The number of Americans 55 and older is expected to skyrocket from 67 million this year to 97 million by 2020.

In many ways, boomers are a different breed altogether than the generations that preceded them. They are healthier, live longer and are more active, mobile and adventurous than prior generations. Trends suggest many will continue working beyond the traditional retirement age of 65, launching second careers, becoming entrepreneurs or focusing more on charitable and volunteer projects.

But in one fundamental way, baby boomers may not be so different from their parents and grandparents. Consider what I call the "Del Boca Vista" migration.

Del Boca Vista is the mythical Florida retirement community Jerry Seinfeld's parents, Helen and Morty called home. Like Helen and Morty, the enduring cliché about older Americans is that, once retired, they pack up their belongings, bid adieu to colder climes, and move to Florida to enjoy rounds of golf and blue-plate specials in Del Boca Vista-like retirement communities.

Like many stereotypes, this one contains a kernel of truth. According to a 2001 American Demographics study based on 2000 census data, Florida registered the highest share of seniors of any state in the country in the19 90s, but other sun-belt centers such as Phoenix, Sacramento, Raleigh-Durham and Las Vegas were also highly attractive "elderly magnets."

William Serow, professor of economics at Florida State University in Tallahassee has been studying migration patterns of the elderly for years, and believes that since the end of World War II younger, more well-off "roving retirees" in their 60s still instinctively seek out warmer climates in "fun" places such as Arizona, North and South Carolina, and Florida.

According to Serow, the other key goal of this more affluent group of retirees is reducing living expenses by moving to sun-belt communities with cheap housing and lower taxes. And therein lies the big conundrum for today's boomer retirees: just as millions of retiring baby boomers are getting ready to migrate to warmer sun-belt states, these attractive retiree destinations are experiencing skyrocketing real estate prices and property tax assessments that may put these locations out of reach for all but the most wealthy boomers.

So, what's the significance of all of this for Central America? Tomorrow's Del Boca Vista migration won't necessarily be to the sun-belt states in the United States. It's just as likely that a large subset of boomer retirees — call them "boomer *gringos*" — will bypass southern sun-belt states altogether for more affordable Central American alternatives such as Nicaragua, Costa Rica, Mexico, Panama, Belize and Honduras. Most Central American countries are still only a two or three hour flight back to the United States and have adequate infrastructures allowing retirees to stay in touch with friends and loved ones back home—good cell phone coverage, broadband Internet connections, even satellite television.

Having recently returned from vacation in Nicaragua and Costa Rica, the anecdotal evidence suggests it's already happening. Costa Rica is experiencing a housing boom that rivals anything here in the United States. and is driven in part by new boomer retirees. Two-or three-bedroom homes that were selling for $270,000 in December of last year are now selling for $350,000 and $400,000 in some parts of the country. While coastal areas may be experiencing their own version of a housing bubble, there are still very reasonable prices for many boomer retirees.

The story to the north in Nicaragua—the second poorest country in the Western Hemisphere, and a country that still conjures up images of right-wing dictators and left-wing revolutionaries—is even more interesting. Small coastal communities such as San Juan del Sur and cities such as Granada are swarming with retired expat boomers who are buying land and building dream retirement beach-front homes for a fraction of what it would cost in the United States.

Costa Rica: Imposes no tax on income earned outside the country, and allows retirees to buy into the national health care system offering care at public hospitals by participating doctors, many of whom are U.S.-educated.

Mexico: Retirees can qualify for "rentista visas" that are renewable annually for five years, and require only that retirees show a minimum income of $1,000 per month. Retirees can join the national HMO for about $200 per person per year.

Nicaragua: The government recently passed Law 306 that includes provisions exempting qualified investors from paying income or property taxes for up to 10 years, and providing generous exemptions from import duties for "pensioners" and investors that qualify.

Panama: Positioning itself as the world's greatest retirement destination. Retirees pay no real estate or property taxes for 20 years.

Honduras: Doctors visits are typically, about $15, and pharmaceutical drugs cost 30 to 50 percent less than in the United States. Honduras offers a one-time exemption from all import duties for retirees, and allows retirees to bring in one car or boat duty-free every five years

RE/MAX and **Century 21** have opened offices in the country, and affordable housing developments on some of the most coveted and pristine coastlines in the Americas are now dotting Nicaragua's Pacific coast. New developments such as Rancho Santana, Iguana Beach and Guacalito have launched sophisticated marketing campaigns to attract boomer retirees, and publications geared toward retirees such as International Living are hosting retirement summits and conferences to sell Nicaragua as a retirement destination.

In Mexico, previously unknown towns such as Ajiic, on the shores of Lake Chapala have attracted tens of thousands of boomer gringos as well. NPR reported last year that here retirees can have a furnished home, cheap dining and the part-time services of a maid and gardener for less than $2000 a month. According to NPR, more than one million Americans now call Mexico home.

While exact figures are difficult to obtain, the U.S. State Department estimates that about 380,000 Social Security checks are delivered to beneficiaries outside the United States each month. Almost 4 million Americans not including embassy officials and the military personnel—are now living overseas, although how many of those expats are retirees is unknown.

What is known is that governments in Central America are luring gringos with new laws that include impressive incentive packages for retirees. And despite the inherent volatility and political risks that remain in many of these countries, boomer gringos (and Central American governments themselves) are betting that the economic benefits of a retiree migration to Central America will be a two-way street. Retirees get a lower cost of living, warm weather and cheap housing and create a virtuous cycle; in return,—more retirees equals more local jobs, resulting in more economic stability and less political instability, resulting in more retirees.

But will this new economic model pay dividends? Serow figures that each retiree household in the United States is responsible for a little more than one job being attracted to the community. While he cautions that such jobs tend to fall into the low-paying, service category here in the United States, for developing economies that are starting at close to zero, service jobs are the best way to get a first foot on the economic ladder.

And it appears that many are already climbing the ladder. The national newspaper in Nicaragua La Prensa, published a story earlier this year about how the boom in tourism and the influx of retirees has benefited the economy. The story described workers who no longer had to look for seasonal work six months out of the year as "illegals" in more developed Costa Rica because they were now employed as full-time laborers close to home, building housing developments for a new wave of foreign investors.

And while the debate rages here at home about the impact of illegal immigration on our own economy and government services, there's no question that "low-paying" service jobs here in the Unites States filled largely by illegal immigrants benefits local communities back home. (Remittances from foreign countries suchas the United States to families in Mexico, are one of the largest sources of foreign currency in the country.)

Wouldn't it be more beneficial to Central American countries if in the future these service jobs were created locally by an influx of American retirees? It's possible that the emigration of wealthy boomer gringos to Central America in the years ahead could slow illegal immigration here as workers become part of a home-grown service economy driven by retirees.

Are American retirees a panacea for Central American economies? Not by a long shot. There are still fundamental economic and political issues that will need to be addressed by the governments themselves that neither an influx of retirees or CAFTA will completely mitigate. Stamping out corruption, increasing government transparency and bolstering education and the rule of law all need to be top priorities at home before the hemisphere can develop strong and sustained economic growth.

But the facts seem to indicate that barring some unexpected political upheaval or economic calamity, the Yanquis are going to keep on coming in larger and larger numbers. Central American governments have already placed their bets. They see our retirees not as a drag on the economy as we here in the Unites States often do, but as a potentially huge source of much-needed capital, investment and job creation. The smart money should be betting that they're right.

Coley Hudgins is a Washington D.C.-based government affairs consultant. He has lived and worked in West Africa, and has traveled extensively throughout Central America and Asia.

If you are a producer or reporter who is interested in receiving more information about this article or the author, please email your request to interview@ techcentralstation.com.

Common business Lingo

A pagos	Payments, buy on time
Abogado, licenciado	Lawyer
Acciones	Stocks
Accionista	Stockholder, shareholder
Activo	Asset
Agrimensor	Surveyor
Al contado	For cash
Anualidad	Annuity
Año fiscal	Fiscal year
Anticipo, prima, depósito	Down payment
Arrendamiento	Lease
Autenticar	Notarize
Avalúo	Appraisal
Certificado de depósito	.CD.
Cheque	Check
Cláusula	Clause
Comprador	Buyer
Contrato	Contract
Corredor	Stockbroker, real estate broker
Costo	Cost
Cuenta	Bank account
Cuenta corriente	Checking account
Déficit	In the red, deficit
Depreciación	Depreciation
Deuda	Debt
Divisas	Foreign exchange (hard currency)
El Justo Valor del Mercado	Fair market value
Embargar, enganchar	Attach assets
En efectivo	Pay in cash
Escritura	Deed
Estado de cuenta	Bank statement, statement
Facilidades de pago	Payment plan
Fideicomiso	Trust
Fidecomisario	Trustee
Financiamiento	Financing

Gastos	Costs, expenses
Giro	Money order
Hipoteca	Mortgage
Impuestos	Taxes
Intereses	Interest
Impuestos prediales	Property taxes
Inversiones	Investments
Justo valor del mercado	Fair market value
Lote	Lot
Montar, poner un negocio	Start a business
Negocios	Business
Notario	Notary
Pagaré	Promissory note
Parcela	Parcel of land
Plazo	Term, period of time
Precio	Price
Préstamo	Loan
Principal	Principal
Propiedad	Property
Registro	Record of ownership
Renta	Income
Rentabilidad	Profitability
Saldo	Balance of an account
Seguros	Insurance
Socio	Partner
Sociedad	Corporation
Subcontratar	To subcontract, farm out
Superávit	In the black, surplus of capital
Tasa de interés	Interest
Testaferro	Person who lends a name to a business
Terreno	Land
Traspaso	Transfer
Timbres fiscales	Tax stamps
Valor..	Value
Vendedor	Seller

RED TAPE

Dealing With Bureaucracy

Just as in the rest of Latin America, Costa Rica is plagued by a more inefficient bureaucratic system than the United States. This situation is exaggerated by the Latin American temperament, the seemingly lackadaisical attitude of most bureaucrats, and the slower pace of life. The concept of time is much different from that in the North America. When someone says they'll do something *"ahorita"* (which literally means "right now"), it will take from a few minutes to a week, or maybe forever. It is not unusual to wait in lines for hours in banks and government offices and experience unnecessary delays.

This situation is very frustrating for foreigners who are used to fast, efficient service. It can be especially irritating if you don't speak Spanish well. Since very few people working in offices speak English, and most North Americans speak little else, it is advisable to study basic Spanish. However, if language is an insurmountable obstacle at first, use a competent bilingual lawyer or ask the Association of Residents of Costa Rica (ARCR) to help you deal with Costa Rica's bureaucracy or "red tape jungle," as it is known. Above all, learn to be patient and remember that you can get the best results if you do not push or pressure people. Try having a good sense of humor and using a smile. You will be surprised at the results.

You shouldn't despair if Costa Rica's "bureaucrazy" gets you down. For a small fee, you can get a person (*gavilán*) to wait in line for you while you run errands or make better use of your time.

A few words of caution: there are some individuals, (*choriceros* in popular jargon), who pass themselves off as lawyers or who befriend you and offer to help you with red tape, claiming they can shortcut the bureaucratic system because of their contacts. As a general rule, avoid such individuals or you will lose valuable time, run the risk of acquiring forged documents, most certainly lose money, and experience indescribable grief.

Since bribery and pay offs are common in most Latin American countries and government employees are underpaid, some people advise paying them extra money to speed up paperwork or circumvent normal channels. This bribery is illegal and not recommended for foreigners, who can be deported for breaking the law. However, in some instances it may be necessary to pay extra money to get things done. Use your own discretion in such matters. A tip here and there for a small favor can accelerate bureaucratic delays. We have a friend who was in the process of getting all of the required paper work to marry a Costa Rican. He was in a hurry and did not have time to waste. He went to the National Registry to get his future wife's birth certificate and was told he would have to wait a week. So, he passed out a little extra money and had it the next morning.

United States Embassy Services

Everyone planning to live, retire or do business in Costa Rica should know that the U.S. Embassy (in the San José suburb of Pavas) can help with Social Security and veterans benefits, notarizing documents, obtaining new U. S. passports, reporting lost or stolen passports, obtaining a marriage license, registering births of your children, registering to vote, complying with Selective Service registration requirements, private mail service, reporting deaths of U.S. citizens abroad, and getting a U.S. visa for your spouse (if you choose to marry a Costa Rican). They also assist in obtaining absentee ballots for U.S. elections and getting U.S. income tax forms and information. However, if you get into any legal trouble in Costa Rica, do not expect help from the U.S. Embassy.

Social Security - In the past there were two ways of receiving your Social Security check if you lived abroad. First, you could have it sent

A Trip Through Costa Rica's Bureaucratic Maze
by Loyd Newton

It's always an adventure in paradise when you have to deal with the bureaucracy in any of it's many forms. Fortunately, it's not something I have to do very often. I've been in Costa Rica for a little over two years now and things are starting to expire and renewal times coming near. My drivers license was due to expire at the end of this week so Monday I went down to the offices in San Jose on Calle 7 to renew it.

I parked my car in one of the public parking lots and they conveniently had a sign posted with the requirements for new and renewed licenses. Besides money, I needed to get a doctors exam for my renewal. I didn't even make it halfway from the parking lot to the drivers license office when I was waved into a doctors office. The exam took about 5 minutes which consisted of answering a few questions and reading the eye-chart above the green line. The doctor also mentioned he had a private practice near my home town and handed me a few business cards to take with me.

At the office I discovered a line that went out the door. Luckily for me, the line that stretched out the door was for new licenses. The one for renewals was doubled around the inside of the offices. I noticed a lot of people armed with newspapers for the long wait. My helper (interpreter, guide, etc.) went to get us a newspaper while I started my hour long wait in line. The people in line near me were very friendly and immediately started up conversations. The man ahead of me spoke English pretty well and was a fountain of information about the process. So instead of reading a newspaper, I spent my hour in line conversing with the ticos and the time went by quickly.

Once I got to the head of the line, I showed my doctors certificate and old license to the man at the first stop. He was very concerned about the fact that my residency card was expiring in June but said I could renew my license. Just use my passport he said and don't show them the residency card. Well, to be honest, I figured out what he was saying at the time but didn't understand what he meant until I hit the last stop.

I took my papers, got back in another line for the bank. There I paid 10,000 *colones* for my 5 year license. I told them the sign said it was only 4000 colones but they explained that was for the 2 year license. Sounded good to me, so I took my receipt and got into another line for the cameras. After about 15 minutes, I made it to the head of the line and went up to have my photo taken for the new license. When I got there, I handed over my papers and receipts and the man asked for my cedula.....mistake, because I gave it to him. He took one look at it and said he would not take my photo. He took me back to the start, "do not pass go, do not collect license". There the man asked me why I should him my *cédula* and I explained because he asked me for it. He told me, that the man would not take my photo or give me the license because my *cédula* was expiring in two months. This didn't make any sense to me, since I don't even need a residency to get a license here.... perhaps it.

When people get a little excited here, they talk very fast so I was having a hard time understanding what they were telling me. My helper had gotten separated between the last stop and the return to go. Fortunately, a tica came over and translated for me. There are some wonderfully helpful people here! While they were explaining the man's reason for not taking my photo, another photographer stepped up and said he would do it. So they took me around to another camera station, and within 5 minutes I had my new drivers license.

A low level bureaucrat that likes to have little power or just doesn't like gringos decided that a cédula that expires in 2 months was a big problem. Fortunately for me, kinder hearted people stepped in and took care of things. "I have always depended upon the kindness of strangers." So I left the place with mixed feelings....distaste for the petty bureaucrat and the hitch after over an hour of waiting and happiness that the good *ticos* and *ticas* won out and I could finish business that day.

I felt so good at not having anything else to do this week, that I went out and played 18 holes of golf today at Valle del Sol. First time I've played golf in a year so I gave up keeping score on the first hole. A great day to be outside and enjoy the weather though so I thoroughly enjoyed it though my golf game needs a lot of work. Guess I'll just have to get out once a week and practice on it.

Pura vida,
Loyd Newton

directly to your P.O. box in Costa Rica through the U.S. Embassy. The only problem with this method was that the checks did not arrive until almost the third week of the month. The other way was to have your check directly deposited into your U.S. account. Now, things are much simpler. After August 2003, your Social Security payments may be deposited electronically to your account in a Costa Rican bank by the third of each month. **Banco Nacional**, **Banco de Costa Rica**, **Banco Interfín** and **Citibank** offer direct deposit of Social Security checks. All you have to do is complete a form and make sure it gets sent to the Federal Benefits Unit of the US Embassy. Call the embassy at 220-3050 if you have any questions. Your bank will charge $6 for this convenient monthly service.

Passports - Effective in 2002, U.S. citizens residing or traveling abroad who need a U.S. passport are issued the latest, state-of-the-art passport incorporating a digitalized photo image and other innovative security features. U.S. embassies and consulates will send the applications to domestic U.S. passport facilities. This increases processing time at some embassies and consulates, but it ensures that U.S. citizens receive secure documents in a timely manner. Therefore, U.S. citizens are encouraged to apply early for renewal of expiring passports.

U.S. embassies and consulates issue passports in emergency situations. Such passports have limited validity and cannot be extended. Bearers are required to exchange their limited validity passports for full-validity digitalized photo passports upon completion of their emergency travel, either through passport facilities in the United States or U.S. embassies abroad.

First-time Passport Applicants - To apply for a U.S. passport, a native-born, U.S. citizen must present a certified copy of his or her birth certificate, two passport photos measuring two inches by two inches (color or black and white with a light background), photo ID and the applicable fee. You will need to present the certificate of naturalization together with the photos, a photo ID, and the fees.

Passport Renewal - You will need your current passport as evidence of citizenship and two passport photos measuring two inches by two inches (color or black and white with a light background). To be eligible, you must have been issued a U.S. passport in your name within the past 12 years. There are different fees for adults and for those under 16.

Lost or Stolen Passport - You will need to report the loss of your passport to the police and obtain a copy of the police report. In addition to the two passport photos, you will need to present proof of identity and proof of U.S. citizenship. The proof of identity could be any photo ID such as U.S. driver's license. Proof of citizenship could be a certified, sealed copy of your U.S. birth certificate and/or an old cancelled U.S. passport.

Report of a Birth Abroad - Children being registered as U.S. citizens must be brought to the embassy or consulate by the U.S. - citizen parent along with the following documents:

1. Child's Costa Rican birth certificate may be obtained from the Civil Registry, or *Registro Civil*.
2. Evidence of parent's U.S. citizenship. This may be in the form of an original U.S. birth certificates, U.S. passports, Certificates of Citizenship or Naturalization Certificates. Military IDs are not proof of U.S. citizenship.
3. Parents' marriage certificate.
4. Evidence of dissolutions of previous marriages. If either parent has been previously married, submit original divorce decrees or death certificates.
5. If only one parent is a U.S. citizen, there are additional requirements. Please check with the embassy.

The Social Security Administration's guide tells you how to receive your Social Security checks while living abroad. See www.ssa.gov/international/your_ss.html

The U.S. State Department provides links and information for U.S. citizens living abroad. See www.travel.state.gov/travel/fed_benefits.html

Purchasing an Automobile

High taxes make the purchase of a new vehicle in Costa Rica more expensive than in many other countries. In the past, people chose to buy new cars in the United States, where prices are much lower. Now, prices of new cars in Costa Rica are more affordable than before, and more people are choosing to purchase locally rather than deal with the paperwork of importing a vehicle and high taxes. Currently a law is (probably) being passed to prevent the importation of vehicles older than five to seven years.

One more reason to buy locally is to ensure your vehicle will be under warranty in case anything goes wrong. Most local dealers offer two to three-year warranties on new cars.

Due to the high price of new cars, used cars are plentiful in Costa Rica. Most of these second-hand cars are priced higher than they would be in the United States or Canada, so Costa Ricans tend to keep them longer and take better care of them. This makes resale value high.

The majority of automobiles in Costa Rica are made in Japan, so most replacement parts are for Japanese automobiles. Spare parts for U.S. cars must be imported, are expensive and sometimes hard to come by. Therefore, you should think twice about bringing an U.S. car to Costa Rica. If you do decide to bring a car from the United States or Canada, it is best to bring a Toyota, Nissan, Honda or other Japanese import for the reasons just mentioned.

If you plan to drive mostly in the country's larger cities, smaller, new or used cars will help reduce fuel consumption and are easier to maneuver on crowded streets. Prices for new small cars are extremely affordable and range between $9,000 and $14,000, while new mid-sized vehicles cost between $13,000 and $20,000. Those of you who plan to drive outside of the city and off-road should consider a sport utility vehicle (SUV), pick-up or jeep. Many of the country's roads are unpaved and filled with potholes, and a solidly built vehicle is absolutely necessary especially during the rainy season. Prices of new SUVs run $20,000 to $75,000, depending on the model and size of the vehicle. Used cars are priced substantially lower.

Here are sample prices of some used cars found in the *The Tico Times'* classified ads.

All prices are in U.S.dollars	
95 Chevy Lumina	$4,900
91 Isuzu Amigo	$2,900
02 Chrysler Caravan	$21,500
00 Mercedes S-500	$30,000
04 Mercedes E240	$48,000
91 Isuzu Rodeo	$5,500
4X4s	
99 4-Runner	$14,000
03 Pathfinder	$27,000
91 Land Cruiser	$13,900
00 GMC Jimmy	$18,500
01 Jeep Wrangler	$22,500
80 Land Cruiser Diesel	$13,900
87 4-Runner	$8,900
03 Dodge Dakota	$25,00
95 Mitsubishi Montero	$11,000

Since new cars are so expensive in Costa Rica, buyers have the option to lease or finance. The dealer can usually arrange financing. If not, many Costa Rican banks offer financing for cars. Interest rates are generally in dollars instead of *colones* and vary according to market rates.

If you decide to bring a car to Costa Rica, there are two ways to do it: by sea or by land. If you ship your car to Costa Rica by boat, contact a shipping company near to where you have your car in the United States or one of the companies mentioned in this chapter. This method of transportation is relatively safe since your car can be insured against all possible types of damage.

If you have all of your paperwork in order, your vehicle should not take more than a month at most to reach Costa Rica, depending on your port of departure. If you send your car from Miami, it takes only one week to reach Puerto Limón on the east coast of Costa Rica and costs about $800 plus taxes. From the west coast or New York, you can expect to pay more than $1,300 plus taxes and some other fees to process your paperwork.

To import a new or used vehicle, you will have to make sure your shipping company sends the following documents: a driver's license for all potential drivers, the original clear title or pink slip (*título de propiedad*), original registration, copy of passport, original bill of lading (*conocimiento de embarque*) if the vehicle has been shipped, and the name of the shipping company. Also make sure your car has Canadian or U.S. plates, or the whole process may be delayed.

Note: ALL VEHICLES, since June 7, 2001, now require an Emissions Control Certificate certified by the Department of Motor Vehicles from your country of origin or by the vehicle's manufacturer if new, dated no later than 30 days prior to the shipping date. The certificate must be translated into Spanish by an official translator and authenticated by the Consulate of Costa Rica nearest to the Emissions Inspection Station that issued your certificate. This applies even to used vehicles, and any car without it will not be able to be registered in the country. This change, in fact, caused many vehicles to be stuck in Customs for a time, as the law passed in December 1999, but was never enforced until the middle of 2001.

To be safe, call the nearest consulate to check what documents are actually required. In many cases, they will ask for a notary public to authenticate the gas emission test and then have the State Department certify that the notary is registered.

If your name does not appear on the original title of the vehicle, you must provide a document from an attorney certifying that the owners allow you to drive their car. Said document must be notarized and approved by the nearest Costa Rican Consulate in your country of origin. Cars that are being financed in the United States and are not fully paid off fall into this category.

If you do not provide all of documents above, including the gas emission certificate, you cannot import the vehicle to Costa Rica.

Make sure that the VIN (vehicle identification number) and all details of the car are correctly typed on all documents. Any errors will void the documents and prevent you from importing the car.

Calculating Taxes on a Vehicle

Long-term imported vehicle duties are calculated by multiplying the Vehicle's Appraised Value (VCAV) at the **Ministerio de Hacienda** by following the percentages according to model year. The VCAV is the sum of the vehicle's market value, freight and freight insurance. Freight is the cost of transporting your vehicle to Costa Rica.

Duties are determined by the age of your vehicle. If your vehicle is a 2006, 2005 or 2004, you pay 52.28 percent of the retail value plus shipping. If your car is a 2003 or 2002, you pay 63 percent of its value plus shipping. For any vehicle older than 2001, a tax of 79.02 percent plus shipping will be charged.

If there is no bill of lading or if you drove your vehicle, freight will equal seven percent of the market value of your vehicle, which could equal thousands of dollars more than actual freight charges. Freight insurance is the amount of money you pay to insure your vehicle. If you did not pay insurance, Customs will multiply the sum of the market value and freight first by 110 percent, then by 1.5 percent.

As you can see, taxes are now higher for used cars. In order to establish the value of a used vehicle, you present the commercial invoice with the purchase value of the vehicle. If you do not have an invoice, you have to declare the value.

Do not think you can fool the Customs inspectors by putting an arbitrary value on your vehicle. They have a list showing the manufacturer's suggested retail price of every vehicle manufactured when it was new, including extra equipment.

In the past, Customs agents would refer to the market value based on the "Black Book," a manual published in the U.S. with a listing of new and used car wholesale auction prices for United States car dealers and loan officers. We were just informed that Customs agents no longer depend on this book. However, if you want to get an idea of the value of your vehicle, contact **National Auto Research** at 2620 Barrett Road, PO Box 758, Gainsville, GA, 30503, Tel: (800) 554-1026, Fax: (770) 532-4792, www.blackbookguides.com. Another good resource is www.crautos.com.

Duties may be checked at the **Ministerio de Hacienda**. (www. hacienda.go.co/autovalor). However, to obtain a better estimate of the duties to be paid, send a fax or E-mail to the Association of Residents or Charles Zeller at E-mail: shiptocostarica@racsa.co.cr, toll- free 1-866-280-9036, Fax: 258-7123. Be sure to include the make of the car, model, serial number (VIN), automatic or stick shift, extras such as air conditioning, power windows or other non-standard equipment. Be sure to specify the country from where you plan to ship the car.

After reading the above, if you still decide to import a used vehicle, we recommend using a Customs broker to run around, obtain all the necessary documents and massive paperwork, and help with the taxes. After going through this process, a friend of ours told us, "A good customs agent can save you money." A bilingual attorney is also important and will save you days of running around from one office to another. He can take you step-by-step through the whole ordeal."

However, if you do decide to do this yourself, you will need to follow the procedure below. First, you have to go to either the east or west coast to pick up your vehicle at the port of entry. This can be a real pain in the neck, requiring a lot of paperwork and patience. It is best to have a Customs agent do all of this for you or go with you in person to pick up the vehicle. A good Customs agent will have all the paper work done and your car out of the *aduana* when you arrive at the port of entry.

When we picked up our 1990 Montero in Limón, we arranged everything beforehand. We took an early-morning bus from San José and arrived in Limón with our agent three hours later. Our car was waiting for us in a private parking lot. We just signed one paper, got in the car and returned to San José. The process would not have gone as smoothly had we not planned carefully and coordinated everything with our Customs agent.

Next, you need to register your car, which usually takes a few working days. First, get your paperwork from customs. Then have your vehicle checked at the nearest **Rieteve SyC Inspection Center** (www.rtv. co.cr). At present there are 11 inspection centers scattered around the country. Call 800-788-0000 to make an appointment and to locate the nearest station to your home. Cars also have to be taken to these stations yearly for general inspections to assure they are roadworthy. Then take the papers they give you to the *Registro Público* or Public Registry vehicle section (*Registro de Vehículos*) in the suburb of Zapote. Call 224-0628 if you need information. The cost of your registration depends on the value of your car. Finally, take the documents from the registry to the Ministry of Public Works (*Ministerio de Obras Públicas y Transportes*) at Plaza Víquez, south of downtown San José. Your temporary paper license plates will be issued a few months later at the *Registro* in Zapote.

You will have to wait for your permanent metal plates. In the meantime, you will be issued a temporary paper plate that you have to affix to the windshield of your vehicle. There is an expiration date on the temporary paper plate. If your metal plates still aren't ready you may renew the paper plate. If you let it expire, there is a fine.

When your permanent metal plates are ready, you'll need to take the following documents to the National Registry (*Registro Nacional*) in Zapote: the temporary paper plate (*placa provisional*), title of ownership (*título de propiedad*), yellow registration card (*tarjeta de circulación*) and resident ID card (*cédula*) or passport.

You can find information about vehicles and property by viewing the National Registry's website at www.registronacional.com.

Every year you have to pay your *marchamo* or sticker indicating you have paid your obligatory liability insurance. It has to be renewed between November 1 and December 31. You also have to pay $10 for an echo *marchamo*. This is a certificate that shows your vehicles emissions are within the legal limit. It is like a smog certificate in the United States. A car without a *marchamo* decal on the windshield after the first of January may be impounded.

You may pay the *marchamo* in person at many banks and even on-line with The **Banco Nacional de Costa Rica**.

Driving an Automobile to Costa Rica

If you have sufficient time and enjoy adventure, drive your automobile to Costa Rica. The journey from the United States to Costa Rica (depending on where you cross the Mexican border), takes about three weeks if driving at a moderate speed. The shortest land distance from the United States to Costa Rica is 2,250 miles through Brownsville, Texas.

Take your time to stop and see some of the sights. We recommend driving only during the day since most roads are poorly lit, if at all. At night, large animals—cows, donkeys and horses— can stray onto the road and cause serious accidents.

Your car must be in good mechanical condition before your trip. Carry spare tires and necessary parts. Take a can of gas and try to keep your gas tank as full as possible, because service stations are few and far between.

Have your required visas, passports and other necessary papers in order to avoid problems at border crossings. Remember, passports are required for all U.S. citizens driving through Central America. You also need complete car insurance, a valid driver's license and vehicle registration.

You can purchase insurance from AAA in the United States., or contacting **Sanborn's Insurance** in the United States Tel: 800-222-0158, Fax: (956)-686-0732 or www.samborns.com. They offer both Mexican and Central American policies.

Instant Auto Insurance offers a 24-hour 800 number and fax service so you can have your policy ready. In the United States and Canada, call 1-800-345-47-01 or Fax: (619)-690-6533.

The web site **www.drivemeloco.com** has information about border crossings and people's experiences making the trip.

You can also buy insurance at the border before entering Mexico. Having an accident in Mexico is a felony, not a misdemeanor. So do not forget to be fully insured.

If you are missing a driver's license, a vehicle registration or insurance, border guards can make your life miserable. Also, remember some border crossings close at night, so plan to arrive at all borders between 8 a.m. and 5 p.m., just to be safe.

When you finally arrive at the Costa Rica-Nicaragua border, expect to be delayed clearing Customs. If you bring many personal possessions to live in Costa Rica permanently, some or all of them may be inventoried and taken to the Custom's warehouse in San José. You may pick them up at a later date after you have paid the necessary taxes. However, if you come in as a tourist you usually will not be hassled by Customs at the border.

As a foreigner in Costa Rica (a non-resident) you are allowed to drive a car with a tourist permit for three months without paying taxes. Your initial three-month permit to drive your car in Costa Rica may be obtained at the Customs office at the port of entry. The documents required are the title, registration of the car and proof of having paid the local minimum insurance (it is important to understand that this insurance does not cover any vehicle damage. You cannot obtain additional insurance locally while driving with this permit.) Mandatory liability insurance from the *Instituto Nacional de Seguros* is $10 for three months.

Another three-month extension is usually granted, but after six months the vehicle must leave the country or the duties must be paid. To get the one-time three-month extension, you will have to leave the country prior to the three-month limit for 48 hours. Upon re-entry, your passport will be restamped, allowing you to drive the vehicle for three more months. Warning: Do not drive the car if the permit has expired—it will be considered an abandoned vehicle and can be confiscated.

When your second three-month extension expires, you have to either leave the country or store the vehicle in a Customs storage facility until you pay the Customs duties and purchase your Costa Rican license plates.

Any person who brings a car to Costa Rica and pays all of the taxes, may keep the car in the country indefinitely once all paperwork is completed. One advantage to bringing your vehicle yourself by land is that you don't have to pay taxes immediately, as you do when you have your vehicle shipped by sea. Warning: If you have permanent residency status and bring a car by sea, you will have to pay all of the taxes almost immediately before you can get your car out of Customs.

If you keep your vehicle in Costa Rica, you will have to apply the corresponding tax formula listed above.

For additional information about driving from the United States to Costa Rica, you can purchase a useful guidebook, *Driving the Pan-American Highway to Mexico and Central America*, by Raymond and Audrey Pritchard, with help from Christopher Howard. You can now order this one-of-a-kind book through **Amazon.com**, **www.drivetocentralamerica.com** or **www.costaricabooks.com**.

Be aware of the following rules if you want to take an automobile out of the country. As one resident who did it pointed out, "Once you have your car in Costa Rica and you want to drive a car across the border from Costa Rica and back, you need to get a *permiso para salida del país* from the *Registro Nacional* in Costa Rica (there is an office in Liberia, I am told), which will require:

1. A certified, written permission from the owner of the vehicle (you will need to see your lawyer for this)
2. A copy of the title

3. The paid and current *marchamo* certificate
4. The current **Riteve** inspection document. They will do a search of the *Registro* files to ensure that there are no unsatisfied liens on the vehicle and the corporation that owns it, if there is one, it is on the up and up regarding liabilities and unpaid taxes.
5. If the vehicle is owned by a corporation, you will also have to supply a certified copy of the corporate constitution.
6. And a recent *personería jurídica*, for the corporation showing that the person seeking authorization to drive the car out is the officer of the corporation and is legally authorized to make such a decision.

Personerías are normally good for only three months, so make sure it is new enough that it will still be valid when you try to come back. The *permiso* document you will receive from the *Registro* is good for one journey of no more than 30 days. The car must leave the country within 30 days of the time the *permiso* is issued for it to be valid. At the border, you will have to have some or all of the above documents examined by Customs on both sides of the border, going each direction.

Be prepared with at least two certified copies of each; you may be asked for them, and if you are and don't have them, you're sunk — there's no copy center at Peñas Blancas. You will be asked for copies of the *personería jurídica* as well as the *marchamo* by the Costa Rican *aduana* going out. Getting across takes about three hours.

Here is what one resident said about his experience at the border. "Going into Panama last year at Paso Canoas, all the officials on both sides were happy with my paperwork, yet I still had to wait in line behind a long line of truck drivers in the Customs office on the Panama side. And when my turn finally came, I had to wait while the Panamanian *aduana* typed out a six-page form, in four copies, hunting and pecking through it on her 40-year old Smith Corona that doesn't advance the ribbon anymore. The document she produced was a *Derecho de Circulación* of which every cop I encountered in Panama wanted to see my copy, as did the *aduanas* on both sides coming back into Costa Rica. I was asked to surrender it to the *aduanas* on the Costa Rican side coming back."

Bringing Your Boat or Plane to Costa Rica

Those of you who own yachts and sailboats will be pleased to know that there are two marinas where you may dock your boats in Costa

Rica, and plans call for a couple more to be built in the future. The country's marinas are the **Flamingo Marina** in the northwest and the **Los Sueños Resort** in the Central Pacific. The latter has 200 slips and is the only marina where you can keep your boat in the country legally for more than 6 months. Slips rent for about $13 to $15 per month, per foot. The marina offers membership in the **Los Sueños Yacht Club**, a full range of sport-fishing charters, day cruises as well as other water sports activities.

In the past the longest you could keep a boat in the country without having to pay taxes on it was six months. Duties can be as high as 57 percent of the boat's real value for brand name boats. This is still the case at the Flamingo Marina in Guanacaste. Most people get around this by taking the boat out every six months and then returning. With all types of vehicles you cannot keep doing this. However, the Los Sueños Marina is the only licensed marina in the country and has a special agreement whereby a boat may be kept in the country under the cover of the marina for up to two years without taking it out of Costa Rica. We understand that you can then renew your permit for another two years. This exemption is only for non-commercial boats and does not apply to those who use their boats for sport fishing. For additional information we urge you to call the Los Sueños Marina at 643-3941/2.

We understand that a new law will be passed soon that will enable owners of small aircraft to keep their planes in the country like boat owners do at present. The government figures anyone who owns a boat or plane will possibly make sizeable investments in the country.

Shipping Your Household Goods to Costa Rica

As previously stated, the old *pensionado* program allowed retirees to import household items including an automobile virtually duty-free. Since most of these privileges were rescinded more than a decade ago, you may well have second thoughts about importing anything.

Keep in mind that most imported used items are also taxed. Taxes range from 40 to 90 percent or more of the value of the article plus your shipping costs. Taxes can be raised at the whim of the Costa Rican government. You can, however, save money by purchasing many imported items at the duty-free zone or *depósito libre* in the southern city of Golfito.

Shopping in Golfito
By Martha Bennett

Appliances are very expensive in Costa Rica because of the import tax. Large appliances are more affordable in Golfito, comparable to U.S. costs. After pricing an American washer in San José at $600, I went to Golfito and bought a washer and dryer for $600. Golfito is near Panamá and used to thrive with the United Fruit Company. When this outfit left, the Costa Rican government allowed the residents to set up a free-zone to maintain their economy.

The procedure for buying appliances is not too difficult but there are steps to follow.

1. There are many excursions which take you there and set up your hotel arrangements. The cost is about $15 round trip plus hotel. You can drive there in about 8 hours. You may also fly, but this uses up your savings. You must stay overnight. This is one of the economy boosting rules. It is hot, but the area away from the freeport complex is quite beautiful.

2. At the shopping complex, get your boleto. This form is your permit to buy about $500 on each passport every six months. If you want to buy more, residents of Golfito will sell you their *boleto* for around $25.

3. Procede in an orderly fashion while shopping. The stores are numbered but they all look alike and you won't want to hit the same one twice. Each shop will give you a paper with their price and store number. Discounts do happen but only for cash. It's worth trying to bargain. Prices vary for the same brand of appliance so throw away papers with higher prices immediately. This saves confusion. If you can decide what you want on the first day, pay for it at once. You can pay the next morning, but lines are long and there are other things to do.

4. Go to your hotel and relax.

5. Return to the stores early, 7:30 a.m., to retrieve your stuff and pay if you haven't. They inspect everything. For big items, there are boys with trolleys to gather everything in a waiting area. Then these boys will take your purchases through the gate where you need to show your passport, *boleto* and sales slip one more time. Do not lose any papers. Your life will be a nightmare. Tips are expected for trolleying your stuff around.

6. Outside, are trucking firms that will deliver your purchases the next day to a warehouse or directly to your house for less than $20. Everything is guaranteed and inspected again. Smaller items can go with you on the bus. If this sounds exhausting, it is. But remember, you can sell these appliances for more than you paid five years down the line. I don't want to do it again, but I'm glad I did it once.

The duty-free zone was designed in 1990 for Costa Ricans and residents. Most popular goods sold there are domestic electrical appliances ranging from refrigerators, freezers and stoves to sound systems and television sets. Many brand names are available in a variety of models. Although you may find many of them cheaper in the United States, they are good buys compared to San José's prices—up to 50 percent on some large appliances. When you add shipping costs from the United States, taxes and possible headaches, it is more practical to buy your appliances at the free port or look for sales at **Importadora Monge**, **Casa Blanca** or **El Gallo** appliance stores.

Some restrictions and paper-work may irk you, but this will be easier for you than importing things from the United States. You can purchase only $500 worth of items every six months. The first period of the year ends on June 30 and the second begins on July 1. You are limited to $500.00 during the first six months. You cannot carry it over to the second period of the year and buy $1,000 worth of merchandise. You can, however, combine your card with a family member and buy $1,000 per period. You must furnish proof that the person you do this with is really a family member.

You may pick up your Purchase Authorization Card or "TAC" (*Tarjeta de Autorización de Compra*), as it more commonly called, at the booth in the duty-free zone in Golfito. You must be over 18 years old and have a Costa Rican ID or passport to do so.

To find out information about shopping, contact **ACODELCO** in San José at Tel: 232-1198, Fax: 232-2692 and in Golfito at 775-0717, Fax: 775-1940. Golfito is open everyday except Monday. Stores open promptly at 8 a.m.

Here is what one resident says about his experience in Golfito: "There are two routes to Golfito: one is through San Isidro de El General through Dominical and Palmar Norte. The other way is along the costal highway through Jacó. I recommend the first route because the second has a stretch of dirt and stone road (40 kilometers) between Dominical and Quepos that is in bad shape.

Travel time is about three hours from San José to San Isidro and three and a half hours from San Isidro to Golfito. If you go through Quepos, add another hour because of the bad road.

"The duty-free shopping is at the far end of the main street going through Golfito,, The main street circles around the duty-free-area, one way. You can't miss it.

"You need to arrive in Golfito one day before you shop because you need to buy a purchase form. You must take your passport if you are a foreigner or your *cédula* if you are Costa Rican. Each person has the right to buy $500 each semester (January through June and July through December). The trip will take approximately seven hours from San José.

"There are many hotels available in Golfito but I recommend one that is very close to the duty-free shops. It is good quality and costs only $50 per room with everything included. Each person can buy a maximum of $500 for one or more products. If you go with a relative (wife, husband, sibling, etc.) you can pay for two cards and buy up to $1,000 worth of articles. There is a wide variety of products, but appliances are really worth buying. They cost about half of what they do in San José. You can also buy articles by using another person's name. There is always someone hanging around the facility waiting to sell you extra tickets.

"One word of caution: Make sure you know the retail prices of what you want to buy, and try not to buy on impulse. Stores are numbered 1 through 50, and if you want something special just ask any of the store clerks; they are happy to direct you to the right place.

"If you need delivery service to San José for stoves, washers, dryers or refrigerators, contract someone directly from a cargo company. Just ask the people where you bought the merchandise. They will be happy to recommend someone. You can find these people close to the stores and if you cannot find them, ask anyone and they can help you out. The cost of delivery is two to three percent of the price of the products. It isn't worth it to take any products back with you that were not bought under your name. There are many police stops and check points along the way and they ask for documentation of the purchase, so make sure to keep all paperwork and receipts. You will need your papers at check out time from the free zone."

For small items, many foreign residents go to the town of David, Panama, near the Panamanian border. Prices on everything including household goods are nearly as low as in the United States. However, because of taxes you will have to pay on large electronic goods and appliances, it is better to shop at the duty-free *depósito* across the border in Golfito. Nevertheless, foreign residents living in Costa Rica on a 90- day tourist visa can go to David for 72 hours to renew their papers for another three months. (Be aware that many frown upon this status of "perpetual tourist," and the government is looking at changing this possibility.)

After taking high shipping costs into consideration, you may be reluctant to ship any household items from the United States. This is a matter of personal choice. Most foreign residents and even Costa Ricans prefer U.S. products because of their higher quality. However, many retirees live comfortably and happily without luxuries and expensive appliances.

You can rent a furnished apartment. If you choose, you can furnish an apartment, excluding stove and refrigerator, for a few hundred dollars. Wooden furniture is inexpensive in Costa Rica. You can also purchase good used furniture and appliances from expatriates and others moving out of the country. Check the local English-language newspapers. What you need to import depends on your personal preference and budget.

Make an effort to get rid of "clutter" and bulky items, and do not ship what can be easily or cheaply replaced in Costa Rica. Try to leave large appliances and furniture at home. You pay more for these items in Costa Rica, but in the long run they turn out to be less expensive when you take shipping costs and taxes into consideration. Talk to other foreign residents and retirees to see what they think is absolutely necessary to bring to Costa Rica. One person who moved here recently told us, "Only bring what you absolutely cannot live without."

If you still want to import your U.S. belongings and household goods and want to save time and money, purchase and ship them from Los Angeles, Houston, New Orleans or, preferably, Miami. The latter is the U.S. port nearest to Costa Rica, and shipping costs are lower. Look in the Yellow Pages of the Miami phone book for a shipping company or call the company listed at the end of this section.

Ways to Bring Your Belongings to Costa Rica

Here are some money-saving tips for bringing small items to Costa Rica. First, when entering the country as a tourist by plane, you can bring in a lot of personal effects and small appliances. A tourist is sometimes waved through Customs without ever having to open any luggage. Costa Rica has become a popular tourist destination.

1. The government understands that tourists come here to enjoy the country and have many different hobbies and reasons for visiting. They know that tourists need such items as surfboards, bicycles, kayaks, musical instruments, photographic equipment, small stereos and more. The government permits items for personal use not intended for resale. The number of these personal items has to be reasonable

in relation to the length of the stay or needed for the exercise of one's profession during his or her trip. Finally, all items have to be portable and considered luggage.

The amount of luggage allowed on the plane by airlines is limited in most cases to two pieces that must not exceed 66 pounds. Sometimes they allow excess luggage for an additional fee. If they do allow you to take more, do so, because it is the cheapest way of bringing items into Costa Rica.

While on the plane, you have to fill out a Customs declaration form. If you are bringing anything that is not considered luggage under the law, declare it at a very low price. Once you have picked up your luggage from the carousel you will have to go through Customs. If they red-light you, you must go through an inspection; otherwise you'll walk through unstopped.

There is a duty-free exemption of up to $500. If you exceed the $500 limit, the back of your passport will be stamped "*bonificado*," which once again means you will be restricted from bringing more imported items into the country for a period of six months. If you bring in more items within six months, you will have to pay the corresponding taxes. Do not think you can get away with bringing more items before then ripping out the last page of your passport. They keep all records on computer.

You have two options if your duty-free $500 exemption is not enough. You can pay the duties right then and there, or you can ask for a receipt and return the following day to pay.

Tourists and residents have the right to bring in $500 in merchandise purchased abroad every six months tax-free, in addition to personal items considered part of a traveler's luggage. There is a long list of personal items you may bring in, such as: clothing, toys, sports equipment, such as surf boards or fishing equipment; a personal computer, photographic equipment; radios, tapes and musical instruments. Personal items are not limited to this list. Almost any article that will be used by the resident or traveler while in the country, whether to work or play, may be considered a "personal item." The $500 tax does not apply to personal items, but is additional to them. Any merchandise that exceeds the $500 limit and cannot be considered a personal article will be retained in Customs until the import duties are paid. Be forewarned that Customs officials will usually stamp the passports of people who bring in obviously new merchandise.

Used clothing and books are not subject to taxes. Do not pack them with taxable articles or you may have to pay taxes on them anyway.

Have friends bring a few things when they come to visit you in Costa Rica. Always try to take as much as possible with you on the plane rather than shipping items by boat, because most used personal things are not taxed at the airport. Even used appliances have a good chance of clearing airport Customs if you can fit them on the plane.

2. If you have a small amount of items (less than 500 pounds) that you cannot take with you as luggage, you should consider sending it as air cargo. One slightly crazy friend of ours, who has moved back and forth between Costa Rica and the United States four times, highly recommends American Airlines Cargo. He always uses them to ship his belongings to Costa Rica.

If you choose to ship your belongings by air, try American Airlines. Call their 800 toll-free number. They will ask you your intended destination. You will then have to give them the number of boxes you are planning to ship, and the respective weight and dimensions of each box.

The operator will then figure out the approximate cost. All items will officially be weighed at the airport cargo facility. The cost is based on either the total weight or the combined dimensions of all your boxes, whichever is greater.

You will then be given the choice of sending your things by express or standard freight. The latter is your best bet if you are not in a hurry. It takes only two to five days to reach Costa Rica from the United States. The only drawback to shipping standard rate is that it will be on a space-available basis, and your merchandise may be slightly delayed. The cost works out to be about a dollar per pound.

It is highly advisable to make your travel plans so as to arrive in Costa Rica before your shipment. This way you can go directly to the Customs house and remove your things after paying the corresponding taxes.

We recommend packing your belongings in unmarked plain boxes, especially if you are shipping computers, stereos or other electronic equipment. Number each box and put the name and address of the person who will be receiving them in Costa Rica. Make a list of the contents of each box for yourself, the airlines and customs. This will help ensure your boxes get there intact. All of your boxes should be made of thick cardboard and have plenty of packing materials to protect any fragile items. Airline employees often heap heavy boxes on top of other cargo. Be sure to write "not for resale" on any paperwork and air bills. This will save you a lot of money when the Customs people figure out how much you will pay in taxes.

If you decide to get your things out of Customs yourself, the process goes like this. First, you will have to go to American Airlines Cargo, located near the airport, pay a small fee and take the paperwork to the Customs house. When you arrive there, you go to a couple of windows. Next, you will sit and wait until they call your name. While you wait you can peek inside of a large glass window and watch the workers load and unload boxes of all sizes and shapes from the 20-foot high storage shelves.

When your name is finally called you go inside and the inspector opens all of your sealed boxes and determines what the contents are worth. Due to a lack of knowledge or because the Customs inspector will want to, they sometimes apply the same rules as luggage and you will pay nothing or very little. Most of the time you do not need a Customs broker to help you with a small shipment.

Finally, you go to a window, which also serves as a branch of one of the national banks, and pay the taxes on the items you have imported.

There are small trucks or *taxis de carga* available outside the Customs building that you can hire to take your belongings to your house or apartment. Prices are quite reasonable. We took a full load to San José and the driver only charged us about $30. He even helped us load and unload.

3. If you have more 500 pounds and large items like refrigerators, it is too expensive to ship by air. Your best option is to send your things by boat in a cargo container. It is more cost-effective to use a large container, and the transit time will be shorter. As a rule of thumb, shipping a quarter of a container will cost as much as a half, and a half will cost as much as a whole container. So it is best to use a whole container. Your Customs agent can get all of your household items and belongings out of Customs.

Here is what one expat said about the experience of shipping his things by container: "I moved down with everything that would fit in a 40-foot container, from the Indianapolis area, and if I remember correctly I paid about $5,500 to $5,800. However, if your location is close to a major seaport, the cost should be a lot lower. My container had to go by truck to Chicago, then by rail to the eastern seaboard (possibly New York or Virginia Beach) before it got onto the ship, and the cost for the land portion was probably greater than the cost of the sea voyage.

"The best part is that they left the container parked in my driveway for several days at no extra charge. It was up on wheels of course, so I had to build a ramp to load it. I loaded it myself with some friends and hired a crew for the real heavy stuff.

"Having that kind of time was key to getting everything to fit right, which was important to me because not a cubic foot was wasted — and there were 2,261 of them. Instead of selling or giving away a ton of stuff in the States, we brought it all down and gave it away here, and brought a lot of additional supplies we needed for our mission work here, in addition to all our household stuff, a couple thousand books and my 17-foot canoe."

4. Driving through Mexico and Central America is another way to bring your household goods and personal belongings to Costa Rica. However, because of the length of the journey, delays at border crossings and other hassles, this method is not recommended. We understand that some trucking companies will ship your belongings overland.

Whether you chose to send some of your possessions by ship or plane as unaccompanied luggage, you will learn to exercise extreme patience. Be prepared to face some unnecessary delays and frustrations when dealing with the Costa Rican Customs house, or *aduana*. Since the new modern Customs warehouse opened near the airport, this process has been somewhat streamlined.

However, it is more usual than not to make several trips to the Customs warehouse to get your belongings. At worst you may spend all day dealing with mountains of paperwork, only to hear at the end of the day that you must come back tomorrow. Furthermore, fickle Customs officials sometimes decide the value of the shipped goods, and two identical shipments can be taxed differently depending on who examines them at the *aduana*.

The documentation required to import personal effects and used household goods are: an original bill of lading, a copy of your passport including the pages with the last entry to Costa Rica, and a list of the value of each item. This list should include brand name, model and serial number of all appliances, large and small. All items have to be used for at least six months before shipping.

Because of this lengthy process and hassles, many people pay a local Customs broker, *Agencia Aduanera*, or hire some other person or their lawyer to do this unpleasant task for them. It may cost a little more this way, but it will save valuable time and hassles.

We recommend the following company (please see their ad in the classified ads section of this guide):

Ship to Costa Rica
Tel: 258-8747
Fax: 258-7123
Toll-Free from the United States or Canada: 1-866-245-6923
E-mail: shiptocostarica@racsa.co.cr

Here is what Susan said about Ship to Costa Rica's services: "Well, finally, we have our stuff! The container arrived a week ago, but we had to store our things because we considered moving to another spot. Then after a hectic week of looking around, we decided we liked our spot just fine and we had a great deal, talked to the neighbors about the reasons we considered leaving and decided to stay here.

"So today was the BIG day. We got a call at 8:30 this morning to say the truck was ready at the warehouse and did we want them to come NOW. That was three hours early—imagine that! And I groaned and said, 'But we're not even dressed.' So we did the Keystone Cops thing and ran around throwing on clothes, throwing cats in the maid's room, throwing the dog in the laundry room, throwing the sheets in with the dog and getting ready for the big day.

"And the truck came and unloaded and the other truck came and unloaded and unloaded, and unloaded. The only space they didn't unload into was the hall bathroom. So that's where we hung out for a moment of peace from the boxes and piles of stuff. Even though we de-stuffed multiple times back in the States we still had so much stuff that I have no idea where it will go.

"Our maid stood wide-eyed through the entire day wondering when the stuff would stop arriving and dreading having to unpack it. She deserves a medal.

"Today I truly felt like an American with many of the undercurrents of what that word means to people who are not and have not got what we have. It was almost embarrassing. But I was assured that we were perfectly normal for Americans moving to Costa Rica.

"After it was all delivered, the guys unwrapped all the furniture and took away the garbage. They helped us bully several dozen boxes into a handy storage area we have under the stairs and smiled the entire time, except for when they delivered my 500-pound fire-proof filing cabinet up a long flight of stairs—we affectionately call this the 'pig'.

"Many thanks to and hats off to Charlie Zeller of Ship to Costa Rica and his son Charlie, Jr., the head of the moving crew. From start to finish, these are the most professional movers I have ever worked with. They are honest, gave me a quote up front and stuck to it right down to when I paid them, delivered on time to my door, arranged all the 'trog' work and paperwork and Customs stuff. Stored my stuff in their warehouse for a week after it arrived in Costa Rica for free and overall did a fantastic job for us. Not one piece of furniture was damaged. I do give myself a little credit because I know how to pack. There have been so far a few little items, mostly dishes, chipped or broken. Nothing that can't be replaced.

"Five stars to Charlie and his crew. If you are looking to move to Costa Rica, I definitely recommend them and you can find them through the ARCR, another wonderful organization that has been immensely helpful.

"So now we are starting the unpack and my animals are sniffing around wondering what the heck went on here all day; they are checking out every box and all the new nooks and crannies and we are all thinking, gee, this looks like home and it don't echo no more in my place."

Be sure to ask the following when choosing a customs agency: Does the agency have English-speaking employees? Talk to them to see if they are customer-service oriented. Find out if they have the resources to access computerized Customs information. Talk to long-time residents who have dealt with reputable agencies and get referrals.

Carlos Bravo of **Servex International** is another good Customs broker. You may contact him at Tel: 253-1152, Cell: 383-2904 or E-mail: servex@racsa.co.cr.

You may also choose to consult the Yellow Pages for a listing of *Agencias Aduaneras* (Custom's brokers). The Association of Residents of Costa Rica (ARCR) can give you the names of several Customs agencies.

How to Find a Lawyer

If you plan to go into business, work, buy or sell property or seek long-term residency status in Costa Rica, you will definitely need the services of a trustworthy and professional attorney.

Your attorney can help you understand the complexities of the Costa Rican legal system, which is based on Napoleonic law. You are guilty until proven innocent, just the opposite of the system in the United States. A lawyer is one of the best investments you can make because he can assist you with bureaucratic procedures and handle other legal matters that arise.

If you are not fully bilingual, be sure to choose a lawyer who is bilingual. The secretary should be bilingual too (Spanish/English). This helps avoid communication problems and misunderstandings and enables you to stay on top of your legal affairs.

It is very important to watch your lawyer closely, since most Costa Rican lawyers tend to drag their feet as bureaucrats do.

Never take anything for granted. Refuse to believe that things are getting done, even if you are assured they are. Check with your lawyer on a regular basis and ask to see your file to make sure he has taken care of business. As you might imagine, paperwork moves slowly in Costa Rica, so you do not want a procrastinating lawyer to prolong the process.

When you first contact a lawyer, make sure he is accessible at all hours. Make sure you have your lawyer's office and home telephone number in case you need him in an emergency. If you are told your lawyer is always "in meetings" or "out of the office," this is a clear sign your work is being neglected and you have chosen the wrong lawyer.

Know your lawyer's specialty. Although most attorneys are required to have a general knowledge of Costa Rican law, you may need a specialist to deal with your specific case. Some people find it is a good idea to have several lawyers for precisely this reason.

Take your time and look around when you are trying to find a lawyer. This should be fairly easy since there are more than 7,000 lawyers from whom to choose. You should ask friends, other people, retirees and other knowledgeable people for the names of their lawyers. Above all, make sure your attorney is recommended by a reliable source. Then try to inquire about your potential lawyer's reputation, his work methods and integrity.

If you find yourself in a jam before finding a lawyer, contact the Association of Residents of Costa Rica (ARCR) for assistance, or you can ask a friend for a recommendation.

All over the world, there are always a few incompetent, unscrupulous attorneys, so be careful with whom you are dealing before you make your final choice. Remember, one of the most important people in your life in Costa Rica is your lawyer, so it is imperative that you develop a good working relationship.

Most attorneys charge from $25 to $50 an hour depending on your problem and their expertise. It is inadvisable to select your lawyer solely on the basis of legal fees. Lawyer's fees, or *honorarios*, vary. Just because a lawyer is expensive does not mean he is good. Likewise, you should not select an attorney because his fees are low. When hiring a

Costa Rica Business and Legal Summary
By Roger A. Petersen
Attorney at Law

Introduction: With the proper guidance and preparation, Costa Rica can be a profitable place to establish a business enterprise while enjoying the tranquility and diversity of the countryside. The business practices, customs and organization that you may be accustumed to in your country of origin may not be applicable to those in Costa Rica.

Be patient, learn the procedures and the local way of doing things before you embark. If you arrive trying to change the country, attitudes and practices you will be in for a surprise. The summary that follows will hopefully assist you in understanding the basic structure of Costa Rican business.

The Costa Rican Political System: Costa Rica is recognized world wide for its stable and democratic political system. All changes of government have occurred by way of free elections which are held every four years. The core of Costa Rica's democratic political system is its Constitution. Originally adopted on November 7, 1949, it remains in effect today establishing a clear system of checks and balances between the three branches of government: the Executive, Judicial and Legislative.

The Legal System: The Costa Rican legal system is based upon the French civil law system as opposed to English common law used in England and the United States. The common law system relies more on case law which is generated by the judicial system and binding on lower courts. In the civil law system the laws passed by the legislature are codified into codes which are then applied by the courts. Only the decisions of the Supreme Court of Costa Rica are binding on the lower courts. The court system is made up of: Lower Courts, trial Level Courts, Appellate Courts and the Supreme Court.

At the present time, delays in processing claims through the legal system are a serious problem. There is a backlog of cases and the government does not have the financial resources to adequately staff and modernize the judicial system to handle those cases.

The country has recently passed legislation which allows for private mediation and arbitration services in the hope that more cases will be resolved by way of alternative dispute.

Foreign investors may also participate or invest in Costa Rica using any of the legal entities recognized by Costa Rican law.

Costa Rican Corporate Law: The most common corporate entity used in Costa Rica is the *Sociedad Anónima (S.A.)* mainly because the liability of the shareholders is limited to their capital contributions and the shares of the corporation may be freely transferred. The corporation must maintain the following three books: (1) Shareholder's minutes book, (2) Board of Directors minutes books, and (3) a Shareholder's log book.

Taxes in Costa Rica: Yes, we have them also. The Costa Rican tax laws were completely overhauled in 1995 with the passage of the new Tax Code. Taxation is based upon source income, in other words, Costa Rica only taxes revenue that is generated within Costa Rica and not worldwide as other countries do.

Personal income taxes range from 10% to 25% depending on the amount earned. Corporate taxation ranges from 10% to 30% depending on the amount. Costa Rica applies a sales tax of 13% and a special consumption tax on selected items which range from 8% to 10%.

The government also collects a property transfer tax of 1.5% which is triggered whenever a property deed is presented at the Costa Rican National Public Registry to record the transfer of ownership of property from one person to another. The same applies to the transfer of ownership of a motor vehicle which triggers a 2.5% transfer tax.

Property taxes are levied and collected by the municipal government where the property is located. The property values on the books of municipalities is far below the actual market value of the property and each municipality is implementing its own property tax program to update its property tax data base.

Mr. Petersen is a partner in the law firm of **Vargas, Petersen & Odio** in San José, Costa Rica where he specializes in commercial and real estate law and litigation. He is a member of both the Florida Bar and the Costa Rican Bar. Mr. Petersen is the author of the well respected and best-selling book, *The Legal Guide to Costa Rica*. He was born in Costa Rica, speaks fluent Spanish and English and attended college and law school in both the United States and Costa Rica.

lawyer to do a job it is advisable to pay a third to a half up front, with the balance to be paid when the job is completed. If the attorney insists on more than 50 percent up front, you should get another attorney.

Check with the Costa Rican version of the Bar Association (*El Colegio de Abogados*) **www.abogados.or.cr** if you have any questions about legal fees. They establish minimum legal fees, however some fees are determined by the amount of the transaction.

In Costa Rica it is not uncommon to hire a lawyer on a full-time basis by paying what amounts to a small retainer. If you find a lawyer who will handle your *pensionado* or residency paperwork for under $500, you have found a bargain.

However, if you speak fluent Spanish and have a lot of patience, you can do your residency or *pensionado* paperwork yourself. Just pick up a list of the requirements from the Immigration office. Outside the Immigration office there are men who will help push your papers through or make sure they are at the "top of the pile." They charge about $10 for this service. There is even a lawyer who works with them on the premises.

Do not pay them all the money up front. If you choose this route you can save yourself hundreds of dollars in attorneys' fees. All a lawyer does is just sign a couple of papers, turn them in at the Immigration office and take your money.

There is a small amount of paperwork involved in giving your lawyer power of attorney (*poder*) so he can take care of your personal business and legal affairs.

This is not a bad idea when you may have to leave the country for a period of time or in the event of an emergency. However, first make sure your lawyer is completely trustworthy and competent. You may either choose to give your attorney *poder general* (general power of attorney) or *poder especial* (special power of attorney). You may revoke both types of power of attorney at any time.

If a foreigner lives or has assets in Costa Rica he or she should have a will. Your lawyer can help you with this.

If you want answers to most of your questions about the complex Costa Rican legal system, purchase *The Legal Guide To Costa Rica* by Roger Petersen. Although this book is no substitute for a good lawyer, it is still very useful for the layman. This guide may be purchased from **Costa Rica Books** (see Chapter 12 for the details). If you have any questions, contact Mr. Peterson at: Tel: 233-5219, Fax: 233-2507 or E-mail: crlaws@racsa.co.cr.

This comprehensive guide contains sample forms and documents. It covers the most common situations you will encounter in Costa Rica: real estate transactions, corporations, commercial transactions, Immigration, labor laws, taxation, wills, marriage and much more.

We suggest you also purchase *The Easy Guide to the Costa Rican Legal System* when it is released in 2007. It was written in conjunction Adolfo Garcia who is in our opinion one of the best legal minds in Costa Rica. This guide will simplify Costa Rica's often confusing legal system, clear up many of your questions and be very user-friendly.

We also recommend purchasing a copy of *Diccionario de Términos Jurídicos* by Enrique Alcaraz. It is a complete English-Spanish dictionary of legal terms.

Here is a partial list of bilingual attorneys who have many North American clients:

Adolfo García
Friendly and astute
Tel: 201-0300 / Cel: 381-3562

Lic. José Fernando Carter Vargas
P.O. Box 5482-1000, San José, Costa Rica
Tel: 257-6646 / Fax: 258-4101,
E-mail: jfcarter@racsa.co.cr

Lic. Ruhal Barrientos Saborio
Apdo. 5576-1000
San José, Costa Rica
Tel: 011-(506) 222-7614 / Cel: 381-5580

Lic. Henry Lang
Tel: 204-7871 / Fax: 204-7872
www.langcr.com

How the Justice System Works in Costa Rica

Let's start with the *tico* system of justice. If you find it strange that *las cortes* (courts) in Costa Rica don't have room for the *jurado* (jury) then you probably haven't heard that Costa Rica practices a justice system based on the Roman and French codes that came to us by way of Spain.

The system has several interesting features that makes it different from the common law system practiced in the United States, Canada and England.

The most outstanding of them all from the gringo perspective, is the lack of a jury. Another is that judges don't have much room for interpretations and must apply the law as a *receta* (recipe); if the crime doesn't fit, they must acquit.

The precept of *inocente hasta que se pruebe lo contrario* (innocent until proven guilty) is also a principle in the Costa Rican system, but whereas in the common law system judges usually are content to set bail for most types of crimes, in Costa Rica judges seem more inclined to deny it.

In fact, there are a good number of other measures at the disposal of a *tico* judge, collectively known as *medidas cautelares* (precautionary measures) that can make the whole process a nightmare for the *imputado* (suspect).

The four most famous *medidas* are: *arresto domiciliario* or *casa por cárcel* (house arrest), *fianza* (bail), *impedimento de salida* (prohibition to leave the country) and last but not least *prisión preventiva* (preventive prison), a measure intended to keep the suspect from obstructing justice.

You can say that *tico* justice guards evidence jealously. If you ever find yourself in hot legal water, by all means try to breathe very carefully and keep a low profile. A certain ex-president of ours did not answer his phone or tell his assistant where he was going for four days, and that cost him an *orden de arresto internacional* (international arrest warrant). He should have known better.

There is some confusion also as to who presses charges, but there should not be as practically anybody with a stake in the matter can do it. For instance, Alcatel is pressing charges against two of its former managers, which are in addition to those already pressed by the government. By the way, in this case there is a difference between *el estado* (the state) and *el gobierno* (the government). The former is represented by the *Ministerio Público* (Attorney's Office) and belongs to the Judiciary, the latter is represented by the *Procuraduría General* (the Government's Lawyer, known as *Procurador*) and belongs to the Executive branch. Together they have most of the powers of what many of you know as a Justice Department, though none have powers as far reaching when it comes to interpreting the law.

The process itself is composed of four phases, and the name of the defendant changes accordingly. When the *Ministerio Público* thinks it has a possible reason to start an investigation, it opens a process called *de instrucción* (instruction) and it is presided by one or several judges, each making decisions apart from the other judges. During this phase the defendant is called *imputado* (suspect), and it is the job of the judge to say if there is *falta de mérito* (lack of merit), else the judge elevates the issue to a higher office known as a *Tribunal*; from here on the defendant is called *indiciado* (indicted), but you can also call him *acusado* (defendant) as well.

A *Tribunal* is made up of three judges, one of whom is the president of the panel. This system is called *colegiado*. This is by all means a process similar to that of common law except for the missing jury. After hearing all the arguments, examining all the *evidencia* (evidence) and listening to all the *testigos* (witnesses), the judges retire to their offices and make their decision alone, then meet up to vote; this is why a verdict by a *Tribunal* in Costa Rica is called a *voto* (vote).

Regardless of the outcome there is a statutory period during which any of the parties can file an *apelación* (appeal); this is the third phase and it is called *casación*. This job belongs to the *Sala III* of the Supreme Court, which confirms the verdict, orders a retrial or even modifies the punishment. From here on, the *acusado* turns into *culpable* (guilty) or *inocente* (innocent) and the big *Cosa Juzgada* seal is put on the whole matter. Reopening it constitutes double jeopardy. If found guilty, there is yet one more phase to go through called *ejecución de la pena* (execution of the verdict), also headed by a full-blown judge who though limited by the penal code, can still change the sentence and even trade it for something else, such as *casa por cárcel* (house arrest).

In the Costa Rican system, unlike the common law system, subtle differences in vocabulary and actions may lead to completely different crimes and equally different lengths of sentences. The operative word in our system is *la tipificación* (the configuration) of the crime.

It all comes down to how Congress worded the law. *Tico* judges must closely observe the letter of that law first, and only then consider whatever *jurisprudencia* (jurisprudence) may already exist.

With that in mind, let's begin our journey into the types of crimes that Mr. District Attorney has at his disposal for doing his job, but just to keep it manageable let's limit that journey to *crímenes económicos* (money related crimes) committed against the state.

Got an easy way to squeeze money out of the government? Did your pal learn about this tip of yours and join in? You want to explore the loophole as far as it takes you? Well then, you are part of a *corruptela*, a type of *actividad* (activity) that may or may not be considered a *crimen* (crime). It all depends.

Let me explain that one again. The squeezing easy money from the government part is definitely a crime, so don't get too excited; what is not a crime is the casual nature of the affair.

In the *tico* system the *dolo* (intent) makes the difference between *cárcel* (doing time) or walking free, in almost all instances. That is why legislators came up with *asociación ilícita* (conspiracy to commit a crime), which to me is sort of like "mail fraud" in the United States, if the DA can't get you for the big crime, he will get you for mail fraud, at least.

The difference between a *corruptela* and *asociación ilícita* is then *dolo* and all it takes is to prove that there was some kind of understanding between the parties. Illicit association carries a six-year sentence.

The current situation of the three *tico* ex-presidents has a lot to do with these type of *tenue* (subtle) differences, with two of them in jail and the other without as much as a formal accusation. At the time this article was written, both presidents were in jail. They have since been released.

Ex-president #1 used to have a rather well-known lawyer's office that was equally well-connected. He was hired by a certain corporation, *supuestamente* (allegedly) for *asesoramiento político* (lobbying). However, he understood differently; to him he was hired to carry out legal work in agreement with his profession. The problem was that the person who paid him says he did it as part of a payment requested by the head of a certain *agencia gubernamental* (government agency) who was part of a large scheme to defraud the state of a $40 million dollar loan given by a certain Scandinavian country. Willingly or unwillingly, he became part of the scheme and therefore is in deep trouble.

What is left to determine, then, is his *grado* (degree) of participation. That is, how much did he actually know? Let's start by giving him el *beneficio de la duda* (benefit of the doubt), as we should, and let's say he was completely unaware of what was going on, thus ruling out intent. This is the lowest degree of participation, in which case he could be charged with *favorecimiento real* (obtaining an actual benefit) from the whole transaction. Being the good lawyer that he is, however, he proceeded to put all of the money he got from the transaction into a *depósito judicial* (escrow account in the hands of the court). He now can go to the court and say he got no benefit since he returned the money. That works, too.

If the fiscal (DA) can find so much as a thread of evidence to prove intent, however, he can then be charged with illicit association and *corrupción*, a crime usually reserved for *servidores públicos* (government employees), but that applies to him by way of the head of the government agency. Just to clarify, contrary to popular belief, an ex-president is not a public servant.

Nevertheless, he has an uphill battle because the head of the government agency involved in the scheme says (allegedly) it was he who organized everything and they were simply following his lead; that could turn him into the *corruptor* (the corrupting party), which is the highest degree of participation and the individual who gets accordingly the biggest prize in real jail time.

Mr. ex-president #2 has sort of a different story, as he was not so close to the action. He considers himself, and he may be right about that, a big shot when it comes to *tecnologías de la comunicación* (communication technologies) and as such he was hired by a friend of his to do some *asesoramiento* (professional consulting). Nothing wrong there, so far.

In another rather friendly transaction, his friend hired another friend, who happened to be a prominent member of a prominent party. Her expertise: *filología* (philology) or correcting papers, essays and the like in the proper usage of the Spanish language. She seems to be an expert on the subject, as she got paid allegedly $900,000 for the job. This is strange because Mr. Big Shot ex-president also got paid exactly the same amount.

In addition, the friend who hired them also kept another $900,000 for himself as payment for his networking abilities that provided Alcatel with so much *talento* (talent) at so high a price. At this point, I should add that the *gerente* (manager) of Alcatel Costa Rica, who hired the friend in the first place is the brother of the *filóloga*.

Remember the definition of *corruptela* above? Well, the *Fiscal General* (DA) is working hard to find out if this situation was a *corruptela*, and, if so if a crime was committed. Nobody is calling anything a crime yet, except Alcatel which seems to believe that its manager for Latin America and its manager for Costa Rica conspired to commit *fraude* (fraud).

This brings us to ex-president #3. His problem is that he apparently is into asking for *préstamos* (loans) from anybody. According to his own declarations he borrowed from a certain former ICE director a total of $140,000; Mr. Director says, instead, the money was allegedly part of the *comisión* (commission) for helping Alcatel get a government contract. In total, that company circulated about $13 million dollars in *pagos* (payments) and the like. So generous they were that even a certain head of a certain government agency, if you catch my drift, who had NOTHING to do with this deal, got money as well. Charges for this case include *corrupción agravada* (aggravated corruption).

That is not all, however. He also allegedly borrowed money from the Taiwanese government and got a contract for *asesoramiento* (consulting) to the Spanish company that is working on the underground electrification project of the city of San José. He did drop the consulting gig and his relationship with the Taiwanese government is not really that clear, either.

Some of these events allegedly took place while he was still in office, which qualifies him for a whole set of crimes that may or may not apply to the other ex-presidents, among them: *enrequicimiento ilícito* (illegal enrichment) and *negociaciones incompatibles* (conflict of interest).

Last but not least is the oldest *crimen económico* on the books: *peculado* (embezzlement), which is nothing but the use of state assets to procure a personal or patrimonial benefit. Which one do you think can be charged with that?

*Courtesy of Guillermo Jiménez from *Tico Speak*

Legal Terms

Accusation	*Denuncia*
Accused person	*Acusado*
Alimony	*Pensión alimenticia*
Appeal	*Apelación*
Appearance in court	*Comparecencia*
Bail	*Fianza*
Case	*Caso*
Civil law	*Derecho civil*
Court	*Tribunal / corte*
Court of appeals	*Corte de apelaciónes*
Criminal law	*Derecho penal*
Custody	*Patria potestad*
Defend	*Defender*
Defense attorney	*Abogado defensor*
District Attorney	*Fiscal*
Embezzlement	*Desfalco*
Eye witness	*Testigo ocular*

False witness	*Testigo falso*
Fees	*Honorarios*
Fight case	*Pelear el caso*
Fine	*Multa*
Fraud	*Fraude*
Guilt	*Culpa*
Guilty	*Culpable*
Hearing	*Audiencia*
Higher court	*Corte superior*
House arrest	*Arresto domiciliario*
Illegal	*Ilegal, prohibido*
Impediment to leave country	*Impedimento de salida*
Innocent	*Inocente*
Judge	*Juez (masc), Jueza (fem)*
Jury	*Jurado*
Law suit	*Demanda*
Lawyer	*Abogado*
Lawyer's bar	*Colegio de Abogados*
Legal	*Legal*
Legal form	*Papel sellado*
Lower court	*Corte inferior*
Not guilty	*No culpable/absuelto*
Plea	*Alegato*
Ruling	*Fallo*
Plaintiff	*Demandante*
Property	*Propiedad*
Prosecutor	*Fiscal/procurador*
Sentence	*Condena/sentencia*
Suit	*Demanda*
Summons	*Citación*
Take the case (lawyer)	*Llevar el caso*
Take to trial	*Llevar a juicio*
Testify	*Declarar*
Testify against	*Testificar / declarar contra*
Testify for	*Testificar / declarar a favor de*
Trial	*Juicio*
Try	*Juzgar / enjuiciar*
Verdict	*Fallo*
Will	*Testamento*
Witness	*Testigo*

*From *Christopher Howard's Guide to Costa Rican Spanish*

Costa Rican Consulates and Embassies Abroad

Costa Rican consulates provide information about visas, work permits, marriage and residency. They can issue tourist visas, authenticate documents and assist Costa Rican citizens living abroad.

Anyone seeking permanent residency in Costa Rica needs to have certain documents notarized by a Costa Rican consulate or embassy in their country of origin. Documents that must be notarized are a birth certificate, police certificate (stating you have no criminal record) and a proof of income statement. All this paperwork should be taken care of before coming to Costa Rica.

If you apply for permanent residency in Costa Rica, it may take months to get notarized documents from your home country, if it's possible at all. If worse comes to worst, you may have to make a trip home to take care of these matters. While you are waiting for papers from abroad, other documents may expire and you will have to start all over again. Bureaucracy is slow enough as it is in Costa Rica, and it is foolish to delay this process any more than necessary.

Each Costa Rican consulate has its own business hours and its area of coverage (jurisdiction) based on the origin of the document. Please locate your nearest consulate for personal attention. If there is no consulate in your state, locate the state or city nearest your residence in the list below.

Consulates in the United States:

Atlanta: 1870 The Exchange Southeast N.W., Suite 100, Atlanta, GA, 30339. Tel: (770) 951-7025 Fax: (770)-951-7073 E-mail: consulate_ga@costarica-embassy.org.

Boston: 175 McClennan Highway, East Boston, MA 02128. Tel: (617) 561-2444, Fax: (617) 561-2461. E-mail: consulate_bos@costarica-embassy.org.

Chicago: (includes Illinois, Indiana, Michigan, Ohio, Iowa, Minnesota, Missouri, North Dakota, South Dakota, Indiana and Wisconsin): 203 North Wabash Avenue, Suite 1312, Chicago, IL 60601. Tel: (312) 263-2772 Fax: (312) 263-5807 E-mail: crcchi@aol.com.

Dallas (Area of coverage: Dallas): 7777 Forrest Ln., Suite C-204, Dallas, TX 75231. Tel: (972) 566-7020, Fax: (972) 566-7943.

Denver: 3356 South Xenia Street, Denver, CO 80231-4542. Tel: (303) 696-8211, Fax: (303) 696-1110, E-mail: crconsul@hypermall.net

Houston: (includes Colorado, Kansas, Nebraska, New Mexico, Oklahoma and Texas): 3000 Wilcrest, Suite 112, Houston, TX 77042. Tel: (713) 266-0484, Fax: (713) 266-1527 E-mail: consulatecr@juno.com.

Los Angeles: (includes Southern California, Arizona, Nevada, Utah and Hawaii): 1605 West Olympic., Suite 400, Los Angeles, CA 90015, Tel: (213) 380-6031 Fax: (213) 380-5639. E-mail: costaricaconsulate la@ hotmail.com.

Miami (area of coverage: Florida): Consulate General, 1101 Brickell Ave., Suite 704-S, Miami, FL 33131, Tel: (305) 871-7487, 871-7485, Fax: (305) 871-0860. After hours emergency phone line: (305) 331-0636 E-mail: consulate_fla@costarica-embassy.org.

New Orleans: (Includes Alabama, Arkansas, Kentucky, Louisiana, Mississippi and Tennessee): World Trade Center Bldg., 2 Canal St., Suite 2334, New Orleans, LA 70130. Tel: (504) 581-6800 Fax: (504) 581-6850. After hours emergency phone line: (504) 256-2027 E-mail: consulno@ aol.com.

New York (includes Connecticut, Maine, Massachusetts, New England, New Hampshire, New Jersey, New York, Pennsylvania, Rhode Island and Vermont): 80 Wall Street, Suite 718, New York, NY 10005. Tel: (212) 623-6310, Fax: 212 509-3068. After hours emergency phone line: (908) 623-6310. E-mail: consulnewyork@hotmail.com.

Phoenix (area of coverage Arizona): 7373 E. Doubletree Ranch Rd.,Suite 200, Scottsdale, Arizona, 85258. Tel: (480) 951-2264 Fax: (480) 991-6606, E-mail: burkeap@aol.com.

Puerto Rico: Avenida Ponce de Leon, Edificio 1510, Oficina P1, Esquina Calle Pelaval, San Juan, Puerto Rico 00909. Tel: (787) 723-6227 Fax: (787) 723-6226. After hours emergency phone line: (787) 627-3220 E-mail: consuladopr@yunque.net.

San Antonio: Continental Building, 6836 San Pedro, Suite 116, San Antonio, TX 78216. Tel: (210) 824-8474, Fax: (210) 824-8489. After hours emergency phone Line: (210) 386-6839 E-mail: mrojasconssulsa@ msn.com.

San Francisco (includes, Alaska, Idaho, Montana, Northern California, Oregon, Washington and Wyoming): P.O. Box 7643, Freemont, Ca 94536. Tel: (510) 790-0785, Fax: (510) 792-5249. After hours emergency phone line: (800) 790-8561 E-mail: consulsfo@hotmail.com.

St. Paul (area of coverage Minnesota): 2424 Territorial Road, St. Paul, MN 55114. Tel: (651) 645-4103,Fax: (651) 645-4684, E-mail: cr-consulate@2424group.com.

Tampa: 2204 Barker Road, Tampa, FL 33605. Tel: (813) 248-6741, Fax: 813) 248-6857 E-mail: crica@integracom.net.

Washington: (includes all U.S. states, District of Columbia, Dela ware, Maryland, Virginia and West Virginia, North Carolina and South Carolina): 2114 "S" Street, NW, Washington, D.C. 20008. Tel: (202) 328-6626 Fax: (202) 265-4795. After Hours emergency phone line: (202) 215-4178, E-mail: consulate@costarica-embassy.org. Web: www.costarica-embassy.org.

Consulates Abroad:

England
14 Lancaster Gate
London, England
K2P 1B7
Tel: 071-723-1772
E-mail: rolomadrigal@hotmail.com

Canada
135 York St., Suite 208
Ottawa, Ontario K1N 5T4
Tel: (613) 562-0842
Fax: (613) 562-22855

Canada
614 Centre A. Street N.W.
Calgary, Alberta

Canada
164 Avenue Road
Toronto, Ontario M5R 2H9
Tel: (416) 961-6773

Canada
145 Chadwik Court
Suite 320
North Vancouver,
V6C 1H2
Tel: (604) 983-2152
Fax: (604) 983-2178
E-mail: consulado@sprint.ca

Canada
1425 René Levexque-West
Suite 602
BC Montreal, H3G 1T7
Tel: (514) 393-1057
Fax: (514) 393-1624

* To obtain a complete list of embassies and consulates visit the Costa Rican Foreign Ministry website at www.rree.go.cr or www.costarica.com/travel/missions-worldwide.

Embassies and Consulates in Costa Rica

If you are planning to travel and explore Latin America and other parts of the world, when you are settled in Costa Rica, you will need the addresses of the embassies and consulates listed below in order to get visas and other necessary travel documents.

Most embassies and consulates are located in downtown San José.

The rest are found in upscale neighborhoods such as Rohrmoser, Los Yoses and San Pedro, about 10 minutes from the center of the city. Before visiting any of the consulates or embassies below, we suggest you find out their hours.

Argentina — Curridabat 234-6520
Austria (consulate) — San José 255-0767
Belgium —Los Yoses 225-6255
Belize — Guadalupe 253-9626
Bolivia — Sabana Sur 290-8844
Brazil — Paseo Colón 383-1904
Canada — Sabana Sur 242-4400
Chile — Los Yoses 224-1547
China — San Pedro 224-8180
Columbia — Barrio Dent 283-6871
Ecuador— Rohrmoser 232-1503
El Salvador — San José 257-7855
France — Curridabat 234-4167
Germany — Sabana Norte 290-9091
Great Britain — Paseo Colón 258-2025
Guatemala —Sabana Sur 220-1297
Honduras — Boulevard Rohrmoser 231-1642
Italy — Los Yoses 234-2326
Israel — Centro Colón 221-6011
Japan — Sabana Norte 232-1255
Mexico — San José.. 257-0633
Nicaragua — Barrio California 257-9006
Panama — San Pedro.. 280-1570
Peru – Curridabat 225-9145
Puerto Rico — Ave. 2, Calle 11-13 257-1769
Spain — Barrio Escalante 222-1933
Switzerland — Centro Colón 221-4829
Taiwan — Barrio Escalante, Guadalupe......................... 224-8180
United States of America, Pavas 220-3050, 519-2000
Venezuela — Los Yoses... 225-8810

RESIDENCY AND RELATED MATTERS

How to Become a Legal Resident of Costa Rica

People find Costa Rica attractive and want to live in the country for a myriad of reasons: good year-round weather, tired of the rat race and hustle-bustle, a new start in life, inexpensive living and retirement, tax benefits, the country's low-cost health care system, to start a business or invest, to learn Spanish, separation or divorce, to enjoy the country's large expatriate community and even to find companionship. Whatever your motives may be for wanting to move to Costa Rica, there are a number of ways to remain in the country on a long-term basis.

Tourists from North America and many countries in Europe may remain legally in the country for three months without having to apply for legal residency. You may own property, start a business or make investments with no more than a tourist visa.

We know many Americans, Canadians and other foreigners who started businesses as tourists (be aware that a tourist cannot legally work in any company, as in most countries). If you plan to reside in Costa Rica full-time, however, one of Costa Rica's residency programs will appeal to you.

Several residency categories permit you to retain your current citizenship and obtain long-term legal status in Costa Rica. They are *pensionado*, *rentista* and *inversionista* (resident investor). Which program you choose depends on your needs and financial position. Becoming a legal resident will by no means affect your U.S. or Canadian citizenship. Be very aware that residency procedures and requirements can change frequently, so always check for current requirements with the ARCR at www.arcr.net.

In March 1992, a change in the *pensionado* law eliminated many tax privileges retirees had enjoyed since the program started in 1964.

Under the old system, foreigners with official *pensionado* or *rentista* (permanent retiree) status were required to live in the country four months a year. They were entitled to the following perks: residency without immigration hassles, all the privileges of Costa Rican citizens except the right to vote and work for hire, and the right to import one of each of the major appliances such as refrigerator, stove, microwave, television, washer and drier, as well as many personal household goods free of taxes.

Pensionados could import a new car every five years duty-free, provided it was worth less than $16,000. In 1992, low taxes on imported cars and duty-free household goods were eliminated. Since then, all *pensionados* have to pay taxes on their automobiles and household goods the same as Costa Rican citizens do.

These benefits were taken away because everyone saw that they were unconstitutionally giving something to foreigners that Costa Ricans could not have themselves. Incentives will always be used to attract people to less attractive countries, but Costa Rica does not have that problem.

Despite this law, Costa Rica is still an attractive retirement haven. People continue to flock to the country because of its high quality of life, peaceful atmosphere, political stability, fantastic climate, friendly people who like foreigners, excellent business environment and natural beauty. In fact, Costa Rica has more American residents per capita than any other country in the world outside of the United States. They can't all be wrong!

The Costa Rican government has reduced taxes on some cars and other imported goods, making them affordable for most Costa Ricans as well as foreign residents. Consequently, the need for a tax-exoneration program has been eliminated.

If you must have an automobile, you can bring a car from the United States, although because of bureaucracy and high duties it is usually better to buy one here. You can also go to Golfito, the free port in southern Costa Rica, and buy a stove, refrigerator or other appliance without paying high import duties.

The practical benefits of obtaining residency in Costa Rica as a foreigner are very tangible, unlike in some other countries:
1. Access to Social Security continued care.
2. Access to checking accounts and credit service from some banks
3. Permission to engage in labor relationships
4. Freedom from worries about immigration checkpoints and possible deportation
5. Ability to purchase personal and business property and real estate
6. Qualify for citizenship and Costa Rican passport once requirements are met
7. Right to purchase telephone lines

Now let's look at the requirements and specific documents you will need to present to the Costa Rican government if you choose to apply for the *pensionado* or *rentista* categories.

A *pensionado* is someone who lives on a pension (a U.S. Social Security check or permanent retirement program). A husband and wife cannot combine their pensions, but the wife can live under the husband's *pensionado* status or visa versa. The individual applying can combine pensions to achieve the total required. If the recipient of the pension dies, the spouse can retain *pensionado* status if the pension is inherited. Some paper work, naturally, is involved.

Here are the requirements for this category:
1. A lifetime income of at least $600 a month generated outside of Costa Rica. Social Security recipients need a certification that can be done at the U.S. Embassy in Costa Rica.
2. A signed letter confirming that you will receive this money in Costa Rica. This is not needed if issued by the U.S. Embassy.
3. A letter from a CPA stating that you will receive at least $600 for life if the pension comes from a company's pension plan.
4. If the money comes from a private company, two letters from bank officials showing that your company is financially sound and that the pension plan has been in existence for at least 20 years.
5. A detailed account of your company's pension plan or a yearly corporate report.

As a *pensionado* you are obligated to exchange $7,200 a year ($600 per month) for colones at a local bank. You need proof of this to update your file. If you cannot prove that you converted enough money during the year, you can lose your status. You also have to renew your *pensionado* I.D. card every two years ($100) and reside in the country for at least four months yearly (not necessarily consecutively). As a *pensionado* you can own and operate your own business but not work. Also, as a *pensionado* you do not have to pay taxes on your income from outside Costa Rica. After three years you may change to permanent residency status. For the same $7,200 per year you can bring your spouse and/or dependent children.

Rentista is a category designed for those who are not retired or receive no government pension. To qualify for *rentista* status, you must have an income of $12,000 a year ($1,000 per month) coming from an investment or annuity outside of the country. A good way to do this is to buy a certificate of deposit for $60,000 from a Costa Rican bank that yields a monthly income of at least $1,000 (from the capital). (Under the new law, this amount is higher if bringing your spouse and/or other dependents).

As a *rentista*, you must prove that this investment will be stable for at least five years. At the end of five years, you have to prove your source of income again or change to permanent residency if possible. Furthermore, every year as a *rentista* you have to prove that you changed $12,000 into colones and show your passport to prove you were in the country at least four months (not necessarily consecutively).

The safest banks are the public banks, which are the Banco Nacional de Costa Rica or the Banco de Costa Rica. You must keep the deposit of your money for five years in a CD and you may withdraw the interest obtained form it. If you decide to withdraw the principal, then you will be charged a penalty and will also be subject to losing your residency, because the bank is required to notify Immigration if the deposit is withdrawn.

As a *rentista*, you can own and operate a business but not work for hire. The disadvantage to being a *rentista* is tying up your funds at relatively low interest. As with *pensionados*, dependents are allowed for an additional amount of income.

We just heard of a new method for obtaining *rentista* status from one of our readers. He said: "If anyone has to get residency under the *rentista* category, they can do it by setting up a business in the States if they already do not have one. The business has to hold $60,000 which is to be dispersed over five years." We urge you to check with a lawyer to see if this method will work before trying it.

In brief, to qualify for *rentista* status, you need:

1. An income of $1,000 per month for the next five years in Costa Rica.
2. Documentation from a bank attesting to income, if the income is from a foreign source.

Inversionista is another resident status for people who are not retired and want to invest in Costa Rica. If you have a lot of money to invest, this might be the best route to go. The government will grant residency under this category if you invest at least $50,000 in high- priority projects such as tourism, $100,000 in reforestation or $200,000 in any other business. No dependents can be included under this category.

The paperwork and requirements are similar to those in the other residency programs, with a few basic differences. Under this program you must reside in Costa Rica at least six months of every year (do not have to be consecutive) and live as a temporary resident for two years. Eventually you may become a permanent resident.

If you plan to start a project, additional paperwork such as a feasibility study and bank references may be needed. If you are going to get involved in tourism, you will need permission from the Costa Rican Tourism Institute (ITC). When investing in an established company, you will have to show the company's books.

Since every circumstance is different and requirements change often, contact the Association of Residents of Costa Rica for a good lawyer to answer your questions.

The following documents are also required for *pensionado*, *rentista*, *inversionista* (resident investor), and all other types of residency in Costa Rica:

Note: All documents usually must be authenticated by the Costa Rican consulate or embassy located closest to the origin of the document (see the list for at the end of the last chapter for the nearest one). The charge is $40 per document. The people at the consulate must affix stamps worth the amount to collect the money. If the documents do not have the required stamps, you can buy them in Costa Rica. Talk to the ARCR before processing documents.

1. **Police Certificate** — From your local area stating that you have no criminal record. (This document is good for only six months, so make sure it is current.) Required for applicant, spouse, and any children ages 14 to 25. The local police in the applicant's usual residence, if different from the applicant's home state, may issue this report, but the police report usually coincides with the applicant's U.S. driver's license number. This document must

also be authenticated by the nearest Costa Rican consulate. Many U.S. state and local law enforcement agencies have websites and special phone numbers to issue such reports, upon request by the applicant.

2. **Birth Certificate** — Required for applicant, spouse and all dependent children (up to 18 years old or up to 25 if a university student; proof of enrollment is required). This document has to be authenticated by the Costa Rican consulate nearest to the issuer authority of the birth certificate.

3. **Marriage Certificate** — If applicable. Proof of divorce is not needed.

4. **Income Certificate** — For *pensionados* and *rentistas* (required only for the applicant). Please see the previous sections for specific details. Talk to the ARCR before processing documents.

5. Certified photocopies of all pages of the applicant's entire passport (Not stamped by consulate),

6. **Photos** — Twelve *cédula*-size photos—six front views and 6 sixprofiles. Do not bring photos, since a specific size is required and passport size will not work. Photos must be matte finish, not glossy.

Translation of Documents: Don't forget that all of these required documents must be translated from English into Spanish by an official translator. Translations from other languages to Spanish have to be either done by the Costa Rican consulate (no one else) in the country where the document was issued or in Costa Rica by an official translator for the specific language to Spanish. The Costa Rican government does not accept translation of the original language to English.

The formal application should have the following information: your mother's maiden name, full name, nationality, passport number, dependent's names, date of entry into Costa Rica, origin and amount of income, address in country of origin or Costa Rica, authentication by a notary public and corresponding stamps.

If you meet the prerequisites for any of the residency categories and have gathered all the required documents, you are ready to apply for your chosen status.

Next, have the ARCR Administration or an attorney present your papers to the proper agency, which will process them in four months or so.

If you want to avoid the many inconveniences of Costa Rica's giant "bureaucrazy" and save time and money in the long run, we suggest you join the ARCR.

Why Belong to ARCR Administration and Association of Residents of Costa Rica?
By Ryan Piercy

- Assistance within Costa Rica before you arrive—advice,contacts and information.
- Recommendation of professional people you can trust, including lawyers, accountants and other specialists.
- Assistance with language.
- Service to establish residency, starting before you arrive.
- Assistance in getting acquainted with the country when you arrive.
- Recommendation of trustworthy real estate firms.
- Assistance with importation of cars, furniture and personal effects through our office.
- Assistance in locating various firms you may require who speak your language.
- Assistance with government agencies and departments, and an explanation of local rules and regulations.
- Assistance in establishing banking contacts.
- Advice about how various investments work in Costa Rica.
- Processing of resident government file updates and I.D. card renewals.
- Full insurance service through our office, including group plans for health, home and vehicles.
- Discount rates for Costa Rica social service medical insurance.
- Safe, inexpensive international mail and courier service.
- ARCR computers are on line with the computers at the Central Registry for property and vehicle title search and company name searches.
- Personal or company credit studies. ARCR computers are on line with the largest checking agencies.
- ARCR is on the Internet; We have a small net cafe for members.
- In the ARCR office, photocopy, fax, postal and document translation services are available to members.
- Hundreds of merchants and professional services provide discounts to members simply by showing the ARCR membership card.
- ARCR can arrange work permits for domestic help in Costa Rica.
- ARCR can assist in rentals and purchases for property and accomodations.
- Membership includes subscription to the bimonthly ARCR magazine, "*El Residente*".

- Participation in the Residents Association's social and cultural events and the opportunity to meet other foreign residents.
- Travel and tourism assistance.
- Access to Costa Rica Assitance or CR Asistencia. ACCR (Automobile Club of Costa Rica)—"AAA-USA".
- Publications about Costa Rica are available from the ARCR office.
- Importing of pets.
- Funeral services.
- Newcomers Seminar. Our informative seminar is held every month,providing vital updates on banking,residency,moving, insurance, medical care and other topics important in making your decision to move here...and it's all FREE!

Who are we?
The ARCR Administration is an organization serving all types of foreign residents in Costa Rica, as well as people living abroad wishing to become residents of Costa Rica.
What do we do?
- Advocate for members before the Costa Rican government in matters of legal and human rights.
- Inform interested persons about procedures for becoming legal residents and to assist and advise them during the process.
- Organize social activities for members.
- Promote member participation in Costa Rican society and culture.

In Costa Rica:
ARCR Administration
Address: Apdo. 1191-1007
   Centro Colón
   San José, Costa Rica
   Tel: (506) 233-8068
   Fax: (506) 255-0061
WebSite:
www.arcr.net
e-mail: arcr@casacanada.net
Street address:
   Casa Canada, corner of Calle 40 and Avenida 4, San José.
   Tico style address:
   200 meters sur del Banco de Costa Rica, Paseo Colón.

The 2,500-member association has been reorganized and revitalized. It now offers services to all legal residents in Costa Rica, not just *pensionados*.

A provisional membership, which entitles you to all information and services, costs $100 yearly. Members with legal Costa Rican residency pay dues of $50 per year. Spouses and dependents of members may join for $10 per year as associate members. The ARCR offices are located at Casa Canada, two blocks south of Centro Colón on the corner of Avenida 4 and Calle 40. They will assist you when you need help applying for *pensionado* or *rentista* status for $870 for the primary applicant, $425 for spouse or dependent and $195 per child. This includes everything except the deposit to the government of $300 to $400 per person and the consular stamps you must obtain on foreign documents ($40 per document, and usually you need three such documents for an individual, or seven for a couple).

The cost for *inversionista* or *representante* status is $1,200 for the primary applicant. These prices are a good deal since many lawyers charge up to $2,000 and take much longer.

The ARCR can also help with buying and selling cars, obtaining a Costa Rican driver's license (see chapter 10 for details), assisting with English-to-Spanish translations of any required documents or papers,

The ARCR's monthly seminar is a must.

and making sure your annual papers are up-to-date. The association can notarize all your important documents, help with the renewal of your ID card or *cédula*, and help you obtain medical coverage with the Costa Rican Social Security System and the new supplemental coverage they now offer (see the section on medical care for details). Should you desire additional information, contact:

ARCR Administration
Apartado 1191-1007, Centro Colón
San José, Costa Rica
Tel: 233-8068 or 221-2053
Fax: 255-0061
E-mail: arcr@casacanada.net
Website: www.arcr.net or www.casacanada.net

Note: Some of the requirements for Costa Rican residency may be subject to change. It is highly advisable to check with the ARCR before applying.

To give readers an idea of what the process of obtaining residency is like, here is an account of one person's experience: "I handled all my own paperwork in the States. That amounted to following very peculiar procedures in New York State (New York City) for my birth certificate, and only slightly less complicated ones in Pennsylvania for my police report, with all of the certifications, etc. Then I took them all to the Costa Rican consulate and had them certified by the Consul in less than an hour.

"I suppose one could go to different consulates for each different document, but it would be a really trying process, as I am sure you are finding out if that's the way you do it. According to the rules, you have to take everything to the consulate assigned to your place of residence in the United States. I lived in south Philly, so New York was the place. In fact, the embassy in Washington said I could bring them all down there if I wanted, when I expressed concern on the phone that I initially had trouble reaching the New York Consul by phone or e-mail.

"I had already gone to the U.S. Embassy in Costa Rica for the paperwork to establish an account for my pension in Costa Rica.

"When I was done all this, my Costa Rican attorney took me by the hand and led me through the police fingerprinting and *Migración*. Each step took less than two hours counting lunch.

"It is really not a big deal — it is more a learning experience in patience than anything else. All told, it took me about three months start to finish, mostly waiting."

New Proposed Immigration Law

A new immigration law has recently been approved, and with it come important changes in many residency categories, as well as in the treatment of illegal residents in the country (TT, Aug. 26, Nov. 4).

Although the new law was opposed by many organizations that deal with immigrants — the Catholic Church and the Ombudsman's Office, among others — it has been promoted as necessary and of vital importance by Immigration authorities.

After many months of debate, and an initial approval that was declared unconstitutional by the Constitutional Chamber of the Supreme Court (*Sala IV*), a final version was approved Oct. 27. The law was recently published on Dec. 12; an eight-month moratorium started on this date, after which the new Immigration law will go into effect in mid-August of next year.

Note: Although the new law has passed, the underlying regulations have not been written yet. Contact ARCR for current changes.

Upon first glance, the categories of *rentista* and *pensionado* remain largely the same; but when you examine the changes carefully, several potentially major problems become evident. A few of the issues pointed out here may be clarified in the regulations for the law, which will be issued at some point in the future but do not exist at this time.

It should be noted that the law is not free of mistakes: what appears to be a clerical error apparently went unnoticed by the legislative system. Articles 77 and 78 both refer to the *rentista* category, and establish different requirements for approval. Article 77 basically keeps the same requirement of $1,000 a month per family for five years (which translates to a $60,000 deposit from which the bank guarantees your annuity). Article 78 then states that the requirement is $2,000 monthly for husband and wife, plus $500 extra for each dependent to be included in the application, which would double the deposit or more. We have yet to learn how this will be solved.

One important change is that the *rentista* and *pensionado* categories become temporary residencies, whereas today they are permanent residencies. Under the new law, holders of temporary residency will be able to change to unconditional permanent residency only after three years. This change is currently not allowed, although it was common practice until a couple of years ago.

The catch is that temporary residencies will only be granted for two years. How the above mentioned benefit will apply is uncertain, because the new rules will not allow any temporary resident to hold this status for more than two years. This is one reason why I would like to emphasize that if you are not currently a legal resident, you should take the necessary steps to legalize your immigration status now, before the new law goes into effect. It is my opinion – yet to be tested by the practice to be adopted by Immigration – that people who currently have or acquire their *rentista* or *pensionado* resident status before the new law goes into application, and keep it for more than three years, will be allowed to change it to unconditional permanent residency.

The new law includes *inversionista* (investor) as a residency category, though no requirements are mentioned. This will leave the list of requirements in the hands of the Executive Branch and subject to change from time to time, as a variable Immigration policy.

Another change is that residencies under all these categories must be filed through Costa Rican consulates abroad, as with other types of residencies. This change may seem simple, but in reality it represents major problems for new applicants.

The first obstacle is that the application must be sent to Immigration by the consulate. There have been many problems with this type of procedure in the past, as the application becomes a two-stage process. In the beginning, the consulate collects and legalizes the basic documents, such as birth certificates, marriage certificate and passport copies. After the file has reached the appropriate department at Immigration, a resolution is drafted asking the applicant to complete the file with a sworn statement, proof of fingerprinting and any document not filed at the consulate. This causes significant delays, as all files have to be reviewed twice, and several appointments have to be obtained to follow up on the file.

While other residency categories have been modified, most of the existing work residencies and permits remain basically the same, even though their classification has changed. In the past, a common practice by Immigration authorities when reviewing work permits and work residencies was to consult the Ministry of Labor regarding the availability of qualified Costa Ricans for the position in question. Now, this consultation will be mandatory, making work-related residencies and permits very restricted.

The law places emphasis on penalizing what is termed "trafficking of people and illegal immigration," and special attention is given to prohibiting people who do not hold working status from performing paid activities. This should concern those "perpetual tourists" who have been "beating the system" by leaving the country for a few days every three months. This common practice, which is not permitted today, will subject these people to the very real possibility of rejection at the border or airport upon their next entry. As per the new law, working as a tourist carries the risk of detention and immediate deportation with a five-year prohibition against entering the country.

The new law defines penalties for those who employ illegal immigrants or tourists, and establishes a legal obligation to cooperate with Immigration by informing about foreigners being employed. Infringement of these obligations will carry significant civil and criminal penalties. Restrictions are also set forth for hotel owners, managers and staff who accommodate foreign citizens: they will be under obligation to keep records of all their guests in a special registry, which must be made available to Immigration authorities at any time, and the hotel may be subject to penalties if it provides its services to illegal immigrants. This may be difficult to check and enforce in reality, but the implications are nonetheless unsettling.

Many changes that we still have no information about will be enacted through the regulations for the law, to be published in the future, to complete the law and include issues that were left out (not necessarily inadvertently).

My advice is to take advantage of the moratorium and legalize your situation in Costa Rica now, as it seems all the changes that have been going on at Immigration, in addition to the new law coming into effect, will make residencies even more complicated and restrictive than they are now.

*Courtesy of Lang & Asociados at 204-7871 or visit www.langcr.com and *The Tico Times*

Additional Methods of Obtaining Costa Rican Residency

As we mentioned in the last section, most of the *pensionado* program's privileges were revoked in 1992, so the only real advantage for becoming a *pensionado* is to be able to stay in the country legally. Now more and more people are looking at other ways of obtaining Costa Rican residency.

The residency program is for people who wish to reside in Costa Rica full-time but who cannot qualify for *pensionado* or *rentista* status. It is also for those who can qualify, but choose not to because some of the advantages were taken away. In the latter case, a $600-per-month *pension* from an approved source is required.

(1) **Residente Inversionista** — There are several other ways for foreigners to obtain legal residency. As we mentioned in the last section, they can become *inversionistas* (resident investors) by investing $50,000 in an approved organization such as a tourism or export

business, $100,000 in a reforestation project or $200,000 in another type of business. With this type of residency you have to live in the country six months a year.

2) **First Degree Relative** — Foreigners can also claim permanent residency if they have an immediate or first-degree relative in Costa Rica, i.e. a child, spouse or parent (mother or father), brother or sister (in this particular case, the applicant must be single) who is a citizen.

They must also prove they have financial means to support themselves while living in Costa Rica (about $600 per month). Relatives of foreigners who have become Costa Rican citizens are also eligible for residency. In all cases you will be asked to prove your relationship. You can usually work under this category. All the documents required for other residency applications must be provided.

(3) **Marriage** — Marrying a Costa Rican also entitles you to residency. This is the fastest way to become a resident. We personally know of many expatriates who have married Costa Ricans for this very reason. Anyone under this category is not required to prove a minimum foreign income.

Retired Residents **PENSIONADO**	Earning Residents **RENTISTA**	Investor Resident **INVERSIONISTA**	Company Visa **REPRESENTANTE**	Permanent Residency
Requires proof of US$600 per month income (equivalent) from permanent pension source or retirement fund. (Combined pensions from one individual qualifies)	Proof of US$1000 monthly income for at least 5 years, guaranteed by a banking institution. (A sample letter with the required wording is available at ARCR) OR a $60,000 deposit in an approved Costa Rican bank.	Investment of US$50,000 in approved sectors such as tourism or export, $100,000 in reforestation, or $200,000 in any other business.	Applicant must be on the board of directors of a company- meeting certain requirements, such as employing a minimum number of local workers (established by law), with certified financial statements	First degree relative status with a Costa Rican Citizen OR marriage, or child that is Costa Rican
Must remain in the country for at least 122 days per year.	Must remain in the country for at least 122 days per year.	Must remain in the country for at least 182 days per year.	Must remain in the country for at least 182 days per year.	Must visit Costa Rica at least once (72 hrs) per year.
Dependants*	Dependants* (+ income)	No	No	No
Cannot work as an employee.	Cannot work as an employee.	Can receive income from the project.	Can earn a salary in the company.	Can work.
Can own a company and receive income.	Can own a company and receive income.	Can own a company and receive income.	Can own a company and receive income.	Can own a company and receive income.
Must exchange $7200 per year within a bank in Costa Rica.	Must exchange $12000 per year within a bank in Costa Rica	No exchange requirement.	No exchange requirement.	No exchange requirement.
Renewable every 2 years.	Renewable every 2 years.	Annual renewal.	Annual renewal.	Variable renewal.
US$300 guarantee deposit for all types of residency				
US$100 + $14 *ID fee*	US$100 + $14 *ID fee*	US$20 *ID fee*	US$20 *ID fee*	US$20 *ID fee*

Courtesy of the Residents Association

In addition, anyone who has lived for several years under another residency category, such as *pensionado* or *rentista*, may apply for Costa Rican residency. Many ex-*pensionados* do this because they can generally qualify for this status easily. With this type of residency you have to visit the country once a year.

As in the other residency categories, you need an application, birth certificate, marital status certificate, police report, several passport photos and in some cases documents proving your relationship to your Costa Rican relatives.

(4) **Working Costa Rican Corporation** — There is a newly added residency status for those who have a working company or *sociedad anónima*. You must have a minimum number of local employees and provide financial statements. Just having a Costa Rican corporation will not qualify a person for this status.

(5) **Residency Under Special Circumstances** — Residency is sometimes to some people who do not fall into any of the previous categories. Not all people who apply under this category will obtain residency. If there are two people with the exact circumstances, one may be granted residency and the other may have it denied. Since each case is different we suggest you talk to Roger Petersen. He is listed in the section on attorneys in this chapter and has helped a few of his clients obtain this type of residency.

(6) **Temporary Residency** — *Residencia temporal* is for students enrolled in a university or language school, Peace Corps volunteers and members of affiliated church service groups, employees of foreign firms, employees of many national companies and other categories. Language teachers at any language institute in San José may obtain temporary residency. Others doing jobs that Costa Ricans cannot do are also eligible for this status.

Temporary residency permits are valid for three months to a year and can be renewed. Temporary residents may enter and leave the country as often as they wish, paying the tourist's rate of exit tax. Once all documents are correctly presented, temporary permits are approved as quickly as possible.

Because each person's situation is different, the procedure is complicated. All residency programs require mounds of paperwork, so we advise you to consult a lawyer to facilitate this process. To find a competent, trustworthy attorney, go to the ARCR office or see the section in the previous chapter entitled, "How to Find a Lawyer."

Cédula Renewal

Renewing *Cédulas*/Residency — In order to renew, you must exchange a total of $7,200 per year as a *pensionado* or $12,000 as a *rentista*. If you spend only part of the year here, you must still exchange this total amount. You can exchange it in as many increments as you like, be it once or 60 times a year. You must keep all exchange receipts for the total required. The only receipts accepted are those you get at a bank every time you change dollars to *colones*. You can use any Costa Rican state or private bank to change your money. The receipt must show your name, amount of dollars exchanged, rate of exchange, and amount of colones received. You can then change it all back into dollars if you wish.

You must renew before your *cédula* expires (*vencimiento*). We also recommend you show your exchange each year, since it means less paperwork. This keeps you correctly up to date at immigration.

Migración has made a few changes to the process of renewing the *cédula de residencia* (don't know about *carnets* for *rentistas* or *pensionados*).

Timbres (stamps) — deposit the money in the **Haciendas general** account at Banco de Costa Rica — *Migración* web page indicates the money can be deposited at Banco Nacional, — but when I tried they send me to Banco de Costa Rica.

Appointments — try to plan ahead if you want to avoid waiting in a huge line, — like four or five months before the expiry date.

Copies of *cédula* — you are required to provide a copy of the inside front cover (your picture, *cédula* no.), inside back cover (*expediente* or file number) and copy of page with latest expiry date.

Renewal without appointment — Thursday and Friday only—get to *Migración* early, — like 6 a.m. (the gates open at 8 a.m.), as it's better to wait a couple of hours early than four hours later. One resident we know renewed his *cédula* in a few hours. He arrived at 7 a.m. and left at noon.

Passport — suggest you carry it with you — they were asking some people for their passport. For more information, see www.migracion. go.cr/residencias/index.html.

Requirements for Renewing Permanent Residency:

1. Present the residency document that needs to be renewed.
2. Pay 1,250 *colones* in the form of an *entero bancario*, special bank deposit form, to account #242480-0 in the Banco de Costa Rica

or to account #215936-6 in the Banco Nacional de Costa Rica, for each year of renewal of the *cédula*.

3. For renewing a residency *cédula* that requires a new document booklet, you must pay, at least one day prior to your appointment, the sum of 1,013 colones in the Banco de Costa Rica account #242480-0 or in the Banco Nacional de Costa Rica account #215936-6. (Note: although not stated, you should have this SEPARATE from No. 2 above, thus if you require a new *cédula*, you will have two *enteros bancarios*).

4. Indicate the place where you can be officially notified, or a fax number. (If it is the place of notification, you must put exact directions to your home or office, or attorneys office.)

5. Resident investors must present financial statements certified by an authorized public accountant. You must also be current with the payment of your national taxes. (Note: Although it does not specify how to be current, your accountant can also certify it.)

6. In the case of loss, theft or complete destruction (of your *cédula*), you must present two passport-size photographs, a certified declaration, "protocolized" — written in his protocol book, before a notary public (apparently about the circumstances of the loss, theft, or destruction of your *cédula*)—and pay (again, with an "*entero bancario*") the sum of 1,013 *colones* in the Banco de Costa Rica account #242480-0 or in the Banco Nacional de Costa Rica, account #215936-6.

Every Costa Rican resident is issued a cédula.

Also, you must pay the sum of 1,250 *colones* into the same accounts. Note: It means only ONE payment into either of the two accounts to cover the cost of replacing the *cédula* document.

7. If the foreigner has stayed away from Costa Rica for a period of more than one year, you must bring a declaration of why and a certification of your penal records (from your country of origin) authenticated by the Costa Rican consulate in your country of origin or where you are a legal resident, and also certified by the Ministry of Foreign Relations in Costa Rica.

8. If you have not renewed the residency document within 30 days after its expiration, conforming to Article 82 of the Regulation of the Immigration Law, you must present a declaration to justify the delay. Note: This probably also requires a certified and protocolized document from your notary public.

9. For each month or fraction thereof after 30 days after the expiration of your *cédula*, a fine of 125 *colones* per month will be collected.

Here is what one couple experienced when they renewed their *cédulas*: "My wife and I arrived at 5:34 a.m. We got into line and began the wait. A man came by and offered a place closer to the front of the line for 4,000 *colones*. This practice is not legal, but is not policed either.

"The man making the offer was selling music CD's, mostly as a cover for the other offer. Having more time than money and sharing the pirate's feelings about all things not legal, I declined the offer. They also offered to rent me a plastic-chair-height stool for 200 *colones*. Later I was sorry I did not take them up on that offer.

"We stood there until a bit before 8:00 a.m., when the line started moving. At the gate they checked to see that we had the necessary papers:

1. My *cédula* (residency document that has to be renewed).

2. A copy of the pages with my picture, the prior validation stamp and the last page.

3. A receipt for the 1,250 colones deposited to the *Migración* account at BCR (Banco de Costa Rica).

4. An application, which was passed out in the line about 7:30 . If you had these items they wrote a number on the copy of your *cédula* and let you inside the gate to proceed to another line, actually the same line in a different place. I was number 80 in the line.

"It took the better part of two hours to get to the window where a person took all my papers and put my copy in their printer and printed my information from their computer on the back of the copy of my *cédula*.

"Next, they instructed me to go to Window 3.

"At window 3 they took four above-mentions items, put them in some order and stapled them together. They told me it would be about an hour and 15 minutes. It was now 9:45.

"We went to the coffee shop and had coffee, talked, read, and at 11:00 returned to Window three. After about five minutes, a person came out with a folder full of papers and began calling names. If you looked remotely like the picture on the *cédula*, they removed the *cédula* from the packet of papers and gave it to you. At 11:17 I had my renewed *cédula* in my hand and we were on our way to the parking lot. We got to the car before the sixth hour was up. So I paid for six hours of parking (3,000 *colones*).

"By around 9 a.m. all of the people in line were inside and I could and I could not tell if they were letting anyone else in. I have heard that they only accept 300 per day without appointments, and only on Thursday and Friday. I also heard that appointments were being made only in person, with a two to three hour window and were for three or four months in the future. Apparently someone else can make the appointment for you. But you have to go to get the renewal."

Long-term residents will have to make many trips to
Costa Rica's Immigrations building in La Uruca.

Immigration and Other Matters

Work Permits

Applicants for work permits must submit the following documents:

1. Letter on certified paper to the Immigration's Temporary Permits Department outlining the reason for the request, with all necessary stamps affixed.
2. Temporary work permit application, available along with the list of requirements at the Immigration information desk in La Uruca district.
3. Four recent passport photographs.
4. A full set of fingerprints, taken at *Puerta* (door) 4 of the Immigration office in La Uruca.
5. Proof of guaranteed income while in the country. This could be provided via a letter from the applicant's employer here.
6. Applicants who will be working for a government or international institution in Costa Rica must provide a confirmation letter from the institution.
7. Photocopy of the photo page and last entry stamp of the applicant's passport.
8. Guarantee deposit of $100 at Immigration's temporary permit department once the permit is approved. If the applicant is also applying for a permit under a residency category, this deposit may be waived. The deposit is refunded when the applicant returns home.

Immigration will approve work permits only for Costa Rican companies authorized by Immigration's Executive Council. Businesses that have a long history of operating in the country are generally considered eligible to receive foreign workers.

Student Permits

For a student permit, an applicant must submit the following:

1. A letter, on certified paper affixed with all necessary stamps, to Immigration's temporary permit department explaining the reason for the permit request as well as the name of the local "sponsor" — a legal resident of Costa Rica, *tico* or foreign, who will accept responsibility for the applicant's actions while he/she is in the country. Letter must be certified by a local attorney or Costa Rican Consul.

2. Application form available at the La Uruca Immigration office's information desk.
3. Four recent passport photographs.
4. A guarantee of $100, which must be deposited with the temporary permit department after the permit is approved. Deposit is refunded when applicant returns home.
5. Proof of the sponsor's income here — a certified letter from the sponsor's employer, financial statements, etc.
6. Photocopy of sponsor's identification card (*cédula*) or residency card (carnet).
7. A full set of the applicant's fingerprints, taken at the Immigration office in La Uruca, *Puerta* (door) 4.
8. Photocopies of the photo page and final entry of the applicant's passport.
9. Registration letter or card from the school where the applicant will study.
10. Minors must present a certified authorization from their parents.

Perpetual Tourist

If you don't want to invest the time and money to become a *pensionado* or resident, you can live as a perpetual tourist in Costa Rica. No paper work or lawyers need to be involved. Just leave for at least 72 hours every three months to renew your tourist visa. Bear in mind that the locals frown upon this, much as we do in our own countries, as this is being done frequently and avoids the "intent of the law." The ARCR recommends you consider some form of residency once you are certain you intend to stay in the country.

You can repeat this process over-and-over again to stay in the country indefinitely. The only disadvantage is that as a tourist you may not work in Costa Rica and it is almost impossible to become a legal resident unless you marry a Costa Rican or have immediate Costa Rican relatives.

If you don't want to bother leaving the country every few months to renew your papers, you can stay in the country illegally. You no longer have to pay the $0.90 fine for each overstayed month. "Perpetual tourists," foreigners who repeatedly overstay their tourist visas, now only pay the country's exit tax. We have personally met many people who have lived as tourists for years without problems; some even started businesses.

Bear in mind that it is always better to have your papers up-to-date because you may be deported almost instantly at the whim of an

Immigration official or if you get into any kind of trouble and are in the country illegally. Costa Rica's Immigration Law gives airport or border officers the right to deport any illegal tourist. We know of a Canadian woman who is now fighting deportation after seven years of being here illegally.

Sometimes airlines give you a hard time if you are not a resident of Costa Rica and try to travel with a one-way ticket.

One of our readers found the solution: "The last time I traveled I was unable to board the flight bound for Costa Rica without an onward ticket. It was the airline that made the fuss, probably because if they bring me to Costa Rica without the onward ticket they can be forced to take me back to where I came from by Immigration (and without pay). Since I was at the counter to collect my boarding pass and ready to "come home," to Costa Rica, I bought a fully refundable ticket to Panama and got a refund in Costa Rica by showing the airline a bus ticket to Panama that I bought for $7."

Extending Your Stay

Every tourist with a valid passport (U.S. citizens, Canadians and most Europeans) has permission to remain in Costa Rica without a visa for up to 90 days.

U.S. and Canadian citizens may enter the country with just a 30-day tourist card or another piece of identification such as a driver's license, passport or birth certificate.

You can get tourist cards from any Costa Rican consulate or embassy prior to your trip or at the airline ticket counter on the day you leave for Costa Rica. Tourist cards can be renewed monthly by applying for an extension called a *prórroga de turismo*. To obtain this extension, you will need your passport, a ticket out of the country (see the section entitled Bus Travel to and from Costa Rica in Chapter 10), three passport-size photos and at least $200 in cash or traveler's checks for each additional month you're staying. Many people opt to pay the fine instead, since this process is such a hassle. It is important to be aware that once you reach the day past your approved visa, you are illegally in the country. Aside from potential deportation, some things this can affect are your right to drive with a foreign license and insurance coverage.

This process takes a couple of days and is a bureaucratic nightmare. To save yourself many headaches, long lines and time, you should go to any local travel agency. Most of the agencies in San José will help extend your tourist card or obtain an exit visa for about $5, even if you didn't purchase your ticket there. This service is worthwhile and usually takes two working days.

The Immigration offices are in the suburb of La Uruca, about a half mile west of the Irazú Hotel. Information may be found online at: www.migracion.go.cr. You may also find information about required passports and visas at www.passportsandvisas.com.

Leaving the Country

Any tourist who has stayed in Costa Rica more than 30 days with just a tourist card will need an exit visa or *visa de salida* to leave the country. Likewise, foreigners who entered Costa Rica using just a passport and overstayed the maximum permitted time of 90 days, will also have to get an exit visa.

To obtain this document, you first need *pensión alimenticia* stamps to prove you have not left dependent children behind. Go to the court buildings or ***Tribunales de Justicia*** (Calle 17, between Avenidas 6 and 8) for these stamps. Then take your passport, the stamps, and your return ticket to the Immigration office to get an exit visa. The whole process takes two working days. As we just mentioned above, most tourist agencies will do all of the running around for a small fee.

One good thing about an exit visa is that it is valid for 10 days from the date it was issued. You can stay in the country another 30 days using this extension, so you can remain in Costa Rica for a total of 100 days.

Costa Rican citizens, retirees and permanent residents must also get an exit visa and *pensión alimenticia* stamps. A foreigner living under any of the three residency categories will pay about $50 for an exit visa.

Everyone has to pay an immigration tax according to their status. You can avoid a lot of hassles and lines at the airport if you pay in San José before going. This tax may be paid in the rear of the basement level of the Bancrédito across from the southwest corner of the Central Park. Take your documents with you, passport or *cédula*, and the cashier will tell you the amount.

Children's Exit Visas

Children under 18, including infants, who remain in Costa Rica for more than 30 days are subject to the country's child welfare laws and will not be permitted to leave the country unless both parents request permission from the National Child Welfare Agency or ***Patronato Nacional de Infancia*** (PANI) (Calle 19 and Avenida 6). This can pose a real problem for a single parent traveling with children who overstay the permitted 90 days. One parent or guardian cannot get exit papers without written permission from the non-accompanying other parent. A Costa Rican Consul in the child's home country must notarize this document.

If you don't adhere to this procedure, your child cannot leave the country. When you go to the airport you have to take your child to a special window where an official form PANI checks to see if the child can be taken out of the country. A travel agent or lawyer may be able to get permission from the PANI if given the child's passport and two extra Costa Rican-sized passport photos.

If your child was born in Costa Rica, the child is automatically a Costa Rican citizen. To exit the country, the child will need an exit permit from the Costa Rican Immigration department if he or she is a minor. The child must have the permission of both parents to leave the country. This can be annoying if the child has to travel a lot with one parent. However, the parents can fill out a special permanent permission form whereby the child can leave country with either parent as many times as necessary until the child is no longer a minor (18). My wife and I did this to make it easier for our son to travel.

Costa Rica's child protection laws can be a real pain in the neck. However, in some cases they can work to your advantage and enable you to stay in the country. All you have to do is have the cooperation of your child's mother.

If you support minor children, you cannot be deported from the country under most circumstances. If a mother wishes, she can ask for an *impedimento de salida*, preventing the father from leaving the country. If the *impedimento* is served, then the only way to leave the country is to pay the equivalent of 13 months' *pensión* (child support) in advance. Although we don't recommend using this method, some foreigners remain in the country indefinitely this way whether they really support their child or not. Your attorney can explain how to use this law to protract your stay in the country.

Here is one resident's experience on leaving the country with minor children: "I am not sure about a non-citizen resident, but for citizens it's just a matter of going down to Immigration with both parents and child and signing a form. Probably better to do this, just in case. The child will need a photograph too, which can be taken there. There are two types of permissions, temporary and permanent. The temporary is only good for certain period of time, say one or three months. It may even only be good for one departure. A permanent one is just that, permanent. The whole idea behind it is to prevent abductions, so if you go with a permanent, it might be a good idea to keep the permission papers separate from the child's passport. When we went, the person working there said that about 75 percent go with a permanent as opposed to the temporary."

By the way, paternity laws are very strict in Costa Rica. If a mother asks for a DNA test and it is positive, the father pays for the test; if it is negative, the mother pays for it. The tests are not cheap, but there is a long waiting list of about three months for these tests.

The *Patronato Nacional de Infancia* handles adoptions in Costa Rica. This process can take a couple of years even for a newborn or child if you satisfy all of the requirements. It is easier and faster if you adopt a child rather than a newborn.

If you father children in Costa Rica, they will be eligible for your Social Security benefits. The U.S. Social Security Administration (SSA) seems to define "natural children" as distinguished from adoptive children. Whether they are born out of wedlock is not an issue.

According to the SSA at: http://www.socialsecurity.gov/pubs/10085. html, "Within a family, a child may receive up to one-half of the parent's full retirement or disability benefit, or 75 percent of the deceased parent's basic Social Security benefit. However, there is a limit to the amount of money that can be paid to a family. The family maximum payment is determined as part of every Social Security benefit computation and can be from 150 to 180 percent of the parent's full benefit amount. If the total amount payable to all family members exceeds this limit, each person's benefit is reduced proportionately (except the parent's) until the total equals the maximum allowable amount."

Costa Rican Citizenship

After living in Costa Rica for a number of years many foreigners decide that they want to acquire Costa Rican citizenship (dual citizenship is permitted.) If you qualify, this is another way to stay in the country legally. As a naturalized citizen, you will have the same rights as a Costa Rican, including the privilege to vote and a Costa Rican passport.

There are some U.S. citizens who give up their citizenship voluntarily to take care of tax benefits for those living abroad. This is an extreme measure and we recommend thinking about the advantages and disadvantages. We heard of one case where the founder of Tupperware moved to Costa Rica about 20 years ago and became a Costa Rican citizen for tax reasons. In this case, millions of dollars were involved. The average person would not benefit from such a move.

There are other benefits of becoming a citizen of Costa Rica for many foreign residents: you can become a member of Costa Rica's Social Security System, the impossibility of extradition of Costa Rican citizens and the mutual visa exemption agreements between Costa Rica and all the European Union countries, Scandinavia, Canada, Japan and Russia.

Naturalization (citizenship) applications are processed and granted by the *Tribunal Supremo de Elecciones y del Registro Civil*, the Costa Rican electoral and civil records. Some consider this institution the fourth most powerful government entity.

You may apply for citizenship if:

1. Married to a Costa Rican for at least 2 years. Article 14, section 5 of the *Constitución Política* and Law 1155 of April 29, 1950, and its reforms, states that a foreigner married to a Costa Rican can apply for citizenship after being married and physically present in Costa Rica for at least two years. The section allows foreigners to reside in Costa Rica without the requirement to become residents under Immigration rules.

Foreign men and women married to Costa Ricans for a minimum of two years, and who have lived in the country for at least two years may also become citizens. The Costa Rican spouse can either be through birth or naturalization. You may also be able to become a naturalized citizen if you have been divorced from a Costa Rica citizen. However, you must comply with both the minimum time requirement for marriage and residence in the country.

2. After five years of residency (accumulated in the country), if Spanish is your first language. More specifically, nationals of other countries of Central America, Spaniards and Ibero-Americans by birth who have resided officially in the country for five years and who fulfill the other requirements that the law requires. Those born in the United States who speak Spanish as a first language do not qualify.

3. After seven years of residency (accumulated in the country) if Spanish is not your first language.

4. Items 2 and 3 require an extensive exam (very difficult and in Spanish) in order to obtain citizenship. Note: Applicants will need to take a written test through the Department of Public Education in geography and the Spanish language. These exams are usually given four times a year. This exam is not easy for most English speakers unless their Spanish is fluent.

Applicants will need to prove they have the financial means to live in Costa Rica. They'll also need a certificate from the computer section of the Department of Immigration showing their exits and entries into Costa Rica from the time they entered Costa Rica to the day they apply for citizenship. Permanent residents and resident investors will need a certificate from the National Immigration Council showing the names of their parents, date of birth and current immigration status.

Residency under the Immigration rules is not required by a foreigner who marries a Costa Rican national and wishes to remain permanently in Costa Rica.

Here is how the process goes:

First, go to the *Tribunal Supremo de Elecciones y Registro Civil*, to the section of *Opciones y Naturalizaciones* in San José.

Ask for an application with all of the instructions, a sample solicitation letter (to be copied verbatim) in Spanish and advice as to where to go for what.

An application must be submitted with:

1. A copy of your *cédula de residencia* (I believe they will make the copy for you at this section).

2. From the Computer Department a certification of the number of passport and list of times you have entered and returned to Costa Rica up to the day you file for Costa Rican citizenship, since your first time from your passport. This can be received from near the bank at *Puerta 7* at *Migración*. It usually takes one week and the cost in stamps is minimal.

3. Certified copy of your birth certificate which is available at *Puerta 2* the same day. Request by 10 a.m. and receive by 2 p.m. This was submitted for your residency initially. (You may use the same one you obtained for Costa Rican residency). In lieu of this last requirement, you may obtain either a certificate from the Immigration Department or from the Tourism Institute showing your date and place of birth, parents' names and a sworn statement of your birth. You will need to have your birth certificate notarized by a Costa Rican Consul.

4. Current copy of marriage documents (*certificado literal de matrimonio*), if using marriage or prior marriage to a *tico(a)*. A birth certificate issued by the Civil Registry for your Costa Rican spouse is also required.

5) A few *timbres fiscales* (stamps) (*19 colones*) *Archivo Nacional* stamps for 5 *colones*.

As far as we know, the United States does not favor dual nationality for its citizens but does recognize its existence. We just checked with the embassy here, and U. S. citizens may obtain Costa Rican citizenship without renouncing U.S. citizenship.

The naturalization process is slow and can take over a year. Once approved, you'll be sworn in at a special ceremony.

Check with the U.S. Embassy in San José for the latest regulations. We know of a number of North Americans who have both U.S. and Costa Rican citizenship. One expatriate friend uses his Costa Rican passport for travel because he claims there are fewer problems than with his U.S. passport.

We suggest consulting a Costa Rican attorney for all the details and specific requirements if you are really interested in this subject. Attorneys charge $700 to $1,000 for this service. However, if you speak fluent Spanish you can do it yourself. There are several people who work outside of the Immigration office who will assist you for a nominal fee.

Once you become a Costa Rican citizen you are entitled to a Costa Rican passport. To obtain a Costa Rican passport you
1. Pay $26 at either Banco de Costa Rica or Banco Nacional before you go to Immigration.
2. Present your national ID card or *cédula* and a photocopy of both sides of it.
3. For children you will need a photocopy of their birth certificate and photocopies of both parent's *cédulas*. You will also have to pay $26 for each child at either of the two banks mentioned above.
4. For children born to foreign parents in Costa Rica, you will need photocopies of their birth certificate, a photocopy of the parent's residency *cédula* or passport and to pay the $26 for each child as above.

Getting Married and Fiancée Visas

Getting married in Costa Rica is really quite simple. All you have to do is complete the required paperwork and have the appropriate documents such as a passport, divorce papers (if you were previously married), birth certificate and any other pertinent information. We suggest consulting your lawyer if you are marrying in Costa Rica to find out exactly what documents are needed and what procedures to follow.

Lawyers can marry people in Costa Rica much like a justice of the peace in the United States. This type of marriage is called *por civil* and is usually quicker than a traditional church wedding or *por la iglesia*. In Costa Rica, people get married either way.

If you choose to have a lawyer marry you, you will need to have two witnesses for the ceremony. Your lawyer will be able to round up a couple of people if you can't find anyone. For additional information about getting married in Costa Rica, go to www.costarica.com/embassy/marriage.

If you are interested in obtaining a fianceé visa, you should be aware of the following process. Marrying a foreign national is a completely different experience than marrying a resident of the United States. In this country, you go down to the license bureau, apply for a marriage license and then tie the knot. When joining your life with an alien spouse, marriage alone does not necessarily allow the married couple to be together in the country. The U. S. government must be petitioned to permit your spouse to live with you in the United States.

When a foreign marriage occurs, the American spouse must file a Petition for Alien Relative and endure many months or even years of separation from his or her new spouse while the petition is approved and finally processed at the foreign consulate abroad.

A citizen of the United States has an additional option available: the fiancée visa. A U.S. citizen can petition for a visa for his or her alien fiancée to allow him or her admission the United States for a period of 90 days, to allow them to prepare for their marriage and life together. The fiancé process can be completed in a much shorter time period than a spousal petition.

Upon entry into the United States, the fiancé(e) is only permitted to remain for a period of 90 days. There are no extensions allowed. During the admission to the United States, the fiancé(e) will receive employment authorization from INS.

The petitioner and beneficiary must marry within the 90-day window or the beneficiary must leave the United States. If marriage to the petitioner occurs, the married couple will then apply for adjustment of status to lawful permanent resident at the INS district office in their area. If the marriage does not occur and the fiance(é) returns to his or her home country within the 90-day period, then the U.S. citizen retains his or her eligibility to pursue options with other potential spouses in the future.

This is intended to provide general information on the visa process. There are many other factors in this complex and ever-changing area of the law. I divorced here several years ago, but as far as I know nothing has changed.

Getting Divorced

1. By mutual consent. This, of course, requires that both parties agree on child support, child custody, dissolution of assets, etc. We believe this can actually be done without a lawyer but wouldn't try it. It may take a year or more for the courts to recognize this, PANI to approve it, etc.

2. The judge can declare divorce by separation if the parties have been approved by the court as separated for one year, which means counting from the date of court approval of the separation. I think you have to attend counseling or reconciliation meetings or something to do this.

3. Separation for at least three years. We are not sure how you prove this.

4. Of course there is divorce for cause, too, but it does not sound like this applies, and is lengthy and usually difficult to prove.

STAYING BUSY AND HAPPY
IN COSTA RICA

Some Sound Advice

Retirement or just living in another country often presents new challenges for people. For the first time, they are confronted with having a plethora of leisure time and the problem of what to do to with it. As you will see throughout this chapter, Costa Rica is a wonderful place to live. In addition to being relatively inexpensive, there are many interesting activities from which to choose. As one of our American friends stated when referring to his busy life in Costa Rica, "My days are so fulfilling that each day in Costa Rica seems like a whole lifetime."

In Costa Rica you have no excuse for being bored or inactive, unless you are just plain lazy. There is a hobby or pastime for everyone regardless of age or interests. Even if you cannot pursue your favorite hobbies, you can get involved in something new and exciting. Best of all, by participating in some of the activities in this chapter, you will meet other people with common interests and cultivate new friendships in the process. You can even spend your time continuing your education or studying Spanish. Most people you meet will also be expatriates, so you probably will not need that much Spanish to enjoy yourself. However, the happiest expats seem to be those who speak Spanish.

They are able to enjoy the culture more fully, mix with the locals and make new friends in the process. If you don't learn the language, you will always be somewhat isolated from the real word here.

Whatever you do, don't make the mistake of being idle. The worst thing you can do is spend all your time drinking in one of the many gringo hangouts in downtown San José. Over the years, we have seen many fellow Americans fail to use their time constructively, and destroy their lives by becoming alcoholics while living in Costa Rica— many have died prematurely. So, use the information we provide in this chapter and take advantage of the many activities Costa Rica offers.

English Books, Magazines and Newspapers

Books, newspapers, magazines and other printed materials in English are available at most leading bookstores, in souvenir shops of larger hotels, and at some newsstands.

Many bookstores carry a large selection of books in English. **7th Street Books**, in downtown San José, is one of the city's best - bookstores (Calle 7, between Ave. 1 and Central, Tel: 256-8251, e-mail: marroca@sol.racsa.co.cr). The North American owners, John and Mark, stock a wide range of new and used books in English

A local bookstore

Why Did You Come Here?
What Do You Do?
By Martha Bennett

There are several species of *extranjeros* living in Costa Rica for a variety of reasons and doing different things. They come to retire, for adventure, to invest or open a business, or to study with one thing in common: changing their life style.

There are tourists. Some come to appreciate the flora and the fauna, volcanoes, beaches and mountains, and observe the Costa Rica culture. Others flock for sports: deep sea fishing, diving, surfing, white water rafting, hiking and hanging out. Everything is available except snow sports. Cultural events may be added on to either group's activities. A third group comes entirely for the bars, casinos and massage parlors. No one comes for the great food which has not inspired restaurants in other parts of the world. No matter, the ingredients are available to create your own cusine.

The people who park here for six months to life do these things and more. Missionaries come for Latin language and culture. Old men come looking for young Ticas. They get them too. This unlikely alliance builds the men's egos and the girls like the upgraded standard of living. Others of all ages earn or supplement their income teaching languages, writing, renting rooms or acting as tour guides. There is a group, usually college educated, who can't find, satisfactory jobs in North America. They are found in the tourist industry or working for international companies. A foreigner can work here if the task is something a Tico can not do. There are regulations, but in Latin countries, these are worked around. A slower pace of life and close family ties appeal to people in high stress jobs who have children. They come for a change of atmosphere. There is crime and substance abuse here, but the tightly knit community provides a healthier climate for raising children.

Retirees participate in many things. Some renovate a dream house. Some persue the World Wide Web. There is a Theater Group, a Canadian Club, Women's club, Scrabble, bridge and T'ai Chi clubs and even a society for refrigeration engineers. The country club set plays golf, graces swimming pools, and dines elegantly. One can study yoga, painting, writing, language, pottery, gardening, holistic medicine and dance.

Remember, living takes longer here. Time is spent finding things, fixing things, cutting red tape and avoiding long lines. But this pace allows more time for reading, observing, listening to music and just being. In Costa Rica, we are more human beings than human doings. *Pura vida*! Pure life!

with an excellent selection of travel, Spanish, nature books and U.S. magazines. They will even special order books for you.

Librería Internacional is a European-style bookstore. This bookstore is not global in name only since it sells books in English, Spanish and German. Locations: Barrio Dent, San Pedro, 300 meters west of Taco Bell, 253-9553; Centro Comercial Multiplaza, second floor, 201-8320; Rohrmoser 200 meters east of El Fogoncito restaurant. 290-3331; Mall Internacional, Alajuela, 442-3800; Plaza Cemaco, second floor, 100 meters north of Garantías Sociales traffic circle, 257-8065; Central Ave., 75 meters west of la Plaza de la Cultura 257-2563; Paseo de las Flores Mall, Heredia.

LibroMax is a discount bookstore chain offering up to 50 percent off on some titles. Locations: second floor Real Cariari Mall; Heredia, across from the parking lot of Ferretería Las 3 Américas; Cartago, across from the Banco Nacional de Costa Rica; Multiplaza Escazú first floor across from Banco Nacional de Costa Rica; Outlet Mall diagonal to the church of San Pedro; Mall San Pedro, main floor; telephone for all stores: 800 LIBROMAX (800-542-7662).

You can also find a good selection of English books in the book section of any of the three **Librería Universal** department stores (Ave. Central, 222-2222) and **Librería Lehmann** (Ave. Central, Calles 1 and 3, 223-1212). **Papyrus** (next to Más x Menos supermarket in Sabana Este, 221-4664) has an excellent selection of magazines, newspapers and paperbacks in English and Spanish. They have another branch in downtown San José.

Mora Books (255-4136, 383-8385) is located in downtown San José in the Omni Building on Avenida 1, between Calles 3 and 5. They have more than 25,000 volumes on display and specialize in used books. **Goodlight Books** (430-4083) in downtown Alajuela offers used books in English.

Some ex-pats order books on line though www.amazon.com and have one of the local private mail services, such as Aerocasillas bring them to Costa Rica. Here is what one expatriate said about importing books this way: "I buy from Amazon, and Aerocasillas would take care of getting it through Customs. If there are any duties to be paid, they ask you to deposit it into their bank account or bring it by their offices prior to them getting it released from Customs. They also will deliver the merchandise to your door. Of course they charge a fee, but I thought it was worth it because once it gets to the address in Miami, it's couriered here to Costa Rica."

Opening an English Language Bookstore in Costa Rica
By Mike Jones

My business partner and I are often asked how we decided to start a bookstore in Costa Rica. We began by listing all the businesses we thought might be interesting to operate and/or potentially profitable. The list we came up with included a pool hall, music store, bar, pharmacy, bagel shop, bookstore and laundromat. As we were mulling over the possibilities, we heard about a bar that was for sale. After talking to the owners of the bar and consulting with our lawyer, we decided to make an offer, contingent upon our being able to discuss with the building's landlord the changes we wanted to make to the bar. When the owners of the bar told us that it wouldn't be possible to talk to their landlord prior to purchase, we balked at the deal, sensing bad faith. A few weeks later, some friends contacted us about an excellent retail location that was becoming available in downtown San José. Because the location is near to the Plaza de la Cultura, a point visited by nearly every tourist, we decided that an English language bookstore, whose main market would be tourists, might work. And so, within the space of two weeks we went from being bar ownwers to bookstore owners.

Our bookstore has now been opened nearly four years, and each year sales have nudged upward. There have been moments of despair, frustration and crisis, but the business appears to have finally left the crawling stage behind and is walking. I never owned a business before in the U.S. and do not think that only four years of business ownership prepares me to give general business advice. What I could instead offer is a handful of tips that relate specifically to expatriate business ownership.

The first relates to your decision about opening a business in Costa Rica. You must decide if you like the country! This is an obvious point, but I have seen many tourists arrive and decide to move here mainly on the basis of having enjoyed their vacation. The rythm of day-to-day existence versus that of tourist life is entirely distinct. If you can pull it off financially, I would recommend first arriving for a six month visit to really test the idea that this is where you would like to live. Even then, you must keep in mind that there is a big difference between living here while not working and living here while running a business; all the things you enjoyed doing when you were free of work obligations, you will find little time for when you are starting up a business.

When you do decide to start a business, be prepared for a dual challenge, you will be facing all the standard problems of business ownership (managing cash, monitoring competition, attempting to increase sales, etc.) at the same time that you are learning a new culture and language.

As you go through the process of trying to decide what kind of business to open, it is common to make a list of kinds of businesses that exist in the home country but do not exist in Costa Rica. For several years we expatriates were clamoring for a bagelry and a micro brewery, and when they did finally arrive they met with considerable success. Nevertheless, it is important to keep in mind the significant cultural differences that exist between the home country and here, and that what works there won't always work here. The expatriate community is not so large that you can succeed simply by targeting that group. You need tico customers too, and disposable income is not too high here. Also, whatever business you choose, it is obviously important as an expatriate to respect the customs and moral standards of this country. One gentleman from Canada entered the store and told me he was planning on opening a topless car wash. I said, "I would suggest doing that in another country."

Expatriate business people need to resist the occasional pull toward paranoia, toward the notion that "they", the locals are all trying to take advantage of me. A more reasonable stance, I think, is to asume that in business everyone is trying to take advantage of everyone, regardless of national origin. So far, our only slightly significant encounters with less than honorable people have been two unfortunate business deals with other expatriate business people, who, because they had no strong family or financial ties to this country, were able to flee the country.

Despite a strong tendency on the part of U.S. media to represent Latin American governments as bureaucratic, inefficient mazes, we have found the opposite to be true in Costa Rica. Nearly all the legal and regulatory issues that we have been required to comply with have generally been handled swiftly and fairly inexpensively by our lawyer. Get a good lawyer whose practice focuses on expatriate clients. A related stereotype about Latin America is that it is rife with corruption. While there are great differences between countries, we have never had anyone approach us and insist that we pay a bribe as a condition for conducting business. True, we have had people offer us the option of a bribe in order to receive faster or better service. I've seen similar things happen in New York. A last word of advice...don't expect to get rich.

Major libraries in the San José area have large collections of English language books and magazines. The place to go for the best selection of books is the **Mark Twain Library** at the **Costa Rican North American Culture Center**, commonly known as the *Centro Cultural*. You can browse all day or check out books. They also have nearly 100 English magazines from which to choose. Call 253-5783 for more information.

The **National Library**, in downtown San José, is not a browsing library but has a large selection of novels and magazines in English. You have to use the card catalog to select your book and then request it at the front desk. Also, the **University of Costa Rica Library** has some materials in English.

There are 55 public libraries in the country. The vast majority of their publications are Spanish language books. Library hours are from 10 a.m. to 6 p.m. In the San José area public libraries can be found in the cities of Desamparados (250-0426), Hatillo (254-1028), Montes de Oca (272-0809), Ciudad Colón (249-3516), Santa Ana (282-9106), Puriscal (416-8300) and Tibás (236-3087).

There is no problem obtaining copies of *New York Times*, *Time* or *Newsweek* in Costa Rica. *The Miami Herald* international satellite edition is now also available in Costa Rica. You can pick up most of these English-language publications at local newsstands, hotels and some bookstores. Other publications available are *Barron's*, *International Herald Tribune*, *Sporting News*, *Sports Illustrated*, *USA Today*, *Wall Street Journal* and *Washington Post*. Obviously you can find almost any publication on line.

Europrensa, S.A. (232-6682), is now offering 320 digitally produced print-on-demand newspapers from 57 countries.

Originally founded in 1992, *Costa Rica Today* is Central America's largest bilingual newspaper (English/Spanish) with more than 100,000 readers. The paper has good information about tourism, retirement and business tips. It is distributed in all of the Central American countries, airports, embassies and consulates abroad and is free. For additional information or to advertise, contact: ***Costa Rica Today***, SJO -117, P.O. Box 0025216, Miami, FL 33102 Tel: 520-0303 Fax: 520-1234, E-mail: editor@costaricatoday.net.

The Tico Times, the largest English-language newspaper published in Central America, is available almost everywhere in Costa Rica. Reading it is an excellent way to keep up with local Costa Rican and Central American news in general. Car sales, cultural activities and other useful information can also be found in this newspaper. The newspaper costs $1 and comes out every Friday.

To subscribe to *The Tico Times* (if you live in the United States), write Dept. 717, P.O. Box 025216, Miami, FL 33102, or e-mail info@ ticotimes.net. If you live in Costa Rica: Apdo. 4362, San José, Costa Rica, Tel: 258-1558. You can read this newspaper on line at: **www. ticotimes.net**.

The *Guanacaste Journal* is a new weekly newspaper with news from the Gold Coast area of Guanacaste.

Inside Costa Rica is another good online publication. It is published daily and has both local and international news articles. *Inside Costa Rica* may be accessed at: **www.insidecostarica.com**.

A.M. Costa Rica is an online newspaper published Monday through Friday. In additional to the usual daily news events and features, there is an excellent classified ads section. You may access this online newspaper at **www.amcostarica.com**. For additional information contact A.M. Costa Rica, Apdo. 6318-1000, San José, Costa Rica, Tel/Fax: 231-7528, E-mail: editor@amcostarica.com.

The Gringo Gazette is a new English-language publication distributed in the western suburbs of San José. You may contact them at gringogazette@yahoo.com.

La Nación, Costa Rica's best Spanish-language daily, has a new online version in English at: **www.nacion.com/In_ee/english**.

Here is a list of all of the Costa Rican newspapers online:

* Al Dia *(Spanish)* .... www.aldia.co.cr
* A.M. Costa Rica *(English)* .... www.amcostarica.com
* Central America Panorama *(Spanish)* ...... www.elpanorama.net
* Costa Rica Today *(English)* ....www.costaricatoday.net
* Cyberprensa *(Spanish)* ....www.cyberprensa.com
* Diario Extra *(Spanish)* ....www.diarioextra.com
* El Financiero *(Spanish)* .... www.capitalfinanciero.com
* El Heraldo *(Spanish)* ....www.elheraldo.net
* Informa-Tico *(Spanish)* ....www.informa-tico.com
* Inside Costa Rica *(Spanish)* ....www.insidecostarica.com
* La República *(Spanish)* .... www.larepublica.net
* Nación *(Spanish)* ....www.nacion.com
* Prensa Libre *(Spanish)* ....www.prensalibre.co.cr
* Semanario Universidad *(Spanish)* ...... www.semanario.ucr.ac.cr
* The Tico Times *(English)* ....www.ticotimes.net

Television and Radio

As in the United States, Costa Rica has satellite cable television, is available in most places in the Central Valley, Liberia, Tilarán, San Carlos, Pérez Zeledón, Orotina and in some beach areas such as Jacó and Quepos. A variety of American television channels provide viewing and entertainment at a low cost from **Amnet** (231-38380, 231-2811 or 231-3939 www.amnetcable.com), **Cable Tica** (254-8858) or **Cable America** (238-1756). You will not miss much TV while living in Costa Rica since these companies offer local channels in Spanish as well as 38 channels in English including CBS, NBC, ABC, FOX, HBO, CNN, ESPN, TNT, the Discovery Channel and more. There is an initial sign up fee of about $25 and a monthly charge of $23. If you want to hook up additional TV in your house or apartment, you will pay only $2.50 extra per month.

Since 1997, **DirectTV** (296-7681, Fax: 296-7684, E-mail: galaxia@racsa.co.cr, www.directv.co.cr) has been available in Costa Rica. With this system you can receive up to 100 channels. The cost has dropped considerably. The basic cost is an $89 installation fee and $23 monthly for the basic package. For the complete movie package including movie and sports channels, the cost is about $45 monthly.

DirectTV systems purchased in the United States will not work with the satellite systems in Costa Rica or the rest of Latin America. NFL and NBA sports packages are now available. Members with DirectTV pay-per-view can now order more than 30 first-run movies per month for about $3 each. Call 201-7171 for more information.

Even better than Direct TV is **Dish TV**, offering digital alternative programming. For a one-time installation fee and a reasonable monthly rate, you get hooked up to digital TV viewing, a "slice of home" so to speak. Some of the many programs offered include Fox, Fox Sports, HBO (10 channels), Showtime (10 channels), NBC, CBS, ABC, Sirius Music and more than a hundred more channels. The programming is from the Dish Network in the United States. You can view what they have to offer at www.dishnetwork.com. We have several friends who have this system and rave about the wide variety of programs. Feel free to contact **Sun Sat TV** (249-0506 or 643-1039, E-mail: chatsbrats@ racsa.co.cr) about any interest or questions you may have concerning satellite TV and the latest technology available in Costa Rica. We have had this system for several years and love it.

Local Spanish-language TV stations are **Teletica** Channel 7 (232-2222), **Repretel** (280-6665) Channels 4, 6 and 11 and **EXTRA TV** 42 (905-398-7288)

Most radio stations play Latin music. However, there are four English language radio stations that play pop, oldies and modern rock. Both foreigners and younger locals listen to these stations since they play a lot of past and present hits. Many of the bus drivers play rock music that the English stations play. **Radio Dos 99.5 FM** plays top -40 music from the 1960s, '70s, '80s and '90s. **Radio 102.3 FM** offers soft rock, classics and oldies. **Radio 107.5 FM**, the country's only all-English radio stations offers 100 percent rock from all decades. **Radio 95.5** plays a great selection of tasty jazz and fusion.

Video and DVD Rentals

Movie buffs will be happy that many video rental shops do business all over the country. For a small initial fee, you can acquire a membership at one of these stores and enjoy many privileges. Most movies you rent are in English with Spanish subtitles.

Video de las Américas (two locations) 253-6545, 257-0303
Video Movies (Curridabat).. 272-5494
Hollywood Video Club (many locations) .. 225-0630, 225-0630
Video Centro Escazú (several locations) 228-8382, 239-4285
Video Happy (Rohrmoser) 231-7295
See the phone book for additional listings.

Shopping

One way to keep active is to go shopping. Although Costa Rica is not as good for shopping as the United States., you can still spend your free time doing some serious shopping, browsing or just window-shopping.

Due to the large number of U.S. and Canadian citizens living in Costa Rica, and a growing number of Costa Ricans exposed to U.S. culture by cable TV and visiting the States, there has been an influx of American products. The only problem is that many of these goods are more expensive in Costa Rica because of import duties.

Everyday, more and more imported goods from the United States are available in Costa Rica. Imported brand name cosmetics, stylish clothing, appliances and some foods can now be found in many stores in San José and other areas catering to foreigners. A number of new stores and shopping centers in or near San José now sell imported items.

In downtown San José, a few specialty shops and a couple of department stores sell American-style clothing and other imported goods. **San José's Central Avenue** or *Avenida Central* has virtually been turned into a pedestrian outdoor mall and walking street. This section begins a block beyond the Central Market and ends at the east end of *Plaza de la Cultura*. **La Gloria** department store, **Lehman** bookstore and the **Universal** department store are all found along this promenade.

A variety of shops around the Central Market offer products at low prices. Prices in this section of town tend to be much more reasonable than in the local mega-malls. Boutiques, a multitude of shoe stores, a record shop, a pharmacy, an outdoor sidewalk café and fast food restaurants such as McDonald's, Burger King and Taco Bell dot both sides of the street.

For you mall-rats or mall-crawlers, there are also a number of local shopping centers that closely resemble U.S.-style malls. **Plaza del Sol**, Costa Rica's first U.S.-style mall, is about five minutes east of San José in Curridabat. A mall is also found at the **Plaza Mayor Shopping Center** in Rohrmoser. It has 21 businesses, including a movie theater, supermarket, bank, pet store, pharmacy and food court. In the suburb of Escazú, home of many foreigners and well-to-do Costa Ricans, a number of U.S.-style mini-malls have sprung up. Most of these newer stores have products that foreigners seek. The **Multiplaza** mega-mall west of Escazú houses a large mall and shopping center. There are the usual chain stores plus a host of specialty shops. **Multiplaza del Este**, in the eastern San José suburb of Curridabat, belongs to the same company. **Terramall**, east of San José on the way to the city of Cartago, is one of the country's newest mall complex.

In Heredia **Paseo de las Flores** has stores, food courts, multiple-screen movie theaters, ample parking and more. A new second section of the mall was added in November of 2006.

The **San Pedro Mall** is one of Central America's largest shopping centers. This mega-mall has more than 260 stores, 35 restaurants, a hotel, a couple of discos, video arcades and parking for 1,200 cars.

A few blocks east of San Pedro Mall is the **American Outlet Mall**. It has more than 150 shops, including a movie theater, a food court and outlet stores. The latter operates like the factory outlets in the United States by selling clothes and other items at discounted prices. **Plaza Real Cariari** has about 125 stores, a food court and theaters.

The **Mall Internacional**, on the main road just before the city of Alajuela, is smaller than the other giant shopping complexes but offers shoppers an ample variety of shops.

Other smaller mini-malls include **Plaza Colonial** in San Rafael de Escazú, Santa Ana 2000 in Santa Ana, San José 2000 near the Hotel Irazú, **Plaza Heredia**, in the neighboring city of Heredia, **Centro Colón** on Paseo Colón, **Centro Comercial Guadalupe** in Guadalupe, the new **Nova Centro** in Moravia, **Plaza América** near Hatillo, **Metrocentro** in the city of Cartago and **Gran Centro Comercial del Sur** south of San José.

There are also music stores, supermarkets and natural food stores located in the San José area. There are even arts and crafts stores and gift shops. Check out **La Casona**, the National Artisan Street Market or the new **International Market of Arts and Crafts** in the suburb of Curridabat to the east of San José.

The newest shopping craze is U.S. warehouse-style mega-stores such as **Wall-Mart** and **Target**. They promise to change local shopping habits and pricing. The new **Hipermás** stores have groceries, furniture, toys, a deli, clothing, appliances and more all under one roof. Best of all, the stores stock a huge amount of U.S. products. Costa Rica's first wholesale shopping club, **PriceSmart**, opened its first store in San José's Zapote district in mid-1999. The chain's stores are similar to the Costco chain in the United States. The company is pioneering the "club" concept in Costa Rica. The store purchases large amounts of imported products, and in turn passes its volume-buying savings on to its club members. They also have stores in Heredia, Escazú and Tibás.

In addition, **GNC** (288-1049) opened several vitamin stores in the San José area. Now all types of vitamins and nutritional products are available.

The **Cemaco** department store chain operates stores in Pavas, Curridabat, Multiplaza, Alajuela and Zapote. The new store in Zapote's **Plaza Cemaco** has 37 departments and more than 60,000 items.

In general, despite the availability of many new imported products and the growing number of malls, mini-malls and specialty shops, shopping in Costa Rica still leaves a lot to be desired if you are used to the North America. Do not expect to find every product you may need in Costa Rica.

As we mention in Chapter 11, if you live in Costa Rica, you have to substitute many local products for items you ordinarily use and do without some things. This is easy due to the variety of similar products available in Costa Rica.

If you absolutely must have products from the States, you can go there every few months—as many foreigners and wealthy Costa Ricans do— to stock up on canned goods and other non-perishable foods, clothing, sundries and cosmetics. We know of one American retiree who goes to Miami every three or four months to buy all the goodies he cannot find in Costa Rica. These frequent trips to the States are unnecessary if you learn to make do with local products.

One thing you may need some time to get accustomed to is the way purchases are handled in some stores. One clerk will wait on you, another will ring up the purchase, and finally you will pick up your merchandise at another window. You find this system in most department stores, pharmacies and older businesses. This system seems to create a lot of extra work for employees and delays for customers. The good news is that every day more and more stores are adopting the American-style one-step self-service system.

A mammoth U.S.-style mall.

Costa Rican Pastimes

Costa Rica has a wealth of indoor and outdoor activities designed for everyone, regardless of sex, age, personal taste or budget. All of us, Costa Ricans, tourists and foreign residents, can participate in river rafting (some of the world's best), camping, walking groups, dancing, racquetball, weight lifting, tennis, baseball, soccer, swimming and surfing, jogging, bicycling, horseback riding and sailing. There are also plays, ceramic classes, movies, bridge clubs, art galleries, social clubs, museums, parks, zoos and more. Dedicated couch potatoes can even stretch out and admire the lovely landscape or work on improving their suntans.

Metro Bowl near the Multiplaza Mall in Escazú is an entertainment center with 20 bowling lanes, restaurants and a pool hall.

There is something for everyone, so enjoy. Check the activities sections of the *Costa Rica Today* or *The Tico Times*. If you read Spanish, there is a listing in the weekend section of *La Nación* called *Buscando Diversión*. You can find activities, cultural events and all sorts of entertainment listed there.

Gyms and health clubs are a good place to socialize and make new friends while working out. Some gyms even have spas, tennis courts and swimming pools. There are more than 32 gyms in the metropolitan area. Call around and visit those in your area to find out which is right for you.

Gold's Gym recently announced that it was going to expand to all of Central America, including Costa Rica. In addition to the gym they already have at the Radisson Hotel, they plan to build a gym in Curridabat, another in Escazú and one more in Rohrmoser. Presently Gold's offers aerobics, Pilates, kick-boxing, yoga, weight training and more. For information, call 256-6689 or E-mail:info2005@ goldsgymcr.co.

If you wish to join a private athletic club, country club or gym, we suggest:

The Indoor Club Curridabat	225-9344
Costa Rican Tennis Club	232-1266
The Spa Corobicí Gym	232-5533
Spa Cariari Hotel Gym	239-0022
Club Olímpico Gym	224-3560
Fitzsimons Gym	296-0264
Hi-Line Gym	232-1464

Soccer is King in Costa Rica
By Chris Howard

If you move to Costa Rica, you will have to learn about soccer or fútbol as it is called here. The game is almost a religion here. Whenever there is a major soccer game, virtually everything comes to a stop and the party begins.

Children of all ages can be seen playing soccer on the weekends. Adults even play informal games during their lunch breaks called mejengas.

Basically, here is how soccer is played:

Using a round ball, a soccer match is played by two teams wearing different colored shirts. Each team consists of not more than 11 players, one of whom is the goalkeeper. An official match may not start if either team consists of fewer than seven players.

Up to a maximum of three substitutes may be used in any match played in an official competition organized under the auspices of the world governing body FIFA, the confederations or the national associations.

In other competition, the rules must state how many substitutes may be nominated, from three up to a maximum of seven. The duration of an official match is 90 minutes played in two halves — each half lasting 45 minutes.

The aim of the game is for one team to score more goals than the opposing team. The winning team is the team that has scored the most goals at the end of the game. Players score a goal when they succeed in moving the whole ball over the opposing team's goal line, between the goalposts and under the crossbar. Players may use any part of their body except their arms and hands.

The ball is out of play when it has wholly crossed the goal line, or touch line - whether on the ground or in the air, and when play has been stopped by the referee.

The game is controlled by one referee on the playing field and two assistant referees placed on opposite touchlines.

The field (or pitch) of play must be rectangular. The length of the touch line must be greater than the length of the goal line.

Length: minimum 90 meters (100 yards), maximum 120 meters (130 yards)

Width: minimum 45 meters (50 yards), maximum 90 meters (100 yards)

International Matches

Length: minimum 100 meters (110 yards) maximum 110 meters (120 yards)

Width: minimum 64 meters (70 yards) maximum 75 meters (80 yards)

The field of play is marked with lines. These lines belong to the areas of which they are boundaries. The two longer boundary lines are called touch-lines. The two shorter lines are called goal lines. The field of play is divided into two halves by a halfway line. The center mark is indicated at the midpoint of the halfway line. A circle with a radius of 9.15 meters (10 yards) is marked around it. A goal area is defined at each end of the field. A penalty area is defined at each end of the field. Goals must be placed on the center of each goal line.

Soccer vocabulary:

árbitro — referee
banda — sideline
cabezazo — header
cancha — field
defensores — defenders
delantero — forward
empate — tie
entrenador — coach
equipo — team
falta — foul
fuera de lugar — offside
fútbol — soccer
jugador — player
Goooooooooooool! — Goal! — Said when some scores.
guardameta, portero, arquero — goalkeeper
marcar — to score
mediocampista — mid-fielder
mejenga — an informal pick-up game
mejengear — to play an informal pick-up game
partido, juego — game
pelota — ball
penal — penalty kick
penales — shoot out
primer tiempo — first half
saque — kick off
saque de banda — side throw-in
segundo tiempo — second half
tarjeta amarrilla — yellow card (warning)
tarjeta roja — red card (expulsion)
tiro de esquina — corner kick
tiro libre — free kick
travesaño — cross-bar

Grupo MultiSpa (Escazú)	289-5051
Grupo MultiSpa (Hotel Radisson)	257-8224
Grupo MultiSpa (Curridabat)	253-0303
Sports Connection	234-9668
Ironman Gym	233-3025
Troyanos Gym (downtown)	222-1641

*Check the phone book for more listings of gyms and private athletic clubs.

Golf

Costa Rica's beautiful scenery and spring-like weather provide a perfect setting for playing golf. It is no surprise the sport has really taken-off over the last couple of years and is on the verge of a boom.

The country promises to become a premier golf travel destination in the future with the opening of public courses. **Golf La Ribera**, the country's first public driving range, recently opened (381-4433) in La Ribera de Belén near a famous water park called *Ojo de Agua*, about 15-20 minutes from downtown. It is a good place to begin your golf experience in Costa Rica. The **Marriott Hotel** has its own range which for now is reserved for the guests. **Parque Valle del Sol** (282-9222) is a nine-hole public course near San José. It is very popular with local expatriates.

Most of Costa Rica's golf courses have rental clubs and provide caddies. There is sometimes a staggering difference in green fees if you are with a member as opposed to showing up at the course as a walk-on. Below is a description of some of the country's courses.

In the Central Valley, the **Cariari Country Club** is one of Costa Rica's two 18-hole course. The Cariari, long considered to be the best course in Central America, has hosted such world-famous golfers as Tom Weiskoff, Ray Floyd and many more. The Cariari is significantly more expensive than Valle de Sol or Los Reyes.

Costa Rica Country Club is a nine-hole course and boasts Central America's most lush clubhouse. You have to be with a member to play but a personal chat with the pro might get you through the gate and on the course. Incidentally, almost all the Costa Rican pros speak English, so a hint at perhaps taking some lessons could help open some doors.

Los Reyes Country Club is just nine-holes for now but designed to be a full 18 eventually. It is about 45 minutes from downtown San José.

Currently there are several places to play golf on Costa Rica's west coast. Over the next few years, more will open. A word of advice: schedule your tee-off for early in the morning or wait for a leisurely, twilight round, because the sun and humidity can be brutal during the day.

Los Sueños Marriott Ocean and Golf Resort is the jewel of the Central Pacific. This beautiful resort is bordered by the Pacific Ocean on one side and rain forest on the other.

Tango Mar Resort and Country Club is a 10-hole course at Playa Tambor on the bottom of the Nicoya Peninsula. You do not have to be accompanied by a member and chances are you will have the course all to yourself.

Garra de León Golf Course at Playa Conchal is one of the best golf courses in Central America. No expense was spared to create a course on a par with the spectacular resort that surrounds it.

Rancho Las Colinas Golf and Country Club, near Flamingo, overlooking Playa Grande in mid-Guanacaste, is one of the newest courses in Costa Rica. This course is the jewel of a quickly developing community.

The Four Seasons Hotel at the Papagayo Peninsula opened its new 18-hole golf course in February of 2004. This course is only opened to guests. Friends who have played there are raving about it.

Golfers may now keep up-to-date on Costa Rica's growing golf scene by subscribing to *Central America's Golf Magazine*, Tel: 231-6931, Fax: 232-1930, E-mail: golftennis@hotmail.com, www.golfmagazine.net.

For golf tours see: **Costa Rica Golf Adventures** at www.golfcr. com.

Museums and Art Galleries

There are more than 30 museums scattered around Costa Rica displaying everything from pre-Columbian artifacts to the history of railways. Many are conveniently located in downtown San José. Most guidebooks have maps showing their locations.

Although not as impressive as museums in the United States or Europe, there is still a lot to see. In general, Costa Rica's museums

A Golfer's Dream
By Landy Blank

My wife Susan and I have lived in Costa Rica for two years. We vacationed here many times before deciding to make our big move. It often feels as though we arrived here just yesterday, at other times I don't remember living anywhere else. However, I will always remember the reaction of family and friends upon being told that we were packing our bags, three large dogs and heading to Costa Rica. I thought everybody would be excited and offer lots of encouragement, but read on to get an idea.

"What will you do on that island?" "We'll bring people to Costa Rica on golf vacations, and actually it's not an island. Oh, I didn't know it was a golf destination, they must have some great courses." "Well, not exactly...They do have one great course, the Cariari, and more are being built." "Landy, they only have one course and you're going to sell golf vacations?" "We're looking ahead and new courses are being built!" "When will they be finished?" "That's a tough question, nobody sems to know, but it will happen! The only way I can find out is to move there, get ourselves settled, and be ready when they do open."

Inevitably at this point in the conversation there was a rolling of the eyes and a small smile would pass across the face of my friend, family member, or golfing buddy.

"Why in the world would you want to leave Charleston? You get to play golf as part of your job at the country club, and then go downtown and eat and drink for free at your restaurant. You must be crazy, I just don't understand."

How do you explain that Costa Rica has gotten into your blood, the people, the beauty, the climate, and despite the bureaucratic hassles, you're determined to live there. It didn't take long for these conversations to become tiresome, and as quickly as possible we made our move to our new home. With dogs, computers, golf clubs, and anything that would fit into a suitcase, we were off to Costa Rica in search of our destiny.

Many of the people we met in Costa Rica expresssed the same incredulity when we told them we were planning to bring groups of golfers here on vacation. The look we got was, "Well, you're not the first crazy gringo to hit Costa Rica, and I wish you all the best luck in the world. Let me buy you a drink!"

(Author's note: In the past two years, two world class championship golf courses have been completed. Costa Rica is quickly becoming known around the world as a golf destination and we are very happy that we made the move!)

provide a good perspective on the history and culture of the country. Here is a list of some of the best museums:

Museums:
Calderón Guardia Museum, Barrio Escalante 255-1218
Costa Rican Scientific and Cultural Center, (for children) 223-7003
Costa Rican Art Museum, Sabana Park 222-7155
Entomological Museum 225-5555
Museum of Criminology. 221-1340
Museum of Contemporary Art 257-7202
Gold Museum 223-0528
Jade Museum 223-5800
National Museum 257-1433
Maritime Museum 661-3666
Juan Santamaría Museum, Alajuela 441-4775

Galleries:
Alterna, Pavas 232-8500
Arte 99, Rohrmoser. 232-4035
Andrómeda, Barrio Amón 223-3529
Café de Artistas, Escazú 228-6045
Contemporary National Art Gallery. 257-5524
Jacob Karpio, San José. 257-7963
José Joaquín García Monge. 221-1329
Kadinsky, San Pedro 234-0478
National Gallery, Children's Museum 258-4929
For more listings, see the yellow pages under *Galerías*.

Excellent Fishing

Costa Rica has some of the world's best sport fishing. Take your choice: fish either the Caribbean or the Pacific, but do not forget those gentle miles of meandering rivers or the fresh water lakes. Lake Arenal is famous for its *guapote* bass. More importantly, most fishing areas are only a few hours' driving time from anywhere in Costa Rica.

Costa Rica is considered one of the best year-round fishing areas in the world. The fishing is outstanding almost all of the time and almost everywhere in Costa Rica. Even when it rains, your chances of catching some excellent sport fish are very good. When it comes to sailfish, tarpon or snook, no place is better than Costa Rica.

If you are really hooked on fishing and want to keep up with the local fishing scene, pick up a copy of the *The Tico Times*. It has an excellent weekly fishing column written by legendary local fishing expert Jerry Ruhlow.

Listed below are some of the better fishing camps, all of which have great accommodations and experienced English-speaking fishing guides.

Caribbean Fishing:
Lucky One	221-0096
Tortuga Lodge	223-0333
Parismina Tarpon Rancho	235-7766
Casamar	381-1380
Río Colorado	232-4063 or 232-8610

Pacific Fishing:
Flamingo Bay Pacific Charters	680-0444 or 680-0620
Papagayo Excursions	680-0859
Oasis del Pacífico (Nicoya)	661-1555
Sports Fishing Quepos	233-9135
Costa Rican Dreams (Quepos)	777-0593

Los Sueños Marina in the Central Pacific.

A Fisherman Finds a Home in Costa Rica
By Todd Staley

A writing assignment first brought me to Costa Rica in 1987. Being an outdoor journalist, I was very excited to test some of the country's "world famous sportsfishing". This trip brought me in contact with the late Archie Fields and we became immediate friends. While sitting on the veranda of his famous Rio Colorado Lodge, I asked Archie if he ever needed someone to run his lodge I would like to be considered. He chuckled and said I was about number 1000 on the list.

I returned to the States and told all that would listen that I didn't know how, but one day I would be living in Costa Rica. In the meantime I sought out other Costa Rican writing assignments and began bringing groups of fishermen down to Costa Rica.

In June of 1991 Archie called my house in the US and asked me to "think" about coming down and managing his fishing lodge. I took less than three seconds to think it over. In the next three months I condensed my life belongings to 7 suitcases and 35 fishing poles and headed for Costa Rica.

In Barra del Colorado where I lived there are no cars. The river, creeks and canals are the streets and avenues. I worked long hours often going as many as three months without a day off and loved every second of it. I used Norman Paperman, the character in Herman Wouk's "Don't Stop the Carnival" as my relief when problems arose concerning employees or guests.

I was awestruck by the culture of the Caribbean side of Costa Rica, especially the stories told to me by the older generations. I met people with zero education but with more wisdom than anyone I had met in my life. The people are a mix of Spanish, African, several types of Indian and Chinese. For the first time in my life, through this experience, I came to believe in "magic" both black and white.

For nearly five years I lived in the jungle. Today I'm in the concrete jungle, but you would have to drag me back kicking and screaming the whole way for me to give up the lifestyle I have grown accustomed to in Costa Rica.

What worked for me is that the first thing I did was throw any American attitude I may have had down the river that flowed in front of the lodge and immersed myself in the culture, language and people. *Tuanis*!

Tango Mar (Tambor)	661-2798
Golfito Sports Fishing	775-0353
Reel'n Release Sportfishing (Dominical)	771-1903
Blue Marlin Fishing (Flamingo Beach)	654-4043

Freshwater Trout Fishing:

Aventuras Tilarán (Arenal)	695-5008
Finca Zacatecales	771-1732

Some of these fishing companies, camps and lodges provide overnight accommodations that include meals. Fishing equipment and boats are also available.

For a listing of other fishing camps and tours, read the *The Tico Times* or consult **Tico Travel** at **www.ticotravel.com**.

Pristine Beaches

Unlike many resort areas in Mexico and Latin America, Costa Rica's beautiful tropical beaches and 767 miles of coastline stretching along two oceans are virtually unspoiled. Water temperatures are very warm so you can stay in the water all day.

There are many white-and dark-sand beaches and numerous resorts along the west coast.

In the northern Guanacaste area, the best beaches include: Playa Naranjo, Playa Panama, Playa Hermosa, Playas del Coco (a favorite gringo hangout), Ocotal, Bahía Pez Vela, Playa Potrero, Playa Flamingo, Playa Brasilito, Conchal, Playa Grande, Playa Tamarindo, Playa Avellanas and Playa Junquillal.

As we move south, the following beaches are scattered along the coast of the Nicoya Peninsula: Playa Azul, Playa Nosara, Playa Sámara, Playa Carrillo, Playa Coyote. Playa Montezuma, on the southeastern tip of Nicoya, is a nice beach.

Moving even farther south, along the central and southern Pacific coast are Puntarenas (Costa Rica's main port), Boca Barranca (good surfing beach), Mata Limón, Playa Tivives, Playa Tárcoles, Playa Escondida, Playa Herradura, Playa Jacó, Playa Hermosa, Esterillos, Quepos, Manuel Antonio (considered by many to be the most beautiful beach in Costa Rica), Playa Dominical and the beaches around the towns of Uvita and Ojochal.

On the Atlantic side, some beautiful beaches are: Playa Bonita (Portete), Punta Cahuita (beautiful beach), Puerto Viejo, Punta Uva and Playa Manzanillo.

Beach safety is very important in Costa Rica. Inexperienced swimmers should only wade in the water. You should also be careful around surfers. Never swim alone. Be aware of rip-tides. If caught in a rip tide, don't panic! Swim parallel to the shore until you are clear of the current. If you cannot break free, let the current take you beyond the breakers. Then swim diagonally toward the shore. Never try to swim against the current.

Do not leave your belongings unattended. If you need to leave your things, ask someone you know to watch them until you return.

Surfing and Diving

Surfers of all ages will be pleased to know that Costa Rica is quickly gaining popularity on the worldwide surf circuit due to its warm weather and great waves. The water is so warm a wetsuit is never needed. Surfing attracts about 250,000 tourists yearly. So, about one out of five tourists come to surf. The sport also generates about $275 million a year in income.

The country boasts close to 40 prime areas for surfing on both the east and west coasts. In Guanacaste, many prime surfing locations line the peninsula from tip to tip. **Roca Bruja** (Witch's Rock) inside Santa Rosa National Park is famous for its tubular waves. Other recommended places to surf in Guanacaste are Playa Grande, Tamarindo, Nosara, Playa Coyote, Malpaís and Manzanillo.

In the Central Pacific region, **Playa Jacó** and the surrounding area is also worth checking out. Nearby **Playa Hermosa** has been host to many surfing tournaments and is steadily gaining popularity. Esterillos Oeste, Esterillos Este, Bejuco, Boca Damas, Playa El Rey and Playa Matapalo are other options in the Central Pacific area. Farther south is Dominical, which is considered a top spot for surfers.

Pavones in the southern Pacific area is a legendary surf spot famous for its endless waves and touted as having the world's longest rideable left break. Try **Matapalo**, located near the Panamanian border. "*Salsa Brava*" at Puerto Viejo and Manzanillo on the east coast have good surfing. There are numerous a surfing schools in Costa Rica, and **Tico Travel** offers surfing tours to the country.

To find out about surfing lessons, see www.wavescr.com, and for information about surfing, see www.crsurf.com.

Schools of fish, turtles, grouper, whales, rays and other species make Costa Rica a great place for divers. Most of the best diving areas are found in Guanacaste around Playas del Coco, Tamarindo, Flamingo and nearby beaches. In the southern Pacific area the diving is good at Isla del Caño just off the Osa Peninsula. The waters teem with many interesting species. We have friends in the area who dive there frequently. The Caribbean coast has famous diving off Cahuita and at Long Shoal off Manzanillo.

During the rainy season, from May to November, visibility may often be obscured in some areas. To find out about the country's diving, see www.costaricadiving.net, www.richcoastdiving.com or www.aquacenterdiving.com.

Boating

With miles of beautiful coastline along the country's Pacific coast, Costa Rica is a boaters paradise. Currently, there are a couple of ports and docking facilities along the coast. **Los Sueños** is the only international marina at this time. It boasts modern docking facilities including potable water, electricity, 24-hour security, mini-self- storage units, a state-of-the-art fuel station, a marine supply store, bar, restaurants and more. For more information, call 637-8886 or 1-866-865-9759toll-free, or visit www.lsrm.com. Information is also available at http://portfocus.com/costa_rica.

Recently the Costa Rican Tourism Institute (ICT) approved new marinas in Quepos and the southern Pacific port of Golfito. The former is under construction; the latter will have more than 200 slips. A new marina is under construction in Flamingo in the north Pacific area, and the ICT is currently studying applications for 15 other marinas on the Pacific Coast.

Parks for Nature Lovers

Costa Ricans take pride in their extensive national park system. The country is rich not only in natural beauty but in all varieties of wildlife. Costa Ricans have set aside 25 percent of their territory and established 36 national parks and preserves to protect the flora and fauna of their country. This is reportedly the largest percentage of any country in the world. In fact, Costa Rica is in first place in ecological tourism in the world.

Five percent of the world's biodiversity can be found in Costa Rica. The variety of birds, butterflies, amphibians, mammals, trees and flowers has to be seen to be believed. The country has 850 species of mammals, 218 species of reptiles, 160 species of amphibians, 845 varieties of birds, 360,000 species of insects and 1000 varieties of orchids as well as 10,353 species of other plants.

Costa Rica's parks are in every region of the country, with some parks more accessible than others.

Additional information and a list of parks may be obtained by calling 233-5673, 233-5284 or 233-4160. Most hotels and tourist information centers can be helpful to nature lovers. Foreigners pay about $6 admission and Costa Ricans and residents $1 to enter Costa Rica's parks. After an international uproar over hikes in park fees, the "Green Pass" was instituted to offer the most affordable way to visit Costa Rica's world-famous parks. For $29, you receive a coupon booklet with four tickets to any national park and one ticket to one of 10 parks.

Costa Ricans take the same pride in their urban parks. Every neighborhood in Costa Rica, from the biggest cities to the tiniest villages, always has a park usually adjacent to the Catholic Church. San

Your whole family can have fun at Waterland aquatic park.

José's **La Sabana Park** is the country's largest city park. The park is crisscrossed by miles of jogging, biking and walking trails. *Ticos* flock by the hundreds to this park to indulge their love of family, children, sports and the outdoors. Go to the park any Sunday and you will see people walking, jogging, picnicking, cycling or playing soccer on one of the many playing fields.

There are also free tennis and basketball courts. The park is located at the site of the old national airport and the terminal building now houses the Costa Rican Art Museum. La Sabana is also the home of the National Stadium and National Gymnasium, where events of all types are held. There is an Olympic-size swimming pool just west of the gymnasium. In the center of the park, a large lake and fountain attracts many people. It is a favorite gathering spot for families.

Another popular weekend destination in San José is **Parque de la Paz**. It does not have the peaceful seclusion of La Sabana, but it still has all the activity. The park is set around three artificial lakes. **Waterland** is the country's first U.S.-style water park. There are several pools, water slides, miniature golf and a soon-to-be-completed pool with artificial waves. An even more spectacular water park is being built a few miles off the coastal highway between Quepos and Dominical. When completed, it will have artificial waves and a whole lot more.

Where to Make New Friends

You should have no problem making new friends of either sex in Costa Rica, but you might have some difficulty meeting Costa Ricans if you speak little or no Spanish. You will be surprised how many *ticos* speak some English and are dying for the chance to perfect their English-language skills while you work on your Spanish. Perhaps you can find someone with whom to exchange language lessons. This is a good way to make new acquaintances and learn how Spanish is really spoken.

You most certainly will find it easier to meet fellow Americans in Costa Rica than in the United States, because Americans living abroad tend to gravitate toward one another. Newcomers have only find an enclave of fellow countrymen to make new friends.

You cannot help bumping-into other Americans since Costa Rica is such a small country (more than 50,000 *gringos* live here permanently). This is especially true if you live in one of the areas where many North Americans reside, such as Escazú, Heredia, Rohrmoser or along the

Pacific beaches. Another good way of contacting other foreign residents is by participating in some of the activities listed in the Weekend section of the *The Tico Times*. This newspaper serves as a vital link within the foreign community, or "*Gringo* Grapevine" and helps to put you in touch with a whole network of expatriates and the services they offer.

At any of the local *gringo* watering holes in downtown San José, such as Nashville South, the New York Bar, the Casino Colonial or Mac's American Bar near the La Sabana Park, you can watch live sporting events from the United States on cable TV or simply shoot the breeze with your compatriots. Many Americans also congregate at the Plaza de la Cultura and at McDonald's across the street, where they linger over coffee every morning and watch the beautiful women pass by.

You have no reason to be lonely unless you want to be. Just be yourself and you will find Costa Rica is just the place for you. Oh yes, we might add that there are poetry readings, art and sculpture exhibitions as well as other activities where people can easily socialize. The Costa Rican-North American Cultural Center has many events where you can also make new acquaintances.

A group of expats having coffee at a local hangout.

Here is a sample of the many organizations.

CLUBS AND ORGANIZATIONS

Aikido Club	289-7479
American Legion Post 11	233-7233
American Legion Post 12	775-0567
Canadian Club	282-5858
Chess Club	384-0936
Democrats Abroad	290-5798
Disabled American Veterans	443-2508
English-Spanish Conversation Club	260-4869
Internet Club	220-0714
Investment Club of Costa Rica	256-5075
Lions Club	670-0447
Mac User Group	257-2160
Mountain Bike Club	290-7870
National Bridge Association	253-2762
Newcomers' Club	232-3999
PC Club	224-9926
Readers Club	228-9167
Republicans Abroad	239-2262
Rotary Club	222-0993
Spanish/English Conversation Club	390-9759
Singles Club	289-8433
Women's Club of Costa Rica	282-6801

* For a complete listing of clubs and related activities, look under the weekly "What's Doing" section in the *Tico Times* or see *Costa Rica Today*. You may also check out the Association of Residents of Costa Rica's community calendar. Call 233-8068 for more information.

Love and Permanent Companionship

If you are looking for someone for romance, Costa Rica might just be the right place for you.

Ladies will find gentleman admirers if they so desire. Due to *machismo*, Costa Rican men are more flirtatious and aggressive than North American men. Most Costa Rican men think foreign women have looser morals and are easier conquests than *ticas* (Costa Rican women). Be careful to take time to develop a long-term, meaningful relationship and do not rush things.

As one local expat pointed out, "*Tico* men have the best *labia* in the world. *Labia* when used in slang, means 'rap.' Costa Rican men are charming, witty, and know how to treat a woman. They can seduce almost any woman, regardless of nationality. I have a few *tico* friends that could get a woman into their car and to a *mirador* overlooking the city within five minutes of meeting them.

"Usually, however, these relationships, if you can call them that, don't last too long. The conquest is a big part of the *tico* male's psyche, and then it's off to the next one. Don't be fooled by these modern-day *Casanovas*, that is of course, unless you want to."

Many single middle-aged women have a tough time finding a mate because they cannot compete with the young curvaceous *ticas*. As one expat woman put it, "We just happen to live in a country of traffic-stopping gorgeous women, — all of whom seem to have been raised in the Geisha School of Relating to Men. If you are planning to move here based on some dream of meeting a Ricky Martin or other Latin stud, think again."

Furthermore, if you do meet a Latin man, he may have a hard time handling an independent American woman. Latin men also like to have a lot of girlfriends on the side. As we mention in Chapter 1 many Latin men measure their virility by the number of women they can seduce.

Men of any age will have no problem meeting Costa Rican women. The women in Costa Rica seem to like older, more experienced men. It is not unusual to see a wife who is 10 to 20 years younger than her spouse. This practice may be frowned on in some countries but is accepted in Costa Rica. Many retirees we know claim to feel rejuvenated and to have a new lease on life after becoming involved with younger women. Costa Rican women have an unparalleled reputation as being the most beautiful, flirtatious and accessible women in Latin America, including Brazil. The ladies of Costa Rica are more warm-hearted and devoted than their North American counterparts. They consider you a joy. One retiree we know boasts, "The women here really know how to treat you like a king!"

A man doesn't even have to be rich to meet women; a $1,500 to $2,000 Social Security check translates to a millionaire's pay in Costa Rica.

Here is what one expat's Costa Rican wife said about her relationship in a recent edition of *The Tico Times*. "Most of the time when a young woman marries an older man, people think she's doing it for the money. I like older men. They are experienced; they've had a lot of fun

How I Found Love in Costa Rica
By Brian

My name is Brian and right now I am about to take a beautiful lady on tour of Southern California. And, at the end of our drive, she will come home with me. She is my lovely *Tica* wife, Yanory and this is her first day in her new home. I met Yanory a year ago in San Jose at an agency called Spanish Eyes.

I first heard of Spanish Eyes through a fellow surfer during one of my trips to Playa Hermosa to surf. He said it was a great way to meet ladies from Costa Rica. Having been a widower 6 years, I was feeling lonely and wanted to find a woman who was kind, sweet, gentle and loving but was not sure how to approach the ladies of Costa Rica.

Once I contacted Spanish Eyes and met Tom and Purita, I felt comfortable and sure that together we would find that perfect lady for me. I met some beautiful women and made some lifetime friends. About a year ago, Purita introduced me to Yanory, a quiet, soft spoken wonderful young woman who captured my mind and heart. We dated and I found myself coming back to

Costa Rica as often as I could to see her. We spent Christmas together and I knew that we were meant for each other so I asked her to marry me. We married in April and began the process for her spousal visa. The process took only 3 months which is unusually fast.

In less than a year, I met my future wife, married her and she is now with me in our home in California. It all seems so easy. But, every step of the way, Purita and Tom were there to answer questions for me, to take my phone calls and answer my questions and to help in any way they could.

Spanish Eyes Introductions is about service. I still do not understand how they find the time to give every client the personalized service that they do. And, how they can recommend the perfect ladies for you to meet. Yanory was not one of my first choices, but a recommendation made by Purita. To this day I do not know how she knew that Yanory would be so perfect for me.

in the past, so they start to think, 'I want to stay now with someone for the rest of my life.' Plus they have their life set up, so they have time to spend with their woman."

With Costa Rican men close to her age, she says, their behavior changes after marriage. With Costa Rican men, you are a princess, but when you get married the whole thing changes: "You are going to have my children. I'm working, so you should make my dinner, wash my clothes." The women get submissive and the men get possessive.

"Costa Rican men don't see their women in the home being the porn star they watch on TV. *Ticos* think the woman at home is pretty, sweet and the mother of their children."

No wonder Costa Rican women are highly sought by foreign men. However, before becoming involved with a Costa Rican woman, you should realize many cultural differences can lead to all kinds of problems, especially if you do not speak Spanish fluently. I have seen so many disasters with people who try to create a relationship without a common language. If a Costa Rican woman is in your future, you are going to have to be able to communicate with her. Even if she speaks some English, the nitty-gritty type of communication that a real relationship requires will definitely require some effort on your part. Men need to seriously consider studying Spanish if they want to have a successful relationship with a native Spanish speaker.

Generally, Latin women are more jealous and possessive than American women, and tend not to understand our ways unless they have lived in North America. Also, be aware that because of their comparative wealth, most Americans, especially the elderly, are considered prime targets for some unscrupulous Latin females.

As we alluded to at the end of the first chapter, in some cases there is another bad side of marrying a Costa Rican woman. You can end up supporting her whole family, either directly or indirectly, as many foreigners complain. There is an out-of-print book, *Happy Aging With Costa Rican Women — The Other Costa Rica*, by James Y. Kennedy. It tells all about the trials and tribulations and experiences many *gringos* have with Costa Rican women. You may be able to find a used copy in a second-hand bookstore in San José or borrow it from a local expatriate.

We advise you to give any relationship time and make sure a woman is sincerely interested in you and not just your money. You will save yourself a lot of grief and heartaches in the long run. Since prostitution is legal and available to men of all ages, be careful of the ladies of ill repute. Many foreigners, after inviting one of these females to spend the night, wake up the next day without the woman and minus wallets and other valuables.

One scam we recently heard of involves a well-dressed woman with a brief case who approaches strangers. She claims to be from another Latin American country and wanting to celebrate her birthday. She says she is alone and has nobody to celebrate it with her. She then invites the unsuspecting victim to accompany her to a bar for a drink. Once in the bar, she slips a drug into the glass of the foreigner. Within minutes he is unconscious. The woman then relieves him of his cash and credit cards. She then takes the credit cards to an accomplice who quickly charges large amounts of money to the cards. So, never drink from a glass or bottle that has been out of your sight.

Most single men can avoid getting involved with gold diggers, prostitutes or other troublesome women if they know where to look for good women. The personals section of the *The Tico Times* is an excellent place to advertise for companionship. It is relatively inexpensive and many Costa Rican women read this section each week. Check out the current or past issues of the *The Tico Times* for ideas on how to write one of these ads.

One American we know ran an ad in the *The Tico Times* and the local Spanish newspapers and ended up screening hundreds of women before finding his ideal mate. As far as we know he is still happily married. Taking classes at the university is another way to meet quality women. The University of Costa Rica in San Pedro is full of beautiful, well-educated females. Cafés, restaurants, bars and other places around the university are good places to meet women. If you have Costa Rican friends, they will usually be able introduce you to someone worthwhile.

The best places for anyone to meet nice women who are sincere and honest tend to be where they would be almost anywhere. Go to church or get involved in a community service project. Most people meet their friends and mates at work. So work at something, even if as a volunteer. If you have Costa Rican friends, they will usually be able introduce you to someone worthwhile.

Meeting people in bars, nightclubs, at the beach, etc., is generally a lousy way to meet someone you really want to have a relationship with anywhere in the world.

Probably the most effective way to meet quality Costa Rica women is through an introduction service. **Spanish Eyes Introductions** provides such a service and screens their women very carefully to protect their clients. In addition to their standard services, they offer parties for their members to meet women. We have several friends who are members and rave about this service. You may contact them at: Tel: 289-5271 or 228-7389, E-mail: info@spanisheyesccostarica.com or see www.spanisheyescostarica.com.

The key is to find a nice, traditional Costa Rican woman and avoid getting involved with "bad" Costa Rican women. Costa Rica has plenty of working girls and hustlers. They hang out at the popular bars and discos specifically to pick up guys. They also go shopping in the malls, ride buses and go to grocery stores. So just because you have met a nice girl in a typical working-girl hang-out does not mean you have met a quality person. If you know what to look for, they are easy to spot.

Many men have knowingly and unknowingly married bad women. Some girls are honest and will directly ask you for money. The hustlers are more dangerous because their *agenda* is to really take you to the cleaners, and they do not rule out marrying you to achieve this objective. Some men say they have lost everything from airline tickets that are cashed instead of used, to large sums of money the girls claim they need to get visas, houses and more. These are the women who contribute to the bad stories you may hear about some Costa Rican women. Unfortunately, the hustlers are the easiest girls to meet in many instances and a good number of men fall into this trap.

A very small number of these women will become good wives, find religion, etc. They are often women who have been sexually or otherwise abused at a very young age, so the problem is very deeply rooted. Your realistic chances of converting them are very slim. No matter how gorgeous the girl is, it is just not worth it.

The best way to spot a bad girl is her profile. They never have a job, never live with their parents, never have phone numbers and never invite you to their home or introduce you to their friends or family. They do not want to leave any trail for you to track them down later. They typically come from very poor backgrounds and have very little education, rarely completing high school.

They are quite aggressive and target older Americans. Often they speak a little English and will start up a conversation with you or smile at you until you make the first move. They will appear friendly and sincerely interested in you. They are always attractive or very young. They will always ask for your phone number.

Perhaps the best way to politely get rid of one of these women is to ask them to loan you a little money. You will immediately see their interest disappear. Actually, a nice woman in Costa Rica might just loan you the money.

Women you see working in stores are usually poorly educated and from poor families. Some may show an interest in an older American who is friendly with them, but the relationship is likely to be overly influenced by a poor woman looking for a rich American husband.

Foreign men should beware of the so-called "Costa Rican set-up." We have heard countless stories where Costa Rican women get pregnant as a ploy to get a foreigner to marry them. We believe it is our duty to alert men about this underhanded and self-centered method of ensnaring them into an unwanted relationship.

In general, a nice Costa Rica woman typically lives with her parents until she gets married. Single daughters are not encouraged to get jobs unless the parents are very poor. Instead, they are expected to help with taking care of the house or study.

Quality Costa Rican women from traditional family backgrounds are raised to take care of their man. They can be quite possessive and jealous at times, but this is only because they are very emotional and deeply in love with their man. They tend to seek out long-term relationships, starting at a very young age. It is quite rare for Costa Rican women to have any interest in casually dating many different men.

One of Costa Rica's beautiful women.

When approached by strangers, they are friendly and helpful by nature; this is their culture. All Costa Ricans value making new friends. Americans often misread this friendliness and think the woman has a romantic interest in them. In order for the woman to develop any romantic interest in you at all, she has to first know from a trusted third party that you are looking for a long-term relationship. After a brief encounter, a decent woman will never ask for your phone number. If you ask for her number, she will always give you the wrong number in order to avoid appearing rude. Nice women live with their parents and would never want to have strange men calling their house. From a romantic interest point of view, quality Latin women are very difficult to meet.

As we alluded to earlier, some Costa Rican women prefer older men. Most Costa Rican women meet a boy in high school and are only interested in men their own age. However, about 40 percent do seriously prefer older men. We have met many Costa Rican friends who are happily married to women 10 to 25 years younger than them.

If the woman is convinced you are seriously looking for a long-term relationship, she will then start to show an interest in getting to know you better. Her initial physical attraction to you will usually be of very minor importance to her. Her main interest will be focused on your personality: Are you are a kind person? Can you offer minimum security to raise a family? Do you sincerely care about her family? Would you make a good father?

Over the years we have encountered a lot of foreigners who end up not using common sense and get involved with people with whom they would probably never associate back home. This brings us to the story of "Dumb and Dumber."

Dumb came to Costa Rica about 12 years ago from the United States, where he was a successful businessman. Almost upon arriving here, he became romantically involved with a woman of ill- repute. He was basically too lazy and busy getting drunk to find a quality mate. Over the course of his relationship, he lost about $300,000 because he entrusted his business dealings to his girlfriend. After splitting up with her and having to give her half of everything he owned because of their common-law situation, he goes and gets involved with another women who will probably "take him to the cleaners" someday.

Dumber is even more stupid than Dumb. He came to the country as a millionaire. The first thing he did was get romantically involved with a woman of the night. Dumber also spent most of his time in bars, like Dumb. Consequently, when he broke up with his lady friend, after a few years together, he had to pay her about $50,000. He is now with another woman and most likely supporting her whole family. He will probably end up broke like Dumb. Neither Dumb nor Dumber speak Spanish nor have made any effort to understand the locals and constantly refer to them in derogatory terms.

The majority of foreign men who come to Costa Rica don't share Dumb and Dumber's fate. Nevertheless, they should learn a lesson from this story.

A Walk on the Wild Side

The author of this guidebook feels it is his responsibility to paint a realistic picture of all of the aspects of living in Costa Rica. He would not be doing a service to our readers if he did not cover the subject of prostitution. However, let it be known that in no way does he condone the sexual exploitation of minors. In this section he only provides information about sexual relationships between consenting adults.

For some people, Costa Rica is a sexual paradise. Like Thailand, the Philippines and many other countries outside of the United States, prostitution is permitted and looked upon with general acceptance in Costa Rica. As in the rest of Latin America, many males have their first sexual experience with prostitutes. In order to control the propagation of venereal disease and AIDS, prostitutes are required by the government to undergo regular health checkups by the Ministry of Health or *Ministerio de Salud* in order to practice their trade legally. Most upscale brothels make sure their employees have their health papers and tests up to date.

It is therefore not surprising that many foreigners are attracted to Costa Rica because of the availability of women. In San José there is a myriad of bordellos, cabarets, escort services, massage parlors and bars where you can find female company. One Costa Rican remarked jokingly when questioned about the number of whorehouses in San José, " In order to put a roof over all of the houses of ill repute, you would have to cover the whole city."

We have interviewed a few tight-fisted residents and retirees who think just because they live here they should pay less for sex than tourists. Consequently, many of them go to the "houses of ill repute" that dot Calle 6, just north of the Central Market. Prices are "rock bottom" and you probably get what you end up paying for. We don't recommend venturing into this area at night. However, none of the people interviewed have ever had problems during the day.

In the *"Gringo* Gulch" area near Morazán Park two places come to mind. **Key Largo** is an institution and has been around for more than 25 years. Located in a beautiful colonial mansion directly across from Parque Morazán, the place looks like a scene taken right out of a Humphrey Bogart movie. It has recently been remodeled and offers live music and dancing nightly.

The Blue Marlin Bar at the Hotel Del Rey is under the same ownership as the Key Largo and is the place to meet women of the night. Most evenings are standing room only in the bar. During the day the bar is a gathering place where local expats and tourists "shoot the bull." The Hotel Del Rey also offers a casino and fine dining

There are a number of cabarets and nightclubs where men can also find female companionship. Most of these establishments try to get you to buy expensive drinks and run up a large tab. It is not unusual to be stuck with a large bill in a short period of time. To avoid surprises, we suggest you do not buy any women more than one or two drinks. The management can be very nasty if you complain about your bill. Here are the most popular cabarets and night clubs: **Club Hollywood** (232-8932), across from the south side of La Sabana Park; **Pure Platinum** (256-9989), Avenida 3 between Calle 10 and 12 and **Night Club Olympus** (233-4058), Central Street, one block north of Hotel Europa. Most of these establishments offer floorshows, Jacuzzis, massage rooms, VIP rooms, exotic dancing and a stable of women from which to choose. **Tango India** (290-1235, www.tangoindia.net), and **KRISIS** (222-7640) are other hot spots worth checking out.

About a dozen escort services operate in the San José area. Most of these services advertise in local newspapers. You may find many of the local escort services by going to search engines like Yahoo, Google or Altavista and typing in the keywords "Costa Rica escorts."

If you are looking for a relaxing massage and steam bath, there are a number of massage parlors to cater to your needs. Prices range from about $15 for a straight hour-long therapeutic massage to $35 for a massage with "the works," or *masaje completo*. As a rule these places are very clean and provide a secure, discret atmosphere. **New Fantasy** (221-4916), located two blocks north of Morazán Park in San José, is very popular among foreign residents. It is located in Barrio Amón, on Avenida 9 and Calle 7, from the Parque Morazán (in front of the Holiday Inn), 200 meters or two blocks to the north, a right turn and you are there. It is frequented by foreign residents, Costa Rican men of means and tourists. The nearby **Sportsmen's Lodge** (221-2533) is another place to find female company. Check out its website at www.sportsmenscr.com. The **747**, located on Calle 6, one block south of Avenida 7, is also a favorite. **Idem**, Avenidas 8-10 and Calle 11, has beautiful women and is considered one of the best massage parlors in the San José area. In western San José you will find **Oasis Masajes** (255-1182) and **Veronica's** (256-7354).

A map of San José's hottest spots can be found at www.dongordo.com/dongordoSJmap.php. There is a better map at www.costaricaticas.com. However, you have to be a member to access it.

There is a good online book that can be used as a guide to all of San José's erotic places, called *Passion in Paradise*. See www.passioninparadise.com to find out how to order this publication. Also check out www.costaricasex.com.

Check out www.costaricamongering.com to get a copy of *Living the Vida Loca in Costa Rica*.

An interesting phenomenon is Central America's famous "love motels." Several dozen are found around San José and the suburbs and do very good business. Many foreigners do not know the difference between a "hotel" and "motel." in Costa Rica and the rest of Central America motels are for making love and serve no other purpose.

These establishments exist for discrete liaisons between adults. Bosses and their secretaries, men with prostitutes, young lovers who still live at home and others enjoy these convenient establishments. Patrons can hide their cars as well as their lovers in one of these places. Rooms may be rented for several hours. Fresh towels, sheets, food, drink and even a condom are provided. Each room also has a small waist-level little window for you to pay and for staff to hand you alcoholic beverages, soft drinks, food, towels, and more. Clients and staff of the motel never see each other's faces.

Most rooms also have a TV, some with pornographic movies, and music. There is a big curtain or door that is closed immediately to hide the identity of the couple and their vehicle. On weekend nights and during lunch, the country's love motels fill up quickly. It is very easy to find one of these motels once you have lived in Costa Rica for a while. Just ask a taxi driver or one of your friends.

Nightlife and Entertainment

There are countless open-air restaurants, bars, dance halls and discotheques all over San José and in most other parts of the country. Costa Ricans love to party and dance. Most of these nightspots will appeal to anyone from 16 to 50, give or take a little for the young at heart.

After you have lived in the country for a while, the dance bug will bite you. There are numerous dance academies in the San José area that offer classes for all levels of experience in various styles of Latin American dance. If you want to learn how to dance like a Costa Rican, call **El Malecón Escuela de Bailes Populares** (255-0378) or **Merecumbé** (220-8511 in Rohrmoser, 289-4774 in Escazú, 240-8511 in Tibás, 237-0851 in Heredia, 442-3536 in Alajuela and 219-8787 in Desamparados). The latter has schools all over the San José area in Alajuela, Heredia, Pavas, Escazú, Tibás and San Pedro. Other dance schools are: **Academia de Bailes Latinos** (233-8938), **Kinesis Academia de Baile** (440-0852), **Inovación Latina** (255-1460) and **Academia Salsabor Estudio** (224-1943).

Once you have mastered the basic dance steps and can dance to the rhythms of *salsa, merengue, cumbia* and other Latin dances, put on your best pair of dancing shoes and go to **El Azteca** dance hall in the suburb of Desamparados. It has large dance floors and really fills up on the weekends. **El Garabaldi** and **El Buen Día** are other dancehalls in the southern part of the city. Here are some more clubs where you can go to dance to Latin music: **El Tobogán**, 200 meters north and 100 meters east of La República (223 -8920), **Castro's Bar**, Calle 22, Barrio México, San José, (256-8789), **El Palenque at Balneario Ojo de Agua** in San Antonio de Belén (441-1309), **Manolo's** Bernardo Soto Highway, Alajuela (433-9001), **Típico Latino**, downtown Heredia, (237-1121), **Nuevo Rancho Garibaldi**, 600 meters west of the Marcial Fallas Clinic in Desamparados, San José (218-1149) and **Picachos**, Paraíso de Cartago, (574-6072). For additional information about Latin dancing, see: www.salsapower.com/cities/costarica.htm

San José´s many discotheques and dance halls play music for all tastes until the wee hours of the morning; admission is inexpensive or free. International liquors and cocktails as well as all local beers and beverages are served. Also, keep in mind that many of these clubs serve food and the traditional heaping plates of delicious local appetizers or hôrs d'oeuvres, called *bocas*.

Most of these establishments are quiet by day and artistically decorated. Many have adjoining restaurants, live music or a disc-jockey and well-lighted dance floors. **El Centro Comercial El Pueblo** has two of the country's best discotheques: **La Plaza** and **Infinito**. Both have huge dance floors and play a mix of American pop, salsa and reggae.

The city of Heredia boasts several excellent watering holes. **El Bulevar**, **Rancho Fofos** and **La Choza** in the vicinity of the National University of Heredia, are the places to party. **Hooligan's Bar** on the road to Heredia, in front of the Atlas Factory, features a Ladies' Night and 2-for-1 nights.

Bohemian types should check out **El Cuartel de La Boca del Monte**. Old hippies and Costa Rican yuppies mingle there. It is one of San José's oldest and most popular bar and restaurant combinations. They have a good mix of Latin and American music. The place really fills up on Mondays and Wednesdays when they feature live music. The bar is known for its truly authentic cuisine.

For lovers of jazz, there are several good clubs in the San José area. **The Jazz Café** in San Pedro is the best spot to hear the rhythms of soul, blues and jazz. The décor will make you feel like you are in a jazz club back home.

The quiet **Shakespeare Bar**, near the Sala Garbo movie theater, is a good place to have a couple of drinks.

If you like the university atmosphere, the college crowd and bar-hopping, then the suburb of San Pedro is just the place for you. Start by checking out the **Planet Mall Disco** located in the San Pedro Mall. **The Sand Rock Bar** around the corner is popular with the younger crowd.

The area around the University of Costa Rica in San Pedro is packed with college-type hangouts. Most of these places are full any night of the week. There is some entertainment here for everyone.

For those of you who do not like loud music, sports bars, large crowds or a boisterous atmosphere, some more sedate establishments let you relax with friends and enjoy conversation. Most hotels bars have a laid-back ambience. The **Hotel Grano de Oro** has a lovely patio where you may sit and nurse your favorite beverage. Also check out the bar on the second floor of the Holiday Inn. It has a great view of Morazán Park.

The Gringo Bar Scene

There are several *gringo* bars that cater almost exclusively to expatriates in downtown San José or nearby. Although we do not recommend hanging out at these places 24-hours a day, there is no better way to hear stories about life in the tropics, keep up on local gossip, meet some colorful local characters and gather tips about living in Costa Rica while you sip your favorite beverage.

The Hotel Presidente's bar, the **News Café**, is the new happening place in San José. The food and drinks are great and it is a fantastic spot to "people watch." Thousands of people walk by this spot each day.

The **New York Bar** is one of our favorite watering holes. The congenial female bartenders will make you feel right at home.

Another *gringo* hangout is the new **Tropix Bar** at the Dunn Inn Hotel in historic Barrio Amón. They offer a variety of drinks and mouth-watering snacks. The atmosphere is quaint.

As previously mentioned a great *gringo* spot is the Blue Marlin Bar Sport enthusiasts frequent this bar. You'll hear a bit of friendly boasting and some tall fish tales at this unique-bar. If you want to make some acquaintances, this bar is worth visiting.

The **Sportsmens Lodge** is a new hang out in downtown San José. They offer satellite TV, pool tables, real Mexican food and rooms. For information, see: www.sportsmenscr.com.

There is always plenty of action in the "Gringo Gulch" area.

Nashville South is a country-western bar in downtown San José with an interesting clientele, western décor and country music in the background.

Mac's American Bar and Restaurant, south of La Sabana Park, is another famous *gringo* hangout. Doña Carmen of Tiny's Tropical bar fame is the cook. You can savor her great cooking and watch major sporting events such as NFL games on DirectTV and the Dish Network. They have a huge Saint Patrick's Day arty every year. We highly recommend this place.

Tex Mex restaurant in Santa Ana is another favorite drinking spot with Americans. A lot of golfers go there after playing at the nearby Valle del Sol golf course.

Rock & Roll Pollo also located in Santa Ana, offers satellite TV for viewing all major U.S. sports. The food is also good.

More Good Bars

Most bars open at 11 a.m. and close at 2 a.m., seven days a week. Some have happy hours.

Antojitos	Good Mexican food
Boulevard	College atmosphere in Heredia
Castro's	Good dancing in Barrio México
Chango	Bar-restaurant in Escazú
Infinito	Has two dance floors, all types of music
Gran Hotel	Nice outdoor patio in the heart of San José
Hotel Corobicí	Good bar
Holiday Inn	Across from Morazán Park
Hooters	Part of the U.S. chain
Hotel Balmoral	Nice quiet bar
K & S Brewery	A micro-brewery in Curridabat
La Cantina	Located at the Hotel Irzazú
La Soda Tapia	Nice place across from Sabana Park
La Plaza	Elegant with large dance floor
Mirador Ram Luna	Family style, jukebox, dancing
Tapachula	Gringo bar near soccer stadium in Alajuela
Tropix Bar	Gringo bar at Hotel Dunn Inn

*See the *The Tico Times* or *La Nación* for more entertainment.

Gambling

Gambling is a pastime enjoyed by both tourists and residents. Costa Rica has about 20 casinos, most in the San José area with a few at beach resorts. Rules differ slightly than in the United States. or Europe, but gambling is fun to learn the Costa Rican way. There are four legal casino games. *Rummy*, a variation of black-jack or 21, is the most popular. The remaining games are craps, roulette (played lottery style rather than with a wheel) and *tute*, a type of poker played against the house. Slot machines are legal. Most casinos give free drinks while you play and are open from 6 p.m. to 3 or 4 a.m. Many casinos offer 24-hour gambling.

Most casinos offer perks for gamblers such as free *bocas* (snacks), drinks and an occasional buffet. Some foreigners gather at casinos on Sundays to watch football games.

The **Fiesta Casino**, the **Gran Hotel Costa Rica Casino** and **Club Colonial** are casinos located in the heart of San José. They are by far the best places to gamble. The casino on the top floor of the Holiday Inn offers a spectacular panoramic view of the city of San José. If for no other reason, you should go to this casino to take in the view and snap a few photos. You may also gamble on the Internet through a local company called **Grand Central Casino** and **Sports Book**.

One of San José's popular casinos.

A Bookmaker in Paradise
By Redstone Brimely

The life I led in the States wasn't working for me. My last business venture ended in failure and I was being evicted from my home. The country health inspector, alerted by my nosey neighbor, posted the notice on my front door citing me with excessive refuse from fast food establishments. If that wasn't enough, I was down to my last pair of pants, I had outgrown Big and Tall. I needed a change.

Watching infomercials at four in the morning, I heard testimony from a West Virginian illiterate expounding of teaching English overseas. I sent for the delux package. The exotic destinations offered were many, but I decided Costa Rica was going to be my new home. There's something about change that gives a young man a bounce to his step. I sensed good things ahead and I was right.

I went to work as an English teacher for a language institute in San José, tutoring local exectives. My first week there I instructed a group of Costa Ricans who spoke excellent English but needed to brush up on their grammar. Interesting work but my biweekly stipend would barely keep me in rice and beans. A compamy called Grand Central Sports, an offshore Las Vegas-style sportsbook operating in San José, had sent their employees to the class. The top student in the class happened to be a supervisor in the wagering department. At the end of the term he offered me a job.

I had never before worked in the gambling business, however I knew something about gambling— my father was a generate gambler.

When I completed my training I was placed in the betting department along with fifty other clerks where the phones were literally "ringing off the hook." Native beauties with cocoa butter skin and pearly white teeth in halter-tops and sarongs answered the phones speaking perfect English. I was in shock!

My main concern when I took this job was whether or not I was breaking any laws. I did some investigating and found out offshore bookmaking is legal and beyond the juristiction of the United States government. The company's growth during the past football season has been phenomenal. In fact, we've both grown. I was made a betting supervisor and was given a couple of weeks off before the start of the basketball season. Until then I'll be at the beach where I've traded in my Oshkosh for Bermuda shorts and a Panama hat with the radio at my feet to keep track of his numerous plays.

The most popular form of gambling in Costa Rica is the national lottery or *lotería*. This game of chance is played a couple of times each week. You can purchase a whole sheet of tickets or a fraction of a sheet from any street vendor.

A substantial amount of money may be won. If you are lucky enough to win the huge annual Christmas Lottery, or *Gordo Navideño*, you will become very rich and will probably be set up for life. To find the results of the lottery, look in the local newspaper. There is also an instant-winner lottery, similar to that played in the United States, *raspa*. In this game you scrape off an area on the ticket with a coin to see if you have matching symbols or numbers.

There is also an illegal underground lottery played the same days as the legal lottery on Tuesday, Friday and Sunday. The game is attractive to some locals because you can win from five to 70 times the amount of your ticket. Also, it is easier to claim the prize in the regular lottery.

There are several types of illegal lottery: **The Changa** is played among Nicaraguans; **La Pulga** is played around the Borbón Market in San José; **La Panameña** works in conjunction with the Panamanian lottery; and **Cuatro Cantos** is played in the port town of Puntarenas.

We don't recommend playing illegal lotteries; we mentioned them only to let our readers know they exist.

Betting on horses is legal in Costa Rica, but the local track closed in 1995 because of financial problems. At the Casino Club Colonial and Hotel Del Rey there is betting on most major sporting events. In November 2001, betting on Costa Rican soccer games was legalized.

Where to Gamble

- Fiesta by far the best casinos in Costa Rica (downtown, Heredia, Alajuela near airport)
- Gran Hotel Costa Rica (another good place to gamble)
- Hotel Del Rey
- Casino Tropical
- Club Colonial (sports betting)
- Holiday Inn
- San José Palacio
- Hotel Cariari
- Balmoral Hotel
- Hotel Corobicí
- Hotel Irazú
- Hotel Herradura

Movies and Theaters in San José and Other Areas

There are movie theaters all over the San José area and in other large cities. Most of these theaters show first-run movies usually within a month after they first are released in the United States. *Ticos* are moviegoers. Last year more than 3.5 million tickets were sold in Costa Rica.

The **Sala Garbo** shows first-rate independent films with Spanish subtitles. About 40 percent of all current hit movies shown in the United States make their way to Costa Rica sooner or later. You should not worry about understanding these movies since they are all in English with Spanish, subtitles except movies for children, which are usually dubbed. You can read the local newspapers to see what movies are currently playing. At present, admission costs about $3. Several theaters have more than one screen. To find out what is playing look in *The Tico Times* or any of the Spanish-language newspapers such as *La Nación*. Information about movies may also be accessed at **www. entretenimiento.co.cr** (in Spanish).

In the Central Valley, you can experience everything from old-time Paramount-style theater palaces to ultra-modern movie complexes in suburban malls. The **Cine Variedades**, up the street from the Plaza

Recently released movies in English are shown here.

de la Cultura, is one of the oldest. The **Cine Magaly** in Barrio La California, is a great theater for that old-time big-movie experience. It has more than 1,000 seats and second-story balconies.

The parent company of the Magaly runs other movie theaters in the country. **Cadena de Cines Magaly**, or CCM, is the country's largest chain with 42 screening rooms located all over the country. They receive about 50 percent of the country's movie viewers.

The Magaly theater chain has a movie theater with three screens on the third floor of the new Outlet Mall in San Pedro. These theaters show nontraditional foreign films and have state-of-the-art DTS Digital and Dolby sound systems. You can purchase and reserve tickets by telephone with a credit card. The Magaly movie chain also recently opened several movie theaters at Mall Internacional in Alajuela, the Paseo de las Flores and Real Cariari shopping centers in Heredia, in Plaza San Carlos and Plaza Liberia in Guanacaste.

In the 1980s there were about 125 independent movie theaters in the country. Today there are 80 theaters with 73 belonging to three major chains and found exclusively in large shopping malls.

The first of Costa Rica's megatheaters was built in the San Pedro Mall. It has five-screens and is located on the second floor of the mall. The opening of this theater complex started a new trend of multiple movie screens located in shopping malls. The idea was to use the movie theaters to draw large numbers of people to the malls.

The Real Cariari shopping center boasts a six-screen movie theater. **Cinemark** is a U.S.-style movie theater with eight screens at the Multiplaza mall, in Escazú. This theater boasts a -top-quality digital sound system and tiered seating . It is one of the best places to see a movie in the country, and serves snacks and candies from the United States and even hot buttered popcorn with real butter and free refills if you purchase the large size. **Cinépolis** at the new Terramall, on the highway to Cartago also has a state- of-the-art theater. It boasts 15 movie screens, three of which have VIP rooms with luxurious seats and George Lucas' THX technology.

San José is purported to have more theaters and theater companies per capita than any other city in the world. Most live plays are in Spanish but there are occasional plays in English at the Costa Rican-North American Cultural Center. The **Little Theatre Group** is Costa Rica's oldest English-language acting troupe and frequently presents plays in English. However, by going to plays in Spanish, you can improve your language skills. Current plays are listed in the activities section of local newspapers.

Movies (*Cines*)

Cinépolis 278-3506
    Terramall
Cine Cariari (six screens) 293-3300
    Plaza Real Cariari, across from the
    Hotel Herradura
Cine Colonial 1 and 2 (two screens) 289-9000
    Centro Comercial Plaza Colonial, Escazú
Cine Magaly 223-0085
    Calle 23, Ave. Central/1 Barrio La California
Cine El Semáforo (alterntive movies) 253-9126
    San Pedro
Cinemark (eight screens) 288-1111
    Multiplaza, Escazú
Cinemark (eight screens) 224-8383
    Multiplaza del Este, Zapote
Cine Variedades 222-6104
    Ave. Central/1, Calle 5
El Observatorio 223-0725
    Calle 23, Ave. Central
Internacional (four screens) 442-6100
    Mall Internacional, Alajuela
Laurence Olivier 222-1034
    Ave. 2, Calle 28
Liberia 223-0085
    Guanacaste
Multicines 234-8868
    San Pedro across from la Plaza Roosevelt and Kennedy Park
Multicines 592-3133
    Cartago at Mall Paraíso
Multicines 665-1515
    Liberia
Multiplex 460-6733
    San Carlos
Pérez Zeledón 772-8780
    San Isidro
Plaza Mayor 1-2 (two screens) 232-3271
    Main Road, Rohrmoser
Plaza Occidente 447-7120
    San Ramón
Sala Garbo 222-1034
    Ave. 2, Calle 28, 100 meters south of
    Pizza Hut Paseo Colón
San Carlos 480-9202

San Pedro Mall (five screens) 221-6272
    Mall San Pedro
Cinematec 207-5732
    Auditorium of the School of General Studies, UCR
Cine Universitario 207-4271
    At the UC. Law School Auditorium
Cine en el Campus, Teatro Centro de Arte del CIDEA,
    Universidad Nacional, 200 meters north of McDonald's,
    Heredia

Theaters (*Teatros*) in and around San José

Teatro de Esquina 257-0223
    100 meters south of the old Atlantic Train Station
Teatro Laurence Olivier 222-1034
    Ave. 2, Calle 28
Teatro Arlequín 222-0792
    Calle 13, Ave. Central
Teatro del Angel 222-8258
    Ave. Central & Plaza de la Democracia
Teatro Melico Salazar 221-4952
    Ave. 2, Calle Central
Teatro de La Aduana 223-4563
    Calle 25, Ave. 3/ 5
Teatro Capra 234-2866
    Calles 29/33, Ave. 1
Teatro Chaplin 223-2919
    Paseo de los Estudiantes
Teatro Máscara 255-4250
    Calle 13, Ave. 2/4
Teatro Nacional 221-5341
    Ave. 2, Calles 3/5
Teatro Giratablas 253-6001
    Diagonal to Kentucky Fried Chicken on
    the road to San Pedro
Teatro Tiempo 222-0792
    Ave. Central/2, Calle 13
Teatro Eugene O'Neill 253-5527
    IN the Costa Rican-North American
    Cultural Center, Barrio Dent

COMMUNICATIONS

Telephone Service

Costa Rica has the most number of telephones in Latin American country and boasts one of the world's best telephone systems, with direct dialing to more than 60 countries. The country has 1.5 million regular telephones, 930,000 cellular phones and 20,000 public phones. The country code for all of Costa Rica is 506. To call any number in the country from North America dial 011 + 506 + the seven-digit number. Calls within the country are a bargain; you can call any place in the country for only a few cents; they are all local calls. If your house or apartment does not have a phone, don't worry. Public telephones are just about everywhere in Costa Rica and use 5, 10, and 20 silver *colón* coins. Phones accepting pre-paid phone cards are slowly replacing coin-operated phones.

If you do not have your own phone and want to make a direct international call, go to the **Radiográfica** (287-0087) telephone office, (open 7 a.m. to 10 p.m.) in downtown San José at Calle 1, Avenida 7. Long-distance calls from may be made from any phone booth by dialing 114. You can also make long distance calls from most hotels. From private phones in homes or offices, the procedure is just like in the United States: by direct dialing or first talking to the operator (*operadora*). The access numbers for calling Costa Rica from North America are 011 + 506 + the number. To call or fax the U.S. from

Costa Rica dial 001+area code+number. You may purchase prepaid phone cards for local or international direct-dial calls. Three types of cards may be purchased from **Costa Rican Electricity Institute** (ICE) offices, **Correos de Costa Rica** or businesses displaying a gold and blue sign that says "*Tarjetas Telefónicas.*" CHIP cards sold in denominations of 300 to 2,000 *colones* may be used for local calls. **Servicio 197** cards come in denominations of 300, 500 and 1000 *colones* and allow domestic calls. **Servicio 199** cards are in $10, $20 or 3,000 and 10,000 *colón* denominations and may be used for international calls and have instructions in English.

Purchasing a telephone can be a real pain in the neck depending on where you live and the number of available lines. You can expect to wait from one to three months for phone installation after paying about $50 for this service.

You can request a number and service from anywhere in Costa Rica by calling 115. Place your request with one of the operators or ask where the nearest ICE office is to order the service. If you need assistance in English, several English-speaking operators available to help you.

To obtain a new phone service call 115 to check for availability. If there are telephone lines available, give the electric meter number of the place where you want your new telephone line installed

You'll also need the telephone number of the nearest building to the place where you want your phone line installed so the phone company can verify if a phone can be installed and how long it will take. Your passport, identification or cellular phone number may be used to identify you for your account information. Finally, a postal address or directions where phone bills and other information about phone service may be sent. When you have given this information to ICE, they will give you a personal identification number to be used for paying the installation fee and to make any change in your service.

The next step is to pay the one-time fee to get on the waiting list for phone service. The fee ranges from $80 to $150, depending on the area for which you are requesting service. This payment can be made at any ICE office, or the phone company will send a messenger at no cost to pick up the payment.

If you are having problems with the line or need to make changes in your service, call 119. No English-speaking operators work at this extension and a lot of transactions are done by computer, so it might be better to go directly to an ICE office for this kind of assistance. Or, you may call the international phone service number at 124, where operators speak English and are often willing to help foreigners having problems with their telephone service. All of this information is clearly explained in Spanish at the beginning of the local phone book.

To have a phone installed, go to one of the following **ICE offices**: north side of the Sabana Park 220-7720; Pavas Centro, 296-0303, La Florida, Tibás, 240-6466; San Pedro, 225-0123; San José, 221-0123. Phone bills may be paid at the ICE office in downtown San José or at any other ICE office in Costa Rica. You can also pay your phone and electric bills (*recibos*) at many supermarkets and online through banks such as, Banco Nacional.

The phone company offers these services with your phone: call waiting, caller ID, rerouting of calls, wake-up calls, restriction of international calls and teleconferencing.

To transfer your telephone line or number to a different location, first you have to find out a telephone number of an office or house that is next to or close by the place where you want your telephone line transferred.

After you have this information, call 115 and give them the telephone number. They will let you know if there are telephone pairs available, or in some cases they might be in the same telephone exchange.

If everything turns out well and the transfer can be done, you need an electric meter number and a photocopy of the owner's ID document.

If it is under a company name, you will need the *personería jurídica* (legal power of attorney) with the corresponding *cédula jurídica* (corporate ID number) and the power of attorney and ID document number of the representative.

The cost of transferring the line is of $37 per line plus sales tax; this amount will be charged to your telephone bill. Fill in the forms sent to you by fax; afterwards you can take this form to the ICE office or send it back by fax, very simple.

When we moved from our old home in Lagunilla de Heredia to San Francisco de Heredia, we had to transfer two telephone lines. The people at the phone company said it would not take too long. With a lot of pushing and shoving, the whole process took six weeks.

Cellular phone service is available in Costa Rica. Cellular phones have become a status symbol here. Most middle and all upper-class *ticos* and many businessmen are using cellular phones. We even saw a street fruit vendor with a cellular phone. The basic monthly fee is about $6, and that includes 60 free minutes of call time. Any additional minutes are 30 *colones* each from 7am to 7pm and 23 *colones* each from 7pm to 7am and holidays. Text messages are 1.5 colones each. The basic rate for calls and text messages may go up slightly soon. See **www. grupoice.com** for additional information.

Phones are more expensive than in the United States, and there are no super deals where you get a free phone by just signing up for a year's service. Nevertheless, business is booming for the companies that sell cell phones here. Stores selling cell phones are found all over the country and in most of the large shopping malls. You can often get hooked up by the store that sells you your phone. You can save money by purchasing your phone in the United States and then getting connected to the service here. However, only certain types of phones from the United States work here.

Cell phone rentals are available in Costa Rica. We recommend the following companies: **Cellular Telephone Rentals** 290-7534, office hours 8:30 a.m.- 5 p.m. CST Monday to Friday, 845-4427, 8:30 a.m. to 9 p.m. CST, toll-free from the United States 800-769-7137, hours 8:30 a.m. to 9 p.m. CST Saturday and Sunday, or E-mail: info@ cellulartelephonerentals.com; and **Rent a Cell Phone**, 800-967-1111, www.costaricarentacellphone.com, toll free from the United States and Canada 1-877-268-2918, in Costa Rica 293-5892 or 379-0676, E-mail: sales@cellphonescr.com.

Sending a fax is very easy in Costa Rica. You can go to **Radiográfica** (Tel: 287-0513, 287-0511) . At the Radiográfica office you can send a fax or have one sent to you. You can call their office to see if they have received a fax for you. They will even call when a fax comes in if they have your phone number. Many private businesses offer fax services to individuals. You can usually find their number in the classified section of *The Tico Times* or *Costa Rica Today* (local English-language newspapers).

Internet Service

Computer buffs will be pleased to know Internet services are available throughout Costa Rica. Costa Rica has Central America's highest Internet connection rate, with 20 of 1,000 citizens regularly going online. The country is second in Internet use in Latin America, surpassed only by Chile. At the beginning 2004, Costa Rica had more than 100,000 Internet accounts. It is predicted that soon one-quarter of the country's population will be frequent users of the Internet.

In Costa Rica, Internet users have several ways of connecting to the national network; by cable modem provided by local cable companies in connection with **RACSA** (*Radiográfica Costarricense*); ADSL and RDSI provided by the *Instituto Costarricense de Electricidad* (ICE) , the telephone company and parent of RACSA; or by dial-up provided by RACSA. Unfortunately, the vast majority of Internet users are limited to the slow dial-up system. Most people complain that it is very slow, difficult to get connected at times and they often get disconnected while online.

To get connected to Internet, just go to the Radiográfica offices and open a RACSAPAC account. Recently, using the Internet became less expensive and the hours more flexible.

Rates for home Internet users are $10 to $15 per month. The new $15 unlimited-hours rate does not include the basic telephone rate of $0.55 per hour online. The extra charge will be added to the Internet client's telephone. For further information about these services, call 287-0321 or 287-0087; Fax: (506) 223-1609, or e-mail: tarifas@sol. racsa.co.cr.

ICE now offers that ADSL broadband Internet. Broadband Internet will eventually enable homes, schools and businesses to connect to the Internet at high speeds at a fraction of the current cost without using regular telephone lines. The monthly cost of this service ranges from $16 for 128-kbps connection with a download speed of 512-kbps, $19 for a 256-kbps connection with a download speed of 2,048-kbps and $25 for a 512-Kbps connection with a download speed of 2,048 kbps. A connection speed of 1,024 with a download speed of 512-kbps costs $38 and 2,048-kbps with a download speed of 768 will run $169. In addition to the ADSL service, ICE also offers a RDSI that comes with two independent phone lines and a greater speed than the regular dial-up service. To find out whether these services are available in your area or to sign up, call 115 or see www.grupoice.com for more details.

Internet service cable TV hookup is also available in Costa Rica through a couple of cable TV companies. This service is faster than regular dial-up service. **Cable Tica** (210-1450) and **Amnet** (210-2929) now offer two-way high-speed cable modem Internet service in some areas, mainly the Central Valley. The monthly cost ranges between $40 and $80 depending on the speed of the connection you choose. At present, this service is available in San José, Heredia, Santa Ana and some of the surrounding suburbs. I live in Heredia and am very happy with the service Amnet provides.

You can also get high-speed satellite Internet service from several companies. The installation cost is about $2,600 and the monthly charge is about $125. In rural areas where there is no broadband

Internet, DSL or cable, this may be the way to go. Call 290-0689 for more information.

Internet users can now make long distance telephone calls using Vonage. They offer an all-inclusive phone service that can bypass the Costa Rican phone system. You can use your existing high-speed Internet connection (broadband) instead of standard phone lines. You will also need a U.S. address to use this system. We know many people who use Vonage from here and are very satisfied. To find out more about their services see www.vonage.com.

Many private Internet companies offer private services such as hosting and Web design.

ICE plans to offer an international Internet phone service by the end of 2006.

For an hourly fee, you may send and receive mail and surf the Web at any of the many local *Internet cafés*. *Internet café* prices can range from anywhere from 200 *colones* ($0.40) to 470 *colones* ($0.90) per hour in the San José area to as much as 2.000 *colones* (US $3.90) at the beach.

Here is our friend Charles Mill's experience at a local *Internet café*: "On my first two trips I used the *Internet café*. They are available almost everywhere. In Heredia you trip over them all the time. They are fast and very reasonable. The main issue that bothered me was that in some *cafés* the keyboards were dirty. You can find *Internet café's* for 150 to 500 *colones* ($0.30 to $1) or more per hour. Last year I was in Branson, Missouri and an *Internet café* was charging $6 per hour. In New York it can cost $12 per hour."

Many hotels now offer free Internet service to their clients, and some of them even have Hot Spots now if you are traveling with your laptop.

The Radiográfica office, in downtown San José, has computers you can use to surf the Web. They even have printers so you can download and print out information from the Web. The central post office in downtown San José offers several computers with Internet and e-mail connection for about $1.50 per hour. Costa Rica's postal services hopes to have nearly 150 post offices branches online over the next few years.

You can pay bills online form here. There is no need to have the paper bill present; you only need to know the last day due and the appropriate account number and name for your bill so you can pay them on time online. IMHO at the Banco Nacional de Costa Rica has the easiest, most complete and best online bill pay here in Costa Rica.

You can have an electronic *colón* and U.S. dollar account on the same page and move funds from one to the other as needed. To pay private parties (such as your landlord) or companies not listed, you need to have their account number and account name, but you can transfer money to them online also within the same bank. They have promised interbank payments coming soon.

As for the U.S. side of online banking, you can use NetBank (www. netbank.com) and pay virtually anyone in the United States either through e-bills, if they are offered, or send them an electronically generated bank check directly. With a PayPal account, you can pay anyone that has an e-mail address anywhere in the world, with some political exceptions.

Mail Service

Costa Rica's postal system, or ***Correos de Costa Rica***, offers postal services comparable to that in many countries abroad. The country's first mail service was officially established in December 1839.

Curbside boxes for mail pickup are almost nonexistent in Costa Rica. You will have to mail your letters from the post office or from a hotel if you are a guest. Just as in the United States, mail may be received and sent from the post office (*correo* or *casa de correos*.) The main post office is in the heart of downtown San José at Calle 2, between Avenidas 1

San José's old post office.

and 3 (223-9766). Other small cities and towns in rural areas have their own centrally located post offices. Airmail between the United States or Europe and Costa Rica usually takes about five to 10 days. At present, an airmail letter to the United States or Canada costs $0.30 or 100 *colones*. A postcard to North America is about $0.20 or 70 *colones*. An airmail stamp to Europe is about $0.35 or 120 *colones*. To save money, the post office is now replacing stamps with adhesive labels that show the amount of postage.

The post office also provides other services, including M-bags for sending large quantities of books or other printed matter abroad, telegrams, fax service, courier services and delivery of documents.

As stated above, mail boxes are few and far between as are house numbers, so we recommend using your nearest post office for all postal- related matters. The country's charming but exasperating "100 meters east of the church" style addresses makes getting a post office box for local mail delivery a necessity. Obtaining a post office box (*apartado*) from your local post office in Costa Rica ensures prompt and efficient mail service.

Getting a post office box is a straightforward process, but vacant boxes can sometimes be hard to come by. P.O. boxes are in great demand, but you can usually get one in January, when most people give up leases on their boxes when annual renewal fees are due. If a box's annual renewal fee isn't paid by mid-February, it is sold to those on the waiting list at that time. Popular branches such as San José's central post office or Escazú have long waiting lists; so it is much easier to find a box in suburban or rural areas.

Many people deal with the shortage of boxes by sharing with friends, neighbors, extended family or business associate. In theory, this practice isn't permitted, but many people do it and nobody seems to check closely.

To apply for a post office box, go to the post office nearest your office or home to fill out an application (*solicitud de apartado*). The annual rental fee costa about $10, $30 or $40 dollars in the San José metropolitan area and provincial capitals, depending on the size of the post office box. There are three sizes: small, medium and large. In rural post offices, the costs are about half these prices.

Once you fill out the paperwork and pay your annual fee, you are given an address that reads something like this: José López, Apdo. 7289-1000, San José, Costa Rica. The number before the hyphen is the *apartado* (P.O. Box) and the number after the hyphen is the post office's code.

An Expat's Adventure at the Post Office
By John Vickery

As posted here earlier, I received 4 M-bags at my apartado in Alejuela in the last week of August. There was one bag that was missing. I'm hoping that this note might help a new person to Costa Rica understand what happens when they are required to report to the main post office in Zapote. I wondered what happened to that last M-bag but figured it would be along shortly.

Sometime in the first week of Sept I received the normal adviso in my apartado telling me to report to the second floor of the correo to retrieve that final M-bag. Upon reporting there the clerk told me I must report to the main post office in Zapote to retrieve my package. When asked why, the clerk responded that he did not know why but suspected there might be a problem.

I hired my trusted pirate taxi driver to take me there. We arrived at 9:30 on Friday morning and the parking lot was almost empty. I still was unsure why I had to report to Zapote but if you follow my adventure, you might find this trip not as intimidating as it might appear.

As you drive into the post office compound you will see the huge post office directly in front of you. This is not the place you need to go. As you enter (through the gate) look off to the right and you'll see a small booth with a guy sitting inside. After you park, go over to that little booth and present the adviso you received from your local post office. The clerk inside the booth will check out your paper, and if all is in order, he will point to the guy sitting next door guarding the pedestrian entrance to the customs area. Here you will need to show your adviso again, then sign into the compound (name, date, passport, cédula number and signature. After this, the guard will ask for your passport, cédula and verify the info. IF you have others with you, they will go through the same process. Once you clear this gate, you will walk about 150 meters towards the back of the building. You will then turn left and enter the building and proceed past a few stations to get to station #1. If there is no one in front of you (I got lucky with only one person in front of me) you will approach this window and pass your adviso to the person on the other side of the glass. This person will check your paperwork on the computer an if you are there (I was), they will print out the paperwork and then grab their handy rubber stamp and stamp like crazy. Then they will hand you one of those papers for you to print your name, date, passport, cédula number and sign it. Then they ask for your passport/cedula to verify the info and if all is OK, they give you one of the papers and they tell you to go across the isle to station number 2. Station 2 is a 20 foot counter and there you'll see a sign in both Spanish and English telling you to wait until your name is called. I waited there about 20 minutes and saw a large cardboard box (too big to fit in an M-bag) delivered to the serious looking guy behind the counter. That can't be mine thought I. Wrong! The guy called my name and put that large box on the counter. I looked at the box and noticed that it had rubber stamps all over it stating that the original package had been damaged in shipment and had be directed to the re-wrapping dept at the USPS post office in Jersey City, New Jersey. The serious looking guy (Customs I later found out) put the package on the counter and found a large knife (not a machete) and proceeded to cut the box open.

A quick aside here: Originally the M-bag I sent contained two of what's called bankers totes. These boxes fold up nicely and have a nice cover which is easy to write on. The USPS office where I mailed them advised that I address the top of each box (in the M-bag) just like a letter. Upper right corner of the box (where a stamp would go)was noted M-bag US postage paid. Upper left hand corner of the box had a return address in the states. Center of the box had the mailing address here in Costa Rica. Well, I looked at that box which was too big to fit in any M-bag and noticed that these re-wrapping folks in New Jersey (I assume) had cut the top of one of my boxes and taped the info to the top of the re-packaged box. Good for them and I'm certainly glad I followed the instructions of my local USPS office!

Back to the serious looking customs agent. He cut the box open and did a quick inspection of the contents. I admit that I cheated just a bit and included a few VHS tapes in amongst the books in the bag. All the guy did was look through the box and say "books". Then he picked up a few of the VHS tapes, shake his head and said "OK". He then signed a paper and asked me for the same info from the previous window (no stamp) and directed me to station number 3. I proceeded to station number 3 which was another window and handed the paper to him. This process took about 15 minutes (signing papers, rubber stamps, etc) and cost me 470 colones. I still do not know why the cost but for less than a $ I wasn't about to ask. The guy at station number 3 then gave me another piece of paper and directed me to station number 4. This was another 20 foot counter and about 10 minutes later I was presented my box and had to sign another number of papers and was allowed to leave carrying my box.

All in all, I think this was a positive Costa Rican experience. I've heard many horror stories dealing with Costa Rican customs. I do not consider this one of those stories!

You may also receive mail in the general delivery section (*lista de correos*) of your local post office. This is especially useful in isolated regions of the country. Register at the nearest post office and they will put your name on the local *lista de correos*. When you pick up your mail, you pay a few cents per letter for this service. All letters must have your name, the phrase *lista de correos* and the name of the nearest post office.

The worst time to receive any correspondence through regular Costa Rican mail is between November 20 and January 1. Letters can be delayed up to a month by the enormous volume of Christmas mail and the vacations of postal workers during the month of December.

You should avoid having anything larger than a letter or a magazine sent to you in Costa Rica. Any item bigger than that will be sent to the customs warehouse (*aduana*) and you will make several trips to get it out. On the first trip to customs your package or parcel is unwrapped so you can fill out a declaration of its contents. On the second trip, you usually will have to pay an exorbitant duty equivalent to the value of the item plus the mailing cost. If you refuse to pay, your package will be confiscated— not sent back, just confiscated.

So, as you can see, due to the costs involved and wasted time, it is better to have friends bring you large items, pick them up when you're visiting the United States, or use one of the private mail companies mentioned in this section.

In an effort to win back some of its customers, the government recently privatized the **Costa Rican Postal Service** (**CORTEL**). The service has officially shed its public status and was reborn as **Correos de Costa Rica S.A**. The overhaul aims to transform the notoriously slow service into an efficient operation. The country's archaic street address system will be changed to a systematic numbering of streets, avenues and buildings.

For information about the **Correos de Costa Rica's** services, contact them at: Tel: 800-900-2000 or 253-3375, extensions 343 and 345, or go to www.correos.go.cr.

Receiving Money from Abroad

Do you plan on having money from abroad sent to you in Costa Rica? Perhaps the cheapest and easiest way to get money are the ATM machines available at almost all banks and supermarkets.

Western Union in Costa Rica boasts that they offer the fastest money transfers in the country. Call Western Union at 1-800-777-7777 or 283-6336, or e-mail: bvib@western-union.co.cr for additional information, or go to one of their local agencies in San José, Liberia, San Isidro de El General, Puntarenas or other parts of the country. You'll have to show some form of valid identification to pick up your money. **Moneygram** 1-800-328-5678, 295-9595, www.moneygram. com, offers similar services.

One of the safest ways to receive money while visiting or residing in Costa Rica is to have an international money order or any other type of important merchandise or document shipped to you by one of the worldwide courier services, such as DHL or UPS. Letters and small packages usually take about two working days (Monday to Friday) to reach Costa Rica from the United States or Canada.

Many worldwide air couriers have offices in San José, such as **DHL** (290-3010), **Federal Express** (255-4567), UPS (257-7447), **TNT** (233-5678), **Jetex** (293-5838) and **Skynet** (232-5678). The latter two are probably the cheapest options. Until recently, Costa Rica's postal service, *Correos de Costa Rica*, was the slowest and least safe option. Its "non-priority" mail was too slow to even consider as a valid option. The Costa Rican postal service does offer priority mail service; call 253-3375 or 800-900-2000 or e-mail: pacc_prioritymail@ correos.go.cr. "Priority" mail (*certificado*) supposedly takes 12 days to reach any destination in the United States and three weeks for Europe and the rest of the world. Rates are very affordable at about $5.35 per kilo and $4.75 for each additional kilo.

However, *Correos de Costa Rica* just inaugurated **EMS Courier**, a national and international courier service with 127 offices throughout the country. It hopes to compete with private courier companies. You may contact them at 221-2136, fax: 221-1737 or e-mail: ems@ correos.go.cr.

U.S. banks can wire money to banks in Costa Rica. This method is safe, but can be slow at times, as many bureaucratic delays can develop while waiting for checks to clear. You are also charged a fee for the transfer. We had a money order sent from England to our account in the Banco Nacional de Costa Rica and didn't experience much delay or any problems. Once we followed the correct procedure our money arrived promptly.

To wire money you will have to use eight-letter codes to your local bank's eight-letter SWIFT account:

Banco Banex S.A. San Jose	BXBACRSJ265951
Banco BAC San Jose	BSNJCRSJ363642
Banco BCT S.A. San Jose	CCIOCRSJ396508
Banco Cuscatlan de Costa Rica San Jose	BACUCRSJ392460
Banco de Costa Rica San Jose	BCRICRSJ019339
Banco Interfin S.A. San Jose	INTECRSJ185480
Banco Internacional de Costa Rica San Jose	COSRCRSJ393955
Banco Lafise, S.A. San Jose	BCCECRSJN/A
Banco Nacional de Costa Rica San Jose	BNCRCRSJ019462
BCT Bank International San Jose	CCIOCRSJ396508
Scotia Bank de Costa Rica San Jose	NOSCCRSJ394833

The Costa Rican postal service is planning to start a money order service allowing money orders to be sent from the United States to Costa Rica. This service promises to be much faster and more economical than getting money wired to your bank in Costa Rica.

You can always have a trustworthy friend or relative bring you up to $10,000 when they come to Costa Rica.

Automatic teller machines (ATMs) are found all over the country. You can't transfer money directly but can get cash advances from one of your credit or debit cards. Use of ATMs, along with cashing a personal check are perhaps the fastest ways to get money.

Another safe way to have checks sent to you is through one of the private mail services we list in the next section.

The worst way to send money is through the regular mail. People report that many checks have been lost or stolen. Postal thieves are very sophisticated in Costa Rica and may work with some unscrupulous black market money changers. The postal system has received numerous complaints and has promised to do something about them.

If you need to file a complaint about lost or stolen mail, go to *Correo de Costa Rica's* complaint department (*Departamento de Reclamaciones*) in downtown San José on Avenida 6, between Calles 17 and 19. If you live outside San José, you can file a complaint at any local post office and it will be forwarded to San José.

If you still choose to use the regular mail system after reading the above, be sure to have your checks or money orders sent to you in secure, non-transparent manila envelopes—ones that can't be seen through when held up to a light.

A rash of postal thefts has prompted more and more people to use the private-mail companies, which offer a variety of postal related services.

Private Mail Services

A few mail companies provide clients with a mail drop and P.O. box in Miami and a physical address where they can send or receive packages. This enables customers living in Costa Rica to have their mail sent to the Miami address from where the companies forward the mail to Costa Rica.

Aerocasillas (P.O. Box 4567-1000, San José, Costa Rica, Tel: 208-4868, Fax: 257-1187, E-mail: servicesjo@aerocasillas.com, www.aerocasillas.com) is the oldest of these companies. Besides their main office, they have branches in the suburbs and in other areas of the country: La Uruca, San José 232-6892; Curridatbat, San José, 224-6381; Novacentro, Guadalupe, 224-9843; Cartago, 592-0000; Limón, 798-0606, ext. 6; Ciudad Quesada, 461-0683; San Ramón 440-8793; Jacó 643-0049 and Quepos 777-1925.

Trans-Express "Interlink" (P.O. Box 02-5635, Miami, FL 33102, Tel: 296-3973/296-3974, Fax; 232-3979); **AAA Express Mail** (Tel: 233-4993, Fax: 221-5056); **Star Box** (P.O. Box 405–1000, San José, Tel: 257-3443, Fax: 233-5624); **Jet Box** (Tel: 231-5592 in Pavas, 253-5400, in Curridabat and 665-0017 in Liberia, see www.jetbox.com); **Daily Mail** (Tel: 233-4993, Fax: 221-5046); and **Air Mail CR** (239-5775) are other companies offering similar services.

Mail Boxes Etc. offers a full ranger of postal related services.

Necessity Begets An
International Mail Service
By Chuck Swett

Back in the good old days, the early sixties Jimn Fendell had been here 10 plus years (arrived with parents in 1951), and I was just getting over the caravan like, Pan-American Airways milk-run through Central America, things were a lot different here. The nearest beach, Puntarenas, was four hours away, via Cambronero, with fog so thick you had to ride on the hood of the car and guide the driver. You could go to the movies for a few *colones*, fill up a VW for almost nothing, and a popuplar priced a liter of milk cost a little over one colón. The train ride to Puntarenas was one big long party. And you could walk down any street in San José at any hour without ever considering yourself to be in danger.

But the one thing you wouldn't even consider doing, unless you really felt generous toward the customs officer population, was subscribe to National Geographic, The Saturday Evening Post or Life Magazine. Playboy would probably not even make it off the plane, much less through the postal system. The custom was to find out who was travelling and ask them to bring that car part or special shampoo or the latest Beatles album, when they came back.

As the country and the expatriate colony grew, communications media began to introduce new goodies and remind the foreigners of things they were accustomed to at home but couldn't easily get on the local market.

Our innovative friend Jim began to recognize the need for an alternative means of establishing and regaining that "link to home" that was missing. A reliable way to get peoples' important mail safely to its destination, and to allow them to enjoy a "taste of home" in their adopted country. That need finally took shape in Aerocasillas, twelve years ago.

Envisioned as becoming "The best personalized network for receiving and sending documents and mechandise between the rest of the world and our country," This way both national and international markets were opened to our clients.

Pioneering the field of private international mail service in this country, Aerocasillas has built a growing user base of 25,000 satisfied customers, with over 3,000 active accounts. This is the result of over twelve years of constant dedication to fulfilling the needs of our clients and seeking ways to improve on the service we provide.

Mail Boxes Etc. (291-0282), has a store in Rohrmoser at Plaza Amistad, Local 8, 400 meters east of Plaza Mayor. They also have branches at Parque Empresarial Forum in Santa Ana (204-7441) and in Curridabat, across from Pops Ice Cream (Tel: 357-9429).

They provide the same services as the companies above plus packing and shipping, office supplies and a photocopy center, as well as selling Hallmark greeting cards and stationery and offer notary and legal services and more.

These companies provide much faster service than the Costa Rican mail system to access mail order products from the United States, to enable clients to subscribe to magazines and newspapers at U.S. domestic rates, to help obtain replacement parts from abroad and to order directly from mail order catalogs such as Land's End, J.C. Penny and L.L. Bean. Large automobile parts may also be ordered from the United States. You can pick up your correspondence directly from their offices or have your letters and packages picked up and delivered to your home or office at any time you choose. They will also get packages out of Customs for you and save you a lot of headaches.

We have used one of these services for more than four years and in general their service has been good. Because of the nature of our book business, we have an unusually high volume of incoming and outgoing mail. Our letters, books, packages, monies and other mail reach their U.S. destinations almost as fast as if they were mailed from another city in the United States. This reliable service makes doing business from Costa Rica very easy.

Most of the private mail companies offer Certified Mail, Registered Mail, Express Mail and FedEx, UPS, DHL or other courier services.

Rates at any of these private mail services run from about $15 to $60 or more per month, depending on the amount of mail you receive and whether you have a business or personal account.

Members of ARCR also have access to these companies, paying no monthly fee, but only for the weight of the mail received. This is very useful for receiving small amounts of mail.

Note: Taxes, Customs charges and restrictions can make shipping goods into Costa Rica a complicated business, but numerous private mail companies offer services that can help residents navigate the sometimes confusing rules for bringing in goods.

There are a few restrictions on what can be brought into Costa Rica. Restricted items such as food and medicine require approval from the Health Ministry. The ministry gives special permission for medicines that treat terminal diseases. Permits can be obtained in person at the

Health Ministry. However, some private mail companies will get the documents for you for a fee.

International goods brought into Costa Rica are subject to taxes and Customs handling charges, which also make international shipping more complicated than sending packages domestically. Taxes vary widely based on the product brought into the country.

Compact disks, for example, are subject to a one percent tax, while car parts are taxed at 30 percent and electronic parts at 50 percent.

Customs handling rates begin at $2 for books and items worth up to $25, and rise up to $50 for items worth $1,000 or more, according to the Aerocasillas website www.aeropost.com.

A recent change in regulations allows Costa Rican residents to bring up to $500 worth of goods into the country tax-free once every six months, though the limit includes the item's cost, the shipping charges according to Customs, and any insurance on the item.

The documents for the tax exemption are available from the Customs office at Juan Santamaría International Airport in Alajuela.

Mail companies, such as Aerocasillas, guide their customers through this process, which requires: an exemption alert form with information about the package and the supplier, to be submitted at least 24 hours before the package arrives; an original identification card or passport and three signed copies; a power of attorney form; and a commercial invoice.

Aerocasillas provides these forms on its website and charges $20 plus sales tax for the service.

For those of you who choose to send something to an address outside Costa Rica, there are certain regulations and options.

You should be aware that many countries restrict what types of items can be sent across their borders. The United States, for example, has special regulations for shipping goods such as coffee, liquor, fruit and other foods, medications and drugs. For shipping these items to the United States, see the website for the U.S. Food and Drug Adminstration. at www.fda.

International couriers such as DHL, UPS and FedEx, which we mentioned earlier in this chapter, can help with shipping items abroad. These companies can handle a wide variety of shipping orders, large or small, and have extensive services to meet individual shipping and tracking needs. Although they offer high-speed, door-to-door shipping of documents and packages, their services can be on the expensive side.

DHL, for example, can ship from Costa Rica to Miami in 24 hours, and anywhere else in the Unites States in 48 hours. To Europe, DHL can get your package or letter there in three or four days.

Shipping through DHL can be done by first calling the company's Costa Rica call center open 8 a.m. to 6 p.m. at 209-6000. Their operators will answer questions and quote prices.

For next-day delivery to Seattle, a four-kilogram box would cost $123.30 and a letter would cost $40.66. To send a box to Miami would cost $83.93 and a letter $19.12. To ship the same size box to London, England would run $198.66 and the letter would cost $68.68.

DHL also provides an array of other services, such as online tracking and shipping and printable Customs forms, the details of which can be found on its Costa Rica-specific website, www.dhl.co.cr/publish/cr/es.high.html.

Jet Box (253-5400, www.jetbox.com), a smaller, Costa Rican-based company that still has a global reach, also offers courier service, with personalized pricing. Senders can set up contracts for $3 to $8 per kilogram to the United States, for example, which is their most common destination. The pricing depends on volume, location and how regularly they ship. In addition, if a person regularly ships small items and wants to ship a large item, the company will offer a special price.

Another shipping company with membership-based rates is Star Box (289-9393), which offers memberships as low as $2.50 a month. With that membership, clients have the right to send a certain weight of goods per month. The per-kilo cost depends on the membership.

Aerocasillas (208-4848, www.aerocasillas.com), focuses mainly on shipping items into Costa Rica; however, it does ship mail and documents to the United States through Miami.

For larger items, a freight company such as Ship to Costa Rica (258-8747 or from the United States or Canada 1-866-245-6923 toll-free) will have to be used. Shipping from Costa Rica to the east or west coast of the United States takes approximately 12 days, and only six days to Miami. To Europe, for example, the shipping time is from 15 to 20 days.

*Part of this section is reprinted with permission of *The Tico Times*. See: www.ticotimes.net.

EDUCATION

How to Learn Spanish

Although many of Costa Rica's well-educated people speak English, (and more than 30,000 English-speaking foreigners live permanently in Costa Rica), Spanish is the official language. Anyone who seriously plans to live or retire in Costa Rica should know Spanish — the more the better. Frankly, you will be disadvantaged, handicapped and be considered a foreigner to some degree without Spanish. Part of the fun of living in another country is communicating with the local people, making new friends and enjoying the culture. Speaking Spanish will enable you to achieve these ends, have a more rewarding life, and open the door for many new, interesting experiences. Knowing some Spanish also saves you money when you're shopping and, in some cases, keeps people from taking advantage of you.

If you take our advice and choose to study Spanish, you can enroll at one of Costa Rica's intensive conversational language schools for a modest fee. Costa Rica has long been a destination of choice for those wishing to learn Spanish. The majority of the schools are located in the cities of San José, Heredia and Alajuela. A few schools are located in beach areas. Most schools offer programs to fit your specific needs. They have classes for beginners as well as intermediate and advanced students. Classes are also offered for business people, teenagers, children, teachers and other professionals. Many of the schools are affiliated with U.S. universities, so college students can receive credit.

In addition to language instruction, most of these schools offer exciting field trips, interesting activities and room and board with local families, all of which are optional. Living with a family that speaks little—or preferably no—English is a wonderful way to improve your language skills, make new friends and learn about Costa Rican culture at the same time. Please check first with the school of your choice for current prices.

Spanish is not a difficult language to learn. With a little self-discipline and motivation, anyone can acquire a basic Spanish survival vocabulary of between 200 and 3,000 words in a relatively short time. Many Spanish words are similar enough to English, so you can guess their meanings by just looking at them. The Spanish alphabet is almost like the English one, with a few minor exceptions. Pronunciation is easier than in English because you say words as they look like they should be said. Spanish grammar is somewhat complicated but can be made easier if you are familiar with English grammar and find a good Spanish teacher. Practicing with native speakers improves your Spanish because you can hear how Spanish is spoken in everyday conversation. You will learn many new words and expressions not ordinarily found in your standard dictionary.

Watching Spanish television and listening to the radio and language cassettes can also improve your Spanish. We suggest that if you have little or no knowledge of spoken Spanish, you purchase the one-of-a-kind *Christopher Howard's Guide to Costa Rican Spanish*. It is designed especially for people planning to retire or live in Costa Rica. It makes learning easy because the student learns the natural way, by listening and repeating as a child does, without the complications of grammar. If you are interested in a deeper study of Spanish, we include a list of language schools at the end of this section.

Need a little motivation to get started learning Spanish as your second language? The following is from a June 2004 news report: "Bilingualism may help keep certain brain functions working better during normal aging, Canadian psychologists say."

"The researchers compared 'executive functions,' such as the ability to ignore distracting information, in 104 monolingual and bilingual adults aged 30 to 59, and 50 adults aged 60 to 88.

"Bilingual adults performed better and the bilingual advantage increased substantially in those over 60, the researchers found. The

Super Tips For Learning Spanish
by Christopher Howard M.A.

1) Build your vocabulary. Try to learn a minimum of five new words daily.
2) Watch Spanish TV programs. Keep a note pad by your side and jot down new words and expressions. Later use the dictionary to look up any words and expressions you don't understand.
(3) Pay attention to the way the locals speak the language.
(4) Listen to Spanish music.
(5) Talk with as many different Spanish speakers as you can. You will learn something from everyone. Carry a small notebook and write down new words when you hear them.
(6) Read aloud in Spanish for five minutes a day to improve your accent.
(7) Try to imitate native speakers when you talk.
(8) Don't be afraid of making mistakes.
(9) Practice using your new vocabulary words in complete sentences.
10) When you learn something new, form a mental picture to go along with it—visualize the action.
11) Try to talk in simple sentences. Remember, your Spanish is not at the same level as your English, so simplify what you are trying to say.
12) If you get stuck or tongue-tied, try using nouns instead of complete sentences.
13) Remember Spanish and English are more similar than different. There are many cognates (words that are the same of almost the same in both languages).
14) Learn all of the basic verb tenses and memorize the important regular and irregular verbs in each tense.
15) Study Spanish grammar, but don't get bogged down in it.
16) Read the newspaper. The comic strips are great because they have a lot of dialog.
17) It takes time to learn another language. Don't be impatient. Most English speakers are in a hurry to learn foreign languages and get frustrated easily because the process is slow. Study a little bit everyday, be dedicated, persist and most of all enjoy the learning process.

¡Buena suerte! Good luck!

* From *Christopher Howard's Guide to Costa Rican Spanish*.

Getting a Head Start
by Christopher Howard M.A.

If you are seriously considering moving to a Latin American country, you should begin to study Spanish as soon as possible.

Here are a few suggestions that will give you a head start in learning the language. Look for some type of Spanish course that emphasizes conversation as well as grammar and enroll as soon as possible. University extension, junior colleges and night schools usually offer a wide range of Spanish classes.

You should also consider studying at a private language school like Berlitz if there is one near where you reside. Many of these schools allow the students to work at their own pace.

Another excellent way to learn Spanish, if you can afford it, is to hire a private language tutor. Like private schools this type of instruction can be expensive, but is very worthwhile. The student has the opportunity of working one-on-one with a teacher and usually progresses much faster than in a large group situation.

If you happen to reside in an area where there are no schools that offer Spanish classes, you should go to your local bookstore and purchase some type of language cassette. This way, at least you will have a chance to learn correct pronunciation and train your ear by listening to how the language is spoken.

Listening to radio programs in Spanish and watching Spanish television are other ways to learn the language, if you are fortunate enough to live in an area where there are some of these stations.

You can also spend your summer or work vacations studying Spanish in Mexico or Costa Rica. This way you will experience language in real life situations. These language vacations can be enjoyable and rewarding experiences.

Finally, try befriending as many native Spainsh speakers as you can who live in the area where you reside. Besides making new friends, you will have someone to practice with and ask questions about the language.

By following the advice above and making an effort to learn the language, you should be able to acquire enough basic language skills to prepare you for living in a Spanish speaking country. Best of all, you will acquire the life-long hobby of learning a new language in the process.

* From *Christopher Howard's Guide to Costa Rican Spanish*.

study appears in the June 2004 issue of the Journal Psychology and Aging.

" 'It shows that a specific experience, bilingualism, has the ability to modify a central aspect of cognitive functioning and keep the brain functioning at a higher level as normal aging inevitably slows us down," said psychology Professor Ellen Bialystok of York University"

The Spanish spoken in Costa Rica is more or less the same as standard Castilian Spanish except for one big difference which confuses beginning students. Spanish has two forms for addressing a person: *usted* and *tú*. However, in Costa Rica, there is third form: *vos*. The verb form used with *vos* is formed by changing the r at the end of a verb infinitive to s and adding an accent to the last syllable. This form is seldom taught because it is considered a colloquial form, used only in some parts of Central America and South America (Argentina and Uruguay, for example). It is not found in most Spanish textbooks. The chart in this chapter provides an explanation of the use of *vos*.

Don't worry! Once you live in Costa Rica for a while and get used to the Costa Rican way of speaking, you will learn to use the *vos* form almost automatically. Costa Ricans appreciate any effort you make to speak their language.

You will notice that Costa Ricans frequently use local expressions called *tiquismos* that are not used in other Latin American countries. Some of these common expressions are *pura vida* (fantastic, super, great), *tuanis* (very good), *buena nota* (good, OK), *salado* (tough luck, too bad), and many others. If Costa Rica were to have a national motto, the choice would most certainly be, *¡Pura Vida!* This expression has become so popular you will see it on T-shirts, in Spanish dictionaries to show appreciation and mostly for greetings. When used as a greeting it can mean "hello" or "How are you doing?" It can also be used to say "good-bye." When you say, *"pura vida"* a person will usually smile. It can also be used to express joy. The expression is infectious.

Another Costa Rican trait is the common use of *don* (for a man) and *doña* (for a woman) when addressing a middle-aged or older person formally. These forms are used with the first name, as in the case of the famous *"don Juan."* However, you will usually hear the more traditional *señor* or *señora* used instead of *don* or *doña*. Teachers in Costa Rica are addressed as *profesor* or *maestro*, an engineer as *ingeniero* and an attorney as *licenciado*. Using these titles is a sign of respect, and not to do so is considered rude. Anyone with a bachelor's degree is also entitled to be addressed as *licenciado*.

The use of *vos* — the other you

The Spanish spoken in Costa Rica is more or less the same as standard Castilian Spanish except for one big difference that confuses many people. Spanish has two forms for addressing a person: *usted* and *tú*. However, in Costa Rica there is a third form, *vos*. This form is seldom taught because it is considered colloquial. In fact, it is not found in most Spanish textbooks or taught to most English-speaking students in their Spanish classes.

Although the use of *vos* varies from region to region and its consideration as standard Spanish varies widely from country to country, you can hear vos used in many countries of Central America, in the countries of the southern South America (Chile, Argentina, Uruguay) and in parts of Colombia, Peru and Ecuador. In areas of America where there was a strong influence of the Spanish Court, places such as Mexico and Peru, the eventual change from *vos* to *tú* and *vuestra merced - usted* mirrored the evolution of the Spanish language in Spain. However, in regions farther away from the centers of power this evolution did not necessarily follow the same pattern. Instead, in some regions tú was displaced by vos in the friendly address and *usted* was used in the polite address.

Vos is used in Latin America in varying ways. It simply replaces *tú* and has its own conjugation. Though it looks similar to the *tú* verbs, there are slight differences in spelling and also in stress/pronunciation. *Vos* is used only with the present indicative tense, present subjunctive and command forms. The verb form used with *vos* is formed by changing the "r" at the end of a verb infinitive to "s" and adding an accent to the last syllable in the present tense. For example: *vos comprás (comprar)*, *vos comés (comer)*, *vos vivís*. In the present subjunctive the forms are exactly the same. For example: *vos comprés (comprar)*, *vos comás (comer)*, *vos vivás*. When *vos* is used in commands, just drop the final "r" off the infinitive ending of the verb. For example: *comprá (comprar)*, *comé (comer)*, *escribí (escribir)*.

Most common set of verb forms with *vos*

Since *vos* came from a different form of the verb than *tú* it is not surprising to see that the *vos* form of the verb often (although not always) uses a different form of the verb than the *tú*.

If you remember your *vosotros* endings of the present tense, you will assume that the endings evolve to áis, éis, and ís, however the most common system of vos endings in the present tense is the following.

Type of verb	ending
ar	-ás
es	-és
ir	-ís

Stem changes such as o to ue, e to ie, e to i, do not occur. For certain one syllable verbs and *estar*, there is no difference between the *tú* form and the *vos* form (since one syllable words do not usually take accents).

For example, compare the following forms:

verb	tú form	vos form
dar	das	dás
ver	ves	vés
estar	estás	estás
ir	vas	vas

However, for most verbs there is a difference:

verb	tú form	vos form
vivir	vives	vivís
hablar	hablas	hablás
ser	eres	sos
tener	tienes	tenés
pedir	pides	pedís
construir	construyes	construís
traer	traes	traés
dormir	duermes	dormís

In most other tenses, the verb forms are the same, except for the affirmative *vos* command. That form is simply the infinitive without the r and with the vowel of the infinitive ending stressed with a written accent if it's more than one syllable or would otherwise need an accent.

verb	+ tú command	+ vos command
tener	ten	tené
ser	sé	sé
venir	ven	vení
tomar	toma	tomá
hablar	habla	hablá
vivir	vive	viví
beber	bebe	bebé
dar	da	da

*From Christopher Howard's Guide to Costa Rican Spanish.

In Costa Rica, as in the rest of Latin America, the father's and mother's surname comes after a person's given name. For example, if <u>Carlos</u> is born to José <u>García</u> López and Marta <u>Lara</u> Pérez, his complete name would be followed by his father's first surname and then by his mother's: <u>Carlos García Lara</u>. All official documents must have both surnames.

For some basic Spanish phrases and more *tiquismos*, see the section entitled "Important Phrases and Vocabulary" in Chapter 12.

Language Schools

To find a language school, start with the list of the list below. Also, check with foreigners who have studied here, visit the school and observe its classes. Perhaps this reader's experience can help you narrow down your choice. "I have found a great school that I am planning on attending this fall. It's called **IPED** and it is located right in downtown Heredia.

"What originally attracted me to this school is the great reviews it received from its former students that I found in various places.

Conversa is one of Costa Rica's

The prices are reasonable compared to other similar schools, and they provide home-stays with *Tico* families.

"Apparently, they will even have someone pick you up at the airport and take you to your *tico* family's house. I plan to get an apartment in Heredia instead of doing a home stay for various reasons including lower costs but, I can see how home-stays can have some great advantages.

"What really cemented my decision is when I e-mailed some questions to the school. They responded to my message within a couple of hours and really took the time to explain things to me. I guess the big advantage to this school is that they have smaller class sizes and give you more personalized attention. They e-mailed me pictures of the school as well — any school with a hammock out back is right up my alley."

This list should start you on your way. Private, individualized language classes are also available. For listings, look in the classified section of *The Tico Times*.

Centro Lingüístico Conversa has an excellent conversational program at the main school in San José and another campus west of town in a rural setting. See their display ad in this book. Write to Apdo. 17-1007, Centro Colón, San José, Costa Rica.Tel: 221-7649,Fax: 233-2418, E-mail: conversa@racsa.co.cr, Web:www.conversa.co.cr.

IPED has an excellent program and is located in the beautiful city of Heredia. Tel: 238-3608 Tel:/Fax: 237-1801 Toll-free from the United States (888)-Si Hablo or 888 744-2256, E-mail: info@learnspanishcostarica.com or ipedcr@racsa.co.cr .

Intercultura is also located in the city of Heredia. P.O Box 1952-3000, Heredia Costa Rica. Tel/Fax: 260- 8480 or 656- 0127. Toll-free number from the United States or Canada: 1-866-363-5421. E-mail: info@interculturacostarica.com.

Instituto de la Lengua Española offers excellent intensive program. Six hours daily for 15 weeks for $635. Terms begin in January, May and September. Apdo. 100-2350, San José, Costa Rica. Tel: 227-7366, Fax: 227-0211.

Forester Institute International offers a variety of classes. Prices range from $600 to $1150 depending on the program. Apdo. 6945-1000, San José, Costa Rica. Tel: 225-1649, Fax: 225-9236, E-mail: forester@racsa.co.cr.

Intensa has two-, three-, and four-week programs with home- stays available. Prices range from $260 to $545. Apdo. 8110-1000, San

Frequently Used Tiquismos (Costa Rican Expressions)

Alimentar las pulgas — To sleep

Birra — Beer

Brete — work

Pura Vida— Great, Fantastic

Caerle la peseta — To get the idea, understand.

Campo — Space (in line, on a bus etc.)

Chepe — Slang for the city of San José

Chile — A joke

Chinamo — A booth or stand where things are sold

Chuica — A rag or old clothes

Cien metros — One city block

Clavar el pico — To fall asleep

Con el moco caído — Sad

¿Diay? — What can be done about it?

Guaro — Moonshine

Harina— Slang for money

Jalado — Dissipated, pale

Jarana— A debt

Jetonear — To lie

lo duda — You said it! You're right!

Macho - Any fair skin or haired person

Montarse en la carreta — To get drunk

Pachuco—A type of street slang

Pinche - A tight-fisted person

Platero —Money hungry person

Porta amí — Who cares

Rajar — To brag

Tata - Father

Torta — An error or screw-up

Vieras — If you only knew; sure; would you believe

Vino — A snoopy person

Volar pico — To talk a lot

José. Tel: 281-1818, Fax: 253-4337, E-mail: intensa@racsa.co.cr, Web: www.intensa.com.

Academia de Español Intercultura has an excellent reputation and is located in Heredia. Tel: 260-8480, Fax: 260-9243, Web: www.interculturacostarica.com.

Centro Cultural Costarricense Norteamericano has eight schools in different parts of the country. Apdo. 1489-1000, San José, Costa Rica. Tel: 207-7500, Fax: 224-1480, Web: www.cccncr.com.

Instituto Universal de Idiomas has various programs . Apdo. 751-2150, San Pedro, Moravia, Costa Rica. Ave. 2, Calle 9 Tel: 223-9917, Fax: 223-9917, E-mail: info@universal-edu.com, Web: www.universaledu.com.

Institute for Central American Development Studies offers one-month programs, five hours a day, for $892, includes classes, lectures, field trips, and home-stay with a Costa Rican family. Apdo. 3-2070 Sabanilla, San José, Costa Rica. Tel: 234-1381 Fax: 234-1337, E-mail: icads@netbox.com.

Centro Panamericano de Idiomas is a new school in a beautiful rural setting. The cost is about $1000 monthly and covers instruction, home-stay and excursions. Apdo. 151-3007, Heredia, Costa Rica. Tel: 265-6866, Fax: 265-6213.

Mesoamerica Language Institute gives four hours of instruction each day for $80 a week. Apdo. 1524-2050, San Pedro, Costa Rica. Tel: 234-7682, E-mail: mesoamer@racsa.co.cr.

Lisa Tec: Tel: 239-2225, Fax: 293-2894, E-mail: mkcarney@itspanish.com, Web: www.itspanish.com.

IPEE Spanish Language School: Tel: 283-7731, Fax: 506-225-7860, E-mail: ipee@gate.net, Web: www.ipee.com.

Academia Tica's various courses and home-stays cost between $120 and $180 for 20 hours of instruction. Apdo. 1294-2100, Guadalupe, San José, Costa Rica. Tel: 229-0013, E-mail: toyopan@intercentro.net.

ILISA, Instituto Latinoamericano de Idiomas: Apdo. 1011, 2050 San Pedro, Costa Rica or Dept. 1420, P. O. Box 25216, Miami, FL 33102-5216. Tel: 225-2495 Fax: 225-4665. In United States and Canada: (800)-454-7248, E-mail: spanish@ilisa.com.

Centro Lingüístico Latinoamericano teaches intensive courses, five hours per day for four weeks, including home-stay for $295 weekly. Apdo. 425-4005, San Antonio de Belen, Costa Rica. Tel: 293-0128, Fax: 239-1869.

Central American Institute of International Affairs (ICAI) specializes in workshops and conferences, all levels of Spanish and also offers deluxe tours and college credits. Apdo. 10302, San José, Costa Rica. Tel: 233-8571, Fax: 221-5238, E-mail: icai@expreso.co.cr, Web: www.expreso.co.cr/icai/index.htm.

University of Costa Rica now offers Spanish courses as a foreign language through the School of Philology, Linguistics and Literature. This program lasts four months and space is limited. The cost is about $450. Tel: 207-5634, Fax: 207-5089, E-mail: espanucr@cariari.ucr.ac.cr.

Berlitz offers different language programs to meet all of your needs. Tel:(506)-204-7555, (506)-253-9191 Fax: 204-7444, 253-1115, Web: http:www.berlitz.com.

There is a Spanish conversational club for foreigners wanting to improve their Spanish skills. Call 254-1433 or 235-7026 for details. **The Instituto Universal de Idiomas** (Avenida 2, Calles 7/9) has an exchange club where you can practice Spanish with a native speaker in exchange for help with English (257-0441). *Centro Cultural* also has free Spanish social- conversation classes through a program called "Simply Spanish"

You can now combine language study with one of **Christopher Howard's Relocation/Retirement Tours**. Please call 800 365-2342 toll free for details.

Costa Rica's Institutions of Higher Learning

If you wish to continue your education, university-level courses are available to foreigners in subjects such as business, art, history, political science, biology, psychology, literature and Spanish, as well as all other major academic areas.

Foreigners can enroll directly as special students for their first two years at the **University of Costa Rica**. Tuition is much lower than at most U.S. universities. Students can also audit classes for a nominal fee. Contact the University of Costa Rica (UCR) at tel: 207-4000, fax: 225-6950 www.ucr.ac.cr. Another excellent public university is **The Nacional University** (UNA) in Heredia, tel: 506-261-0101, fax: 237-7593, e-mail: webmaster@una.co.ac.cr, www.una.accr. **National Correspondence University** (UNED) offers correspondence,

programs,tel; 253-2121, fax: 506-253-4990, e-mail: cendocu@arenal.
uned.ac.cr, www.uned.ac.cr.

During the last 10 years there has been a proliferation of private
universities. They are mainly for students who can't qualify academically
for the University of Costa Rica or National University of Heredia.
These schools are more expensive than the public universities and
their degrees aren't quite as prestigious. **Autonomous University of
Central America**, or UACA as it is more commonly known here, is
the oldest of these private universities and has an excellent reputation,
tel: 234-0701, fax: 224-0391, e-mail: lauaca@racsa.co.cr. Please see
the local phone book for a listing of the many private universities
found in the San José area.

Some U.S. universities offer programs in Costa Rica for which you
can get university credit. We understand the University of California
offers one such program. However, you are better off surfing the
Internet to see what is available if you want to continue your education
here and receive credits towards a degree in the United States or
Canada.

The University of Costa Rica in San Pedro.

Public Universities

- University of Costa Rica (Universidad de Costa Rica)- The main campus is located in San José. There are also other campuses in Cartago, Turrialba, Puntarenas and Alajuela. Tel: 207-5535, Web: www.ucr.ac.cr.
- National University (Universidad Nacional). The main campus is in the city of Heredia. There are branches in Liberia and Pérez Zeledón. Tel: 277-3317. Web: www.una.ac.cr.
- Institute of Technology (Instituto de Tecnología) Located in the city of Cartago. Tel: 552-5333. Web: wwwitcr.ac.cr
- The State University's Extension Program (Universidad Estatal a Distancia). The main school is in San José. There are more than 30 branches in other parts of the country. Tel: 253-2121. Web: www.uned.ac.cr.

Private Universities

- Adventist University of Central America. Tel: 441-5622, Fax: 441-3465. E-mail: unadeca@racsa.co.cr.
- Escuela de Agricultura de la Región Tropical Húmedo (EARTH). Tel: 255-2000, Fax:255-2726. E-mail: relext@ns.earth.acca. Web: www.earth.accr.
- Latin American University of Science and Technology (ULACIT). Tel: 257-5767, Fax: 222-4542. E-mail: info@ulacit.ac.cr.
- Inter-American University of Costa Rica. Apdo. 6495-1000, San José. Tel: 234-6262, Fax: 253-8744.
- International University of the Americas (UIA). Apdo. 1447-1002, San José. Tel: 233-5304, Fax: 222-3216, E-mail: infomatri@uia.ac.cr. Web: www.uia.ac.cr.
- Instituto Centroamericano para la Administración de Empresa (INCAE). Apdo. 960-4050, Alajuela. Tel: 433-0506, Fax: 433-9101.
- University for Peace, Apdo. 138, Ciudad Colón.Tel: (506) 249-1072, Fax: (506) 249-1929
- University Mundial. Tel: 240-7057, Fax: 236-6537.

Of course, certain requirements for these schools of higher learning must be met. Once again, remember that private universities are generally more expensive than public universities. Please see the telephone book for a more extensive list of private universities.

Outstanding Private Schools

Before I talk about Costa Rican schools, I would like to share with you what one foreign resident said motivated him to move here to educate his children:

"One of the many ills of our American society is, simply we are TOO affluent. I know many are starving and have no shelter. I am not addressing this segment of our society. Rather, I am addressing the great masses in the middle and upper strata. We have too much house, too many cars, too many things, too much stuff. Add to this, the influence of the reactionary baby-boomer parents who wish to give their children everything they didn't have, and you end up with a population of children who have unrealistic expectations of what life is, who are disenchanted, listless, confused, depressed, and seeking an out. They grew up in unstructured environments with too much stuff and not enough rules, or any kind of life ethic that would help them to grow into successful human beings. In short, they weren't optimally deprived of money, free time, privileges, etc.

Costa Rica isn't as affluent as the United States in the ways that many measure, but I'll bet the kids truly understand the principle of working to attain a goal, and I'll bet more of them have real purpose, respect, and discipline than American children. The United States has become too affluent and now complacent. We are seeing the ills of this everywhere. Costa Rica is looking pretty good."

If you have small children or teenagers, you will be pleased to know that Costa Rica has a variety of schools from which to choose. There are many public schools, numerous private bilingual schools and four English-language or American schools. The location of the school you chose will also determine your choice of where to live. Your educational options are much greater in the Central Valley than in rural or outlying areas. Living out side of the Central Valley will most certainly limit your choice of schools. Public schools in rural areas most often offer instruction only through the ninth grade.

Public schools tend to be crowded, but legal foreign residents are entitled to attend public schools. However, since all instruction is in Spanish, you should not even think of enrolling an older child in a public school unless they speak, read and write Spanish fluently. Children younger then 10 usually can pick up the language quickly. If your children are not Spanish speakers, you also have the option of enrolling them in a private school if there is one in your area.

All schools in Costa Rica that go beyond the ninth grade have to offer the **National Baccalaureate** or *Bachillerato de Educación Diversificada*. This degree is required to enroll in university in Costa Rica. With this *diploma* alone, however, it is very difficult if not impossible to enter a university in the United States.

The **International Baccalaureate** is a second type of *diploma* offered by Costa Rica's European schools. To earn this *diploma*, students must complete and test in six subjects; write an extended 4,000 word essay of independent research guided by a faculty mentor; complete 150 hours of creative, action and service (CAS) activities; and participate in a critical thinking course called **Theory of Knowledge**. The program begins in the 11th grade and is completed in the 12th grade. Admittance to universities in the UUnited States, Europe and Latin America is possible with this degree.

The third type of degree is the **United States Diploma**, with which students may be admitted to universities in the United States or Europe and other parts of the world. But you cannot enter university in Costa Rica with this *diploma* alone. All of the American Schools in Costa Rica offer the United States Diploma. The Southern Association of Colleges and Schools, (SACS), accredits all of these schools.

Where the International Baccalaureate is not offered, in the American Schools, many students opt for two *diplomas* to create more opportunities when choosing a university. They work for the National Baccalaureate, then go onto the 12th grade for the United States

Group of students at a Costa Rican private school.

Diploma. In the 12th grade many students take advanced placement courses, to get college credit.

All Costa Rican students whether they attend private or public schools, are required to take **Public Education Ministry** (MEP) testing in the sixth, ninth and 11th grade.Even if they have perfect grades, students have to pass these tests to move on to the next level.

The school week is Monday through Friday, and the day begins about 7:30 a.m. and ends about 2 p.m. in private schools. Schedules vary according to the school and age of the students. Public schools are on a similar schedule unless they are operating two shifts, in which case the second shift may not end before 5 or 6 p.m.

Most schools include pre-kinder to 12th grade. The school structure is further divided into pre-kinder, kinder, primaria (grades one to six), secundaria (seventh to 12th grades). Some private schools have a middle school (grades seven and eight) and high school (grades nine through 12). Class size in private schools ranges from 20 to 30 students, depending on the age of the students and the school. Public schools tend to have much larger classes, ranging from 40 to 60 students.

Students are graded on a scale with 100 being the highest possible score and 70 being the minimum passing grade. The grading system is not on an ABCDF system as in many schools in the United States.

Students from pre-kinder through 12th grade are required to wear uniforms established by each school. Even private schools require the use of uniforms. There is usually an emblem on the chest of each school's shirt with the name of the particular institution.

Costa Rica's private English-language American schools are exceptional, and have high academic standards. Four are accredited in the United States: Lincoln School, Marian Baker School, Country Day School and American International School. Some follow the U.S. school year schedule with vacations in June, July and August.

Others follow the Latin American academic calendar, which begins sometime in February and ends in November or December. Changing from the U.S. calendar to one of these schools may require that your children move back half a year and start the grade over. Schools are also free to move students up a half-year if they are academically and mature enough to handle the change.

These schools are academically oriented and prepare students for admittance to colleges in the United States as well as in Costa Rica. They teach English as a primary language and offer Spanish as a second language. In some ways these schools are better than similar institutions in the United States because not as many harmful distractions or bad influences exist in Costa Rica. Children also have the opportunity to learn a new language, which is of great value to them. The cost of some of these private schools can be more than $300 per month.

It is a good idea to visit a number of schools before deciding which one is right for your child. You should ask to visit a couple of classrooms as well as see all of the facilities. This way you may view the school's infrastructure.

Make a list of the pros and cons of each school before making your final decision. Do not forget to see if the school is accredited in the United States Also find out about the teacher-student ratio. Be sure to see what percentage of the students graduate and go on to universities in Costa Rica and the United States. Finally, try to talk to other foreigners who have children enrolled in private schools to see if they are satisfied with the quality of education their children receive.

We talked with one U.S. couple who did not have the resources to afford a private school, so they opted for home schooling. They recommended several programs that you can find on the Internet: www.calvertschool.edu, www.unl.edu and www.keystonehighschool.com.

Our son attends the Lincoln School in Moravia. He has learned more than at the private school he attended in the United States. All subjects are taught in English except for an hour a day of Spanish. There are special courses of Spanish as a second language for students new to the country and advanced classes for foreign students who have mastered the language and Costa Ricans. We have seen children who move to the country learn to speak fluent Spanish in a couple of years. Conversely, Costa Rican children are able to master English in a short period of time. If you listen to the high school students speak English, you would think they grew up in North America. It must be pointed out that, generally, the younger the student, the more quickly a second language can be learned. Junior and senior high school students take much longer to learn a new language than preschool and elementary students.

The following schools are accredited in the United States. Some follow the U.S. schedule, September to June. Others follow the Costa Rican academic year which, begins in March and ends in November:

Lincoln School: Pre-kindergarten through grade 12 with classes in English. Tuition about $450 monthly: Apdo. 1919, San José, Costa Rica. Tel: 247-0800, Fax: 247-0900, E-mail: director@lincoln.ed.cr, Web: www.lincoln.ed.cr. Follows the U.S. academic year.

American International School: Pre-kindergarten through grade 12. Classes taught in English, U.S.-style education. Annual tuition: $1,070 pre-kindergarten, $3,130 for kindergarten to grade 12. Apdo. 4941-1000, San José, Costa Rica. Tel: 239-2567, Fax: 239-0625 E-mail: aiscr@cra.ed.cr. Follows the U.S. school year.

Country Day School: (Escazú) Kindergarten through grade 12. Annual tuition: $3,245 pre-kindergarten, $6,510 grades one to 12. Apdo. 8-6170, San José, Costa Rica. Tel: 289-8406, Fax: 228-2076, E-mail: codasch@racsa.co.cr, Web: www.cds.ed.cr. Follows the U.S. school year.

Country Day School Guanacaste: This new branch of the Country Day School offers a curriculum similar to the main campus in Escazú. Since the school is located near Flamingo, a surfing class is available for high school students. All subjects are taught in English except for Spanish. Future boarding facilities are being considered. Tel: 654-5042, Fax: 654-5044, E-mail: cdsgte@costarica.net, Web: www.cds.ed.cr.

Marian Baker School: Kindergarten through grade 12. U.S. curriculum with classes in English. Annual tuition: $3,550 kindergarten, $6,610 preparatory to grade six and grades seven to 12. Apdo. 4269, San José, Costa Rica, Tel: 273-3426, Fax: 234-4609; E-mail: mbschool@racsa.co.cr. Web: www.marianbakerschool.com. Follows the U.S. school year.

Blue Valley School: Preschool to grade 12. Tel: 215-2203,Fax: 228-8653, E-mail: bvschool@racsa.co.cr., Web: www.bluevalley.ed.cr. Follows both U.S. and Costa Rican calendars.

The European School: Pre-kindergarten through six. Apdo. 177, Heredia, Costa Rica. Tel: 261-0717, Fax: 237-4063, E-mail: eurschool@cafebritt.com or aaronson@racsa.co.cr, Web: www. eupeanschool.com

The less expensive bilingual private schools below also prepare students for U.S. colleges and universities, but follow the Costa Rican academic year that begins in March and ends in November.

Anglo American School: Kindergarten through grade six. Costs about $100 a month. Apdo. 3188-1000, San José, Costa Rica. Tel: 225-1723.

British School: Kindergarten through grade 12. Tel: 2200131, Fax: 506-232-7822,E-mail:director@britishschoolcr.com,Web: www.britishschoolscr.com.

Canadian International School Pre-kindergarten through grade two. About $100 monthly. Apdo. 622-2300, San José, Costa Rica. Tel: 272-7097; Fax: 272-6634.

Colegio Bilingue Santa Cecilia: Preschool to grade 11. Tel: 237-7733, Fax: 237-4557, colsuper@racsa.co.

Colegio Humboldt: Kindergarten through grade 12. Classes half in German, half in Spanish. Apdo. 3749, San José, Costa Rica. Tel: 232-1455, Fax: 232-0093, E-mail: humboldt@racsa.co.cr, Web: www.infoweb.co.cr/humbolt.

Colegio Internacional: Grades seven through 10. Apdo. 963, 2050 San Pedro, Costa Rica. Tel: 224-3136 Fax: 253-9762, E-mail: sekerdir@racsa.co.cr, Web: www.sek.net.

Colegio Metodista: Kindergarten through grade 12. Classes in English and Spanish. Apdo. 931-1000, San José, Costa Rica. Tel: 225-0655, Fax: 225-0621.

Escuela Británica: Kindergarten through grade 11, classes half in English, half in Spanish. $150 per month. Apdo. 8184-1000 San José, Costa Rica. Tel: 220-0131 Fax: 232-7833, E-mail: british@racsa.co.cr, Web: www.infoweb.co.cr/british..

Liceo Franco-Costarricense: Classes in French, English and Spanish. Concepción de Tres Ríos. Tel: 273-4543, Fax: 279-6615, E-mail: lyfrancos@racsa.co.cr, Web: www.lefranco.ac.cr.

International Christan School: Pre-kindergarten through grade 12. Annual tuition: $990 pre-kindergarten, $1,300 preparatory and kindergarten, $2,200 grades one to six, $2,300 grades 7 - 8 , $2,500 grades 9 - 12. Apdo. 3512-1000, San José, Costa Rica. Tel: 241-1445 Fax: 241-4944, E-mail: intchris@racsa.co.cr, Web: wwwicscr.net.

Pan American School: Pre-kinder through 12. Tel: 293-7393, Fax: 298-5700, E-mail: cpcrsa@racsa.co.cr, Web: www.panam.ed.cr. Located in San Antonio de Belén.

Saint Anthony School: Pre-school through grade 6. Classes half in English, half in Spanish. Apdo. 29-2150, Moravia, Costa Rica. Tel: 235-1017, Fax: 235-2325, E-mail: santhony@racsa.co.cr.

Saint Francis: Kindergarten through grade 11, classes in English and Spanish. Inquire about rates. Apdo. 4405-1000, San José Costa Rica. Tel: 297-1704 Fax: 240-9672, E-mail: sfc@stfrancis.ed.cr.

Saint Mary's: Pre- kindergarten through grade six, about $100 monthly. Classes in English and Spanish. Apdo. 229-1250, Escazú, Costa Rica. Tel: 228-2003.

Summerhill Latinoamericano: Pre-school, elementary school and weekend camp programs. Tel: 280-1933, Fax: 283-0146.

*See the yellow pages for more listings.

Here are some links to online Spanish courses.

Some of them are free:

http:// www.pimsleurapproach.com

http://www.rosettastone.com

http://www.bbc.co.uk/languages/spanish/

http://www.donquijote.org/online/

http://www.docnmail.com/learnmore/language/spanish.htm

http://www.ihspain.com/madrid/online_spanish.html

http://www.studyspanish.com/

http://www.learn-spanish-online.de/

http://www.spanish-online.com/

http://www.speakteacher.com/

http://www.spanishprograms.com/

http://www.learnspanishtoday.com/

* From Christopher Howard's Guide to Costa Rican Spanish.

Excellent Books for Learning Spanish

Christopher Howard's Guide to Costa Rican Spanish, by Christopher Howard. This book is especially designed to help you speak like a Costa Rican native. More than 25 years of research went into the preparation of this guide. It contains one section explaining Costa Rican slang. This material cannot be found anywhere else.

Madrigal's Magic Key to Spanish, by Margarita Madrigal. Dell Publishing Group , 666 Fifth Avenue, New York, NY 10103. Provides an easy method of learning Spanish based on the many similarities between Spanish and English. This book is a "must" for the beginner.

Open Door to Spanish - A Conversation Course for Beginners by Margarita Madrigal. Regent Publishing Company. (books 1 and 2). Two more great books for the beginner.

Spanish for Gringos, by William C. Harvey. Barron's Press. This is an amusing book that will help you improve your Spanish.

Barron's Spanish Idioms, by Eugene Savaia and Lynn W. Winget. This book has more than 2,000 idiomatic words and expressions. It is a helpful handbook for students of Spanish, tourists and business people who want to increase their general comprehension of the language.

Barron's Basic Spanish Grammar, by Christopher Kendris. An in-depth study of Spanish grammar.

A New Reference Grammar of Modern Spanish, by John Butt and Carmen Benjamin. NTC Publishing Group. This one of the best reference books ever written about Spanish grammar. It is very easy to use and understand.

Barron's Spanish Vocabulary, by Julianne Dueber. A good book for building vocabulary.

Household Spanish, by William C. Harvey. Barron's Press. A user-friendly book especially for English-speakers who need to communicate with Spanish-speaking employees.

Useful Reference Books

Dictionary of Spoken Spanish Words, Phrases and Sentences. Dover Publications Inc., New York, NY. ISBN 0-486-20495-2. This is the best of all phrase dictionaries. It contains more than 18,000 immediately useable sentences and idioms. We recommend it highly.

The New World English/Spanish Dictionary, by Salvatore Ramondino. A Signet Book. Another excellent dictionary of Latin American Spanish.

Latin-American Spanish Dictionary, by David Gold. Ballantine Books. A good dictionary of Spanish used in Latin America.

Business Books

Just Enough Business Spanish, Passport Books. Full of phrases to help the businessman.

Talking Business in Spanish, by Bruce Fryer and Hugo J. Faria. Barron's Educational Series. Has more than 3,000 business terms and phrases. A must for any person planning to do business in the Spanish-speaking world.

2007 - 2008
Costa Rica Books Catalog
More Great Books to Buy!

These highly specialized guides are availables through our catalog.
On special request some can be ordered from bookstores
in the U.S. Canada or Europe

Christopher Howard's Living & Investing in the New Nicaragua
By Tim Rogers

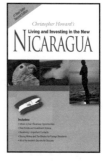

"This visionary work will help anyone thinking of living or making money in Nicaragua. It promises to become a Classic.".

This one-of-a-kind guidebook provides you with all the tools for living and investing in Nicaragua - Central America's "Sleeping Giant" and Land of Oportunity.

Living and Investing in Panama
By Christopher Howard

This one-one-of-a-kind definitive guidebook will tell you everything you need know about living and investing Latin America's most underrated country. Panama best benefits for retires of any country south of the border. It also has the most attractive financing for real estate purchases.

Christopher Howard's Guide to Costa Rican Spanish
By the author of **The Golden Door to Retirement and Living in Costa Rica**, Christopher Howard

*"A must if you plan to live in Costa Rica.
The ONLY book that teaches you Costa Rican slang!"*

FAST, EASY, PROVEN METHOD!
GUARANTEED RESULTS!
BEST SELLER

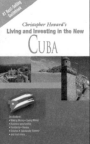

10

GETTING AROUND

Air Travel to-in-and around Costa Rica

Most direct flights from Miami cost less, however there are flights from your home city to San José by way of Los Angeles, Houston, Atlanta, Chicago, Washington D.C., New Orleans or Panama.

Most flights arrive at **Juan Santamaría International Airport** (Tel: 443-2622) the country's main airport, located about a half-hour northwest of San José. The airport now boasts a new terminal with restaurants and many shops. Many travelers choose to fly into **Daniel Oduber International Airport**, the country's other major airport, located near the city of Liberia. The main attraction here is the airport's proximity to the excellent Pacific beaches in the northern province of Guanacaste. Many U.S. carriers now offer daily flights to this area. Delta, Air Canada and American West are now flying to Guanacaste. About 200,000 passengers enter yearly through this new airport.

However, the vast majority of flights continue to land at Juan Santamaría Airport. About 3 million passengers entered through this airport in 2004. The airlines currently offering service from the United States to San José, Costa Rica, are **Aviateca** (800-327-9832), **Sasha** (800-327-1225), **Continental** (800-231-0856), **Mexicana** (531-7921), **Grupo Taca** (800-535-8780), **American** (800-433-7300), **Delta** (800-241-4141), **United** (800-538-2929) and **LACSA** Costa

Rica's national airline. Lacsa's toll-free number is 800-225-2272 in the United States and 800-663-2444 in Canada.

Some airline tickets are good for a year, but you need permission from Costa Rican Immigration to stay in the country longer than 90 days unless you are a resident or *pensionado*. Most airlines offer excursion rates and three-or-four week packages. Others, especially Canadian airlines, offer special group and charter rates. Fares are subject to availability, change and restrictions including advance purchase requirements, minimum stops or cancellation penalties. Remember, the main tourist season in Costa Rica runs from about Thanksgiving to Easter. This period coincides approximately with local vacations, so it is hard to find available space at this time of year. If you are planning to travel to or from Costa Rica during December, you may have to buy a ticket months in advance because of the Christmas holidays. However, if you get into a jam you can sometimes find space on a flight via Panama.

If you plan to travel or explore South America from Costa Rica, you can usually save money by flying to Miami and then buying a round-trip ticket to your destination. For instance, a one-way ticket from San José to Buenos Aires, Argentina can cost more than a round trip ticket from Miami to Buenos Aires.

The Travel Store (www.allcostaricatravel.com e-mail: travel@ costaricatravelstore.com) and **Tico Travel** (800-493-8426) specialize in trips to Costa Rica. Retirement/Relocation Tours may be booked through **Live in Costa Rica Tours** (800-365-2342).

International Airlines Located in San José Costa Rica	
Airport Information	441-6069/443-2622
American Airlines, La Sabana	257-1266
Avianca	233-3066
Aviateca	257-9444
Continental	296-4911
Copa	222-6640
Delta	257-4141
Grupo Taca	257-9444
Iberia	257-8266
KLM	220-4119
Luthansa	221-7444
LTU	243-9292
Martin Air	232-3246
Mexicana	257-6334
United	220-4844

A Travel Business is Born
By Robert Hodel

So there I was, preparing for the culmination of three years of law when I realized that sinking feeling just was not going to go away.

That feeling I was referring to was the fact that I did not want to spend the rest of my life, nor even one minute for that matter, as a lawyer.

As soon as I accepted that fact I was in a quandry. What was I to do?

It was then I remembered from somewhere that the key to any successful business venture one may choose is to: 1) do what you like and 2) do what you know or do well.

With that in mind I pondered my future both day and night. Finally, I realized the thing I liked most to do was travel and the place I knew best, other than my home town, was Costa Rica.

I knew where was the best place to go and when. I also knew how to get the best prices on airfare, rental cars and hotels. So after a long phone call with my brother, who was even more knowledgeable than myself, I had a plan.

We would start a travel company dedicated primarily to Costa Rica and we would call it Tico Travel. I would move back to Costa Rica and introduce myself to the hotels, car rental companies and tour operators that we wanted to work with plus stay on top of any new developments that would be of interest to our clients. My brother moved to Florida and opened our office and was able to give our clients expert information on Costa Rica with a "gringo" point of view.

Within a short amount of time we became the agency of choice for people that travel frequently to Costa Rica and also for the first time visitor.

Along the way we learned many things. For instance, just because it makes sense does not mean it works that way.

We also found no matter how much we advertised, that over 80% of our clients were either clients' referals or repeat customers, as a testimony to how important one's reputation is in this part of the world.

I have been told many times that one could make many times more money with the same effort if we were in the United States.

That may be so but I have been told something else by a longtime resident here,"We are not here for the money, we are here for the lifestyle."

See Tico Travel on the Internet at www.ticotravel.com.

Domestic Airlines

Smaller domestic airlines such as Sansa, Nature Air or chartered planes called air taxis, are used for flights within the country. Domestic airlines use four-to-15-passenger planes. The latter can cost up to a few hundred dollars an hour. Sansa, the national airline, is more reasonably priced ($15 to $30, depending on your destination). Sansa flies to the beach cities of Golfito, Quepos, Barra del Colorado, Sámara, Nosara, and Tamarindo. We recommend purchasing your tickets in advance, especially during the heavy tourist season (December to May.) These flights get you to your designation quickly and economically, save you time, and give you the thrill of viewing Costa Rica's spectacular landscape from above.

Sansa's office is in the **Grupo Taca** building diagonal to the northeast corner of the Sabana Park. Call 221-9414, or e-mail; info@ flysansa.com or sansa@lacsa.atlas-com or see www.flysansa.com for flight times and reservations. Some travel agencies in San José also make reservations. **Nature Air** offers domestic flights. Call 220-3054 or see www.natureair.com. Charters are available at 257-0766 or www. costaricacharters.com. Also look in the yellow pages under *"Taxis Aereos."*

Traveling by City Bus

Bus fares from San José to the surrounding suburbs are very cheap. On urban and inter-urban buses, you pay the driver as you board.

Here is a list of where to catch a bus from the center of San José to surrounding neighborhoods.

Alajuela	Ave. 2 across from Parque La Merced
Alajuelita	Ave. 6/8, Calle 8
Aserrí	Ave. 4/6, Calle 7
Barrio México	Ave. 3, Calle 3
Barrio Luján	Ave 2, Calles 5 /7
Calle Blancos	Ave. 5, Calles 1/3
Coronado	Ave. 7, Calle 0
Curridabat	Ave. 6, Calles 3/5
Desamparados	Ave. 4, Calles 5/7
Escazú	Ave. 0/1, Calle 16
Guadalupe	Ave.3, Calle 0
Hatillos	Ave. 2/6 Calle 6, Ave. 4 Calle 2

Traveling by bus around San José or to the surrounding suburbs may seem quite difficult to a newcomer. However, once you get the hang of it, you will find it a surprisingly easy and affordable way to travel. Most expatriates who do not have cars use the city's excellent bus system. A few who own cars prefer taking buses to avoid traffic and paying for parking.

If you do not know where to catch a specific city bus to your destination, then you will have to ask someone. If you cannot find an English speaker who knows or your Spanish is not adequate, then go to the tourism office below the Plaza de la Cultura in the heart of San José. They will provide you a free map of San José's bus stops. Also, you might want to ask a policeman who can usually help.

Buses provide inexpensive transportation to any destination in the country.

When you finally find your bus stop, you should not assume that every bus that stops there goes to your destination. It is not unusual to have several buses with different routes using the same bus stop. When in doubt, try to ask someone who is waiting, "*¿A dónde va este autobús?*" (Where does this bus go?). Another thing you can do is look at the sign displayed horizontally above the windshield or at the lower left-hand-corner of the front window. These signs will list the final destination of the bus.

Once you figure out which bus to take, have your change in hand and be ready to pay the bus fare. You can usually find out how much the fare is by asking one of the people waiting or by looking at the sign in the bus's window. Do not be in a hurry to board, since some passengers may exit through the front door.

When you get inside the bus, hand the driver your fare. If you do not have the exact amount the driver will make change. Try to avoid giving the driver anything larger than a 2,000 *colón* bill. Be careful not to stand between the electronic counter or the driver will get mad. They were installed to replace the turnstiles most *buses* used to have. These devices have an electric eye and count the number of people who use the bus. Once, a friend of mine boarded a bus, and his young son accidentally stood in front of the electric counter. The driver made my friend pay an extra fare or he would have had to pay the amount out of his own pocket.

Next, you will need to find a seat. It is advisable not to sit on the sunny side of the bus. A large number of buses have large windows with no curtains. If you sit on the side the sun hits, you may feel like you are under a magnifying glass. However, many of the newer buses have curtains you can draw to keep out the sun.

During rush hour, buses tend to be very crowded and you often have to stand if you cannot find a seat. In this case, take hold of one of the horizontal bars. Most buses start and stop with a jerky motion and it is easy to fall if you are standing and not holding on to something.

Be sure to let the driver know about a block before you want to get off. You can do this by pulling the horizontal cord next to the window or by pressing an overhead button. *Buses* usually have one these devices. If you cannot locate the cord or button, or if either one of them does not work, then yell, "*Parada!*" (Stop!), so the driver will know to let you off at the next stop. If you do not know at which bus stop to get off, ask the driver or someone else on the bus. Usually the name of a street, neighborhood or landmark will suffice. If you let the driver know where you want to be let off upon boarding, he will usually remember to tell you when you reach your stop.

Bus Travel Around Costa Rica

For a very low cost ($2 to $8, or about $1 per hour of driving time) you can take a bus to almost anywhere in the country. Most Costa Ricans do not own cars, so they depend on buses for traveling to other parts of the country. Riding a bus provides the perfect opportunity to get to know people on a personal basis, see the lovely countryside and learn something about the country and the culture. Most buses used for these longer trips are modern and very comfortable. Unlike some parts of Latin America, Costa Rica's buses are not filled with chickens and other small animals and standing is not allowed. Buses are crowded on weekends and holidays, so buy your tickets in advance or get to the station early. Be sure to check for schedule changes.

Alajuela (a bus every 20 minutes or so), Ave. 2,
Calle 12/14...222-5325
Arenal (buses at 4:15, 8:40, 11:30 am), Calle 16, Ave. 1/3
Cartago (a bus every 10 minutes), Calle 5,
Ave. Central, Calles18/20 233-5350
Golfito (get tickets in advance), Ave. 3/5, Calle 14........221-4214
Heredia (a bus every five minutes), Calle 1, Ave. 7/9 233-5350
Heredia (small buses or busetas), Ave.2, Calles 12/14.. 261-7171
Liberia (get tickets in advance), Calle 14, Ave. 1/ 3.......222-1650
Limón (hourly get tickets in advance on holidays),
Calle Central, six blocks north of the Metropolitan
Cathedral..221-2596 or 223-7811
Nicoya (get tickets in advance), Calle 14, Ave. 3/5 222-2666
Puntarenas (every 30 minutes; be early on holidays),
Calle16, Ave. 10/12..222-0064
Quepos (get tickets in advance inside the market),
Coca Cola Terminal...223-5567
San Carlos (a bus every hour), Coca Cola Terminal......255-4318
Santa Cruz, Calle 20, Ave.3/4....................................221-7202
San Isidro El General (get tickets in advance),
Calle 16, Ave. 1/3.. 222-2422
San Ramón Calle16, Ave. 10/12 222-0064
Sarchí (Coca Cola Terminal, every hour),

Calle 16/18, Ave. 1/5	494-2139

Southern Border (Paso Canoas, leaves daily)

Ave. 3/5, Calle 14	221-4214
Tilarán (daily) Calle 12, Ave. 7/9	222-3854
Turrialba, Calle 13, Ave. 6/8	556-0073

*If your destination is not listed, check with a local travel agency or some knowledgeable person who is familiar with bus schedules and knows the different bus stops. An Intercity Buses website gives a complete bus schedule at www.yellowweb.co.cr/crbuses.hmtl.

Bus tickets may be purchased online at www.CostaRicaBusTicket. com. This company covers most areas north and west of San José. You may contact them at 365-9678.

Interbus (tel. 283-5573, fax 283-7655, e-mail vsftrip@racsa.co.cr, www.interbusonline.com) and **Fantasy Tour/Gray Line** (tel. 220-2126, fax 220-2393, e-mail fantasy@racsa.co.cr, www.graylinecostarica. com) offer direct tours between many of the country's major tourist attractions. Both companies offer transportation to more than 40 destinations and have offices around the country. *Costa Rica by Bus* is a great new book that covers bus routes, fares and more. To purchase a copy, see www.costaricabybus.com.

Bus Travel to and from Costa Rica

If you want to travel to Guatemala, Panama or other Central American countries, you can use the bus services listed. If you want to live in Costa Rica permanently without being a legal residents, you can take a bus to Panama or Nicaragua, return to Costa Rica after 72 hours, and thus renew your papers so you can remain legally in the country for another 90 days. Many foreigners living as perpetual tourists in Costa Rica go through this procedure every few months in order to avoid Immigration hassles.

From time to time, the Immigration asks to see a return ticket before extending tourist cards. So it is a good idea to buy an inexpensive bus ticket to a neighboring country to prove you can leave the country.

Tica Bus (tel: 2218954), Avenidas 2 and 4 between Calles 9 and 11, offers bus service to the rest of Central America.

San José to Panama City leaves daily at 10 p.m. from the **Tica Bus** Terminal. The 542-mile journey takes 18 hours.

San José to David (Panama) leaves daily at 7:30 a.m. from Avenida 5 , Calle 14. It makes the 240 mile-trip in nine hours.

San José to Managua leaves the **Sirca Bus Company** at 6 a.m. The 270-mile trip takes about 10 hours.

San José to Guatemala leaves daily at 6 a.m. from Avenida 4, between Calles 9 and 11. This trip takes two and a half days.

San José to Honduras leaves at 6 a.m. daily.

Traveling by Train

Costa Rica's rail system was originally built in the late 1800s to serve the coffee and banana industry. One line ran from San José to Puntarenas on the Pacific coast and another from San José to Puerto Limón on the Caribbean. In 1995 regular passenger train service on Costa Rica's two main rail lines was shut down due to economic losses. The famous "Jungle Train" that ran from San José to the Caribbean port of Limón was discontinued because of earthquake-caused landslides. Starting in 2002, the **Railroad Institute** (**INCOFER**) offered twice weekly passenger service to Puntarenas. With any luck, full train service to both coasts will resume soon.

Due to an effort to reduce traffic in the metropolitan San José area two interurban commuter lines were started in the last year. One train runs from east to west from Pavas to the Universidad Latina in San Pedro. Another line runs for about eight miles from San Vicente de Paul Hospital in the city of Heredia to the Universidad Latina. In the future the commuter routes could be expanded to Alajuela and Cartago.

Costa Rica's Taxis

As we mentioned in Chapter 3, it is not necessary to own an automobile if you live in or near San José because taxis are plentiful and inexpensive. San Jose's buses are cheaper, but taxis are the best way to get from point A to point B.

Taxis registered with the **Ministry of Public Works and Transportation** (MOPT) are red with a yellow triangle on both front doors. The triangle contains the taxi's license number, which begins with the letter(s) of the province where the cab is licensed and registered, followed by a "P" for province. For example, a taxi registered in San José province has a license plate number beginning with "SJP."

Tico Train Tour
By John Vickery

About a month ago I was walking down the train tracks over in Sabana Sur when I thought I heard a train whistle (horn?). Must have been the previous evenings cerveza confusing my hearing as I'd only seen one train in 6 months. I checked behind me and here was a 6 car train bearing down on me at the incredible speed of maybe 35 kph. I stepped off the tracks with plenty of time spare and watched it pass. There were people (old & young) hanging out the windows waving and smiling. Hmmmmm... I thought it would be fun to ride a train sometime. Where would this train be going, and how could I get a ride? I thought I'd done my homework after moving here. Obviously I'd missed something. Finding new experiences in a new land is exciting.

The next weeks *Tico Times* had a small article about the train I saw. I visited their web page http://www.ticotraintour.com/ and liked what I saw and fired off an Email. I received an almost instant reply in English and they sent 5 or 6 pictures of the train ride which are not on the website. Two small problems with the web page. Page says the train goes to the East coast but it goes to Caldera (west coast) and two of the Email addresses (both RACSA) do not work . The working address is: americatravel@ice. co.cr Anyway, we along with 4 friends took that train ride yesterday (8th of May) and had a good time. This was a spur of the moment decision. I received a phone call around noon on Saturday (7th of May) from a Tico friend asking if we'd be interested in taking the train the next day if he could get tickets? "Of course", I said. Less than an hour later I received another call saying everything was set and a taxi would be picking us up at 7:15 am at our front door. It was on time and we were off! I had no idea where the train station was in Alajuela but the taxi driver did and when we were dropped off, another group was waiting on the platform at the (seemingly) deserted train station. It's difficult to describe but everyone on that platform appeared quite exited for the upcoming train ride. I know I was and my expectations were rewarded nicely.

The company has an office in Alajuela in addition to the one at the Pacific train station in San Jose and they claim tickets must be purchased in advance. One of our party joined us at the last minute and purchased her ticket on the train. Since we all reside in Alajuela we really did not wish to go into San Jose to catch that train at 7:00, we asked for another pick up location. The train stopped and picked us (and 6 others) up at the station in Ciruelas (spelling) here in Alajuela at 7:45.

It is a very pleasant ride through countryside and towns that is not seen from the highways. Most times you can hang out the widows taking pictures or just observing the passing countryside. Beware that this is not a routine train and there are places the trees and scrub is not trimmed back. I had a few tree branches hit my head (no bigee) and there were a few gorges (through the rock walls) where the clearance between the train and the wall is measured in inches. Just watch where you are going when you dangle out the window. Huge bridge just before Atenas that anyone afraid of heights should not look out the widow as you cross. Fantastic sight! If you are not afraid of heights, get your camera out and take pictures. Quick one minute stop just before

Atenas for people to observe and take pictures of an old turn of the centuryelectric locomotive. You'll never feel any uphill grade during this ride, but think about it. How do you get out of the central valley without going over the mountains? Carefully keep sticking your head out the window and watch where you're going.

Quick aside here: I would advise not choosing a passenger car directly behind the locomotive as the engineer is constantly blasting the horn and it is very loud.

Attention: If you pick the absolute last car from San Jose, (kinda quiet) You'll then be in the absolute first car (right behind the locomotive) on the return trip. That's a hint for you. Think about it. I'm betting only about 50% of those horn blasts are required for intersections and the other 50% is to alert everyone that we are coming through so they can come out and wave to us. All ages come out but the smiles on the kids are contagious. You can't help but wave and smile back! It's unbelievable as to the number of folks who come out to wave & smile.

No alcohol is allowed on the train and smoking is only permitted on the little walkway between the cars. (be careful)

This is one example of the personal responsibility that I love CR for. If you wish to stand on that platform and smoke. It is your responsibility to hold onto the hand rail. If not, you could fall off the train very easily and you might not be missed for miles or hours. There is NO big brother govt watching you here. Adjust!

After passing through Atenas (no stop) you get some nice views of three of the bridges that someday may be part of that long talked about new road. One bridge appears be having quite a bit of excavation work being done at one end. I have seen very nice views up in the Atenas area from the highway (?) but those views pale compared to the scenes from the train.

Next stop (maybe 5 minutes) is in the middle of some street in downtown Orotina.

The train ride continues and everyone is watching out the windows when it appears that the train somehow has left the tracks and is driving down the road. Pavement on both sides of the train and pulperias and shops on both sides. WOW!

Nothing happening at this stop until the return trip when the train is swamped by people selling many different food stuffs. After this stop we continue on with more horn blasts and more people coming out to wave at us. (smile!)

Lovers take note: Just before arriving in Caldera you will spend about a minute in absolute darkness (you literally cannot see your hand in front of your face) traveling through a tunnel. It's fun! Arriving in Caldera around 11:00 you have two options. You can hang around Caldera without much (that I saw) to do (quick aside for anyone who likes to fish. There is a bridge here that quite a few people fish off. Don't know what you might catch and have no idea of bait/lures, but that bridge appears to be quite popular). or you can buy a round trip ticket on one of the buses already there at the train stop for 1,000 colones for the round trip ride into Puntarenas. . I was not thrilled with Puntarenas. I have since learned that if I had read up on Puntarenas I would have many activities to occupy me while the women went shopping.

Us males found other things to do for the 4 1/2 hours (bars etc) Perhaps I'm a little spoiled from Manuel Antonio, but I wasn't impressed by the beach in Puntarenas. Swimable but I'd not go out of my way to swim there.

Got back on the bus at 3:45 and back to the train. I wonder how they turned that train around. The passenger cars were in the same position as when we arrived but the locomotive and caboose had switched ends. My simple mind wonders about these little things. Ride back was fun too except for about an hour in the rain. Had to shut the windows and it got hot and stuffy during this period.

Odds & Ends:

Round trip fare is $12.50 for residents and $30 for tourists. Obviously this is a touristoperation but I'm guessing 90% of the riders were Ticos. Each car has a host with a smallmegaphone to inform of points of interest etc. Free coffee, juice and snacks are providedon the morning ride and other soft drinks/water and food may be purchased. The ride eachway is approx 4 hours. For females: I would not even consider sitting on the toilet seat.

Once we entered darkness there were only two (very weak) lights in our car. Enough to see around you but don't even consider trying to read anything! OK! Just about the time all you exhausted travelers decided to take a quick nap, you wonder what that loud annoying noise from the next car back is. It keeps getting louder & louder and seems to be coming closer. What is it?! Now it is in your car and you can't get away from it! Can you say mini-carnival? A bunch of fools (I say that lovingly) in costumes and masks comes up the aisle in your car singing and playing music and attempting to get you out in the aisle dancing. There is no arguing with them.... either you loudly applaud them or you dance with them. Does anyone have a camera? I do! It is a fun wake up call!

Taxis charge 365 *colones* ($.70) for the first kilometer and 340 *colones* ($0.60) per kilometer thereafter. You can rent cabs by the hour or by the day. There is a "delay" fare of 3,200 *colones* ($6.20) an hour when a taxi is going less than 10 km an hour (in case of traffic jams or bad roads) for more than six minutes. Drivers cannot legally charge more to pick up or drop off a passenger at a hotel or mall, if the service is at night or if the passenger is a foreigner.

If you want the driver to wait while you do an errand or some other business, there is an hourly rate of about 1,555 *colones* ($3). There is an official rate/fare sheet published and the taxi drivers usually have a copy. You may be able to get him to show it to you or even make you a copy.

If you have to go more than 12 kilometers outside the metropolitan area, there is another rate. A trip of about five kilometers will cost 2,500 *colones* ($2.50), 10 kilometers will cost 5,000 *colones* ($10.00) and 20 kilometers will cost 10,000 *colones* ($20.00). In this case the driver and the passenger should negotiate the fare (do this in advance).

If you are planning to use a driver/taxi for say, half a day, you may be able to agree upon a flat rate for the time. Once decided you could ask the driver to write down the amount on a piece of paper 'so you can be sure you understand correctly' how much it is. A rate based on a certain number of hours agreed upon in advance is more likely to be honored without the driver trying to gouge a little more at the end.

If you have had your *taxista* help with loading a bunch of things or several heavy things or he has been extra helpful, you may want to include a modest tip at the end. Just remember, taxis generally don't get tips (except maybe the orange taxis from the airport), so don't overdo the tipping.

Nearly all taxis have computerized meters called *marías*. Always insist that your taxi driver use his meter, and be sure to ask about rates before traveling anywhere. Even if you negotiate a flat rate, drivers are required to put on the meter. The meter should display the starting fare on its face. Drivers are required by law to use their meters, even if they tell you they are not. The meter must be in working order. If the *maría* is missing or broken, you might be overcharged for the trip. Always tell the driver, "*Ponga la maría por favor* or "*Con la maría, por favor.*" (Please turn on the meter). If the driver won't, get out and take another cab. Don't worry; there will almost always be another nearby.

Many city cab drivers get upset if you try to pay with large bills. If you intend to pay with a big bill, ask the driver if he has change before boarding the cab to avoid last minute misunderstandings. If you tell a driver beforehand you are going to pay with a large bill, he'll usually stop along the way to get change at a gas station.

Be aware that some unscrupulous taxi drivers will take a circuitous route to your destination, which will rack up extra fare.

Here are some tips you may want to follow under certain circumstances when traveling alone by taxi:

1. Check license plates.
2. Don't get into taxis with polarized windows.
3. Don' t get into taxis without license plates.
4. Check that the identification coincides with the driver and is up-to date.
5. Don' t wait for a taxi in the street at night.
6. Once inside the car, call home by phone (cellular), giving the license plates and a description of the vehicle, and how long it will take you to arrive. If there is nobody at home, fake the conversation.

Most taxi drivers are polite, but if you are overcharged or dissatisfied with service, you can take the driver's permit number, usually on the visor of his taxi or his license number and complain to the MOPT Office at Plaza Víquez. You can do this in person, by letter or over the telephone (257-7798, ext. 2512).

Taxies can be found around every public square and park, outside discotheques, on most busy streets, and in front of government buildings and most hotels.

Be careful, since many taxis parked in front of hotels may overcharge. Some of the drivers claim they work exclusively for the hotel and will overcharge you. Taxi drivers at hotels justify their high rates because they sometimes have to wait for customers.

WARNING: Many of the taxi drivers who work in front of hotels will try to sell you property, offer you seemingly good contacts or other services. Your best bet is to deal only with professionals in your area of interest and not depend on taxi drivers for these services.

They will try to double the fare to account for driving back to the hotel, their home base, empty. Many times the explanation is fair and the driver is honest. Also, if you have a complaint and the driver works for the hotel you have immediate recourse: the hotel's management.

It is difficult to find a taxi during the rainy season, especially in the afternoon, which is when it usually rains. You may also have trouble getting a cab on weekdays or during rush hour between 7 to 9 a.m. and from 4:30 to 6:30 p.m., as in most cities.

To hail a taxi just yell, "Taxi!" If a taxi is parked just ask the driver, "¿*Libre*?" (free) to see if he is available. If the taxi is available, he will usually nod or say, "*Sí*" (yes). If you want to stay on a taxi driver's good side, NEVER slam the taxi's doors; taxis are expensive in Costa Rica and drivers try to keep them in good shape.

Some people moonlight as taxi drivers using their own unmarked cars. Many look like regular cabs but without the yellow triangles on the front doors. They are called *piratas* (pirates) by the locals, and will often approach if they see you looking for a taxi. Since they do not have meters, we advise you not to hire any of these vehicles for transportation. Most do not have insurance to cover their passengers in the event of an accident. If you do have to take one, remember there is no meter, so negotiate the fare before you get in or you may run the risk of being overcharged.

A lot of working-class locals depend on informal taxis called *colectivos*. What they do is take an unmarked mini-van instead of a bus. They pay less and get to their destinations more quickly. These collective pirate taxis operate only during rush hour and in the areas of Desamparados, Hatillo, Escazú, Vázquez de Coronado, Tres Ríos and Pavas.

If you call a taxi, be able to give your exact location in Spanish so the taxi driver knows where to pick you up. If your command of Spanish is limited, have a Spanish speaker write down directions to your destination. We know one old grouchy gringo who has never made an effort to learn a word of Spanish. He has all the directions of the places he has to go written in Spanish for taxi drivers. If you phone for a taxi, the driver can turn on the meter when he gets the call and charge for the driving time to your location.

Taxis are a bargain in Costa Rica.

Airport pick-ups can be arranged in advance by calling one of the taxi companies. We recommend doing this, especially during the rainy season, when it is difficult to get a taxi when you need one.

Telephone numbers of the local taxi companies are in the yellow pages of the telephone book under the heading "Taxi." **Alfaro** (221-8466), **Coopeguaria** (226-1366), **Coopeirazú** (254-3211) and **Coopetico** (224-7979) have taxis available 24-hours a day. (See the directory in the back of this book for a list of taxi companies.)

Many of these companies also rent big trucks, or *taxis de carga*, at a low hourly rate. These vehicles can be very helpful if you ever have to move furniture.

Automobile Rentals

Major international car rental agencies and private car rentals are conveniently located all over San José. Most rental agencies operate like those in the United States. The cost of renting a vehicle depends on the year, model and make of car. You must be at least 21 years old and have a valid driver's license, an American Express, Visa or Master Card or be able to leave a large deposit. Remember, insurance is extra, mandatory by law and quite expensive.

Always phone or make arrangements for car rentals well in advance. For a list of car rental agencies, see the phone directory we have provided in the back of this book, the yellow pages or *The Tico Times* for ads. We recommend **Prego Rent-A-Car**, which offers all kinds of vehicles to meet your every need. Unlike many car rental companies, they give generous discounts.

The Tico Times has ads for private drivers or chauffeurs. This is a good alternative to taxis but can be expensive. We know quite a few people who do not like to drive and prefer to hire private drivers instead of taking taxis whenever they have to do errands or other business.

Driving in Costa Rica

You may use your current driver's license for up to 90 days if you are a tourist. After 90 days you must have a Costa Rican driver's license, but obtain it before your 90 days is up. This is because, at present foreigners can obtain a Costa Rican license if they possess a valid foreign license, "valid" meaning during the 90 days after entry. All permanent residents and *pensionados* must have a Costa Rican license to drive in Costa Rica.

It is relatively easy to obtain a license if you meet the requirements. First, go to San José's central driver's license office where licenses are issued. It is located one block west of Plaza Víquez on the southwest corner (Ave. 18 and Calle 5, 227-2188). You can also obtain a license from the regional offices in Liberia, Limón, Perez Zeledón, San Carlos and San Ramón.

Good news! The days of long lines to renew a Costa Rican driver's license are over, thanks to new digital equipment that now processes licenses in a few minutes.

If you have a license from your own country, it is only a matter of taking an eye exam, transferring information, paying a small processing fee and, having a little—or a lot of— patience and you will have your license in an hour. First, go across the street to one of the businesses with a sign outside saying, *"Dictamen or Examen Médico."* You will have to fill out a questionnaire about your medical history, read an eye chart and pay about $10 dollars to a doctor to get a "medical certificate." In the past, only people over 50 had to go through this cursory medical exam. Now people of all ages have to take it in order to get a license.

Next, cross the street and go to a window where you show a clerk your driver's license from your country and pay about $20. You also have to leave your passport or residency card with the clerk. Then go to the next window and wait until your name is called. The employee hands you a piece of paper and you go to have your photo taken for your license, at which time your passport or residency card is returned. Finally, you sit and wait for about 15 minutes to a half-hour. When your name is called you go to the counter and receive your Costa Rican license "hot off the press." It is actually hot from the laminating machine. The license is valid for three years. To renew, the procedure is similar to the steps described above.

If you do not have a current license or if your license has expired, you have to take a driver's test and written exam as in the United States. The first step involves learning the basic traffic laws, road signs and driver's etiquette which are slightly different here. There are several courses through MOPT designed to help you learn about driving in Costa Rica and pass the written test.

Courses cost about $5.00 and the required test costs a little over $3.00. After passing the written exam, you have to take the driving test. Once you pass both tests you may get your license. To find out

On Driving in Costa Rica
By Carlos Morton

After nearly two years of living (and Driving) on Costa Rica's scenic highways, I feel inspired to submit the following wisdom to my fellow gringos. I speak with the voice of experience, having been a taxi driver in Chicago and New York City. I've also lived in Mexico, driven there and other parts of Central America.

So, without any hyperbole whatsoever, I give the following advice.

1. DON'T WORRY ABOUT THE POTHOLES: Three are too many of them! Trying to avoid the potholes will only cause you to crash into other cars and/or pedestrians.Best thing to do is buy yourself a monster Sports Utility Vehicle (or Hum-vee, tank, dump truck, etc.) and drive over all obstacles, including beaches, ditches and animals.

2. IGNORE ALL STOP SIGNS, TRAFFIC LIGHTS AND SIGNS: Everyone else does! Besides, the traffic lights are usually positioned in awkward places too hard to see. Stop signs are bent, broken, faded or hidden behind shrubbery. Translations: *"Alto"* "means speed," *"Ceda el paso"* means "get the hell out of my way!" If you find yourself in a *rotunda*, pretend you are in the bumper-car rides at the *Parque de Diversiones* (local amusement park).

3. PARK WHERE YOU WANT: That's right! In the middle of the street, on the sidewalk, anywhere your little heart desires. No one will give you a ticket; no one will tow your car away. Continue talking with your car in idle to Don Profundo while other frustrated motorists honk their horns and curse.

4. DRIVE AS FAST AS POSSIBLE: When in Rome, do as the Romans do. You may pass on the right, drive on the sidewalk, pass on the left going up hills against oncoming traffic, it's all fair game. Furthermore, this is a free country, and you don't have to wear a seatbelt if you don't want!

5. DO NOT TRY TO BRIBE A TRAFFIC COP: It will cost you more! Yes, he'll think your just another rich Gringo who overstayed your tourist visa. Wait until he offers to let you give him the *propina* (tip). The barter, always barter. Show him the certified Tico driver's license you procured from a cereal box.

6. DISCARD YOUR MAPS: Maps are useless without street signs or addresses. If you want directions, stop and ask three or four different people, who will probably tell you three or four different ways to get there.

7.DON'T LET THE PEDESTRIAN HAVE THE RIGHT OF WAY: People think they own the roads! Run them over! That also includes kamikazes on motorbikes, people on bicycles, horseback riders and oxen pulling colorful oxcarts.

about courses and test sites nearest you call the ministry at 226-4201, 226-4213, 226-7944, 227-5158 or 228-9297. This is all worthwhile if you plan to live and drive in Costa Rica.

One thing we would like to point out is that in most cases a driver's license is not a valid form of identification as in the United States. In order to cash checks or identify yourself, you need a passport or a *cédula*. The latter is issued only when you have permanent residency in Costa Rica.

Here is what one resident experienced when he went to get his driver's license: "My wife and I arrived here in November and renewed our visa as required but waited until last May to go to the MOPT office in San José for our first Costa Rican drivers license.

The lady who approves your U.S. license was only there from 7:30 a.m. until 1:30 p.m., but she does take well over an hour for lunch. These hours may have changed by now. We visited one of the many nearby doctor's offices and purchased our 5,000 *colón* medical certificate or *dictamen*, which is the first step before even entering the driver license building. If I remember correctly, upon entering the building, you will pass to the right of the existing lines and wait by a door for the lady to call you in. If the lady is in her office it will not take long. She checks the expiration date on your U.S. license but not much else. She might check to see if you have your physical paperwork and look at your passport. If all is satisfactory to her, she will take her rubber stamp out and have a little fun. Then she will scratch her initials on some scraps of paper and send you on your way. Next, you will go stand in that first line you already bypassed. When you get to one of the clerks, you' ll hand over all your paperwork, including your passport. They will check everything over, ask you your address here in Costa Rica, do some more rubber stamping and pass you along to the line at the indoor bank so you can pay the 4,000 *colónes* license fee. Make certain you save your receipt and move off to stand in the line to get your picture taken. The day we were there, this was the longest line and went out the back door into a parking lot. It moved surprisingly fast though.

"The first license will be for only two years but renewals can be for five years. Both of us were on our second visa renewal and it never caused us any problems or questions. I do not know if renewals can be made in other places. Would like to know if anyone has first-hand knowledge."

Whether you are renting a car or using your own automobile, always keep the proper documents in your car. Check with your lawyer to see

Round Trip Back to Paradise
By Jay Trettien

"I never had more money or had more fun than when I lived in Costa Rica," was my response when a fellow bartender friend from southern California suggested we open a bar in Baja California.

"If you're heading South of the Border, you may as well go to Costa Rica, where the weather is nicer and the people more friendly," I said.

I was first invited to Costa Rica in 1973 by a college friend who worked for the Bank of America. Through the bank he had met an American who needed help with a bar he had just bought. My friend suggested that maybe I would come to Costa Rica to help out. A late-night phone call, and two weeks later I arrived from New York. After a few weeks of working together, the bar owner and I had developed trust and a friendship and, on the strength of a handshake, I became a partner in what was to become Central America's most popular "*Gringo*" rock and roll bar, Ye Pub. *Gringos* and *ticos* loved the place. After living in Costa Rica for a while , I was granted a *cédula*, or Costa Rican "green card."

But the time came to sell. Costa Rica had been enjoying a spectacular boom but with small countries as fast as it goes up, it can go down. After three years we sold.

With a girlfriend that was driving me nuts it was easy to leave Costa Rica. I visited every country in South America. I had already seen almost all of Europe, most of the United States and Canada. So, I ended up in Australia and New Zealand for about four years, finally washing up on the shores of southern California.

I began thinking about Costa Rica again and made a brief visit about 12 years ago to be pleasantly surprised that I still had friends in the country. I returned to California, loaded up the old Pontiac and ended up back in Costa Rica.

A lucky coincidence got me my *cédula* back when the Costa Rican government declared an amnesty for all foreigners, trying to get a grip on all the illegal Nicaraguans in the country.

Now I'm working at a popular San José hotel bar. I think I have about $150 under my mattress, but I have a good time and a lot of fun.

When guests ask me how long I've been in Costa Rica, I say, " I don't remember...10-12 years." And that's the truth, I don't really remember.

Guest, "Do you like Costa Rica?" "NO! I'm here on the United States Witness Protection Program, but they could only find this low-profile job for me!"

what documents are required. If you are a *pensionado* and your car has special *pensionado* plates, the police will occasionally stop you to see if your paperwork is in order. If a policeman should stop you, above all be polite, stay calm, and do not be verbally abusive. Most traffic police are courteous and helpful. However, if you commit a traffic violation, some policemen will try to have you pay for your ticket on the spot. Be advised this is not the standard procedure. If this happens to you, there are two offices where you can complain. You can file your complaints with the **Judicial Police** (OIJ) or with the Legal Department of the **Transit Police** (227-2188). Finally, if you are involved in a traffic accident, do not move your car! Be sure to contact the local traffic police (222-7150, 227-8030) so they can make out a report.

If you have an accident, be sure and follow this procedure:

1. **Find out where you are** *tico*-style. You are going to have to summon maybe the Red Cross, but definitely the traffic cops and the National Insurance Institute (INS) inspector — so get the location right.

2. **Severe injuries**. Call Cruz Roja ambulance at 128 or 911. Find out where the ambulance is going to take the injured persons.

3. **Call the police**. Call the traffic police (222 -9245, 222 -9330 or 911 in the Central Valley), who will go to the scene of the accident. Be patient and don't move your car until the cops tell you. Note: it is not enough to wave to a cop on a nearby corner— the police are not the ones who report on accidents — you have to call the special traffic accident squad.

4. **Call INS** at 800-800-8000 (toll-free, 24 hours) and ask them to send an inspector. The INS inspector usually gets there more quickly than the cops. He will fill out an accident report and give you instructions on how to proceed with the claim. (If the INS operator tells you that an inspector can't go, take the name and number of the operator; — these calls are taped, so this gives you a recourse if need arises. Later, contact your insurance agent to find out how to do the paperwork.)

5. **Witnesses**. Take down their names, addresses and phone numbers — also of the driver of the other car. Take note of particulars of his vehicle, and the license number.

6. **Drinking**. If you think the other driver has been drinking, ask the cop to give the driver a Breathalyzer test (*alcolemia*). Also point this out to the INS inspector.

7. **Tow truck**. If your car needs towing, ask the INS man to call one. Most INS auto policies include free towing as part of the "*INS*

Asistencia" roadside assistance program. If you don't have the right to free towing, ask the cop to radio for a tow truck. Remember to bargain with the tow truck operator, get a receipt, and make sure you know where he's taking your car. Left to his own devices, he will take your car to a shop that offers him a commission — often an expensive one. Give him your input. Body shops "authorized by INS" will do most of the tedious paperwork relating to the claim, and they usually finance the repair, — but they often overcharge; other body shops tend to charge less, but you may have to finance the repair and do the claim paperwork yourself.

8. **Do not assume any obligations or responsibility**, — or make a deal with other parties involved in the accident. Body shops do excellent work, but they are expensive — and sometimes the "decent chap" you had your prang against and made a deal with, will become less "decent" when he finds the cost of repairing his car is more than he thought; then he may conjure up all sorts of fairy stories and false witnesses saying you hit and ran and are therefore to blame for the accident. If you stand your ground and summon the cops and the INS inspector, this is unlikely to happen.

9. **Summons**. At the scene of the accident, the cop will give each driver an illegible blue/green ticket, which is a summons to appear at the corresponding traffic court (*Tribunal de Tránsito*) or municipal office (*Alcaldía*) to make a deposition concerning the accident. IMPORTANT! Ask the cop which traffic court, and when to go. He will usually tell you to go eight-10 days after the accident; don't go sooner — as the paperwork will not be ready. Do not fail to react to the summons lest you be found guilty by default. The deposition is fairly straightforward, and no great command of Spanish is required. People don't usually take attorneys to the traffic court unless there was serious injury or death resulting from the accident. Don't be alarmed if you find that the other driver's deposition is not accurate; — the ungodly often tell plausible lies to try to get themselves off the hook — here is where the value of the traffic cop's report of the accident becomes important, for the judge to separate truth from fiction. Ask for a copy of your deposition, and also ask when the *sumaria* (sentence) will be ready. You will need these in the claim process.

*Courtesy of David Garret, insurance agent, e-mail: info@ segurosgarrett.com.

Be very careful when driving in San José or any other city. Most streets in San José are narrow, one-way and very crowded due to heavy traffic. Names of streets are not on signposts on the street corners as in the United States. Many streets' names are on small blue signs on the sides of buildings. Some streets do not even have signs.

One thing that gets on foreigners nerves is "honking." It seems that most Costa Rican drivers are born with a horn in their hand. If traffic slows just a little, they are quick to honk. This can be extremely nerve-racking and annoying but is a well-ingrained custom here. So get use to it, and do not get upset when honked at. There is no reason to go into road-rage mode when honked at. Furthermore, male Costa Ricans have the habit of honking when they see a beautiful woman on the street.

There is some car theft in Costa Rica. To discourage thieves, you should always park your car in your garage or in public parking lots. If you park on the street, make sure there is someone like a guard who can watch your car. Always lock your car and set the alarm system.

When driving in the countryside, drive only during the day, watch out for livestock and be sure to use some kind of map. Do not get off the main paved road unless absolutely necessary during the rainy season if your car does not have four-wheel drive. You may end up getting stuck in the mud. Unfortunately, the only way to many of Costa Rica's best beaches and mountain resorts is by unpaved roads. So be careful!

While on this subject, let us say a word about potholes, or *huecos*, as they are called here. The Costa Rican government tries to keep its paved roads in good shape but cannot keep up with the workload. So watch out for potholes and ruts in the pavement. Your car's shocks and suspension system will be grateful.

This is one resident's experience of driving in Costa Rica: "Driving is Costa Rica can be dangerous and you had better believe it. The *ticos* pass on curves, drive the wrong way on one way streets, tailgate, weave in traffic, run red lights, make illegal turns and you name it. The buses and trucks will run one off the road. The trick here is to know what to expect. Give the guy room to pass, expect the bus to change into your lane, slow down and let the guy tailgating and flashing his headlights pass. When you have a green light, make sure a car is not running a red light in front of you.

"The roads can be bad, very bad and terrible. One night I hit a hole and bent a wheel. The tire went flat and it was raining hard. I stopped a taxi and he put my spare on for me. I gave him a few dollars and we were both happy. When I took the damaged wheel to a shop, the man knew what to do. He took a sledge hammer and beat it back into shape. I suspect he has done that many times. As others have pointed out, it is very difficult to see holes in the road when it is raining."

Things could be better if the traffic cops would patrol more. As a rule they just stand by the side of the road."

Here is a brief summary of Costa Rica's traffic laws and some advice.

1. Avoid accidents by driving carefully and defensively.

2. Unless otherwise indicated, the minimum speed on highways is 40 kilometers per hour. The speed limit varies and is posted on the side of the road.

3. On highways and secondary roads, the speed limit is 60 kilometers per hour, unless otherwise indicated.

4. In urban areas, the speed limit is 40 kilometers per hour, unless otherwise indicated.

5. Around school zones and in front of hospitals and clinics the speed limit is 25 kilometers per hour.

6. Driving on beaches is strictly prohibited everywhere, except when there is no other path connecting two towns.

7. Driving under the influence of alcohol and/or drugs is strictly prohibited. The law permits police officers to perform alcohol tests on drivers.

8. The law requires all car passengers to wear a seat belt, even when riding in a taxi.

9. Pull over if any police officer signals you to do so. Police officers may ask you to stop if there is an accident ahead, a checkpoint or if you are violating the law by not having a license plate or exceeding the speed limit.

10. Your personal documents and the vehicle's registration papers are private property and may not be retained by a police officer for any reason.

11. If you are involved in an accident, always wait until a police officer arrives. Do not move your vehicle. The officer will prepare a report. You may also report the accident by calling 911 or 800-0123456.

12. Under no circumstances give money to traffic police or other police officers.

13. If a police officer insists on stopping you and retaining your documents for no apparent reason, ask him to escort you to the nearest police station to resolve the problem.

14. If you believe a traffic policeman or any other police officer acted inappropriately or you have questions regarding their behavior,

call 257-7798, ext. 2506, and ask to be referred to the nearest police station.

15. Drive confidently and stay alert. Do not stop for people signaling you and never stop for hitchhikers.

16. Do not drive through or park your car in poorly lit areas. Do not leave any belongings in the car where they might be spotted by a passerby.

17. Check your car and make sure you are carrying the proper documents before you begin to drive. If you are given a ticket, pay it at the nearest state bank. If you are renting a car, present a copy of the receipt for the ticket you paid to the car rental agency when you return the car.

For information about traffic laws and other related matters call **800-TRANSITO** or see www.transito.go.cr or www.cav.go.cr (traffic tickets). For your information, *The Essential Road Guide for Costa Rica* by Bill Baker, is designed to make driving easier. This book is also available through Costa Rica Books. *Driving the Pan-American Highway to Mexico and Central America* is another helpful publication. You may order it through Amazon.com or see www.drivetocentralamerica. com.

Driving Times in and around Costa Rica

Driving times from San José are based on 43 km an hour which is about 27 mph.

LOCATION	DISTANCE (KM)	TIME
Alajuela	18	25 minutes
Atenas	45	1 hour 10 minutes
Cahuita	195	3 hours 15 minutes
Cartago	20	25 minutes
Cañas	182	2 hours 50 minutes
Cd Quesada	100	2 hours 40 minutes
Golfito	330	8 hours 30 minutes
Grecia	43	1 hour
Heredia	12	25 minutes
Jacó	102	2 hours
Liberia	228	3 hours 30 minutes
Limón	153	2 hours 15 minutes
Monteverde	162	4 hours
Nicoya via Liberia	318	4 hours
Parrita via Jacó	243	3 hours 15 minutes

Paso Canoas	349	8 hours
Peñas Blancas	292	4 hours
Playas del Coco	262	4 hours
Puntarenas	105	1 hour 15 minutes
Quepos via Jacó	268	3 hours 15 minutes
San Isidro de El General	131	3 hours
Tamarindo	301	4 hours 15 minutes
Tilarán	209	3 hours 15 minutes
Volcán Irazú	53	1 hour 40 minutes
Volcán Poás	55	1 hour 30 minutes

Keeping Your Bearings Straight

You can get confused in Costa Rica trying to find your way around especially in San José. Except for the center of San José, most streets have no names or numbers, or they are not in a visible place. People use known landmarks to get around, to locate addresses and give directions. If you are unfamiliar with this system. it is almost impossible to find your way around, and easy to get lost. Don't worry. After you have lived in Costa Rica awhile, you will get used to this system. In the event you get lost, you can always ask Costa Ricans for directions—provided you understand a little Spanish or they speak some English.

As you know, Costa Ricans are generally very friendly and are usually happy to help you find the address you are seeking. However, it is always a good idea to ask a second person, because most *ticos* are embarrassed to admit they don't know an address and will sometimes give you directions whether they know where you want to go or not.

Here are some basic tips on how to get around Costa Rica and understand how the street numbering works. It is somewhat easier to find your way in downtown San José because of the layout of the city. Avenues, or *Avenidas*, run east west. All the odd-numbered avenues are north of Central Avenue (*Avenida Central*). The even-numbered avenues are south. Streets, or *Calles*, run north south, with odd-numbered streets east of *Calle Central* and even-numbered streets to the west.

If you get lost, looking for a street sign on the side of a building and counting by two's will usually help you get your bearings. Keep in mind that the word avenue is often abbreviated as A and streets as

Memorize the Spanish survival phrases below and you should be able to find your way around, located addresses and hopefully not get lost.

¿A qué distancia queda...? - How far is...?
¿Dónde está...? - Where is...?
Tome la primera calle... - Take the first street
a la derecha - to the right
a la izquierda - to the left
directo/derecho - straight ahead
diagonal - diagonal to
a la par de - next to in Costa Rica
al lado de, contiguo - also next to
¿Hay un...por aquí? - Is there a ...around here?
Doble a la derecha - turn right
Doble a la izquierda - turn left
a la vuelta - around the corner
una cuadra - a block
cien metros - a block in Costa Rica
cien varas - also a block in Costa Rica
una teja - also one block in Costa Rica
entrada - driveway
la esquina - corner
cerca de - near
lejos de - far
largo - far in Costa Rica (incorrect Spanish)
enfrente de - opposite
en el cruce - at the intersection
estoy perdido - I'm lost
¿Puede indicarme el camino? - Can you show me the how to get to...?
norte - north
sur - south
este - east
oeste - west

* From *Christopher Howard's Guide to Costa Rican Spanish*

C when you get written directions. To find your way around Costa Rica, you also need to know that 100 meters (*cien metros*) is another way of saying one block. Likewise, 50 meters (*cincuenta metros*) is a half-block and 150 meters (*ciento cincuenta metros*) a block and a half. The word *varas* (an old Spanish unit of measurement, almost a yard) is slang and often used instead of the word *metros* (meters) when giving directions.

Landmarks, such as corner grocery stores (*pulperías*), churches, schools and other buildings, are usually used with this metric block system to locate addresses. For example, in finding a house someone might say, "From Saint Paul's Church, 200 meters west and 300 meters south." In interpreting written directions you should also know that M stands for meters.

An old trick Costa Ricans often use for finding the four compass points may make it easier for you to get your bearings straight. The front doors of all churches in Costa Rica face west. So, if there is a church nearby, imagine yourself with your back to the entrance of the church—you are facing west.

If you live in San José, there is another method for finding the compass points. Poás Volcano is north, the Cruz de Alajuela mountain approximately south, the direction of Cartago is east and the general direction of the La Sabana or Rohrmoser is west. This system of using landmarks should make it easier for you to find your way around the city.

The time wasted searching for a house or building in Costa Rica may be a thing of the past. The Costa Rican postal system plans to initiate a new plan that will introduce a uniform system of street and house numbers.

Signs will be posted on street corners following a coordinated system of colors, sign sizes and symbols. Blue signs will mark international thoroughfares, yellow will be used to indicate inter-provincial highways and white will denote interurban roads. Homeowners will be told where to place their number signs. This system will be tested in several areas with the hope of extending it to all parts of the country within three years. Let us hope this system becomes a reality to make everyone's life easier.

MORE USEFUL INFORMATION

Where to Find Affordable Foods

A wide variety of delicious tropical fruits and vegetables grow in Costa Rica. It is amazing that every fruit and vegetable you can think of in addition to exotic native varieties flourish here. More common tropical fruits such as pineapples, mangoes and *papayas* cost about a third what they do in the United States. Bananas can be purchased at any local fruit stand or street market for about five cents each.

Once you live in Costa Rica, you can do as many Costa Ricans do and eat a few slices of mouth-watering fruit for breakfast at one of the many sidewalk *fruterías* or fruit stands all over the country. For people living on a tight budget, this healthy, fresh fruit breakfast will cost about $0.50 to $0,60. There are also many *sodas*, or small cafes, where you can eat a more typical Costa Rican breakfast for about $1.

Besides fruits and vegetables, many other bargain foods are available in Costa Rica. Bakeries sell fresh homemade breads and pastries. Other foods such as eggs, chicken, meat and honey are available at most small neighborhood grocery stores, *pulperías*, as well as large supermarkets. These supermarkets are much like markets in the United States; everything is under one roof, but the selection of products is smaller. There are even 24-hour mini-markets in gas stations like the 7-Eleven, Circle-K types found in the United States.

Some imported packaged products found in Costa Rican supermarkets can be expensive. It is usual to pay more for your favorite breakfast cereal, certain canned foods or liquor. Do not worry because there are local products to substitute for your favorite U.S. brand. However, if you absolutely cannot live without your foods from the States, you can usually find them at the **AutoMercado** supermarkets and **Hipermás** stores. You can stock-up on these items on shopping trips to the States and bring them back with you by plane.

Since most foods are so affordable in Costa Rica, you will be better off changing your eating habits and buying more local products so you can keep your food bill low. You can save more money by shopping at the Central Market or *Mercado Central* in Heredia or in San José, as many cost-conscious Costa Ricans do. The latter covers a whole city block in the heart of downtown San José, near the banking district. Under one roof are hundreds of shops where you can buy fresh fruits, vegetables, grains and much more. You can also go to an open-air street market found in most every large town, called *feria del agricultor*, on any Saturday or Sunday morning. Farmers bring their fresh produce to these street markets each week, so you can find a variety of produce, meats and eggs at low prices. There is a weekly list that appears in *La Nación* newspaper listing the suggested prices of all fruits and vegetables sold at the various *ferias*.

Inexpensive fruits and vegetables can be found at
any of the country's weekend outdoor markets or *ferias*.

Ceviche de Corvina
(Marinated White Seabass)

1 lb. seabass, cut in small pieces
3 tablespoons omion, finely chopped
1 tablespoon celery, finely chopped
2 tablespoons fresh coriander, chopped
2 cups lemon juice
Salt, pepper and Tabasco Sauce
1/2 teaspoon Worcester Sauce

Combine all ingredients in a glass bowl.
Let it stand for at least four hours in the refrigerator.
Serve chilled in small bowls topped with catsup and soda crackers on the side. Serves 8.

TRES LECHES
(Three Milk Cake)

Cake Base
5 eggs
1 teaspoon baking powder
1 cup sugar
1/2 teaspoon vanilla
1 1/2 cups of flower

Preheat oven at 350 F. Sift baking powder. Set aside. Cream butter and sugar until fluffy. Add eggs and vanilla and beat well. Add flour to the butter mixture 2 tablespoons at a time, until well blended. Pour into greased rectangular Pyrex dish and bake at 350 F for 30 minutes. Let cool. Pierce with a fork and cover. For the filling combine 2 cups of milk, 1 can of condensed milk and one can of evaporated milk. Pour this mixture over the cool cake. To make the topping, mix 1 1/2 cups of half & half, 1 teaspoon vanilla and a cup of sugar. Whip together until thick. Spread over the top of the cake. Keep refrigerated. Serves 12.

Gallo Pinto
(Rice and Beans)
The Traditional Costa Rican Dish

Gallo Pinto is eaten nationwide.
Most people eat it for breakfast.
Others for lunch or dinner. Makes 3 to 4 servings

Preparation Time: 10 minutes

Ingredients
2 cups of cooked long grain rice
1 cup of red or black small cooked beans ("frijol criollo")
1/2 cup of finely diced white onions
3 teaspoons of vegetable oil
2 tablespoons of chopped cilantro ("Culantro de Castilla")
Salt to taste
Lizano Sauce ("Salsa Lizano" is a mild sauce used on every day
cooking in Costa Rica)

Instructions
Place vegetable oil on a frying pan and heat for approximately 1 minute.
Saute onions until caramelized. Add entire pot of cooked beans and
its gravy into the sautéed onions. Stir over low-medium heat for a
minute. Combine cooked rice to sautéed bean mix well and simmer
for 5 minutes. Add salt to taste. Add cilantro. Cook on high heat and
quick.Serve immediately and add the Lizano Sauce to taste.

A few words about Costa Rica's excellent seafood. With oceans on both sides, Costa Rica has a huge variety of fresh seafood. Tuna, maahi-mahi and corvina, abound as do lobster, shrimp of all sizes and some crab. All of these can be purchased at any *pescadería* (fish market) in the country at low prices. If you haven't done so, try a heaping plate of *ceviche* (fish cocktail) at one of the many fish restaurants called *marisquerías*.

Typical Costa Rican food is similar to that of Mexico and other Central American countries. *Tortillas* often, but not always, are eaten with a meal of rice, beans, fruit, eggs, vegetables and a little meat. The most common dish, *gallo pinto*, is made with rice and black beans as a base and fried with red bell peppers and cilantro.

Some other popular Costa Rican foods include *casado*, the blue-plate special (fish, chicken or meat with beans and chopped cabbage), *empanadas* (a type of stuffed bread turnover), *arreglados* (a kind of sandwich) and *palmito* (heart of palm), which is usually eaten in salads.

The major supermarkets in the Central Valley are **Perimercados** (several locations in the San José area), **Más x Menos** (a large chain also with home delivery at 800-MASYMAS), **Auto Mercado** (upscale, also with home delivery service), and **Palí Supermercados** (discount warehouses). **Megasuper** is the newest chain with huge stores all over the Central Valley.

Modern U.S.-style supermarkets abound in Costa Rica.

For food prices on-line, see: www.hipermas.co.cr/ofertas1.htm, www.masxmenos.co.cr/folleto.htm and www.maxibodega.co.cr/ofertas.htm. For home delivery of groceries: www.amidomicilio.com/servlet/catalogo and www.expressmart.net/version3/index.php. For home delivered organic and natural foods see www.NaturaStyle.com tel: 235-7654 or 386-0092.

Where to Eat

Many excellent restaurants serving a wide variety of international foods are scattered all over the San José area. Most of these restaurants are incredible bargains when compared to similar establishments in the United States. You will be happy to know that Costa Rica's restaurants are clean, and health codes are strictly enforced by the **Health Ministry** (*Ministerio de Salud*). For your convenience we have included a list of our favorite places to eat, but you are sure to discover many on your own or by word of mouth once you have lived in Costa Rica for a while.

Some of the best sea food you will ever savor may be found at **La Fuente de los Mariscos** behind the Hotel Irazú in the San José 2000 Shopping Center. **El Banco de Mariscos** in Santa Barbara de Heredia and **El Balcón de Mariscos** in Curridabat round out our list of affordable seafood eateries. **Machu Picchu**, **Ceviche del Rey** and the **Inka Grill** serve delicious Peruvian-style seafood.

There are also many Italian restaurants. The **Balcón de Europa** serves about the best *pasta* dishes in San José. If you like U.S.-style food and beer served in foot-tall mugs, try **Fridays** near the university in San Pedro. **La Soda Tapia** is famous for its gigantic fruit salads and typical breakfasts. **Restaurante Grano de Oro**, in the charming hotel of the same name, offers an excellent menu.

You can dine, watch TV and read an assortment of newspapers at the **News Café** in the Hotel Presidente. They just installed a new street-side bar that is a great spot for people watching. **Chelles** (Ave. Central, Calle 9) serves great sandwiches. **Café Parisien**, in the Gran Hotel Costa Rica, never closes and is one of the best locations in town to people watch. The **City Café** is one of many all-night restaurants and a popular North American hangout. If you get a case of the munchies and want to grab a late-night snack, there is a lot of action here with the adjacent gambling area and swinging bar. Rounding out our list of all-night eateries is **Manolo's** outdoor café .

Chinese restaurants abound in the San José area. It seems as if there is one on every block. The Asian food served here is not as tasty as what you will find in San Francisco's Chinatown, but it is inexpensive. If you want something other than chopsuey, chow mein and rice dishes, try **Tin Jo** (221-7605) restaurant. It has a wide selection including tasty Mandarin, Szechuan and even Thai food. **Shil La** is a new restaurant in the suburb of Rohrmoser that features authentic Korean and Japanese food including sushi, sashimi and tempura. **Villa Bonita** in Pavas is famous for its Asian food.

Lovers of Mexican food should try any of the **El Fogoncito** locations, **Antojitos** (four locations), **Las Tunas** in Sabana Norte and **Los Panchos** in Zapote. The latter has a great atmosphere together with roving mariachis to serenade you. **Tex Mex** in Santa Ana has become very popular with foreigners.

Excellent French cuisine is available at **El Refugio del Chef Jacques** in Heredia.

The Pops ice cream parlors sell every imaginable flavor of your favorite ice cream. **Haagaen Dazs** now has stores in Escazú and Curridabat and is available in many super markets. **TCBY**, the U.S. frozen yogurt chain, even has a couple of stores here. **Spoon** pastry shops sell the best cakes and pastries in the country many locations in the San José area.

Bagels can even be found in Costa Rica. **Bagelmens'** in San Pedro, Curridabat, Belén and Escazú offers a wide selection of fresh baked bagels, sandwiches and excellent coffee.

La Fuente de Mariscos hasf thbest seafood you will ever savor.

Coffee connoisseurs can savor a cup of their favorite local brew and grab a bite to eat at the **Café Parisien** in the Gran Hotel Costa Rica. The new **Port City Java** chain of gourmet Cafés is very similar to Starbucks. **Café Britt** offers a great coffee tour of its farm in the hills of Heredia. We recommend this excursion to tourists as well as permanent residents. They explain every step of how coffee is grown and processed and relate the history of coffee in Costa Rica.

If you like to eat-on-the-run, you can; all of the American fast food restaurant chains operate in Costa Rica. **Pizza Hut**, **Papa John's**, **McDonald's**, **Taco Bell**, **Burger King**, **Kentucky Fried Chicken**, **Quizno's** and Subway sandwiches all have restaurants conveniently located in San José, the suburbs and several shopping malls.

However, the best chicken is served at the **Rosti-Pollos** restaurants in downtown San José, San Pedro, Escazú, Heredia, Alajuela and Guadalupe. They cook their chicken over coffee branches, which gives it an incredibly delicious flavor.

Denny's has one 24-hour restaurant next to the Hotel Irazú and another by the airport with more restaurants scheduled to open in the next couple of years. The chain offers breakfast specials just as they do in the United States.

Meat lovers will be pleased to know that **Tony Roma's**, famous for its ribs, opened a restaurant in Escazú. The same owners just opened the first **Wendy's** hamburger chain in Costa Rica.

Most U.S. fast-food chain can be found in San Jose

Goya in downtown San José and **La Masía de Triquell** in Sabana Norte offer a wide variety of Spanish and international dishes. **Zermatt** (222-0604) serves European- style dishes.

For the best Costa Rican style cooking try **La Casa de Doña Lela** with restaurants in Escazú, Belén and in Tibás about a mile past the Saprissa Soccer Stadium. The food is delicious and a steal. **Rústico**, a local chain, also offers a wide selection of Costa Rican style dishes. They have restaurants in Multiplaza, San Pedro Mall. Paseo de las Flores and Real Cariari Mall. **La Casona del Cafetal** is a real find. This restaurant is located about 45 minutes from San José in the heart of the Orosi Valley and has a great Sunday buffet. The setting is incredible. It is located next to a lake and surrounded by a coffee plantation.

Sodas are plentiful and found all over. You can be assured that almost any small shop displaying the sign *soda* serves affordable food, since the majority of working-class *ticos* eat in these establishments. Most big towns and cities have a central market where a lot of *sodas* can be found. Both San Jose's and Heredia's central markets have dozens of *sodas* where you can find almost every imaginable dish at rock bottom prices. We have eaten at the market in Heredia and many a time couldn't finish the huge amount of food that was served to us. The bill usually never runs more than three dollars.

There are a number of vegetarian restaurants all over San José and surprisingly in remote areas of the country such as Montezuma Beach. As more and more Costa Ricans become health conscious

The Vishnu Natural Food Restaurants offer affordable cusine.

these establishments grow in popularity. Prices are generally low and the servings are huge. One establishment in San José offers soups, salad, rice, a vegetable dish, dessert and a natural fruit juice drink for under $3. **Restaurante Vegetariano** of San Pedro, located near the University of Costa Rica, is one of our favorites and popular with the college crowd. **SIGLO XXI**, 300 meters west of Pops ice -cream in west Sabana, is a vegetarian Chinese food restaurant. **Vishnu** has a couple of locations in downtown San José and another in Heredia. **The Mango Verde**, also in downtown Heredia completes our list of vegetarian eateries.

The Tico Times and *Costa Rica Today* both carry advertisements for restaurants and feature occasional restaurant reviews. In addition, *The Tico Times Restaurant Guide* lists hundreds of restaurants.

Home Delivery

Many establishments that would offer home delivery in the United States do so in Costa Rica. We have listed a few below. Please consult the phone bookor information for more locations near you.

Fast Food:

Pizza Hut	290-9595
Domino's Escazú	228-8650
Papa John's	258-9999
Dos por Uno Pizza	800-621-2121, 281-2121
McDonald's	286-0101
Burger King	257-7777

Chicken:

RostiPollos	218-1212
Pollos Campero	256-6363

Others

Spoon Escazú	288-3145 (many other locations)

Religion

Although 90 percent of Costa Ricans are Roman Catholic, there is freedom of religion and other religious views are permitted.

We hope the list of churches we have provided below will help you. Call the number of your denomination to be directed to your nearest house of worship in the San José area. Some churches in the San José area have services in English.

Baptist (San Pedro)	253-7911
Beit Menschem	296-6565
Bilingual Christian Fellowship	442-3663
B'nai Israel	257-1785
Catholic (Downtown Cathedral)	221-3820
Catholic (Escazú)	228-0635
Catholic (Los Yoses)	225-6778
Catholic (Rohrmoser)	232-2128
Catholic (Barrio San Bosco)	221-3748
Catholic (San Rafael)	232-6847
Christian Science	221-0840
Episcopal	225-0209
International Baptist Church	253-7911
Jehovah's Witness	221-1436
Methodist	222-0360
Mormon (Santos de Los Ultimos Días)	234-1945
Protestant	228-0553
Quaker	233-6168
Seventh Day Adventists	223-7759
Saint Mary's (Catholic)	239-0033

One of Costa Rica's houses of worship.

Synagogue Shaare Zion	222-5449
Unitarian	228-1020 or 228-4196
Union Church	235-6709
Unity	228-6051
Unity Church (Escazú)	228-6051

Costa Rica's Holidays

Costa Ricans are very nationalistic and proudly celebrate their official holidays, called *feriados*. During some holidays, the country virtually comes to a standstill and many banks, public institutions, government and private offices and stores close. Plan your activities around these holidays and do not count on getting business of any kind done. In fact, the whole country shuts down during *Semana Santa* (the week before Easter) and the week between Christmas and New Year's Day. San José turns into a pleasantly quiet city as many Costa Rican families spend their holidays at the beach. Asterisks indicate paid holidays and days for workers.

January 1	New Year's Day*
March 19	Saint Joseph's Day
Holy Week	Holy Thursday and Good Friday*
April 11	Juan Santamaría's Day (local hero)*
May 1	Labor Day
May	University Week (held in San Pedro)
June	Father's Day (the third Sunday)
July 25	Annexation of Guanacaste Province*
August 2	Virgin of Los Angeles Day
August 15	Mother's Day*
September 15	Independence Day*
October 12	Columbus Day - (Discovery of America)
October 12	Limón Carnival
October 31	Halloween
November 2	Day of the Dead
December 8	Immaculate Conception
December 25	Christmas*
December 25	Feria de Zapote (December 25 to January 2)
December 25	Fiestas de Fin del Año

Bringing Your Pets to Costa Rica

We did not forget those of you who have pets. There are procedures for bringing your pets into the country that require very little except patience, some paperwork and a small fee.

Dogs and cats entering Costa Rica must have a health certificate issued by a licensed veterinarian. The examination for the certificate must be conducted within the two weeks prior to travel to Costa Rica.

A registered veterinarian from your hometown must certify that your pets are free of internal and external parasites. It is necessary that your pet have up-to-date vaccinations against rabies (the rabies vaccination must not be older than one year), distemper, leptospirosis, hepatitis and parvovirus within the last three years. Remember, all of these required documents are indispensable and must be certified by the Costa Rican consulate nearest your hometown. These papers are only good for 30 days. If you do not renew them within this period of time, you will have to make another trip to the vet's office and the airline will not accept your animal. If you are bringing an exotic animal to Costa Rica —parakeet, macaw or other—you will need special permits from the Convention of International Species in Danger of Extinction and the Costa Rican Natural Resources Ministry.

If all of this paperwork is too much for you, the Association of Residents of Costa Rica (ARCR) can take care of everything, including airport pick up, for about $100. If you have no place to keep your pet, they offer boarding at $20 a day.

If you fail to comply with these regulations and do not provide the required documents, your pet(s) can be refused entry, placed in quarantine or even put to sleep. But don't worry, if worse comes to worst, there is a 30-day grace period to straighten things out.

If the animal is traveling with you as part of your luggage, the average rate is $50 from one destination to the next (i.e. Los Angeles—Miami—San José). If your pet travels alone, depending on size and weight, the average rate is $100 to $200. Please consult your airline for the actual price. Call the 800 toll-free cargo section of American Airlines and they will tell you the cost.

Whether your pet is traveling with you or separately, be aware that the weather can delay your animals arrival in Costa Rica. U.S.D.A. Department of Agriculture regulations on flying animals say that you may not fly a pet as baggage or cargo if during any part of the trip the temperature will rise above 80 degrees or below 40 degrees at either your point of departure or a layover. Some airlines, such as Delta, will not fly any pets from May 15 to September 15. We know of several people who have arrived at the airport only to find out their animals could not travel due to a change in the weather. Call your airline the day you intend to ship your animal and again an hour or two before departure to see if your animal will be allowed to travel. This way you can avoid unpleasant surprises.

Also, make sure your dog or cat has an airline-approved portable kennel. These rules are very strict and the kennel must be the appropriate size for your animal or it will not be allowed to travel. Some airlines rent kennels. Make sure your kennel has a small tray so your pet can have food and water during the journey. Two to eight hours is a long time to go without food or water.

If there is a layover involved, the baggage handlers will give water to your pet. The operator at American Airlines told us about a special service that will walk your dog for an extra charge at some airports. Some people suggest tranquilizing dogs and cats when shipping them by plane. We talked to our vet when we were going to ship our large Siberian husky, and he did not seem to think it was a good idea. We also asked a friend who ships show dogs all over the United States and he said to use our own judgment since tranquilizers can make an animal ill.

Some airlines allow small pets to travel in kennels in the passenger cabin. You can bring one per passenger on the plane and often the airlines will only allow one pet per cabin, so reserve early. They must fit in these tiny little carriers. A few airlines have restrictions on certain breeds of dogs, including Doberman pinschers, rottweilers and pit bulls. Be sure to check with the airline if you have one of these breeds.

One foreigner shared the following story about when he brought his pet: "I used US Air when I brought my small dog here last month. It was a good experience and he was with me on the plane the entire trip. The price was $100 and other than the USDA vet's certification and shot record (which must not be more than two weeks old), the pet must be cleared for import by a vet here in Costa Rica."

Another expat and animal lover hired a charter to bring her many pets to Costa Rica: "After doing major research on this, I realized that the cost of my 12 pets in cargo, renting a vehicle that could transport them, us and 20 odd pieces of luggage, driving for almost three hours to get to the airport and waiting at the airport for many, I found it wasn't going to be a whole lot less expensive than doing a private charter."

There are also pet transport services such as www.airanimal.com and www.pettransporter.com, which have contracts with the airlines allowing them to make things easier for you.

If you want to take your pet out of Costa Rica, you will need a special permit, a certificate from a local veterinarian, and proof that all vaccinations are up-to-date. When you obtain these documents, take them to the Ministry of Health and your pet is free to leave the country. The day you leave, plan on being at the airport at least two and a half hours early, since all your pet's papers must be stamped before departure. Do not for get to make sure that your papers comply with the rules and regulations of your home country or destination.

These requirements and additional information are available from the Agriculture Ministry's Animal Sanitation Department (260-9046).

Veterinarians

Dr. Federico Patiño (Rohrmoser) 231-5276
Clínica Echandi 223-3111
Dr. Adrián Molina 228-1909
Dr. Federico Piza 248-7166
Dr. Douglas Lutz.. 225-6784
Dr. L. Starkey.. 253-7142
Tecnología Veterinaria (clinic, pharmacy, and boarding). 228-9347
Dr. Lorena Guerra (makes house calls, also boarding).... 228-9887

If you have to travel, the **Clínica Echandi** will care for your dog, cat or other pet. They charge about $7 per day for this boarding service. For additional veterinarians, look under the heading "*Veterinaria*" in the yellow pages. See www.costarica-embassy.org/consular/travel/pets.htm or www.puppytravel.com.

If you would like to adopt a pet contact the AHPPA refuge in Heredia (267-7158) where you can adopt a pet.

Services for the Disabled

Getting around in the United States or Canada is hard enough when a person is disabled, but it can be even harder in a foreign country.

Handicapped and disabled persons should find living in Costa Rica not much of an obstacle. Presently, some places have wheel-chair access. A few hotels such as the Hampton Inn in Alajuela and the Hotel del Sur in San Isidro, have fully equipped rooms for disabled persons.

During the rainy season, the terrain can sometimes be hard to negotiate. Recently the government has increased the construction of sidewalk ramps, special marked parking spaces and telephones for people with physical limitations. In 1998, the Costa Rican Law for the Equality of Opportunities for Persons with Disabilities went into effect. It mandates every public space in the country to be wheelchair-accessible by 2008, thus improving accessibility for the disabled.

As we mention in Chapter 3, medical care is affordable in Costa Rica and should not be a problem. Also, keep in mind that taxis are inexpensive and the best way to travel for people with physical impediments. Since hired help is such a bargain, a full-time employee may be hired as a companion or as a nurse for a very reasonable price. We even know several men confined to wheelchairs who have found love and married in Costa Rica. There is a social club for disabled veterans that meets once a month. Call 443-9870 for more information.

We suggest you pick up the book, *Access to the World: A Travel Guide for the Handicapped*, by Louise Weiss, published by Chatham Square Press, 401 Broadway, New York, NY 10013. This book contains good information and suggestions for disabled travelers. Also check out www.disabilitytravel.com/independent/accessible-costa-rica.html.

For Our Canadian Readers

In order to escape Canada's cold winters, many Canadians live in Costa Rica on a full or part-time basis. It is therefore not surprising that many businesses and services catering to Canadians have been created.

Canadians may stay in Costa Rica for up to 90 days without a visa, however a passport is required. Extensions may be obtained from the office of Immigration office. If you overstay your visa or entry stamp, you will have to pay a nominal fine for each extra month you've stayed.

The **Canadian Club** helps make life easier for Canadians living or planning to live in Costa Rica. By attending club meetings people can make new friendships and establish some good contacts.

This organization provides information about acquiring residency, starting a business, transferring ownership of a car, names of doctors and lawyers and will assist with purchasing medical, automobile and home insurance in Costa Rica. All Canadian visitors and residents are urged to attend. They meet at the King's Garden Restaurant over the

Más x Menos supermarket in east Sabana, the third Wednesday of every month at noon. You can find a schedule of their activities and meetings in *The Tico Times*.

The **Canada Costa Rica Trust Company Limited** (CCTC) offers a variety of financial services for Canadians. It is located in Casa Canada, Avenida 4, Calle 40 in San José. For more information, you may contact them at P.O. Box 232-1007, Centro Colón, San José, Costa Rica, tel: 255-1723 or 255-1592, fax: 255-0061.

If you are a Canadian non-resident living in Costa Rica, you should think about receiving the *CRA Magazine's Canadian Expat Quarterly*. It sends out a periodic update newsletter covering topics of tax and financial interest to Canadians overseas. If you should have an expatriate-related tax or investment question, send it to them and they will try to research the answer for you. Contact **Canadians Residents Abroad Inc.**, 305 Lakeshore Road East, Oakville, Ontario L6J 1J3, tel: (905)-842-0080, fax:(905)-842-9814, e-mail: cra@canadiansresidentabroad.com, www.canadiansresidentabroad.com.

The Canadian Embassy is now located in the Oficentro office complex, in building 5, third floor, in the Sabana Sur area of San José, behind the Contraloría. Their address and phone are Apartado 351-1007 Centro Colón, San José, Costa Rica, tel: 296-4149, fax: 296-4270.

If you have any questions about Costa Rica or need a visa, you may contact any of the following Costa Rican Embassies and Consulates in Canada:

Montreal,
1155 Dorchester Blvd. West, Suite 2902,
Montreal, Quebec H3B 2L3,
Tel: (514) 866-8159.

Ottawa,
15 Argule St., Ottawa,
ON K2P 1B7,
Tel: (613) 234-5762 or 562-2855 fax: 230-2656.

Toronto,
164 Avenue Rd., Toronto,
ON M5R 2H9,
Tel: (416) 961- 6773, fax: 961-6771.

Understanding the Metric System

If you plan to live in Costa Rica, it is in your best interest to understand the metric system. You will soon notice that automobile speedometers, road mileage signs, the contents of bottles, and rulers are in metric. Since you probably did not study this system when you were in school and it is almost never used in the United States, you could become confused.

The conversion guide below will help you:

To Convert:	To:	Multiply by:
Centigrade	Fahrenheit	1.8, then add 32
Square km	Square miles	0.3861
Square km	Acres	247.1
Meters	Yards	1.094
Meters	Feet	3.281
Liters	Pints	2.113
Liters	Gallons	0.2642
Kilometers	Miles	0.6214
Kilograms	Pounds	2.205
Hectares	Acres	2.471
Grams	Ounces	0.03527
Centimeters	Inches	0.3937

PARTING THOUGHTS
AND ADVICE

Personal Safety in Costa Rica

Living in Costa Rica is much safer than residing in most large cities in the United States or Latin America, but you should take some precautions and use common sense to ensure your own safety. Remember, you should be careful in any third-world country.

According to an August edition of *USA Today*, "Costa Rica is one of the five safest places in the world for women travelers. Only Amsterdam and Thailand are safer."

In Costa Rica, the rate for violent crimes is very low, but there is a problem with theft, especially in the larger cities. If you are from a quiet rural town in the United States, you will probably find Costa Rica has more crime. If you are from a large city like Newark, you will think you are in heaven in Costa Rica.

Thieves tend to look for easy targets, especially foreigners, so you cannot be too cautious. Make sure your house or apartment has steel bars on both the windows and garage. The best bars are narrowly spaced because some thieves use small children as accomplices, as they can squeeze through the bars to burglarize your residence or open doors.

Make sure your neighborhood has a night watchman if you live in the city. Some male domestic employees are willing to work in this capacity. However, ask for references and closely screen any person you hire. Also, report suspicious people loitering around your premises. Thieves are very patient and often case a residence for a long time to observe your comings and goings. They can and will strike at the most opportune moment.

You should take added precautions if you live in a neighborhood where there are many foreigners. Thieves associate foreigners with wealth and look for areas where they cluster together. One possible deterrent, in addition to a night watchman, is to organize a neighborhood watch group in your area. If you leave town, get a friend or other trustworthy person to house-sit.

Mountain areas offer some spectacular views and tranquility but are less populated and usually more isolated. This makes them prime targets for burglars and other thieves. We have a friend who moved to a beautiful home in the hills, but was burglarized a couple of times. Out of desperation he had to hire a watchman and buy guard dogs. Unfortunately, a few weeks later he was robbed while doing an errand in town. This is the down side to living off the beaten path.

If you are really concerned about protecting your valuables, you would be better off living in a condominium complex or an apartment. Both are less susceptible to burglary due to their design and the fact that, as the saying goes, there is safety in numbers.

Private home security patrols can provide an alarm system and patrol your area for a monthly fee. A few companies here specialize in security systems for the home and office. Some even offer very sophisticated monitored surveillance systems. You should contact **ADT** at 257-7373 if interested in one of these services. We just installed a complete ADT security system in our home in Heredia for less than $600.

The National Insurance Institute offers insurance policies that protect your home against burglary. However, the coverage is limited to certain items; there are stipulations, a lot of paperwork involved and there is a 10 percent deductible on the value of stolen items. All items must be listed as well as their serial numbers. Premiums run from 1 to 1.5 percent of the total on the list depending on where you live. Homes in more secure areas receive the lower rates. Less protected homes in remote areas have higher rates. If your home is to be unoccupied for more than 48 hours, it must be placed under the care of a guard and you must notify the insurance company one week in advance.

According to world crime statistics the probability of losing your car in good old safe North America is a mere 750 percent greater than in Costa Rica. Nevertheless, if you own an automobile, you should be especially careful. Thieves can pop open a locked trunk and clean it out in a few minutes. Make sure your house or apartment has a garage with iron bars so your car is off the street.

When parking away from your house, always park in parking lots or where there is a watchman or cuidacarros. He will look after your vehicle for 100 colones (about 20 U.S. cents) or whatever change you have handy when you park on the street. It is not difficult to find watchmen since they usually approach and offer their services as soon as you park your car.

Never park your vehicle or walk in a poorly lit area. Avoid walking alone at night and during the day, and stay alert for pickpockets. Pickpockets like to hang around bus stops, parks and crowded marketplaces, especially the **Central Market** (between Calles 6 and 8, Avenidas. 1 and Central).

Here are some safety tips:

1. Dress simply.

2. Never flaunt your wealth by wearing expensive jewelry or carrying cameras loosely around your neck because they make you an easy mark on the street. Keep a good watch on any valuable items you may be carrying.

3. Find a good way to conceal your money and never carry it in your back pocket. It is best to carry money in front pockets. It is also a good idea to always carry small amounts of money in several places rather than all your money in one place. If you carry large amounts of money, use traveler's checks.

4. Be very discreet with your money. Do not flash large amounts of money in public. When withdrawing cash at the bank, ask the cashier to count the money again slowly; it is not advisable to count it again in front of others. Every time you finish a transaction in a bank or store, put away all money in your purse or wallet before going out into the street. Carry a single credit card and at least 10,000 colones. Don't carry bank credentials unless you are thinking of effecting some banking or another movement

5. Don't show your cellular telephone in the street. Should the cellular ring and you are walking in the street, stick to the wall, look both ways, answer and ask the person calling to ring back later.

6. Always look at the hands and eyes of anyone walking towards you, if they have their hands in their pockets, it is possible they are carrying a weapon.

7. Never carry any original documents, such as passports or visas. Make a photocopy of your passport and carry it with you at all times. The authorities will accept most photocopies as a valid form of identification.

Avoid the dangerous parts of San José, especially the area near the Coca-Cola bus terminal and the Zona Roja south of Parque Central. Keep alert. Be aware of who is around you and what they are doing. Thieves often work in teams. One will distract you while the other makes off with your valuables. Never accept help from strangers and or business propositions or other offers from people you encounter on the street. Never pick up hitchhikers.

Men should also watch out for prostitutes who are often expert pickpockets and can relieve the unsuspecting of their valuables before they realize it. Men, especially when inebriated or alone, should be careful—or avoid—the Gringo Gulch area in the vicinity of Morazán Park, the Holiday Inn and the Key Largo Bar. Many muggings have been reported in this area at night.

If you are a single woman living by yourself, never walk alone at night. If you do go out at night, be sure to take a taxi or have a friend go along.

White-collar crime exists in Costa Rica, and a few dishonest individuals—Americans, British, Canadians, Costa Ricans and other nationalities included—are always waiting to take your money. Just because he or she speaks good English does not make the individual a good person. Over the years, many unscrupulous individuals have set up shop here. We have heard of naive foreigners losing their hard-earned savings to ingenious schemes. Con men prey on newcomers. One crook bilked countless people out of their money by selling a series of non-existent gold mines here and abroad. The guy is still walking the streets today and dreaming up new ways to make money.

One "dangerous breed of animal" you may encounter are a few foreigners between 30 and 60 years of age who are in business but do not have pensions. Most such people are struggling to survive and have to really hustle to make a living in Costa Rica. In general, they are desperate and will go to almost any means to make money. They may even have a legitimate business but most certainly try to take advantage of you to make a few extra dollars. Most complaints we hear concerning people being "ripped off" are caused by individuals who fit this description.

On your first trip to Costa Rica you will probably be besieged by con- artists anxious to help you make an investment. Be wary of blue ribbon business deals that seem too good to be true, or any other get-rich-quick schemes i.e. non-existent land, fantastic sounding real estate projects, phony high-interest bank investments or property not belonging to the person selling it. If potential profit sounds too good to be true, it probably is.

Always do your homework and talk to other expats before you make any type of investment. There seems to be something about the ambience here that causes one to trust total strangers. The secret is to be cautious without being afraid to invest. Before jumping into what seems to be a once-in-a-lifetime investment opportunity, ask yourself this question: Would I make the same investment in my hometown?

Do not do anything with your money in Costa Rica that you wouldn't do at home. A friend and long-time resident here always says jokingly when referring to the business logic of foreigners who come to Costa Rica: "When they step off the plane they seem to go brain-dead."

Most people in Costa Rica are honest, hard-working individuals. However, do not assume people are honest just because they are nice. Remember, it does not hurt to be overly cautious.

If you are robbed or swindled under any circumstances, contact the police or the **O.I.J.** (*Organización de Investigación Judicial*), a special, highly efficient investigative unit like the FBI (Avenidas 8 and 10, Calles 15 and 17, in the middle building of the court-house complex, 295-3271). The O.I.J. has 20 more offices around the country. All of them are open 24 hours a day. You may also want to contact the **Ministry of Public Security**, (*Ministerio de Seguridad Pública*) at 227-4866. You may not recover your money, but you may prevent others from being victimized.

Despite all this talk of safety and crime Costa Rica is still one of the safest countries in the world. The firm AON Corp. in its study *The Risk of Terrorism Worldwide*, ranks Costa and a handful of other countries as the safest in the world. You may find Costa Rica crime statistics at: http://www.rohan.sdsu.edu/faculty/rwinslow/namerica/costa_rica.html.

HANDGUNS

We have received numerous requests for information about Costa Rica's handgun laws.

The admission of firearms and ammunition into the territory of Costa Rica is subject to restrictions and import permits approved by Costa Rican authorities.

Applications to import non-military weapons into the country may be filed by or through a licensed importer, authorized dealer or a particular person. The Congress of Costa Rica strongly restricts the import of any war weapons into the country; therefore any war weapon in the hands of a non-authorized individual is illegal.

First check with your airline about its policy on packing guns in your luggage. If you want to bring a handgun, *revolver*, or pistol in to Costa Rica, you must follow the required procedure:

1. Inform the airline that you are traveling with a weapon.

2. Once you arrive in Costa Rica, your weapon will remain at the Customs office until you register the weapon at the Ministry of Public Security's Department of Firearms and Ammunitions. There, you must provide the following documents:

3. Official registration of the firearm with the corresponding authorities of your state of residence (Secretary of State and or Police Department). This document must be duly certified by the Costa Rican consulate; please follow the authentication procedure.

4. Police record from the pdolice precinct where you have legally reside for the last six months. This document must be no older than six months, and must be duly certified by the Costa Rican consulate; please follow the authentication procedure.

5. Weapon Entrance Proof of Receipt issued by the Customs/airport authorities in Costa Rica.

6. Take a psychological test in Costa Rica to evaluate your personality traits.

7. Once you obtain the required permits, bring them to the Customs office and your weapon will be released.

If you are caught traveling with a weapon without the appropriate permits and registrations in Costa Rica, your weapon will be confiscated and you will be fined, arrested or deported.

In order to legally have a handgun it must be registered with the **Departmamento de Armas y Explosivos** (Department of Weapons and Explosives). If you bring your weapon from the United States you will have to pay taxes. They can range sometimes from 50 to 100 percent of the new value of the weapon.

If you don't have proof or a receipt of ownership or you want to reduce the taxes on an imported weapon , you should obtain a sworn statement (*declaración jurada*) from a lawyer saying someone gave you your weapon. This way you will not have to pay the taxes. However, if you purchase your weapon in Costa Rica, the taxes are included in the price. Expect to pay about double for a handgun in Costa Rica. If you fail to register your gun, there will be serious legal repercussions if you are caught with an unregistered weapon. To register your handgun take the proof of purchase/declaration of ownership papers and your residency *cédula* to the **Departamento de Armas y Explosivos** in Zapote. Once you have registered a handgun, it is illegal to carry it unless you have a special permit or *Permiso de Portación de Armas*. In order to get a permit you have to be a legal resident or have a Costa Rican corporation. You may register the gun through the latter.

You have to take both the theoretical and practical exams to get your gun carry permit. The former is a psychological test in Spanish to see if you are suited to own a gun. The cost of this exam is about 5,000 to 7,000 *colones*. If you pass this exam, you can then take the practical exam. Finally, you take the practical exam to show a qualified instructor that you know how to use your gun by shooting at some targets. You need to score 80 percent (10 rounds fired from 10 meters).

The cost of this exam is 5,000 *colones*. You may take shooting lessons from a certified instructor at the **Club de Tiro** (220-0188) next to the national Soccer Stadium at the west end of La Sabana Park. Exams are held there on Monday, Wednesday and Friday at 8 a.m. Get there at least an hour early with your ID (*cédula* or passport) because they only accept 40 people per day. The results of both the psychological and shooting test will be filed with the *Departamento de Armas y Explosivos*.

Once you are done, they will give you a document that you need to save; wait 8 working days and then go to the *Departamento de Armas y Explosivos del Ministerio de Seguridad Pública* in San Pedro, 150 meters south of La Fuente de la Hispanidad or 100 meters south of the San Pedro Cemetery, right on the highway. Give them the document you saved and they will give you your carnet (ID permit).

Once you have your permit, you can go and buy your gun. In some gun shops they will make you a nice offer that includes a registration (recommeded).

After you buy your gun, you will need to return to **El Polígono** with the gun papers and carry out the registration. All this is assuming you want to buy the gun here. It is easier to buy a gun locally than to bring one from the United States.

DEATH OF A FRIEND OR LOVED ONE OVERSEAS

Facing the death of a friend or loved one is difficult under any circumstances, let alone when it occurs in a foreign country. Since the majority of Americans living in Costa Rica are middle-aged or seniors, it is advisable that they know what procedures to follow if their spouse or a friend passes away.

First, you should contact the U.S. Embassy to report the death of an American citizen. The American Citizen Services section of the U.S. Embassy may be reached at 519-2000, ext. 2452. If necessary, they will contact family members, hold valuables for the family, act as a liaison to help the family make funeral and/or cremation arrangements, and help with repatriation of the body (this cost is covered by the government if the deceased was an active member of the military, if so desired). They will also issue a Certificate of Death Abroad, an official copy of which is sent to the State Department in Washington, D.C. This document may be important for both insurance, tax and probate purposes.

Note: If your spouse or a friend passes away anywhere else except in a hospital, the body has to undergo an autopsy. A police report will also have to be made. You will have to get a death certificate from a doctor before the body can be sent to a funeral home. Without a death certificate the body will be taken to the judicial morgue, no matter the circumstances under which your relative died. Then you'll have to go though a bureaucratic process to get it released. If your relative dies in the hospital, you do not have to worry about this. You can find out additional information by calling the U.S. Embassy at 220-3050.

Cremation is not that common in Costa Rica. **Jardines de Recuerdo** has a monopoly on cremations. The cost is about $2,000. All bodies tobe cremated must under go an autopsy. Jardines de Recuerdo can take care of this. It also provide authorization to ship the sealed urn out of the country. A regular burial is a lot more affordable.

By the way, you can prepay either cremation or burial at today's rates for these services.

Here is a person's recent experience with the cremation of a member of the family: "A relative passed away late on a Monday night, the autopsy was completed around noon on Tuesday, and the funeral home refrigerated the remains until they could schedule the cremation at their facility on Saturday morning.

"Three local funeral homes offer cremation, all about $1,600 plus $500 for the autopsy, and I selected Jardines de Recuerdo (www. jardinesdelrecuerdo.co.cr/cremacion_y_cenizarios.htm) in San José. The cremation was in their cemetery on the way to the city of Heredia.

"I was present and viewed my relative's remains immediately prior to the cremation, which is attached to the chapel. I also viewed the crematory unit and it was void of any previous remains. I needed to do this for peace of mind.

"The funeral home obtained all permits, including the Consular Mortuary Certificate from the U.S. Embassy. If you are returning the ashes to the United States for burial, you need to allow time for this to meet airline regulations."

Life as an Expatriate

Throughout this book we have provided the most up-to-date information available on living and retirement in Costa Rica. We have also provided many useful suggestions to make your life in Costa Rica more enjoyable and help you avoid inconveniences. Adjusting to a new culture can be difficult for some people. Our aim is to make this transition easier so you can enjoy all of the marvelous things that Costa Rica offers.

Before moving permanently to Costa Rica, we highly recommend spending time here on a trial basis to see if it is the place for you. We are talking about a couple of months or longer, so you can experience Costa Rican life as it is. Remember visiting Costa Rica as a tourist

Advice for Living in Costa Rica
By Loyd Newton

I'm from the DFW area but I've lived in Costa Rica for four years now. On balance, it's definitely worth the move to Costa Rica. I thought I'd see if I could address the issues you mentioned. I lived many years in Arlington, Irving and my last house was up in Lewisville.

1. There is regulation of real estate but the laws are very different from the United States. There are a few horror stories here, but for the most part there really aren't any problems. You just have to be careful and take time to understand the laws here. Squatting can be a problem for absentee landlords, but if you plan to buy property and then not even look at it for three years, you may have a problem. If you live on the property and keep an eye on anybody trying to build on it, you won't have any problems. If buying property, it's best to get a good lawyer; the *gringos* here can recommend many, or join the ARCR and let them help.

2. If you live out in the boondocks where there's never been a phone connection, you may have to wait awhile to get a phone hookup. If you live in towns where there is a phone line already existing, you will be able to get dial-up-quality depends on the condition of the phone lines. If you live in the towns, many will have access to RDSI at a minimum and ADSL in a growing number of locations. I use the Internet everyday and I complain about the dial-up quality, so I decided to go get RDSI, because, as yet, ADSL isn't available in my area.

3 and 4. Get a *tico* friend to help find the property you want. If you buy from a *gringo* or use a *gringo* real estate agent, or buy from an Internet site, you're going to pay a lot more than a *tico* would. I've always used *tico/tica* friends to help me find my rental houses and I pay about $150 to $200 less for a similar property than some of my *gringo* friends.

5. Get a 4x4 or vehicle with high ground clearance. I've been all over Costa Rica in a little Dodge Colt but decided finally to buy an Isuzu Trooper 4x4. I've never had to use 4x4, but it's nice to have. High ground clearance will get you just about anywhere. However, if you are planning to buy a property that is at the end of a long dirt road that's uphill, definitely go with a 4x4 for the rainy season. As for the potholes, drive a reasonable speed and learn to dodge them.

6. Yep, they will try to take advantage of gringos. Again, get recommendations from the *gringos* who have lived here awhile. You should plan to socialize whenever you can with the gringo community here to get contacts. Fortunately, the gringo community here is friendly and has a lot of get togethers. Several married couples I know in the Heredia area have parties or get-togethers every couple of months, and then there are the ARCR and *Gallo Pinto* groups.

7. Nothing is easy in Costa Rica when you have to deal with the government or beureacracy, but you have to bring three things with you when do: patience, patience and patience. It's not like the United States, and if you can adapt to it, it's not that bad. I've learned to carry a book with me whenever I have to deal with government offices. Don't expect it to function logically, though.

8. Fortunately it's a small country and you learn how to get around okay. My first year here, I didn't have a car and used buses and taxis. It didn't take long to learn the area. My recommendation is to buy a cheap but good GPS and build up your knowledge of the areas before buying a car. I thought the same when I first got here watching how the people drive and the lack of directions or road signs, but I can get around as well as a tico these days. It helps to learn a little Spanish, too so you can ask directions if you get lost or are in doubt.

As for me, I love it here. Great weather, beautiful country, friends both *gringo* and *tico*, low cost of living, good cheap health care, interesting culture, beaches, mountains, dancing, etc. Come on down, the water's fine.

Regards,
Loyd

is quite another thing from living here on a permanent basis. It is also good to visit for extended periods during both the wet and dry seasons, so you have an idea of what the country is like at all times of the year. During your visits, talk to many retirees and gather as much information as possible before making your final decision. Get involved in as many activities as you can during your time in the country. This will help give you an idea of what the country is really like.

It is a good idea to attend one of the monthly Newcomer's Seminars offered by the Association of Residents of Costa Rica (ARCR). Besides gathering information, you will learn from other residents and make some good contacts. Please see page 474 for more details.

The final step in deciding if you want to make Costa Rica your home is to try living there for at least a year. That's sufficient time to get an idea of what living in Costa Rica is really like and what problems may confront you while trying to adapt to living in a new culture. It may also allow you to adjust to the climate and new foods. You can learn all the dos and don'ts, ins and outs and places to go or places to avoid before making your final decision.

You may decide to try seasonal living for a few months a year. Many people spend the summer in the United States or Canada and the winter in Costa Rica (which is its summer), so they can enjoy the best of both worlds—the endless summer. As we mentioned in Chapter 6, it's easy to do, since you can legally stay in the country up to six months as a tourist without having to get any type of permanent residency.

Whether you choose to reside in Costa Rica on a full- or part-time basis, keep in mind the cultural differences and new customs. First, life in Costa Rica is very different. If you expect all things to be exactly as they are in the United States, you are deceiving yourself. The concept of time and punctuality are not important in Latin America. It is not unusual and not considered in bad taste for a person to arrive late for a business appointment or a dinner engagement. This custom can be incomprehensible and infuriating to North Americans but will not change since it is a deeply rooted tradition.

As we previously mentioned, in most cases bureaucracy moves at a snail's pace in Costa Rica that can be equally maddening to a foreigner. In addition, the Latin mentality, machismo, seemingly illogical reasoning, traditions, different laws and ways of doing business seem incomprehensible to a newcomer.

You will notice countless other different customs and cultural idiosyncrasies after living in Costa Rica for a while. No matter how psychologically secure you are, some culture shock in the new living situation will confront you. The best thing to do is respect the different cultural values, be understanding and patient, and go with the flow. Learning Spanish will ease your way.

The fastest way to fit in with the locals is to speak the native language. You do not have to be fluent in Spanish. The locals will recognize your interest; doors will open and friendships will blossom.

Whatever you do, try to avoid being the Ugly American. We know cases where Americans have caused themselves a lot of problems by their obnoxious behavior and by trying to impose their American ways on the locals.

You should also read *Survival Kit for Overseas Living*, by L. Robert Kohls, Intercultural Press, P.O. Box 700, Yarmouth, Maine 04096. This guide is filled with useful information about adjusting to life abroad.

Costa Rica is an exciting place to live but poses many obstacles for the newcomer. Don't expect everything to go smoothly or be perfect at first. By taking the advice we offer throughout this book and adjusting to the many challenges, you should be able to enjoy all of Costa Rica's wonders.

Our recommendation is not to burn your bridges or sever your ties with your home country; you may want to return home.

Try taking the adaptability test in this section to see if you are suited for living abroad.

Here are one foreign resident's observations about adapting to life here. "I have been here 15 years. I guess most people would say I have prospered here, although I sure have had my ups and downs. Nevertheless, I am still here and I love this country for many reasons. I notice and observe incoming souls because it is my business to do so. Here are some observations:

1) Culture shock can be hard the first year here. Make yourself as comfortable as you can. This is not the time to hole up in a one room cold water place after leaving your comfy nest in the United States. or elsewhere. You are dealing with language differences, cultural differences, perhaps work change. Be physically comfortable.

2) Affiliate with something. Attend language school, church, clubs or other activities. You can be alone in a crowd, and you are far from home. Reach out to friends.

3) Have something to do. I have seen the Hammock Syndrome affect many: nothing to do, tip the rum bottle, hang out looking for women (or men), lose goals and lose focus. Volunteer, build a house, have a pet, but build a life.

4) You must learn the language. If you don't, you are not really living here; you are just existing here. Listen to people speak and copy them. It is the way a child learns his native language. Get a best friend who is tico and cut a deal. I teach you, you teach me.Hey, one hour a day.

Getting Past Culture Shock
by Eric Liljenstrope

Unlike twenty years ago, the majority of people (especially travelers) know the term Culture Shock. However, there still exists an "it won't happen to me" attitude in many who move overseas. The symptoms can be severe, including difficulty sleeping, loss of appetite, paranoia and depression. Denial of the possibility of Culture Shock and ignorance of its symptoms can result in increased difficulty in adjusting to a new life overseas. A basic understanding of the reasons why it happens and what you can do about it are essential when making an international transition.

Culture shock occurs when people find that their ways of doing things just don't work in the new culture. It is a struggle to communicate, to fulfill the most basic needs, and many find that they are not as effective or efficient as before in their jobs and in their personal lives. All this loss of competence threatens a person's sense of identity.

The abilities and relationships that we relied on to tell us who we are, are absent, and we find ourselves a little lost in our new homes. To re-establish ourselves in a new context requires proactive planning in a number of different areas of life.

There are four basic areas of Culture Shock, like four legs to a chair. They are the physical, intellectual, emotional and social. To have the smoothest possible transition, one needs to employ a balanced approach in each of the areas.

After a transition such as an overseas move, the rhythms of everyday life are interrupted, including our exercise and eating habits. Often people neglect their exercise regiment because they don't know where to find a gym or they don't feel safe running or exercising in public places. Similarly, diets are neglected or some begin drinking too much alcohol. The way that our bodies feel physically directly affects our emotional health. A healthy diet and consistent exercise can help balance our emotional lives when confronting the difficulties of an international move.

The second area of concern is the intellectual dimension. When we step into a new culture we often find that we understand very little about the local customs and history. Due to our lack of understanding we sometimes assume that people think like us and value the same things we do. Reading and inquiring about the history and the culture of Costa Rica can help one to see things from a Costa Rican's perspective and develop greater empathy for their culture and ways of thinking.

Tending to emotional needs when moving overseas will help us to weather the ups and downs of the adjustment period. Finding people that are in similar positions that you can talk to and confide in helps to alleviate some of the loneliness that one feels.

When a person begins to feel down, sometimes they are listening to negative "tapes" in their head. One's "tapes" consist of the things we tell ourselves or the conversations that we have in our own mind. The negative tapes need to be consciously changed to positive hopeful messages. From "I am a failure and I hate this place" to "things are getting better every day." It may seem somewhat Pollyanna, but it really works.

Finding a group of friends, learning the language, and getting involved in clubs or activities helps to fill the social needs that we have when changing our latitude. This requires time and dedication, especially if one wants to meet locals. Meeting locals is essential for long-term happiness overseas, but it can take a long period of time and a great deal of proactive planning. It may sound harsh, but it's important to remember that the locals don't really need you. They have their families and friends from their whole lives. You need to insert yourselves in their lives.

In my time working with people in international transition I have seen may cases of fabulous success, but I have also seen many spectacular failures. If a person develops a plan and proactively carries it out, it is very probable that you will find success and happiness in your new Latin home.

Eric Liljenstolpe is president and founder of the GLOBALSOLUTIONS GROUP (GSG), an organization based in San José, Costa Rica, is committed to enhancing intercultural understanding. GSG offer seminars and workshops to help people during the cultural adjustment process. You can check out upcoming events and learn more about what GSG offers at www.gsgintercultural.com.

5) Let yourself fall in love with this country. There are a million wonderful things about it. Avoid people who fuss and complain; it is so very boring but it reinforces negativity. Ever meet a Frenchman or a German in the United States who sits around all day talking about the potholes in Texas? I bet you would avoid that guy after a while or suggest that he go back to Stuttgart or Timbuketu. I allow myself only one tiny complaint a day. It is usually about service in public places.

6) Do what successful expatriates do. They all have created real lives here and have goals.

7)A controversial comment, but I feel I must make it: men seem to "make it" here better than women who come here from abroad. There are many reasons for this and many exceptions, I suppose. However, American women and other women: be aware of this tendency and do all you can to ameliorate it. Find a way to belong here aside from your life with mate or husband. This is probably sage advice in any country, but more so here. "

If you're thinking of moving here, insightful Costa Rican, Guillermo Jiménez has some interesting advice about foreigners who prosper and those who fail. He states:

"1. *Ticos* have disarming smiles and their accent is so sweet it is ridiculous (I know; I am a *tico*), so much so that you can't tell good from bad, so be ready for the learning curve.

2. Costa Rica is not Disneyland. Disney is fake; Costa Rica is real and much more beautiful and fun but without the liability. If you feel like jumping inside a volcano, be our guest, but then don't blame us for it. If you want to go out with that girl or guy who looks kind of suspicious, be our guest, but please leave a message for your folks saying it was not the fault of the Costa Ricans when they have to come looking for you.

3. Observe the *ticos*, then do as they do, except when driving. If you are the only *gringo* on a road in the middle of nowhere with no *Tico* in sight, then try to get out of there quickly because it is either a banana plantation or a place you shouldn't be. If you see *ticos* building their roofs a certain way and using certain materials, unless you can hire a *tico* architect or an expert in tropical construction yourself, then build yours the same way.

4. Be honest always. Getting a smile from a *tico* is free; earning his trust is next to impossible. We are wired that way. Set limits and stick to them. Try to enjoy yourself. If there is one thing we *ticos* do well, is to enjoy ourselves.

5. You are allowed to experiment all you want, but remember, we are the locals and we have the upper hand.

6. When you meet *ticos*, keep in mind you are not the only one going through culture shock. We are trying to figure you out as well.

7. Leave the S.C.C. (Second Coming of Columbus) syndrome at home. No matter what you think of us, we do not need another European-type to come save us from ourselves or to help civilize us. Get involved in the community, but avoid the rich *gringo* role."

Here are some reasons why some people don't adjust to living in Costa Rica. These observations are from foreigners who already live here.

"This is not a definitive list, but in my experience the expats I've known who return to their home countries in North America or Europe do so for the following reasons, in order of frequency:

"1. Need more money. I have known many who don't have the ability to make chunks of money in Costa Rica like they did in their home country, but still are able to spend large amounts of it just the same. So they go back, make a chunk of money, return, do that a few times, then either settle down up there, or stop spending so much here and settle down here.

"2. Can't adjust to the culture. Many people I know who can't adjust, get totally wiped out emotionally from a robbery and become sure-fire cynical. The education-by-fire regarding Napoleonic law is just too much for them. And the number of people who couldn't live without the consumer power, options and protection they were accustomed to, really, those are the quickies — in and out in a year. I've also known some who've suffered crimes and wrongs against them that were far worse than robbery, and still stayed.

"A few I have known who have gone back to their homes were not sufficiently prepared for a different culture. I had one acquaintance who complained bitterly that Costa Ricans should speak English. She was angry all the time about banks, stores etc. She wanted an American city with Costa Rican prices and climate. Illogical and crazy, yes. Things here are done on a different time schedule and that drove another person I knew nuts. He wanted things done yesterday, which will not happen in Costa Rica.

"3. Missed family and friends. Grandparents seem to fit into this category, and might repatriate after years lof iving here. Then there's the youngsters who were just trying out living abroad and had no intentions of leaving friends and family behind for long anyway. But the old saying around here was quite true for a very long time: 'Costa Rica is for the wanted, and the unwanted.' Most people I've known who've stayed were getting the heck away from something or someone in their home country, searching to be wanted by someone, or hoping not to be found.

"4. Death of a spouse, severe health reasons and a few years ago, loss of income are reasons for a few folks I knaow going back. In a couple of instances, the move to Costa Rica was mainly the dream of only one-half of the couple, and the other half was never happy here."

"5. Not realizing you are a guest, no matter how long you live here. You must be prepared to adjust to the culture, learn the language (or improve your ability to communicate in their tongue), realize not everything is 100 percent (is it in the United States or wherever you came from?), not treating yourself to something that reminds you of home (a trip to Denny's) and doing whatever it takes to make a life here. Not finding a purpose for your life. Retirees, and I realize not everyone who comes here is one, haven't been trained for retirement for the most part. Time weighs heavy; some drink more, some find more things to complain about because they haven't anything to do.

"6. Couples who don't see eye to eye about living here don't last. It takes unique people to move to a foreign country and couples should have a common goal to build a new life in this wonderful country.

"If he or she can't leave papa or momma or the kids, don't move to Costa Rica. If he or she doesn't want to adapt to a new culture, don't move to Costa Rica. If your marriage is on the rocks and you think a geographic cure is needed, don't move to Costa Rica."

You really need to do your homework moving to any foreign country.

Communicating with Costa Ricans
by Eric Liljenstrope

On many occasions I have been engaged in a conversation with a Costa Rican friend or acquaintance when a very basic conversational miscue occurs. I ask a question and my friend responds by saying yes. I assume that the yes I receive meant an affirmative response, i.e. Yes, I'll be there, yes, I'll do it, or Yes you can dress like that in public without people laughing at you. However, my experience in Costa Rica and other Latin American countries has taught me a different meaning of the word yes of which I was not previously aware . Yes, can be merely an acknowledgement of the fact that I am talking, that the listener has heard me, or a reflection of what I want to hear. Yes does not necessarily mean an affirmative, positive response. The person may not show up, may not do what you thought they would do, and you may be dressed ridiculously and shouldn't be allowed to go out in public.

Costa Rican playwright Melvin Méndez from the book, The Ticos, expands on this point. He writes of his fellow Costa Ricans, "We beat around the bush to avoid saying 'No', a syllable which seems almost rude to us. And rather than hurt someone, we say one thing and do another." I had an experience recently that illustrates this point. I was supposed to meet a friend at a party and when I called him after arriving at the party he assured me that, yes, he'd be right over. When I called again, an hour later, he said, yes, he was almost ready and was just leaving the house. He never showed up. The truth was that he was waiting for a phone call from a girl that he wanted to go out with but didn't want to tell me that he was choosing her over me, so in order not to hurt my feelings he just told me what I wanted to hear. This was not the first time I had experienced such difficulties in basic communication, and experience has taught me to take such snubs in stride. Remembering that no disrespect or injury was intended. My friend was doing the culturally acceptable, correct and polite thing by expressing to me that he wanted to be at the party with me and that he liked me. He was answering a different question than the one I was asking. I was literally asking, "Are you coming to the party?" But he was answering a question much like, "Would you like to come to the party with me if you could?"

So, how in the world can a person adjust to such conversational conundrums? Understanding the basic differences between the communication styles of indirect culture direct culture can be helpful. A person from a culture with direct communication style values "putting all the cards on the table" and "cutting to the chase." Direct communicators do not place as much emphasis on context or on body language to get their point across. For direct communicators, if it is not verbally stated, it is not communicated. In contrast, indirect communicators place a heavy emphasis on context and often consider stating what appears to be obvious as insulting. It is assumed that an intelligent person will read the context and body language in communication, whereas direct communicators assume that if something is important then it will be stated clearly with no room from misinterpretation.

Perhaps you are left feeling a little overwhelmed at the prospect of having to reinterpret what people are saying to you with the added complexity of communication in a foreign language. The good news is that one gets better at interpreting indirect speech patterns as well as adjusting expectations appropriately. In the example above, I knew after the second phone call that my friend was not going to be coming. or at least I knew there was a strong possibility he wouldn't be there. Something in his tone of voice tipped me off. Of course, the ability to read those subtleties took years to develop, so one must have patience during the process.

What well-adapted Costa Rican residents know adapting their communication style.

(1) Give people an option. Sometimes one doesn't know *Ticos* are sincere until you give another option.

(2) Ask in another way, using qualified speech. You might try to say something like, "Is it difficult for you to come tonight?"

(3) Ask a third party. Sometimes a friend of a friend or someone else who is familiar with the situation is the only way to get accurate information.

(4) Ask a Costa Rica. Costa Ricans will always be able to interpret their compatriots much better than foreigners.

Cultural Differences
You know you are living in Costa Rica when:
Author Unknown

1. You try to walk across the street on a green light and the cars use you for target practice.

2. Foreigners refer to the pervasive sound of car alarms as "The Costa Rican National Anthem."

3. All of the street signs are invisible.

4. When the highway department puts up signs telling you construction is about to begin on the new highway and then three years later they take down the signs.

5. When your address won't fit in any of the forms that ask for it.

6. You go to the bank and there are 15 teller windows and only two are open.

7. You get your phone bill and find out you are paying for cell phone calls and you don't own a cell phone.

8. You invite your Tico friends for dinner at 7:00 and they show up at 10:00.

9. All of the road maps have highway numbers but none of the highways have signs with those numbers.

10. When a cup of coffee costs more than your local coffee shop back home and there are no refills.

11. When you are stopped at a red light and the car behind you honks.

12. They build the bridges for a new highway and five years later start planning the road.

13. You go to the government doctor, learn you need surgery, and find out it is scheduled for 2010.

14. You build a new house, get good news and learn that your phone will be installed in "less than three years".

15. The national pastime is "standing in line".

16. The most popular number is one. One phone company, one oil company, one beer company, one insurance company, one ....

17. When every intersection that has a stop light also has a stop sign.

18. You ask how long it takes to go from one place to another, someone tells you half an hour, and an hour later you still are not there.

M.R.T.A. Overseas Living Adaptability Test

Using the figures 1 (below average), 2 (average) or 3 (above average), ask yourself the following questions and rate your answer accordingly. Couples should take the test separetly. As you take the test, write your selected numbers down, then add them together. When completed, refer to the Score Comments Box at the bottom of this page.

1) Open to new adventures..1 2 3
2) Flexible in your lifestyle...1 2 3
3) Enthusiastic to new things in a new and different culture...........1 2 3
4) Able to make and enjoy new friends 1 2 3
5) Willing to learn at least basic phrases in a new language...........1 2 3
6) Healthy enough mentally and physically not to see family, friends and favorite doctor for occasional visits........................1 2 3
7) Confident enough to be in a "minority" position as a foreigner in a different culture 1 2 3
8) Independent and self-confident enough not to be influenced by negative and often ignorant comments against a possible move to a foreign country 1 2 3
9) Patient with a slower pace of life..................................1 2 3
10) Usually optimistic 1 2 3
11) Eager to travel to a new country...................................1 2 3
12) Open mind to dealing with a different type of bureaucracy 1 2 3
13) Understand enought to look at things in a different light without being critical and accepting the differences 1 2 3
14) Financially stable without needing to work.........................1 2 3

Score Comments:

Your Score	Evaluation
37-45	Great move abroad
30--36	Will have a few problems
22-32	Some problems but possible
Less than 22	Forget it, stay home!

Courtesy of Opportunities Abroad. This test taken from the book "Mexico Retirement Travel Assistance." To order wrtie M.R.T.A., 6301 S. Squaw Valley Rd., Suite 23, Pahrump, NV 89648-7949

23 Things Every Prospective Expatriate Should Know
by Shannon Roxborough

When moving to a foreign country, making adequate pre-departure preparations is essential. Here are some tips to make your international move easier.

1) Be sure to undergo a complete medical check-up before leaving to avoid dealing with a major health issue overseas.
2) Take one or more advance trips to your destination to familiarize yourself. It's worth the investment.
3) Take the appropriate documents on the advance trip to start the immigration paperwork. Consulate personnel in the country can secure the visa and residency permit more efficiently than those working thousands of miles away.
4) If you have dependent children, in your pre-departure research, be thorough in seeking the availability of education in your host country.
5) Make sure you and your family understand the country's culture so that they know what will be accepted in terms of volunteer and leisure activities at your new home.
6) In case of health emergencies, make sure you know good health-care providers and how to contact them.
7) Use a travel agency for booking en-route travel so you may search for low-cost fares.
8) Check into purchasing round-trip tickets for en-route travel. They may be less expensive than one-way. And the return ticket may be used for other travel.
9) Remember the sale of your Stateside home increases year-end tax costs due to lost interest deduction.
10) Cancel regular services and utilities. Pay the closing bill for garbage collecting, telephone, electricity, water, gas, cable TV, newspapers, magazines (or send them a change of address), memberships such as library and clubs, store accounts (or notify them that your account is inactive), and credit or check - cashing cards that will not be used.
11) Leave forwarding address with the Post Office or arrange for a mail forwarding service to handle all your U.S. mail.
12) Give notice to your landlord or make applicable arrangements for the sale of your home.
13) Have jewelry, art, or valuables properly appraised, especially if they will be taken abroad. Register cameras, jewelry and other

similar items with customs so that there will be no problem when reentering the U.S.

14) Make sure a detailed shipping inventory of household and personal effects (including serial numbers) is in the carry-on luggage and a copy is at home with a designated representative.

15) Obtain extra prescriptions in generic terms and include a sufficient supply of essential medicine with the luggage.

16) Obtain an international driver's license for all family members who drive. Some countries do not recognize an international driver's license but they issue one of their own, provided you have a valid home country license. Bring a supply of photographs as they may be required in the overseas location for driver's licenses and other identification cards.

17) Bring a notarized copy of your marriage certificate.

18) Arrange for someone to have power of attorney in case of an emergency.

19) Close your safety deposit box or leave your key with someone authorized to open it if necessary.

20) Notify Social Security Administration or corporate accounting department (for pensions) where to deposit any U.S. income. Make sure the bank account a d routing numbers are correct.

21) Bring copies of the children's school transcripts. If they are to take correspondence courses, make arrangements prior to departure and hand-carry the course material.

22) At least learn the Language basics prior to going to a foreign country. Trying to integrate with the new culture without the ability to communicate can be frustrating if not impossible.

23) Learn about the country's people and way of life before moving there. Go to your library, call your intended destination's tourism board and read all of the travel publications (magazines and travel guidebooks) you can to educate yourself.

Though this short article only provides a brief overview of the essentials, use it as a guide to prepare yourself for a smooth transition abroad.

Useful Resources:
Transitions Abroad Magazine 800 293-9373
A Guide to Living Abroad 609-924-9302

Costa Rica Movers Checklist
by Tim
(Courtesy of www.realcostarica.com)

An international move is considerably different than a move within the same state or country. The rules are very different, and the planning can seem daunting.

I moved to Costa Rica from Illinois several years ago, and I was blessed to have some great assistance from the moving companies (yes, there were more than one involved) and from the ARCR. Since my move, I have been part of the development of the ARCR Forums which would have been a great help to me as so many questions are answered there.

To assist those of you who are making the "big move", I have compiled a check list to help you. I welcome your input and suggestions, and from the feedback I receive, I will be constantly adding to or revising this list. Your ideas are welcome here! I am going to break this down by period of time, from several months before the move date right up to the big day.

Start planning at least four to six months prior to the time you wish to leave.

2-4 Months Prior

Start collecting a list of all the people you will need to notify that you are moving. Right now, this is just a list, but I guarantee that you will be adding to it for the next two to three months as you think of people, businesses, etc. that will need to be notified. I started with 15 and ended up with 52 just before the move. You will be amazed!

If you don't already know how to do Internet banking, now is the time to set up accounts and learn how to do this. Also read about banking and paying bills in Costa Rica. It is rare that you will not need to manage money, pay bills, etc even after you are living here. In fact, start learning how the Internet works. It will be your primary means of contact. Learn to transfer funds, pay bills, review statements, etc.

Start to plan what you will bring to Costa Rica and what you will leave behind or sell. Some items you may wish to buy here

Create a Moving Planner. Your mover may have one to use. If not, make one. It should include every step you will be making and a time line to start and finish each task.

Plan where you will be living either permanently or temporarily in Costa Rica.

Hobbies and Activities. This may be the only time in your life when you won't be working, because you can't. Will you be able to do the things you enjoy? Finding your own outlets will prevent overdependence on your spouse. Seek out diverse activities that involve members of the local community and thus maximize your international experience. Interact with the user groups. You WILL need social support to make this move successfully.

Get maps of Costa Rica. Learn about the country.

Got those documents yet? Don't let this slide! I know of many couples who live in one state or province but were married in another, the wife born in still another state and the husband born in yet another or overseas! Then they were married in a totally different location or country.

Many Costa Rican embassies may need to be involved. This job can be time-consuming and enormous when living in your home country, but trying to gather this stuff while living here can be a nightmare. Get on this NOW! Don't forget the kids; you need their records too.

Medical stuff. Update the family on vaccinations. The only one I recommend is the standard tetanus vaccination, but your personal health may require others. Get a family checkup before you come. Also, begin investigating heath insurance; the public health insurance is available only to legal residents. Private insurance is available, but it is a crummy policy. There are many international health insurance policies available, and you should research those early on. Do a Web search on "international health insurance". Dental care here is much cheaper than in the United States, so you may wish to get those cavities or other pricey dental work done here. Glasses are not cheap here, but the exams are, so it might be a good idea to upgrade your eyeglass prescription.

1-2 Months Prior

Set up a reliable email account. AOL, Hotmail, and some others are NOT reliable as many block email from Costa Rica. Get one that is 100 percent reliable for international use. Google mail (for now) has been very reliable.

Contact your banks and credit card companies. Let them know of your move. Banks and credit card companies need to know you are leaving or you will surely run afoul of their security measures. This can waste time and be very embarrassing. Arrange to begin receiving your bank and credit card statements via e-mail. Get set up so you can pay them on time to avoid costly charges.

Select a mover and work with them to get organized. The right mover can save you a TON of money by assisting on the valuation of the goods you will be moving. I know people who have moved entire households and paid $600 in import duties. I know others who paid

$3,800 for about the same amount of stuff at the same value. Choose wisely.

Pick your departure date, remembering pet black-out periods, and other factors. Start planning what you will do when you get off the plane in Costa Rica.

Selling stuff? Get started NOW. Place the newspaper ads and get the stuff out of the house. You will be paying to have stuff packed, and it is silly to bring items you will not use. Be ruthless in this process, but not too ruthless. Take what you NEED. Start getting recommendations from the movers with whom you are communicating. Make a list with three columns: items to leave behind, items for the mover to move, and items you'll move by yourself. Remember to stay in close contact with your mover in Costa Rica as they can advise what items to carry on to save duties.

For each item you aren't going to take with you, decide whether you'll sell it, give it away to charity, or otherwise dispose of it before your move. There may be tax implications for the charity stuff, so get receipts and chat with your tax person.. Also, many charities will pick up the stuff for free which saved me a ton of time.

Talk to your lawyer. Are your wills up to date? If you are selling a lot of property or goods prior to the move, your will may need to be updated to reflect the changes in assets. Also, if this is a permanent move, start thinking about how you will handle wills made here! Also, if you are over 60, you may wish to read this. In any case, start thinking about which country will control the probating of your assets. Clearly, this is a job for an attorney.

Moving with pets? Costa Rica has many rules about moving animals and birds, and these rules change frequently. Learn the current rules. You will need to get vaccinations for the animals and some of these need to be within 30 days of the move. Some must have special documents. This is covered elsewhere on this web site, but you should make sure you know the current rules. Airlines have a lot of rules regarding shipping of animals. All have blackout dates where noanimals can be flown. Get the facts. Start investigating this now. ARCR is a good source. Do not move animals when the closest Costa Rican Embassy is closed. If you have airline problems, they will not permit you to move animals until they speak with the embassy. If it is closed, you are not leaving.

Plan where you will be living, either permanently or temporarily in Costa Rica.

Start collecting the receipts for major items you will be taking with you so you have some idea as to their age and value at purchase.

Time to check the process for getting your police report. Contact your local police department and see what they require and how much time it takes. The report may need to be certified by an embassy, so check current law and budget sufficient time.

1 Month Prior

Set up a U.S. mail address for use after your move. See the section on private mail services. Most of these companies are located in Miami and will forward your e-mail to you in Costa Rica. Depending on where you live, the mail will be delivered to your home. Do not depend on regular mail. It can takes weeks to get a letter from the United States. Your credit card companies will not find this an acceptable excuse for non payment. I know people who inadvertently caused themselves credit issues because they did not plan this. You do not want to return to the United States with credit issues should your permanent move not be so permanent.

Note to ARCR members: If you are an ARCR member, you can use their private mail services for free. You pay only for the weight.

Start canceling your utilities. Let your electric, gas, telephone and other companies know your plans. Final bills should be emailed (if possible) or sent to your U.S. forwarding address. Since you will want to have your utilities still connected on moving day, arrange to have them disconnected from your present home after your scheduled move-out. Will you need a phone on moving day?

Cell phone contracts may not be easily cancelled if contracted for long periods. Deal with this now.

Cable TV, DirectTV, etc. are also contract services. Contact those suppliers about how best to terminate service.

By now, you should pretty much know what you are taking and what you are not. Once again, take an objective look at what you own, and decide what must go and what can be left behind. You are paying to move this stuff do you really need it?

Set up mail forwarding. Get the forms from the post office.

Cancel magazine and other subscriptions that you may not need. Change the mailing address for those you will still want.

Remember to return library books and anything else you have borrowed. Also remember to collect all items that are being cleaned, stored or repaired.

Certain documents needed for residency should be last-minute (in this case, last month) items, including police reports. Some may have to be certified by the nearest Costa Rica embassy. Others may need to be certified by the Secretary of State where you live (or equivalent office) BEFORE submission to the embassy. This is much harder to do once you are here in Costa Rica, so check with your residency advisor or residency attorney, and don't let this sneak up on you.

Consider renewing your driver's license if it is expiring soon. In most states, it is not a good idea to let it expire, and you may not want to make a special return trip to your home country in order to renew it (though some U.S. states now allow for renewal by e-mail). Find out what your state's laws are so your license does not expire.

Get copies of all of your family's medical and dental records, including histories of vaccinations. Explain clearly that you are leaving the country. These records may be invaluable to you here in Costa Rica. Get X-ray photos as well, if possible.

Moving with kids? Get copies (certified, if needs be) of all their school records.

2 Weeks Prior

Finalize plans regarding your new location where you will be living in Costa Rica.

Did you set up private mail service?

Clean and clear your home, including closets, basements and attics.

Dispose of flammables such as fireworks, cleaning fluids, matches, acids, chemistry sets, aerosol cans, paint, ammunition and poisons such as weed killer. These cannot be shipped in any form to Costa Rica. Guns can be imported here, but many movers will not do this. Check with your mover.

Get letters of reference from your U.S. banks. If possible, these letters should be addressed directly to the banks you will be using here in Costa Rica. If that is not possible, then use the old "To whom etc." Note, though, that some banks will not accept "To whom" letters.

Return any borrowed items including library books. Now is also a good time to ask for the return of any items you have lent!

1 Week Prior

If you have young children, arrange for someone to watch them on moving day. You'll be concentrating your efforts on the move, and a sitter can keep your children occupied and make sure they remain safe during the busy loading process. I guarantee your patience level will not be at an all time high... so plan to have them kept safe and out of your hair.

Start searching the house. You will need to carry valuable jewelry with you. If you've hidden any valuables around the house, be sure to collect them before leaving. Almost everyone has silly hiding places for stuff don't leave home without checking them.

This is your week to tie up loose ends. Check back through your Moving Planner to make sure you haven't overlooked anything.

Pack your suitcases and confirm your personal travel arrangements (flights, hotel, rental cars, etc.) for your family. Try to keep your plans as flexible as possible in the event of an unexpected schedule change or delay.

Prepare a Trip Kit for moving day. This kit should contain the things you'll need while your belongings are in transit, including first aid stuff.

Many people leave without clearing their safety deposit boxes. Don't be one of them.

Empty, defrost and clean your refrigerator and freezer if they are staying behind, and clean your stove, all at least 24 hours before moving, to let them air out.

Plan meals that will use up the food in your refrigerator/freezer.

Consider taking movies and/or photos of everything you are moving. Surprisingly, it is often difficult to remember all the things we have. Once you get to Costa Rica and unpack, the photos or movies can help refresh your memory. They can also be invaluable for insurance purposes.

The property valuation thing is really important. Work with your Costa Rica mover to value items as they tell you.

2-3 Days Prior

Start dismantling your furniture, taking down curtains, pictures and light fixtures, unless the moving company is going to provide this service.

Clean and let dry all kitchen appliances to avoid the appearance of mildew during shipping. Disconnect all electrical and cover naked wires where necessary.

If necessary, reserve a parking spot for the removal van or container as close as possible to your residence. Loading operations will be much easier. Often, moves such as this use shipping containers that are dropped off.

Put aside a few soft drinks and munchies for the packing crew in order to optimize their working conditions. They work much better if your attitude is friendly.

Put away all important documents and articles of value (passports, airline tickets, cash, travel addresses, destination country contact details, portable computers, phones, keys etc.) that you wish to carry personally. This will avoid having them packed accidentally. Once packed for an international move, it will be incredibly hard and costly to retrieve them.

Any travel arrangements that need to be re-confirmed?

The Big Day

When I moved, every box had to be hand-packed by the mover and the contents therein certified. Anything I had placed in a box had to be removed, inspected, placed back into the box and resealed. I now believe this has changed and you are once again allowed to pack your own boxes, containers, etc. Check with your mover as to what the current U.S. government policy. However, just because you can do it does not mean you should. Packing a container can be a job for pros, so unless you really know how to pack, insulate and protect your valuables, think about having it done for you.

Upon arrival of the packing crew, you should go around your home with the crew foreman and point out all that needs to be packed. If you have any special requests, i.e. packing of your beds last, now is the time to mention that to them.

Before the truck or container departs, walk around your home with the crew foreman to be sure nothing was forgotten.

Take a few minutes to sit down and just think. Look around. Your life is going to change beyond comprehension beginning in less than a few hours or days.

After you are here - just things to think about.

Your current driver's license expires on the day your tourist visa expires. Get a Costan Rica driver's license now. It is easy, though it can be a bit time-consuming. Go to the nearest MOPT (Ministry of Public Transportation, but just say MOPT). Take your passport and your current (valid) drivers license. You will need to get a physical at any of about 50 doctor's offices within two blocks of the MOPT. Then you will take the results of your physical and enter the MOPT building to begin the process. You will need about 15,000 colones and patience.

You are likely to arrive considerably ahead of your shipment. Take this time to look things over and to ensure your utilities have been connected. They were probably never disconnected anyway.

Check existing appliances and systems to ensure all are working properly, and arrange for repairs if necessary

Open your bank accounts

Get social and maybe arrange to meet some of those folks you have been corresponding with.

Residency Checklist
Courtesy of the ARCR

Below is a list of questions often asked by people who are considering moving to Costa Rica.

1. What is required to obtain legal residency? Can I meet these requirements? What is the cost? How often does residency have to be renewed, what are the conditions of renewal and what is the cost?

   Residency Requirements (see Chapter 6 for specific information): $600 per month pension from an approved source: or investment income of $1,000 per month from an approved source - orInvest between $50,000 and $200,000 in an approved sector of the economy.Regular, unrestricted residency can be applied for after two years on one of the above plans. The cost to process residency is approximately $870 per family head plus $425 for dependent spouse and $195 per dependant child. Residency renewals are usually every other year. General conditions for renewal are four months residence in Costa Rica, that the required amount of monthly income was changed into Costa Rican currency or that the terms of the investor residency are met. Renewal cost is $150 to $200.

2. What is required to visit, or while you are waiting for residency (visas, length of stay permitted, restrictions on residents on visa or in tourist or temporary resident categories)?

   North Americans can stay in Costa Rica legally for up to three months. They must then leave for a period of 72 hours, and can then return to the country for another three months. If the three-month period is overstayed, a travel agency or ARCR can arrange payment of a small fine and prepare the travel documents required to leave the country for the required 72 hours. Tourists can own vehicles, property and businesses and generate income from self-employment.

3. What is the political situation (dictatorship, democracy, monarchy, etc.) ?

   Costa Rica is a very democratic republic, headed by a president who is in power for one four-year term. Ministers are appointed and there is an elected Congress. There has been no military since 1948, when it was constitutionally banned.

4. How stable is the country (history of coups, potential for future unrest)?

Costa Rica has a history of stable government that stretches back to when the country was founded. It had one brief civil war in 1948, when a president wanted a second term in power. At this time, a new constitution was drawn to ensure that such a situation could not occur again.

5. Weather Do you like 4 seasons? Hot weather? Temperate all year? Snow?

Weather in Costa Rica is largely a matter or choice, unless someone is looking for snow. There is none, even on the 13,000-foot high-mountains. It varies from hot coastal lowlands, where rainfall varies according to location and season, to very cool mountainous regions. There are plains that go months without rain, and areas where it rains daily. The average temperature in the Central Valley is ideal, with evenings of 17 to 18 Celsius and days averaging 25 to 28 Celsius year-round. The dry season is usually from the end of November until past Easter. The amount of rain in the rainy season depends on the climate zone, with heaviest rains usually in October. Rainfall is usually in the afternoon, if it is going to rain.

6. Income taxes Are you taxed on income brought into the country? Are you allowed to earn income in the country? If yes, how is it taxed?

There is no income tax on money earned outside of Costa Rica by residents. Personal income taxes are low compared to North America, with many personal expenses deductible from locally earned income. Corporate taxes are also low.

7. Other taxes (sales taxes, import duties, exit taxes, vehicle taxes, property taxes, etc.)
   - Sales tax — 13 percent
   - Import duties are being decreased in Costa Rica in compliance with the GATT agreements. Duties are high however, ranging from 50 to 90 percent of the vehicle's current value (blue book rates).
   - Tourists pay an exit duty of approximately $17, while residents pay more.
   - License plate fees are paid annually for vehicles, and depend upon the value. They are not excessive.
   - Property taxes are very low in comparison with North America.

8. How much will it cost in fees, duties and taxes to bring your personal possessions into the country? (cars, boats, appliances, electronic equipment, personal effects, artwork, etc.)?

New residents will be charged import duty on cars and boats at the same rate as would be paid by a resident. Personal effects and artwork are not taxed. Electronic equipment and appliances will be valued and a duty charged.

9. Rental property - (rental rates, laws protecting tenants, lease laws, rental taxes).

Rental rates depend on the area. Any rental agreement is assumed to be for three years, during which time the landlord may not raise the rent. Lease contracts are honored by the courts provided they are drawn according to the law of rentals. Landlords may not evict tenants for reasons other than non-payment of rent or illegal activities.

10. Purchase of property - (property value, taxes, restrictions on foreign ownership, purchase taxes, legal and registration fees, laws about foreign property owners, history of government respect for these laws, expropriation laws, squatters rights. If you are going to build: building regulations, how are local construction companies, is there any guarantee on construction once finished, what are construction costs?)

Property prices vary from area to area. There is a computerized central registry system similar to that in North America, and lawyers or others, such as the ARCR, who subscribe to the service can search title from their office computers. Foreign residents and non-residents have the same property ownership rights as citizens, with the exception of leasing land from the municipality and purchasing land close to the frontiers. Registration, taxes and legal fees will be approximately 5.5 percent of the declared value of the land on purchase. The government has an excellent history of respecting foreign ownership of land. Construction is less costly than usually found in North America. A finished luxury house currently would cost about $500 to $1,000 per square meter ($50-$100 per square foot) to build (2006). The contractor is responsible for defects in construction for five years.

11. Communications - (Are there reliable phone and fax lines, cellular phones, connections to Internet and other computer communication services, are there local newspapers, radio and TV in a language you understand? Is there cable TV or is satellite TV available?)

Costa Rica has a state owned hydro/telephone company. Phone installation can be slow, but once installed they function well. Touch-tone international dialing for phone and fax is in place, as is a well-developed cellular system. Costs are competitive. Internet was introduced in 1995 and use has become widespread. There are several Spanish language and one English- language daily newspaper, two English-and one German-language weekly, and various magazines. Foreign newspapers can be purchased readily. There are several Spanish-language television stations, and different cable TV companies offering English-language channels. Satellite TV dishes and DirectTV are readily available.

12. Transportation - (How are the roads? Are flights available to places you wish to go? How are the bus, train, ferry services? How costly is it to travel to and from your chosen country to frequent destinations to bring in or visit family, business interests, etc.)
    Costa Rican roads are in generally poor condition. Potholes are common, and an endless chain of patching is underway. Air service from Costa Rica is well developed, with many direct flights daily to Mexico, United States, Central and South America, and also direct flights to Europe (Italy, Spain, Germany, England, Holland), Canada and Cuba. Average return airfare to a destination in the United States is about $550. Bus service is excellent, frequent and inexpensive. Deluxe buses are operated on many runs with air conditioning and video movies. There is no passenger train service except for commuter trains near San José.

13. What time zone is your proposed country of residence in compared to areas with which you may want to be in frequent telephone communication, such as where there are family or business interests?
    Costa Rica is within 2 hours of most North American cities for time zone. There is no daylight saving time, so it varies seasonally.

14. Shopping - (Would you have a choice of items you wish to purchase to compare prices? In case of malfunction, are parts and service available locally? {Appliances, electronics, photographic equipment, computers, vehicles, furniture and fixtures, etc.}. Is computer software support and repair service available?)
    Most things are offered for sale in and around San José, much less so in the rest of the country. The Central Valley boasts many large, enclosed malls and there is little one could want that is not readily available at competitive prices. There is a wide range of warranty, service and repair companies to choose from. Computer software sales and services are common, as are hardware repair facilities. There is a duty-free zone in Golfito in the southwest of the country, where everyone is permitted to purchase up to $600 in goods from some 80 stores at low prices twice a year.

15. Are the types of food to which you are accustomed readily available, both in restaurants and markets?
    There are thousands of restaurants in the Central Valley offering cuisine from most countries of the world. Giant supermarkets offer most familiar items. Items imported from North America are

usually more expensive, however, many familiar name brands are manufactured in Central America and the prices are reasonable. Also, many items will be available inexpensively from local manufactures with as good or better quality than the brand name you are used to.

16. If you have hobbies, are clubs, supplies and assistance available? Almost all hobbies are represented by clubs and suppliers locally.

17. What cultural activities are available (Art, music, theater, etc.)? There is an excellent symphony orchestra, several live theaters and many local or visiting musical, dance and entertainment groups. There is an active art community and several galleries.

18. What entertainment is available (sports, cinemas, night clubs, dancing, fiestas, etc.)? Fútbol (soccer) is the most popular local sport. Every region, no matter how small, has a soccer field. There are dozens of cinemas, and most films are in English with Spanish sub-titles. San José never sleeps, with a large number of night clubs, discos, bars, casinos and dance halls. Fiestas are popular and frequent throughout Costa Rica.

19. What recreational facilities are available (golf courses, tennis, health clubs, recreation centers, other participatory sports)? There are many recreation and health centers, private and public, and 18- and nine-hole golf courses. Many courses are under construction by various resort developers. Tennis and basketball are popular. Whitewater rafting, kayaking, horseback riding, water sports, hiking, bicycling and many other sports are popular and well provided for.

20. Will your appliances, electronics and electrical equipment work on the available power supply? Costa Rica has 110-115 volt electricity and the NTSA television system, as in North America.

21. If you like the beach, are good beaches available? What is the water temperature? There are hundreds of miles of world-class sandy beaches in various colors. The ocean temperature is warm — well over 80 F — year-round. Surfing is world-famous.

22. What is the situation with poisonous growth, insects, snakes, dangerous animals? There are few dangerous animals. There are several varieties of poisonous snakes, but they are not usually seen. Insects are few in the Central Valley, more on the coast and in the rain forest.

23. What is the violent crime rate? Sneaky crime (theft, car and house break-ins)? What support can be expected from the police

department? How helpful are the police to local residents and foreign residents?

Violent crime is low. In the San José area, break-ins of unoccupied cars and buildings are common, and care is necessary. The police do not differ in their treatment of foreigners and citizens. Generally the police will not come to a break-in until the victim goes to their office and files a report.

24. How do the local residents treat foreign visitors and residents?

Costa Ricans are a very welcoming and friendly people who welcome foreigners.

25. What are the local investment opportunities? Is there any consumer or investment protection legislation for investors? What return can you expect on investments?

There are two stock markets in Costa Rica, and all banks issue Certificates of Investment (as do many private companies and licensed finance companies). OPAB's are available (similar to money market funds) and yield about 5 percent annually. Private and national banks have savings accounts with interest rates in the two to four percent range. Mortgages, investments in private companies and investments in stock, bond and commodity markets outside of Costa Rica are easily arranged through local investment brokers. There is no consumer protection legislation.

26. Is the banking system safe and reliable? Can they transfer funds and convert foreign currency checks, drafts and transfers? Are checking, savings and other accounts you may need available to foreigners? Is there banking confidentiality? Exchange controls? Can money brought into the country be taken back out again?

There are four national (government owned) and about 23 private banks operating in Costa Rica, including Citibank from the United States and Scotiabank from Canada. All deposits in national banks are guaranteed without limit by the government of Costa Rica. Banking is both safe and reliable, although the national banks can be bureaucratic. Checking, savings and investment services are available from all of them. It is also possible to operate accounts in the United States or elsewhere through Costa Rican private banks. Banking in Costa Rica is protected by secrecy legislation. Foreigners may have bank accounts. There are no exchange controls or restrictions on removing funds from the country.

27. Are good lawyers, accountants, investment advisors and other professionals available?

There is a wide variety of professionals available in all fields. Lawyer-client relations are protected by confidentiality laws. Many of the major international accounting firms have offices in Costa Rica.

28. How is the health care system? Are there diseases that are dangerous to foreigners, and if so does the local health care system address the problem? What is the quality of hospitals, doctors, dentists? What is the availability of specialists? How is the ambulance service? Is dentistry up to the standards you are used to?

The health care system is excellent. There is a plan for citizens and residents who have work permits covering medical care, hospitalization and prescription drugs. Citizens are also covered for dental care. This is funded by employers contributing 22 percent of wages paid, and the employee contributing 9 percent. There is also private medical insurance, through the state owned insurance monopoly, which is inexpensive and covers 80 percent of medical costs. Medical services and hospitals are available on a "pay as you go" system for those without medical insurance. Medical care costs are very low compared to North America. Hospitals regularly do high-tech operations such as heart and organ transplants. There are many specialists in Costa Rica, and doctors have their home phone numbers in the yellow pages for emergencies. There is an ambulance service in almost every town in the country, operated by the Red Cross. There is also a wide choice in dental care. No special shots are required to come to Costa Rica.

29. How is sanitation? Can you drink the water? Do restaurants have good sanitation standards? Are pasteurized milk and dairy products available? Do meat, fish and vegetable markets have satisfactory sanitary standards?

Water can be drunk from the tap throughout Costa Rica. Sanitary standards are very high for a third-world country. Pasteurized milk and dairy products are normal everywhere.

30. How is the education system? If you have children, are good private schools available in the language in which you would like them educated? What is the school year?

There is a free education system for all, through high school. The official literacy rate is over 93 percent. There are many universities and technical training schools. Many university students have their tuition paid by grants. English is taught in the public school system but the main language is Spanish. There are excellent bilingual and trilingual schools available with a principal language of English, French or German. Some schools are on the North American school year.

31. If you are interested in having domestic staff, what is the cost of cooks, housekeepers, gardeners, etc.?

The current cost for domestic staff is about $1.00 per hour. This will vary if second-language ability is required, and may be dependent upon specific conditions, such as whether room and board are provided.

32. What legislation is there to protect foreign residents? What rights do foreign residents have in comparison to citizens? What is the government's past record in respecting the rights of foreign citizens?

Foreign residents are protected by the constitution, and have most of the rights of citizens. The record of the government historically has been excellent in honoring these rights. They do not have the right to:

- Vote or participate in political activities
- Work for wages without a permit
- Own land close to national borders

33. What natural dangers are there (hurricanes, tornadoes, typhoons, volcanoes, earthquakes, droughts, floods)?

Costa Rica is in an earthquake zone. While there are many recorded earthquakes per year, only about half a dozen can be felt. There are no hurricanes, but heavy rainsmay cause flooding. There are several active volcanoes, the most active of which is Arenal. It erupts almost continuously, without causing damage. Loss of life and damage have been caused by volcanic eruptions in the past.

34. Where does the country stand environmentally? What are the environmental issues? What is the history in dealing with environmental concerns?

Costa Rica, in comparison with other third world countries, is very environmentally conscious. Twenty-seven percent of the area of the country has national park or protected reserve status, the 50 meters above the high-tide-line is public property and cannot be privately owned or developed and the next 150 meters inland in approximately 85 percent of the country is owned by the local municipality and cannot be sold. This land can be leased from the municipality for approved projects or residences. There are strict environmental guidelines in place for all developments and mining activity. Logging is closely monitored. Most international ecological groups are represented in Costa Rica, so even where the government overlooks an infringement of the environmental laws, the legal mechanisms are in place for concerned organizations or individuals to halt development with cause. Coastal construction is limited to low rise buildings. Attempts are being made to address pollution in rivers and streams, and vehicle emissions are now being tested to keep them within set standards. There are many privately funded research facilities, as may be expected in a country with more bird and insect species than all of North America, more than 200 types of hardwood tree,1,500 varieties of orchids and so on.

35. Is there controlled growth and well managed development?
Development is planned to a certain extent, although in much of the country private land can be used as the owner wishes. Subdivisions must meet government standards, including paved roads, power, water and park land, and they must be maintained by the developer for several years after being sold out. Free zones and industrial areas are well defined, and government policy has been to encourage business to take jobs providing factories to the villages to allow people to travel short distances to work and to slow the spread of large cities. All construction must meet strict earthquake standards. Most industry in Costa Rica is of a non-polluting type. Examples would be electronics, pharmaceuticals and clothing manufacturing. Agriculture is still the largest export sector, led by traditional bananas and coffee, but with non-traditional items such as ferns, flowers and tropical plants gaining rapidly. Huge refrigerated facilities are in place to encourage new agricultural exports.

36. Can pets be brought to the country?
Pets can be brought to Costa Rica. A veterinary certificate is required. Ask the ARCR office for more details on how we can assist you.

Frequently Asked Questions

How can I teach school or volunteer in Costa Rica?

There are several U.S.-curriculum and English-medium schools in Costa Rica, and some of them recruit teachers in the United States. If you are interested in teaching school in Costa Rica or another foreign country, see the U.S. Department of State's Overseas Schools page for a list of recruiting organizations and for information on schools that are supported by the U.S. government overseas.

The Peace Corps has a small number of volunteers in Costa Rica. Other U.S. non-profit programs such as WorldTeach have placed volunteers in Costa Rica in past years. The Embassy has no specific information on volunteer opportunities at this time. The Embassy of Costa Rica in Washington, DC (202-234-2945) may have additional information about volunteer programs.

Can I receive my Social Security checks at the U.S. Embassy?

Only military personnel can receive their Social Security checks at the U.S. Embassy. The recipient should have at least 20 years of service. In order to receive checks at the embassy, you must fill out a registration form to be submitted to and approved by the Office of the Defense Representative in the embassy.

At one time, all other beneficiaries could receive checks in Costa Rica by registering with the Federal Benefits Unit. You needed to provide the embassy with your home and mailing addresses, phone number, identification document and Social Security number. The checks were received through Diplomatic Pouch and were mailed via "registered mail" to the address indicated in your registration document. The problem was the checks did not reach your post office box until the middle of the month.

The good news is that a couple of Costa Rican banks now offer direct deposit to your account by the third of each month. Please check with the embassy to see which banks provide this service and what forms have to be filled out.

For information about all of Social Security's programs, see their website at www.socialsecurity.gov.

What inoculations do I need for Costa Rica? How is medical care in Costa Rica?

There are no required inoculations for Costa Rica, but it is a good idea to check with your physician for recommendations of optional inoculations and health precautions. Costa Rica is suffering an outbreak of dengue fever, although the incidence remains lower than in other

Central American countries. Dengue is transmitted by mosquito bite and there is no vaccine. Anyone planning to travel in affected areas should take steps to avoid mosquito bites. These include wearing long sleeves and pants, using insect repellent on exposed skin, and sleeping under mosquito netting.

Medical care in the capital city of San José is adequate. However, in areas outside of San José medical care is more limited. Doctors and hospitals often expect immediate cash payment for health services. U.S. medical insurance is not always valid outside the United States. Supplemental medical insurance with specific overseas coverage, including provision for medical evacuation, has proven useful in many emergencies.

How can I register with the U.S. Embassy?

All travelers should register with the embassy in case an emergency occurs in Costa Rica or at home.

Go to the Embassy Consular Section, Window C, Mondays 8 a.m. and 11:30 a.m. and 1:00 p.m. and 3:00 p.m.

Tuesday to Friday between 8:00 a.m. and 11:30 a.m.

You can also send the embassy your information on-line: include name, passport number, travel plans, local contact in Costa Rica, and next-of-kin contact information in the United States. Registration on-line will not serve to prove citizenship in case of passport loss, but will provide a basis for which an emergency passport may be issued.

In person registration is necessary to be entered in embassy records as an American citizen.

Those American citizens who are living in Costa Rica, whether or not they are official residents, should also register.

Do I have access to APO privileges in the U.S. Embassy?

If you are a holder of a U.S. military identification card, you may use the embassy's Army Post Office privileges.

Whay if I Work Outside the United States?

If you work or own a business outside the U.S. and are younger than full retirement age, notify the nearest U.S. Embassy or consulate or Social Security office right away. If you do not, it could result in a penalty that could cause the loss of benefits. This loss of benefits is in addition to benefits that may be withheld under one of the work tests explained on the following pages.

For people born in 1937 or earlier, full retirement age is 65.

Beginning with people born in 1938, full retirement age increases gradually until it reaches age 67 for those born in 1960 or later.

Report your work even if the job is part-time or you are self-employed. Some examples of the types of work which should be reported are work as an apprentice, farmer, sales representative, tutor, writer, etc. If you own a business, notify us even if you do not work in the business or receive any income from it.

If a child beneficiary (regardless of age) begins an apprenticeship, notify the nearest U.S. Embassy or consulate or the Social Security Administration. An apprenticeship may be considered work under the Social Security program.

The following work tests may affect the amount of your monthly benefit payment. Work after full retirement age does not affect the payment of benefits.

The Foreign Work Test

Benefits are withheld for each month a beneficiary younger than full retirement age works more than 45 hours outside the U.S. in employment or self-employment not subject to U.S. Social Security taxes. It does not matter how much was earned or how many hours were worked each day.

A person is considered to be working on any day he or she:

- Works as an employee or self-employed person;
- Has an agreement to work even if he or she does not actually work because of sickness, vacation, etc.; or
- Is the owner or part owner of a trade or business even if he or she does not actually work in the trade or business or receive any income from it.

Generally, if a retired worker's benefits are withheld because of his or her work, no benefits can be paid to anyone else receiving benefits on his or her record for those months. However, the work of others receiving benefits on the worker's record affects only their own benefits.

*Courtesy of the U.S. Embassy

INDISPENSABLE SOURCES OF INFORMATION ABOUT LIVING IN COSTA RICA

LIVE IN COSTA RICA is a time-proven company offering well-organized introductory trips from the United States for people interested in moving to Costa Rica. For more information, contact them toll-free at: 800-365-2342 E-mail: liveincostarica@cox.net or christopher@costaricabooks.com or see **www.liveincostarica.com**. All trips are led by Christopher Howard, the author of this best-selling guidebook and renowned expert on living and doing business in Costa Rica. See Chapter 2 and this chapter for a sample itinerary.

RELOCATION AND RETIREMENT CONSULTANTS have helped newcomers find success and happiness in Costa Rica for more than 25 years. They offer an extensive network of contacts and insider information for potential residents and investors. See **www. liveincostarica.com** or contact them at: SJO 981, P.O. Box 025216, Miami, FL 33102-5126, Tel/Fax: 261-8968, E-mail: crbooks@racsa. co.cr.

ARCR SEMINARS ON LIVING IN COSTA RICA are given once a month by the Association of Residents of Costa Rica (ARCR). Do not miss the opportunity to get informed about living in Costa Rica. The topics covered are: Costa Rican Laws and Regulations, Health Care System in Costa Rica, Real Estate (buying, selling and renting), Insurance in Costa Rica, Banking in Costa Rica, Moving and Customs, and Living and Retiring in Costa Rica. Call 221-2053 or 233-8068 or fax 255-0061 for more information.

EL RESIDENTE is published by the ARCR and not for sale to the general public. If you join the association, your membership will include a bi-monthly copy of their newsletter.

TICO TRAVEL also offers trips to Costa Rica. Their trips are designed to introduce retirees, investors and entrepreneurs to the exciting opportunities that await them abroad.They remain committed to individual and high-quality service, offering un-biased information about Costa Rica. They offer shorter tailor-made tours for individuals, couples and small groups. Their trips are also led by Christopher Howard. Call toll-free 800 493-8426, Fax (954) 493-8466, E-Mail: tico@gate.net or see www.ticotravel.com.

YOUNG EXPATS OF COSTARICA is a social club for expatriates under the age of 40 living in Costa Rica. This club will help younger expatriates living in or moving to Costa Rica to meet other expats in their age group for friendship, romance, travel and activity partners, and professional networking. (**www.YoungExpatsOfCostaRica. org**)

The club's primary organizing tool is the Yahoo Groups e-mail list/forum foundat the club's website. Members can use this list to coordinate social activities such as parties, movies, clubbing, trips and other outings, and to discuss issues of particular interest to younger singles, couples, and families, including Costa Rican colleges, ways to make a living here, dating and starting families in Costa Rica, etc. This is in contrast to other expat organizations, events and Internet forums in Costa Rica, which currently consist mostly of retirees and middle aged people and thus are more focused on topics of interest to older people.

Discussion Groups

Over the last few years, online Costa Rican discussion groups have begun to flourish. Joining one or more of these forums is an excellent way to see what issues residents of Costa Rica face on a daily basis and to keep up with a lot of what is happening in the local expatriate community. Members can express their problems or concerns and receive a lot of constructive feedback. Many residents contribute daily while others add something occasionally or just simply read what their fellow members have to say. Another reason to follow these groups is that many friendships have been made online. Not a week goes by without numerous activities being mentioned for the group's members.

If you are thinking of moving to Costa Rica a lot of value can be derived from the groups below. What follows is a brief description of each of the major discussion groups. Membership in all of these groups is free.

CostaRicaLiving@yahoogroups.com

CostaRicaLiving is an English-language e-mail group dedicated to the exchange of information about living in or visiting Costa Rica. Its approximately 1,000 members are welcome to ask questions, share tips and opinions, make recommendations, network and share experiences about retirement, travel, establishing businesses, bringing up families or virtually any other issue related to Costa Rica. Membership to the group is open. The list is unmoderated, non-commercial, non-religious and non-political. Promotion of personal businesses, sales, rentals and recommendations are accepted. Costa Rica Living maintains a separate bulletin board for descriptions of areas of Costa Rica, FAQs, ads, legal advice, announcements and photos.

Association of Residents of Costa Rica Forum (www.arcr.com)

This forum is for general discussion, questions, news and comments pertaining to living in Costa Rica. Posts include discussion of questions on health care, working in Costa Rica, housing, cost of living environment, social commentary or any other topic that pertains to life in Costa Rica.

Choose Costa Rica Bulletin Board (www.discoverypress.com)

This group was started as an experiment, a copy of the very successful Mexico Connect forum that deals with living and retiring in Mexico. John Howells, the site's founder, says, "I am continually amazed at the number of hits our bulletin board receives, and worry that some day it will be too much to handle. My administrator tries to keep things under control by steadfastly refusing to accept commercial advertising and by encouraging forum participants to stay on the topic (living and travel in Costa Rica) and to observe rules of common courtesy. That doesn't always happen, but we try."

GalloPinto@yahoogroups.com

Gallo Pinto translates as speckled or spotted rooster, and is the name of a flavored and garnished black bean and rice dish normally served at breakfast. Gallo Pinto is a different kind of Internet discussion group, one that welcomes stories, discussions and questions about Costa Rica and is open for discussion of most all other topics, as long as good taste is observed. The founder of the group states, "The prime focus is Costa Rica, by expatriates living here, those exploring doing so in the future and ticos (Costa Ricans). We try to dig a bit deeper into all facets of Costa Rican life, and to break many off the old Internet rules along the way. We welcome Q and A's, stories and discussions on the history, culture, politics, religion and everything else about Ticolandia encouraging HTML, lucid thinking and writing and discovering "piggybacking" and short "chat room" type messages. Gallo Pinto also fosters a friendly club-like atmosphere, where members can delve into all things interesting to curious, intelligent, self-disciplined people."

Central Valley Living (costaricacentralvalleyliving@yahoo.com)

As the name indicates this group specializes in news about the Central Valley.

Escazú News (escazunews@yahoo.com)

Specializing in news about Escazú.

Costa Rica Pages Forum (www.costaricapages.com)

This group was founded by Casey Halloran. He is an expert in the field of Internet marketing and runs several successful Internet-based tour companies in Costa Rica and Panama. His site offers a moderated forum on travel, living, retirement, investment and working in Costa Rica. The site features educated discussion and debate on the pros and cons of life in Costa Rica, information and tips on how to find a job and live happily from those who have done it. Several renowned local experts participate in the forum and will be happy to answer all of your questions.

www.costaricaretirementvacationproperties.com — good retirement homes and excellent investments
www.primecostaricaproperty.com— good retirement homes
www.liveincostarica.com — tours for living here
www.retireincostarica.net — tours for living here
www.costaricabooks.com — books about Costa Rica
www.costaricagolfproperties.com — real estate
www.costaricaspanish.net — learning Spanish
www.drivetocentralamerica.com— making the trip by car
www.investincentralamerica.com — investment information
www.blujeweltravel.com — more information on Costa Rica
www.ticotravel.com — tour information
www.escapeartist.com — excellent information for expats
www.costaricapages.com — excellent directory
www.arcr.net — Association of Residents of Costa Rica
www.interbusonline.com — bus information
www.gallopinto.com — A forum, news group
www. CostaRicaLiving@yahoogroups.com — a forum
www.discoverypress.com — a forum, news group
www.registronacional.go.cr — hall of records
wwww.hospitalsanjose.net — Cima private hospital
www.clinicabiblica.com — another private hospital
www.clinicacatolica.com — another good private hospital
www.fischel.co.cr — largest pharmacy chain
www.racsa.co.cr — telecommunications site
www.filetax.com/expat.hmtl — expat tax site
www.orcag.com — Panamanian corporations
www.drivemeloco.com—car insurance
www.sanborns.com — car insurance
www.aerocasillas.com — private mail service
www.liveinnicaragua.com — living in Nicaragua
www.primenicaraguaproperty.com. — retirement property
www.liveinpanama.com — living in Panama
www.panamaretirementproperties.com — real estate

SUGGESTED READING

BOOKS ABOUT COSTA RICA

* *Christopher Howard's Guide to Costa Rican Spanish*, by Christopher Howard. A one-of-a-kind guidebook for travelers and full-time residents of Costa Rica. A "must" if you plan to make the move and want to speak Spanish like a Costa Rican. There are translations in English Costa Rican expressions found no where else.It may be ordered from Costa Rica Books.

* *Christopher Howard's Offical Guide to Costa Rican Real Estate*, by Costa Rica Books. Another one-of-a-kind guide from Costa Rica books. Costa Rica's premier experts have collaborated to make this book essential reading if you plan to invest in Costa Rican real estate. Scheduled to be released in June 2007.

* *Christopher Howard's Guide to the Costa Rican Legal System*, by Adolfo Garcia. This forthcoming, easy-to-use guide promises to simplify Costa Rica's complex and often confusing legal system. Sceduled to be released in 2007.

Butterfly in the City, by Jo Stuart. Former contributor to The Tico Times newspaper and current columnist for Am Costa Rica. This guide offers a great view of living in Costa Rica. To order: jostuart@amcostarica.com.

At Home in Costa Rica: Adventures in Living the Good Life, by Martin Rice. This anecdotal guide tells a fascinating tale of the trials and tribulations of learning a new way of life, a new language, making new (and unusual) friends, building two homes, rehabilitating animals and surviving the machinations of an alien institutional bureaucracy. To order, see: www.homeincostarica.net/thebook.

Living Abroad in Costa Rica, by Erin Van Rheenen. Another fine publication from Avalon Publications. An excellent complement to this guidebook. The author has done her research.

Choose Costa Rica, by John Howells. Discovery Press. A long-time favorite with people who want to make the move. Mr. Howells has been a part-time Costa Rican resident for many years. Another must-read if you plan to move here.

Costa Rica Handbook, by Christopher D. Baker. Moon/Avalon Publications. The longest, most extensive and best guidebook for exploring the country, with more than 750 pages of invaluable information.

* *Driving the Pan-American Highway to Mexico and Central America*, by Raymond and Audrey Pritchard, $18.95. This is the only book available if you are planning to drive from the U.nited States to Costa Rica via the Pan-American Highway.

The Essential Road Guide for Costa Rica, by Bill Baker, $19.95. A good guide book if you plan to do a lot of driving in the country.

The Legal Guide to Costa Rica, by Roger Petersen, $29.95. Everything you need to know about Costa Rica's complex legal system.

The Costa Ricans, by Richard, Karen, and Mavis Biesanz. Waveland Press, Prospect Heights, IL.

The Southern Costa Rica Guide, by Alexander del Sol. An excellent guidebook for the southern part of the country. To order: alexdelsol@yahoo.com or from amazon.com.

Amcham's Guide to Investing and Doing Business in Costa Rica, by the American Chamber of Commerce of Costa Rica. AMCHAM, P.O. Box, 4946, San José, Costa Rica. An updated guide containing good information on Costa Rica's business and investment climate.

Insurance in Costa Rica, by David R. Garrett. Garrett and Asociados, SJO 450, P.O. Box 025216, Miami, FL 33102-5216.

Bell's Walking Tour of Downtown San José, by Vernon Bell. A good guide for exploring the downtown area. P.O. Box 185, 1000, San José, Costa Rica. E-mail: home-stay@racsa.co.cr.

Guía Integral de la Salud. A complete guide to medical services in Costa Rica. It includes the names of many doctors, laboratories and hospitals. To order contact info@rhsaludintegral.com or see www.saludintegral.com.

BOOKS FOR EXPATRIATES

A Travelers Guide to Latin American Customs and Manners, by Elizabeth Devine. Published by St. Martin's Press. Helps the newcomer understand the Latin way of life.

Escape from America, by Roger Gallo. See http://www.escapeartist.com. This book is a must-read for anyone who wants to relocate overseas. It has the answers to all of your questions, plus profiles of the best countries in which to live. This book may be out of print.

How I Found Freedom in an Unfree World, by Harry Browne, Liam Works — Dept. FB, P.O. Box 2165, Great Falls, MT 59403-2165, or toll- free 1-888-377-0417. This book will revolutionize your life.

The World's Retirement Havens, by Margret J. Goldsmith. This guide briefly covers the top retirement havens in the world. Most of the material is still current since it was published in 1999. You may obtain this guide from John Muir Publications, P.O. Box 613, Santa Fe, NM 87504.

PERIODICALS

Costa Rica Today is a free travel oriented newspaper published twice a month. However, it does have information for residents. Two columns are very informative for people who live here: "Learning the Language" and "Living in Costa Rica." Contact information: Tel: 520-0303, E-mail: info@costaricatoday.com

The Tico Times newspaper is published weekly. It is worth subscribing to if you plan to live in Costa Rica. See Chapter 7 for subscription details.

Costa Rica Outdoors, is a magazine that covers almost all of the country's outdoor activities. To subscribe write to: Costa Rica Outdoors, Dept. SJO 2316, P.O. Box 025216, Miami, FL 33102-5216. You can also call or fax -282-6743.

VIDEOS

Costa Rica Unica, is an informative video dealing with history, the people, archeology, ecology and touring. It provides an in-depth view of the country. This fine video may also be ordered from our company. The price is $22.95.

*All of the titles above with an asterisk are available through **Costa Rica Books** by calling toll-free 800-365-2342. You may also order the same titles from **Amazon.com** or by viewing **www.costaricabooks. com**.

IMPORTANT SPANISH PHRASES
AND VOCABULARY

You should know all of the vocabulary below if you plan to live in Costa Rica.

What's your name?	*¿ Cómo se llama usted?*
Hello!	*¡Hola!*
Good Morning	*Buenos días*
Good Afternoon	*Buenas tardes*
Good night	*Buenas noches*
How much is it?	*¿Cuánto es?*
How much is it worth?	*¿Cuánto vale?*
I like	*Me gusta*
You like	*Le gusta*
Where is...?	*¿Dónde está...?*
Help!	*¡Socorro!*
What's the rate of exchange	*¿Cuál es el tipo de cambio?*
I'm sick	*Estoy enfermo*

where	*dónde*	week	*la semana*
what	*qué*	Sunday	*domingo*
when	*cuándo*	Monday	*lunes*
how much	*cuánto*	Tuesday	*martes*
how	*cómo*	Wednesday	*miércoles*
which	*cuál or cuáles*	Thursday	*jueves*
why	*por qué*	Friday	*vienes*
now	*ahora*	Saturday	*sábado*
later	*más tarde*		
tomorrow	*mañana*	month	*mes*
tonight	*esta noche*	January	*enero*
yesterday	*ayer*	February	*febrero*
day before		March	*marzo*
yesterday	*anteayer*	April	*abril*
day after		May	*mayo*
tomorrow	*pasado mañana*	June	*junio*

July	*julio*	bored	*aburrido*
August	*agosto*	happy	*contento*
September	*septiembre*	sad	*triste*
October	*octubre*	expensive	*caro*
November	*noviembre*	cheap	*barato*
December	*diciembre*	more	*más*
		less	*menos*
spring	*primavera*	inside	*adentro*
summer	*verano*	outside	*afuera*
fall	*otoño*	good	*bueno*
winter	*invierno*	bad	*malo*
		slow	*lento*
north	*norte*	fast	*rápido*
south	*sur*	right	*correcto*
east	*este*	wrong	*equivocado*
west	*oeste*	full	*lleno*
		empty	*vacío*
left	*izquierda*	early	*temprano*
right	*derecha*	late	*tarde*
easy	*fácil*	best	*el mejor*
difficult	*difícil*	worst	*el peor*
big	*grande*		
small	*pequeño, chiquito*	I understand	*comprendo*
		I don't	
a lot	*mucho*	understand	*no comprendo*
a little	*poco*	Do you speak	
there	*allí*	English?	*¿Habla usted*
here	*aquí*		*inglés?*
nice, pretty	*bonito*	hurry up!	*¡apúrese!*
ugly	*feo*	O.K.	*está bien*
old	*viejo*	excuse me!	*¡perdón!*
young	*joven*	Watch out!	*¡cuidado!*
fat	*gordo*		
thin	*delgado*	open	*abierto*
tall	*alto*	closed	*cerrado*
short	*bajo*	occupied	
tired	*cansado*	(in use)	*ocupado*

free (no cost)	*gratis*	red	*rojo*
against the		yellow	*amarillo*
rules or law	*prohibido*	pink	*rosado*
exit	*la salida*	orange	*anaranjado*
entrance	*la entrada*	brown	*café, castaño*
stop	*alto*	purple	*morado,*
breakfast	*el desayuno*		*púrpura*
lunch	*el almuerzo*		
dinner	*la cena*	0	*cero*
cabin	*la cabina*	1	*uno*
bag	*la bolsa*	2	*dos*
sugar	*el azúcar*	3	*trés*
water	*el agua*	4	*cuatro*
coffee	*el café*	5	*cinco*
street	*la calle*	6	*seis*
avenue	*la avenida*	7	*siete*
beer	*la cerveza*	8	*ocho*
market	*el mercado*	9	*nueve*
ranch	*la finca*	10	*diez*
doctor	*el médico*	11	*once*
egg	*el huevo*	12	*doce*
bread	*el pan*	13	*trece*
meat	*el carne*	14	*catorce*
milk	*la leche*	15	*quince*
fish	*el pescado*	16	*diez y seis*
ice cream	*el helado*	17	*diez y siete*
salt	*la sal*	18	*diez y ocho*
pepper	*la pimienta*	19	*diez y nueve*
post office	*el correo*	20	*veinte*
passport	*pasaporte*	30	*treinta*
waiter	*el salonero*	40	*cuarenta*
bill	*la cuenta*	50	*cincuenta*
		60	*sesenta*
blue	*azul*	70	*setenta*
green	*verde*	80	*ochenta*
black	*negro*	90	*noventa*
white	*blanco*	100	*cien*

200	doscientos	1000	mil
300	trescientos	1,000,000	un millón
400	cuatrocientos		
500	quinientos		
600	seiscientos		
700	setecientos		
800	ochocientos		
900	novecientos		

* If you want to perfect your Spanish, we suggest you purchase our best-selling Spanish book, *Christopher Howard's Guide to Costa Rican Spanish*. It is a one-of-a-kind pocket-sized course designed for people who want to learn to speak Spanish the Costa Rican way.

TIQUISMOS

Here are some Costa Rican expressions you should be familiar with if you plan to spend a lot of time in Costa Rica.

¡Buena Nota!	Fantastic! Great!	*maje*	pal
camaronear	work an extra job	*pachanga*	party
		paja	B.S.
chapa	a coin or stupid person	*panga*	a small boat
		pulpería	corner grocery store
chicha	anger		
chumeco	dark skin	*queque*	cake
chunche	a thing	*roco*	old person
color	shame	*¡Salado!*	Too bad! Tough luck!
dar pelota	flirt		
fila	line	*soda*	a small cafe
gato	blue-eyed person	*Tico*	a Costa Rican
goma	hangover	*timba*	big stomach
harina	money	*tiquicia*	Costa Rica
jalar una torta	get in trouble	*vos*	you, informal equivalent of *tú*
jamar	to eat		
¡Jale!	Hurry up!		

IMPORTANT TELEPHONE NUMBERS

GENERAL EMERGENCY..911
BILINGUAL TOURIST INFORMATION 800-343-6332
MUNICIPALITY OF SAN JOSE 223-4655, 223-4640
COLLECT CALLS WITHIN COSTA RICA................................110
TIME OF DAY 112
INFORMATION 113
AT&T (INTERNATIONAL CALLS) 114
AT&T 9 COLLECT-CREDIT CARD CALLING........ 0-800-011-4114
UNLISTED NUMBERS...115
IMMIGRATION 220-0355
OIJ (Judicial Police) 295-3271
TRANSIT POLICE (ACCIDENTS) ....227-4866 EXT. 205-265
POLICE 117
PARAMEDICS 118
FIRE DEPARTMENT...118
CHAMBER OF COMMERECE......................... 221-0005,221-0389
INTERNATIONAL COLLECT CALLS 116
TELEPHONE OUT OF ORDER 119
TELEGRAMS 123
ELECTRIC COMPANY...126
RURAL GUARD 127
AMBULANCE...128
BILINGUAL EMERGENCY SERVICE (Like our 911) 122
MCI...162
ELECOM CANADA..161
U. S. SPRINT (INTERNATIONAL CALLS)..........................163
NATIONAL PARKS 192
TOURISM INTITUTE (ICT)............................. 223-1733, 257-6057
TRAVELER'S INFORMATION 800-0123456
RED CROSS AMBULANCE 221-5818
PUBLIC MEDICAL CENTERS
    HOSPITAL MEXICO... 232-6122
    HOSPITAL NACIONAL DE NIÑOS........................... 222-0122
    HOSPITAL SAN JUAN DE DIOS 257-6282
    HOSPITAL CALDERON GUARDIA 257-7922
CLINICA BIBLICA (private hospital with
    24 hour pharmacy) 257-5252
CLINICA CATOLICA (private hospital)................... 283-6616
PSIQUIATRICO (Psychiatric Hospital) 232-2155
AMERICAN EXPRESS assistance................................ 0-800-120-039
DIRECT DIALING TO U.S.A. ....001+area code and number
U.S. EMBASSY (3 a.m.–4:30 p.m., M–F) 220-3939
U.S. EMBASSY (after hours, weekends) 220-3050

CANADIAN EMBASSY (anytime) 255-3522
AIRPORT INFORMATION (24 hours) 441-0744

PHONE NUMBERS FOR SPECIAL SERVICES

Accountants
HOUSEMAN, DAVID ....223-2787 or 239-2045

Alarms
ADT... 257-7373

Automobile Repair
H.M.S. (English spoken, reliable and honest) 223-0348

Banks
BANCO CREDITO AGRICOLA DE CARTAGO 251-3011
BANCO DE COSTA RICA.. 255-1100
BANCO NACIONAL DE COSTA RICA 223-2166
BANCO BANEX (PRIVATE) 221-6344
BANCO LYON (PRIVATE).. 221-2212

Bottled Water
ALPINA. 256-2020
CRISTAL... 442-5453

Business and Secretarial Services
BILINGUAL SECRETARIAL SERVICES 228-4367
TEMPO 222-7844

Car Rentals
EUROCAR (our first choice) 257-1158
AVIS RENT-A-CAR. 232-9922
HERTZ 221-1818

Car Services
EMERGENCY AUTOSERVICES............................... 221-2053
TOWING ....381-6534 or 258-4248

Credit Card Companies
AMERICAN EXPRESS... 233-0044
DINNERS CLUB... 233-0455

VISA.. 223-2211

Customs Agents
ABC MOVERS... 227-2645, 226-9010

Dentists
ACOSTA, ARTURO 228-9904
SANDRA FERNANDEZ... 257-3382
HIRSCH, RONALD (CHILDREN'S DENTIST) 222-1081

Doctors
AGGERO, ROLANDO.. 255-4476
ARCE, LUIS R. (EAR, NOSE AND THROAT) 235-5653
ARELLANO, ALFONSO (CARDIOLOGIST) 233-5435
BOLAÑOS, PEDRO (ACUPUNTURE) 231-3165
ESQUIVEL, JULIO (GYNECOLOGY) 220-1010
GABRIEL,PATRICK (CHIROPRACTOR)................. 296-0020
KOGEL, STEVEN (AMERICAN PSYCHIATRIST)... 253-4502
or 225-7149
LABORATORY LABIN.. 222-1987
MURRAY, CHARLES
(PSYCHOLOGICAL COUNSELING)........................ 260-9902
NUNEZ, RODOLFO (DERMATOLOGY) 222-6265
PARDO, ROGELIO (INTERNAL MEDICINE) 222-1010

Errands
RAPHA NISSI MULTISERVICES 250-5940, 257-0305

Handyman Services
MARIDOS DE ALQUILER..................438-7070 or 438-7949

Interpreters and Translators
TRANSLATION SERVICES....................................... 228-4367
TEMPO 222-7844

Laundry
DRY CLEANERS USA (many locations) 220-1570,231-7396
Maids
CINDERELA DOMESTIC SERVICES......TEL/FAX 262-2834,
BEEPER 256-7890 CODE 2084

Mailing Services (private)
AEROCASILLAS 255--4567
TRANS-EXPRESS INTERLINK 296-3973/296-3974
STAR BOX 221-9092

Real Estate
COSTA RICA RETIREMENT VACATION PROPERTIES
(e-mail: robert@costaricaretirementvacationproperties.com)
toll-free 1-888-581-1786

Self-Storage
BODEGA AMERICA 392-1921,2821579, 265-0445

Taxis
AEROPUERTO 241-0333
COOPETAXI 235-9966
COOPETICO 224-7979
TAXI ALFARO 221-8466
TAXI COOPEGUARIA 226-1366
TAXIS DE CARGA Y MUDANZAS (For moving) 223-0921

Tours and Travel Agencies
LIVE IN COSTA RICA TOURS 800-365-2342
TICO TRAVEL 800-493-8426
TRAVEL STORE 279-8927

BCR (*Banco de Costa Rica*) - Bank of Costa Rica

BCCR (*Banco Central de Costa Rica*) - Central Bank

BCAC (*Banco Crédito Agrícola de Cartago*) - Bank of Cartago

BNCR (*Banco Nacional de Costa Rica*) - National Bank

CCSS (*Caja Costarricense del Seguro Social*) -Social Security system for medical care and retirement

CONICIT (*Consejo Nacional de Investigaciones Científicas y Tecnológicas*) - Scientific and technological research

CONAPE (*Consejo Nacional de Prestamos para la Eduicación*) - Loans for students

DIS (*Dirección de Intelegencia y Seguridad Nacional*) - Internal security

ICAA (*Instituto Costarricense de Acueductos y Alcantarillados*) - Company that supplies water to your home.

ICE (*Instituto Costarricense de Electricidad*) - Telephone and electric company

INCOFER (*Instituto Costarricense de Ferrocarriles*) - In charge of the railroad

INCOP (*Instituto Costarricense de Puertos del Pacífico*) - In charge of the Pacific ports

ICT (*Instituto Costarricense de Turismo*) - In charge of tourism

IMAS (*Instituto Mixto de Ayuda Social*) - Provides a variety services and help to poor families

IMN (*Instituto Meteorologico Nacional*) - National Weather Institute

INA (*Instituto Nacional de Aprendizaje*) - Trade schools

INEC (*Instituto Nacional de Estadística y Censos*) -Census Bureau

INAMU (*Instituto Nacional de las Mujeres*) -Institute for Women

INS (*Instituto Nacional de Seguros*) - State-run insurance company

INVU (*Instituto Nacional de Vivienda y Urbanismo*) - Housing department

ITCR (*Instituto Tecnológico de Costa Rica*) - Technological schools

JAPDEVA (*Junta Administrativa Portuaria y de Desarrollo Económico de la Vertiente Atlántica*) - In charge of Atlantic port

JPSSJ (*Junta de Protección Social de San José*) - Runs the state lottery whose profits go for social welfare

MINAE (*Ministerio de Ambiente y Energía*) - Protects the environment

MCJD (*Ministerio de Cultura, Juventud y Deportes*) - Ministry that promotes cultural events and sports for the youth.

MOPT (*Ministerio de Obras Públicas y Transporte*) - Transportation Department

OIJ (*Organismo de Investigacion Judicial*) - Like our F.B.I.

PANI (*Patronato Nacional de Infancia*) - Child welfare association.

PROCOMER (*Promotora del Comercio Exterior de Costa Rica*) - Promotes trade abraod

SENARA (*Servicio Nacional de Aguas Subterráneas, Riego y Avenamiento*) - Promotes and regulates the country's water supply

SUGEF (*Superintendencia General de Entidades Financieras*) - Regulates banks, money exchange houses and other financial businesses but not pensions or stockbrokerages.

SUGEVAL (*Superintendencia General de Valores*) - Regulates , supervises and oversees Costa Rican securities markets, the activities of private individuals or corporate entities.

UCR (*Universidad de Costa Rica*) - University of Costa Rica

UNED (*Universidad Estatal a Distancia*) - University extension

UNA (*Universidad Nacional*) - National University

Zip Codes by City

Office Name	Zip Code	Fax	Tel	Location of the Postal Office
Administración Central	1000	233-1909	233-9766	Diagonal a la Fishel, San Jose
Aeropuerto	4003	279-5418	441-1278	Aeropuerto Internacional Juan Santamaria.
Aguas Zarcas	4433	474-4062	474-4062	100 E y 25 S. De la Iglesia Catolica
Alajuela	4060	441-0122	441-9107	Avenida 5, Calle 1, Alajuela
Alajuelita	1400	254-6072	254-6826	50 Sur de la Iglesia Católica
Asamblea Legislativa	1013	233-1656	243-2528	Edificio Asamblea Legislativa
Aserri	1450	230-4115	230-4115	De la Iglesia 100 Este 125 Sur
Atenas	4013	446-5140	446-5140	Esquina sureste del mercado
B. San José, Alajuela	4030	433-9991	433-9991	Contiguo a G.A.R.
Bagaces	5750	671-1119	671-1119	De la bomba de gasolina 200 oeste
Barra del Tortuguero	7311	N/A	383-7886	Tortuguero Centro
Barranca	5460	663-2636	663-2636	Frente Bodegas del INCOP
Barrio Mexico	1005	222-2713	233-3713	Esquina Norte Plaza, 50 N 25 E
Barva de Heredia	3011	260-6622	260-6622	Avenidas 4 y 6, Calle 1
Batán	7251	718-6130	472-2075	25 Norte del Hospedaje Batáan
Boca Arenal	4407	N/A	N/A	200 Sur de la Iglesia Católica
Boca de Nosara	6233	682-0100	682-0100	Contiguo al Centro de Salud
Bribrí	7312	N/A	758-3014	Contiguo a la Municipalidad
Buenos Aires	8100	730-0003	730-0003	Contiguo a la G.A.R.
Cahuita	7302	755-0096	755-0096	Contiguo a la SubComisaria
Cañas	5700	669-0309	669-1701	Frente a Coopecompro
Cariari	7212	767-7198	767-7198	25 Este de la Escuela de Campo Kennedy
Carmona de Nandayure	5313	N/A	657-7366	Contiguo a la Municipalidad
Cartago	7050	551-0070	552-4595	Avenida 2 entre Calle 15 y 16
CATIE	7170	ext.286	556-6431	Turrialba CATIE
Centro Colón	1007	223-6674	223-6574	Calle 38 AV 0 y 1, Ed. Centro Colón
Ciudad Colón	6100	249-1966	249-1966	Costado Norte de la Casa Cural
Ciudad Quesada	4400	460-1576	460-3399	100 Norte Cruz Roja
Cobano	5361	642-0047	642-0047	Contiguo a la G.A.R.
Coco Beach (Playas del Coco)	5019	670-0418	670-0418	Frente al parque
Coronado	2200	229-1151	292-2684	200 N 50 O Iglesia
Correo Interno	2020	223-6521	223-6521	Centro Postal Zapote
Corte Suprema de Justicia	1003	223-6780	223-6780	Calle 15 y 17 AV 8 Edif. Corte
Cuidad Cortéz	8153	788-8210	788-8210	150 Oeste del Hospital Tomas Casas
Cuidad Neilly	8250	783-3140	783-3500	Costado Suroeste del Mercado
Curridabat	2300	272-0360	272-0360	300 O. Esquina suroeste Iglesia
Desamparados	2400	259-3573	259-2357	100 Sur Bomberos
El Roble	5461	663-0995	663-0995	De la entrada principal del Roble 400 norte
Escazú	1250	289-5298	289-4308	100 N. Palacio Municipal
Esparza	5500	635-5138	636-6666	100 este del Liceo Diurno Esparza
Fecosa	1009	N/A	255-1610	AV. 20 Calle E. Edif. Ferrocariles
Filadelfia	5050	688-8213	688-8213	De Coopecompro 100 sur y 25 este
Florencia	4401	475-5005	475-5005	Contiguo a la G.A.R.
Frailes	2414	N/A	544-0099	Frente Banco Nacional
Golfito	8201	775-0373	775-1911	Frente a la Plaza
Grecia	4100	444-5661	494-4501	Avenida 1, entre calles 1 y 3
Guácimo	7213	716-5028	716-5028	200 Este del Edificio Municipal
Guadalupe	2100	224-0379	253-5349	Costado Oeste Parque
Guápiles	7210	710-6161	710-7203	Costado Norte de la Municipalidad
Hatillo	1300	254-7607	254-7607	Centro Comercial Hatillo
Heredia	3000	260-6767	260-0461	Avenida Central entre Calle central y 2
Hojancha	5251	659-9186	659-9186	Costado suroeste del parque
Ipis	2110	229-0016	229-0016	Contiguo Plaza
Jaco	4023	643-3479	643-3479	Frente a la G.A.R.
Jicaral	5353	650-0114	650-0114	150 norte de la G.A.R.
Juan Viñas	7160	532-2285	532-2285	Enfrente al parque
La Cruz	5009	679-9329	679-9329	50 este del parque
La Fortuna	4417	479-9178	479-9178	50 O. De la Bomba de Gasolina
La Uruca	1150	223-0917	223-6492	100 O Lanner y Saenz
La Y Griega	1011	227-2737	227-2737	Frente Centro Comercial del Sur
Las Juntas de Abangares	5600	662-0767	662-0076	25 norte del Kinder
Liberia	5000	666-0359	666-1649	200 norte del Banco Crédito Agrícola
Limón	7300	758-1543	758-3471	Diagonal de la esquina Norte del Mercado
Los Chiles	4450	471-1061	471-1061	Local Nº 06 Mercado Municipal

Miramar	5550	639-9451	639-9451	Costado norte de la iglesia principal
Moravia	2150	236-1506	235-9936	Costado Parque
Naranjo	4200	450-0644	450-0644	A la par de la estación de bomberos
Nicoya	5200	685-5004	685-5088	Diagonal al parque
Nuevo Arenal	5717	N/A	694-4310	Contiguo a la G.A.R.
Orotina	4021	428-8481	428-8481	Contiguo a la G.A.R.
Palmar Norte	8150	786-6291	786-6291	Contiguo a la G.A.R.
Palmares	4300	452-0274	453-1954	Calle Central entre calles 6 y 8
Paquera	5357	641-0060	641-0060	Contiguo a la G.A.R.
Paraíso	7100	574-7660	574-7660	Avenida 1 , Calle Central
Parque Industrial Cartago	7052	766-6242	766-6509	Parque Industrial Cartago
Parrita	6300	779-9108	779-9108	150 oeste de la Municipalidad de Parrita
Paseo Estudiantes	1002	233-0692	233-0692	Calle 9 AV. 10 y 12
Paso Canoas	8255	732-2021	732-2021	Frontera con Panamá
Pavas	1200	232-8745	232-0333	Contiguo Escuela Pavas
Pital	4437	473-3097	473-3097	Diagonal a la Plaza de Deportes
PIZFA	4002	N/A	N/A	Parque Industrial Alajuela
Plaza Mayor	1235	N/A	N/A	Pavas Centro
Puerto Jiménez	8203	735-5045	735-5045	Frente a la Plaza
Puerto Viejo de Sarapiquí	3069	766-6247	766-6509	Frente al Banco Nacional
Puntarenas	5400	661-0440	661-2156	Frente al Banco Costa Rica
Puriscal	6000	416-6073	416-7656	50 N. Esquina Noroeste Parque
Quepos	6350	777-0279	777-1471	Frente a la Plaza Rancho GDR costado Oeste
Río Claro	8200	789-9420	789-9420	200 Norte del Aserradero Impala
Río Frío	3071	764-1019	472-2075	Costado oeste del Taller Eladio
Sabanilla	2070	253-6302	253-6302	Costado Oeste Parque
Samara	5235	666-0368	656-0368	Contiguo a la G.A.R.
San Antonio Belen	4005	239-2254	293-0360	Avenida Central, Calle 6
San Francisco de Dos Ríos	2350	227-6355	227-6355	100 Sur de la Iglesia
San Francisco Guadalupe	2120	N/A	221-5041	De la Iglesia 100 Este 125 Norte
San Gerardo de Chomes	6659	N/A	N/A	Contiguo a Servicentro San Gerardo
San Ignacio de Acosta	1500	410-0095	410-0095	Costado Este Parque
San Isidro Heredia	3017	258-7692	268-7692	100 norte y 15 al este de la clínica católica.
San Isidro P.Z.	8000	771-3060	771-0346	Detrás del Colegio la Asunción.
San Joaquin de Flores	3007	265-5692	265-5692	A la par de la municipalidad
San José 2000	1017	232-3843	232-3843	Planta Baja C.C. S.J.2000
San Marcos de Tarrazú	8055	546-6325	546-6325	Contiguo a la Municipalidad
San Mateo de Alajuela	4017	N/A	N/A	Costado oeste Palacio Municipal
San Pablo de Heredia	3019	237-2269	237-2269	Esquina sur del parque
San Pablo de León Cortéz	8059	546-7679	546-7679	Fte. Parque
San Pedro de Montes de Oca	2050	225-4852	283-5138	Costado Oeste de la Plaza
San Pedro Poas	4059	448-5344	448-5344	200 sur y 25 este de la escuela.
San Rafael de Guatuso	4500	464-0132	464-0132	50 Sur de la Estación de Gasolina
San Rafael Heredia	3015	238-0461	238-0461	100 este de la iglesia
San Ramon	4250	445-5718	445-7606	Avenida 2 Calles 2 y 4
San Sebastián	1350	226-5072	226-5072	400 N. De la Iglesia
San Vito	8257	773-3130	773-3830	Contiguo a la G.A.R.
Santa Ana	6150	282-7403	282-7403	Costado Norte de la Plaza
Santa Ana 2000	6151	282-4687	282-4687	Centro Com. Sta. Ana 2000
Santa Barbara Heredia	3009	N/A	N/A	50 sur esquina noroeste del parque
Santa Cruz	5150	680-0280	N/A	Frente a la empresa Alfaro
Santa María de Dota	8051	541-1020	541-1020	Costado Norte del Parque
Santa Rosa de Pocosol	4409	477-6065	477-6065	Frente al Costado Sur del Parque
Santo Domingo	3100	244-2113	244-2113	Avenida Central, Calles 2 y 4
Sarchi Norte	4150	454-4300	454-4533	Diagonal plaza deportes costado sur
Siquirres	7200	768-8229	768-6006	Frente a la G.A.R.
Tibas	1100	235-1764	297-0767	100 E. 10 S. Parque
Tilaran	5710	695-5387	695-6230	Del estadio 150 Oeste
Tres Ríos	2250	279-5418	279-5418	Costado Oeste Escuela Central
Turrialba	7150	556-0427	556-7670	Avenida 6 Calle 0
Upala	5707	470-0545	470-0174	Del parque 100 Norte
Veintisiete de Abril	5153	N/A	N/A	Contiguo a la G.A.R.
Venecia	4443	472-2075	472-2075	100 Este de la Soda Matute
Villareal	5159	653-0676	653-0676	Frente a la plaza de deportes
Zapote	2010	224-5747	283-5585	Frente Liceo de Zapote
Zarcero	4350	463-3276	463-3276	Costado Norte del Parque
Zona Franca Met. Barreal	3006	239-0236	239-0236	Zona Franca Metropolitana Barreal

INDEX

NOTES

Special Services for Newcomers

The time-tested business listed in this special section provide excellent services. We have interviewed hundreds of foreigners who have utilized these services and are very pleased with them.

Thank you!